Theories of Personality

ELEVENTH EDITION

Theories of Personality

DUANE P . SCHULTZ
University of South Florida

SYDNEY ELLEN SCHULTZ

CENGAGE
Learning®

Australia • Brazil • Mexico • Singapore • United Kingdom • United States

CENGAGE
Learning

Theories of Personality, Eleventh Edition
Duane P. Schultz and
Sydney Ellen Schultz

Product Director: Jon-David Hague

Content Developer: Michelle Clark

Product Assistant: Kimiya Hojjat

Marketing Manager: Melissa Larmon

Art and Cover Direction, Production
Management, and Composition:
Lumina Datamatics, Inc.

Manufacturing Planner: Karen Hunt

Cover Image: ©Alan Bailey/Shutterstock;
©Rusian Guzov/Shutterstock; ©sianc/
Shutterstock, ©Jochen Schoenfeld/Shut-
terstock, ©Konstantin Sutyagin/Shutter-
stock; ©PT Images/Shutterstock; ©Jason
Stitt/Shutterstock; ©beboy/Shutterstock;
©TalyaPhoto/Shutterstock; ©knikola/
Shutterstock

Unless otherwise noted all items
©Cengage Learning®

For product information and technology assistance, contact us at
Cengage Learning Customer & Sales Support, 1-800-354-9706.

For permission to use material from this text or product, submit all
requests online at **www.cengage.com/permissions.**
Further permissions questions can be e-mailed to
permissionrequest@cengage.com.

Library of Congress Control Number: 2015915554

Student Edition:
ISBN: 978-1-305-65295-8

Cengage Learning
20 Channel Center Street
Boston, MA 02210
USA

Cengage Learning is a leading provider of customized learning
solutions with employees residing in nearly 40 different countries
and sales in more than 125 countries around the world. Find your local
representative at **www.cengage.com.**

Cengage Learning products are represented in Canada by
Nelson Education, Ltd.

To learn more about Cengage Learning Solutions, visit
www.cengage.com.

Purchase any of our products at your local college store or at our
preferred online store **www.cengagebrain.com.**

Printed in the United States of America
Print Number: 07   Print Year: 2019

brief Contents

contents

The Life-Span Approach   157

preface to the Eleventh Edition

Each edition of a textbook must be as vital, dynamic, and responsive to change as the field it covers. To remain an effective teaching instrument, it must reflect the development of the field and continue to challenge its readers. We have seen the focus of personality study shift from global theories, beginning with Sigmund Freud's 19th-century psychoanalytic theory of neuroses, to 21st-century explorations of more limited personality facets or dimensions. And we have seen the basis of personality exploration change from case studies of emotionally disturbed persons to more scientifically based research with diverse populations. Contemporary work in the field reflects differences in gender, age, and sexual orientation as well as ethnic, racial, religious, and cultural heritage.

New and Expanded Coverage

New biographical material has been included for the theorists, to suggest how the development of their theory may have been influenced by events in their personal and professional lives. This approach shows students that the development of science through theory and research is not always totally objective. It may also derive from intuition and personal experience later refined and extended by more rational, analytic processes. Social and cultural influences on the theorists' beliefs about human nature are also described.

The sections on personality research have been updated with nearly 400 new references to maintain the emphasis on current issues. Research findings have been summarized throughout the text in "Highlights" boxes; this feature presents bullet point lists to help the student organize and compare the results of research studies.

Some of the topics with new and expanded coverage include the following:

- Do we present our true selves on social media? How does the use of social media influence our personality? How does our personality influence our use of social media? Do selfies show the real you?
- Updated work on the MMPI, the Rorschach, and the Thematic Apperception Test.
- The Mechanical Turk—a new way to conduct personality research online.
- New findings on the Freudian concepts of ego resilience, the Oedipus complex, and defense mechanisms. New findings on dreams, and the use of computers to interpret dreams.
- Social companion robots to facilitate psychoanalysis.
- Research on Jung's Psychological Types conducted in Arab cultures.
- Post-traumatic stress disorder (PTSD) as a result of neglect in childhood.
- New findings on Adler's concept of birth order.
- Over 30 new studies on Erikson's concepts of ego identity, gender preference, virtual ethnic identity, gender differences in toy preferences, and his stages of development.
- Cultural differences from Allport's work extended to the facial expression of emotions.
- More on the five-factor model of personality and the Dark Triad—an approach that includes narcissism, machiavellianism, and psychopathy.
- The Smartphone Basic Needs Scale—a self-report inventory designed to measure how Maslow's hierarchy of needs can be satisfied by smartphone use.

- New research findings on self-efficacy and locus of control.
- Techniques to measure sensation seeking. The relationship between sensation seeking and cyberbullying.
- More on Seligman's life and his development of positive psychology. Defining and finding happiness. The concept of flourishing. And how learned helplessness was used in developing techniques of torture in the war on terror.

Organization of the Text

The eleventh edition of *Theories of Personality* retains its orientation toward undergraduate students who have had little previous exposure to personality theories. Our purpose is to reach out to beginning students and ease their task of learning about the study of personality. We have chosen theorists who represent psychoanalytic, neopsychoanalytic, lifespan, genetics, humanistic, cognitive, behavioral, and social-learning approaches, as well as clinical and experimental work. The concluding chapter reviews these perspectives that describe personality development and suggests ways to help students draw conclusions and achieve closure from their studies.

Each theory in the text is discussed as a unit. Although we recognize the value of an issues or problems approach that compares theories on specific points, we believe that the issues-oriented book is more appropriate for higher-level students. The theories-oriented text makes it easier for beginning students to grasp a theory's essential concepts and overall flavor. We try to present each theory clearly, to convey its most important ideas, assumptions, definitions, and methods. We discuss each theorist's methods of assessment and empirical research and offer evaluations and reflections. Except for placing Freud first in recognition of his chronological priority, we have not arranged the theories in order of perceived importance. Each theory is placed in the perspective of competing viewpoints.

A Note on Diversity

The first person to propose a comprehensive theory of the human personality was Sigmund Freud, a 19th-century clinical neurologist who formulated his ideas while treating patients in Vienna, Austria. His work, called *psychoanalysis*, was based largely on sessions with wealthy White European women who came to him complaining of emotional distress and disturbing thoughts and behaviors. From his observations of their progress, or lack of it, he offered a theory to explain everyone's personality. Freud's system was important for the concepts he proposed—many of which are now part of popular culture—as well as for the opposition he provoked, inspiring other theorists to examine and promote their own ideas to explain personality.

Today, personality theorists and researchers recognize that an explanation based on a small, homogeneous segment of the population cannot be applied to the diverse groups of people sharing space in our world. The situation is similar in medicine. Medical researchers recognize, for example, that some medications and treatments appropriate for young adults are not suitable for children or elderly people. Diseases prevalent in certain ethnic groups are rare in others, requiring differences in medical screening and testing for diverse populations. Contemporary personality theory strives to be inclusive, studying the influences of age, gender, race, ethnic origin, religious beliefs, sexual orientation, and child-rearing practices. We see examples of this diversity throughout the text.

Features

For the student, we offer chapter outlines, summaries, research highlights, review questions, annotated reading lists, margin glossary terms, a cumulative glossary, tables and figures, a reference list, and referrals to relevant Web sites.

For instructors, the instructor's manual with test bank has been thoroughly revised and offers lecture outlines, ideas for class discussion, projects, useful web links, and test items. The test bank is available in digital formats. PowerPoint Lecture Slides and electronic transparencies are available on eBank. The transparencies feature select figures and tables from the text loaded into Microsoft PowerPoint. Contact your local sales representative for details.

Duane P. Schultz
Sydney Ellen Schultz

chapter 1

Personality: What It Is and Why You Should Care

Take a Look at the Word

Let's start by examining the word you're going to be dealing with this semester. It not only defines this course, but it will also help define your life as well.
Here are three standard dictionary definitions of the word taken at random:

- The state of being a person.
- The characteristics and qualities that form a person's distinctive character.
- The sum total of all the physical, mental, emotional, and social characteristic of a person.

You get the idea. It's everything about you that makes you what you are—a unique individual who is different, in large and small ways, from everybody else. It's a simple word, but a difficult concept to truly comprehend, which is why it takes a book and a semester to begin to come to grips with it. We're going to try to understand it, or at least learn something about it, by exploring the various ideas that psychologists have advanced over the years to try to explain it.

We have organized those ideas—those theories—in terms of their different outlooks on human nature, beginning with Sigmund Freud. We will deal with extensions that grew out of his theory of psychoanalysis and talk about the men and women who revised his ideas or rebelled against them. After that, we will move on to what is called the life-span approach, tracking personality development from birth all the way to old age. We'll then discuss theories that focus on individual personality traits, on psychological health, on predetermined behavior patterns, and on cognitive learning from social situations. We will also introduce current ideas for the 21st century and offer some suggestions and conclusions from our exploration of personality.

It's important to recognize that personality theorists from the last century rarely considered the importance of ethnic and cultural differences. We will see that it is not meaningful to generalize to all people from, for example, ideas that one theorist based on clinical observations of neurotic European women, or that another theorist based on tests given to American male college students. Therefore, when we discuss research conducted on these theories, and describe their use for real-world problems of diagnosis and therapy, we'll also try to show the influence of age, gender, race, ethnic and national origin, religious beliefs, and sexual orientation.

To make your study easier, we will include Highlights sections, giving brief summaries of research findings, as well as chapter outlines, summaries, review questions, and reading lists. Important words will be defined in the margins, and these definitions will also be listed in the glossary in the back of the book. In addition, check out the Web sites in our "Log On" features included in each chapter. For direct links, log on to the student companion site at www.cengagebrain.com.

Everybody Has One

Everybody has one—a personality, that is—and yours will help determine the boundaries of your success and life fulfillment. It is no exaggeration to say that your personality is one of your most important assets. It has already helped shape your experiences up to now, and it will continue to do so for the rest of your life. Everything you have accomplished to date, all of your expectations for the future, whether you will make a good husband, wife, partner, or parent, even your health can be influenced by your personality and the personalities of those around you. Your personality can limit or expand your options and choices in life, prevent you from sharing certain experiences, or enable you to take full advantage of them. It restricts, constrains, and holds back some people and opens up the world of new opportunities to others.

How often have you said that someone has a *terrific* personality? By that you typically mean the person is affable, pleasant, nice to be around, and easy to get along with—the kind of person you might choose to be a friend, roommate, or colleague at work. If you are a manager, you might choose to hire this person. If you are ready to commit to a relationship, you might want to marry this person, basing your decision on your perception of his or her personality. You also know people you describe as having a *terrible* personality. They may be aloof, hostile, aggressive, unfriendly, unpleasant, or difficult to get along with. You would not hire them or want to associate with them, and they may also be shunned, rejected, and isolated by others.

Keep in mind that, while you are making judgments about the personalities of other people, they are making the same kinds of judgments about you. These mutual decisions that shape the lives of both the judged and the judges are made countless times, every time we are in a social situation that requires us to interact with new people. Of course, the number and variety of social situations you are involved in are also determined by your personality—for example, your relative sociability or shyness. You know where you rate on that characteristic, just as you no doubt have a reasonably clear picture of what your overall personality is like.

Describing Your Personality

Of course, it's glib and overly simple to try to sum up the total constellation of someone's personality characteristics by using such fuzzy terms as *terrific* and *terrible*. The subject of personality is too complex for such a simplified description, because humans are too complex and changeable in different situations and with different people. We need to be more precise in our language to adequately define and describe personality. For that reason, psychologists have devoted considerable effort to developing tests to assess, or measure, personality, as we'll see throughout the book.

You may think you don't need a psychological test to tell you what your personality is like, and, in general, you may be right. After all, you probably know yourself better than anyone else. If you were asked to list the words that best describe your personality, no doubt you could do it without too much thought, assuming you were being honest with yourself.

Try it. Write down as many adjectives as you can think of to describe what you are really like—not how you would like to be, or what you want your teachers or parents or Facebook friends to think you are like—but the real you. (Try not to use the word *terrific*, even if it does apply in your case.) How many words did you find? Six? Ten? A few more? A widely used personality test, the Adjective Check List, offers an astonishing 300 adjectives that describe personality.

People taking the test choose the ones that best describe themselves. No, we're not going to ask you to go through all 300 adjectives, only the 30 listed in Table 1.1. Place a check mark next to the ones you think apply to you. When you're done, you'll have a description of your personality in greater detail, but remember that in the actual test, you would have another 270 items to pick from.

How Does Personality Develop?

Our focus here is not on what *your* personality is like. You don't need a psychology course to learn that. What we will be studying are the forces and factors that shape your personality. Later in this chapter, and throughout the book, we will deal with

---

TABLE 1.1   Adjective check list

Make a check mark next to the words you believe apply to your personality.

_____	affectionate	_____	ambitious	_____	assertive
_____	boastful	_____	cheerful	_____	cynical
_____	demanding	_____	dominant	_____	fearful
_____	forceful	_____	generous	_____	high-strung
_____	impatient	_____	insightful	_____	meek
_____	moody	_____	optimistic	_____	opinionated
_____	persistent	_____	prudish	_____	relaxed
_____	sarcastic	_____	sensitive	_____	sociable
_____	submissive	_____	tolerant	_____	trusting
_____	uninhibited	_____	vindictive	_____	withdrawn

some basic questions about the nature of personality—for example, whether we are born with a certain type of personality or learn it from our parents, whether personality is influenced by unconscious forces, and whether it can change as we get older.

We will cover a variety of theories that have been proposed to help answer these and related questions about human nature. After we have discussed them—what they are, how they came about, and what their current status is—we will evaluate how useful they are in answering our questions and contributing to our understanding of how personality develops. We may think of each of these theorists as contributing individual pieces to a huge online jigsaw puzzle, which is why we study their ideas, even though some of their concepts are decades old. Psychologists continue to try to fit these pieces together to bring forth a clearer image, a more complete picture of what makes us the way we are and determines how we look at the world.

Personality Project – Northwestern University

Discusses major approaches to personality theory and offers links to resources, advice for students, and information about personality tests.

Personality Theories e-textbook – Professor C. George Boeree

Downloadable chapters about major personality theorists and links to relevant web sites.

Society for Personality and Social Psychology

The world's largest organization of personality and social psychologists; a division of the American Psychological Association. Members work in academics, industry and government. The site offers information on training and careers.

Ways of Looking at Personality

We talked about formal definitions of personality earlier. Now let's get away from dictionary definitions and take a look at how we use the word in our everyday lives. We use it a lot when we are describing other people and ourselves. One psychologist suggested that we can get a very good idea of its meaning if we examine our intentions—what we mean—whenever we use the word *I* (Adams, 1954). When you say *I*, you are, in effect, summing up everything about yourself—your likes and dislikes, fears and virtues, strengths and weaknesses. The word *I* is what defines you as an individual, separate from everybody else.

How Others See Us

Another way of trying to understand personality is to look to its source. The word goes back to about the year 1500, and derives from the Latin word *persona*, which refers to a mask used by actors in a play. It's easy to see how persona came to refer to our outward appearance, the public face we display to the people around us. Based on its derivation, then, we might conclude that personality refers to our external and visible characteristics, those aspects of us that other people can see. Our personality would then be defined in terms of the impression we make on others—that is, what we appear to be. Viewed from that perspective, personality is the visible aspect of one's character,

Our personality may be the mask we wear when we face the outside world

Cristian Baitg/Photographer's Choice/Getty Images

as it impresses others. In other words, our personality may be the mask we wear when we face the outside world.

But is that all we mean when we use the word *personality*? Are we talking only about what we can see or how another person appears to us? Does personality refer solely to the mask we wear and the role we play? Surely, when we talk about personality, we mean more than that. We mean to include many different attributes of an individual, a totality or collection of various characteristics that goes beyond superficial physical qualities. The word encompasses a host of subjective social and emotional qualities as well, ones that we may not be able to see directly, that a person may try to hide from us, or that we may try to hide from others.

Stable and Predictable Characteristics

We may in our use of the word *personality* refer to enduring characteristics. We assume that personality is relatively stable and predictable. Although we recognize, for example, that a friend may be calm much of the time, we know that he or she can become excitable, nervous, or panicky at other times. Thus, sometimes our personality can vary with the situation. Yet although it is not rigid, it is generally resistant to sudden changes. In the 1960s, a debate erupted within psychology about the relative impact on behavior of such enduring personal variables as traits and needs versus variables relating to the situation (see Mischel, 1968, 1973).

The controversy continued for some 20 years and concluded with the realization that the "longstanding and controversy-generating dichotomy between the effect of the situation versus the effect of the person on behavior … is and always was a fake" (Funder, 2001, p. 200). And so the issue was resolved by accepting an interactionist approach, agreeing that enduring and stable personal traits, changing aspects of the situation, and the interaction between them must all be considered in order to provide a full explanation for human nature.

Unique Characteristics

personality
The unique, relatively enduring internal and external aspects of a person's character that influence behavior in different situations.

Our definition of personality may also include the idea of human uniqueness. We see similarities among people, yet we sense that each of us possesses special properties that distinguish us from all others. Thus, we may suggest that **personality** is an enduring and unique cluster of characteristics that may change in response to different situations.

Even this, however, is not a definition with which all psychologists agree. To achieve more precision, we must examine what each personality theorist means by the term. Each one, as we will see, offers a unique version, a personal vision, of the nature of personality, and that viewpoint has become his or her definition. And that is what this book is all about: reaching an understanding of the different versions of the concept of personality and examining the various ways of defining the word *I*.

Personality and the Social Media

Our increasing, almost constant use of the various social media to interact with other people in a virtual reality rather than in person has led to a great deal of recent research which attempts to relate our personalities to the online world in which we now live. There are at least three ways in which social media and personality may interact to affect one another, leading to three questions to which psychologists are increasingly seeking answers.

1. Do we present our real selves on social media?
2. Does the use of social media influence or change our personalities?
3. Do people with different personalities use social media in different ways?

Are You the Same Person Online?

We saw earlier that one way of defining personality is in terms of the mask we wear, the public face we display to the people around us. Increasingly, many of us display another face, not in person, but through the Internet on social networking Web sites such as Facebook. As a result, another way of defining our personality may include how others see us online.

But are they seeing us as we really are, or are we creating online some idealized self-image that we want to display to other people? Are we pretending to be someone we are not, or are we conveying an accurate description of our personality? Some research suggests that most people are honest about their online faces. Studies conducted in the United States and in Germany found that social networking sites do convey accurate images or impressions of the personality profiles we offer. The researchers concluded that depictions of personalities presented online are at least as accurate as those conveyed in face-to-face interactions (Gosling, Gaddis, & Vazire, 2007; Back et al., 2010).

A more recent large-scale study in Germany, however, found that many people have a tendency to present themselves online as being much more emotionally stable than they really are (Blumer & Doring, 2012). Other later studies have found that those who are introverted, neurotic, lonely, and socially awkward find it easier to express their true selves (their real personalities) online instead of in person (Marriott & Buchanan, 2014). It has also been found that those who feel they are able to express their true selves are more active on Facebook and other social media sites than those who do not feel that way about themselves (Seidman, 2014).

And what about selfies, those photos we take of ourselves? How accurate are they in showing our true selves? Or are they merely posing and posturing for effect, to impress others—to make our own little "reality shows?" Research has found that more women than men send selfies and that excessive use of them can make the sender less likeable and even reduce the intimacy or closeness of friendships. They can even reinforce the idea that how people look is more important than how they actually behave in real life toward their friends (Drexler, 2013; Rutledge, 2013).

Of course, as you know, we are not always honest in how we depict ourselves in person either, particularly when we meet new people we want to impress, like a date or an employer. With people we have known for a while, with whom we feel secure, and who represent no threat, we may be less likely to pretend to be something we are not. Perhaps the major difference with social networking sites is that there is a much wider and more instantly reachable audience than in our everyday offline lives.

In addition, we now know that what we post about ourselves can also have great potential consequences to our careers and future when prospective employers find "inappropriate content" such as drunkenness, sexual display, and use of profanity on a candidate's social media sites. One study found that evaluations of Facebook pages containing negative content resulted in false perceptions of that person's personality. Sites of those with no inappropriate displays resulted in more accurate evaluations of the person's personality, which, in the real world, can make the difference between being hired for a job or accepted by a graduate school (Goodman, Smith, Ivancevich, & Lundberg, 2014).

How Does the Social Media Influence Our Personality?

Psychologists have found that the use of online social networking sites like Facebook can both shape and reflect our personalities. One study of adolescents in China aged 13 to 18 found that excessive time spent using the Internet resulted in significant levels of anxiety and depression when compared to teenagers who spent considerably less time online (Lam & Peng, 2010). Other research found that high levels of social media use can reduce psychological well-being (how happy we feel) and decrease the quality of relationships with friends and romantic partners (Blais, Craig, Pepler, & Connolly, 2008; Huang, 2010a; Kross et al., 2013).

An online survey of college students in the United States showed that those who spent time talking with their parents on the telephone had more satisfying personal and supportive relationships with them than students who kept in touch with the parents through social networking sites. In addition, college students who communicated with their parents on social networking sites reported greater loneliness, anxiety, and conflict in their relationships with their parents (Gentzler, Oberhauser, Westerman, & Nadorff, 2011).

Studies conducted in such diverse countries as the Netherlands, Serbia, Hong Kong, and Korea have demonstrated that those who reported excessive use of social media tend to be more lonely, introverted, and low in self-esteem than those who use it less (Baek, Bae, & Jang, 2013; Milosevic-Dordevic & Zezelj, 2013; Muusses, Finkenauer, Kerkhof, & Billedo, 2014; Yao & Zhong, 2014). Spending too much time online can also lead to addiction, which can be just as obsessive and excessive as addiction to alcohol, drugs, or gambling. Excessive online use has also been shown to change portions of the brain that are linked to depression and increased irritability (Mosher, 2011).

How Does Our Personality Influence Our Use of Social Media?

In addition to affecting our personalities, social networking sites can also reflect them. Studies in both Eastern and Western cultures found that those who were more extraverted and narcissistic (who had an inflated, unrealistic self-concept) were much more likely to use Facebook than those who did not score high on those personality characteristics. The more narcissistic teenagers were also more likely to update their Facebook status more frequently (Kuo & Tang, 2014; Michikyan, Subrahmanyam, & Dennis, 2014; Ong et al., 2011; Panek, Nardis, & Konrath, 2014; Winter et al., 2014).

Other studies suggest that those who report high use of social networking sites tend to be more extraverted, more open to new experiences, lower in self-esteem and socialization skills, less conscientious, and lower in emotional stability than those who report lower levels of usage (Blackhart, Ginette, Fitzpatrick, & Williamson, 2014; Correa, Hinsley, & de Zuniga, 2010; Mehdizadeh, 2010; Papastylianou, 2013; Ross, Orr, Sisic, Arseneault, Simmering, & Orr, 2009; Weiss, 2014; Wilson, Fornasier, & White, 2010).

Personality differences among cell phone users have also been found. Research involving teenagers and adults in Australia found that extraverts and those with a strong sense of self-identity spent much more time making calls and changing their ring tones and wallpaper than those scoring lower on these personality characteristics. The studies also found that those who were more neurotic and less conscientious and shy spent more time texting on their phones than those who were less neurotic and more conscientious (Bardi & Brady, 2010; Butt & Phillips, 2008; Walsh, White, Cox, & Young, 2011).

Finally, what about the personalities of people who engage in Internet trolling— deliberately hurting, harassing, and upsetting others by posting hateful, inflammatory, and derogatory comments about them. What are they like? The evidence shows that trolls are mostly male with an average age of 29, who, as you might expect, score high in sadism. They take pleasure in degrading others. It makes them feel good (Buckels, Trapnell, & Paulhus, 2014; Lewis, 2014).

The Role of Race and Gender in Shaping Personality

The personality theorists we cover in this book offer diverse views of the nature of the human personality. Despite their disagreements and divergences, however, they all share certain defining characteristics in common. All are White, of European or American heritage, and almost all are men. There was nothing unusual about that, given the period during which most of these theorists were developing their ideas. At the time, nearly all of the great advances in the arts, philosophy, literature, and the sciences, including the development of the scientific methods, were propounded and promoted by White men of European or American background. In most fields, educational and professional opportunities for women and people of ethnic minority groups were severely limited.

In addition, in the field of personality theory, virtually all the patients and subjects the earlier theories were based on were also White. Even the laboratory rats were white. Also, the majority of the patients and subjects were men. Yet, the personality theorists confidently offered theories that were supposed to be valid for all people, regardless of gender, race, or ethnic origin.

None of the theorists stated explicitly that his or her views applied only to men or to Whites or to Americans, or that their ideas might not be useful for explaining personality in people of other backgrounds. Although the theorists accepted, to some degree, the importance of social and environmental forces in shaping personality, they tended to ignore or minimize the influence of gender and ethnic background.

We know from our own experiences that our brothers, sisters, and friends were exposed to different childhood influences than we were and that, as a result, they grew up to have different personalities. We also know from research in social psychology that children from different environments—such as a predominantly White Midwestern town, a Los Angeles barrio, an Appalachian mountain village, or an affluent Black suburb—are exposed to vastly different influences. If the world in which people live and the factors that affect their upbringing are so different, then surely their personalities can be expected to differ as a result. They do.

We also know that boys and girls are usually reared according to traditional gender stereotypes, and this upbringing also influences personality in different ways. Research has documented many differences between men and women on specific personality factors. For example, one large-scale study of the intensity of emotional awareness and expression compared male and female college undergraduates at two American universities and male and female students at medical schools in the United States and in Germany.

The results showed that women from both countries displayed greater emotional complexity and intensity than did men (Barrett, Lane, Sechrest, & Schwartz, 2000). A study of more than 7,000 college students in 16 Islamic nations found that women measured significantly higher in anxiety than men did in 11 of the 16 samples studied (Alansari, 2006). We will see many examples throughout the book of gender and sex differences in personality.

The Role of Culture in Shaping Personality

The influence of cultural forces on personality is widely recognized in psychology. A specialty area called cross-cultural psychology has fostered a great deal of research supporting the conclusion that personality is formed by both genetic and environmental influences. "Among the most important of the latter are cultural influences" (Triandis & Suh, 2002, p. 135).

This was demonstrated in a study of Japanese who emigrated to the United States, compared to those who stayed in Japan. Those who moved became much more "American" in their personalities. They changed in significant ways in response to their changed culture (Gungor, Bornstein, De Leersnyder, Cote, Ceulemans, & Mesquita, 2013).

Other research showed that recent Chinese immigrants to Canada demonstrated the same low level of introversion as the Hong Kong Chinese who did not emigrate. However, Chinese immigrants who had lived in Canada at least 10 years and thus had greater exposure to Western culture, scored significantly higher in extraversion than did more recent immigrants or the Hong Kong subjects. Cultural forces had exerted a significant impact on this basic personality characteristic (McCrae, Yi, Trapnell, Bond, & Paulhus, 1998).

Anxiety and other negative emotions may also be related to cultural differences. When the experiences of Asian-American students were compared with those of European-American students in a daily diary study, it was found that the Asian Americans reported a far greater number of negative emotions in social situations than the European-Americans did (Lee, Okazaki, & Yoo, 2006). Western people in general, and Americans, in particular, also exhibit greater optimism and view themselves and their future more positively. They even consider their sports teams, cities, and friends to be superior, when compared to those of Asian cultures (Endo, Heine, & Lehman, 2000).

There are even large-scale cultural differences in brain activity and genetic makeup, which have been demonstrated in the field of cultural neuroscience (Azar, 2010). Using measures of brain wave activity, researchers found differences in brain function between people in Eastern and Western cultures when responding to the same stimuli (Park & Huang, 2010). One study found brain wave activity of Japanese and Americans to differ in reaction to the same visual stimuli; the differences paralleled each culture's measured level of submissiveness or dominance (Freeman, Rule, & Ambady, 2009).

We will see a number of other examples in this section, and throughout the book, of the many ways in which the culture we live in shapes and molds our personalities.

Different Cultural Beliefs about Destiny

The concept of *karma* has for centuries shaped the outlook of the people of India and other countries that accept Hinduism or Buddhism. It may be seen as a fatalistic and deterministic view of human nature. The consequences of our present and past actions are believed to determine our destiny or fate, our happiness or unhappiness in the future. In other words, events don't occur because we make them happen but because they were destined to happen.

Thus, in this view, our fortune or misfortune, health or sickness, happiness or unhappiness are preordained and independent of our own actions. You can see how this belief may lead to a passive, resigned personality type, accepting of whatever comes one's way and not being motivated to take action to change it. Contrast this with a view more typical of American culture that emphasizes free choice and action, and the role of our own personal effort and initiative in bringing about our personal success or failure.

Research shows substantial cultural differences between East and West in this notion of fate attribution or destiny (Norenzayan & Lee, 2010). However, there is also evidence that as Eastern cultures such as China modernize and become more Westernized, that cultural belief is reduced (Wong, Shaw, & Ng, 2010).

Individualism

Individual competitiveness and assertiveness are often seen as undesirable and contrary to Asian cultural standards. Western cultures are typically depicted as the opposite. For example, when college students in Australia were compared with college students in Japan, the Australians were found to emphasize the importance of individuality much more than the Japanese, who were more oriented toward the collective or the group (Kashima, Kokubo, Kashima, Boxall, Yamaguchi, & Macrae, 2004). In another example, an Asian-American job applicant who is a recent immigrant to the United States and not yet fully acculturated to American values and beliefs is likely to score low on a personality test measuring such factors as competitiveness, assertiveness, and self-promotion. This person would probably be judged as deficient—as not measuring up to American standards—and thus unlikely to be offered a job.

In an individualistic society, the focus is on personal freedom, choice, and action. In a collectivist society, the focus is on group norms and values, group role expectations, and other cultural constraints on behavior. People in individualistic cultures show greater extraversion, self-esteem, happiness (or subjective well-being), optimism about their future, and a belief in their ability to control and direct it. For example, one massive study of over 400 million people in 63 countries found that the personality trait of individualism was strongly and consistently related to positive well-being (Fischer & Boer, 2011).

Genetic differences between people in collectivistic versus individualistic cultures have been linked to lower levels of anxiety and depression in collectivistic cultures and higher levels in individualistic cultures (Chiao & Blizinsky, 2010).

College students in the United States scored significantly higher than college students in Japan on measures of self-efficacy—the feeling of being adequate, efficient and competent in coping with life and in exerting control over life events (Morling, Kitayama, & Miyamoto,

2002). College students in Australia were found to be significantly more agreeable, conscientious, optimistic, and satisfied with their lives than students in Singapore (Wong, Lee, Ang, Oei, & Ng, 2009).

Other research found differences in subjective well-being between Asian-American students and European-American students at the same university in the United States. The European-American students attained their feeling of well-being by pursuing goals for the purpose of personal satisfaction. The Asian-American students seemed to "attain and maintain their well-being by achieving goals that they pursue to make important others [such as their parents] happy and [to] meet the expectations of others" (Oishi & Diener, 2001, p. 1680).

Thus, the motivations and satisfactions of these students and their corresponding images of human nature differed with their cultural backgrounds. In addition, a comparison of Japanese and American college students revealed that the American students were far more likely to use positive terms to describe themselves. The Japanese students were more likely to use negative terms (Kanagawa, Cross, & Markus, 2001).

Thus, the degree to which a culture focuses on and encourages individualism has a powerful effect on the personality of its citizens.

Child-Rearing Practices

The impact on behavior and personality of cultural differences in child-rearing practices is also substantial. In the individualistic culture of the United States, parents tend to be noncoercive, democratic, and permissive in their child-rearing techniques. In collectivist cultures, such as Asian and Arab societies, parental practices tend to be more authoritarian, restrictive, and controlling.

Studies of adolescents in several Arab countries showed that they felt a greater connection with their parents than did American adolescents. The researchers noted that Arab adolescents "follow their parents' directions in all areas of life, such as social behavior, interpersonal relationships, marriage, occupational preference, and political attitudes.... they do not feel that they suffer from their [parents'] authoritarian style and are even satisfied with this way of life" (Dwairy, Achoui, Abouserie, & Farah, 2006, p. 264). The study concluded that these authoritarian parental practices did not adversely affect the mental health and emotional well-being of the Arab teenagers as they would in more liberal Western cultures.

Chinese mothers living in Canada were found to be more authoritarian in raising their children than non-Chinese mothers in Canada (Liu & Guo, 2010). Turkish mothers living in Germany who were more assimilated into the German culture emphasized individualistic goals for their children much more than Turkish mothers who were not so assimilated (Durgel, Leyendecker, Yagmurlu, & Harwood, 2009).

Clearly, such differences in child-rearing practices and their resulting values will influence the development of different kinds of personalities.

Self-Enhancement

Self-enhancement is defined as the tendency to promote oneself aggressively and make one conspicuous. The opposite of that, self-effacement, is considered to be more in agreement with the cultural values of Asian societies. This was supported in a laboratory study comparing Canadian and Japanese college students. Self-enhancement was far more prevalent among the Canadian students; self-criticism was significantly more evident among the Japanese students (Heine, Takata, & Lehman, 2000).

Similar results were obtained in three additional studies comparing self-ratings and questionnaire responses in collectivist versus individualistic cultures. The subjects in these instances were Japanese college students compared with American college students, and Chinese high school and college students in Singapore compared with Jewish high school and college students in Israel. The results from both studies showed that those from collectivist cultures (Japan and China) showed significantly greater self-criticism and significantly lower self-enhancement than those from individualistic cultures (the United States and Israel) (Heine & Renshaw, 2002; Kurman, 2001). A study comparing people in the United States, Mexico, Venezuela, and China found that the Chinese demonstrated the strongest tendency toward self-effacement than those in the other cultures (Church et al., 2014).

Nordic cultures such as Norway, Sweden, and Denmark provide another example of cultures encouraging self-effacement. The cultural concept of *Janteloven* enjoins people not to place their own interests above those of their community and to show humility in the presence of others. A comparison of college students in the United States and Norway found that the Americans rated themselves significantly higher than average on positive personality traits and lower than average on negative traits than the Norwegian students did. This tendency to self-enhancement among the U.S. students, which was not found to the same degree among the Norwegian students, appears to be culturally induced, determined by the values taught in the different countries (Silvera & Seger, 2004).

Large differences in individualism have also been found in cultures that are not so far apart geographically. One might reasonably expect differences between Eastern cultures such as Japan and Western cultures such as the United States, as we have seen. But differences have also been reported between European cultures, such as Spain and the Netherlands. A comparison using a self-report inventory of people found that the Spanish people were more concerned with matters of honor and family-related values, such as family security, respect for parents, and recognition from others. In contrast, the Dutch people scored much higher on individualistic values such as ambition, capability, and independence (Rodriguez-Mosquera, Manstead, & Fischer, 2000).

If you consider yourself to be self-enhancing, take heart. Maybe it's not so bad. Research in various countries in Europe found that self-enhancers were rated by others as being emotionally stable, socially attractive, and socially influential (Dufner, Denissen, Sediilides, Van Zalk Meeus, & Van Aken, 2013). And finally, a study of American college students found that those high in self-esteem and self-enhancement look for mates who share their own characteristics. In other words, self-enhancers are looking for someone who is as great as they think they are (Brown, Brown, & Kovatch, 2013).

A Diversity of Cultures

As we have just seen, there have been major advances in exploring a wide range of cultural differences in personality research in recent years. However, it still remains true that much less research has been conducted on personality in African and South American nations than in English-speaking countries, or in many of the countries of Europe and Asia. Also, much of the research that has been conducted among those populations has not been made widely available in English-language sources.

Another problem limiting the applicability of cross-cultural personality research is that the majority of studies in personality use American college students as subjects. One of the goals of this book is to cover research results from a more diverse and representative selection of people. The studies you will read about here are from more than 40 different countries, all of which are listed on the inside back cover, and from a variety of age groups, cultures, religions, and ethnic backgrounds. We will not be dealing only with the personalities of White American college students.

Race, Ethnicity, and Multicultural Issues

The Social Psychology Network provides links to diverse sites related to racial, ethnic, and multicultural issues, especially African, Asian, Hispanic, Jewish, and Native American cultures.

Assessing Your Personality

To assess something means to measure or evaluate it. The assessment of personality is a major area of application of psychology to a number of real-world concerns. For example, clinical psychologists try to understand the symptoms of their patients or clients by assessing their personalities, by differentiating between normal and abnormal behaviors and feelings. Only by evaluating personality in this way can clinicians diagnose disorders and determine the best course of therapy.

School psychologists evaluate the personalities of the students referred to them for treatment in an attempt to uncover the causes of adjustment or learning problems. Industrial/organizational psychologists assess personality to select the best candidate for a particular job. Counseling psychologists measure personality to find the best job for a particular applicant, matching the requirements of the position with the person's interests and needs. Research psychologists assess the personalities of their subjects in an attempt to account for their behavior in an experiment or to correlate their personality traits with other measurements.

No matter what you do in your life and your working career, it is difficult to avoid having your personality assessed in some way at some time. Indeed, much of your success in the workplace will be determined by your performance on various psychological tests. Therefore, it is important that you have some understanding of what they are and how they work.

The Concepts of Reliability and Validity

reliability The consistency of response to a psychological assessment device.

validity The extent to which an assessment device measures what it is intended to measure.

The best techniques of personality assessment adhere to the principles of **reliability** and **validity**.

Reliability   Reliability involves the consistency of response to an assessment device. Suppose you took the same test on two different days and received two widely different scores. How would you know which score is the most accurate one? A test like that would not be considered reliable because its results were so inconsistent. No one could depend on that test for an adequate assessment of your personality. It is common to find some slight variation in scores when a test is taken a second time, but if the variation is large, then something is wrong with the test or with the method of scoring it.

Validity   Validity refers to whether an assessment device measures what it is intended to measure. Does an intelligence test truly measure intelligence? Does a test of anxiety actually evaluate anxiety? If a test does not measure what it claims to, then it is not valid and its results cannot be used to predict behavior. For example, your score on an invalid intelligence test, no matter how high, will be useless for predicting how well you will do in college or in any other situation that requires a high level of intelligence. A personality test that is not valid may provide a totally misleading portrait of your emotional strengths and weaknesses and will be of no value to you or a potential employer.

Methods of Assessment The personality theorists discussed in this book devised different methods for assessing personality that were the most useful for their theories. By applying these methods, they obtained the data on which they based their formulations. Their techniques vary in objectivity, reliability, and validity, and they range from dream interpretation and childhood recollections to computer-administered objective tests. The major approaches to personality assessment are:

- Self-report or objective inventories
- Projective techniques
- Clinical interviews
- Behavioral assessment procedures
- Thought and experience sampling procedures

Self-Report Personality Tests

self-report inventory A personality assessment technique in which subjects answer questions about their behaviors and feelings.

The **self-report inventory** or test approach involves asking people to report on themselves by answering questions about their behavior and feelings in various situations. These tests include items dealing with symptoms, attitudes, interests, fears, and values. Test-takers indicate how closely each statement describes themselves, or how much they agree with each item. There are a number of self-report personality tests in use today as we will see in later chapters, but one of the most useful is the Minnesota Multiphasic Personality Inventory (MMPI).

Minnesota Multiphasic Personality Inventory (MMPI) The MMPI has been translated into more than 140 languages and is the world's most widely used psychological test (see Butcher, 2010; Cox, Weed, & Butcher, 2009). First published in 1943, the MMPI was revised in 1989 to make the language more contemporary and nonsexist. The latest revision is the MMPI-2-RF (Restructured Form), which appeared in 2008. The MMPI is a true-false test that consists of 567 statements.

The test items cover physical and psychological health; political and social attitudes; educational, occupational, family, and marital factors; and neurotic and psychotic behavior tendencies. The test's clinical scales measure such personality characteristics as gender role, defensiveness, depression, hysteria, paranoia, hypochondriasis, and schizophrenia. Some items can be scored to determine if the test-taker is deliberately faking or careless, or misunderstood the instructions.

For example, research has shown that the MMPI-2-RF can successfully distinguish between those who have genuine physical pain and those who are faking it in order to claim disability payments (Crighton, Applegate, Wygant, Granacher, & Ulauf, 2013). The test has also been shown to distinguish between those who are faking symptoms of post-traumatic stress disorder (PTSD) and those whose symptoms are genuine (Mason et al., 2013). It has also been found that those who are mentally ill can learn (through online instruction) how to respond on the MMPI so as to hide their symptoms and appear to be mentally healthy (Hartmann & Hartmann, 2014).

Examples of the types of statements in the MMPI are shown in Table 1.2.

The MMPI-2 is used with adults in research on personality as a diagnostic tool for assessing personality problems, for employee selection, and for vocational and personal counseling. In 1992, the MMPI-A was developed for use with adolescents. The number of questions was decreased from 567 to 478, to reduce the time and effort needed to administer it.

Both forms of the test have their shortcomings, however, one of which is length. It takes a lot of time to respond attentively to the large number of items. Some people

TABLE 1.2   Simulated items from the Minnesota Multiphasic Personality Inventory (MMPI)

ANSWER "TRUE" OR "FALSE."
At times I get strong cramps in my intestines.
I am often very tense on the job.
Sometimes there is a feeling like something is pressing in on my head.
I wish I could do over some of the things I have done.
I used to like to do the dances in gym class.
It distresses me that people have the wrong ideas about me.
The things that run through my head sometimes are horrible.
There are those out there who want to get me.
Sometimes I think so fast I can't keep up.
I give up too easily when discussing things with others.

lose interest and motivation long before they finish. Also, some of the items on this and other self-report personality tests deal with highly personal characteristics, which some people consider an invasion of privacy, particularly when being required to take the test to get a job. Nevertheless, despite the length and privacy issues, the MMPI in its various forms is a valid test that discriminates between neurotics and psychotics and between the emotionally healthy and the emotionally disturbed. Thus, it remains a highly valuable diagnostic and research tool.

Assessment of Self-Report Inventories   Although there are self-report inventories to assess many facets of personality, as we will see in later chapters, the tests are not always appropriate for people whose level of intelligence is below normal, or for those with limited reading skills. Even minor changes in the wording of the questions or the response alternatives on self-report measures can lead to major changes in the results. For example, when adults were asked what they thought was the most important thing for children to learn, 61.5 percent chose the alternative "to think for themselves." But when adult subjects were asked to supply the answer themselves—when no list of alternatives was provided—only 4.6 percent made that or a similar response (Schwarz, 1999).

There is also the tendency for test-takers to give answers that appear to be more socially desirable or acceptable, particularly when they are taking tests as part of a job application. Suppose you were applying for a job you really wanted and were asked this question on a test—"I am often very tense on the job." Would you answer "yes" to that question? We wouldn't either.

When a group of college students took a self-report test with instructions to make themselves appear as good, or as socially acceptable, as possible, they were more careful with their answers and took longer to complete the test than students who were not deliberately trying to look good (Holtgraves, 2004). Similar results have been shown with other self-report inventories. Most subjects find it easy to give false answers when asked to do so in research studies (McDaniel, Beier, Perkins, Goggins, & Frankel, 2009).

Despite these problems, self-report inventories remain the most objective approach to personality assessment. Their greatest advantage is that they are designed to be scored objectively and quickly through automated personality assessment programs, providing a complete diagnostic profile of the test-taker's responses.

Online Test Administration

Self-report inventories, like everything else now, can be taken online. Many employers prefer that job applicants take tests this way as a prescreening method, rather than taking up time and space at the company's office. The advantages of computerized test administration include the following:

- It is less time-consuming for both the applicant and the organization
- It is less expensive
- The scoring is more objective
- The method is readily accepted by younger members of the workforce
- It prevents test-takers from looking ahead at questions (which they can do with a traditional paper-and-pencil test), and it prevents them from changing answers already given

A sizable body of research has confirmed the usefulness of this approach. No significant differences in responses to most self-report inventories have been found between paper-and-pencil tests and the same tests administered online (see, for example, Chuah, Drasgow, & Roberts, 2006; Clough, 2009; Luce, Winzelberg, Das, Osborne, Bryson, & Taylor, 2007; Naus, Philipp, & Samsi, 2009).

It has also been found that most of us are significantly more likely to reveal sensitive, even potentially embarrassing, information when responding online to self-report inventories than to paper-and-pencil tests given in person by a live test administrator. Understandably, many people feel a greater sense of anonymity and privacy when interacting with a computer and so reveal more personal information.

Projective Techniques

projective test A personality assessment device in which subjects are presumed to project personal needs, fears, and values onto their interpretation or description of an ambiguous stimulus.

Clinical psychologists developed **projective tests** of personality for their work with the emotionally disturbed. Inspired by Sigmund Freud's emphasis on the importance of the unconscious, projective tests attempt to probe that invisible portion of our personality. The theory underlying projective techniques is that when we are presented with an ambiguous stimulus, like an inkblot or a picture that can be interpreted in more than one way, we will project our innermost needs, fears, and values onto the stimulus when we're asked to describe it.

Because the interpretation of the results of projective tests is so subjective, these tests are not high in reliability or validity. It is not unusual for different people giving the test to form quite different impressions of the same person, based on the results of a projective test. In such a case, the inter-scorer reliability of the test is low. Nevertheless, these tests are widely used for assessment and diagnostic purposes. Two popular projective tests are the Rorschach Inkblot Technique and the Thematic Apperception Test (TAT).

Rorschach and His Inkblots   The Rorschach was developed in 1921 by the Swiss psychiatrist Hermann Rorschach (1884–1922), who had been fascinated by inkblots since childhood. As a youngster, he had played a popular game called *Klecksographie*, or *Blotto*, in which children gave their interpretations of various inkblot designs. Rorschach was known to be so intensely interested in inkblots that as a teenager, he acquired the nickname *Klecks*, which means, in German, blot of ink. Later, when Rorschach was serving a hospital residency in psychiatry after receiving his M.D., he and a friend played Blotto with patients to pass the time. Rorschach noticed consistent differences between the responses of patients and the responses offered by school children to the same inkblots.

In developing his test, Rorschach created his own inkblots simply by dropping blobs of ink on blank paper and folding the paper in half (see Figure 1.1). After trying a variety

FIGURE 1.1

An inkblot similar to a Rorschach inkblot.

of patterns, he settled on 10 blots for the very practical reason that he could not afford to have more than 10 printed. He wrote about his work with inkblots, but the publication was a failure. Few copies were sold, and the few reviews it received were negative. Although the test eventually became immensely popular, Rorschach became depressed and died 9 months after his work was published.

Using the Rorschach   The inkblot cards (some black, others in color) are shown one at a time, and test-takers are asked to describe what they see. Then the cards are shown a second time, and the psychologist asks specific questions about the earlier answers. The examiner also observes behavior during the testing session, including the test-takers' gestures, reactions to particular inkblots, and general attitude.

Responses can be interpreted in several ways, depending on whether the patient reports seeing movement, human or animal figures, animate or inanimate objects, and partial or whole figures. Attempts have been made to standardize the administration, scoring, and interpretation of the Rorschach. The most successful of these, the Comprehensive System, claims, on the basis of considerable research, to lead to improved reliability and validity (see Exner, 1993).

There is no universal agreement about the Rorschach's usefulness and validity, even with the Comprehensive System for scoring. Some researchers have concluded that there is no scientific basis for the Rorschach; others insist that the test is as valid as any other personality assessment measure. Nevertheless, the Rorschach continues to be a popular assessment technique in personality research and clinical practice.

The Rorschach is also widely used in research in Europe and South America. Overall, validity research is generally more supportive of the MMPI than of the Rorschach. Thus, the MMPI can be used with greater confidence, especially for ethnic minority groups and diverse cultural groups (see, for example, Wood, Garb, Lilienfeld, & Nezworski, 2002).

Hermann Rorschach and the Rorschach Test
Serious information sources about Hermann Rorschach and the Rorschach test.

Thematic Apperception Test (TAT)   Henry Murray and Christiana Morgan developed the TAT (Morgan & Murray, 1935). The test consists of 19 ambiguous pictures, showing one or more persons, and 1 blank card. The pictures are vague about the events depicted and can be interpreted in different ways. People taking the test are asked to tell a story about the people and objects in the picture, describing what led up to the situation shown, what the people are thinking and feeling, and what the outcome is likely to be. In clinical work, psychologists consider several factors in interpreting these stories, including the kinds of personal relationships involved, the motivations of the characters, and the degree of contact with reality shown by the characters.

There are no objective scoring systems for the TAT, and its reliability and validity are low when used for diagnostic purposes. However, the TAT has proven useful for research purposes, and scoring systems have been devised to measure specific aspects of personality, such as the needs for achievement, affiliation, and power. It also continues to be useful in clinical practice. (Gieser & Wyatt-Gieser, 2013).

Other Projective Techniques   Word association and sentence completion tests are additional projective techniques that psychologists use to assess personality. In the word-association test, a list of words is read one at a time to the subject, who is asked to respond to each with the first word that comes to mind. Response words are analyzed for their commonplace or unusual nature, for their possible indication of emotional tension, and for their relationship to sexual conflicts. Speed of response is considered important.

The sentence-completion test also requires verbal responses. Subjects are asked to finish such sentences as "My ambition is …" or "What worries me is …" Interpretation of the responses with both of these approaches can be highly subjective. However, some sentence-completion tests, such as the Rotter Incomplete Sentence Blank, provide for more objective scoring.

Clinical Interviews

In addition to specific psychological tests used to measure an individual's personality, assessment often includes clinical interviews. After all, it is reasonable to assume that valuable information can be obtained by talking to the person being evaluated and asking relevant questions about past and present life experiences, social and family relationships, and the problems that led the person to seek psychological help. A wide range of behaviors, feelings, and thoughts can be investigated in the interview, including general appearance, demeanor, and attitude; facial expressions, posture, and gestures; preoccupations; degree of self-insight; and level of contact with reality.

Armed with the results of psychological tests like the MMPI, which are usually administered before or during a series of interview sessions, the psychologist can focus on problems indicated by the test results and explore those areas in detail. Interpretation of interview material is subjective and can be affected by the interviewer's theoretical orientation and personality. Nevertheless, clinical interviews remain a widely used technique for personality assessment and a useful tool when supplemented by more objective procedures.

Behavioral Assessment

In the behavioral assessment approach, an observer evaluates a person's behavior in a given situation. The better the observers know the people being assessed and the more frequently they interact with them, the more accurate their evaluations are likely to be (Connelly & Ones, 2010). Psychologists Arnold Buss and Robert Plomin developed a questionnaire to assess the degree of various temperaments present in twins of the same sex (Buss & Plomin, 1984). The mothers of the twins were asked, on the basis of their observations of their children, to check those items on the questionnaire that best described specific and easily discernible instances of their children's behavior. Sample items from the questionnaire are listed in Table 1.3.

As we noted in the section on clinical interviews, counselors routinely observe their clients' behavior—considering, for example, facial expressions, nervous gestures, and general appearance—and use that information in formulating their diagnoses. Such observations are less systematic than formal behavioral assessment procedures, but the results can provide valuable insights.

Thought and Experience Assessment

In the behavioral approach to personality assessment, we saw that specific behavioral actions are monitored by trained observers. In the thought-sampling approach to assessment, a person's thoughts are recorded systematically to provide a sample over a period of time. Because thoughts are private experiences and cannot be seen by anyone else, the only person who can make this type of observation is the individual whose thoughts are being studied.

In this procedure, then, the observer and the person being observed are the same. The thought-sampling assessment procedure is typically used with groups, but it has also been applied to individuals to aid in diagnosis and treatment. A client can be asked to write or record thoughts and moods for later analysis by the psychologist.

A variation of thought sampling is the experience sampling method. This is conducted very much like thought sampling, but the participants are asked also to describe the social and environmental context in which the experience being sampled occurs. For example, subjects might be asked to note whether they were alone or with other people when an electronic beeper sounded, alerting them to record their experiences. Or they

TABLE 1.3   Sample items from the Buss and Plomin EASI Temperament Survey
Child tends to cry easily.
Child has a quick temper.
Child cannot sit still long.
Child makes friends easily.
Child tends to be shy.
Child goes from toy to toy quickly.

might be asked precisely what they were doing or where they were. The goal of this method is to determine how one's thoughts or moods may be influenced by the context in which they occur.

Thought sampling research relies on technological developments such as smartphones to allow participants to record their assessments quickly and easily. Electronic entries can be timed and dated. Thus, researchers can determine whether assessments are being recorded at the times and intervals requested. If they are entered sometime after the experience, they could be influenced by the vagaries of memory.

An example of the experience sampling approach to personality assessment involved a group of college students who kept daily Internet diaries for 28 days. Each entry described their moods as well as stressful events and how they coped with them. It may not surprise you to learn that the primary type of negative event involved academic issues. The second most reported type of negative issue dealt with interpersonal issues—getting along with others (Park, Armeli, & Tennen, 2004). Other approaches to personality assessment might not have uncovered this information so easily.

An experience sampling study of Japanese students found that those who reported having repetitive thoughts at night and obsessing about something in their lives had problems going to sleep, slept fitfully, and for not as long as compared to students who did not report having repetitive thoughts (Takano, Sakamoto, & Tanno, 2014).

A possible limitation of the experience sampling approach is that subjects might be so busy doing other things that they forget to record their activities when signaled to do so. As a result, the useful data might be restricted only to the most conscientious research participants. It is also possible that emotions or moods—such as anger or sadness—affect the nature of the information reported (Scollon, Kim-Prieto, & Diener, 2009). Overall, however, the method is useful to researchers and provides data comparable to those from self-report inventories.

Gender and Ethnic Issues That Affect Assessment

Gender   The assessment of personality can be influenced by a person's gender. For example, women tend to score lower than men on tests measuring assertiveness, a difference that may result from sex-role training that traditionally teaches girls and young women in some cultures not to assert themselves. Whatever the cause, personality test results often show differences between males and females on a number of characteristics and at every age. For example, a study of 474 children, median age 11, reported that girls showed a higher level of depression and a greater concern with what other people thought of them than boys did (Rudolph & Conley, 2005).

In addition, considerable data from personality tests, clinical interviews, and other assessment measures indicate differential rates of diagnosis based on gender for various emotional disorders. Women are more often diagnosed with depression, anxiety, and related disorders than are men. Several explanations have been offered. There actually may be a higher incidence of these disorders among women, or the differential rate may be related to gender bias or gender stereotyping in interpreting the assessment results.

Also, the therapists who recommend treatment options based on the assessment results may exhibit a bias against women. The average course of therapy for women tends to be longer than that for men, and doses of psychoactive medications prescribed for women tend to be higher than those for men.

Asians   The Asian-American population in the United States is a complex, heterogeneous group, which includes people of Chinese, Japanese, Filipino, Thai, Korean, and Vietnamese extraction, among others. A psychological test such as the MMPI, which has been validated in a major city in China, may not be valid for Chinese people living in the United States, or even for Chinese people living in other parts of China. Although the MMPI and other personality tests have been translated into Asian languages, little research has been conducted on their reliability and validity for use with Asian Americans.

We saw earlier that there are substantial and consistent cultural differences in personality between people of Asian and non-Asian background. Asian cultures also differ from Western societies in their attitudes toward having and being treated for mental illness, one of the major reasons for assessing personality.

Asian Americans tend to view any form of mental disorder as a shameful condition that they are embarrassed to admit. As a result, they are less likely to seek treatment from a therapist or counselor for emotional problems. Research consistently shows that Asian Americans, particularly first-generation immigrants, underutilize mental health treatment services. Those born in the United States are almost twice as likely to seek treatment as those born outside the United States (Meyer, Zane, Cho, & Takeuchi, 2009). First-generation Chinese students in the United States were found to be significantly less likely to seek treatment for emotional issues than first-generation European students in the United States (Hsu & Alden, 2008). Asian Americans also tend to wait until the disturbance is severe before seeking help and less likely to benefit from it (Hwang, 2006).

A psychologist in New York City reported that her immigrant Chinese patients initially complained only about physical symptoms such as backache or stomachache, and never about depression. Several sessions were required before they built up enough trust to venture to describe a problem such as depression. Some Asian languages, such as Korean, do not even have a specific word for depression. The psychologist reported that one Korean client finally struck his chest with his fist and said he had a "down heart," thus describing the mental condition in physical terms (Kershaw, 2013). Asian Americans are also far less likely to take antidepressant medications as compared to Whites (Gonzalez, Tarraf, Brady, Chan, Miranda, & Leong, 2010).

With such contrasting beliefs about the nature of a particular disorder, it is easy to understand why people of diverse cultural backgrounds may score differently on assessment measures of personality. In addition, the practice of using American values, beliefs, and norms as the standard by which everyone is judged may help explain much research that shows that Asian Americans tend to receive different psychiatric diagnoses than American patients of European heritage.

Blacks Research conducted in the 1990s showed generally consistent differences between Black and White subjects on self-report personality tests. Based on such test score differences, some psychologists concluded that popular and frequently used personality tests, such as the MMPI, are biased against African Americans and should not be used to assess their personalities. Evidence to support this viewpoint has been contradicted by later research using the MMPI. For example, in a study of psychiatric patients (both Blacks and Whites) who were hospitalized at a Veterans Administration (VA) center, no significant differences were found on any of the test's scales (Arbisi, Ben-Porath, & McNulty, 2002).

However, Black and White college students were found to differ on a test designed to measure paranoia. Black students scored significantly higher on items measuring a lack of trust in other people, a suspicion of their motives, and a tendency to be on guard with others. Similar results, showing a higher level of distrust and paranoid personality patterns, were shown in later research using older Black subjects between the ages of 55 and 64 (Iacovino, Jackson, & Oltmanns, 2014).

Do these consistent findings mean that Blacks are more paranoid than Whites? No. We must evaluate and interpret these and similar findings within the appropriate racial and ethnic context. Thus, the researchers noted that "the group differences may reflect mistrust or interpersonal wariness caused by pervasive discrimination and perceived racism" (Combs, Penn, & Fenigstein, 2002, p. 6). The same conclusion was reached in the 2014 study.

Other research found that African-American college students who identified strongly with Black cultural values had lower levels of depression and hopelessness than those without a strong cultural identification (Walker, Alabi, Roberts, & Obasi, 2010). However, Black teenagers who scored high in perceived discrimination reported greater depression and lower self-esteem and life satisfaction than teens who scored low in perceived discrimination against them (Seaton, Caldwell, Sellers, & Jackson, 2010).

What about the effect of race on the interpretation of MMPI test results? Do White researchers interpret test results differently when they know the person who took the test is Black or White? The answer seems to be consistently "No," as shown by two recent studies, which found no differences in interpretations between Black or White test-takers (Knaster, 2013; Knaster & Micucci, 2013).

Research on the effects of counseling and therapy conducted with Black college students showed that they rated Black therapists more favorably than they did White therapists. The students were also more accepting and understanding of the treatment options when they met with Black therapists, and they were more likely to believe that the therapy would benefit them (Thompson & Alexander, 2006; Want, Parham, Baker, & Sherman, 2004).

Hispanics Studies show that scores obtained on the MMPI by people of Hispanic origin are similar to those obtained by Whites (see, for example, Handel & Ben-Porath, 2000). With projective techniques, however, the situation is different. Rorschach scores for subjects from Mexico and from Central American and South American countries differ significantly from the norms of the comprehensive scoring system. Thus, it is questionable whether these norms are useful with Hispanic populations (Wood et al., 2002).

It has also been found that Hispanics are less likely than other minority groups to seek psychological counseling or treatment. Among Hispanics who do seek counseling, half never follow up on their first visit by returning for additional sessions (Dingfelder, 2005). A study of White and Hispanic adolescents found that significantly more Whites received adequate mental health care than Hispanics (Alexandre, Martins, Silvia, & Richard, 2009). Foreign-born Hispanics are even less likely to use mental health services than Hispanics born in the United States (Bridges, deArellano, Rheingold, Danielson, & Silcott, 2010).

Hispanic adolescents who do seek mental health treatment are typically seen by clinicians for shorter periods of time than White adolescents (Edman, Adams, Park, & Irwin, 2010). However, a study of Mexican-American college students found that as they became more integrated in the mainstream U.S. culture, their attitudes toward counseling became more favorable (Ramos-Sanchez & Atkinson, 2009). One confounding factor is the shortage of Spanish-speaking clinical psychologists and other mental health personnel.

Hispanic Americans tend to be more satisfied with mental health personnel who understand their culture, which typically is highly collectivist in nature and thus more group-oriented than individual-oriented (see, for example, Malloy, Albright, Diaz-Loving, Dong, & Lee, 2004). And they are more likely to benefit from therapy with Hispanic psychologists, who, unfortunately, account for only 1 percent of the psychologists in the United States. That may explain why older Hispanic people (ages 65 and up) prefer to seek mental health advice from their family physician rather than counselors, psychologists, or psychiatrists who are not likely to speak Spanish (Dupree, Herrera, Tyson, Jang, & King-Kallimans, 2010).

HIGHLIGHTS: Personality Assessment

Asians tend to score:

- High in collectivism
- Low in individual competitiveness and assertiveness
- Low in self-enhancement and optimism
- Low in the tendency to seek mental health treatment

African Americans tend to score:

- Low on trust of other people
- Low on hopelessness and depression (if they identify with Black cultural values)
- High on depression
- Low on self-esteem if they perceive discrimination against them

Hispanics tend to score:

- Low in tendency to seek mental health treatment
- High in collectivism
- High in PTSD symptoms following injuries

The collectivist orientation may help explain the higher rates of PTSD found in a study of Hispanic police officers when compared to Black officers and non-Hispanic White officers. The Hispanic officers reported receiving significantly less social support following critical incidents on the job that lead to PTSD. The researchers noted that for the Hispanic officers, "their culturally valued collectiveness may have left these officers particularly sensitive to social isolation, thus exacerbating their symptoms" (Pole, Best, Metzler, & Marmar, 2005, p. 257). A study of civilian survivors with physical injuries also found a higher rate of PTSD symptoms among Hispanics as compared to Whites (Marshall, Schell, & Miles, 2009).

Other Cultural Issues in Assessment   Hermann Rorschach was one of the first to recognize the effects of cultural differences in performance on personality assessment techniques. In 1921, he found differences in responses to his Inkblot Test from people living in two culturally distinct areas of Switzerland. He wrote that such responses "should be very different in various people and races" (quoted in Allen & Dana, 2004, p. 192). A study of American Indians using the MMPI-2 demonstrated how responses to test questions reflected behavior that was considered normal in that culture but pathological in the mainstream White culture (Hill, Pace, & Robbins, 2010). Other research reinforces this idea that what is normal in one culture may be judged undesirable, wrong, sick, or just plain weird in other cultures (Cheung, 2009).

Although some personality tests have been translated for use in other cultures, there are potential problems with their cross-cultural application (see, for example, Gudmundsson, 2009). This is particularly crucial when a test designed for the population of a Western culture is administered to people in a non-Western culture, such as Chinese or Filipino. For example, among traditional Chinese people, important personality characteristics include being gracious, having a family orientation, emphasizing harmony with others, and showing frugality in everyday behavior. None of these factors is typical of those measured by American personality inventories.

When the MMPI-2 was first translated into Arabic, the issue arose of how to treat questions about one's sex life. In Arab countries, any open discussion of sex is considered inappropriate, even offensive. The researchers decided to retain the sex questions in the test but to specify in the instructions that the subjects' responses to these items were optional. A study of college students in Iran showed that more than 90 percent chose not to respond to items relating to sex (Nezami, Zamani, & DeFrank, 2008).

The TAT cannot be used in Islamic cultures because of the Muslim prohibition against representing humans in pictorial form. When groups of European women and Muslim women were asked to make up stories in response to the TAT pictures, the European women did so readily and easily, whereas the Muslim women hesitated. The researcher noted that the Muslim women "consistently refused to give coherent interpretations. They refused to invent or fictionalize [the pictures]" (Bullard, 2005, p. 235).

Translators of American personality tests for use in other cultures also face the problem of American slang and colloquial expressions. Phrases such as "I often get the blues," or "I like to keep up with the Joneses" might have little meaning or relevance when translated into another language. It should be noted that there are a growing number of examples of personality tests developed in America being successfully translated into Arabic. This is particularly true for personality characteristics that are common to both cultures such as Internet addiction among the young. The Internet Addiction Test developed in the United States has been shown to be an equally valid predictor of such addiction in teenagers in Arab countries (Hawi, 2013).

Even the way people in the United States answer test questions may differ from other cultures. Responding to items in a true-false format or multiple-choice format seems natural to American college students, who have been taking these types of tests since childhood. To others, it may be an awkward and alien way of answering questions. When the MMPI was first introduced in Israel in the 1970s, many people there found it difficult to respond because they were unfamiliar with the true-false answer format. The test instructions had to be rewritten to explain to the respondents how they were supposed to record their answers (Butcher, 2004). The reworking of personality tests to ensure that they accurately reflect and measure relevant personality variables is difficult and requires knowledge of and sensitivity to cultural differences.

Research in the Study of Personality

Psychologists conduct research on personality in different ways. The method used depends on which aspect of personality is under investigation. Some psychologists are interested only in overt behavior—what we do and say in response to certain stimuli. Other psychologists are concerned with feelings and conscious experiences as measured by tests and questionnaires. Such self-report inventories are among the most frequently used research techniques. Still other investigators try to understand the unconscious forces that may motivate us. A method useful for examining one aspect of personality may be inappropriate for another aspect.

The major methods used in personality research are the clinical method, the experimental method, virtual research, and the correlational method. Although different in their specifics, these methods depend in varying degrees on objective observation, which is the fundamental defining characteristic of scientific research in any discipline.

case study A detailed history of an individual that contains data from a variety of sources.

The Clinical Method

The primary clinical method is the **case study** or case history, in which psychologists probe their patients' past and present lives for clues to the source of their emotional problems.

Undertaking a case study is similar to writing a mini-biography of a person's emotional life from the early years to the present day, including feelings, fears, and experiences.

Freud used case studies extensively in developing his theory of psychoanalysis, as we will see in Chapter 2. He probed into his patients' childhood years, looking for those events and conflicts that may have caused their present neuroses. One such patient was Katharina, an 18-year-old woman suffering from anxiety attacks and shortness of breath. In reconstructing what he considered to be the relevant experiences in her childhood, Freud traced Katharina's symptoms to several early sexual experiences she reported, including a seduction attempt by her father when she was 14. With another patient, Lucy, Freud linked her reported hallucinations to events in her past that related to her love for her employer that had been rebuffed.

It was through such case studies that Freud developed his theory of personality, with its focus on sexual conflicts or traumas as causal factors in neurotic behavior. Freud and later theorists who used the case study method searched for consistencies and patterns in their patients' lives. On the basis of what they perceived as similarities among the reports of their patients, these theorists generalized their findings to everyone.

Psychologists also use a variety of other clinical methods in addition to case studies, including tests, interviews, and dream analysis. Although the clinical method attempts to be scientific, it does not offer the precision and control of the experimental and correlational methods. The data obtained by the clinical method are more subjective, involving mental and largely unconscious events and early life experiences.

Such data are open to different interpretations that may reflect the therapist's own personal biases, more so than data obtained by other methods. Also, memories of childhood events may be distorted by time, and their accuracy cannot easily be verified. However, the clinical method can provide a window through which to view the depths of the personality, and we shall see many examples of its use, especially by the psychoanalytic and neo-psychoanalytic theorists.

The Experimental Method

An experiment is a technique for determining the effect of one or more variables or events on behavior. We are constantly exposed to stimuli going on around us in our everyday world—lights, sounds, phone screens, voices, sights, odors, instructions, and trivial conversations. When psychologists want to determine the effect of just one stimulus variable, they arrange an experimental situation in which only that variable is allowed to operate.

All other variables are eliminated or held constant during the experiment. Then, if the behavior of the subjects changes while only that one stimulus variable is in operation, we can be certain that it alone is responsible for that changed behavior. The change could not have been caused by another variable because no other variable was allowed to influence the subjects during the experiment.

There are two kinds of variables in an experiment. One is the **independent** or stimulus **variable**, which is the one manipulated by the experimenter. The other is the **dependent variable**, which is the subjects' behavior in response to that manipulation. To be certain that no variable other than the independent variable can affect the results, researchers study two groups of subjects: the experimental group and the control group. Both groups are chosen at random from the same population of subjects.

The **experimental group** includes those subjects to whom the experimental treatment is given. This is the group exposed to the stimulus or independent variable. The **control group** is not exposed to the independent variable. Measures of the behavior being studied are taken from both groups before and after the experiment. In this way, researchers can determine if any additional variables might have influenced the subjects' behavior.

independent variable In an experiment, the stimulus variable or condition the experimenter manipulates to learn its effect on the dependent variable.

dependent variable In an experiment, the variable the experimenter desires to measure, typically the subjects' behavior or response to manipulation of the independent variable.

experimental group In an experiment, the group that is exposed to the experimental treatment.

control group In an experiment, the group that does not receive the experimental treatment.

If some other variable was operating, then both groups would show the same changes in behavior. But if no other variable was in operation—if the independent variable alone influenced the subjects—then only the behavior of the experimental group would change. The behavior of the control group would remain the same.

Applying the Experimental Method   Here's an example of the experimental method in action, using data from Albert Bandura's social-learning theory of personality (see Chapter 13). Bandura wanted to find out if children would imitate the aggressive behavior they saw in adults. He could have observed children on neighborhood streets or at a playground, hoping to catch their reactions if they happened to witness a violent incident. He could then have waited to see whether the children would imitate the aggressive behavior they had seen.

That approach is obviously unsystematic and uncontrolled. Observing children who just happened to be present on a street corner would not provide an appropriate sample of subjects. Some of the children might already possess a tendency to behave aggressively, regardless of the violent behavior they observed. Therefore, it would be impossible to decide whether their aggressive behavior resulted from witnessing that violent act or from some factor that had been part of their personality long before the observation took place.

Also, observing children at random would not allow the researcher to control the type of aggressive act to which the subjects might be exposed. Children see many kinds of violence every day—on video games, movies, and television as well as on the streets or in playgrounds. In the experiment Bandura wanted to run, it was necessary that all the children he observed be exposed to the same instance of aggressive behavior. He approached the problem systematically by designing an experiment in which children whose preexperiment levels of aggression had been measured were then exposed to the same display of adult aggression. Children in the control group witnessed nonaggressive adults in the same setting. Both groups of children were watched by trained observers to see how they would behave.

The results showed that those children who watched the aggressive adult behaved aggressively, while children in the control group showed no change in aggressiveness. Bandura therefore concluded that aggressiveness can be learned by imitating the aggressive behavior of others.

Limitations of the Experimental Method   There are situations in which the experimental method cannot be used. Some aspects of behavior and personality cannot be studied under rigorously controlled laboratory conditions because of safety and ethical considerations. For example, psychologists might be better able to treat emotional disturbances if they had data from controlled experiments on different child-rearing techniques to determine what kinds of early experiences might lead to problems in adulthood. Obviously, however, we can't take groups of children from their parents at birth and expose them to various child-rearing manipulations to see what happens.

Another difficulty with the experimental method is that the subjects' behavior might change simply because they know they are being observed. They might behave differently if they thought no one was watching their responses. When people know they are participating in an experiment, they sometimes try to guess the purpose of it and behave in ways to either please or frustrate the experimenter. This kind of response defeats the purpose of the experiment because the resulting behavior (the dependent variable) has been influenced by the subjects' attitudes rather than by the experimental treatment. This is quite a different response from what the researcher intended to study.

Experimental research has its limitations, but when it is well controlled and systematic, it provides excellent data. We will see examples throughout the book of how the experimental method applies to understanding many aspects of personality.

Virtual Research

Psychologists routinely conduct research online, including administering psychological tests, taking opinion surveys, and presenting experimental stimuli and recording the subjects' responses. They are doing much the same kinds of research they once could conduct only in person in the laboratory. Now, through crowd-sourcing and other online employment services, they can rapidly and inexpensively find enough subjects for their studies. One highly popular source is the Mechanical Turk on Amazon, on which people are paid modest amounts for a variety of services including serving as subjects in psychological surveys and experiments (see Emanuel 2014; Mason & Suri, 2012; Paolacci & Chandler, 2014).

Virtual research offers advantages over traditional experimental research. Studies conducted on the Web produce faster responses, are less costly, and have the potential to reach a broader range of subjects of different ages, levels of education, employment, income, social class, and ethnic origin. Online research can assess a population far more diverse than that found on a typical college campus (Crump, McDonnell, & Gurieckis, 2013).

However, online research also has disadvantages. Web users tend to be younger, more affluent, and better educated than nonusers, thus limiting the chances that an online sample will be truly representative of the population as a whole (though still likely to be more representative than a group of college student subjects). Those not likely to be represented in online research include older adults, low-income people, visually impaired, or non-English speakers (Buhrmester, Kwang, & Gosling, 2011; Suarez-Balcazar, Balcazar, & Taylor-Ritzler, 2009).

People who respond to online research may also differ from nonresponders on important personality characteristics. Research conducted in Germany and in the United States found that people who failed to respond to an online survey were judged, on the basis of their personal Web sites, to be more introverted and disagreeable, less open to new experiences, and lower in self-esteem than those who did respond to the survey (Marcus & Schutz, 2005).

A study in which American college students were given the choice of participating in psychological research online or in person found that the more extraverted chose to participate in person and the more introverted chose the online method (Witt, Donnellan, & Orlando, 2011). Other research found no significant differences between online and telephone survey respondents in their willingness to disclose sensitive personal information. The average response rate for online participants was approximately 10 percent lower than for telephone or mail surveys. Also, some 10 percent of online survey participants were found to engage in excessive clicking and mouse movements when responding (Fan & Yan, 2010; Hines, Douglas, & Mahmood, 2010; Stieger & Reips, 2010).

It is difficult to determine how honest and accurate online subjects will be when they provide personal information on factors such as age, gender, ethnic origin, education, or income. Nevertheless, a significant number of studies comparing online and traditional laboratory research methods show that the results are, in general, consistent and similar.

The Correlational Method

In the **Correlational method**, researchers investigate the relationships that exist among variables. Rather than manipulating an independent variable, the experimenters deal with the variable's existing attributes. For example, instead of experimentally creating stressful

correlational method
A statistical technique that measures the degree of the relationship between two variables, expressed by the correlation coefficient.

situations in subjects in the psychology lab and observing the effects, researchers can study people who already function in stressful situations—such as police officers, race car drivers, or college students suffering from test anxiety.

Another way the correlational method differs from the experimental method is that in the correlational approach subjects are not assigned to experimental and control groups. Instead, subjects who differ on an independent variable—such as age, gender, order of birth, level of aggressiveness, or degree of neuroticism—are compared with their performance on some dependent variable, such as personality test responses or job performance measures.

Applying the Correlational Method   Researchers applying the correlational method are interested in the relationship between the variables—in how behavior on one variable changes or differs as a function of the other variable. For example, is birth order related to aggressiveness? Do people who score high on an IQ test make better computer scientists than people who score low? Do people with high anxiety use social media to a greater extent than those low in anxiety? The answers to such questions are useful not only in research but also in real-world situations where predictions have to be made about a person's chances of success. The college entrance examinations you took are based on correlational studies that show the relationship between the two variables of standardized test scores and classroom success.

Suppose a psychologist wanted to determine whether people high in the need for achievement earn higher grades in college than people low in the need for achievement. Using the correlational method, the psychologist would measure the achievement-need levels of a group of already admitted college students using a self-report inventory and compare them with their grades. The independent variable (the different levels of the need for achievement, from high to low) was not manipulated or changed in this case. The researcher worked with existing data and found that students high in the need for achievement did earn higher grades than students low in the need for achievement (Atkinson, Lens, & O'Malley, 1976).

We will see many examples of the use of the correlational method in personality research throughout the book, especially in discussions of the development of assessment techniques. The reliability and validity of assessment devices are typically determined through the correlational method. In addition, many facets of personality have been studied by correlating them with other variables.

The Correlation Coefficient   The primary statistical measure of correlation is the correlation coefficient, which provides precise information about the direction and strength of the relationship between two variables. The direction of the relationship can be positive or negative. If high scores on one variable accompany high scores on the other variable, the direction is positive. If high scores on one variable accompany low scores on the other variable, the direction is negative (see Figure 1.2). Correlation coefficients range from +1.00 (a perfect positive correlation) to −1.00 (a perfect negative correlation). The closer the correlation coefficient is to +1.00 or −1.00, the stronger the relationship and the more confidently we can make predictions about one variable from the other.

Cause and Effect   The primary limitation of the correlational method relates to the matter of cause and effect. Just because two variables show a high correlation with each other, we cannot conclude that one has caused the other. There may indeed be such a relationship, but researchers cannot automatically conclude that one exists, as they can with a well-controlled, systematic experiment.

Suppose a psychologist found a strong negative relationship between the two personality variables of shyness and self-esteem: The higher the level of shyness, the lower the

FIGURE 1.2
Graphs of high positive
and high negative
correlations.

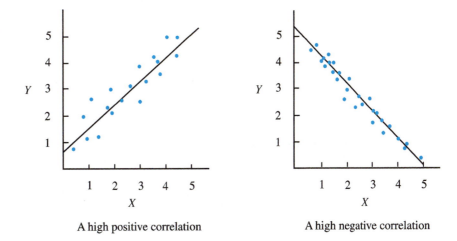

A high positive correlation   A high negative correlation

level of self-esteem. Conversely, the lower the level of shyness, the higher the level of self-esteem. The relationship is clear and straightforward: People who are shy tend to score low on measures of self-esteem. We cannot conclude with certainty, however, that being shy causes people to have low self-esteem. It could be the other way around. Maybe low self-esteem causes people to be shy. Or perhaps some other variable, such as physical appearance or parental rejection, could cause both shyness and low self-esteem.

This restriction on drawing conclusions from correlational research presents problems for researchers, whose goal is to identify specific causes. However, for practitioners, whose goal is to predict behavior in the real world, the correlational method is extremely satisfactory. To be able to predict success in college on the basis of the need for achievement, for example, we need only establish that the two variables have a high correlation.

If a college applicant scores high on a test of the need for achievement, we can predict that he or she will earn good grades in college. In this case, we are not concerned with determining whether the level of the achievement need causes good academic performance, only with whether the two variables are related and whether one can be predicted from the other.

The Role of Theory in Personality Theories

Theories are sometimes referred to in dismissive and contemptuous terms. "After all," people may say, "it's only a theory!" It is popular to assume that a theory is something very vague, abstract, and speculative—really no more than a hunch or a guess and quite the opposite of a fact. It is true that a theory without research evidence to support it is speculation. However, a mass of research data can be meaningless unless and until it is organized into some sort of explanatory framework or context. A theory provides that framework for describing empirical data in a meaningful way. A theory can be considered a kind of map that represents and explains all the data in their interrelationships. It attempts to bring order to the data, to fit them into a meaningful pattern.

Theories are sets of principles used to explain a particular class of phenomena—in our case, the behaviors and experiences relating to personality. If personality theories are to be useful, they must be testable, capable of stimulating research on their various propositions. Researchers must be able to collect data through one or more of the research methods we talked about earlier to determine whether aspects of the theory should be accepted or rejected.

Personality theories must be able to clarify and explain the data of personality by organizing those data into a coherent framework. Theories should also help us understand and predict behavior. Those theories that can be tested and can explain, understand, and predict behavior may then be applied to help people change their behaviors, feelings, and emotions from harmful to helpful, from undesirable to desirable.

The Autobiographical Nature of Personality Theories

We saw that the intent of theories is toward greater objectivity. However, psychologists have long recognized that some personality theories have a subjective component, which may reflect events in the theorist's life as a sort of disguised autobiography. The theorist may draw on these events as a source of data to describe and support his or her theory. No matter how hard scientists try to be impartial and objective, their personal viewpoint is likely to influence their perception to some degree. This should not surprise us. Personality theorists are human too, as we will see, and like most of us they sometimes find it hard to accept ideas that diverge from their own experience.

In order to understand a personality theory fully then, we should learn something about the life of the person who proposed it. It is important to consider how the development of a theory may have been influenced by specific events in a theorist's life. In cases where sufficient biographical information is available, we will see examples of how a theory reflects those events. At least initially, the theorist may have been describing himself or herself. Later, the theorist may have sought appropriate data from other sources to support the generalization of that personal view to others.

The significance of personal events in a theorist's life has long been recognized. William James, who is considered by many to have been the greatest American psychologist, believed that biography was a crucial subject for anyone who attempts to study human nature. He argued that it was even more important to understand eminent persons' lives than it was to know their theories or systems if we wanted to learn about the different ways people approach human experience. Freud put it succinctly and clearly, when he wrote that his most important patient—the one from whom he learned the most about personality—was himself.

One historian noted that "More than any other professional discipline, psychologists have sought to publish biographical and autobiographical sketches of those in their calling.... At some level, at least, they seem to have acknowledged that their lives and values are the key to their 'scientific knowledge'" (Friedman, 1996, p. 221).

We shall see many examples of the autobiographical nature of personality theories, but we must also introduce a note of caution into this intriguing relationship between theory and real life. Perhaps it is not the person's life experiences that influence the development of the theory. Maybe it's the other way around. Perhaps the theory influences what the theorists remember and choose to tell us about their lives. Much of our information about a theorist's life comes from autobiographical recollections. These accounts are usually written late in life, after the person has proposed and defended the theory.

The time spent developing a theory and affirming a public commitment to it may distort the theorist's memories of his or her earlier years. Does the person recall only those life events that support the theory? Are contradictory or troublesome events conveniently forgotten? Are experiences invented to enhance a theory's credibility? Although we cannot always answer these questions, we should keep them in mind while we explore the notion that personality theories may be at least partly autobiographical.

In the end, it may be a question you will have to answer for yourself, recognizing that perhaps experiences in your own life may influence how you come to understand and judge the lives of others—and their theories of personality.

Questions about Human Nature: What Are We Like?

An important aspect of any personality theory is the image of human nature it represents. Each theorist has a conception of human nature that addresses the basic issues of what it means to be human. For centuries, poets, philosophers, and artists have phrased and rephrased these questions, and we see their attempts at answers in our great books and paintings. Personality theorists, too, have addressed these troubling questions and have reached no greater consensus than artists or writers.

The various conceptions of human nature offered by the theorists allow for a meaningful comparison of their views. These ideas are frameworks within which the theorists perceive themselves and other people and then construct their theories. The following text describes the issues that define a theorist's image of human nature. As we discuss each theory, we will consider how the theorist deals with these fundamental issues.

Are We in Charge of Our Lives? Free Will versus Determinism

A basic question about human nature concerns the age-old controversy between free will and determinism. Theorists on both sides of the issue ask, can we consciously direct the course of our actions? Can we spontaneously choose the direction of our thoughts and behavior, rationally selecting among alternatives? Do we have a conscious awareness and a measure of self-control? Are we masters of our fate, or are we victims of past experience, biological factors, unconscious forces, or external stimuli—forces over which we have no conscious control?

Have external events so shaped our personality that we are incapable of changing our behavior? Some personality theorists take extreme positions on this issue. Others express more moderate views, arguing that some behaviors are determined by past events and some can be spontaneous and under our control.

What Dominates Us? Our Inherited Nature or Our Nurturing Environment?

A second issue has to do with the nature–nurture controversy. Which is the more important influence on behavior: inherited traits and attributes (our nature or genetic endowment) or features of our environment (the nurturing influences of our upbringing, education, and training)? Do the abilities, temperaments, and predispositions we inherit determine our personality, or are we shaped more strongly by the conditions under which we live? Personality is not the only topic affected by this issue. Controversy also exists about the question of intelligence: Is intelligence affected more by genetic endowment (nature) or by the stimulation provided by home and school settings (nurture)?

As with the free will–determinism issue, the alternatives are not limited to extreme positions. Many theorists assume that personality is shaped by both sets of forces. To some, inheritance is the predominant influence and environment of minor importance; others hold the opposite view.

Are We Dependent or Independent of Childhood?

A third issue involves the relative importance of our early childhood experiences, compared with events that occur later in life. Which is the more powerful shaper of personality? If we assume, as some theorists do, that what happens to us in infancy and childhood is critical to personality formation, then we must consequently believe that

historical determinism
The view that personality is basically fixed in the early years of life and subject to little change thereafter.

our later development is little more than an elaboration of the basic themes laid down in the early years of life. This view is known as **historical determinism**. Our personality (so this line of thought goes) is mostly fixed by the age of 5 or so and is subject to little change over the rest of our life. The adult personality is determined by the nature of these early experiences.

The opposite position considers personality to be more independent of the past, capable of being influenced by events and experiences in the present as well as by our aspirations, hopes, and goals for the future. An intermediate position has also been proposed. We might assume that early experiences shape personality but not rigidly or permanently. Later experiences may act to reinforce or modify early personality patterns.

Is Human Nature Unique or Universal?

Is human nature unique or universal? This is another issue that divides personality theorists. We may think of personality as so individual that each person's action, each utterance, has no counterpart or equivalent in any other person. This obviously makes the comparison of one person with another meaningless. Other positions allow for uniqueness but interpret this within overall patterns of behavior accepted as universal, at least within a given culture.

Our Life Goals: Satisfaction or Growth?

A fifth issue involves what we might call our ultimate and necessary life goals. Theorists differ on what constitutes our major motivation in life. Do we function like machines, like some sort of self-regulating mechanism, content as long as some internal equilibrium or balance is maintained? Do we act solely to satisfy physical needs, to obtain pleasure and avoid pain? Is our happiness totally dependent on keeping stress to a minimum? Some theorists believe that people are little more than tension-reducing, pleasure-seeking animals. Others consider us to be motivated primarily by the need to grow, to realize our full potential, and to reach for ever-higher levels of self-actualization, development, and fulfillment.

Our Outlook: Optimism or Pessimism?

One final issue reflects a theorist's outlook on life—optimism versus pessimism. Are human beings basically good or evil, kind or cruel, compassionate or merciless? Here we are dealing with a question of morality, a value judgment, which supposedly has no place in the objective and dispassionate world of science.

However, several theorists have dealt with the question and, as we shall see, it has spawned a vital body of research. Some theorists' views of the human personality are more positive and hopeful, depicting us as humanitarian, altruistic, and socially conscious. Other theorists find few of these qualities in human beings, either individually or collectively.

Our general image of human nature is the lens through which we perceive, assess, judge, and interact with other people in our culture. It also represents how we define ourselves. The significance of this is to point out to you that there are many sources of influence on the growth and development of the human personality, and diverse ways of explaining human nature. Perhaps one or more of the explanations we describe in this book will be congenial to you, or perhaps they will clash with your views and your own image of human nature. Few of us can approach this topic without preconceptions because it is, after all, the study of ourselves.

Chapter Summary

Personality can be defined as an enduring, unique cluster of characteristics that may change in different situations. Differences in gender, ethnicity, and cultural background can influence personality development and the results of personality assessment tests. Research in cross-cultural psychology shows how personality can vary from one culture or country to the next. The Internet shapes and reflects personality primarily through social networking sites such as Facebook.

Techniques for assessing or measuring personality must be reliable (defined as the consistency of responses on a test) and valid (the degree to which the test measures what it is intended to measure). The resulting assessment of personality can be influenced by the subject's gender and ethnic identity and by the test administrator's attitudes and beliefs.

Self-report inventories, in which people report on their own behavior and feelings in various situations, are objective in that scores are not influenced by personal or theoretical biases. Most self-report inventories can be administered online. Projective techniques attempt to probe the unconscious by having people project their needs, fears, and values into their interpretation of ambiguous figures or situations. Projective techniques are subjective, low in reliability and validity, and usually poorly standardized.

Clinical interviews are used to assess personality, but the interpretation of interview results is subjective. In behavioral assessment, an observer evaluates a subject's responses in specific situations. In thought and experience sampling, people record their thoughts, feelings, and experiences over a period of time.

People from collectivist societies, such as Asian countries, tend to score lower on factors such as self-enhancement and higher on pessimism, negative affectivity, and psychological distress than people from more individualistic societies such as the United States. Studies of the responses of Blacks and Whites on the MMPI reveal no significant differences as a function of race. Hispanics tend to obtain scores similar to those of Whites on the MMPI but not on projective techniques.

Translations of personality tests must take into account the nature of other cultures with regard to the questions that may be asked, the translated wording, and the way in which the questions are to be answered.

Psychological research methods include the clinical, experimental, virtual, and correlational approaches. Research requires objective observation, controlled and systematic conditions, and duplication and verifiability. The clinical method relies on case studies, in which psychologists reconstruct patients' lives to find clues to their present emotional problems. The clinical approach does not satisfy the requirements of psychological research as well as the experimental and correlational methods do.

The experimental method is the most precise research method. Using this method, psychologists can determine the effect of a single variable or stimulus on the subjects' behavior. The variable being studied (i.e., the stimulus to which the subjects are exposed) is the independent variable; the subjects' responses or behavior is the dependent variable. Internet research offers a faster and less expensive alternative as well as access to a broader range of subjects. Online research has limitations but studies show that it produces results similar to those of laboratory research.

In the correlational method, psychologists study the relationship between two variables to determine how behavior on one variable changes as a function of the other. The correlation coefficient, the primary statistical measure of correlation, indicates the direction and intensity of the relationship.

A theory provides a framework for simplifying and describing data in a meaningful way. Some personality theories may be partly autobiographical, reflecting a theorist's life experiences. Personality theorists present different images of human nature. Some of the issues on which they differ are: free will versus determinism, nature versus nurture, the importance of the past versus the present, uniqueness versus universality, equilibrium versus growth, and optimism versus pessimism. Cultural factors, such as child-rearing practices, can lead to different images of human nature.

Review Questions

1. In what ways does our personality influence our eventual success in interpersonal relations, in our career, and in our general level of health and happiness?

2. Describe various ways of defining personality.
3. Give examples of how the Internet can both shape and reflect our personality.

4. In what ways do the personalities of those who spend considerable time using Facebook differ from the personalities of those who spend less time using it?

5. In what ways may gender and ethnic factors affect the study and assessment of personality?

6. Describe cross-cultural psychology and its impact on the study of personality.

7. Give examples of everyday situations that involve the assessment of personality. Recount your own experience of having your personality evaluated.

8. How would low reliability and validity of an assessment technique affect its usefulness in selecting new employees for a job?

9. Distinguish between self-report techniques and projective techniques for assessing personality. What are the advantages and disadvantages of each approach?

10. How did Hermann Rorschach develop his inkblots? Why did he use only 10 of them?

11. Discuss the advantages of online test administration.

12. Give examples of the behavioral and the thought sampling procedures for assessing personality.

13. What are some limitations of the experience sampling method? How do the data this method provides compare with data from self-report inventories?

14. Give examples of ways in which the personality assessment process can be influenced by a subject's ethnic background.

15. What problems are involved in translating a self-report test developed in the United States for use in a different culture? Give an example of one such problem.

16. Describe the advantages and disadvantages of the case study approach.

17. What three requirements of scientific research are met by the experimental method?

18. Discuss the advantages and limitations of using the Internet for psychological research as compared to more traditional research conducted in a laboratory.

19. Give an example of personality research that uses the correlational method.

20. How might cultural factors affect our image of human nature? Give examples.

21. We asked six questions in our discussion of human nature. Write down your thoughts on these issues. At the end of the book, you will be asked to reconsider these questions to see how your views might have changed.

Suggested Readings

Archer, R., & Smith, S. (2014). *Personality assessment* (2nd ed.). New York: Routledge. An introduction to ways of assessing personality, including the MMPI and other self-report inventories, as well as projective techniques such as the Rorschach and the TAT.

Elms, A. C. (1994). *Uncovering lives: The uneasy alliance of biography and psychology.* New York: Oxford University Press. Contains insightful psychological portraits of writers, political leaders, and personality theorists, including Freud, Jung, Allport, and Skinner.

Funder, D. (2012). *The personality puzzle* (6th ed.). New York: Norton. An easy-to-read introduction to personality, covering all aspect of the field, including applications and theories.

Gosling, S., & Johnson, J. (2010). *Advanced methods for conducting online behavioral research.* Washington, DC: American Psychological Association. A primer for conducting online research, including recruiting subjects, research ethics, data security, and data tracking. Deals with surveys and experimental approaches; for sophisticated computer users.

Kaplan, R., & Saccuzzo, D. (2012). *Psychological testing: principles, applications and issues* (8th ed.). Belmont, CA: Cengage. All you need to know about psychological assessment and testing. Covers correlations, interviewing techniques and various forms of assessment in real-world situations such as counseling and job applications.

Robins, R., Fraley, R., & Krueger, R. (2007). *Handbook of research methods in psychology.* New York: Guilford. A clear introduction to the wide range of research approaches to the study of personality, including experimental, longitudinal, biographical, genetic, self-report, projective, neuroscience, and online research.

The Psychoanalytic Approach

The earliest approach to the formal study of personality was psychoanalysis, the creation of Sigmund Freud, who began his work in the closing years of the 19th century. Nearly every personality theory developed in the years since Freud's work owes a debt to his position—either building on it or opposing it.

Psychoanalysis as Freud conceived it emphasized unconscious forces, biologically based drives of sex and aggression, and unavoidable conflicts in early childhood. These were considered the rulers and shapers of our personality.

Freud's views had an impact not only on psychology but also on the general culture. He succeeded in redefining the human personality and revolutionizing our ways of thinking about human nature—about who we are.

chapter 2

Sigmund Freud: Psychoanalysis

Fair Use

Turn your eyes inward, look into your own depths, learn to first know yourself.

—*Sigmund Freud*

---

psychoanalysis
Sigmund Freud's theory of personality and system of therapy for treating mental disorders.

It is no exaggeration to say that personality theory has been influenced more by Sigmund Freud than by anyone else. His system of **psychoanalysis** was the first formal theory of personality and is still the best known. Not only did Freud's work affect thinking about personality in psychology and psychiatry, but it also made a tremendous impact on the way we look at human nature in general. Few ideas in the history of civilization have had such a broad and profound influence. When he died in 1939, the *New York Times* noted his passing in an editorial stating that Freud was "the most effective disturber of complacency in our time" (quoted in Bakalar, 2011, p. D7).

Many of the personality theories proposed after Freud are derivatives of or elaborations on his basic work. Others owe their impetus and direction in part to their opposition to Freud's psychoanalysis. It would be difficult to comprehend and assess the development of the field of personality without first understanding Freud's system.

The Life of Freud (1856–1939)

The Early Years

Freud was born in 1856, in Freiberg, Moravia, which is now the town of Pribor, in the Czech Republic. His father was a relatively unsuccessful wool merchant. When his business failed in Moravia, he moved the family to Leipzig, Germany, and then later, when Freud was 4, to Vienna, where Freud remained for almost 80 years.

When Freud was born his father was 40 years old and his mother (his father's third wife) was only 20. The father was strict and authoritarian. Freud later remembered how much hostility and anger he felt toward him when he was growing up. He also felt superior to his father as early as age 2. Freud's mother was very attractive and she was extremely protective and loving toward Sigmund, her first son. Freud felt a passionate, even sexual attachment to her, a relationship that set the stage for his concept of the Oedipus complex. As we will see, much of Freud's theory reflected and built on his own experiences as a child.

Freud's mother took pride in young Sigmund, convinced he would become a great man. Among Freud's lifelong personality characteristics were a high degree of self-confidence, an intense ambition to succeed, and dreams of glory and fame. Showing the impact of his mother's continuing attention and support he wrote: "A man who has been the indisputable favorite of his mother keeps for life the feeling of a conqueror, that confidence of success that often induces real success" (quoted in Jones, 1953, p. 5). There were eight children in the Freud family, two of them his adult halfbrothers with children of their own. Freud resented them all and grew jealous whenever another competitor for his mother's full-time attention and affection was born.

From an early age he exhibited a high level of intelligence, which his parents helped to foster. His sisters were not allowed to practice the piano lest the noise disturb Freud's studies. He was given a room of his own; he often took his meals there so as not to lose time from his studies. The room was the only one in the apartment to contain a prized oil lamp; the rest of the family had to use candles.

Freud entered high school a year earlier than was typical and was frequently at the head of his class. He was fluent in German and Hebrew, and mastered Latin, Greek, French, and English in school and taught himself Italian and Spanish. As a youngster he enjoyed reading Shakespeare in English. Freud had many interests, including military history, but when it came time to choose a career from among the few professions that were open to Jews in Vienna, he settled on medicine.

It was not that he wanted to become a physician but rather he believed that the study of medicine would lead to a career in scientific research, which would in turn bring him the fame he so strongly wanted and felt he deserved.

The Cocaine Episode

While in medical school, Freud began to experiment with cocaine, which at that time was not an illegal substance. He took the drug himself and persuaded his fiancée, sisters, and friends to try it. Freud called cocaine a miracle drug and claimed it eased his depression and chronic indigestion. He "continued to use cocaine to make bad days good and good days better. Cocaine thrilled him in a manner that everyday life could not. He wrote romantic, often erotic letters to his fiancée [and] dreamed grandiose dreams of his future career" (Markel, 2011, p. 81).

In 1884, he published an article about cocaine's beneficial effects, thinking it would make him famous. But that was not to be. This article was later judged to be a major contributor to the epidemic of cocaine use which swept over Europe and the United States, lasting well into the 1920s. Freud was strongly criticized for his part in unleashing the cocaine plague.

The publicity later brought him infamy rather than fame, and for the rest of his life he tried to erase his earlier endorsements of cocaine, deleting all references to it from his own bibliography. However, he continued to use cocaine well into middle age (Freud, 1985). He apparently took it from 1884 to 1896, and then switched to wine. In June 1899, he wrote to a friend, "I am gradually becoming accustomed to the wine; it seems like an old friend. I plan to drink a lot of it in July" (quoted in Markel, 2011, p. 177).

Finding the Sexual Basis of Neurosis

Freud was discouraged from pursuing his intended career in scientific research when his major professor told him that it would be many years before he could obtain a professorship and support himself financially. Because he lacked an independent income, he believed his only choice was to enter private practice. A further impetus was his engagement to Martha Bernays, which lasted 4 years before they could afford to marry. Freud established practice as a clinical neurologist in 1881 and began his exploration of the personalities of people suffering from emotional disorders.

He studied several months in Paris with the psychiatrist Jean Martin Charcot, a pioneer in the use of hypnosis, who alerted Freud to the possible sexual basis of neurosis. Freud overheard Charcot say that a particular patient's problem was sexual in origin. "In this sort of case," Charcot said, "it's always a question of the genitals—always, always, always" (Charcot quoted in Freud, 1914, p. 14).

Freud noted that while Charcot was discussing this issue he "crossed his hands in his lap and jumped up and down several times.... for a moment I was almost paralyzed with astonishment" (Freud quoted in Prochnik, 2006, p. 135).

When Freud returned to Vienna, he was again reminded of the possible sexual origin of emotional problems. A colleague described a woman patient's anxiety, which the therapist believed stemmed from her husband's impotence. The husband had never had sexual relations with his wife in 18 years of marriage.

"The sole prescription for such a malady," Freud's colleague said, "is familiar enough to us, but we cannot order it. It runs: *Penis normalis dosim repetatur!*" (quoted in Freud, 1914, p. 14). As a result of these incidents, and his own sexual conflicts, Freud was led to consider the possibility of a sexual basis for emotional disturbance.

Childhood Sexual Abuse: Fact or Fantasy?

After several years in clinical practice, Freud was increasingly convinced that sexual conflicts were the primary cause of all neuroses. He claimed that the majority of his women patients reported traumatic sexual experiences from their childhoods. These events resembled seduction, with the seducer usually being an older male relative, typically the father. Today we call such experiences child abuse, and they often involve rape or incest. Freud believed that it was these early sexual traumas that caused neurotic behavior in adulthood.

About a year after he published this theory, Freud changed his mind and announced that in most cases the childhood sexual abuse his patients told him about had never really happened. They had been telling him fantasies, Freud claimed. At first, this was a stunning blow, for it seemed that the foundation of his theory of neurosis had been undermined. How could childhood sexual traumas be the cause of neurotic behavior if they had never happened?

On further reflection, Freud concluded that the fantasies his patients described were quite real to them. They believed that the shocking sexual events had actually happened. Because the fantasies still focused on sex, then sex remained the cause of adult neuroses. In 1898, he wrote that "the most immediate and most significant causes of neurotic illness are to be found in factors arising from sexual life" (quoted in Breger, 2000, p. 117).

It is important to note that Freud never claimed that all the childhood sexual abuses his patients reported were fantasies; what he did deny was that his patients' reports were *always* true. It was, Freud wrote, "hardly credible that perverted acts against children were so general" (Freud, 1954, pp. 215–216).

Today we know that childhood sexual abuse is much more common than once thought, which led contemporary scholars to suggest that Freud's original interpretation of the seduction experiences may have been correct. We do not know whether Freud deliberately suppressed the truth, perhaps to make his theory more acceptable, or whether he genuinely believed that his patients were describing fantasies. It may well be that "more of Freud's patients were telling the truth about their childhood experiences than [Freud] was ultimately prepared to believe" (Crewsdon, 1988, p. 41).

Ten years after Freud changed his mind and announced that childhood seduction scenarios were fantasies, he admitted in a letter to a friend that such traumatic experiences were frequently genuine. A few years later he confided to another friend that "I have myself analyzed and cured several cases of real incest (of the most severe kind)" (quotes from Kahr, 2010, p. 4).

The conclusion that child sexual abuse occurred more often than Freud was willing to admit publicly was reached by one of Freud's disciples in the 1930s, and Freud tried to suppress the publication of his ideas. It has also been suggested that Freud changed his position on the seduction theory because he realized that if sexual abuse was so widespread, then many fathers (including perhaps his own) would be considered suspect of perverse acts against their children (Krüll, 1986).

Freud's Own Sex Life

It is a paradox that Freud, who emphasized the importance of sex in emotional life, experienced so many personal sexual conflicts. He "had no contact with members of the opposite sex throughout [his early years]. He was decidedly shy and afraid of women and was a virgin when he married at age 30" (Breger, 2009, p. 11). His attitude toward sex was negative. He wrote about the dangers of sex, even for those who were not neurotic, and urged people to rise above what he called the common animal need for sex.

The sex act was degrading, he wrote, because it contaminated both mind and body. He apparently ended his own sex life at the age of 41, writing to a friend: "sexual excitation is of no more use to a person like me" (Freud, 1954, p. 227). He occasionally had been impotent during his marriage and had sometimes chosen to abstain from sex because he disliked condoms and *coitus interruptus*, the standard birth control methods of the day.

Freud blamed his wife, Martha, for the termination of his sex life, and for many years he had dreams involving his resentment toward her for forcing him to abandon sex. "He felt resentful because she became pregnant so easily, because she often became ill during her pregnancies, and because she refused to engage in any kind of sexual activity beyond [procreative acts]" (Elms, 1994, p. 45). Thus, Freud's periods of impotence may also have been related to his fear that Martha would become pregnant again.

Freud's Neurotic Episode

Freud's personal frustrations and conflicts about sex surfaced in the form of neuroses, in the same way he believed sexual difficulties affected his patients. In his 40s, he experienced a severe neurotic episode, which he described as involving "odd states of mind not intelligible to consciousness—cloudy thoughts and veiled doubts, with barely here and there a ray of light…. I still do not know what has been happening to me" (Freud, 1954, pp. 210–212). He was also troubled by a variety of physical symptoms, including migraine headaches, urinary problems, and a spastic colon. He worried about dying, feared for his heart, and became anxious about travel and open spaces. It was not a happy time for him.

Freud diagnosed his condition as anxiety neurosis and neurasthenia—a neurotic condition characterized by weakness, worry, and disturbances of digestion and circulation. He traced both disturbances to an accumulation of sexual tension. In his writings, he proposed that neurasthenia in men resulted from masturbation, and anxiety neurosis arose from abnormal sexual practices such as *coitus interruptus* and abstinence. By so labeling his symptoms, "his personal life was thus deeply involved in this particular theory, since with its help he was trying to interpret and solve his own problems…. Freud's theory of actual neurosis is thus a theory of his own neurotic symptoms" (Krüll, 1986, pp. 14, 20).

Despite Freud's personal conflicts about sex (or perhaps because of them), he was fascinated by beautiful women. A friend noted that "among [Freud's] students there were so many attractive women that it began to look like more than a matter of chance" (Roazen, 1993, p. 138).

Analyzing Freud's Dreams

Freud psychoanalyzed himself through the study of his own dreams, a process he continued for the rest of his life. When he started, he wrote to a friend that "The chief patient I am busy with is myself" (quoted in Kandel, 2012, p. 63). It was during this period that he performed his most creative work in developing his theory of personality. Through the exploration of his dreams, he realized, for the first time, how much hostility he felt toward his father. He recalled his childhood sexual longings for his mother and dreamed of a sex wish toward his eldest daughter. Thus, he formulated much of his theory around his own neurotic conflicts and childhood experiences, as filtered through his interpretations of his dreams. As he perceptively observed, "The most important patient for me was my own person" (Freud quoted in Gay, 1988, p. 96).

Freud's Ideas Attract Attention

As his work became known through published articles and books as well as papers presented at scientific meetings, Freud attracted a group of disciples who met with him once a week to learn about his new system. The topic of their first meeting was the psychology of cigar making. One writer referred to the group as a second-rate "collection of marginal neurotics" (Gardner, 1993, p. 51). Freud's daughter Anna described the early disciples a bit more charitably as the "unconventional ones, the doubters, those who were dissatisfied with the limitations imposed on knowledge; also among them were the odd ones, the dreamers, and those who knew neurotic suffering from their own experience" (quoted in Coles, 1998, p. 144).

The disciples included Carl Jung and Alfred Adler, who later broke with Freud to develop their own theories. Freud considered them traitors to the cause, and he never forgave them for disputing his approach to psychoanalysis. At a family dinner, he complained about his followers' disloyalty. "The trouble with you, Sigi," said his aunt, "is that you just don't understand people" (quoted in Hilgard, 1987, p. 641).

At home, Freud led a disciplined and regimented life. His daughter-in-law remarked, "The Freuds had their noontime meal, the main meal in Vienna, at the stroke of one, and war or no war, you had to be there on time or not eat" (quoted in Berman, 2008, p. 561).

Freud Comes to America

In 1909, Freud received formal recognition from the American psychological community. He was invited to give a series of lectures at Clark University in Worcester, Massachusetts, and to receive an honorary doctoral degree. Although grateful for the honor, Freud did not like the United States, and complained about its informality, bad cooking, and scarcity of bathrooms. Although he had been troubled by gastrointestinal problems for many years prior to his visit, "he blamed the New World for ruining his digestion" (Prochnik, 2006, p. 35).

Freud's system of psychoanalysis was warmly welcomed in the United States. Two years after his visit, American followers founded the American Psychoanalytic Association and the New York Psychoanalytic Society. Over the next few years, psychoanalytic societies were established in Boston, Chicago, and Washington DC.

In 1920, only 11 years after his visit to America, more than 200 books on his work had been published in the United States (Abma, 2004). Leading U.S. magazines such as *Time, Ladies' Home Journal*, and *The New Republic* featured articles about Freud. Dr. Benjamin Spock's phenomenally successful baby and child care books that influenced the raising of several generations of America children were based on Freud's teachings. Freud's work on dreams even inspired a popular song that included the line: "Don't tell me what you dream'd last night—For I've been reading Freud" (quoted in Fancher, 2000, p. 1026). America may have made Freud sick, so he claimed, but it also helped bring him worldwide fame.

The Final Years

During the 1920s and 1930s, Freud reached the pinnacle of his success, but at the same time his health began to deteriorate seriously. From 1923 until his death 16 years later, he underwent 33 operations for cancer of the mouth, perhaps as a result of his smoking 20 cigars daily. Portions of his palate and upper jaw were surgically removed, and he experienced almost constant pain, for which he refused medication. He also received X-ray and radium treatments and even had a vasectomy, which some physicians thought would halt the growth of the cancer.

When the Nazis came to power in Germany in 1933, they expressed their feelings about Freud by publicly burning his books, along with those of other so-called "enemies of the state," such as the physicist Albert Einstein and the writer Ernest Hemingway. "What progress we are making," Freud wrote. "In the Middle Ages they would have burnt me; nowadays they are content with burning my books" (Freud quoted in Jones, 1957, p. 182).

In 1938, the Nazis occupied Austria, but despite the urgings of his friends, Freud refused to leave Vienna. Several times gangs of Nazis invaded his home. It was not until his daughter Anna was arrested (and later released) that Freud agreed to leave for London. Four of his sisters died in Nazi concentration camps.

Freud's health became even worse, but he remained mentally alert and continued to work almost to the last day of his life. By late September 1939, he told his physician, Max Schur, "Now it's nothing but torture and makes no sense any more" (quoted in Schur, 1972, p. 529). The doctor had promised that he would not let Freud suffer needlessly. He administered three injections of morphine over the next 24 hours, each dose greater than necessary for sedation, and brought Freud's long years of pain to an end.

Sigmund Freud

Various sites provide biographical information, discussions of his theory, research on relevant concepts, and links to other resources.

The Sigmund Freud Museum, London

Visit the Freud Museum in London to see photos, depictions of Freud's years in England, and furnishings from his home in Vienna, including the famous psychoanalytic couch. You can also purchase a Freud T-shirt, coffee mug, mouse pad, jigsaw puzzle, or beanie.

Library of Congress: Freud Exhibition

The exhibition on Freud displayed at the Library of Congress in Washington DC, in 1998, contains many photographs and other items of interest.

Instincts: The Propelling Forces of the Personality

instincts In Freud's system, mental representations of internal stimuli, such as hunger, that drive a person to take certain actions.

Freud wrote that **instincts** were the basic elements of the personality, the motivating forces that drive behavior and determine its direction. Freud's German term for this concept is *Trieb*, which is a driving force or impulse (Bettelheim, 1984). Instincts are a form of energy—transformed physiological energy—that connects the needs of the body with the wishes of the mind.

The stimuli for instincts—hunger and thirst, for example—are internal. When a need such as hunger is aroused in the body, it generates a state of physiological excitation or energy. The mind transforms this bodily energy into a wish. It is this wish—the mental representation of the physiological need—that is the instinct or driving force that motivates the person to behave in a way that satisfies the need. A hungry person, for example, will look for food. The instinct is not the bodily state itself (the hunger). Rather, it is the bodily need transformed into a mental state, a wish.

When the body is in such a state of need, the person experiences a feeling of tension or pressure. The aim of an instinct is to satisfy the need and thereby reduce the tension. Freud's theory is therefore a homeostatic approach, meaning that we are motivated to restore and maintain a condition of physiological equilibrium, or balance, to keep the body free of tension.

Freud believed that we always experience a certain level or amount of instinctual tension and that we must continually act to reduce it. It is not possible to escape the pressure of our physiological needs as we might escape some annoying stimulus in our external environment. This means that instincts are always influencing our behavior, in a cycle of need leading to reduction of need.

People may take different paths to satisfy their needs. For example, the sex drive may be satisfied by heterosexual behavior, homosexual behavior, or autosexual behavior, or the sex drive may be channeled into a totally different form of activity. Freud believed that psychic energy could be displaced to substitute objects, and this displacement was of primary importance in determining an individual's personality.

Although the instincts are the exclusive source of energy for human behavior, the resulting energy can be invested in a variety of activities. This helps explain the diversity we see in human behavior. All the interests, preferences, and attitudes we display as adults were believed by Freud to be displacements of energy from the original objects that satisfied the instinctual needs.

Two Types of Instincts

Freud grouped the instincts into two categories: life instincts and death instincts.

life instincts The drive for ensuring survival of the individual and the species by satisfying the needs for food, water, air, and sex.

libido To Freud, the form of psychic energy, manifested by the life instincts, that drives a person toward pleasurable behaviors and thoughts.

cathexis An investment of psychic energy in an object or person.

The Life Instincts   The **life instincts** serve the purpose of survival of the individual and the species by seeking to satisfy the needs for food, water, air, and sex.

The life instincts are oriented toward growth and development. The psychic energy manifested by the life instincts is the **libido**. The libido can be attached to or invested in objects, a concept Freud called **cathexis**. If you like your roommate, for example, Freud would say that your libido is cathected to him or her.

The life instinct Freud considered most important for the personality is sex, which he defined in broad terms. He was not referring exclusively to the erotic, but also included almost all pleasurable behaviors and thoughts. He described his view as enlarging or extending the accepted concept of sexuality. He considered the sexual impulses to include "all of those merely affectionate and friendly impulses to which usage applies the exceedingly ambiguous word 'love'" (Freud, 1925, p. 38).

Freud regarded sex as our primary motivation. Erotic wishes arise from the body's erogenous zones: the mouth, anus, and sex organs. He suggested that people are predominantly pleasure-seeking beings, and much of his personality theory revolves around the necessity of inhibiting or suppressing our sexual longings.

death instincts The unconscious drive toward decay, destruction, and aggression.

aggressive drive The compulsion to destroy, conquer, and kill.

The Death Instincts   In opposition to the life instincts, Freud postulated the destructive or **death instincts**. Drawing from biology, he stated the obvious fact that all living things decay and die, returning to their original inanimate state, and he believed that people have an unconscious wish to die. One component of the death instincts is the **aggressive drive**, which he saw as the wish to die turned against objects other than the self. The aggressive drive compels us to destroy, conquer, and kill. Freud came to consider aggression as compelling a part of human nature as sex.

Freud developed the notion of the death instincts later in his life, as a reflection of his own experiences. He endured the physiological and psychological debilitations of age, his cancer got worse, and he witnessed the large-scale carnage of World War I. In addition, one of his daughters died at the age of 26, leaving two young children. All these events affected him deeply, and, as a result, death and aggression became major themes in his theory, and in his own life as well. In his later years, Freud dreaded his own death, and exhibited high levels of hostility, hatred, and aggressiveness toward those colleagues and disciples who disputed his views and left his psychoanalytic circle.

The concept of the death instincts achieved only limited acceptance, even among Freud's most dedicated followers. One psychoanalyst wrote that the idea should be "relegated to the dustbin of history" (Sulloway, 1979, p. 394). Another suggested that if Freud were a genius, then the suggestion of the death instincts was an instance of a genius having a bad day (Eissler, 1971).

The Levels of Personality

Freud's original conception divided personality into three levels: the conscious, the preconscious, and the unconscious. The conscious, as Freud defined the term, corresponds to its ordinary everyday meaning. It includes all the sensations and experiences of which we are aware at any given moment. As you read these words, for example, you may be conscious of the sight of the page, a message you want to send to a friend, and someone playing loud music next door.

Freud considered the conscious to be a limited aspect of personality because only a small portion of our thoughts, sensations, and memories exists in conscious awareness at any one time. He likened the mind to an iceberg. The conscious is that part above the surface of the water—the tip of the iceberg.

More important, according to Freud, is the unconscious, that larger, invisible portion below the surface. This is the focus of psychoanalytic theory. Its vast, dark depths are the home of the instincts, those wishes and desires that direct our behavior. The unconscious contains the major driving power behind all behaviors and is the repository of forces we cannot see or control.

Between these two levels is the preconscious. This is the storehouse of all our memories, perceptions, and thoughts of which we are not consciously aware at the moment but that we can easily summon into consciousness. For example, in the unlikely event your mind strays from this page and you begin to think about what you did last night, you would be summoning up material from your preconscious into your conscious. We often find our attention shifting back and forth from experiences of the moment to events and memories in the preconscious.

The Structure of Personality

The Id

id To Freud, the aspect of personality allied with the instincts; the source of psychic energy, the id operates according to the pleasure principle.

Freud later revised this notion of three levels of personality and introduced in its place three basic structures in the anatomy of the personality: the id, the ego, and the superego (see Figure 2.1). The **id** corresponds to Freud's earlier notion of the unconscious (although the ego and superego have unconscious aspects as well). The id is the reservoir for the instincts and libido (the psychic energy manifested by the instincts). The id is a powerful structure of the personality because it supplies all the energy for the other two components.

Because the id is the reservoir of the instincts, it is vitally and directly related to the satisfaction of bodily needs. As we saw earlier, tension is produced when the body is in a state of need, and the person acts to reduce this tension by satisfying the need. The id

FIGURE 2.1
Freud's levels and structures of personality.

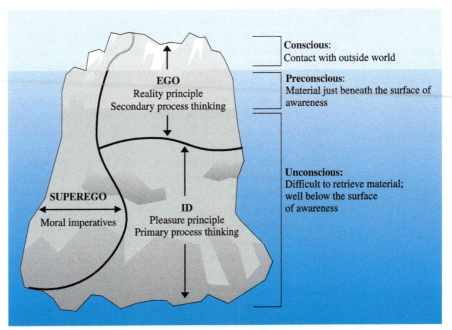

Source: From Weiten, *Psychology: Themes and Variations*, 2E. © 1992 Cengage Learning.

pleasure principle The principle by which the id functions to avoid pain and maximize pleasure.

operates in accordance with what Freud called the **pleasure principle**. Through its concern with tension reduction, the id functions to increase pleasure and avoid pain.

The id strives for immediate satisfaction of its needs and does not tolerate delay or postponement of satisfaction for any reason. It knows only instant gratification; it drives us to want what we want when we want it, without regard for what anyone else wants. The id is a selfish, pleasure-seeking structure—primitive, amoral, insistent, and rash.

primary-process thought Childlike thinking by which the id attempts to satisfy the instinctual drives.

The id has no awareness of reality. We might compare the id to a newborn baby who cries and frantically waves its legs and arms when its needs are not met but who has no knowledge of how to bring about satisfaction. Hungry infants cannot find food on their own. The only ways the id can attempt to satisfy its needs are through reflex action and wish-fulfilling hallucinatory or fantasy experience, which Freud labeled **primary-process thought**.

The Ego

Most children learn that they cannot grab food from other people unless they are willing to face the consequences. For example, kids learn that they have to postpone the pleasure obtained from relieving anal tensions until they get to a bathroom, or that they cannot indiscriminately give vent to sexual and aggressive longings. The growing child is taught to deal intelligently and rationally with other people and the outside world and to develop the powers of perception, recognition, judgment, and memory—the powers adults use to satisfy their needs. Freud called these abilities **secondary-process thought**.

secondary-process thought Mature thought processes needed to deal rationally with the external world.

We can sum up these characteristics as reason or rationality, and they are contained in Freud's second structure of personality, the **ego**, which is the rational master of the personality. Its purpose is not to thwart the impulses of the id but to help the id obtain the tension reduction it craves. Because the ego is aware of reality, however, it decides when and how the id instincts can best be satisfied. It determines appropriate and socially acceptable times, places, and objects that will satisfy the id impulses.

ego To Freud, the rational aspect of the personality, responsible for directing and controlling the instincts according to the reality principle.

The ego does not prevent id satisfaction. Rather, it tries to postpone, delay, or redirect it in order to meet the demands of reality. It perceives and manipulates the environment in a practical and realistic manner and so is said to operate in accordance with the **reality principle**. (The reality principle stands in opposition to the pleasure principle, by which the id operates.)

reality principle The principle by which the ego functions to provide appropriate constraints on the expression of the id instincts.

The ego thus exerts control over the id impulses. Freud compared the relationship of the ego and the id to that of a rider on a horse. The raw, brute power of the horse must be guided, checked, and reined in by the rider; otherwise the horse could bolt and run, throwing the rider to the ground.

The ego serves two masters—the id and reality—and is constantly mediating and striking compromises between their conflicting demands. Also, the ego is never independent of the id. It is always responsive to the id's demands and derives its power and energy from the id.

It is the ego, the rational master, which keeps you working at a job you may not like, if the alternative is being unable to provide food and shelter for your family. It is the ego that forces you to get along with people you dislike because reality demands such behavior from you as an appropriate way of satisfying id demands.

This controlling and postponing function of the ego must be exercised constantly. If not, the id impulses might come to dominate and overthrow the rational ego. A person controlled by the id can easily become a danger to society, and might end up in treatment or in prison. Freud argued that we must protect ourselves from being controlled by the id and proposed various unconscious mechanisms with which to defend the ego.

So far, we have a picture of Freud's view of the human personality as being in a constant state of battle. It's trying to restrain the id while at the same time serving it, perceiving and manipulating reality to relieve the tensions of the id impulses. Driven by instinctual biological forces that it strives to satisfy, the personality walks a tightrope between the demands of the id and the demands of reality, both of which require constant vigilance.

The Superego

The id and the ego do not represent Freud's complete picture of human nature. There is also a third set of forces—a powerful and largely unconscious set of dictates or beliefs—that we acquire in childhood: our ideas of right and wrong. In everyday language we call this internal morality a conscience. Freud called it the **superego**.

He believed that this moral side of the personality is usually learned by the age of 5 or 6 and consists initially of the rules of conduct set down by our parents. Through praise, punishment, and example, children learn which behaviors their parents consider good or bad. Those behaviors for which children are punished form the **conscience**, one part of the superego. The second part of the superego is the **ego-ideal**, which consists of good, or correct, behaviors for which children have been praised.

In this way, Freud believed, children learn a set of rules that earn either acceptance or rejection from their parents. In time, children internalize these teachings, and the rewards and punishments become self-administered. Parental control is replaced by self-control. We come to behave at least in partial conformity with these now largely unconscious moral guidelines. As a result of this internalization, we feel guilt or shame whenever we perform (or even think of performing) some action contrary to this moral code.

As the ultimate arbiter of morality, the superego is relentless, even cruel, in its constant quest for moral perfection. It never lets up. In terms of intensity, irrationality, and insistence on obedience, it is not unlike the id. Its purpose is not merely to postpone the pleasure-seeking demands of the id, as the ego does, but to inhibit them completely, particularly those demands concerned with sex and aggression.

The superego strives neither for pleasure (as the id does) nor for attainment of realistic goals (as the ego does). It strives solely for moral perfection. The id presses for satisfaction, the ego tries to delay it, and the superego urges morality above all. Like the id, the superego admits no compromise with its demands.

The ego is caught in the middle, pressured by these insistent and opposing forces. Thus, the ego has a third master, the superego. To paraphrase Freud, the poor ego has a hard time of it, pressured on three sides, threatened by three dangers: the id, reality, and the superego. The inevitable result of this friction, when the ego is too severely strained, is the development of anxiety.

Anxiety: A Threat to the Ego

You already have a general idea of what the word *anxiety* means because you know how you feel when you're anxious about something. Anxiety is not unlike fear, but we may not know what we're afraid of. Freud described **anxiety** as an objectless fear, meaning that we cannot point to its source, to a specific object that caused it.

Freud made anxiety an important part of his personality theory, asserting that it is fundamental to the development of all neurotic and psychotic behavior. He suggested that the prototype of all anxiety is the birth trauma.

The fetus in its mother's womb is in the most stable and secure of worlds, where every need is satisfied without delay. But at birth, the organism is thrust into a hostile environment. Suddenly, it is required to begin adapting to reality because its instinctual demands may not always be immediately met. The newborn's nervous system, immature and ill prepared, is bombarded with diverse sensory stimuli.

Consequently, the infant engages in massive motor movements, heightened breathing, and increased heart rate. This birth trauma, with its tension and fear that the id instincts

superego To Freud, the moral aspect of personality; the internalization of parental and societal values and standards.

conscience A component of the superego that contains behaviors for which the child has been punished.

ego-ideal A component of the superego that contains the moral or ideal behaviors for which a person should strive.

anxiety To Freud, a feeling of fear and dread without an obvious cause; **reality anxiety** is a fear of tangible dangers; **neurotic anxiety** involves a conflict between id and ego; **moral anxiety** involves a conflict between id and superego.

won't be satisfied, is our first experience with anxiety, according to Freud. From it, the pattern of reactions and feelings that will occur every time we are exposed to some threat in the future develops.

When we cannot cope with anxiety, when we are in danger of being overwhelmed by it, the anxiety is said to be traumatic. What Freud meant by this is that the person, regardless of age, is reduced to a state of helplessness like that experienced in infancy. In adult life, infantile helplessness is reenacted to some degree whenever the ego is threatened. Freud proposed three different types of anxiety: reality anxiety, neurotic anxiety, and moral anxiety.

Reality Anxiety

The first type of anxiety, the one from which the others are derived, is **reality anxiety** (or objective anxiety). This involves a fear of real dangers in the real world. Most of us justifiably fear fires, hurricanes, earthquakes, and similar disasters. We run from wild animals, jump out of the paths of speeding cars, and run out of burning buildings.

Reality anxiety serves the positive purpose of guiding our behavior to escape or protect ourselves from actual dangers. Our fear subsides when the threat is no longer present. These reality-based fears can be carried to extremes, however. The person who cannot leave home for fear of being hit by a car or who cannot light a match for fear of fire is carrying reality-based fears beyond the point of normality.

Neurotic Anxiety

The other kinds of anxiety, neurotic anxiety and moral anxiety, are more consistently troublesome to our mental health. **Neurotic anxiety** has its basis in childhood, in a conflict between instinctual gratification and reality. Children are often punished for overtly expressing sexual or aggressive impulses. Therefore, the wish to gratify certain id impulses generates anxiety.

This neurotic anxiety is an unconscious fear of being punished for impulsively displaying id-dominated behavior. Note that the fear is not of the instincts themselves, but of what might happen as a result of gratifying the instincts. The conflict becomes one between the id and the ego, and its origin has some basis in reality.

Moral Anxiety

Moral anxiety results from a conflict between the id and the superego. In essence, it is a fear of one's conscience. When you are motivated to express an instinctual impulse that is contrary to your moral code, your superego retaliates by causing you to feel shame or guilt. In everyday terms, you might describe yourself as conscience-stricken.

Moral anxiety is a function of how well developed the superego is. A person with a strong inhibiting conscience will experience greater conflict than a person with a less stringent set of moral guidelines. Like neurotic anxiety, moral anxiety has some basis in reality.

Children are punished for violating their parents' moral codes, and adults are punished for violating society's moral code. The shame and guilt feelings in moral anxiety arise from within; it is our conscience that causes the fear and the anxiety. Freud believed that the superego exacts a terrible retribution for violation of its tenets.

The Purpose of Anxiety

Anxiety serves as a warning to the person that something is amiss within the personality. Anxiety induces tension in the organism and thus becomes a drive (much like hunger or thirst) that the individual is motivated to satisfy. The tension must be reduced.

Anxiety alerts the individual that the ego is being threatened and that unless action is taken, the ego might be overthrown. How can the ego protect or defend itself? There are a number of options: running away from the threatening situation, inhibiting the impulsive need that is the source of the danger, or obeying the dictates of the conscience. If none of these rational techniques works, the person may resort to defense mechanisms—the nonrational strategies designed to defend the ego.

Defenses against Anxiety

We saw that anxiety is a signal that impending danger, a threat to the ego, must be counteracted or avoided. The ego has to reduce the conflict between the demands of the id and the strictures of society as represented by the superego. According to Freud, this conflict is ever present because the instincts are always pressing for satisfaction, while the taboos of society are always working to limit such satisfaction.

Freud believed that the defenses must, to some extent, always be in operation. All behaviors are motivated by instincts; similarly, all behaviors are defensive in the sense of defending against anxiety. The intensity of the battle within the personality may fluctuate, but it never stops. Freud postulated several **defense mechanisms** (see Table 2.1) and noted that we rarely use just one; we typically defend ourselves against anxiety by using several at the same time. Also, some overlap exists among the mechanisms.

Although defense mechanisms vary in their specifics, they share two characteristics in common: (1) they are all denials or distortions of reality—necessary ones, but distortions nonetheless, and (2) they all operate unconsciously. We are unaware of them, which means that on the conscious level we hold distorted or unreal images of our world and ourselves.

Repression **repression**, which is the most fundamental and frequently used defense mechanism, is an involuntary removal of something from conscious awareness. It is an unconscious type of forgetting of the existence of something that brings us discomfort or pain. Repression can operate on memories of situations or people, on our perception of the present (so that we may fail to see some obviously disturbing event right in front of us), and even on the body's physiological functioning. For example, a man can so strongly repress the sex drive that he becomes impotent.

Once repression is operating, it is difficult to eliminate. Because we use repression to protect ourselves from danger, in order to remove it, we would have to realize that the idea or memory is no longer dangerous. But how can we find out that the danger no

defense mechanisms
Strategies the ego uses to defend itself against the anxiety provoked by conflicts of everyday life. Defense mechanisms involve denials or distortions of reality.

repression A defense mechanism that involves unconscious denial of the existence of something that causes anxiety.

TABLE 2.1   Some Freudian defense mechanisms

Repression: Involves unconscious denial of the existence of something that causes anxiety

Denial: Involves denying the existence of an external threat or traumatic event

Reaction Formation: Involves expressing an id impulse that is the opposite of the one truly driving the person

Projection: Involves attributing a disturbing impulse to someone else

Regression: Involves retreating to an earlier, less frustrating period of life and displaying the childish and dependent behaviors characteristic of that more secure time

Rationalization: Involves reinterpreting behavior to make it more acceptable and less threatening

Displacement: Involves shifting id impulses from a threatening or unavailable object to a substitute object that is available

Sublimation: Involves altering or displacing id impulses by diverting instinctual energy into socially acceptable behaviors

denial A defense mechanism that involves denying the existence of an external threat or traumatic event.

reaction formation A defense mechanism that involves expressing an id impulse that is the opposite of the one that is truly driving the person.

projection A defense mechanism that involves attributing a disturbing impulse to someone else.

regression A defense mechanism that involves retreating to an earlier, less frustrating period of life and displaying the usually childish behaviors characteristic of that more secure time.

rationalization A defense mechanism that involves reinterpreting our behavior to make it more acceptable and less threatening to us.

displacement A defense mechanism that involves shifting id impulses from a threatening object or from one that is unavailable to an object that is available; for example, replacing hostility toward one's boss with hostility toward one's child.

sublimation A defense mechanism that involves altering or displacing id impulses by diverting instinctual energy into socially acceptable behaviors.

longer exists unless we release the repression so we can once again be aware of the memory? The concept of repression is the basis of much of Freud's personality theory and is involved in all neurotic behavior.

Denial   The defense mechanism of **denial** is related to repression and involves denying the existence of some external threat or traumatic event that has occurred. For example, a person with a terminal illness may deny the imminence of death. Parents of a child who has died may continue to deny the loss by keeping the child's room unchanged.

Reaction Formation   In **reaction formation**, we defend ourselves against a disturbing impulse by actively expressing the opposite impulse. For example, a person who feels threatened by sexual longings may become a rabid crusader against pornography. Someone who is disturbed by extreme aggressive impulses may become overly solicitous and friendly. Thus, lust becomes virtue and hatred becomes love, in the unconscious mind of the person using this mechanism.

Projection   Another way of defending against disturbing impulses is to project them on to someone else. This defense mechanism is called **projection**. Lustful, aggressive, and other unacceptable impulses are seen as being possessed by other people, not by oneself. The person says, in effect, "I don't hate him. He hates me." Or a mother may ascribe her sex drive to her adolescent daughter. The impulse is still manifested, but in a way that feels less threatening to the individual.

Regression   In **regression**, the person retreats or regresses to an earlier period of life that was more pleasant and free of the current level of frustration and anxiety. Regression usually involves a return to one of the stages of childhood development. The individual returns to this more secure time of life by behaving as they did at that time, such as being childish and dependent.

Rationalization   **Rationalization** is a defense mechanism that involves reinterpreting our behavior to make it seem more rational and therefore more acceptable. We excuse or justify a threatening thought or action by persuading ourselves that there is a rational explanation for it. The person who is fired from a job may rationalize by saying that they really didn't like the job anyway. The loved one who turns you down now appears to have many faults. It is less threatening to blame someone or something else for our failures than to blame ourselves.

Displacement   If an object that satisfies an id impulse is not available, the person may shift the impulse to another object. This is known as **displacement**. For example, children who hate their parents or adults who hate their bosses, but are afraid to express their hostility for fear of being punished, may displace the aggression onto someone else—usually someone who is less likely to fight back or retaliate.

The child may hit a younger brother or sister, or the adult may shout at the dog. In these examples, the original object of the aggressive impulse has been replaced by an object that is not a threat. However, the substitute object will not reduce the tension as satisfactorily as the original object would. If you are involved in a number of displacements, a reservoir of undischarged tension accumulates, and you will be increasingly driven to find new ways of reducing that tension.

Sublimation   Whereas displacement involves finding a substitute object to satisfy id impulses, **sublimation** involves altering the id impulses themselves. The instinctual energy is thus diverted into other channels of expression, ones that society considers acceptable and admirable. Sexual energy, for example, can be diverted or sublimated into artistically creative behaviors.

Freud believed that a variety of human activities, particularly those of an artistic nature, are manifestations of id impulses that have been redirected into socially acceptable outlets. As with displacement (of which sublimation is a form), sublimation is a compromise. As such, it does not bring total satisfaction but leads to a buildup of undischarged tension.

Lying to Ourselves

As we have seen, these defense mechanisms are unconscious denials or distortions of reality. We are lying to ourselves when we use these defenses, but we are not aware of doing so. If we knew we were lying to ourselves, the defenses would not be so effective. If the defenses are working well, they keep threatening or disturbing material out of our conscious awareness. As a result, we may not know the truth about ourselves. We may have a distorted picture of our needs, fears, and desires.

There are situations in which the truth about ourselves emerges, when our defenses break down and fail to protect us. This occurs in times of unusual stress (or when undergoing psychoanalysis). When the defenses fail, we are stricken with overwhelming anxiety. We feel dismal, worthless, and depressed. Unless the defenses are restored, or new ones formed to take their place, we are likely to develop neurotic or psychotic symptoms. Thus, according to Freud, defenses are necessary to our mental health. We could not survive long without them.

Psychosexual Stages of Personality Development

Freud believed that all behaviors are defensive but that not everyone uses the same defenses in the same way. All of us are driven by the same id impulses, but there is not the same universality in the nature of the ego and superego. Although these structures of the personality perform the same functions for everyone, their content varies from one person to another. They differ because they are formed through experience, and no two people have precisely the same experiences, not even siblings raised in the same house.

Thus, part of our personality is formed on the basis of the unique relationships we have as children with various people and objects. We develop a personal set of character attributes, a consistent pattern of behavior that defines each of us as an individual.

Growing up Is Not Easy

psychosexual stages of development To Freud, the oral, anal, phallic, and genital stages through which all children pass. In these stages, gratification of the id instincts depends on the stimulation of corresponding areas of the body.

Freud argued that a person's unique character type develops in childhood, largely from parent–child interactions. The child constantly tries to maximize pleasure by satisfying the id demands, while parents, as representatives of society, try to impose the demands of reality and morality. So important did Freud consider childhood experiences that he said the adult personality was firmly shaped and crystallized by the age of 5

What persuaded him that these early years are so crucial were his own childhood memories along with the memories revealed by his adult patients. Invariably, as his patients lay on his psychoanalytic couch, they reached far back into their childhoods. Increasingly, Freud perceived that the adult neurosis had been formed in the early years of life.

Freud also sensed strong sexual conflicts in the infant and young child, conflicts that seemed to revolve around specific regions of the body. He noted that each body region assumed a greater importance as the center of conflict at a different age. From these observations he derived his theory of the **psychosexual stages of development**; each stage is defined

TABLE 2.2 Freud's psychosexual stages of development

STAGES	AGES	CHARACTERISTICS
Oral	Birth–1	Mouth is the primary erogenous zone; pleasure derived from sucking: id is dominant.
Anal	1–3	Toilet training (external reality) interferes with gratification received from defecation.
Phallic	4–5	Incestuous fantasies; Oedipus complex; anxiety; superego development.
Latency	5–Puberty	Period of sublimation of sex instinct.
Genital	Adolescence–Adulthood	Development of sex-role identity and adult social relationships.

by an erogenous zone of the body (see Table 2.2). In each developmental stage a conflict exists that must be resolved before the infant or child can progress to the next stage.

Sometimes a person is reluctant or unable to move from one stage to the next because the conflict has not been resolved, or because the needs have been so supremely satisfied by an indulgent parent that the child doesn't want to move on. In either case, the individual is said to be fixated at this stage of development. In **fixation**, a portion of libido or psychic energy remains invested in that developmental stage, leaving less energy for the following stages.

Central to the psychosexual theory is the infant's sex drive. Freud shocked his colleagues and the general public when he argued that babies are motivated by sexual impulses. Recall, however, that Freud did not define sex in a narrow way. He believed that the infant is driven to obtain a diffuse form of bodily pleasure deriving from the mouth, anus, and genitals, the erogenous zones that define the stages of development during the first 5 years of life.

The Oral Stage: Taking In or Spitting Out

The oral stage, the first stage of psychosexual development, lasts from birth until some time during the second year. During this period, the infant's principal source of pleasure is the mouth. The infant derives pleasure from sucking, biting, and swallowing. Of course, the mouth is obviously used for survival—for the ingestion of food and water—but Freud placed a greater emphasis on the erotic satisfactions derived from oral activities.

During this stage, the infant is totally dependent on the mother or caregiver who becomes the primary object of the child's libido. In more familiar terms, we might say the infant is learning, in a primitive way, to love the mother. How the mother responds to the infant's demands, which at this time are solely id demands, determines the nature of the baby's small world. The infant learns from the mother to perceive the world as either a good or bad, satisfying or frustrating, safe or perilous place to be.

There are two ways of behaving during this stage: oral incorporative behavior (taking in) and oral aggressive or oral sadistic behavior (biting or spitting out). The oral incorporative mode occurs first and involves the pleasurable stimulation of the mouth by other people and by food. Adults fixated at the oral incorporative stage become excessively concerned with oral activities, like eating, drinking, smoking, and kissing.

If, as infants, they were excessively gratified during this stage, their adult oral personality will be predisposed to a high degree of optimism and dependency. Because they

fixation A condition in which a portion of libido remains invested in one of the psychosexual stages because of excessive frustration or gratification.

In the oral stage of psychosexual development, pleasure is derived from sucking, biting, and swallowing.

Philip Nealey/Photodisc/Jupiter Images

were overindulged in infancy, they continue to depend on and expect others to gratify their needs. As a consequence, they become overly gullible, swallow or believe anything they are told, and trust other people inordinately. Such people are labeled oral passive personality types.

The second oral behavior, oral aggressive or oral sadistic, occurs during the painful, frustrating eruption of teeth. As a result of this experience, infants come to view the mother with hatred as well as love. After all, she has been responsible for everything in the infant's life so far, so she must also be responsible for the pain.

Those who become fixated at this level are prone to excessive pessimism, hostility, and aggressiveness. They are likely to be argumentative and sarcastic, making so-called biting remarks and displaying cruelty toward others. They tend to be envious of other people and try to exploit and manipulate them in an effort to dominate them.

The oral stage concludes at the time of weaning, although some libido remains if fixation has occurred. Then the infant's focus shifts to the other end.

The Anal Stage: Letting Go or Holding Back

Society, in the form of parents, tends to defer to the infant's needs during the first year of life, adjusting to its demands and expecting relatively little adjustment in return. This situation changes dramatically around the age of 18 months, when a new demand, toilet training, is made of the child. Freud believed that the experience of toilet training during the anal stage had a significant effect on personality development.

Defecation produces erotic pleasure for the child, but with the onset of toilet training, the child is put under pressure to learn to postpone or delay this pleasure. For the first time, gratification of an instinctual impulse is interfered with as parents attempt to regulate the time and place for defecation.

As any parent can attest, this is a time of conflict for everybody. Children learn that they have a weapon that can be used against their parents. The child has control over something and can choose to comply or not with the parents' demands. If the toilet training is not going well—for example, if the child has difficulty learning or the parents are excessively demanding—the child may react in one of two ways.

One way is to defecate whenever and wherever the parents don't want them to, thus defying their attempts at regulation. Children who find this a satisfactory technique for reducing frustration and use it frequently may develop an anal aggressive personality. To Freud, this was the basis for many forms of hostile and sadistic behavior in adult life, including cruelty, destructiveness, and temper tantrums. Such a person is likely to be disorderly and to consider other people as objects to be possessed.

A second way the child may react to the frustration of toilet training is to hold back or retain the feces. This produces a feeling of erotic pleasure (derived from a full lower intestine, Freud said) and can be another successful technique for manipulating the parents. They may become worried, even frantic, if the child goes days without a bowel movement. Thus, the child discovers a new method for securing parental attention and affection.

This behavior is the basis for the development of an anal retentive personality. Such a person becomes stubborn and stingy, and hoards or retains things because feelings of security depend on what is saved and possessed, and on the order and in which possessions and other aspects of life are maintained. The anal retentive person is likely to be rigid, compulsively neat, obstinate, and overly conscientious.

The Phallic Stage

A new set of problems arises around the fourth to fifth year, when the focus of pleasure shifts from the anus to the genitals. Again the child faces a battle between an id impulse and the demands of society, as reflected in parental expectations.

Children at the phallic stage display considerable interest in exploring and manipulating the genitals, their own and those of their playmates. Pleasure is derived from the genital region not only through behaviors such as masturbation but also through fantasies. The child becomes curious about birth and about why boys have penises and girls do not. The child may talk about wanting to marry the parent of the opposite sex.

The phallic stage is the last of the pre genital or childhood stages, and phallic conflicts are the most complex ones to resolve. They are also difficult for many people to accept because they involve the notion of incest, a taboo in many cultures. Between incestuous desires and masturbation we can see the seeds of shock, anger, and suppression being sown in the parents of the typical 4 year old. Reality and morality come to grips with the evil id once again.

The Oedipus Complex in Boys   The basic conflict of the phallic stage centers on the unconscious desire of the child for the parent of the opposite sex. Accompanying this is the unconscious desire to replace or destroy the parent of the same sex. Out of Freud's identification of this conflict came one of his best-known concepts: the **Oedipus complex**. Its name comes from the Greek myth described in the play *Oedipus Rex*, written by Sophocles in the fifth century B.C. In this story, young Oedipus kills his father and marries his mother, not knowing who they are.

The Oedipus complex operates differently for boys and girls; Freud developed the male part of the complex more fully. In the Oedipus complex, the mother becomes a

Oedipus complex During the phallic stage (ages 4–5), the unconscious desire of a boy for his mother, accompanied by a desire to replace or destroy his father.

The boy comes to resolve the Oedipus complex by identifying with his father.

Radius Images/Jupiter Images

love object for the young boy. Through fantasy and overt behavior, he displays his sexual longings for her. However, the boy sees the father as an obstacle in his path and comes to look upon him as a rival and a threat.

He also perceives that the father has a special kind of relationship with the mother in which he, the boy, is not allowed to participate. As a result, he becomes jealous of and hostile toward the father. Freud drew his formulation of the Oedipus complex from his own childhood experiences. He wrote, "I have found love of the mother and jealousy of the father in my own case, too" (Freud, 1954, p. 223).

Accompanying the boy's desire to replace his father is the fear that the father will retaliate and harm him. He interprets his fear of his father in genital terms, becoming fearful that his father will cut off the offending organ (the boy's penis), which is the source of the boy's pleasure and sexual longings. And so **castration anxiety**, as Freud called it, comes to play a role, as it may have done in Freud's childhood. "There are a number of indications that [Freud's father] enjoined little Sigmund not to play with his genitals, and even threatened him with castration if he did" (Krüll, 1986, p. 110).

Additional evidence to support this contention comes from Freud's later writings on masturbation, in which he saw such threats from fathers as common. Freud also reported that his adult dreams contained material relating to the fear of castration by his father.

Two other childhood events may have reinforced Freud's fear of castration. At around the age of 3, he and his nephew engaged in some rough sex play with his niece and discovered she did not have a penis. For a 3-year-old boy, this may have been enough

castration anxiety A boy's fear during the Oedipal period that his penis will be cut off.

evidence to prove that penises can be cut off. In the opinion of one biographer, "the threat of castration is particularly realistic to a Jewish boy, since it is easy to establish a connection between ritual circumcision and castration" (Krüll, 1986, p. 110). Freud confirmed this in his later writings.

So strong is the boy's fear of castration that he is forced to repress his sexual desire for his mother. To Freud, this was a way of resolving the Oedipal conflict. The boy replaces the sexual longing for the mother with a more acceptable affection and develops a strong identification with the father. In doing that, the boy experiences a degree of vicarious sexual satisfaction. To enhance the identification, he attempts to become more like his father by adopting his mannerisms, behaviors, attitudes, and superego standards.

The Oedipus Complex in Girls

Electra complex During the phallic stage (ages 4–5), the unconscious desire of a girl for her father, accompanied by a desire to replace or destroy her mother.

Freud was less clear about the female phallic conflict, which some of his followers termed the **Electra complex**. The name was derived from another happy family story by Sophocles in which Electra persuades her brother to kill their mother, whom she hated.

According to Freud, a girl's first object of love, like the boy's, is the mother, because she is the primary source of food, affection, and security in infancy. During the phallic stage, however, the father becomes the girl's new love object. Why does this shift from mother to father take place? Freud said it was because of the girl's reaction to her discovery that boys have a penis and girls do not.

The girl blames her mother for her supposedly inferior condition and consequently comes to love her mother less. She may even hate the mother for what she imagines the mother did to her. She comes to envy her father and transfers her love to him because he possesses the highly valued sex organ. Freud wrote: "Girls feel deeply their lack of a sexual organ that is equal in value to the male one; they regard themselves on that account as inferior and this envy for the penis is the origin of a whole number of characteristic feminine reactions" (Freud, 1925, p. 212). Thus, a girl develops **penis envy**, which is a counterpart to a boy's castration anxiety. She believes she has lost her penis; he fears he will lose his.

penis envy The envy the female feels toward the male because the male possesses a penis; this is accompanied by a sense of loss because the female does not have a penis.

This female Oedipus complex, Freud suggested, can never be totally resolved, a situation he believed led to poorly developed superegos in women. Freud wrote that an adult woman's love for a man is always tinged with penis envy, for which she can partially compensate by having a male child. The girl comes to identify with the mother and repress her love for her father, but Freud was not specific about how this occurs.

The Phallic Personality

Phallic conflicts and their degree of resolution are of major importance in determining adult relations with the opposite sex. Poorly resolved conflicts can cause lingering forms of castration anxiety and penis envy. The so-called phallic character or personality type evidences strong narcissism.

Although continually acting in ways to try to attract the opposite sex, they have difficulty establishing mature heterosexual relationships. They need constant recognition and appreciation of what they see as their attractive and unique qualities. As long as they receive such support they function well, but when it is lacking they feel inadequate and inferior.

Freud described the male phallic personality as brash, vain, and self-assured. Men with this personality try to assert or express their masculinity through repeated sexual conquests. The female phallic personality, motivated by penis envy, exaggerates her femininity and uses her talents and charms to overwhelm and conquer men.

The tense drama of the phallic stage is repressed in all of us according to Freud. Its effects motivate us as adults at the unconscious level, and we remember very little, if anything, about the conflict.

The Latency Period

The storms and stresses of the oral, anal, and phallic stages of psychosexual development form the basic material out of which most of the adult personality is shaped. The three major structures—the id, ego, and superego—have been formed by around the age of 5, and the relationships among them are being solidified.

Fortunately, because the child and parents certainly could use some rest, the next 5 or 6 years are quiet. The **latency period** is not a psychosexual stage of development. The sex instinct is dormant during this time, Freud believed, and is temporarily sublimated in school activities, hobbies, and sports and in developing friendships with members of the same sex.

The Genital Stage

The genital stage, the final psychosexual stage of development, begins at puberty. The body is becoming physiologically mature, and if no major fixations have occurred at an earlier stage of development, the individual may be able to lead a normal life. Freud believed that the conflict during this period is less intense than in the other stages. The adolescent must conform to societal sanctions and taboos that exist concerning sexual expression, but he believed that conflict is minimized through sublimation.

The sexual energy pressing for expression in the teenage years can be at least partially satisfied through the pursuit of socially acceptable substitutes and, later, through a committed adult relationship. The genital personality type is able to find satisfaction in love and work, the latter being an acceptable outlet for sublimation of the id impulses.

The Importance of Childhood

Freud stressed the vital importance of the early childhood years in determining the adult personality. According to Freud, the first 5 years are the crucial ones. His personality theory pays less attention to later childhood and adolescence, and he was little concerned with personality development in adulthood. To Freud, what we are as adults—how we behave, think, and feel—is determined by the conflicts to which we are exposed and with which we must cope before many of us have even learned to read.

Questions about Human Nature

Freud did not present us with a flattering or optimistic image of human nature. Quite the opposite. He argued that each person is a dark cellar of conflict in which a battle is continually raging. Human beings are depicted in gloomy, pessimistic terms, condemned to a struggle with our inner forces, which we are almost always destined to lose. Doomed to anxiety, to the thwarting of at least some of our driving impulses, we experience continuing tension and conflict. We are endlessly defending ourselves against the forces of the id, which stand ever alert to topple us. Not a happy prospect.

In Freud's system, there is only one ultimate and necessary goal in life: to reduce tension. On the nature–nurture issue, Freud adopted a middle ground. The id, the most powerful part of the personality, is an inherited, physiologically based structure, as are the stages of psychosexual development. However, other parts of our personality are learned in early childhood, from parent–child interactions.

Although Freud recognized universality in human nature, in that we all pass through the same stages of psychosexual development and are motivated by the same id forces, he asserted that part of the personality is unique to each person. The ego and superego perform the same functions for all of us, but their content varies from one person to another because they are formed through personal experience. Also, different character types can develop during the psychosexual stages.

latency period To Freud, the period from approximately age 5 to puberty, during which the sex instinct is dormant, sublimated in school activities, sports, and hobbies, and in developing friendships with members of the same sex.

On the issue of free will versus determinism, Freud held a deterministic view: Virtually everything we do, think, and even dream is predetermined by the life and death instincts, the inaccessible and invisible forces within us. Our adult personality is determined by interactions that took place before we were 5, at a time when we had limited control. These experiences forever hold us in their grip.

Freud also argued, however, that people who undergo psychoanalysis could achieve the ability to exercise increased free will and take responsibility for their choices. "The more the individual is able to make conscious what had been unconscious, the more he or she can take charge of his or her own life" (Solnit, 1992, p. 66). Thus, Freud suggested that psychoanalysis had the potential to liberate people from the constraints of determinism.

Freud's overall picture of human nature, painted in these bleak hues, reflects his own personal view of humanity, which darkened with age and declining health. His judgment of people in general was harsh. "I have found little that is 'good' about human beings on the whole. In my experience, most of them are trash" (Freud, 1963, pp. 61–62). We can see this stern judgment of us in his personality theory.

Assessment in Freud's Theory

Freud considered the unconscious to be the major motivating force in life. It is the repository of all of our childhood conflicts which have been repressed out of conscious awareness. The goal of Freud's system of psychoanalysis was to bring those repressed memories, fears, and thoughts back into conscious awareness. How can the psychoanalyst evaluate, assess, or even find this invisible portion of the mind, this dark arena that is otherwise inaccessible to us? Over the course of his work with patients, Freud developed two methods of assessment: free association and dream analysis.

Free Association

free association A technique in which the patient says whatever comes to mind. In other words, it is a kind of daydreaming out loud.

catharsis The expression of emotions that is expected to lead to the reduction of disturbing symptoms.

Freud's development of the technique of **free association** owes much to Josef Breuer, a Viennese physician who befriended Freud during Freud's early years in private practice. In treating a young woman who showed symptoms of hysteria, Breuer found that hypnotizing her enabled her to remember repressed events. Recalling the events—reliving the experiences—brought relief from the disturbing symptoms.

Freud then started using hypnosis with some degree of success and called the process **catharsis**, from the Greek word for purification. However, he later abandoned hypnosis, partly because he had difficulty hypnotizing some of his patients. Also, some patients revealed disturbing events during hypnosis, but were unable to recall them when he questioned them later.

Looking for a technique other than hypnosis for helping a patient recall repressed material, Freud asked patients to lie on a couch while he sat behind it, out of sight. His reason for staying out of sight and hidden from the patients was both personal and professional. "I cannot put up with being stared at by people for eight hours a day or more," he wrote. Also, "Since while I am listening to the patient, I too give myself over to the current of my unconscious thoughts, I do not want with my expressions of face to give the patient the material for interpretations or to influence him in what he tells me" (quoted in Lingiardi & De Bei, 2011, p. 301).

Freud encouraged his patients to relax and concentrate on events in the past. They were supposed to engage in a kind of daydreaming out loud, saying whatever came to mind. Patients were told to express spontaneously every idea and image exactly as it occurred, no matter how trivial, embarrassing, or painful the thought or memory might seem. The memories were not to be omitted, rearranged, or restructured.

Freud believed there was nothing random about the information uncovered during free association and that it was not subject to a patient's conscious choice. The material revealed by patients in free association was predetermined, forced on them by the nature of their conflict.

Free Association Is Not Always so Free

Freud also found that sometimes the technique did not operate so freely. Some experiences or memories were evidently too painful to talk about, and the patient would be reluctant to disclose them. Freud called these moments **resistances**. He believed they were significant because they indicated that the analysis was getting close to the source of the patient's problems. Resistance is a sign that the treatment is heading in the right direction and that the analyst should continue to probe in that area. Part of the psychoanalyst's task is to break down or overcome resistances so the patient can confront the repressed experience.

resistance In free association, a blockage or refusal to disclose painful memories.

Dream Analysis

Freud believed that dreams represent, in symbolic form, repressed desires, fears, and conflicts. So strongly have these feelings been repressed that they can surface only in disguised fashion during sleep.

He argued that there were two aspects of dreams: the manifest content, which refers to the actual events in the dream; and the latent content, which is the hidden symbolic meaning of the dream. Over the years, Freud found consistent symbols in his patients' dreams, events that signified the same thing for nearly everyone (see Table 2.3).

TABLE 2.3 Dream symbols or events and their latent psychoanalytic meaning

SYMBOL	INTERPRETATION
Smooth-fronted house	Male body
House with ledges, balconies	Female body
King and queen	Parents
Small animals	Children
Children	Genital organs
Playing with children	Masturbation
Baldness, tooth extraction	Castration
Elongated objects (e.g., tree trunks, umbrellas, neckties, snakes, candles)	Male genitals
Enclosed spaces (e.g., boxes, ovens, closets, caves, pockets)	Female genitals
Climbing stairs or ladders; driving cars; riding horses; crossing bridges	Sexual intercourse
Bathing	Birth
Beginning a journey	Dying
Being naked in a crowd	Desiring to be noticed
Flying	Desiring to be admired
Falling	Desiring to return to a state such as childhood where one is satisfied and protected

For example, steps, ladders, and staircases in a dream represented sexual intercourse. Candles, snakes, and tree trunks indicated the penis; and boxes, balconies, and doors signified the female body. Freud warned that despite this apparent universality of symbols, many symbols are specific to the person undergoing analysis and could have a different meaning for someone else.

Dreams reveal conflicts in a condensed, intensified form. Dream events rarely result from a single cause, and any event in a dream can have many sources. Dreams may also have mundane origins. Physical stimuli, such as the temperature of the bedroom or contact with one's partner, can induce a dream, and dreams can also be triggered by internal stimuli, such as a fever or an upset stomach.

A study in Hong Kong found that people who slept prone, lying flat on their stomach, were more likely to have dreams involving sexual activities, being smothered, locked up, tied, and unable to move than those who slept in other positions (Yu, 2012). A large-scale study in Germany found that the five most typical dreams involved flying, trying something repeatedly, being chased, having sexual experiences, and matters related to school (Goritz, 2014).

It is interesting that of the more than 40 of his own dreams Freud described in his book *The Interpretation of Dreams*, only a few had a sexual content, despite his conviction that dreams typically involve some infantile sexual wish. The dominant theme in Freud's reported dreams was ambition, a characteristic he vigorously denied having.

Uncovering the Conflicts

Both of these Freudian assessment techniques—free association and dream analysis—reveal to the psychoanalyst a great deal of repressed material, but all of it is in disguised or symbolic form. The therapist then must interpret or translate the material for the patient. Freud compared this procedure with the task of an archeologist reconstructing a community that has been destroyed and buried under the accumulation of centuries. Just as the archeologist attempts to reconstruct a building from broken fragments, so a psychoanalyst reconstructs an experience from buried, fragmented memories. Thus, the evaluation or assessment of a patient's personality, the uncovering of his or her unconscious conflicts, depends on the skill, training, and experience of the analyst.

Criticisms of Freud's Research

case study A detailed history of an individual that contains data from a variety of sources.

Freud's major research method was the **case study** which, as we saw in Chapter 1, has several limitations. It does not rely on objective observation, the data are not gathered in systematic fashion, and the situation (the psychoanalytic session) is not amenable to duplication and verification. In addition, we cannot systematically vary the conditions of childhood in which patients are reared, nor can we replicate in the laboratory a person's home environment. Thus, clinical observations cannot be repeated, as they can in controlled psychological experiments.

A fundamental criticism of freud's case studies involves the nature of his data. He did not keep verbatim records of the therapy sessions, and he warned analysts against taking notes during the sessions, believing it would distract their attention from their patients' words. Freud made notes several hours after seeing each patient. Describing his technique for recording his patients' comments, Freud said, "I write them down from memory in the evening after work is over" (quoted in Grubrich-Simitis, 1998, p. 20). As a result, it's possible that his data were incomplete, consisting only of what he remembered hours later.

It is also possible that his memory of the sessions was selective and that he recorded only experiences that supported his theory, or that he interpreted those experiences in ways that would support his theory. Of course, Freud's notes may have been highly accurate, but we cannot be certain because we are unable to compare his case reports with what his patients said. And even if Freud had kept a complete record of his therapy sessions, we cannot determine the validity of the patients' comments. Freud made few attempts to verify the accuracy of a patient's stories, which he might have done by questioning the patient's friends and relatives about the events described. Therefore, the first step in Freud's research, the collection of data, must be characterized as incomplete and possibly inaccurate.

Some critics also suggest that Freud's patients did not actually reveal childhood sexual experiences because, in most cases, those experiences had never occurred. These writers argue that Freud inferred the stories of sexual seduction in childhood from his analysis of the patients' symptoms. For example, although Freud claimed that virtually all his women patients said they had been seduced by their fathers, his case notes do not show that any patient ever claimed that this had occurred (Kihlstrom, 1994).

Other critics agree that Freud was suggesting accounts of childhood seduction, without really hearing his patients say so, because he had already formed the hypothesis that such seductions were the true cause of adult neuroses. Still others charge that Freud may have used the power of suggestion to implant alleged memories of childhood seduction that had never taken place (McCullough, 2001). "Where patients did not of their own accord provide material which could be construed in sexual terms, Freud did not hesitate to point them in the 'right' direction" (Webster, 1995, p. 197).

Another criticism of Freud's research is that it is based on a small and unrepresentative sample of people, restricted to himself and those who sought psychoanalysis with him. Only a dozen or so cases have been detailed in Freud's writings, and most of these were of young, unmarried, upper-class women of good education. It is difficult to generalize from this limited sample to the population at large.

In addition, there may be discrepancies between Freud's notes on his therapy sessions and the case histories he published, which supposedly were based on these notes. Several investigators compared Freud's notes with the published case study of the Rat Man, one of his most famous patients. They found a lengthening of the period of analysis, an incorrect sequence of events disclosed by the patient, and unsubstantiated claims that the analysis resulted in a cure (Eagle, 1988; Mahoney, 1986).

Thus, the published version of the case did not agree with the notes Freud made after his sessions with the patient. It is not possible to determine whether Freud deliberately made these changes to bolster his theory (or his ego) or whether they were the products of his unconscious. Nor do we know if such distortions characterize other Freudian case studies. It may remain a mystery forever because Freud destroyed most of his patient files not long after he compiled them.

Finally, it has been argued that none of Freud's handful of published case histories provides compelling supporting evidence for his theory. One of Freud's biographers concluded: "Some of the cases present such dubious evidence in favor of psychoanalytic theory that one may seriously wonder why Freud even bothered to publish them" (Sulloway, 1992, p. 160).

We will see in later chapters that these kinds of criticisms leveled against Freud also apply to later personality theorists who used the case study as their primary research method, and based their theories on their patients' reports. This does not automatically mean that their work is devoid of merit. Freud and other analysts offered a wealth of material about the human personality. If we accept their views as valid, however, we must do so on some basis other than experimental verification.

Freud's Negative Views on Experimental Research

Although Freud was familiar with the experimental method, he had little confidence in it, believing that "scientific research and psychoanalysis are inherently incompatible"

(Chiesa, 2010, p. 99). An American psychologist once sent him information about experiments that had been conducted to validate Freudian concepts. Freud "threw the reprints across the table in a gesture of impatient rejection" and wrote to the psychologist that he did not "put much value on such confirmation" (Rosenzweig, 1985, pp. 171, 173). He believed there was no need for the kinds of experiments published in the psychology journals of the day because "they told him nothing more than he had already learned from his clinical encounters with patients" (Holzman, 1994, p. 190).

Freud insisted that his work was scientific, that he had amassed ample proof for his conclusions, and that only psychoanalysts who used his techniques were qualified to judge the scientific worth of his work. Freud wrote that psychoanalysis was based on "an incalculable number of observations and experiences, and only someone who has repeated those observations on himself and on others is in a position to arrive at a judgment of his own upon it" (Freud, 1940, p. 144).

Difficulty arises because Freud's observations cannot be repeated. As we have seen, we have no way of knowing exactly what he did in collecting his data and in translating his observations into hypotheses and generalizations.

Scientific Testing of Freudian Concepts

In the years since Freud's death in 1939, many of his ideas have been submitted to experimental testing. An analysis of some 2,500 studies evaluated the scientific credibility of some of Freud's ideas. In this evaluation, case histories were not considered. Every effort was made to restrict the investigation to data thought to have a high degree of objectivity (Fisher & Greenberg, 1977, 1996).

The researchers found that some Freudian concepts—notably the id, ego, superego, death wish, libido, and anxiety—could not be tested by the experimental method. Concepts that could be tested, and which evidence appeared to support, however slightly, included the oral and anal character types, the basic concept of the Oedipal triangle, castration anxiety, and the notion that females resolve the Oedipal dilemma by having a child as compensation for the lack of a penis.

Concepts not supported by research evidence include those of dreams as disguised expressions of repressed wishes, resolution of the male Oedipus complex by identification with the father and acceptance of the father's superego standards out of fear, and the idea that women have inadequately developed superegos. In addition, researchers found no evidence to support the psychosexual stages of development or a relationship between Oedipal variables and sexual problems later in life.

The Unconscious   The notion that unconscious forces can influence conscious thought and behavior is now well established. Current research shows that unconscious influences may be even more pervasive than Freud suggested (Custers & Aarts, 2010; Scott & Dienes, 2010; Gafner, 2012). One personality researcher observed that "today there is agreement that much [psychological] functioning occurs without conscious choice and that some of our behavior actually occurs in opposition to what is consciously desired" (Pervin, 2003, p. 225). Psychologists also recognize that much of the information processing involved in cognitive activities is unconscious (Armstrong & Dienes, 2014). Some even propose that the causal mechanisms underlying all behavior and thought may be unconscious (Bargh & Chartrand, 1999; Wegner & Wheatley, 1999).

> It now appears that the unconscious is "smarter" than first thought, capable of processing complex verbal and visual information and even anticipating (and planning for) future events.... No longer simply a repository for drives and impulses, the unconscious appears to play a role in problem solving, hypothesis testing, and creativity. (Bornstein & Masling, 1998, pp. xiii–xxviii)

subliminal perception
Perception below the
threshold of conscious
awareness.

Subliminal Perception   Much research on the nature of the unconscious involves **subliminal perception** in which stimuli are presented to people below their level of conscious awareness. (The word *subliminal* derives from *sub*, meaning below, and *limen*, meaning threshold.) Despite their inability to perceive the stimuli, their conscious processes and behavior are activated by the stimuli. In other words, people can be influenced by things they are not consciously aware of seeing.

In one study, subjects were shown a series of words and pictures for such a brief time that they could not consciously perceive them (Shevrin, 1977). Then, when they were asked to free-associate, what they talked about reflected the stimuli they had been shown but had not actually been able to see. For example, when the stimulus was a picture of a bee, the associations included the words *sting* and *honey*. The subjects' thought processes were affected by the stimuli, even though they were unaware of having seen them. Many such studies using subliminal perception support the idea that cognitive activity is *influenced* by the unconscious (Westen, 1998).

Effects on Behavior   A series of experiments on college students in the United States and in Germany showed that goals could be aroused, or activated, outside of conscious awareness. In addition, behaviors to satisfy these goals were then displayed, even though the students were not consciously aware of doing so. For example, the subliminally aroused goal of performing better on an experimental task led them to actually perform better. In another instance, the unconsciously activated goal of being cooperative on an experimental task led to cooperative behaviors. The authors of the study concluded that "behavioral goals can become activated without any consciously made choice required" (Bargh, Gollwitzer, Lee-Chai, Barndollar, & Troetschel, 2001, p. 18).

When college students in the United States were shown happy faces, below the level of conscious awareness, they consumed more of a beverage that was made available to them than did students who were exposed to images of angry faces. The happy-face group also indicated a greater willingness to pay for their drink and to want more of it than did the angry-face group. Although none of the students consciously saw the faces, the stimuli had registered in their unconscious and acted to influence their behavior (Winkielman, Berridge, & Wilbarger, 2005).

Effects on Emotional Processes   Other imaginative research has demonstrated that the unconscious can influence emotional as well as cognitive and behavioral processes. In one such study, the words *Mommy and I are one* were flashed for 4 milliseconds to research participants, along with a picture of a man and a woman joined together at their shoulders.

Male schizophrenic patients exposed to this subliminally presented stimulus showed a greater improvement than did a control group not exposed to that message. Female schizophrenic patients showed no improvement when exposed to that message but did show improvement when presented with the subliminal message: *Daddy and I are one* (Silverman & Weinberger, 1985).

In other studies, the *Mommy and I are one* message was effective in helping a variety of research peoples stop smoking and drinking, become more assertive, eat a more healthful diet, and reduce fears. Thus, a subliminally presented message has been shown to have therapeutic value (Weinberger & Silverman, 1990).

A study of adults in England found that those who scored high in anxiety sensitivity were far more likely to see anxiety-related words that were presented below the level of conscious awareness than were adults who scored low in anxiety sensitivity. The sensitivity of the first group made them more vigilant and thus more likely to perceive anxiety-related words, even though the words were presented so rapidly that the people did not consciously see them (Hunt, Keogh, & French, 2006).

Other research has shown that subliminally presented stimuli—in this case, fearful faces—actually raised the physiological stress levels of the subjects, even though they did not actually see the stimuli (Hansel & von Kanel, 2013).

The Ego We noted that Freud viewed the ego's role as constantly mediating between reality and the insistent demands of the id. The ego is the rational part of the personality that must control and postpone the id's demands, balancing them against the circumstances and demands of the real world. Psychoanalytic researchers have identified two components of the ego: ego control and ego resiliency.

Ego control, as you would expect from the name, is close to Freud's original conception. It refers to the amount of control we are able to exert over our impulses and feelings. The degree of ego control ranges from under-controlled (in which we are unable to restrain any impulses and feelings) to over-controlled (in which we tightly inhibit the expression of our impulses). Both extremes are considered maladaptive.

Ego resiliency refers to our flexibility in adjusting or changing our typical level of ego control to meet the daily changes in our environment. Persons with little ego resiliency are referred to as "ego brittle," meaning they are unable to alter their level of ego control to meet challenges or difficult life situations. Those high in ego resiliency are flexible and adaptable, able to tighten or loosen their degree of ego control as the situation warrants.

Mothers between the ages of 21 and 27 who rated their mothering experiences as positive and satisfying were found to have high ego resiliency. Mothers who rated their mothering experiences as negative were found to have decreased ego resiliency. The researchers suggested that difficult life situations, setbacks and failures, or other negative experiences tend to lower ego resiliency (Paris & Helson, 2002).

Ego Control among Children Children who score low on measures of ego control are rated by their teachers as being more aggressive and less compliant and orderly than children who score high on ego control. Children who score high on ego resiliency are rated by their teachers as better able to cope with stress, lower in anxiety, and less in need of reassurance than children low in ego resiliency.

A study of 5-year-old children in the Netherlands found that those with low ego resiliency showed physiological signs of greater stress during negative situations, typically interactions with their parents. Children high in ego resiliency did not show such evidence of stress in similar situations (Smeekens, Riksen-Walraven, & van Bakel, 2007).

High ego resiliency also correlated positively with general intelligence, good grades in school, popularity with peers, greater life satisfaction, and better social functioning. Low ego control in boys and girls, and low ego resiliency in girls, was related positively to drug abuse in adolescence. Thus, important aspects of personality and behavior can be linked to ego control and ego resiliency (Block & Block, 1980; Chung, 2008; Hofer, Eisenberg, & Reiser, 2010; Shiner, 1988).

Research using college students found that those low in ego control tended to be unpredictable, assertive, rebellious, moody, and self-indulgent. Those very high in ego control were described as bland, consistent, dependable, and calm. Students rated high in ego resilience were assertive, poised, socially skilled, and cheerful (Letzring, Block, & Funder, 2005).

A longitudinal study that periodically assessed these personality characteristics in American subjects ranging in age from 3 to 23 found that both ego control and ego resiliency were generally stronger later in life than in childhood. Individual differences in ego control were seen at various ages, suggesting that one's level of ego control could be identified early (Block & Block, 2006).

Research in Italy found a marked stability in ego resilience from ages 16 to 20 for both male and female subjects. In contrast, studies in Sweden found that boys tended to become less ego resilient in adolescence while girls became more ego resilient. These results suggest the possibility of cultural and gender differences in ego resiliency (Chuang, Lamb, & Hwang, 2006; Vecchione, Alessandri, Barbaranelli, & Gerbino, 2010).

Finally, it probably will not surprise you to learn that ego resiliency is also related to positive mental health. Research in a variety of countries including the United States, Italy, Spain, Portugal, South Korea, and Pakistan, using subjects ranging from college students to the elderly to amputee war veterans, showed clearly that those who score high in ego resiliency also score high in subjective well-being, extraversion, and agreeableness. (Alessandri, Vecchione, Caprara, & Letzring, 2012; Gunsung, 2013; Seaton, 2014; Zeb, Naqvi, & Zonash, 2013).

Catharsis   To Freud, catharsis involved the physical expression of an emotion by recalling a traumatic event, which often led to relief of the disturbing symptom. In popular culture, the term catharsis has come to refer to expressing one's emotion as a way of reducing hostility and aggression. Self-help books urge us to give vent to anger by taking it out on some inanimate object—beating a pillow, breaking a dish, or hitting a punching bag. Does this work? Does acting out aggressions reduce negative emotions? The answer is no.

In one study of catharsis, two groups of college students were exposed to messages that either supported or disputed the notion that cathartic behavior is a good way to relieve anger. Next, some of the students were experimentally provoked to anger; an essay they had written was severely criticized. They were told that their paper was one of the worst essays ever written.

Students who were thus provoked and who had read the pro-catharsis message were significantly more prone to act out their aggression by hitting a punching bag. In a second experiment, those who received the pro-catharsis message not only hit the punching bag but also behaved aggressively toward the person who had annoyed them by criticizing their writing. They even displayed heightened aggression toward innocent people who had played no role in promoting their anger.

So, hitting the punching bag had not been cathartic. It had not dissipated their anger but might even have increased it (Bushman, Baumeister, & Stack, 1999). Other research confirmed that venting anger served to increase the likelihood of expressing more anger, and did not reduce negative emotions (Bushman, 2002; Lohr, Olatunji, Baumeister, & Bushman, 2007). Other research has shown that people who believed venting anger was good for them were more attracted to violent video games than were those who did not believe in the value of catharsis (Bushman & Whitaker, 2010).

Displacement   Displacement involves shifting one's id impulses from a disturbing object that is not available to a substitute object or person. An analysis of 97 studies supported the contention that displaced aggression is a viable and reliable phenomenon. The analysis found that the more negative and stressful the setting or context in which displacement occurs, the greater the intensity of that displacement (Marcus-Newhall, Pedersen, Miller, & Carlson, 2000).

A study of college students found that those in a group that was experimentally provoked to anger, and then left to spend 25 minutes focusing their attention on their angry thoughts and feelings, were far more likely to demonstrate displaced aggression than those whose experimental condition did not include the 25 minutes of brooding. The researchers concluded that dwelling on our anger maintains the feeling and is likely to cause it to be expressed outwardly in aggressive behavior (Bushman, Bonacci, Pedersen, Vasquez, & Miller, 2005).

Repression   Research has provided support for the Freudian defense mechanism of repression. In one study, subjects memorized two lists of words that were flashed on a screen. Some words on the lists were conceptually similar; for example, *cats* and *dogs* are both animals. The subjects were then given an electric shock with some words on the first list. No shocks were administered with the words on the second list.

Then they were tested on how well they remembered the words. They forgot the words that had been accompanied by the shock but recalled those not accompanied by the shock. They also repressed words on the second list that were conceptually similar to the words on the first list that had been accompanied by a shock. The researchers concluded that the threatening words had been pushed out of conscious awareness (Glucksberg & King, 1967).

Repressors and Non-Repressors   A number of differences have been found between those of us who habitually repress bad experiences and memories and those who do not. It is not as though repressors are simply forgetful and have trouble remembering much of anything. Rather, they only have problems remembering specific experiences that they found negative, stressful, fearful, and traumatic (Saunders, Worth, Vallath, & Fernandes, 2014).

Repressors tend to be low in anxiety and high in defensiveness, and to have significantly poorer recall of negative memories from childhood (Davis, 1987; Myers & Derakshan, 2004). In addition, repressors are far more likely to avoid romantic attachments than are non-repressors (Davis, 1987; Vetere & Myers, 2002). Repressors are also less likely to smoke and drink, and to score higher than non-repressors on the belief that excessive drinking would not lead to harmful personal consequences (Shirachi & Spirrison, 2006).

Repressors have also been shown to be much more likely than non-repressors to deny possessing personality traits they had identified as personally emotionally threatening, such as selfishness, laziness, rudeness, and dishonesty. Repressors also had fewer unpleasant or threatening emotional memories available for retrieval than did non-repressors because they had repressed them (Newman, Duff, & Baumeister, 1997; Newman & McKinney, 2002; Schimmack & Hartmann, 1997).

Repressors and non-repressors have been compared on a number of experimental tasks. When some were shown pictures of neutral, nonthreatening stimuli and pictures of embarrassing, threatening stimuli, the repressors avoided even looking at the threatening ones. When repressors were asked to free-associate to phrases with sexual or aggressive content (presumably threatening material), physiological measurements showed them to be highly emotionally aroused, yet their verbal responses gave no hint of anger or sexual arousal because they had repressed their emotional reactions. Non-repressors did not inhibit their emotional reactions, and this was evident in their verbal responses (Davis, 1987).

In another study, repressors and non-repressors were shown a grisly and disturbing film about animal mutation and lingering death from the effects of nuclear testing. When they were asked to recall a personal experience that made them happy, repressors remembered more pleasant events and thoughts than did non-repressors.

The researchers concluded that the repressors coped with the negative stimuli in the film by accessing positive memories. Thus, repressors did not experience to the same frequency and degree as non-repressors the distressing emotional states engendered by the film. The repressors were not merely pretending to be unaffected; they had repressed the experience successfully (Boden & Baumeister, 1997).

Repression was also studied in two groups of children in the United States. Some of the children were healthy while others had cancer or other chronic debilitating illnesses. The sick children were more likely to be repressors and less likely to express anger than the healthy children (Phipps & Steele, 2002).

Projection   Research on projection—attributing one's negative traits and behaviors to someone else—have found that accusing another person of lying and cheating in a game increased the amount of blame placed on that person and reduced the amount of blame the subjects placed on themselves for showing the same negative behaviors (Rucker & Pratkanis, 2001). Adults who were of a higher social class as children are more likely to use projection than those who were raised in lower-class families (Cramer, 2009).

Projection can also influence our judgments about our spouses or partners. A study of unemployed job seekers found that they projected their feelings of depression about the stresses of unemployment onto their partners when asked to make everyday judgments about them. In addition, the more alike the partners were on a psychological measure of depression, the greater was the tendency for one to project that feeling when judging the other.

The researchers noted: "Individuals seem more likely to assume that their spouses are like them when their spouses actually are like them" (Schul & Vinokur, 2000, p. 997). Thus, in this instance, the subjects were accurate in projecting their own characteristics onto their spouses or partners.

A Hierarchy of Defense Mechanisms   Studies have found a hierarchy among the Freudian defense mechanisms in which the simpler ones are used earlier in life and the more complex ones emerge as we grow older. For example, denial, which is a simple, low-level defense mechanism, is used mostly by young children and less often by adolescents. Identification, a more complex defense, is used considerably more by adolescents than by younger children. Denial is also used more frequently by boys. Girls are more likely to use the more complex mechanisms of regression, displacement, and reaction formation (Tallandini & Caudek, 2010).

In research on students from grades 2, 5, 8, 11, and first-year college classes, responses to the Thematic Apperception Test pictures supported the notion of clear age differences in defense mechanisms. The use of denial and projection decreased with age whereas identification increased with age (Porcerelli, Thomas, Hibbard, & Cogan, 1998). A longitudinal study of 150 students ages 11 to 18 found that the projection and identification defenses were used more often than denial, and that their use increased from early to late adolescence (Cramer, 2007).

A longitudinal study of people who were first tested in nursery school and later at age 23 found a link between preschool personality and the use of denial as young adults. As we noted earlier, denial tends to be used as a defense mechanism mostly by children and its use typically declines with age. In this study, however, the male subjects who at age 23 were still using denial had a number of psychological problems that had been identified when they were in nursery school.

Their childhood personalities were high in emotional immaturity and unworthiness and low in personal competence and ego resiliency. For women subjects, no such clear relationship was found between childhood personality and the continued use of denial at age 23. The authors of the study suggested that boys might be more vulnerable to stress than girls (Cramer & Block, 1998).

A study of American adults found that the use of displacement and regression as defense mechanisms decreased from adolescence to early old age in the mid-60s. Subjects older than that, however, reverted to the more maladaptive defenses they had used when they were younger (Diehl, Chui, Hay, Lumley, Gruhn, & Labouvie-Vief, 2014).

Two studies conducted in Canada demonstrated that adolescent girls with anorexia nervosa (an eating disorder), and older women who had been victims of spouse abuse, were far more likely to use denial as a coping mechanism than were girls or women who were not in these categories. The researchers suggested that by unconsciously denying their difficulties, the girls and women were attempting to minimize or distance themselves from their situations (Arokach, 2006; Couturier & Lock, 2006).

A study of adult men found that those who tried to protect themselves from feelings of weakness by being more powerful and competitive and avoiding emotional expression tended to use more immature defense mechanisms. Those men who did not feel so great a need to be more powerful than others and who could express their emotions more freely used more mature defense mechanisms (Mahalik, Cournoyer, DeFrank, Cherry, & Napolitano, 1998). Research has also found that parents who abuse their children tend to use the immature defense mechanism of denial (Cramer & Kelly, 2010).

Defense Mechanisms in Asian Cultures   The notion of defense mechanisms was proposed and developed in a European setting from studies of White middle-class patients. Much of the ensuing research conducted on defense mechanisms was performed using American or European subjects. In an unusual study of Asians and Americans, a group of Americans was compared with a group of Asian Buddhists living in Thailand. The researchers found a strong similarity between people in the two cultures in their use of regression, reaction formation, projection, repression, denial, and compensation (Tori & Bilmes, 2002).

Later research on college students in China diagnosed with borderline personality disorders showed that they used more immature defense mechanisms than students without such disorders (Xiang, Li, & Shen, 2010).

Dreams   Early research on dreams confirmed Freud's idea that dreams in disguised or symbolic form reflect emotional concerns. However, research does not support his idea that dreams represent a fulfillment of wishes or desires. His ideas on dreams have nonetheless spurred a large number of studies on various aspects of dreams and dreaming.

Effect of Traumatic Experiences on Dreams   It seems clear that dreams are often characterized by highly emotional content from the dreamers' own lives, both past and present. For example, large-scale surveys of Germans between the years 1956 and 2000 showed that those old enough to have been affected directly by World War II (1939–1945) were experiencing highly emotional war-related dreams more than 50 years after the war ended (Schredl & Piel, 2006).

The same was found in studies of British soldiers who had been prisoners of the Germans in World War II. The themes of their dreams centered on being in battle, imprisonment, attempts to escape, and hunger (Barrett, Sogolow, Oh, Panton, Grayson, & Justiniano, 2014). Studies of survivors of 21st century wars in Iraq and Afghanistan showed that the soldiers' dreams were also characterized by flashbacks to traumatic scenes of battle and other forms of combat stress (Phelps & Forbes, 2012).

Studies of Kurdish and of Palestinian children exposed to physical danger in their everyday lives showed that they dream about threatening and traumatic situations far more than children of these and other cultures reared in more peaceful surroundings (Valli, Revonsuo, Palkas, & Punamaki, 2006).

More Ordinary Dream Content   A great deal of research confirms that dreams also reflect mundane, ordinary, everyday experiences, and that the emotional intensity of these experiences, as well as the person's mood, influences the dream stories (see, for example, Schredl, 2006; Schredl, Funkhouser, & Arn, 2006). It apparently often happens that if you are having a bad day, you may well have bad dreams that night. And if something in your room smells bad, even that can affect your dreams. Research in a sleep laboratory in Germany found that a mere 10 seconds' exposure to the smell of roses when the subjects were asleep resulted in more pleasant dreams than being exposed to the smell of rotten eggs (Hutson, 2010).

Studies of adults in the United States and in Germany found that women recall their dreams far more than men do, perhaps because women wake up more frequently during the night. Men dream more about male characters, while women dream more or less equally about both male and female characters. Men have many more aggressive dreams than women do (Blume-Marcovici, 2010; Schredl, 2010a).

A long-term study of adults in Canada who kept diaries of their dreams showed a significant correlation between the nature of their dreams and their psychological well-being. Those with lower levels of psychological well-being (thus presumably less happy) reported more dreams of aggression toward others, negative emotions, and failure and misfortune. Those with higher levels of psychological well-being reported dreams of friendly interactions with others, positive emotions, and success and good fortune (Pesant & Zadra, 2006).

Finally, it may not surprise you to learn that college students often dream about sex. In addition, male students dream more about bonding with friends, while female students dream more about pregnancy, weddings, and shopping (Rainville & Rush, 2009).

Effects of Electronic Media on Dreams Exposure to electronic media such as cell-phones, smartphones, computers, DVDs, and video games, as well as interactive Internet use, have all been shown to influence the content and frequency of dreams (Gackenbach, Kuruvilla, & Dopko, 2009). People who spend a great deal of time playing video games tend to have more bizarre dreams containing dead and imaginary characters than people who spend considerably less time playing video games (Gackenbach, Kuruvilla, & Dopko, 2009; Schneider & Domhoff, 2006).

Large-scale studies of children in Britain showed clearly that what they watched on television, as well as what they read, affected the contents of their dreams. It was also found that the more time the kids spent on any one activity, the more it influenced their dreams (Lambrecht, Schredl, Henley-Einion, & Blagrove, 2013; Stephan, Schredl, Henley-Einion, & Blagrove, 2012).

When Chinese college students were asked whether they dreamed in color or in black and white, those who had watched black-and-white television and films as children answered that they dreamed in black and white. Those who had greater exposure to color TV and movies dreamed in color (Schwitzgebel, Huang, & Zhou, 2006).

Did you ever think playing video games might protect you against nightmares? Some researchers thought so and they found that among students who had experienced traumas, those who played a lot of video games were less troubled by nightmares than those who did not. However, the protection of video games only worked for men, not women (Gackenbach, Darlington, Ferguson, & Boyes, 2013).

Cultural Differences in Dreams Cultural differences in dreaming have been studied in several populations. Research on the Parintintin Indians of Brazil's Amazon rain forest showed that they believe dreams are a means of telling the future. They take dreams seriously, their own and those of relatives and friends (Kracke, 2010).

A comparison of the dreams of college students in the United States and China revealed that the Chinese students reported more familiar people in their dreams and fewer aggressive situations than did the American students (Xian-Li & Guang-Xing, 2006). The dreams of Chinese were found to contain such sex symbols (according to Freud) as knives, swords, and daggers, much more than the dreams of American subjects (Yu, 2010).

A study of White and Asian-American college students showed that in childhood, the Whites were much more likely to tell their parents about their dreams. They were also more likely as they got older to describe their dreams to friends and to place a high value on their dreams. The Asian-American students were more secretive about their dreams and were highly reluctant to talk about them (Fiske & Pillemer, 2006).

Research comparing the contents of dreams reported by Iranian and American college students found that the Iranians were far more likely to dream about people they know, to dream about events taking place indoors, and to experience more positive emotions in their dreams than the American sample (Mazandarani, Aguilar-Valaje, & Domhoff, 2013).

Interpreting Our Dreams People in both Eastern and Western cultures tend to agree that dreams may contain hidden personal truths that can provide useful information about themselves and their environment (Morewedge & Norton, 2009). As a result, many people are interested in dream interpretation. A study of Islamic students in the United Arab Emirates found that approximately two-thirds of the female students and one-third of the male students expressed a great interest in interpreting their dreams (Salem, Ragab, & Abdel, 2009; Schredl, 2010b). Other research has found that Muslims in the United Arab Emirates are far more interested in dream interpretation than a sample of Canadians of the same age (Salem, 2014).

A group of Japanese researchers have determined that it is possible for computers to interpret and recognize the visual images that are taking place in dreamers' minds when they are asleep. They awakened sleeping subjects every 6 minutes to ask them to describe what they were seeing just before they woke up. They then wrote a computer program to sort through the different patterns of brain activity recorded on an MRI (Magnetic Resonance Imaging) of the subjects' brain activity while they were both awake and asleep. The computers "learned" to decode the images that appeared in the dreams with an average accuracy rate of 66 percent. The researchers claim that this is the first step toward the day when computers will interpret and analyze our dreams for us (Horikawa, Tamaki, Miyawaki, & Kamitani, 2013).

The Oedipus Complex Most psychological research leads to the conclusion that there is no validity at all to Freud's concept of the Oedipus complex (Kupfersmid, 1995). However, there have been a number of studies dealing with the behavior and attitudes of children toward parents of the same and opposite sex, which is a major ingredient of Freud's notion of the Oedipal relationship.

For example, parents of boys and girls ages 3 to 6 were asked to record affectionate behaviors and aggressive or hostile behaviors their children directed toward them. The results showed that acts of affection toward the parent of the opposite sex and aggression toward the parent of the same sex occurred much more frequently than the reverse. These types of Oedipal-related behaviors were greatest around age 4 and began to decline by age 5 (Watson & Getz, 1990). A classic study found that significantly more men reported dreams reflecting castration anxiety; significantly more women reported dreams reflecting castration wishes or penis envy (Hall & Van de Castle, 1965).

Freud proposed that penis envy in girls leads them to view the father as a love object, a desire later supplanted by the wish for a baby. In an experimental test of this proposal, college-age women were exposed to subliminal messages containing pregnancy themes. Their later responses on an inkblot test were found to contain significantly more phallic imagery than the responses of women in the control group or of college-age men exposed to the same stimuli. The researchers claim that these results support Freud's belief that pregnancy has phallic significance for women (R. L. Jones, 1994).

A study conducted in Wales of boys and girls ages 12 to 14 assessed their attitudes toward their parents. The results showed that children who were ambivalent toward their fathers (who viewed them with a mixture of both love and hatred) displayed a less secure attachment toward other people than did children who did not feel ambivalent about their fathers. The researchers noted that this finding supports Freud's insistence on the importance of the father in influencing the child's later relationships (Maio, Fincham, & Lycett, 2000).

Oral and Anal Personality Types An investigation of the oral personality type showed a strong relationship between the oral orientation, as identified by the Rorschach, and obesity (Masling, Rabie, & Blondheim, 1967). This supports Freud's contention that oral types are preoccupied with eating and drinking. Another study found oral personality types to be more conforming to the suggestions of an authority figure than anal personality types (Tribich & Messer, 1974). According to Freud, oral personalities are dependent and submissive and should be more conforming than anal personalities; anal types tend to be hostile and can be expected to resist conformity.

Freud also contended that women were more orally dependent than men were, but later research found no such difference between the sexes (O'Neill & Bornstein, 1990). In general, then, there is some research support both for the oral and anal personality types (Westen, 1998). There is little empirical evidence for the phallic personality type.

It has been suggested that Freud's anal character keeps resurfacing or recycling in psychology under different names, such as conscientiousness, orderliness, obstinacy, and the obsessive-compulsive personality disorder (Haslam, 2011).

Age and Personality Development Freud proposed that personality was formed by about the age of 5 and was subject to little change after that. Later research on personality development over time indicate that the personality characteristics of preschool children changed dramatically, as shown by follow-up studies conducted over 6 to 7 years (Kagan, Kearsley, & Zelazo, 1978). Other studies suggest that the middle childhood years (ages 7–12) may be more important in establishing adult personality patterns than the early childhood years.

Noted child development psychologist Jerome Kagan reviewed the literature and concluded that personality appears to depend more on temperament and experiences in later childhood than on early parent–child interactions, as Freud had suggested (Kagan, 1999). Although there is no denying that our first 5 years of life affect our personality, it is now obvious that personality continues to develop well beyond that time.

The Freudian Slip According to Freud, what appears to be ordinary forgetting or a casual lapse in speech is actually a reflection of unconscious motives or anxieties. In research to test this phenomenon, two groups of men were shown the same pairs of words flashed on a computer screen (Motley, 1987). When a buzzer sounded, they were asked to say the words aloud. One group had electrodes attached to their bodies; they were told that during the experiment they would receive a painful electric shock. This situation was an experimental way of engendering anxiety. In the second group, the experimenter was an attractive, sexy woman. This group was given a test of sexual anxiety.

Men anxious about the electric shock made verbal slips such as *damn shock* when the words on the screen were *sham dock*. Those in the sexual anxiety condition revealed that anxiety in verbal slips such as *nude breasts* for *brood nests*. Those who scored high on the sexual anxiety test made the greatest number of sex-related Freudian slips.

Men in a control group exposed to the same words but to neither anxiety-arousing condition did not make verbal slips. Not all lapses in speech are Freudian slips, of course, but research suggests that at least some may be what Freud said they were—hidden anxieties revealing themselves in embarrassing ways.

A recent American president speaking before a teacher's group said "I'd like to spank all teachers." Clearly he meant to say that he wanted to *thank* all teachers. Another well-known American politician said he wanted to encourage "the breast," when referring to "the best and the brightest" (quoted in Pincott, 2013). Do you think these might have been Freudian slips?

> ## HIGHLIGHTS: Research on Freud's Ideas
>
> People who score low in *ego control* tend to be:
>
> - Aggressive and noncompliant
> - Unpredictable and assertive
> - Moody and self-indulgent
>
> People who score low in *ego resiliency* tend to be:
>
> - Stressed during negative interactions with parents
> - Anxious and in need of reassurance
> - Unassertive, sad, and lacking social skills
>
> People who vent anger through *catharsis* tend to be:
>
> - Even angrier afterward
> - Attracted to violent video games
>
> Research supports Freud's concepts of:
>
> - The influence of the unconscious
> - Displacement
> - Repression
> - Denial
> - Projection
> - Dreams as a reflection of emotional concerns
> - The so-called Freudian slip

Repressed Memories of Childhood Sexual Abuse   In the late 1980s, the issue of repressed memories resurfaced in sensational legal proceedings involving people who claimed they suddenly recalled incidents of abuse that had occurred years earlier. Women brought criminal charges against fathers, uncles, and family friends; men brought charges against priests, coaches, and teachers. Some of the accused were convicted and imprisoned on the basis of memories of incidents said to have taken place as long as 20 years before. Such accusations and subsequent trials are still taking place today.

Research on repressed memories of childhood sexual abuse has found ample evidence that such abuse can be forgotten for many years before being recalled (Delmonte, 2000). A study of women who had either repressed their memories, recovered such memories, or had never forgotten the experiences found that those who reported recovered memories scored higher on measures of fantasy proneness and dissociation (a splitting off of mental processes into separate streams of awareness) (McNally, Clancy, Schacter, & Pitman, 2000). Such states could, of course, be attributed to the childhood trauma.

Despite evidence to support the existence of repressed memories of childhood sexual abuse that did occur, research has also demonstrated how easily false memories can be implanted and recollections distorted, to the point where something that never occurred can be made conscious and appear to be genuine (Loftus & Ketcham, 1994; Ofshe & Watters, 1994).

In one study, young children were interviewed 4 years after they had spent 5 minutes playing with a man sitting across a table. The man never touched the children. During follow-up interviews, researchers created a climate of accusation by telling the children they would be questioned about an important event in their lives. "Are you afraid to tell?" they were asked. "You'll feel better once you've told" (Ceci & Bruck, 1993, p. 421). One-third of the children agreed with the interviewer's suggestion that they had been hugged and kissed by the man. Two of the children agreed with the suggestion that they had been photographed in the bathroom; one agreed that the man had given her a bath.

A study involving college students in Italy showed that dream interpretation could be used to implant false memories. Half of the students were told by a psychologist who was also a popular radio celebrity that their dreams were manifestations of repressed memories of traumatic childhood events. Examples of these incidents included being abandoned by their parents or lost in an unfamiliar place. The other group of subjects did not receive such interpretations of their dreams.

All the subjects had been selected on the basis of questionnaire responses completed weeks earlier in which they had stated that no traumatic events had occurred during their childhood. When questioned 10 to 15 days after the dream interpretations, the majority of the experimental subjects agreed that the traumatic experiences had really happened and that they had repressed the memories for years (Mazzoni, Lombardo, Malvagia, & Loftus, 1999).

Elizabeth Loftus, a pioneering researcher in the area, concluded that overall, "there is little support for the notion that trauma is commonly banished out of awareness and later reliably recovered by processes beyond ordinary forgetting and remembering.... There can be no doubt that 'memories' for factually fake as well as impossible, or at least highly improbable, horrific traumatic events were developed [or implanted], particularly among persons subjected to suggestive memory recovery procedures" (Loftus & Davis, 2006, pp. 6, 8).

However, it is important to keep in mind that childhood sexual abuse does occur. It is a haunting reality for many people and far more widespread than Sigmund Freud envisioned in the 19th century. The effects can be debilitating. Men and women who were sexually abused as children have strong tendencies toward anxiety, depression, self-destructiveness, low self-esteem, and suicide (see, for example, McNally, Perlman, Ristuccia, & Clancy, 2006; Pilkington & Lenaghan, 1998; Westen, 1998).

Extensions of Freudian Theory

Several theorists we will cover in the chapters to follow developed positions in opposition to Freud's. Other theorists remained faithful to some of Freud's basic assumptions but attempted to expand, extend, or elaborate on his views. One of the most important of this group was Freud's daughter Anna, who set out to counteract what were seen as weaknesses or omissions in the Freud's psychoanalysis and to build on those weaknesses.

Ego Psychology: Anna Freud

Anna Freud (1895–1982) said she never would have been born if a safer contraceptive method been available to her parents. Despite that beginning she became the only one of Freud's six children to follow in his path (Young-Bruehl, 1988). She was an unhappy child who was jealous of the older sister favored by her mother and was ignored by her other siblings. She later lamented "the experience of being ... only a bore to them, and of feeling bored and left alone" (Appignanesi & Forrester, 1992, p. 273).

But Anna was not ignored by her father. She became his favorite, and by the age of 14 was dutifully attending meetings of his psychoanalytic group, listening attentively to the case histories being presented and discussed. At 22, Anna began 4 years of psychoanalysis with her father, who was later sharply criticized for analyzing his daughter.

One historian called it "an impossible and incestuous treatment.... an Oedipal acting-in at both ends of the couch" (Mahoney, 1992, p. 307). But another explained: "No one else would presume to undertake the task, for Anna's analysis would inevitably call into question Freud's role as her father" (Donaldson, 1996, p. 167). To analyze one's child was a serious violation of Freud's own rules for the practice of psychoanalysis, and the situation with Anna was kept secret for many years.

In her analysis Anna reported violent dreams involving shooting, killing, and dying, as well as defending her father from his enemies. Nevertheless, "she shared with him her sexual fantasies and her forays into masturbation and emerged from the analysis grateful to her father and more committed to him than ever" (Edmundson, 2007, p. 61).

Anna Freud joined the Vienna Psychoanalytic Society, presenting a paper entitled *Beating Fantasies and Daydreams*. Although she claimed to be describing the experiences of a patient, she was actually relating her own fantasies. She spoke of an incestuous love relationship between father and daughter, a physical beating, and sexual gratification through masturbation.

She devoted her life to the care of her father and to his system of psychoanalysis. Several years after he died she described a series of dreams she had about him. "He is here again. All of these recent dreams have the same character: the main role is played not by my longing for him but rather his longing for me.... In the first dream of this kind, he openly said: 'I have always longed for you so' " (Anna Freud, quoted in Zaretsky, 2004, p. 263).

And while Anna was close to death, some 40 years after her father died, she would sit in a wheelchair wearing his old wool coat, which she had kept all those years (Webster, 1995).

Anna Freud's Approach to Psychoanalysis   Whereas the elder Freud had worked only with adults, attempting to reconstruct their childhoods by eliciting their recollections and analyzing their fantasies and dreams, Anna worked only with children. She established a clinic and a center to train analysts in the building next door to her father's home in London. In 1927 she published *Four Lectures on Child Analysis*. Sigmund Freud approved of her work: "Anna's views on child analysis are independent of mine; I share her views, but she has developed them out of her own independent experience" (Freud quoted in Viner, 1996, p. 9).

Anna Freud substantially revised orthodox psychoanalysis by greatly expanding the role of the ego, arguing that the ego operates independently of the id. This was a major extension of the Freudian system that involved a fundamental and radical change.

She proposed those refinements in *The Ego and the Mechanisms of Defense*, published in 1936 (while her father was still alive), in which she clarified the operation of the defense mechanisms. The book received widespread praise and is considered a basic work on ego psychology. The standard defense mechanisms discussed earlier in this chapter owe their full development and articulation to Anna Freud. This is only one of her significant contributions to psychoanalytic theory.

The Anna Freud Centre

The Anna Freud Centre in London carries on her work with emotionally disturbed children and adolescents.

Reflections on Freud's Theory

Freud's system of psychoanalysis has had a phenomenal impact on theory and practice in psychology and psychiatry, on our image of human nature, and on our understanding of personality. His influence has also been felt in the general culture and his work has been featured in many popular books, magazines, and newspapers. One article called him an "inescapable force," exerting an impact even 65 years after his death (see Adler, 2006, p. 43).

Psychoanalysis contributed to the growing interest of American psychologists in the study of personality beginning in the 1930s. In the 1940s and 1950s, the ideas of psychoanalysis influenced the emerging study of motivation in psychology. Contemporary psychology has absorbed many Freudian concepts, including the role of the unconscious, the importance of childhood experiences in shaping adult behavior, and the operation of the defense mechanisms. As we have seen, these and other ideas continue to generate a great deal of research.

We will see further evidence of Freud's importance in the chapters about personality theorists who built on Freud's system or used it as a source of opposition for their ideas. Great ideas inspire not only by being considered valid but also by being perceived as incorrect, thus stimulating the development of other viewpoints.

The Decline of Freudian Psychotherapy

Freud's theory of personality remains more influential than his system of psychoanalytic therapy. Although research on Freud's ideas and experimental tests of his concepts continue to be plentiful, psychoanalysis as a therapeutic technique has declined in popularity, particularly in the United States.

In China, however, psychoanalysis as a method of therapy has become more popular. Using Skype, the Internet videoconferencing service and software application, Freudian psychoanalysts in the United States have been offering training programs to a growing number of Chinese psychoanalysts (Osnos, 2011; Wan, 2010). In some European countries, conducting traditional psychoanalytic sessions over the Internet has also been growing rapidly with initial reports of successful results (Migone, 2013).

In addition, some research has found that the use of social robots can enhance the effectiveness of psychoanalysis, particularly among the elderly. These so-called "companion robots" have been successful in enhancing physical and cognitive impairments and in improving well-being among patients (Costescu, Vanderborght, & David, 2014).

Growing numbers of people are seeking therapy for behavioral and emotional problems, but fewer are choosing the expensive, long-term approach Freud developed. Briefer courses of therapy, lasting from 1 to 15 sessions, have become the norm, along with the increasing use of psychotherapeutic drugs.

The trend away from orthodox psychoanalysis in the United States has also been reinforced by the managed-care approach to total health care. It is considerably less costly for insurance companies to approve a treatment regimen that involves simply prescribing a drug rather than a course of psychoanalysis that might last several years. In addition, managed care demands empirical evidence of the effectiveness of therapeutic treatment before providing insurance reimbursement and the evidence for the effectiveness of psychotherapy is weak (see, for example, Mayes & Horwitz, 2005).

Criticisms of Psychoanalysis

We have already noted the flaws in the case study approach, Freud's primary method of research. In addition to those issues, raised mainly by experimental psychologists, there are also questions asked by other personality theorists. Some argue that Freud placed too great an emphasis on instinctual biological forces as determinants of personality.

Others challenge Freud's focus on sex and aggression as major motivating forces and believe that we are shaped more by social experiences than by sexual ones. Some theorists disagree with Freud's deterministic view of human nature, suggesting that we have more free will than Freud acknowledged, and that we can choose to act and grow spontaneously, and to be in at least partial control of our fate.

Another criticism focuses on Freud's emphasis on past behavior to the exclusion of our goals and aspirations. These theorists argue that we are also influenced by the future, by our hopes and plans, as much as or more than by our experiences before age 5. Still other personality theorists think Freud paid too much attention to the emotionally disturbed, to the exclusion of the psychologically healthy and emotionally mature.

Critics suggest that, if we wish to develop a theory of human personality, why not study the best and the healthiest, the positive human qualities as well as the negative ones? Theorists also take exception to Freud's views on women, specifically to the concepts of penis envy, women's poorly developed superegos, and women's inferiority feelings about their bodies.

Ambiguous definitions of certain Freudian concepts have also been questioned. Critics point to confusion and contradiction in such terms as id, ego, and superego. Are they distinct physical structures in the brain? Are they fluid processes? In his later writings Freud addressed the difficulties of defining some of his concepts precisely, but the questions remain.

Freud's Lasting Influence

This book is a history of modern insights into personality. In our personal and social growth we are never free of our past, nor should we want to be. The past offers the foundation on which to build, as later personality theorists have built on Freud's work. If psychoanalysis has served no other purpose than to inspire others and provide a framework within which to develop new insights, then Freud's importance to the world of ideas is secure. Every structure depends on the soundness and integrity of its foundation. Sigmund Freud gave personality theorists a highly original, stimulating, and challenging base on which to build.

Chapter Summary

Freud's theory is at least partly autobiographical in that he based some of his major concepts on his childhood experiences, dreams, and sexual conflicts.

Instincts are mental representations of stimuli that originate within the body. Life instincts serve the purpose of survival and are manifested in a form of psychic energy called libido. Death instincts are an unconscious drive toward decay, destruction, and aggression.

The three structures of the personality are the id, ego, and superego. The id, the biological component of personality, is the storehouse of instincts and libido. It operates in accordance with the pleasure principle. The ego, the rational component of personality, operates in accordance with the reality principle. The superego, the moral side of personality, consists of the conscience (behaviors for which the child is punished) and the ego-ideal (behaviors for which the child is praised). The ego mediates among the demands of the id, the pressures of reality, and the dictates of the superego.

Anxiety develops when the ego is pressured too greatly. Reality anxiety is a fear of dangers in the real world. Neurotic anxiety is a conflict between instinctual gratification and reality. Moral anxiety is a conflict between the id and the superego. Defense mechanisms operate unconsciously. They are distortions of reality that protect the ego from the threat of anxiety. Defense mechanisms include repression, reaction formation, projection, regression, rationalization, displacement, and sublimation.

Children pass through psychosexual stages of development defined by the erogenous zones of the body. The oral stage involves two modes of behavior: oral incorporative and oral aggressive. The anal stage involves the first interference with the gratification of an instinctual impulse. The phallic stage involves the Oedipus complex, the child's unconscious sexual longings for the parent of the opposite sex and feelings of rivalry and fear toward the parent of the same sex.

Boys develop castration anxiety; girls develop penis envy. Boys resolve the Oedipus complex by identifying with their father, adopting their father's superego standards, and repressing their sexual longing for their mother. Girls are less successful in resolving the complex, which leaves them with poorly developed superegos. During the latency period, the sex instinct is sublimated in school activities, sports, and friendships with persons of the same sex. The genital stage, at puberty, marks the beginning of heterosexual relationships.

Freud's image of human nature is pessimistic. We are doomed to anxiety, to the thwarting of impulses, and to tension and conflict. The goal of life is to reduce tension. Much of human nature is inherited, but part is learned through parent–child interactions.

Two methods of personality assessment are free association and dream analysis. In free association, a patient spontaneously expresses ideas and images in random fashion. Sometimes resistances develop in which a patient resists talking about disturbing memories or experiences. Dreams have both a manifest content (the actual dream events) and a latent content (the symbolic meaning of those events).

Freud's research method was the case study, which does not rely on objective observation. It is not controlled and systematic, nor is it amenable to duplication and verification. Freud's data are not quantifiable, may be incomplete and inaccurate, and were based on a small and unrepresentative sample.

Some Freudian concepts have been supported by empirical research: the unconscious, repression, projection, displacement, verbal slips, and some characteristics of oral and anal personality types. Major portions of Freud's theory (the id, superego, death wish, libido, catharsis, and anxiety) have not been scientifically validated. Two components of the ego have been identified: ego control and ego resiliency. With regard to repressed memories of childhood sexual abuse, some may be real, whereas others may be implanted and distorted.

Freud's theory has been modified by Anna Freud, who elaborated on the role of the ego. Personality theorists criticize Freud for placing too much emphasis on biological forces, sex, aggression, emotional disturbances, and childhood events. They also criticize his deterministic image of human nature, his negative views of women, and the ambiguous definitions of some of his concepts. However, there is no denying Freud's phenomenal impact on Western culture and on later personality theorists, who either elaborated upon or opposed his system.

Review Questions

1. In what ways did Freud's theory reflect his childhood experiences and his own conflicts about sex?
2. How did Freud define instincts? How do instincts connect the body's needs with the mind's wishes?
3. Distinguish between the life instincts and the death instincts. How do they motivate behavior.
4. Define the id, the ego, and the superego. How are they interrelated.
5. What did Freud mean when he said that the ego is caught in the middle, pressured by three insistent and opposing forces?
6. What are the three types of anxiety Freud proposed? What is the purpose of anxiety? How do we defend ourselves against anxiety?
7. Describe how each of the following defense mechanisms protects us against anxiety: reaction formation, projection, sublimation.
8. In what ways do the oral and anal stages of psychosexual development differ from one another and contribute to personality development?
9. What behaviors characterize an adult fixated at the oral incorporative phase? At the anal retentive phase?
10. How do boys and girls resolve the conflicts of the phallic stage of psychosexual development?
11. In your opinion, how would boys and girls reared by a single mother resolve these conflicts?
12. What are Freud's views on the relative influences of heredity and environment? What is Freud's position on the issue of free will versus determinism?
13. What kind of information can be revealed by free association? What are resistances?
14. Describe two aspects or contents of dreams. Discuss research conducted to test Freud's ideas about dream contents.
15. Which of the propositions in Freud's theory have received empirical support?
16. What criticisms have been made of Freud's case study method?
17. Give examples of research conducted on the concepts of the Freudian slip, the ego, and catharsis.
18. How does research on subliminal perception support Freud's views on the unconscious?

19. What is the difference between ego control and ego resiliency? Describe some personality characteristics of people who score high in ego control.
20. In what ways do repressors differ from non-repressors? Which of the two repressive coping styles is associated with happier and healthier behavior?
21. At what ages are the defense mechanisms of denial, identification, and projection most likely to be used? Why?
22. Does the Freudian defense mechanism of repression explain all instances of repressed memories of childhood abuse? What other factors might account for such memories?
23. Describe some of the ways in which Anna Freud extended and modified traditional Freudian theory.
24. Discuss the current status and acceptance of psychoanalysis as a personality theory and as a method of psychotherapy.

Suggested Readings

Cohen, D. (2012). *The escape of Sigmund Freud.* New York: Overlook Press. An account of Freud's escape from the Nazis in Vienna with the help of a German official, and the last two years of his life in London.

Coles, R. (1993). *Anna Freud: The dream of psychoanalysis.* New York: Addison-Wesley. Describes Anna Freud's life, her work on defense mechanisms, and her hopes for the future of psychoanalysis.

Ellenberger, H. F. (1970). *The discovery of the unconscious: The history and evolution of dynamic psychiatry.* New York: Basic Books. Traces the study of the unconscious from primitive times to Freudian psychoanalysis and its derivatives.

Gafner, G. (2012). *Subliminal: How Your Unconscious Mind Rules Your Behavior.* New York: Pantheon. A physicist's account summarizing research in neuroscience and psychology showing how much of our behavior, emotions and cognitive processes are influenced by unconscious processes.

Krüll, M. (1986). *Freud and his father.* New York: Norton. Examines the lives of Sigmund Freud and his father and analyzes the influences of Freud's experiences as a son on the development of psychoanalysis.

Lerman, H. (1986). *A mote in Freud's eye: From psychoanalysis to the psychology of women.* New York: Springer-Verlag. Describes how Freud's negative bias toward women developed from his personal experiences and permeated his theory of psychoanalysis. Shows how Freud's stages of psychosexual development, as they apply to females, have been largely disproved, and offers criteria for a woman-based personality theory.

Markel, Howard. (2011). *An Anatomy of Addiction: Sigmund Freud, William Halstead, and the Miracle Drug Cocaine.* New York: Vintage. An account of the uses and abuses of cocaine in the 19th century, as recounted through the lives of two users, Freud and the noted American physician William Halstead.

Roazen, P. (1975). *Freud and his followers.* New York: Knopf. A lively, well-written account of Freud's life and of the men and women who became his disciples, some of whom later broke away to form their own schools of thought.

Sulloway, F. J. (1979). *Freud, biologist of the mind: Beyond the psychoanalytic legend.* New York: Basic Books. A biography that places Freud's work in the context of its times and disputes the legend that Freud was a lonely hero working in isolation.

The Neo-psychoanalytic Approach

Several personality theorists, who initially were loyal to Freud and committed to his system of psychoanalysis, broke away because of their opposition to certain aspects of his approach. Carl Jung and Alfred Adler were associates of Freud's before they rebelled against him and offered their own views of personality. Karen Horney did not have a personal relationship with Freud but was also an orthodox Freudian before marking out a different path. Erik Erikson's work is also derived from Freudian psychoanalysis.

These neo-psychoanalytic theorists differ from one another on a number of issues but they were equally opposed to Freud's emphasis on instincts as the primary motivators of human behavior, as well as his deterministic view of personality. These neo-psychoanalytic theorists presented more optimistic and flattering images of human nature than Freud did. Their work shows how quickly the field of personality diversified within only a decade after it formally began.

Carl Jung: Analytical Psychology

Fair Use

My life is a story of the self-realization of the unconscious. Everything in the unconscious seeks outward manifestation, and the personality too desires to evolve out of its unconscious conditions.

—**Carl Jung**

Sigmund Freud once designated Carl Jung as his spiritual son and heir, but Jung went on to develop his own theory of personality that differed dramatically from orthodox psychoanalysis. He fashioned a new and elaborate explanation of human nature quite unlike any other which he called **analytical psychology**.

The first point on which Jung came to disagree with Freud was the role of sexuality. Jung broadened Freud's definition of libido by redefining it as a more generalized psychic energy that included sex but was not restricted to it.

analytical psychology
Jung's theory of personality.

The second major area of disagreement concerned the direction of the forces that influence personality. Whereas Freud viewed human beings as prisoners or victims of past events, Jung believed that "man is not necessarily doomed forever to be shoved about by traumas over which he could exercise little control" (Obituary, *New York Times*, June 7, 1961). Jung argued that we are shaped by our future as well as our past. We are affected not only by what happened to us as children, but also by what we aspire to do in the future.

The third significant point of difference revolved around the unconscious. Rather than minimizing the role of the unconscious, as did the other neo-psychoanalytic dissenters we will discuss, Jung placed an even greater emphasis on it than Freud did. He probed more deeply into the unconscious and added an entirely new dimension: the inherited experiences of all human and even prehuman species. Although Freud had recognized the influence of inherited primal experiences, Jung made it the core of his system of personality. He brought together ideas from history, mythology, anthropology, and religion to form his own image of human nature.

The Life of Jung (1875–1961)

An Unhappy Childhood

Jung's difficult and unhappy childhood years were marked by deaths and funerals, neurotic parents in a failing marriage, religious doubts and conflicts, bizarre dreams and visions, and a wooden doll for his only companion. Born in Switzerland into a family that included nine clergymen (eight uncles and his father), Jung was introduced at an early age to religion and the classics. He was close to his father but considered him weak and powerless. Although kind and tolerant, Jung's father experienced periods of moodiness and irritability and failed to be the strong authority figure his son needed.

Jung's mother was by far the more powerful parent, but her emotional instability led her to behave erratically. She would change in an instant from being cheerful and happy to suddenly mumbling incoherently and gazing vacantly into space. As a boy, Jung came to view his mother as being two different people inhabiting the same body. Not surprisingly, this disturbed him. One biographer suggested that "the whole maternal side of the family appeared to be tainted with insanity" (Ellenberger, 1978, p. 149).

As a result of his mother's odd behavior, Jung became wary of all women, a suspicion that took many years to dispel. He later described his mother as being fat and unattractive, which may explain why he totally rejected Freud's notion that every boy has a sexual longing for his mother. Clearly, that did not reflect his childhood experience.

To avoid his parents and their continuing marital problems, Jung spent many hours alone in the attic, carving a doll out of wood, a figure in whom he could confide his innermost thoughts and fears. A sister was born when Carl was 9 years old, but her presence in the house did nothing to ease his loneliness and feeling of isolation.

Strange Dreams and Fantasies

Distrustful of his mother and disappointed in his father, Jung felt cut off from the external world, the world of conscious reality. As an escape, he turned inward to his unconscious, to the world of dreams, visions, and fantasies, in which he felt more secure. This choice would guide Jung for the rest of his life. Whenever he was faced with a problem, he would look for a solution through his dreams and visions.

The essence of his personality theory was shaped in essentially the same way. When Jung was three, he dreamed he was in a cavern. In a later dream, he saw himself digging down beneath the earth's surface, unearthing the bones of prehistoric animals. To Jung, such dreams represented the direction of his approach to the human personality. They directed him to explore the unconscious mind, which lies beneath the surface of behavior.

So strongly was he guided by these manifestations of his unconscious that he entitled his autobiography *Memories, Dreams, Reflections* (1961). He believed that his approach to personality resembled a subjective, personal confession. Thus, like Freud's work, Jung's personality theory was intensely autobiographical. In a lecture given at the age of 50, he acknowledged the influence of his life events on his theory.

As a child, Jung deliberately avoided other children, and they avoided him. A biographer wrote: "Carl usually played alone for parents of the village children deliberately kept them away from the odd little boy whose parents were so peculiar" (Bair, 2003, p. 22). In describing his solitary childhood, Jung wrote, "The pattern of my relationship to the world was already prefigured; today as then I am a solitary" (Jung, 1961, pp. 41–42).

Jung's loneliness is reflected in his theory, which focuses on the inner growth of the individual rather than on relationships with other people. In contrast, Freud's theory is concerned more with interpersonal relationships, perhaps because Freud, unlike Jung, did not have such an isolated and introverted childhood.

The Study of Medicine

Jung disliked school and resented the time he had to devote to formal studies rather than to ideas that interested him. He much preferred to read on his own, particularly about religious and philosophical issues. To his delight, he was forced to miss 6 months of school as a result of a series of fainting spells. He returned to school but his presence was disruptive. His teachers sent him home because his classmates were more interested in "waiting for Carl to faint than in doing their lessons" (Bair, 2003, p. 31).

When Jung overheard his father say, "What will become of the boy if he cannot earn his living?" his illness suddenly disappeared, and he returned to school to work more diligently than before (Jung, 1961, p. 31). Jung later wrote that the experience taught him about neurotic behavior. He recognized that he had unconsciously arranged the situation to suit himself, to keep him out of school, and that realization made him feel angry and ashamed.

Jung chose to study medicine at the University of Basel and decided, to the disappointment of his professors, to specialize in psychiatry, a field then held in low repute. He believed that psychiatry would give him the opportunity to pursue his interests in dreams, the supernatural, and the occult.

Beginning in 1900, Jung worked at a mental hospital in Zurich, under the direction of Eugen Bleuler, the psychiatrist who coined the term *schizophrenia*. When Jung married the second-richest heiress in all of Switzerland, he quit his job at the hospital and spent his spare time riding around the countryside in his much-loved red Chrysler convertible. He also gave lectures at the University of Zurich and developed an independent clinical practice.

The Years with Freud

By the time Jung became associated with Sigmund Freud in 1907, Jung had already established a significant professional reputation on his own. When Jung and Freud met for the first time, they were so congenial and had so much to share that they talked for 13 hours. Their friendship became a close one. "I formally adopted you as an eldest son," Freud wrote to Jung, "and anointed you as my successor and crown prince" (Freud & Jung, 1974, p. 218). Jung considered Freud a father figure. "Let me enjoy your friendship not as one between equals," he wrote to Freud, "but as that of father and son" (Freud & Jung, 1974, p. 122). Their relationship appeared to contain many of the elements of the Oedipus complex, with its inevitable wish of the son to destroy the father.

Also, their relationship may have been tainted, even doomed, by a sexual experience Jung said he had at the age of 18. A family friend, an older man who had been a father figure and confidant, made physical overtures to Jung, seeking a homosexual encounter. Repelled and disappointed, Jung broke off the relationship. Years later, when Freud, who was nearly 20 years older than Jung, attempted to designate Jung as his son and heir, Jung may have felt Freud was, in a sense, forcing himself on Jung and changing the nature of their relationship. Because of Jung's earlier encounter with the older man, he may have been similarly disappointed in Freud and unable to sustain an emotionally close relationship with him.

For a time, however, the two men remained close. Jung continued to live in Zurich, but he met with Freud periodically and maintained a voluminous correspondence. In 1909, he traveled with Freud to the United States to lecture at Clark University. Freud was grooming Jung to take over the presidency of the International Psychoanalytic Association. Concerned that psychoanalysis would be labeled a Jewish science (as it came to be called during the Nazi era), Freud wanted a non-Jew to assume titular leadership of the movement.

Contrary to Freud's hopes, Jung was not an uncritical disciple. Jung had his own ideas and unique view of the human personality, and when he began to express these notions, it became inevitable that they would part. They severed their relationship in 1913.

Jung's Neurotic Episode

That same year, when Jung was 38 years old, he suffered a severe neurotic episode that lasted for 3 years. He believed he was in danger of losing contact with reality and was so distressed that he resigned his lectureship at the University of Zurich. At times he considered suicide. He "kept a revolver next to his bed in case he felt he had passed beyond the point of no return" (Noll, 1994, p. 207). Although he felt unable to continue with his scientific work, he somehow continued to treat his patients.

During the crisis Jung experienced vivid and violent dreams and visions involving large-scale disasters such as ice covering the earth, flowing rivers of blood, even the destruction of all civilization (see Elms, 2010). Other dreams were more personal but equally terrifying. "Jung travels the land of the dead, falls in love with a woman he later realizes is his sister, gets squeezed by a giant serpent and ... eats the liver of a little child" (Corbett, 2009, p. 5).

During those years he was haunted by visions of a bloody apocalypse and widespread carnage and desolation. He meticulously recorded those dreams in calligraphy and elaborate drawings in some 200 pages of what became known as *The Red Book,* so called because it was bound in red leather. The journal was kept secret in a Swiss bank vault and was not published until 2009, nearly 50 years after his death (see Harrison, 2009). The book received widespread publicity and quickly became an international sensation.

Freud, as we saw, had also suffered a neurotic episode at approximately the same age and resolved it by analyzing his dreams, which formed a basis for his personality theory. Jung's situation offers a remarkable parallel. Jung overcame his disturbance by confronting his unconscious through the exploration of his dreams and fantasies. Although Jung's self-analysis was less systematic than Freud's, his approach was similar.

Out of Jung's confrontation with his unconscious he fashioned his approach to personality. "The years when I was pursuing my inner images," he wrote, "were the most important in my life—in them everything essential was decided" (Jung, 1961, p. 199). He concluded that the most crucial stage in personality development was not childhood, as Freud believed, but middle age, which was the time of Jung's own crisis.

Like Freud, Jung established his theory on an intuitive base, which derived from his personal experiences and dreams. It was then refined along more rational and empirical lines by data provided by his patients. Nearly two-thirds of them were middle-aged and suffering from the same difficulties Jung faced.

Jung's Sex Life

Jung, who minimized the importance of sex in his personality theory, maintained a vigorous, anxiety-free sex life and enjoyed a number of extramarital affairs. One of these relationships endured, with his wife's knowledge, for many years. He surrounded himself with adoring women patients and disciples who typically fell deeply in love with him. A biographer noted that this "happened with all of his female disciples sooner or later, as he often told them at the beginning of their treatment" (Noll, 1997, p. 253).

Contrast Jung's active sex life with Freud's troubled attitude toward sex and his cessation of sexual relations at the time he was fashioning a theory that focused on sex as the cause of neurotic behavior. "To Jung, who freely and frequently satisfied his sexual needs, sex played a minimal role in human motivation. To Freud, beset by frustrations and anxious about his thwarted desires, sex played the central role" (Schultz, 1990, p. 148).

Fame and Weird Behavior

The rest of Jung's long life was personally and professionally successful, although he did behave in some really bizarre ways. In the mornings he would greet the kitchen utensils, saying " 'greetings to you' to the frying pans or 'good morning to you' to the coffee pot" (Bair, 2003, p. 568). He also worried needlessly about money even though he was quite wealthy. He hid large amounts of cash inside books and then forgot the secret code he had devised to help him remember which books contained the money. He stuffed money into vases and jars and buried them in his garden and then forgot the elaborate system he had concocted to help him find them. After his death, his family recovered much of the money from his books but it is likely that the cash in his garden remains there today.

Jung and his wife adopted a cold, formal manner for dealing with their three daughters. There was limited physical contact, no hugging or kissing. "When they said hello or goodbye, they shook hands, if they touched at all" (Bair, 2003, p. 565).

Jung remained productive in research and writing for most of his 86 years. His books became popular, and his analytical psychology attracted increasing numbers of followers. His ideas spread to the English-speaking world, and particularly to the United States, primarily through the generous financial support of the wealthy and prominent Rockefeller, McCormick, and Mellon families. A number of the family members sought analysis with Jung and in return arranged for the translation and publication of his books into English. It is interesting to speculate whether Jung's works might have remained little known without their help, inaccessible to all but the German-speaking community (Noll, 1997).

Carl Jung

Various sites provide biographical information, discussions of his theory, research on relevant concepts, and links to other resources.

The C. G. Jung Institute

Leads to informational web sites for various Jung Institutes, describing training requirements and educational opportunities.

Psychic Energy: The Basis of Jung's System

One of the first points on which Jung disagreed with Freud involved the nature of libido. Jung did not believe that libido was primarily a sexual energy; he argued instead that it was a broad, undifferentiated life energy.

libido To Jung, a broader and more generalized form of psychic energy.

psyche Jung's term for personality.

Jung used the term **libido** in two ways: first, as a diffuse and general life energy, and second, from a perspective similar to Freud's, as a narrower psychic energy that fuels the work of the personality, which he called the **psyche**. It is through psychic energy that psychological activities such as perceiving, thinking, feeling, and wishing are carried out.

When a person invests a great deal of psychic energy in a particular idea or feeling, it is said to have a high psychic value and can strongly influence the person's life. For example, if you are highly motivated to achieve power, then you will devote most of your psychic energy to devise ways of obtaining it.

Principles of Psychic Energy

opposition principle Jung's idea that conflict between opposing processes or tendencies is necessary to generate psychic energy.

Jung drew on ideas from physics to explain the functioning of psychic energy. He proposed three basic principles: opposites, equivalence, and entropy (Jung, 1928). The **principle of opposites** can be seen throughout Jung's system. He noted the existence of opposites or polarities in physical energy in the universe, such as heat versus cold, height versus depth, creation versus decay. So it is with psychic energy, he argued. Every wish or feeling has its opposite. This opposition—this conflict between polarities—is the primary motivator of behavior and generator of energy. The sharper the conflict between polarities, the greater will be the energy produced.

equivalence principle The continuing redistribution of energy within a personality; if the energy expended on certain conditions or activities weakens or disappears, that energy is transferred elsewhere in the personality.

For his **principle of equivalence**, Jung applied the physical principle of the conservation of energy to psychic events. He stated that energy expended in bringing about some condition is not lost but rather is shifted to another part of the personality. Thus, if the psychic value in a particular area weakens or disappears, that energy is transferred elsewhere in the psyche. For example, if we lose interest in a person, a hobby, or a field of study, the psychic energy formerly invested in that area is shifted to a new one. The psychic energy used for conscious activities while we are awake is shifted to dreams when we are asleep.

The word *equivalence* implies that the new area to which energy has shifted must have an equal psychic value; that is, it should be equally desirable, compelling, or fascinating. Otherwise, the excess energy will flow into the unconscious. In whatever direction and manner energy flows, the principle of equivalence dictates that energy is continually redistributed within the personality.

entropy principle A tendency toward balance or equilibrium within the personality; the ideal is an equal distribution of psychic energy over all structures of the personality.

In physics, the **principle of entropy** refers to the equalization of energy differences. For example, if a hot object and a cold object are placed in direct contact, heat will flow from the hotter object to the colder object until they are in equilibrium at the same temperature. In effect, an exchange of energy occurs, resulting in a kind of homeostatic balance between the objects.

Jung applied this law to psychic energy by proposing that there is a tendency toward maintaining a balance or equilibrium in the personality. If two desires or beliefs differ greatly in intensity or psychic value, energy will flow from the more strongly held to the weaker. Ideally, the personality has an equal distribution of psychic energy over all its aspects, but this ideal state is never achieved. If perfect balance or equilibrium were attained, then the personality would have no psychic energy because, as we noted earlier, the opposition principle requires conflict for psychic energy to be produced.

Aspects of Personality

Jung believed that the total personality, or psyche, is composed of several distinct systems or aspects that can influence one another.

The Ego

ego To Jung, the conscious aspect of personality.

The **ego** is the center of consciousness, the part of the psyche concerned with perceiving, thinking, feeling, and remembering. It is our awareness of ourselves and is responsible for carrying out all the normal everyday activities of waking life. The ego acts in a selective way, admitting into conscious awareness only a portion of the stimuli to which we are exposed.

The Attitudes: Extraversion and Introversion

extraversion An attitude of the psyche characterized by an orientation toward the external world and other people.

introversion An attitude of the psyche characterized by an orientation toward one's own thoughts and feelings.

Much of our conscious perception of our environment, and how we react to it, is determined by the opposing mental attitudes of **extraversion** and **introversion**. Jung believed that psychic energy could be channeled externally, toward the outside world, or internally, toward the self. Extraverts are open, sociable, and socially assertive, oriented toward other people and the external world. Introverts are withdrawn and often shy, and tend to focus on themselves, on their own thoughts and feelings.

According to Jung, all of us have the capacity for both attitudes, but only one becomes dominant in our personality. The dominant attitude then tends to direct our behavior and consciousness. The nondominant attitude still remains influential, however, and becomes part of the personal unconscious, where it can affect behavior. For example, in certain situations an introverted person may display characteristics of extraversion, and wish to be more outgoing, or be attracted to an extravert.

Psychological Functions

As Jung came to recognize that there were different kinds of extraverts and introverts, he proposed additional distinctions among people based on what he called the psychological functions. These functions refer to different and opposing ways of perceiving both the external real world and our subjective inner world. Jung posited four functions of the psyche: sensing, intuiting, thinking, and feeling (Jung, 1927).

Sensing and intuiting are grouped together as nonrational functions because they do not use the processes of reason. These functions accept experiences and do not evaluate them. Sensing reproduces an experience through the senses the way a photograph copies an object. Intuiting does not arise directly from an external stimulus. For example, if we believe someone else is with us in a darkened room, our belief may be based on our intuition or a hunch rather than on actual sensory experience.

The second pair of opposing functions, thinking and feeling, are rational functions that involve making judgments and evaluations about our experiences. Although thinking and feeling are opposites, both are concerned with organizing and categorizing experiences. The thinking function involves a conscious judgment of whether an experience is true or false. The kind of evaluation made by the feeling function is expressed in terms of like or dislike, pleasantness or unpleasantness, stimulation or dullness.

Just as our psyche contains some of both the extraversion and introversion attitudes, so do we have the capacity for all four psychological functions. Similarly, just as one attitude is dominant, only one function is dominant. The others are submerged in the personal unconscious. Further, only one pair of functions is dominant—either the rational or the irrational—and within each pair only one function is dominant. A person cannot be ruled by both thinking and feeling or by both sensing and intuiting, because they are opposing functions.

Psychological Types

psychological types To Jung, eight personality types based on interactions of the attitudes (introversion and extraversion) and the functions (thinking, feeling, sensing, and intuiting).

Jung proposed eight **psychological types**, based on the interactions of the two attitudes and four functions. (See Table 3.1.)

The *extraverted thinking types* live strictly in accordance with society's rules. These people tend to repress feelings and emotions, to be objective in all aspects of life, and to be dogmatic in thoughts and opinions. They may be perceived as rigid and cold. They tend to make good scientists because their focus is on learning about the external world and using logical rules to describe and understand it.

The *extraverted feeling types* tend to repress the thinking mode and to be highly emotional. They conform to the traditional values and moral codes they have been taught and are unusually sensitive to the opinions and expectations of others. They are emotionally responsive, make friends easily, and tend to be sociable and effervescent. Jung believed this type was found more often among women than men.

The *extraverted sensing types* focus on pleasure and happiness and on seeking new experiences. They are strongly oriented toward the real world and are adaptable to different kinds of people and changing situations. Not given to introspection, they tend to be outgoing, with a high capacity for enjoying life.

The *extraverted intuiting types* find success in business and politics because of a keen ability to exploit opportunities. They are attracted to new ideas, tend to be creative, and are able to inspire others to accomplish and achieve. They also tend to be changeable, moving from one idea or venture to another, and to make decisions based more on hunches than on reflection. Their decisions, however, are likely to be correct.

TABLE 3.1 Jung's psychological types

Extraverted thinking	Logical, objective, dogmatic
Extraverted feeling	Emotional, sensitive, sociable; more typical of women than men
Extraverted sensing	Outgoing, pleasure seeking, adaptable
Extraverted intuiting	Creative, able to motivate others, and to seize opportunities
Introverted thinking	More interested in ideas than in people
Introverted feeling	Reserved, undemonstrative, yet capable of deep emotion
Introverted sensing	Outwardly detached, expressing themselves in aesthetic pursuits
Introverted intuiting	Concerned with the unconscious more than everyday reality

Extraverts channel the libido externally, toward the outside world.

Age Fotostock/SuperStock

The *introverted thinking types* do not get along well with other people and have difficulty communicating ideas. They focus on thoughts rather than feelings and have poor practical judgment. Intensely concerned with privacy, they prefer to deal with abstractions and theories, and they focus on understanding themselves rather than other people. Others see them as stubborn, aloof, arrogant, and inconsiderate.

The *introverted feeling types* repress rational thought. They are capable of deep emotion but avoid any outward expression of it. They seem mysterious and inaccessible and tend to be quiet, modest, and childish. They have little consideration for others' feelings and thoughts and appear withdrawn, cold, and self-assured.

The *introverted sensing types* appear passive, calm, and detached from the everyday world. They look on most human activities with benevolence and amusement. They are aesthetically sensitive, expressing themselves in art or music, and tend to repress their intuition.

The *introverted intuiting types* focus so intently on intuition that they have little contact with reality. They are visionaries and daydreamers—aloof, unconcerned with practical matters, and poorly understood by others. Considered odd and eccentric, they have difficulty coping with everyday life and planning for the future.

The Personal Unconscious

personal unconscious
The reservoir of material that was once conscious but has been forgotten or suppressed.

The **personal unconscious** in Jung's system is similar to Freud's concept of the preconscious. It is a reservoir of material that was once conscious but has been forgotten or suppressed because it was trivial or disturbing. There is considerable two-way traffic back and forth between the ego and the personal unconscious. For example, your attention might wander away from this page to a memory of something you did yesterday. All kinds of experiences are stored in the personal unconscious, which has been likened to a filing cabinet. Little mental effort is required to take something out, examine it for a while, and then put it back, where it will remain until the next time we want it or are reminded of it.

Complexes

complex To Jung, a core or pattern of emotions, memories, perceptions, and wishes in the personal unconscious organized around a common theme, such as power or status.

As we file more and more experiences in our personal unconscious, we begin to group them into what Jung called **complexes**. A complex is a core or pattern of emotions, memories, perceptions, and wishes organized around a common theme. For example, we might say that some people have a complex about power or status, meaning that they are preoccupied with that theme to the point where it influences behavior. They might try to become powerful by running for elective office, or to identify or affiliate with power by driving a motorcycle or a fast car. By directing thoughts and behavior in various ways, the complex determines how that person perceives the world.

Complexes may be conscious or unconscious. Those that are not under conscious control can intrude on and interfere with consciousness. The person with a complex is generally not aware of its influence, although other people may easily observe its effects.

Some complexes may be harmful, but others can be useful. For example, a perfection or achievement complex may lead a person to work hard at developing particular talents or skills. Jung believed that complexes originate not only from our childhood and adult experiences, but also from our ancestral experiences, the heritage of the species contained in the collective unconscious.

The Collective Unconscious

collective unconscious The deepest level of the psyche containing the accumulation of inherited experiences of human and pre-human species.

The deepest and least accessible level of the psyche, the **collective unconscious**, is the most unusual and controversial aspect of Jung's system. Jung believed that just as each of us accumulates and files all of our personal experiences in the personal unconscious, so does humankind collectively, as a species, store the experiences of all our human and pre-human ancestors in the collective unconscious. This heritage is passed to each new generation.

He believed that whatever experiences are universal—that is, are repeated by each generation—become part of our personality. Our primitive past thus becomes the basis of the human psyche, directing and influencing our present behavior. To Jung, the collective unconscious was the powerful and controlling repository of ancestral experiences. Thus, Jung linked the personality of each of us with the past, not only with childhood but also with the history of the species.

We do not inherit these collective experiences directly. For example, we do not inherit a fear of snakes. Rather, we inherit the potential to fear snakes. We are predisposed to behave and feel the same ways people have always behaved and felt. Whether the predisposition becomes reality depends on the specific experiences we encounter in life.

Jung believed that certain basic experiences have characterized every generation throughout human history. People have always had a mother figure, for example, and have experienced birth and death. They have faced unknown terrors in the dark, worshipped power or some sort of godlike figure, and feared an evil being. The universality of these experiences over countless evolving generations leaves an imprint on each of us at birth and determines how we perceive and react to our world. Jung wrote, "The form of the world into which [a person] is born is already inborn in him, as a virtual image" (Jung, 1953, p. 188).

A baby is born predisposed to perceive the mother in a certain way. If the mother behaves the way mothers typically behave, in a nurturing and supportive manner, then the baby's predisposition will correspond with its reality.

Because the collective unconscious is such an unusual concept, it is important to note the reason Jung proposed it and the kind of evidence he gathered to support it. In his studies of ancient cultures, both mythical and real, Jung discovered what he believed to be common themes and symbols that appeared in diverse parts of the world. As far as he could determine, these ideas had not been transmitted or communicated orally or in writing from one culture to another.

In addition, Jung's patients, in their dreams and fantasies, recalled and described the same kinds of symbols he had discovered in ancient cultures. He could find no other explanation for these shared symbols and themes over such vast geographical and temporal distances than that they were transmitted by and carried in each person's unconscious mind.

Archetypes

archetypes Images of universal experiences contained in the collective unconscious.

The ancient experiences contained in the collective unconscious are manifested by recurring themes or patterns, which Jung called **archetypes** (Jung, 1947). He also used the term *primordial images*. There are many such images, as many as there are common human experiences. By being repeated in the lives of succeeding generations, archetypes have become imprinted in our psyches and are expressed in our dreams and fantasies.

Among the archetypes Jung proposed are the hero, the mother, the child, God, death, power, and the wise old man. A few of these are developed more fully than others and influence the psyche more consistently. These major archetypes include the persona, the anima and animus, the shadow, and the self.

The Persona   The word *persona* refers to a mask that an actor wears to display various roles or faces to the audience. Jung used the term with basically the same meaning.

persona archetype The public face or role a person presents to others.

The **persona archetype** is a mask, a public face we wear to present ourselves as someone different from who we really are. The persona is necessary, Jung believed, because we are forced to play so many roles in life in order to succeed in school and on the job and in getting along with a variety of people.

Although the persona can be helpful, it can also be harmful if we come to believe that it reflects our true nature. Instead of merely playing a role, we may then become that

In the fully developed personality, a person will express behaviors considered characteristic of the opposite sex.

Zero Creatives/Cultura/Corbis

role. As a result, other aspects of our personality will not be allowed to develop. When this happens, the ego may come to identify with the persona rather than with the person's true nature, resulting in a condition known as inflation of the persona. Whether the person plays a role or comes to believe that role, he or she is resorting to deception. In the first instance, the person is deceiving others; in the second instance, the person is deceiving himself.

The Anima and Animus   The anima and animus archetypes refer to Jung's recognition that humans are essentially bisexual. On the biological level, each sex secretes the hormones of the other sex as well as those of its own sex. On the psychological level, each sex manifests characteristics, temperaments, and attitudes of the other sex by virtue of centuries of living together. The psyche of the woman contains masculine aspects (the **animus archetype**), and the psyche of the man contains feminine aspects (the **anima archetype**). (See Figure 3.1.)

Animus archetype
Masculine aspects of the female psyche.

Anima archetype
Feminine aspects of the male psyche.

These opposite sex characteristics aid in the adjustment and survival of the species because they enable a person of one sex to understand the nature of the other sex. The archetypes predispose us to like certain characteristics of the opposite sex and guide our behavior with reference to the opposite sex.

Jung insisted that both the anima and the animus must be expressed. A man must exhibit his feminine as well as his masculine characteristics, and a woman must express her masculine characteristics along with her feminine ones. Otherwise, these vital aspects will remain dormant and undeveloped, leading to a one-sidedness of the personality.

shadow archetype The dark side of the personality; the archetype that contains primitive animal instincts.

The Shadow   The most powerful archetype has the sinister and mysterious name of **shadow**, which contains the basic, primitive animal instincts and therefore has the deepest roots of all archetypes. Behaviors that society considers evil and immoral reside in the shadow, and this dark side of human nature must be tamed if people are to live in harmony. We must at all times restrain, overcome, and defend against these primitive impulses. If not, society will very likely punish us.

But that presents us with a dilemma because not only is the shadow the source of evil, it is also the source of vitality, spontaneity, creativity, and emotion. Therefore, if the shadow is totally suppressed, the psyche will be dull and lifeless. It's the job of the ego to repress the animal instincts enough so that we are considered civilized while allowing sufficient expression of the instincts to provide creativity and vigor.

If the shadow is fully suppressed, not only does the personality become flat, but the person also faces the possibility that the shadow will revolt. The animal instincts do not disappear when they are suppressed. Rather, they lie dormant, waiting for a crisis or a weakness in the ego so they can gain control. When that happens, the person becomes dominated by the unconscious, which is not a good thing.

FIGURE 3.1

The Yin-Yang symbol illustrates the complementary sides of our nature. The dark right side represents feminine aspects (the anima archetype) and the light left side represents masculine aspects (the animus archetype). The dot of the opposite color in each portion indicates the expression of the characteristics of the opposite archetype.

self archetype To Jung, the archetype that represents the unity, integration, and harmony of the total personality.

The Self   The **self archetype** represents the unity, integration, and harmony of the total personality. To Jung, the striving toward that wholeness is the ultimate goal of life. This archetype involves bringing together and balancing all parts of the personality. We have already noted Jung's principle of opposites and the importance of polarities to the psyche. In the self archetype, the opposites of conscious and unconscious processes must become assimilated so that the self, which is the center of the personality, shifts from the ego to a point of equilibrium midway between the opposing forces of the conscious and the unconscious. As a result, material from the unconscious comes to have a greater influence on the personality.

The full realization of the self lies in the future. It is a goal—something to always strive for but which is rarely achieved. The self serves as a motivating force, pulling us from ahead rather than pushing us from behind (as our past experiences do).

The self cannot begin to emerge until all the other systems of the psyche have developed. This occurs around middle age, a crucial period of transition in Jung's system, as it was in his own life. The actualization of the self involves goals and plans for the future and an accurate perception of one's abilities. Because development of the self is impossible without self-knowledge, it is the most difficult process we face in life and requires persistence, perceptiveness, and wisdom.

The Development of the Personality

Jung believed that personality is determined by what we hope to be as well as by what we have been in the past and by what happened to us then. He criticized Freud for emphasizing only past events as shapers of personality, to the exclusion of the future. Jung believed we develop and grow regardless of age and are always moving toward a more complete level of self-realization (see Table 3.2).

Jung took a longer view of personality than Freud, who concentrated on the early years of life and foresaw little development after the age of 5. Jung did not posit sequential stages of growth in as much detail as Freud, but he wrote of two general periods in the overall developmental process (Jung, 1930).

Childhood to Young Adulthood

The ego begins to develop in early childhood, at first in a primitive way because the child has not yet formed a unique identity. What might be called children's personalities are, at this stage, little more than a reflection of the personalities of their parents. Obviously, then, parents exert a great influence on the formation of the child's personality. They can enhance or impede personality development by the way they behave toward their child.

TABLE 3.2 Jung's developmental stages	
Childhood	Ego development begins when the child distinguishes between self and others.
Puberty to young adulthood	Adolescents must adapt to the growing demands of reality. The focus is external, on education, career, and family. The conscious is dominant.
Middle age	A period of transition when the focus of the personality shifts from external to internal in an attempt to balance the unconscious with the conscious.

Parents might try to force their own personalities on their children, wanting them to be an extension of themselves. Or they might expect their children to develop personalities quite different from their own as a way of seeking vicarious compensation for their own deficiencies. The ego begins to form substantively only when children become able to distinguish between themselves and other people or objects in their world. In other words, consciousness forms when the child is able to say "I."

It is not until puberty that the psyche assumes a definite form and content. This period, which Jung called our psychic birth, is marked by difficulties and the need to adapt. Childhood fantasies must end as the adolescent confronts the demands of reality. From the teenage years through young adulthood, we are concerned with preparatory activities such as completing our education, beginning a career, getting married, and starting a family.

Our focus during these years is external, our conscious is dominant, and, in general, our primary conscious attitude is that of extraversion. The aim of life is to achieve our goals and establish a secure, successful place for ourselves in the world. Thus, young adulthood should be an exciting and challenging time, filled with new horizons and accomplishments.

Middle Age

Jung believed that major personality changes occur between the ages of 35 and 40. This period of middle age was the time of personal crisis for Jung and for many of his patients. By that age, the adaptation problems of young adulthood have usually been resolved. The typical 40-year-old is established in a career, a marriage, and a

Middle age is a time of transition, when one's focus and interests change.

Tetra Images/Alamy

community. Jung asked why, when success has been achieved, so many people that age are gripped by feelings of despair and worthlessness. His patients all told him essentially the same thing: They felt empty. Adventure, excitement, and zest had disappeared. Life had lost its meaning.

The more Jung analyzed this period, the more strongly he believed that such drastic personality changes were inevitable and universal. Middle age is a natural time of transition in which the personality is supposed to undergo necessary and beneficial changes. Ironically, the changes occur because middle-aged people have been so successful in meeting life's demands. They had invested a great deal of energy in the preparatory activities of the first half of life, but by age 40 that preparation was finished and those challenges had been met. Although they still possess considerable energy, it now has nowhere to go, and so, Jung believed, it has to be rechanneled into different activities and interests.

Jung noted that in the first half of life we must focus on the objective world of reality—education, career, and family. In contrast, the second half of life must be devoted to the inner, subjective world that heretofore had been neglected. The attitude of the personality must shift from extraversion to introversion. The focus on consciousness must be tempered by an awareness of the unconscious. Our interests must shift from the physical and material to the spiritual, philosophical, and intuitive. A balance among all facets of the personality must replace the previous exclusive focus on consciousness.

Thus, at middle age we must begin the process of realizing or actualizing the self. If we are successful in integrating the unconscious with the conscious, then we are in a position to attain a new level of positive psychological health which Jung called individuation.

Individuation: How to Reach Fulfillment

individuation A condition of psychological health resulting from the integration of all conscious and unconscious facets of the personality.

Simply stated, **individuation** involves becoming an individual, fulfilling one's capacities, and developing one's self. The tendency toward individuation is innate and inevitable, but it can be helped or hindered by environmental forces, such as one's educational and economic opportunities and the nature of the parent–child relationship. There are several stages or steps through which we must proceed before we can reach Jung's ideal of self-fulfillment.

Confront the Unconscious   To strive for individuation, middle-aged people must abandon the behaviors and values that guided the first half of their lives and confront their unconscious, bringing it into conscious awareness and accepting what it tells them to do. They must listen to their dreams and follow their fantasies, exercising creative imagination through writing, painting, or some other form of expression. They must let themselves be guided not by the rational thinking that drove them before, but by the spontaneous flow of the unconscious. Only in that way can the true self be revealed.

Jung cautioned that admitting unconscious forces into conscious awareness does not mean being dominated by them. The unconscious forces must be assimilated and balanced with the conscious. At this time of life, no single aspect of personality should dominate. An emotionally healthy middle-aged person is no longer ruled by either consciousness or unconsciousness, by a specific attitude or function, or by any of the archetypes. All are brought into harmonious balance when individuation is achieved.

Dethrone the Persona   Of particular importance in the midlife process of individuation is the shift in the nature of the archetypes. The first change involves dethroning the persona. Although we must continue to play various social roles if we are to function in the real world and get along with different kinds of people, we must recognize that our public personality may not represent our true nature. Further, we must come to accept the genuine self that the persona has been covering.

Accept Our Dark Sides   Next, we become aware of the destructive forces of the shadow and acknowledge that dark side of our nature with its primitive impulses, such as selfishness. That does not mean that we submit to them or allow them to dominate us, but simply accept their existence. In the first half of life, we use the persona to shield this dark side from ourselves, wanting people to see only our good qualities. But in concealing the forces of the shadow from others, we also conceal them from ourselves. That must change as part of the process of learning to know ourselves. A greater awareness of both the destructive and the constructive aspects of the shadow will give the personality a deeper and fuller dimension, because the shadow's tendencies bring zest, spontaneity, and vitality to life.

Once again we see this central theme in Jung's individuation process, that we must bring each aspect of the personality into harmony with all other aspects. Awareness of only the good side of our nature produces a one-sided development of the personality. As with other opposing components of personality, both sides of this dimension must be expressed before we can achieve individuation.

Accept Our Anima and Animus   We must also come to terms with our psychological bisexuality. A man must be able to express his anima archetype, or traditionally feminine traits such as tenderness, and a woman must come to express her animus, or traditionally masculine traits such as assertiveness. Jung believed that this recognition of the characteristics of the other sex was the most difficult step in the individuation process because it represents the greatest change in our self-image. Accepting the emotional qualities of both sexes opens new sources of creativity and serves as the final release from parental influences.

Transcend   Once the psyche's structures are individuated and acknowledged, the next developmental stage can occur. Jung referred to this as transcendence, an innate tendency toward unity or wholeness in the personality, uniting all the opposing aspects within the psyche. Environmental factors, such as an unsatisfactory marriage or a frustrating job, can inhibit the process of transcendence and prevent the full achievement of the self.

Questions about Human Nature

Jung's image of human nature is quite different from Freud's. Jung did not hold such a deterministic view, but he did agree that personality may be at least partly determined by childhood experiences and by the archetypes. However, there is ample room in Jung's system for free will and spontaneity, the latter arising from the shadow archetype.

On the nature–nurture issue, Jung took a mixed position. The drive toward individuation and transcendence is innate, but it can be aided or thwarted by learning and experience. The ultimate and necessary goal of life is the realization of the self. Although it is rarely achieved, we are continually motivated to strive for it.

Jung disagreed with Freud on the importance of childhood experiences. Jung thought they were influential but did not completely shape our personality by age 5. We are affected more by our experiences in middle age and by our hopes and expectations for the future.

Each individual is unique, in Jung's view, but only during the first half of life. When some progress toward individuation is made in middle age, we develop what Jung designated as a universal kind of personality in which no single aspect is dominant. Thus, uniqueness disappears, and we can no longer be described as one or another particular psychological type.

Jung presented a more positive, hopeful image of human nature than Freud did, and his optimism is apparent in his view of personality development. We are motivated to grow and develop, to improve and extend our selves. Progress does not stop in childhood, as Freud had assumed, but continues throughout life. Jung believed that we always have the hope of becoming better. Jung argued that the human species also continues to improve. Present generations represent a significant advance over our primitive ancestors.

Despite his basic optimism, Jung expressed concern about a danger he saw facing Western culture. He referred to this danger as a sickness of dissociation. By placing too great an emphasis on materialism, reason, and empirical science, we are in danger of failing to appreciate the forces of the unconscious. We must not abandon our trust in the archetypes that form our heritage. Thus, Jung's hopefulness about human nature was a watchful, warning kind.

Assessment in Jung's Theory

Jung's techniques for assessing the functioning of the psyche drew on science and the supernatural, resulting in both an objective and a mystical approach. He investigated a variety of cultures and eras, studying their symbols, myths, religions, and rituals. He formed his personality theory on the basis of his patients' fantasies and dreams (as well as his own), and his explorations of ancient languages, alchemy, and astrology. Yet, the work that first brought Jung to the attention of psychologists in the United States involved empirical and physiological assessments. His techniques were an unorthodox blend of opposites, which is not surprising for a theory based on a principle of opposition.

Jung's Assessments of His Patients

His sessions with patients were unusual and often chaotic. His patients did not lie on a couch. "I don't want to put the patient to bed," he remarked. Usually, Jung and the patient sat in comfortable chairs facing each other, although sometimes Jung faced a window so he could look out at the lake near his house. Occasionally, he took patients out on his sailboat.

One patient recalled that Jung "paced back and forth, gesturing as he talked, whether about a human problem, a dream, a personal reminiscence, an allegorical story, or a joke. Yet he could become quiet, serious, and extremely personal, sitting down almost too close for comfort and delivering a pointed interpretation of one's miserable personal problem so its bitter truth would really sink in" (quoted in Bair, 2003, p. 379).

Sometimes Jung could be rude. When one patient appeared at the appointed time, he said, "Oh no. I can't stand the sight of another one. Just go home and cure yourself today" (quoted in Brome, 1981, pp. 177, 185). When a patient began to talk about her mother, a topic Freud would have encouraged, Jung silenced her abruptly: "Don't waste your time" (Bair, 2003, p. 379).

Jung believed that his patients' fantasies were real to them and he accepted them at face value. When Marie-Louise von Franz (1915–1998), who later became a lifelong disciple, first met Jung, he told her about a patient who lived on the moon. She replied that surely Jung meant the patient *acted* as though she lived on the moon. Jung said no, the woman truly did live on the moon. Von Franz decided that "either [Jung] was crazy or I was" (obituary for Marie-Louise von Franz, *New York Times*, March 23, 1998).

Three more formal techniques Jung used to evaluate personality were the word-association test, symptom analysis, and dream analysis. A widely used self-report personality test, the Myers-Briggs Type Indicator, was developed later by others to assess Jung's psychological types.

Word Association

word-association test
A projective technique in which a person responds to a stimulus word with whatever word comes to mind.

The **word-association test**, in which a subject responds to a stimulus word with whatever word comes immediately to mind, has become a standard laboratory and clinical tool in psychology. In the early 1900s, Jung used the technique with a list of 100 words he believed were capable of eliciting emotions (see Table 3.3). Jung measured the time it took for a patient to respond to each word. He also measured physiological reactions to determine the emotional effects of the stimulus words.

Jung used word association to uncover complexes in his patients. A variety of factors indicated the presence of a complex, including physiological responses, delays in responding, making the same response to different words, slips of the tongue, stammering, responding with more than one word, making up words, or failing to respond.

Symptom Analysis

symptom analysis
Similar to catharsis, the symptom analysis technique focuses on the symptoms reported by the patient and attempts to interpret the patient's free associations to those symptoms.

Symptom analysis focuses on the symptoms reported by the patient and is based on the person's free associations to those symptoms. It is similar to Freud's cathartic method. Between the patient's associations to the symptoms and the analyst's interpretation of them, the symptoms will often be relieved or disappear.

Dream Analysis

dream analysis A technique involving the interpretation of dreams to uncover unconscious conflicts.

Jung agreed with Freud that dreams are the "royal road" into the unconscious. Jung's approach to **dream analysis** differed from Freud's, however, in that Jung was concerned with more than the causes of dreams, and he believed that dreams were more than unconscious wishes. First, dreams are prospective; that is, they help us prepare for

TABLE 3.3 Normal and neurotic responses to Jung's word-association test

STIMULUS WORD	NORMAL RESPONSE	NEUROTIC RESPONSE
Blue	Pretty	Color
Tree	Green	Nature
Bread	Good	To eat
Lamp	Bright	To burn
Rich	Beautiful	Money; I don't know
To sin	Much	This idea is totally alien to me; I do not acknowledge it
Needle	To prick	To sew
To swim	Healthy	Water

Source: Jung, C. G. (1909/1973). The association method. In *The collected works of C. G. Jung* (Vol. 2, pp. 442–444). Princeton, NJ: Princeton University Press. Used by permission.

experiences and events we anticipate will occur. Second, dreams are compensatory; they help bring about a balance between opposites in the psyche by compensating for the overdevelopment of any one psychic structure.

Instead of interpreting each dream separately, as Freud did, Jung worked with a series of dreams reported by a patient over a period of time. In that way, Jung believed he could discover recurring themes, issues, and problems that persisted in the patient's unconscious.

Jung also used amplification to analyze dreams. In Freudian free association, the patient begins with one element in a dream and develops a chain of associations from it by reporting related memories and events. Jung focused on the original dream element and asked the patient to make repeated associations and responses to it until he detected a theme. He did not try to distinguish between manifest and latent dream content, as Freud did.

The Myers-Briggs Type Indicator

Myers-Briggs Type Indicator (MBTI) An assessment test based on Jung's psychological types and the attitudes of introversion and extraversion.

An assessment instrument related to Jung's personality theory is the **Myers-Briggs Type Indicator (MBTI)**, developed in the 1920s by Katharine Cook Briggs and Isabel Briggs Myers (Briggs & Myers, 1943, 1976). Today, the MBTI is the most popular and most frequently used personality test ever devised and is taken by more than two million people every year for hiring and promotion decisions (Cunningham, 2012). It is highly likely that in the business world you will have to take this test to get a job or a promotion (see Table 3.4).

TABLE 3.4   Sample items from the Myers-Briggs Type Indicator

Which answer comes closer to telling how you usually feel or act?

1. When you go somewhere for the day, would you rather

   (a) plan what you will do and when, or

   (b) just go?

2. Do you tend to have

   (a) deep friendships with a very few people, or

   (b) broad friendships with many different people?

3. When you have a special job to do, do you like to

   (a) organize it carefully before you start, or

   (b) find out what is necessary as you go along?

4. When something new starts to be the fashion, are you usually

   (a) one of the first to try it, or

   (b) not much interested?

5. When the truth would not be polite, are you more likely to tell

   (a) a polite lie, or

   (b) the impolite truth?

Source: Modified and reproduced by special permission of the publisher, CPP, Inc., Mountain View, CA 94043 from Myers-Briggs Type Indicator® assessment by Katharine D. Meyers Isabel Briggs Myers. Copyright 1943, 1944, 1957, 1962, 1976, 1977, 1983, 1984, 1987, 1991, 1993, 1998, 2012 by Peter B. Myers and Katharine D. Myers. All rights reserved. Further reproduction is prohibited without the publisher's written consent.

The test was developed in Washington DC, by Katharine Briggs, who doted on her teenage daughter Isabel. Katharine wrote a book-length manuscript about her remarkable home-schooled daughter, calling her a genius, even a "little Shakespeare." When Isabel went to college at Swarthmore, near Philadelphia, Pennsylvania, mother and daughter corresponded almost daily. And then one day Isabel brought home a law student, Clarence Myers.

"Katharine and Isabel were bold and imaginative and intuitive. Myers was practical and logical and detail-oriented" (Gladwell, 2004, p. 45). Katharine was so shocked by the personality differences between her daughter and her future son-in-law that she embarked on an intensive program of self-study in psychology to try to understand him.

In 1923, she read Jung's book, *Psychological Types*, and found what she was looking for, a way to categorize people and to explain the differences among them. And so, without any research grant support, university affiliation, or graduate students, she developed, with Isabel's help, a test to measure those differences.

In 1975, Isabel Briggs Myers and Mary McCaulley, a psychology professor at the University of Florida, established the Center for Applications of Psychological Type for MBTI training and research. In 1979, the Association for Psychological Type was founded. Two journals published research reports on applications of the test. The MBTI is considered the most visible practical outgrowth of Jung's work on the human personality.

Research on Jung's Theory

life-history reconstruction Jung's type of case study that involves examining a person's past experiences to identify developmental patterns that may explain present neuroses.

Jung, like Freud, used the case study method, which Jung called **life-history reconstruction**. It involved an extensive recollection of a person's past experiences in which Jung sought to identify the developmental patterns he believed led to the present neurotic condition. The criticisms of Freud's data and research methods also apply to Jung's work. Jung's data did not rely on objective observation and were not gathered in a controlled and systematic fashion. Also, the situations in which they were obtained, the clinical interviews, were not amenable to duplication, verification, or quantification.

Like Freud, Jung did not keep verbatim records of his patients' comments, nor did he attempt to verify the accuracy of their reports. Jung's case studies involved (as did Freud's) a small, unrepresentative sample of people, making it difficult to generalize to the population at large.

Jung's analysis of the data was subjective and unreliable. We do not know how he analyzed his data because he never explained his procedures. It is obvious that the data were subjected to some of the most unusual interpretations of any personality theory. We noted earlier that Jung studied a variety of cultures and disciplines. It was on this basis, and that of his own dreams and fantasies, that he interpreted the information gathered from his patients.

His work has been criticized for dealing with conclusions he may have slanted to fit his theory. It is also alleged that his visions, which he claimed to have experienced during his midlife confrontation with his unconscious, can be traced to the material he had read (Noll, 1993, 1994).

As was the case with Freud's propositions, many of Jung's observations cannot be submitted to experimental test. Jung himself was indifferent to this criticism and commented that anyone who "wishes to know about the human mind will learn nothing, or almost nothing, from experimental psychology" (quoted in Ellenberger, 1970, p. 694).

Research on Psychological Types

Despite Jung's negative view of experimental psychology, researchers have been able to submit some aspects of Jungian theory to experimental test, with results that are supportive of some of Jung's propositions. Most of this research uses the MBTI and focuses on the attitudes of introversion and extraversion. However, not all research supports Jung's delineation of the psychological types (Pittenger, 2005).

Studies of College Students

One study of college students found that their job interests were closely related to Jungian attitudes and psychological types (Stricker & Ross, 1962). Introverts showed strong interests in occupations that did not involve personal interaction, such as technical and scientific work. Extraverts were more interested in jobs that offered high levels of social interaction, such as sales and public relations. Other research found that introverted feeling and judging types had higher grade point averages than the other psychological types (DiRienzo, Das, Synn, Kitts, & McGrath, 2010).

Different psychological types may be drawn to different professions (Hanewitz, 1978). The MBTI was given to a large sample of police officers, schoolteachers, and social work and dental school students. The teachers and social work students showed high levels of intuiting and feeling. Police officers and dental school students, who deal with people in different ways from teachers and social workers, scored high in extraversion and in sensing and thinking.

College students who scored high in intuiting were inclined toward more creative vocational interests. Those who scored high in sensing favored more conventional vocational interests (Apostal, 1991). A study of women admitted to the U.S. Naval Academy who took the MBTI found that the extraverted-sensing-thinking-judging types were the most likely to graduate. In contrast, the women most likely to drop out scored higher in feeling and perceiving (Murray & Johnson, 2001). A 10-year research program on students at liberal arts colleges also found that those most likely to drop out before graduation scored high on the MBTI in perceiving (Barrineau, 2005).

MBTI scores of medical school students showed that those who became primary care physicians scored high in feeling and introversion. Those who became surgeons had been labeled extraverted and thinking types (Stilwell, Wallick, Thal, & Burleson, 2000). Another sample of college students who took the MBTI, extraverts scored higher than introverts in psychological well-being and general life satisfaction (Harrington & Loffredo, 2001).

Studies of Cognitive Functioning

Jungian personality types appear to differ in their cognitive or mental functioning. People categorized as introverted thinking types have better memories for neutral or impersonal stimuli, such as numbers. Persons labeled extraverted feeling types have better memories for human stimuli with emotional overtones, such as facial expressions (Carlson & Levy, 1973). It was also found that brain wave activity, as measured by the EEG, differed for each of the psychological types, as assessed by the MBTI (Gram, Dunn, & Ellis, 2005).

Also, introverted thinking and extraverted feeling types differ in their ability to recall significant personal experiences (Carlson, 1980). When subjects were asked to recall their most vivid experiences involving such emotions as joy, anger, and shame, extraverted feeling types most often reported memories involving other people. Introverted thinking types more frequently recalled events that occurred when they were alone. In addition, extraverted feeling types recalled highly emotional details, whereas introverted thinking types remembered more emotionally neutral and factual experiences.

Studies of Diverse Cultures

The MBTI has been translated for use in a number of different countries, including Turkey, Syria, and other Arab countries (Atay, 2012; Ayoubui & Ustwani, 2014). A study of Muslims living in England found that "within a Muslim context religious participation is associated with extraversion rather than introversion and with thinking rather than feeling" (Francis & Datoo, 2012, p. 1037). A study of Greek Orthodox churchgoers living in London showed that they scored high in introversion, sensing, thinking, and judging (Lewis, Varvatsoulias, & George, 2012). Research on women college students in Israel found that extraverts and feeling types scored higher on measures of happiness than introverts and thinking types (Francis, Yablon, & Robbins, 2013).

Among college students in Singapore, extraverts preferred to communicate with other people in person, whereas introverts preferred online contacts (Goby, 2006). When students in Bulgaria (ages 13–16) were given the MBTI, the results showed that those who scored high on intuiting and sensing had greater self-esteem. Those who scored low on sensing and judging had lower self-esteem (Papazova & Pencheva, 2008).

Research on junior and mid-level managers in India showed that those who scored very high on the thinking function tended to be collaborative in their efforts to manage conflict. Those who scored high in feeling tended to avoid dealing with conflicts. The men in this study scored higher on thinking, whereas the women scored higher on feeling (Mathew & Bhatewara, 2006).

A study of managers in China, however, did not find any significant differences between men and women in scores on the MBTI (Huifang & Shuming, 2004). Additional research on managers in China found that their MBTI scores were much more similar to the scores of managers in the United States than to the general population in China (Yang & Zhao, 2009).

Perhaps not surprisingly, a study of Australians and Canadians found that the fundamental motivating feature for people who scored high in extraversion was the social attention their behavior brought them (Ashton, Lee, & Paunonen, 2002).

Research on Dreams

In research on dreams to study the occurrence of archetypes, subjects were asked to recall their most recent dream, their most vivid dream, and their earliest dream over a period of 3 weeks (Cann & Donderi, 1986). They were also given the MBTI and another personality test. Introverts were more likely than extraverts to recall everyday dreams that bore no relation to archetypes. Intuiting types recalled more archetypal dreams than did sensing types. Persons who scored high in neuroticism recalled fewer archetypal dreams than those who scored low in neuroticism. The researchers concluded that these findings agreed with predictions made on the basis of Jung's personality theory.

Individuation

An intensive investigation of men and women aged 37 to 55, who held senior executive positions, found that they displayed behaviors that corroborate Jung's concept of individuation. The study involved interviews with the executives, their colleagues, and their family members as well as observations of their behavior on the job. They were also evaluated on the TAT, the MBTI, and the Adjective Check List. The researcher concluded that the executives "looked within [themselves] for direction and energy, questioned their inherited values, relinquished outmoded aspects of their selves, revealed new dimensions of who they are, and allowed themselves to be more playful and spontaneous" (Lyons, 2002, p. 9). The executives also took actions according to their own wishes and desires instead of simply reacting to external demands and pressures. These behavioral and emotional characteristics correspond to Jung's description of the individuation process.

The Midlife Crisis in Women

We saw that the onset of middle age, around age 40, was a time of personal crisis for Jung and many of his patients. Jung, and others who have studied this so-called midlife crisis, initially viewed it as a phenomenon far more likely to affect men than women. More recently, however, the idea that women undergo a similar crisis has been recognized.

One national survey of women in the United States found that they were in worse health than men, felt they had little or no control over their marriages, and had fewer opportunities to find employment (Barrett, 2005). Women at midlife who experienced more stressful changes in their lives reported lower levels of satisfaction with their lives (Darling, Coccia, & Senatore, 2012).

Lesbian women reported less emotional turmoil at midlife than did heterosexual women. Black women had more positive self-perceptions at middle age than did White women (Brown, Matthews, & Bromberger, 2005; Howell & Beth, 2004). A survey of women in their 50s, who had been studied periodically since their senior year in college, asked them to describe the most difficult period in their lives since graduation. A variety of self-ratings revealed that the early 40s were the time of greatest conflict (Helson, 1992).

Other research demonstrated that many women in midlife undergo an intense period of self-evaluation, reviewing their lives and judging their relative success or failure. One study found that the midlife transition was less difficult for women who had actively pursued careers than for women who stayed at home and focused on marriage and family. Many subjects in the latter group concluded that their marriages had been a partial or complete failure. Their regret over their choice led them to consider drastic changes. The career women felt significantly less need to make major changes at midlife (Levinson, 1996).

Making Life changes

Research involving two samples of college-educated women confirmed these rather bleak findings. The women were studied initially as students and later when they were in their late 30s or early 40s. The majority of the women experienced a period of life reevaluation around age 40, as Jung had predicted. Approximately two-thirds made major life changes between the ages of 37 and 43 as a direct result of their self-evaluation.

When asked at age 37 if they would opt again for the same life choices they had made when younger, 34 percent from an affluent private college and 61 percent from a large state university said they would not. If they could do it all over again, these women said they would pursue educational and career opportunities instead of family goals. Another sample of women studied at midlife also showed that two-thirds of them believed they had been less successful in life than their adult daughters who worked outside the home (Carr, 2004).

A sense of dissatisfaction at midlife motivated many women to change, but not all were able to go back to school or find a job that made full use of their abilities. Those women who were able to make satisfactory life changes by age 43 reported significantly greater feelings of general well-being than those women who were unable to make such changes. The changed group experienced an increased sense of personal identity and an enlarged view of their own capabilities. Thus, regret about their earlier choices led to make positive changes in midlife (Stewart & Ostrove, 1998; Stewart & Vandewater, 1999).

Personal Growth or Stagnation?

A longitudinal study followed women for 20 years after they graduated from college. The results showed that the personalities of the women at midlife, based on ratings by independent judges, could be divided into three levels or prototypes: conflicted, traditional, and individuated. The lowest level, the conflicted prototype, was characterized by personal conflicts, psychological problems, poor relationships with others, anxiety, hostility, and rigidity. The women at this level were considered to be psychologically immature.

The second level, the traditional prototype, was characterized by devotion to others, feelings of guilt, an emphasis on fulfilling duties and obligations at the expense of their own self-development and self-expression, and a concern for societal standards and getting the approval of others. They were also described as competent adults and good citizens who focused on marriage rather than career but lacking a high degree of psychological maturity and self-understanding.

The third level, the individuated prototype, corresponds to Jung's concept of individuation, the ideal outcome of the midlife personality crisis. Women at this level were described as high in autonomy, creativity, responsiveness and closeness to others, self-actualization, individual achievement orientation, empathy, tolerance, ego resilience, and intellectual and cultural sophistication (John, Pals, & Westenberg, 1998).

Studies of women in the United States and in Australia confirmed that for some, middle age is a time of increasing personal growth, moving in new directions, ridding themselves of past problems, and experiencing the freedom to be themselves (Arnold, 2005; Leonard & Burns, 2006). In other words, they had reached a higher level of psychological maturity, a finding that supports Jung's view of individuation as the supreme state of psychological health and self-development.

HIGHLIGHTS: Research on Jung's Ideas

Research on *psychological types* has found that:

- Introverts are drawn to technical and scientific jobs
- Extraverts prefer jobs with a lot of social interaction
- Introverted, feeling, and judging types tend to get high grades in school
- Extraverts score higher on happiness and life satisfaction
- Introverts prefer online rather than personal social contact

Research on the *midlife crisis in women* has found that:

- Homosexual women experience fewer emotional difficulties than heterosexual women
- Black women feel greater self-satisfaction in middle age than White women
- The midlife crisis is resolved more easily by women with independent careers than by those more focused on marriage and family
- The concept of individuation applies to women as well as to men

Reflections on Jung's Theory

Contributions

Jung's complex and unusual approach to the human personality has had considerable impact on a broad range of disciplines, notably psychiatry, sociology, economics, political science, philosophy, and religion. Recognized by the intellectual community at large, Jung received honorary degrees from Harvard and Oxford and has been acknowledged as a powerful influence on the work of many scholars.

Jung made several important and lasting contributions to psychology (see, for example, Summerville, 2010). The word-association test became a standard projective technique and inspired the development of the Rorschach inkblot test and the so-called lie-detection techniques. The concepts of psychological complexes and of introverted versus extraverted personalities are widely accepted in psychology today. The personality scales that measure introversion and extraversion are standard diagnostic and selection devices. A great deal of research is being conducted on the introversion–extraversion personality dimensions, as we will see in Chapter 8.

In the following chapters, we will also see evidence of Jung's influence on the work of some other theorists. Jung's notion of individuation, or self-actualization, anticipated the work of Abraham Maslow. Jung was the first to emphasize the role of the future in determining behavior, an idea adopted by Alfred Adler. Maslow, Erik Erikson, and Raymond Cattell embraced Jung's suggestion that middle age is a time of crucial personality change. The idea of a midlife crisis is now seen by many as a necessary stage of personality development and has been supported by considerable research.

Criticisms

Despite the significance of these formulations, the bulk of Jung's theory was not received enthusiastically by psychologists. One reason concerns the difficulty of understanding Jungian concepts. Sigmund Freud, Alfred Adler, and others wrote in a clear style that allows their books to be easily read and understood. Jung did not write for the general public. Reading his work can be frustrating, because his books contain many inconsistencies and contradictions.

Jung once said, "I can formulate my thoughts only as they break out of me. It is like a geyser. Those who come after me will have to put them in order" (quoted in Jaffé, 1971, p. 8). One Jungian scholar described one of Jung's major books as only partly intelligible. "The connection between one thought and the next is not clear and … there are many internal contradictions" (Noll, 1994, p. 109). This criticism can be applied to many of Jung's writings. They are difficult to comprehend and lack internal consistency and systematization.

Jung's embrace of the occult and the supernatural is probably the source of most of the criticism directed at his theory. Evidence from mythology and religion is not in favor in an era when reason and science are considered the most legitimate approaches to knowledge and understanding. Critics charge that Jung accepted as scientific evidence the mythical and mystical occurrences his patients reported.

Despite these problems, a surge of interest in Jung's work began in the late 1980s and continues today. Formal training in Jungian analysis is available in New York, Chicago, Boston, San Francisco, Los Angeles, and several other major cities in the United States and Canada. There are also Jungian training institutes in South America, Europe, and Israel. The Society of Analytical Psychology, founded in 1947, publishes the Jungian *Journal of Analytical Psychology*.

Chapter Summary

Parts of Jung's personality theory were influenced by his unhappy childhood experiences and his dreams and fantasies. Jung broadened Freud's definition of libido, redefining it as a more generalized dynamic force. Jung argued that personality is shaped by the future as well as the past, and he placed even greater emphasis on the unconscious than Freud did.

Jung used the term *libido* in two ways: as a diffuse, generalized life energy and as a narrower energy that fuels the psyche. The amount of energy invested in an idea or feeling is called a value. Psychic energy operates in accordance with the principles of opposites, equivalence, and entropy. The principle of opposites states that every aspect of the psyche has its opposite and that this opposition generates psychic energy. The principle of equivalence states that energy is never lost to the personality but is shifted from one part to another. The principle of entropy states that there is a tendency toward equilibrium in the personality.

The ego is the center of consciousness and is concerned with perceiving, thinking, feeling, and remembering. Part of our conscious perception is determined by the attitudes of introversion and extraversion, in which libido is channeled internally or externally.

The psychological functions include thinking, feeling, sensing, and intuiting. Thinking and feeling are rational functions; sensing and intuiting are nonrational. Only one attitude and function can be dominant. The eight psychological types are formed by combinations of the attitudes and functions.

The personal unconscious is a reservoir of material that was once conscious but has been forgotten or suppressed. Complexes, which may be conscious or unconscious, are patterns of emotions, memories, perceptions, and wishes centering on common themes. The collective unconscious is a storehouse of the experiences of humankind transmitted to each individual. Archetypes are recurring themes that express these experiences. The most powerful archetypes are the persona, anima, animus, shadow, and self.

Psychic birth occurs at puberty, when the psyche assumes a definite content. Preparatory activities mark the time from adolescence through young adulthood. In the period of middle age, when success has been achieved, the personality undergoes changes. Psychic energy must be rechanneled into the inner world of the unconscious, and the attitude must shift from extraversion to introversion.

Individuation (the realization of one's capabilities) does not occur until middle age, when people must confront their unconscious and abandon the behaviors and values that guided the first half of their lives. Transcendence involves the unification of the personality.

Jung's image of human nature was more optimistic and less deterministic than Freud's view. Jung believed that part of personality is innate and part is learned. The ultimate life goal is individuation. Childhood experiences are important, but personality is more affected by midlife experiences and hopes for the future. Personality is unique in the first half of life but not in the second.

Jung's methods of assessment include the investigation of symbols, myths, and rituals in ancient cultures; the word-association test, used to uncover complexes; symptom analysis, in which patients free-associate to their symptoms; and dream analysis. The Myers-Briggs Type Indicator, an assessment instrument deriving from Jung's approach, is a highly popular employee selection technique and is also used for research on Jung's system.

Jung's case study method, called life-history reconstruction, did not rely on objective observation, was not systematic and controlled, and was not amenable to duplication and verification.

Research has supported some of Jung's ideas on attitudes, functions, and psychological types, but broader aspects of his theory have resisted attempts at scientific validation. His work has had considerable influence in several fields. Widely accepted Jungian ideas include the word-association test, complexes, introversion-extraversion, self-actualization, and the midlife crisis.

Review Questions

1. How would you describe the ways in which Jung's personality theory was influenced by his childhood experiences?

2. What are the principles of opposites, equivalence, and entropy? How do they relate to the concept of psychic energy?

3. Describe the three major points of difference between Jung's theory of analytical psychology and Freud's theory of psychoanalysis.

4. How does the principle of opposites apply to the attitudes and functions?

5. Explain how the eight psychological types derive from the attitudes and functions.
6. In what ways do introverts differ from extraverts?
7. Why are thinking and feeling considered to be rational functions while sensing and intuiting are said to be nonrational functions?
8. What is the relationship between the ego and the personal unconscious?
9. How does the personal unconscious differ from the collective unconscious?
10. What is a complex? How can a complex be helpful? (Do you have any?)
11. Distinguish between the persona archetype and the self archetype.
12. Explain the similarities and the differences between Jung's concept of the shadow archetype and Freud's concept of the id?
13. What are the anima and animus archetypes? In Jung's view, are they supposed to be suppressed or expressed? Why?
14. Discuss Jung's ideas on the development of personality throughout the life span, especially the periods of adolescence and middle age.
15. What is individuation? How must our archetypes change if we are to achieve individuation?
16. In what ways does Jung's image of human nature differ from Freud's?
17. What is the purpose of the word-association test? What are the purposes of dreams?
18. Describe Jung's approach to his sessions with his patients. How did his typical sessions differ from those of Freud?
19. Discuss the research findings using the MBTI that show the occupational preferences of extraverts and introverts.
20. Describe the criticisms and the contributions of Jung's personality theory.

Suggested Readings

Bair, D. (2003). *Jung: A biography*. Boston: Little, Brown. A thoroughly researched biography that assesses Jung's complex personality throughout the life span and shows its impact on his theories. Also notes the censorship the Jung heirs maintain over significant amounts of Jung's correspondence, suggesting that the definitive work has yet to be written.

Bishop, P. (2014). *Carl Jung*. London: Reaktion books. A concise biography of Jung that follows his life from childhood through his years with Freud and beyond, portraying him as one of the most important European theorists of the 20th century.

Crellin, C. (2014). *Jung's Theory of Personality: a Modern Reappraisal*. New York: Routledge/Taylor & Francis Group. A thorough and scholarly critical analysis of Jung's approach to understanding personality, emphasizing its continuing relevance.

Ellenberger, H. F. (1970). *The discovery of the unconscious: The history and evolution of dynamic psychiatry*. New York: Basic Books. Traces the study of the unconscious from primitive times to Freudian psychoanalysis and its derivatives. See Chapter 9, "Carl Gustav Jung and Analytical Psychology."

Freud/Jung letters. (1974). Princeton, NJ: Princeton University Press. Contains some 360 letters, dating from 1906 to 1913, that show the development and dissolution of the friendship between Sigmund Freud and Carl Jung. Edited by William McGuire.

Hannah, B. (1976). *Jung: His life and work*. New York: Putnam. A biographical memoir by a Jungian analyst who was a friend of Jung's for more than 30 years.

Jung, C. G. (1961). *Memories, dreams, reflections*. New York: Vintage Books. Jung's recollections of his life, written at the age of 81.

Kerr, J. (1993). *A most dangerous method: The story of Jung, Freud, and Sabina Spielrein*. New York: Knopf. The story of a woman patient who became involved in a long-standing relationship with her analyst, Carl Jung.

Roazen, P. (1975). *Freud and his followers*. New York: Alfred A. Knopf. A lively, well-written account of Freud's life and of the men and women who became his disciples, some of whom later broke away to form their own schools of thought. See Part 6, "The 'Crown Prince': Carl Gustav Jung."

Schultz, D. (1990). *Intimate friends, dangerous rivals: The turbulent relationship between Freud and Jung*. Los Angeles: Jeremy Tarcher. Describes the personal and professional relationship between Freud and Jung and the parallels and differences in their childhood, midlife crises, and relationships with women.

chapter 4

Alfred Adler: Individual Psychology

Fair Use

The goal of the human soul is conquest, perfection, security, superiority. Every child is faced with so many obstacles in life that no child ever grows up without striving for some form of significance.

—*Alfred Adler*

individual psychology
Adler's theory of personality.

Alfred Adler fashioned an image of human nature that did not portray people as victims of instincts, biological forces, or childhood experiences. He called his approach **individual psychology** because it focused on the uniqueness of each person and denied the universality of biological motives and goals ascribed to us by Sigmund Freud.

In Adler's view, each of us is primarily a social being. Our personalities are shaped by our unique social environments and interactions, not by attempts to satisfy biological needs. Unlike Freud, who saw sex as being of primary importance in shaping our personalities, Adler minimized the role of sex. To Adler, the conscious, not the unconscious, was at the core of personality. Rather than being driven by forces we cannot see and control, we are actively involved in creating our unique selves and directing our own futures.

With Adler and Freud, we see two vastly different theories created by two men, only 14 years apart in age, who were brought up in the same city in the same era and educated as physicians at the same university. As with Freud, certain aspects of Adler's childhood seemed to have influenced his way of looking at human nature.

The Life of Adler (1870–1937)

Childhood and Adolescence

Adler's early childhood was marked by illness, an awareness of death, and intense jealousy of his older brother. He suffered from rickets (a vitamin D deficiency characterized by softening of the bones), which kept him from playing with other children. At age 3, his younger brother died in the bed next to his. At 4, Adler himself almost died from pneumonia. When he heard the doctor tell his father, "Your boy is lost," he decided to become a doctor (Orgler, 1963, p. 16).

Adler was pampered by his mother initially, but then was suddenly dethroned at the age of 2 by the arrival of another baby. Biographers have suggested that Adler's mother may have then rejected him, but he was clearly his father's favorite. Therefore, his childhood relations with his parents were quite different from Freud's, who was much closer to his mother than to his father. As an adult, Adler had no use for the Freudian concept of the Oedipus complex because it was so foreign to his childhood experiences.

Adler was always jealous of his older brother, who was vigorous and healthy and could engage in the physical activities and sports in which Alfred could not take part. "I remember sitting on a bench, bandaged up on account of rickets, with my healthy elder brother sitting opposite me. He could run, jump, and move about quite effortlessly, while for me, movement of any sort was a strain and an effort" (Adler quoted in Bottome, 1939, pp. 30–31).

Adler felt inferior to his brother and to the other neighborhood children, who all seemed healthier and more athletic. As a result, he resolved to work hard to overcome his feelings of inferiority and to compensate for his physical limitations. Despite his small stature, clumsiness, and unattractiveness, the legacies of his illness, he forced himself to join in games and sports.

Gradually he achieved a sense of self-esteem and social acceptance. He also developed a fondness for the company of other people and retained this sociability all his life. In his personality theory, Adler emphasized the importance of the peer group and suggested that childhood relationships with siblings and with children outside the family were much more significant than Freud believed.

In school (the same one Freud had attended), Adler was initially unhappy and only a mediocre student. Believing him to be unfit for anything else, a teacher advised Adler's father to apprentice him to a shoemaker, a prospect Adler found frightening. He was particularly bad in mathematics but persisted and eventually rose from being a failing student to the top of his class through sheer hard work.

In many ways, the story of Adler's childhood reads like a tragedy, but it is also a textbook example of his theory of overcoming childhood weakness and inferiority to shape one's destiny. The theorist who would give the world the notion of inferiority feelings spoke from the depths of his own childhood. "Those who are familiar with my life work will clearly see the accord existing between the facts of my childhood and the views I expressed" (quoted in Bottome, 1939, p. 9).

Adulthood

Fulfilling his childhood ambition, Adler studied medicine at the University of Vienna but graduated with no better than a mediocre academic record. He first went into private practice as an ophthalmologist but soon shifted to general medicine. He was interested in incurable diseases but became so distressed at his helplessness to prevent death, particularly in younger patients, that he decided to specialize in neurology and psychiatry instead.

Relations with Freud

Adler's 9-year association with Freud began in 1902, when Freud invited Adler and three others to meet once a week at Freud's home to discuss psychoanalysis. Although their relationship never became close, Freud initially thought highly of Adler and praised his skill as a physician who was able to gain the trust of his patients.

It is important to remember that Adler was never a student or disciple of Freud's and was not psychoanalyzed by him. One of Freud's colleagues charged that Adler did not have the ability to probe the unconscious mind and psychoanalyze people. It is interesting to speculate on whether this supposed lack led Adler to base his personality theory on the more easily accessible consciousness and to minimize the role of the unconscious.

By 1910, although Adler was president of the Vienna Psychoanalytical Society and coeditor of its journal, he was also an increasingly vocal critic of the Freudian theory. He soon severed all connection with psychoanalysis and went on to develop his own approach to personality.

Freud reacted angrily to Adler's defection. He belittled Adler's physical stature (Adler was 5 inches shorter than Freud) and called Adler loathsome, abnormal, driven mad by ambition, filled with venom and meanness, paranoid, intensely jealous, and sadistic. He also described Adler's theory as worthless (Fiebert, 1997; Gay, 1988; Wittels, 1924).

Adler showed similar hostility toward Freud, calling him a swindler and denouncing psychoanalysis as filth (Roazen, 1975). Adler became irate whenever he was introduced or referred to as a student of Freud's. In his later years, Adler became just as embittered toward defectors from his own approach as Freud had been toward those, like Adler, who deviated from psychoanalysis. Adler was known to "flare suddenly into heated anger when he felt his authority challenged" (Hoffman, 1994, p. 148).

Becoming a Celebrity in America

In 1912, Adler founded the Society for Individual Psychology. He served in the Austrian army during World War I (1914–1918) and later organized government sponsored child-counseling clinics in Vienna. In his clinics, Adler introduced group training and guidance procedures, forerunners of modern group therapy techniques. In 1926, he made the first of several visits to the United States, where he taught and gave extremely popular lecture tours.

He moved to New York City in 1929 and continued to develop and promote his individual psychology. A biographer noted that Adler's "personal traits of geniality, optimism, and warmth coupled with an intensely ambitious drive ... soon catapulted him to American prominence as a psychological expert" (Hoffman, 1994, p. 160). Adler's books and lectures brought him recognition on a national scale, and he became America's first popular psychologist, a celebrity of the day. In 1937, while on an exhausting 56-lecture tour of Europe, Adler suffered a heart attack and died in Scotland.

Alfred Adler

Various sites provide biographical information, discussions of his theory, research on relevant concepts, and links to other resources.

North American Society of Adlerian Psychology

An organization formed to foster and promote the research, knowledge, training, and application of Adlerian Psychology, maintaining its principles and encouraging its growth.

Inferiority Feelings: The Source of All Human Striving

inferiority feelings The normal condition of all people; the source of all human striving.

Adler believed that **inferiority feelings** are a constant motivating force in all behavior. "To be a human being means to feel oneself inferior," Adler wrote (1933/1939, p. 96). Because this condition is common to all of us, then, it is not a sign of weakness or abnormality.

compensation A motivation to overcome inferiority, to strive for higher levels of development.

Adler proposed that inferiority feelings are the source of all human striving. Individual growth results from **compensation**, from our attempts to overcome our real or imagined inferiorities. Throughout our lives, we are driven by the need to overcome this sense of inferiority and to strive for increasingly higher levels of development.

The process begins in infancy. Infants are small and helpless and are totally dependent on adults. Adler believed that infants are aware of their parents' greater power and strength and of their own hopelessness to resist or challenge that power. As a result, infants develop feelings of inferiority relative to the larger, stronger people around them.

Although this initial experience of inferiority applies to everyone in infancy, it is not genetically determined. Rather, it is a function of the environment, which is the same for all infants, a climate of helplessness and dependence on adults. Inferiority feelings are inescapable, but more important they are necessary because they provide the motivation for us to strive and grow.

The Inferiority Complex

inferiority complex A condition that develops when a person is unable to compensate for normal inferiority feelings.

Suppose a child does not grow and develop as it gets older. What happens when the child is unable to compensate for those feelings of inferiority? An inability to overcome inferiority feelings intensifies them, leading to the development of an **inferiority complex**. People with an inferiority complex have a poor opinion of themselves and feel helpless and unable to cope with the demands of life. Adler found such a complex in the childhood of many adults who came to him for treatment.

Causes of Inferiority Complexes

An inferiority complex can arise from three sources in childhood: organic inferiority, spoiling, and neglect.

Organic Inferiority   Adler argued that defective parts or organs of the body shape personality through the person's efforts to compensate for the defect or weakness, just as Adler compensated for rickets, the physical inferiority of his childhood years. A child who is physically weak, as Adler was, might focus on that weakness and work to develop superior athletic ability.

Many people with physical disabilities strive to compensate for their weaknesses.

History records many examples of that kind of compensation. In ancient times the Greek statesman Demosthenes overcame a stutter to become a great orator. The sickly Theodore Roosevelt, 26th president of the United States, became a model of physical fitness as an adult. Efforts to overcome organic inferiority can result in striking artistic, athletic, and social accomplishments, but if those efforts fail, they can lead to an inferiority complex.

Adler saw examples of people who had successfully compensated for physical weaknesses in his practice. His office in Vienna was located near an amusement park, and his patients included a number of circus performers and gymnasts. They possessed extraordinary physical skills that, in many cases, they developed as a result of hard work to overcome childhood disabilities.

Spoiling Spoiling or pampering a child can also bring about an inferiority complex. Spoiled children are the center of attention in the home. Their every need or whim is satisfied, and little is denied them. Such children naturally develop the idea that they are the most important people in any situation and that others should always defer to them.

The first experience at school, where these children are no longer the focus of attention, comes as a shock for which they are unprepared. Spoiled children have little social feeling and are impatient with others. They have never learned to wait for what they want, nor have they learned to overcome difficulties or adjust to others' needs. When confronted with obstacles to gratification, spoiled children come to believe that they must have some personal deficiency that is thwarting them; hence, an inferiority complex develops.

Neglecting   It is easy to understand how neglected, unwanted, and rejected children can develop an inferiority complex. Their infancy and childhood are characterized by a lack of love and security because their parents are indifferent or hostile. As a result, these children develop feelings of worthlessness, or even anger, and view others with distrust. Indeed, today, neglect has come to be considered a major form of child abuse (Hickman, 2009).

The Superiority Complex

superiority complex A condition that develops when a person over-compensates for normal inferiority feelings.

Whatever the source of the complex, a person may attempt to overcompensate and so develop what Adler called a **superiority complex**. This involves an exaggerated opinion of one's abilities and accomplishments. Such persons may feel inwardly self-satisfied and superior and show no need to demonstrate their superiority with actual accomplishments. Or the person may feel such a need and work hard to become extremely successful. In both cases, persons with a superiority complex are given to boasting, vanity, self-centeredness, and a tendency to denigrate others.

Striving for Superiority, or Perfection

Inferiority feelings are the source of motivation and striving, but to what end? Are we motivated simply to be rid of inferiority feelings? Adler believed that we work for something more; however, his view of our ultimate goal in life changed over the years.

At first, he identified inferiority with a general feeling of weakness or of femininity, in recognition of the inferior standing of women in the society of his day. He spoke of trying to compensate for this feeling as the masculine protest. The goal of the compensation was a will or a drive toward power in which aggression, a supposedly masculine characteristic, played a large part. Later he rejected the idea of equating inferiority feelings with femininity and developed a broader viewpoint in which we strive for superiority, or perfection.

striving for superiority The urge toward perfection or completion that motivates each of us.

Adler described his notion of **striving for superiority** as the fundamental fact of life (Adler, 1930). Superiority is the ultimate goal toward which we strive. He did not mean superiority in the usual sense of the word, nor did the concept relate to the superiority complex. Striving for superiority is not an attempt to be better than everyone else, nor is it an arrogant or domineering tendency or an inflated opinion of our abilities and accomplishments.

What Adler meant was a drive for perfection. The word *perfection* is derived from a Latin word meaning to complete or to finish. Thus, Adler suggested that we strive for superiority in an effort to perfect ourselves, to make ourselves complete or whole.

This innate goal, the drive toward wholeness or completion, is oriented toward the future. Whereas Freud proposed that human behavior is determined by the past (that is, by the instincts and by our childhood experiences), Adler saw human motivation in terms of expectations and aspirations for the future. He argued that instincts and primal impulses were insufficient as explanatory principles. Only the ultimate, final goal of superiority or perfection could explain personality and behavior.

Fictional Finalism

Adler applied the term *finalism* to the idea that we have an ultimate goal, a final state of being, and a need to move toward it. The goals for which we strive, however, are potentialities, not actualities. In other words, we strive for ideals that exist in us subjectively. Adler believed that our goals are fictional or imagined ideals that cannot be tested against reality. We live our lives around ideals such as the belief that all people are created equal or that all people are basically good. Adler's life goal was to conquer the death he faced at the age of 4 from pneumonia. His way of striving for that goal, which of course is fictional because ultimately it cannot be won, was to become a physician (Hoffman, 1994).

These beliefs influence the ways we perceive and interact with other people. For example, if we believe that behaving a certain way will bring us rewards in a heaven or an afterlife, we try to act according to that belief. Belief in the existence of an afterlife is not based on objective reality, but it is real to the person who holds that view.

fictional finalism The idea that there is an imagined or potential goal that guides our behavior.

Adler formalized this concept as **fictional finalism**, the notion that fictional ideas guide our behavior as we strive toward a complete or whole state of being. We direct the course of our lives by many such fictions, but the most pervasive one is the ideal of perfection. He suggested that the best formulation of this ideal developed by human beings so far is the concept of God. Adler preferred the terms *subjective final goal* or *guiding self-ideal* to describe this concept, but it continues to be known as "fictional finalism" (Watts & Holden, 1994).

There are two additional points Adler made about striving for superiority. First, it increases rather than reduces tension. Unlike Freud, Adler did not believe that our sole motivation was to reduce tension. Striving for perfection requires great expenditures of energy and effort, a condition quite different from equilibrium or a tension-free state.

Second, the striving for superiority is manifested both by the individual and by society as a whole. Most of us are social beings. We strive for superiority or perfection not only as individuals but also as members of a group. We try to achieve the perfection of our culture.

In Adler's view, individuals and society are interrelated and interdependent. People must function constructively with others for the good of all. Thus, to Adler, human beings perpetually strive for the fictional, ideal goal of perfection. How in our daily lives do we try to attain this goal? Adler answered this question with his concept of the style of life.

The Style of Life

Adler stated that the ultimate goal for each of us is superiority or perfection, but we try to attain that goal in many different ways. Each of us expresses the striving differently. We develop a unique pattern of characteristics, behaviors, and habits, which Adler called a distinctive character, or **style of life**.

style of life A unique character structure or pattern of personal behaviors and characteristics by which each of us strives for perfection. Basic styles of life include the dominant, getting, avoiding, and socially useful types.

To understand how the style of life develops, we must go back to the concepts of inferiority feelings and compensation. Infants are afflicted with inferiority feelings that motivate them to compensate for helplessness and dependency. In these attempts at compensation, they acquire a set of behaviors. For example, the sickly child may strive to increase physical prowess by running or lifting weights. These behaviors become part of the style of life, a pattern of behaviors designed to compensate for inferiority.

Everything we do is shaped and defined by our unique style of life. It determines which aspects of our environment we attend to or ignore and what attitudes we hold. The style of life is learned from social interactions and is so firmly crystallized by the age of 4 or 5 that it is difficult to change thereafter.

The style of life thus becomes the guiding framework for all of our later behavior. Its nature depends on social interactions, especially the person's order of birth within the family and the nature of the parent–child relationship. Recall that one condition that can lead to an inferiority complex is neglect. Neglected children may feel inferior in coping with the demands of life and therefore become distrustful of and hostile toward others. As a result, their lifestyle may involve seeking revenge, resenting others' success, and taking whatever they feel is their due.

The Creative Power of the Self

You may have spotted an apparent inconsistency between Adler's notion of style of life and our earlier observation that his theory is less deterministic than Freud's. Adler said we are in control of our fate, not victims of it. But now we find that the style of life is determined by social relationships in the early years and subject to little change after that.

This seems almost as deterministic as the Freudian view, which emphasized the importance of early childhood in the formation of the adult personality. However, Adler's theory is not as deterministic as it may seem at first. He resolved this seeming dilemma by proposing a concept he called the **creative power of the self**.

creative power of the self The ability to create an appropriate style of life.

Adler believed that we create our *selves*, our *personality*, our *character*; these are all terms Adler used interchangeably with *style of life*. We are not passively shaped by childhood experiences. Those experiences themselves are not as important as our conscious attitude toward them. Adler argued that neither heredity nor environment provides a complete explanation for personality development. Instead, the way we perceive and interpret these influences forms the basis for the creative construction of our attitude toward life.

Adler believed in the existence of individual free will that allows each of us to create an appropriate style of life from the abilities and experiences given us by both our genetic endowment and our social environment. Although unclear on specifics, Adler insisted that our style of life is not determined for us. We are free to choose and create it ourselves. Once created, however, the style of life remains constant throughout life.

Four Basic Styles of Life

Adler described several universal problems and grouped them into three categories: problems involving our behavior toward others; problems of occupation; problems of love. Further, he proposed four basic styles of life for dealing with these problems: the dominant type, the getting type, the avoiding type, and the socially useful type.

The *dominant type* displays a dominant or ruling attitude with little social awareness. Such a person behaves without any regard for other people. The more extreme of this type attack others and become sadists, delinquents, or sociopaths. The less virulent become alcoholics, drug addicts, or suicides; they believe they hurt others by attacking themselves. The *getting type* (to Adler, the most common human type) expects to receive satisfaction from other people and so becomes dependent on them. The *avoiding type* makes no attempt to face life's problems. By avoiding difficulties, the person avoids any possibility of failure.

These three types are not prepared to cope with the problems of everyday life. They are unable to cooperate with other people and the clash between their style of life and the real world results in abnormal behavior, which is manifested in neuroses and psychoses. They lack what Adler came to call social interest.

The *socially useful* type, in contrast, cooperates with others and acts in accordance with their needs. Such persons cope with problems within a well-developed framework of social interest.

Social Interest

social interest Our innate potential to cooperate with other people to achieve personal and societal goals.

Adler believed that getting along with others is the first task we encounter in life. Our level of ability to get along with other people becomes part of our style of life, and therefore influences how well or poorly we will deal with all of life's problems. He described this as the concept of **social interest**, which is the individual's innate potential to cooperate with other people in order to achieve personal and societal goals. Adler's term for this concept in the original German, *Gemeinschaftsgefühl*, is best translated as "community feeling" (Stepansky, 1983, p. xiii). However, *social interest* has become the accepted term in English.

Although we are influenced more strongly by social than biological forces, in Adler's view, the potential for social interest is innate. In that limited sense, then, Adler's approach has a biological element. However, the extent to which our innate potential for social interest is developed depends on our early social experiences.

No one can entirely avoid other people or obligations toward them. From earliest times, people have congregated in families, tribes, and nations. Communities are indispensable to human beings for protection and survival. Thus, it has always been necessary for people to cooperate with others to express their social interest. The individual must cooperate with and contribute to society to realize personal and communal goals. Adler believed that people have a fundamental need to belong in order to be healthy, well-functioning individuals (Ferguson, 2010).

The Role of the Mother in Developing Social Interest

Adler noted the importance of the mother as the first person with whom a baby comes in contact. Through her behavior toward the child, the mother can either foster social interest or thwart its development. Adler believed that the mother's role was vital in developing the child's social interest as well as all other aspects of the personality. He wrote:

> This connection [between mother and child] is so intimate and far reaching that we are never able in later years to point to any characteristic as the effect of heredity. Every tendency which might be inherited has been adapted, trained, educated and made over again by the mother. Her skill or lack of skill will influence all the child's potentiality. (Adler quoted in Grey, 1998, p. 71)

The mother must teach the child cooperation, companionship, and courage. Only if children feel a kinship with others will they be able to act with courage in attempting to cope with life's demands. Children (and later, adults) who look upon others with suspicion and hostility will approach life with the same attitude. Those who have no feeling of social interest may become neurotics or even criminals. Adler believed that a host of evils ranging from war to racial hatred to public drunkenness stemmed from a lack of community feeling.

The Role of Adler's Life Experiences in Developing Social Interest

Early in his career, Adler suggested that people were driven by a lust for power and a need to dominate. He proposed this idea at the time when he was struggling to establish his own point of view within the Freudian circle. After he broke with Freud and achieved recognition for his own work, he changed and said that people are motivated more by social interest than by the needs for power and dominance.

When Adler was part of Freud's group, he was considered cantankerous and ambitious, quarreling over the priority of his ideas. But in later years, he mellowed and his system also changed, from emphasizing power and dominance as motivating forces to stressing the more benign force of social or community interest. Here we see another example of how Adler's theory reflected his own life experiences.

Birth Order

One of Adler's most enduring contributions is the idea that order of birth is a major social influence in childhood, one from which we create our style of life. Even though siblings have the same parents and live in the same house, they do not have identical social environments. Being older or younger than one's siblings and being exposed to differing parental attitudes create different childhood conditions that help determine different kinds of personalities.

Adler liked to amaze lecture audiences and dinner guests by correctly guessing people's order of birth on the basis of their behavior. He wrote about four situations: the first-born child, the second-born child, the youngest child, and the only child. Think about your own order of birth within your family and see how you think it compares with Adler's views.

The First-Born Child

First-born children are in a unique and enviable situation, at least for a while. The parents are usually very happy at the birth of their first child and devote a great deal of time and attention to the new baby. First-borns typically receive their parents' instant and undivided attention. As a result, first-borns have a very happy and secure existence, until the second-born child appears.

Dethronement   Suddenly, no longer the focus of attention, no longer receiving constant love and care, first-borns are, in a sense, dethroned. The affection and attention first-borns received during their reign will now have to be shared with the new baby. They must often submit to the outrage of waiting until after the newborn's needs have been met, and they are admonished to be quiet so as not to disturb the new baby.

No one could expect first-borns to suffer this kind of drastic displacement without putting up a fight. They will try to recapture their former position of power and privilege. The first-born's battle to regain supremacy in the family is lost from the beginning, however. Things will never be the same, no matter how hard the first-born tries.

For a time, first-borns may become stubborn, ill behaved, and destructive and may refuse to eat or go to bed. They are striking out in anger, but the parents will probably strike back, and their weapons are far more powerful. When first-borns are punished for their troublesome behavior, they see that as more proof of their fall and may come to hate the second child, who is, after all, the cause of the problem.

Adler believed all first-borns feel the shock of their changed status in the family, but those who have been excessively pampered feel a greater loss. Also, the extent of the loss depends on the first-born's age at the time the rival appears. In general, the older a first-born child is when the second child arrives, the less dethronement the first-born will experience. For example, an 8-year-old will be less upset by the birth of a sibling than will a 2-year-old.

Characteristics of First-Borns

Adler found that first-borns are often oriented toward the past, locked in nostalgia, and pessimistic about the future. Having once learned the advantages of power, they remain concerned with it throughout life. They can exercise power over younger siblings, but at the same time they are more subject to the power of their parents because more is expected of them.

One's order of birth within the family—being older or younger than one's siblings—creates different conditions of childhood that can affect personality.

Denise Hager, Catchlight Visual Services/Catchlight Visual Services/Alamy

There are advantages to being the first-born child, however. As the children age, the first-born often has to play the role of teacher, tutor, leader, and disciplinarian, expected by parents to help care for younger siblings. These experiences often enable the first-born to mature intellectually to a higher degree than the younger children. As one psychologist put it:

> Second-born children might ask older siblings about the meanings of words, about how some things work and why, about the whereabouts of candy or of a parent who is late in coming back home, and about countless other matters that older siblings must now explain…. In this role of tutor, first-born children gain an intellectual advantage. By virtue of rehearsal, by virtue of having to articulate an explanation or offer the meaning of a word, firstborns gain more verbal fluency more quickly than the second-borns. (Zajonc, 2001, p. 491)

Adler believed that first-borns also take an unusual interest in maintaining order and authority. They become good organizers, conscientious and scrupulous about detail, authoritarian and conservative in attitude. Sigmund Freud was a first-born; Adler described him as a typical eldest son. First-borns may also grow up to feel insecure and hostile toward others. Adler believed that neurotics, perverts, and criminals were often first-borns.

The Second-Born Child

Second-born children, the ones who caused so much upheaval in the lives of first-borns, are also in a unique situation. They never experience the powerful position once occupied by the first-borns. Even if another child is brought into the family, second-borns do not suffer the sense of dethronement felt by the first-borns.

Also, by this time the parents have usually changed their child-rearing attitudes and practices. A second baby is not the novelty the first was; parents may be less concerned and anxious about their own behavior and may take a more relaxed approach to the second child.

From the beginning, second-borns have a pacesetter in the older sibling. The second child always has the example of the older child's behavior as a model, a threat, or a source of competition. Adler was a second-born child who had a lifelong competitive relationship with his older brother (whose name was Sigmund). Even when Adler became a famous analyst, he still felt overshadowed by his brother.

> Alfred [Adler] always felt eclipsed by his "model brother" and resented his favored status in the family.... Even in middle age, he would feel moved to comment wearily that wealthy businessman Sigmund, "a good industrious fellow [who] was always ahead of me—is still ahead of me!". (Hoffman, 1994, p. 11)

Characteristics of Second-Borns

Competition with the first-born may serve to motivate the second-born, who may try to catch up to and surpass the older sibling, a goal that spurs language and motor development in the second-born. Not having experienced power, second-borns are not as concerned with it. They are more optimistic about the future and are likely to be competitive and ambitious, as Adler was.

Other less beneficial outcomes may also arise from the relationship between first-borns and second-borns. If, for example, the older siblings excel in sports or scholarship, the second-borns may feel that they can never surpass the first-borns and may give up trying. In this case, competitiveness would not become part of the second-borns' lifestyles, and they may become underachievers, performing below their abilities in many facets of life.

The Youngest Child

Youngest or last-born children never face the shock of dethronement by another child and often become the pet of the family, particularly if the siblings are more than a few years older. Driven by the need to surpass older siblings, youngest children often develop at a remarkably fast rate. Last-borns are often high achievers in whatever work they undertake as adults.

The opposite can occur, however, if the youngest children are excessively pampered and come to believe they needn't learn to do anything for themselves. As they grow older, such children may retain the helplessness and dependency of childhood. Unaccustomed to striving and struggling, used to being cared for, these people find it difficult to adjust to adulthood.

The Only Child

Only children never lose the position of primacy and power they hold in the family. They remain the focus and center of attention. Spending more time in the company of adults than a child with siblings, only children often mature early and manifest adult behaviors and attitudes.

Only children may experience problems when they find that in areas of life outside the home, such as school, they are not the center of attention. Only children have learned neither to share nor to compete. If their abilities do not bring them sufficient recognition and attention, they are likely to feel keenly disappointed.

With his ideas about order of birth, Adler was not proposing firm rules of childhood development. A child will not automatically acquire a particular kind of character based solely on his or her position in the family. What Adler was suggesting was the likelihood that certain styles of life will develop as a function of order of birth combined with one's early social interactions. The creative self in constructing the style of life uses both influences.

Questions about Human Nature

Adler's system provides a hopeful, flattering image of human nature that is the antithesis of Freud's dreary, pessimistic view. Certainly it is more satisfying to our sense of self-worth to consider ourselves capable of consciously shaping our own individual development and destiny rather than being dominated by instinctual forces and childhood experiences over which we have no control.

Adler's image of human nature is optimistic in his belief that people are not driven by unconscious forces. We possess the free will to shape the social forces that influence us and to use them creatively to construct a unique style of life. This uniqueness is another aspect of Adler's flattering picture. Freud's system, in contrast, offered a depressing universality and sameness in human nature.

Although Adler argued that some aspects of human nature are innate—for example, the potential for social interest and striving for perfection—it is experience that determines how these inherited tendencies will be realized. Childhood influences are important, particularly order of birth and interactions with our parents, but we are not victims of our childhood experiences. Instead, we use them to create our style of life.

Adler saw each person as striving to achieve perfection, and he viewed humanity in similar terms. He believed in the creative power of the individual and was optimistic about social progress.

Assessment in Adler's Theory

Like Freud, Adler developed his theory by analyzing his patients; that is, by evaluating their verbalizations and behavior during therapy sessions. Adler's approach was more relaxed and informal than Freud's. Whereas Freud's patients lay on a couch while he sat behind them, Adler and his patients sat in comfortable chairs facing each other. The sessions were more like chats between friends than the more formal relationships maintained by Freud.

Adler also liked to use humor in his therapy, sometimes teasing his patients in a lighthearted, friendly way. He had a storehouse of jokes appropriate for various neuroses and believed that making a joke would sometimes lead a patient to "see how ridiculous his sickness is." When an adolescent patient told Adler he felt guilty when he masturbated, Adler replied: "You mean to say you masturbate and feel guilty? That is too much. One would be enough: either masturbate or feel guilty. But both is too much" (Hoffman, 1994, pp. 209, 273).

Adler assessed the personalities of his patients by observing everything about them: the way they walked and sat, their manner of shaking hands, even their choice of which chair to sit in. He suggested that the way we use our bodies indicates something of our style of life. Even the position in which we sleep is revealing.

For example, according to Adler, restless sleepers and those who sleep flat on their back want to seem more important than they are. Sleeping on one's stomach shows a stubborn and negative personality. Curling in the fetal position shows that the person is fearful of interacting with others. Sleeping with the arms outstretched reveals a need to be nurtured and supported.

Adler's primary methods of assessment, which he referred to as the entrance gates to mental life, are order of birth, early recollections, and dream analysis. In addition, psychologists have developed psychological assessment tests based on Adler's concept of social interest. Adler's purpose in assessing personality was to discover the patient's style of life and to determine whether it was the most appropriate one for that person.

Early Recollections

early recollections
A personality assessment technique in which our earliest memories, whether of real events or fantasies, are assumed to reveal the primary interest of our life.

According to Adler, our personality is created during the first 4 or 5 years of life. Our **early recollections**, our memories from that period, indicate the style of life that continues to characterize us as adults. Adler found that it made little difference whether his clients' early recollections were of real events or were fantasies.

In either case, the primary interest of the person's life revolved around the remembered incidents and so, in Adler's view, early recollections are "the most satisfactory single indicators of lifestyle" (Manaster & Mays, 2004, p. 114). Adler also found that many early memories contained references to actual physical objects as part of the memory they were drawing forth (Clark, 2009).

Although Adler believed that each early memory should be interpreted within the context of the patient's style of life, he found commonalities among them. He suggested that memories involving danger or punishment indicated a tendency toward hostility. Those concerning the birth of a sibling showed a continued sense of dethronement. Memories that focused on one parent showed a preference for that parent. Recollections of improper behavior warned against any attempt to repeat the behavior.

Adler believed that:

> People remember from early childhood (a) only images that confirm and support their current views of themselves in the world ... and (b) only those memories that support their direction of striving for significance and security. [His] focus on selective memory and lifestyle emphasize what is *remembered*. In contrast, Freud's approach to interpreting early memories emphasizes what is *forgotten* through the mechanism of repression. (Kopp & Eckstein, 2004, p. 165)

Adler's Strange Early Memory

An early memory Adler recalled as an adult was from when he was 5 years old and had just started school. He remembered being terribly afraid every day because the path to school led through a cemetery (Adler, 1924/1963). He was frightened every time he walked to school but was also confused because other children seemed not to notice the cemetery.

Since he was the only one who was afraid, this heightened his sense of inferiority. One day he decided to put an end to his fears. He ran through the cemetery a dozen times until he felt he had overcome his feelings. From then on, he was able to go to school without being afraid.

Thirty years later Adler met a former schoolmate and asked him if the old cemetery was still there. The man expressed surprise and told Adler there had never been a cemetery near their school. Adler was shocked; his recollection had been so vivid! He sought out other classmates and questioned them.

They all told him the same thing: There had been no cemetery. Adler finally accepted that his memory of the incident was faulty. Nonetheless, it symbolized the fear and inferiority, and his efforts to overcome them, which characterized his style of life. That early recollection had revealed an important and influential aspect of his personality.

Dream Analysis

Adler agreed with Freud about the value of dreams in understanding personality but disagreed on the way in which dreams should be interpreted. Adler did not believe that dreams fulfill wishes or reveal hidden conflicts. Rather, dreams involve our feelings about a current problem and what we intend to do about it.

One of Adler's own dreams illustrates this point. Before his first visit to the United States, Adler felt anxious and worried, concerned about how he and his theory of personality would be received. The night before he was scheduled to cross the Atlantic Ocean by ship, he dreamed that the ship, with him aboard, capsized and sank.

> All of Adler's worldly possessions were on it and were destroyed by the raging waves. Hurled into the ocean, Adler was forced to swim for his life. Alone he thrashed and struggled through the choppy waters. But through the force of will and determination, he finally reached land in safety. (Hoffman, 1994, p. 151)

This dream revealed Adler's fear about what he would face in the United States and his intention to land safely, in other words, to achieve success for himself and for his theory of individual psychology.

In the fantasies of our dreams (both night dreams and daydreams), we believe we can surmount the most difficult obstacle or simplify the most complex problem. Thus, dreams are oriented toward the present and future, not toward conflicts from the past.

Adler believed that dreams should never be interpreted without knowledge of the person and his or her situation. The dream is a manifestation of a person's style of life and so is unique to the individual. Adler did find common interpretations for some dreams, however. Many people reported dreams involving falling or flying. Freud interpreted such dreams in sexual terms.

According to Adler, a dream of falling indicates that the person's emotional view involves a demotion or loss, such as the fear of losing self-esteem or prestige. A flying dream indicates a sense of striving upward, an ambitious style of life in which the person desires to be above or better than others.

Dreams that combine flying and falling involve a fear of being too ambitious and thus failing. A dream of being chased suggests a feeling of weakness in relation to other people. Dreaming one is naked indicates a fear of giving oneself away. Additional Adlerian dream interpretations are shown in Table 4.1.

Measures of Social Interest

Adler had no desire to use psychological tests to assess personality. He argued that tests create artificial situations that provide ambiguous results. Instead of relying on tests, Adler thought therapists should develop their intuition. He did, however, support tests of memory and intelligence; it was tests of personality he criticized.

TABLE 4.1 Dream events and their latent meanings

DREAM EVENT	ADLERIAN INTERPRETATION
Being paralyzed	Facing insoluble problems
School exams	Being unprepared for situations
Wearing the wrong clothes	Being disturbed by one's faults
Sexual themes	Retreating from sex or inadequate information about sex
Rage	An angry or hostile style of life
Death	Unresolved issues about the dead person

Source: Adapted from Grey, 1998, p. 93.

Psychologists have developed tests to measure Adler's concepts of social interest and style of life. The Social Interest Scale (SIS) consists of pairs of adjectives (Crandall, 1981). Subjects choose the word in each pair that best describes an attribute they would like to possess. Words such as *helpful*, *sympathetic*, and *considerate* are thought to indicate one's degree of social interest.

The Social Interest Index (SII) is a self-report inventory in which subjects judge the degree to which statements represent themselves or their personal characteristics (Greever, Tseng, & Friedland, 1973). The items, such as *I don't mind helping out friends*, were selected to reflect Adler's ideas and to indicate a person's ability to accept and cooperate with others.

People who score high on the SII, indicating a high degree of social interest, tend to be high in friendliness, empathy, cooperation with others, tolerance, and independence. They have also been found to be lower in anxiety, hostility, depression, and neuroticism (Leak 2006a, 2006b).

The Basic Adlerian Scales for Interpersonal Success (BASIS-A), is a 65-item self-report inventory designed to assess lifestyle as well as degree of social interest. The five personality dimensions measured are social interest, going along, taking charge, wanting recognition, and being cautious (Peluso, Peluso, Buckner, Curlette, & Kern, 2004).

Research on Adler's Theory

Adler's primary research method was the case study. Unfortunately, little of Adler's data survived. He did not publish case histories except for two fragments: one written by a patient, the other written by a patient's physician. Adler did not know the patients involved, but he analyzed their personalities by examining their writings.

Adler's data and research method are subject to the same criticisms we discussed for Freud and Jung. His observations cannot be repeated and duplicated, nor were they conducted in a controlled and systematic fashion. Adler did not attempt to verify the accuracy of his patients' reports or explain the procedures he used to analyze the data, and he had no interest in applying the experimental method. A follower wrote: "Adler wanted his psychology to be a science, but it has not been a psychology easily verified by the scientific method" (Manaster, 2006, p. 6).

Although most of Adler's propositions have resisted attempts at scientific validation, several topics have been the subject of research. These include dreams, inferiority feelings, early recollections, pampering and neglect in childhood, social interest, and order of birth.

Dreams   Adler's belief that dreams help us solve current problems was investigated by exposing subjects to situations in which the failure to solve a puzzle was considered a threat to the personality. They were then allowed to sleep. Some were permitted to dream but were awakened only during non-rapid-eye-movement (NREM) sleep. Others were awakened during rapid-eye-movement (REM) sleep so that they could not dream.

Those who dreamed later recalled significantly more of the uncompleted puzzle than those who did not dream. The researchers concluded that dreaming enabled the subjects to deal effectively with the current threatening situation—that is, the failure to solve the puzzle (Grieser, Greenberg, & Harrison, 1972).

In another study, the dreams of two groups were reported (Breger, Hunter, & Lane, 1971). One group consisted of college students who were anticipating a stressful psychotherapy session. The other group consisted of patients about to undergo major surgery. Both groups recalled dreams that focused on their conscious worries, fears, and hopes. They dreamed about the current problems they were facing.

Inferiority Feelings   Research has found that adults who scored low on inferiority feelings tended to be more successful and self-confident and more persistent in trying to achieve their goals than adults who scored high on inferiority feelings. A study of American college students showed that those with moderate inferiority feelings had higher grade point averages than those with low or high inferiority feelings (Strano & Petrocelli, 2005).

Research on teenagers and young adults in China showed that they felt inferior about different aspects of their life at different ages. Younger teens experienced inferiority feelings about poor grades; older teens had inferiority feelings about physical attractiveness. College students reported inferiority feelings about their lack of social skills (Kosaka, 2008).

Early Recollections Early memories of people diagnosed as anxiety neurotics were concerned with fear; early memories of depressed persons centered on abandonment; and early memories of those with psychosomatic complaints involved illness (Jackson & Sechrest, 1962). Early memories of alcoholics contained threatening events, as well as situations in which they were controlled by external circumstances rather than by their own decisions. The early memories of a control group of non-alcoholics showed neither of these themes (Hafner, Fakouri, & Labrentz, 1982).

A study of police officers in the United States found that those who had traumatic early recollections experienced more pronounced symptoms of post-traumatic stress disorder than those who did not have those kinds of early memories (Patterson, 2014). Early recollections of adult criminals dealt with disturbing or aggressive interactions with other people. They contained more unpleasant events than the early recollections of a control group (Hankoff, 1987). The early memories of adolescent delinquents

Our earliest memories of childhood help reveal our lifestyle.

Fancy/Jupiter Images

involved breaking rules, having difficulty forming social relationships, and being unable to cope with life on their own. They also perceived their parents as untrustworthy and as more likely to hurt than to help. These themes were not present in the early memories of a control group (Davidow & Bruhn, 1990).

Recollections of psychiatric patients considered dangerous to themselves and to others showed more aggressive early memories than did recollections of non-dangerous psychiatric patients. The recollections of the dangerous patients revealed that they felt vulnerable and powerless and saw others as hostile and abusive (Tobey & Bruhn, 1992).

The Nature of Early Recollections

Research using objective scoring systems for early recollections has shown that these memories tend to be subjective recreations rather than events that actually occurred, much like Adler's memory of the cemetery (Statton & Wilborn, 1991).

One study reported that when people were asked to make up early recollections that might have happened to someone else, the themes were similar to those revealed by their own recollections (Buchanan, Kern, & Bell-Dumas, 1991). This study also provided research support for Adler's contention that early recollections reveal one's current style of life and therefore can be used as a therapeutic device. (Table 4.2 summarizes possible themes of early recollections.)

Early recollections studied in adults in the United States and in Israel have been shown to predict career preferences. For example, the early memories of physicists, mathematicians, and psychologists included themes such as curiosity, independent thought, and skepticism about information from authority figures (Clark, 2005; Kasler & Nevo, 2005).

Neglect in Childhood   Adler suggested that children who were neglected or rejected by their parents developed feelings of worthlessness. A study of adults hospitalized for depression found that the patients rated their parents as having been hostile, detached, and rejecting (Crook, Raskin, & Eliot, 1981). Interviews with siblings, relatives, and friends of the patients confirmed that the parents had indeed behaved in hostile and neglectful ways.

In another study, parents of 8-year-old children completed a questionnaire to assess their child-rearing behaviors and their level of satisfaction with their children (Lefkowitz

TABLE 4.2	Early recollections and style of life themes
RECOLLECTION	**POSSIBLE THEME**
First school memory	Attitudes toward achievement, mastery, and independence
First punishment memory	Attitude toward authority figures
First sibling memory	Evidence of sibling rivalry
First family memory	Functioning in social situations
Clearest memory of mother	Attitudes toward women
Clearest memory of father	Attitudes toward men
Memory of person you admire	Basis for role models
Happiest memory	Basis for how your strongest needs are best gratified

Source: Adapted from Bruhn, A. R. (1992). The early memories procedure. *Journal of Personality Assessment, 58*(1), 1–15.

& Tesiny, 1984). Ten years later the children, then age 18, were given the depression scale of the Minnesota Multiphasic Personality Inventory (MMPI). Those whose test scores showed they were more depressed had been neglected in childhood by their parents. Those whose parents had not been indifferent or unloving scored lower on the depression scale.

More recent research has found that neglected children have also been found to experience more shame, depression, symptoms of PTSD, and lower socialization skills than children who were not neglected (Bennett, Sullivan, & Lewis, 2010; Lowell, Viezel, Davis, & Castillo, 2011; Milot, Plamondon, Ethier, Lemelin, St-Laurent, & Rousseau, 2013).

Children and adolescents in China (ages 5–17) who experienced neglect were far more likely to develop high anxiety than those who were not neglected (Guan, Deng, & Luo, 2010). Neglected children may also be more prone to acts of violence and excessive alcohol use later in life (Widom, Czaja, Wilson, Allwood, & Chauhan, 2013). It does appear, then, that children who are neglected in childhood pay a high price for it as they grow up.

Pampering in Childhood Adler argued that pampering in childhood could lead to a pampered style of life in which the person shows little or no social feelings for others. Research supports this idea and also suggests that pampering can lead to excessive narcissism, which involves a lack of responsibility or empathy for other people, as well as an exaggerated sense of self-importance, and a tendency to exploit others. Studies have identified four types of pampering.

- Overindulgence, which involves the persistent parental gratification of a child's needs and desires, leading to feelings of entitlement as well as tyrannical and manipulative behavior
- Overpermissiveness, which involves allowing children to behave as they please with no consideration for the effects of their behavior on other people, leading to a disregard of social rules and the rights of others
- Overdomination, which involves exclusive parental decision-making, leading to a child's lack of self-confidence and a tendency to become dependent on others in adulthood
- Overprotection, which involves parental caution, excessively warning children of potential dangers in their environment, leading to generalized anxiety and a tendency to avoid or hide from social situations

Studies with college students found that children of over-domineering mothers were more likely to seek psychotherapy while in college. Students who rated their parents as both overindulgent and overprotective tended to be low in self-esteem. Students whose parents were considered to be overindulgent and over-domineering scored high in narcissism (Capron, 2004).

Social Interest Research using the SIS found that those high in social interest reported less stress, depression, anxiety, and hostility than those low in social interest. High social interest scorers scored higher on tests assessing cooperation with others, empathy, responsibility, and popularity (Crandall, 1984; Watkins, 1994; Watkins & St. John, 1994). Research with college students found that those high in social interest scored high in spirituality and religiosity. However, their spirituality was of a positive, tolerant, and helping nature, not necessarily religious ethnocentrism or fundamentalism (Leak, 2006a).

Other studies in the United States and China showed that those high in social interest were also high in subjective well-being, hope and optimism, agreeableness, self-identity, self-determination, and a strong sense of purpose in life (Barlow, Tobin, & Schmidt, 2009; Foley, Matheny, & Curlette, 2008; Leak & Leak, 2006).

A study of high school adolescents in grades 9 to 12 found that those high in social interest scored significantly higher in overall life satisfaction, as well as satisfaction with friends and family, than did those who scored low in social interest (Gilman, 2001). Other research, conducted with male criminal offenders ranging in age from 18 to 40, showed that those who scored high in social interest were far less likely to commit additional crimes following their release from jail than were those who scored low in social interest (Daugherty, Murphy, & Paugh, 2001). Juvenile delinquents scored lower on social interest than did those who were not identified as delinquents (Newbauer & Stone, 2010).

Studies with the SII showed that women who scored high in social interest were significantly higher in self-actualization, a characteristic of the healthy personality described by Maslow (see Chapter 9). Other research found that social interest was higher in women than in men and that it increased with age for both sexes (Greever, Tseng, & Friedland, 1973).

A study of Latino men and women living in the United States found that those who were well-adjusted to both cultures scored higher on social interest measures than those primarily acculturated to only the Latino or the U.S. lifestyle (Miranda, Frevert, & Kern, 1998).

High social interest may also be good for your health. Social interest, with its related feelings of belonging, cooperation, and a sense of contributing to or receiving support from a social network has been positively associated with physical and mental well-being. For example, people who scored high in social interest tended to have stronger immune systems, fewer colds, lower blood pressure, and greater subjective well-being (Nikelly, 2005).

Birth Order A great deal of research has been conducted on the effects of one's order of birth within the family (Eckstein & Kaufman, 2012). In one survey of 200 birth-order studies, the authors concluded that first-borns had higher success and achievement levels and were more likely to become accountants, lawyers, architects, surgeons, college

HIGHLIGHTS: Research on Adler's Ideas

Children who are neglected tend to develop

- Feelings of worthlessness and shame
- Depression
- Anxiety

Children who are pampered tend to

- Have low self-esteem
- Become narcissistic
- Lack empathy for others

People who score high in social interest tend to

- Score low on depression, anxiety, and hostility
- Develop feelings of empathy for others
- Become happy and agreeable

professors, or astronauts. Later-borns, on the other hand, were more likely to become firefighters, high school teachers, musicians, photographers, social workers, or stuntmen (Eckstein, et al., 2010).

Obviously, being the first-born, second-born, last-born, or an only child can influence personality in a variety of ways. Simply having older or younger siblings, regardless of one's own order of birth, can affect personality. For example, studies of nearly 20,000 people in England, Scotland, and Wales, and some 3,500 people in the United States, found that the number of older brothers a man had could predict his sexual orientation. Boys with older brothers were more sexually attracted to men than boys who did not have older brothers. The greater number of older brothers a man had, the greater the attraction to the same sex. Having older sisters did not appear to predict sexual orientation in women (Bogaert, 2003).

Birth order can also affect our choice of friends. First-borns are more likely to associate with other first-borns, second-borns with other second-borns, and so on. Only children tend to associate with other only children. These preferences held for friendships as well as for romantic relationships (Hartshorne, 2010; Hartshorne, Salem-Hartshorne, & Hartshorne, 2009).

First-Born Children A study in Finland found that the behavior and characteristics of first-borns can influence whether the parents decide to have other children, within 5 years of the birth of the first. Parents whose first child showed high intelligence, few behavior problems, and the ability to adapt to new situations were more likely to have additional children (Jokela, 2010).

According to Adler, first-borns are concerned with power and authority. One way for them to gain power and authority as adults is through achievement in their work. In many areas, from college attendance to high-level management, first-borns are over represented relative to their proportion of the population. More first-borns than later-borns become eminent, and they tend to attain greater intellectual achievement in academic settings and greater power and prestige in their careers (Breland, 1974; Schachter, 1963).

Studies in the United States and in Poland found that first-borns scored higher on measures of intelligence, completed more years of formal education, and worked in more prestigious occupations than later-borns (Herrera, Zajonc, Wieczorkowska, & Cichomski, 2003). Research on adults in Sweden showed that first-borns scored higher than later-borns on tests of managerial or executive functioning (Holmgren, Molander, & Nilsson, 2006). A study of more than 240,000 male army recruits in Norway showed that older siblings scored higher on IQ tests than younger siblings (Kristensen & Bjerkedal, 2007).

British research has found that first-borns are far less likely to suffer from PTSD than those who are the fifth child or younger in large families. The later-borns were found to be more subject to stress and adjustment disorders (Green & Griffiths, 2014). These research results in general are supportive of Adler's views.

Evidence suggests that first-borns may be more intelligent than later-borns, but not all researchers agree (see Rodgers, 2001). The IQ scores of 400,000 European men were analyzed with respect to birth order (Belmont & Marolla, 1973). The results showed that first-borns had higher IQ scores than second-borns, second-borns had higher scores than third-borns, and so on.

These findings were confirmed for men and women in several nations (Zajonc, Markus, & Markus, 1979). A possible explanation relates not to genetic differences but to the first-born's exclusive exposure to adults. Consequently, first-borns may have a more stimulating intellectual environment than later-borns.

Although first-borns may be more intelligent than later-borns, they do not always earn higher grades in school. Studies of U.S. high school students confirm that first-borns have higher IQ scores but later-borns tend to work harder and achieve higher grade point averages (Frank, Turenshine, & Sullivan, 2010; Rettner, 2010).

First-borns tend to be more suggestible and dependent on other people. They are anxious in stressful situations and have a higher need for social relationships (Schachter, 1963, 1964). These findings can be predicted from Adler's theory. He noted that first-borns experience anxiety when dethroned by a sibling and attempt to regain their position by conforming to parental expectations. Thus, first-borns rely more on the standards of others to guide their behavior and form the basis of their self-concept (Newman, Higgins, & Vookles, 1992).

Other research found that first-borns scored lower than later-borns on tests of depression and anxiety and higher on self-esteem (Gates, Lineberger, Crockett, & Hubbard, 1988). First-borns may also be more extraverted and conscientious (Sulloway, 1995). However, later research in the Netherlands found the opposite: Later-borns were more extraverted in that they were more dominant and assertive (Pollet, Dijkstra, Barelds, & Buunk, 2010).

First-born girls were found to be more obedient and socially responsible than later-borns and to feel closer to their parents (Sutton-Smith & Rosenberg, 1970). Studies in France, Croatia, Canada, and England showed that first-borns were more closely supervised in childhood, rated by their mothers as less fearful, reported more frightening childhood dreams, and scored higher on measures of dominance in college (Beck, Burnet, & Vosper, 2006; Begue & Roche, 2005; Kerestes, 2006; McCann, Stewin, & Short, 1990).

Second-Born Children   Less research has been conducted on second-born children. A study of first-born and second-born siblings, conducted over 3 years, found that the attitudes, personalities, and leisure activities of second-born children were influenced more by their older siblings than by their parents (McHale, Updegraff, Helms-Erikson, & Crouter, 2001). Research on major league baseball players found that those who were younger brothers were 10 times more likely than older brothers to attempt the high-risk action of stealing bases during a game. They also had higher batting averages than those who were older brothers (Sulloway & Zweigenhaft, 2010).

Last-Born Children   Adler predicted that last-born children, if excessively pampered, would have adjustment problems as adults. One popular explanation for alcoholism is that some people cannot cope with the demands of everyday life. According to Adler's theory, then, more last-borns than early-borns would become alcoholics. This prediction has been supported by considerable research dealing with alcoholism and birth order. Binge drinking in college has been found to be significantly higher among last-borns than first-borns (Laird & Shelton, 2006). Other research suggests that last-borns may feel a greater degree of academic rivalry with their siblings than first-borns do (Badger & Reddy, 2009).

Only Children   To Adler, only-born adults are overly concerned with being the center of attention, as they were in childhood. He also considered only-borns to be more selfish. Research has not consistently supported this notion. One study found that only children were more cooperative than first-borns or last-borns (Falbo, 1978). Another study found that they were more self-centered and less popular than were children reared with siblings (Jiao, Ji, & Jing, 1986).

HIGHLIGHTS: Research on Birth Order

First-borns tend to be:

- Intelligent and hardworking
- Successful in college and career
- Low on measures of depression and anxiety
- High in self-esteem

Second-borns tend to be:

- Influenced by older siblings
- More likely to take risks when playing baseball

Last-borns (the youngest child) tends to be:

- High in social interest and agreeableness
- Can also be rebellious

Only-borns tend to be:

- High in achievement and intelligence
- Industrious and perform well in school
- High in self-esteem

An analysis of 115 studies of only-borns reported higher levels of achievement and intelligence and comparable social and emotional adjustment with people who have siblings (Falbo & Polit, 1986). Later research (Mellor, 1990) confirmed those results and reported that only children had greater initiative, aspiration, industriousness, and self-esteem. In addition, they have been found to be strongly motivated toward achievement and to score high in confidence and organizational skills (Siribaddana, 2013).

An analysis of several studies shows that the number of siblings in a family is a consistent predictor of educational success; people with fewer siblings do perform better in school (Downey, 2001). Only-borns may also have more educational opportunities and parental resources, enabling them to perform better than children with siblings.

Birth-Order Effects: A Matter of Belief?

And now, after you have read about those studies showing the differences among people related to their order of birth, we come to one other piece of research. Those who believe in the effects of birth order were found to be different from those who do not believe that order of birth affects people in different ways. Believers in birth-order effects, one study suggests, score significantly lower in being open to new experiences and significantly higher in neuroticism than those who do not believe in differential effects of their order of birth (Gundersen, Brown, Bhathal, & Kennedy, 2011).

Reflections on Adler's Theory

Contributions

Adler's influence within psychology has been substantial. In later chapters we will see examples of his ideas in the work of other personality theorists. Those contributions make Adler's personality theory one of the most enduring. He was ahead of his time, and his cognitive and social emphases are more compatible with trends in psychology today than with the psychology of his own day (LaFountain, 2009). Abraham Maslow wrote over 30 years after Adler's death that: "Alfred Adler becomes more and more correct year by year. As the facts come in, they give stronger and stronger support to his image of man" (1970a, p. 13).

Adler's emphasis on social forces in personality will be seen in the next chapter in the theory of Karen Horney. His focus on the whole person and the unity of personality is reflected in the work of Gordon Allport. The creative power of people to shape their own styles of life, and the insistence that future goals are more important than past events, influenced the work of Abraham Maslow. A social-learning theorist, Julian Rotter, wrote that he "continues to be impressed by Adler's insights into human nature" (Rotter, 1982, pp. 1–2).

Adler's ideas also reached into Freudian psychoanalysis. It was Adler who proposed the aggressive drive more than 12 years before Freud included aggression with sex as primary motivating forces. The neo-Freudian ego psychologists, who focus more on conscious and rational processes and less on the unconscious, follow Adler's lead rather than Freud's.

Adler disputed Freud's views on women, arguing that there was no biological basis, such as penis envy, for women's alleged sense of inferiority. Such a notion, Adler charged, was a myth invented by men to maintain their alleged sense of superiority. He acknowledged that women may feel inferior but believed that was due to social conditioning and sex-role stereotyping. He also believed in the idea of equality for the sexes and supported the women's emancipation movements of the day.

Specific Adlerian concepts of lasting importance to psychology include the early work on organic inferiority, which has influenced the study of psychosomatic disorders; the inferiority complex; compensation; and order of birth. Adler is also considered a forerunner of social psychology and group therapy (see Figure 4.1).

Criticisms

As influential as Adler's work has been, however, it does have its critics. Freud charged that Adler's psychology was oversimplified and would appeal to many people because it eliminated the complicated nature of the unconscious, had no difficult concepts, and ignored the problems of sex. Freud remarked that it could take 2 years or more to learn about his psychoanalysis, but "Adler's ideas and technique can be easily learned in two weeks, because with Adler there is so little to know" (quoted in Sterba, 1982, p. 156).

It is true that Adler's theory seems simpler than Freud's or Jung's, but that was Adler's deliberate intention. He wrote that it had taken him 40 years to make his psychology simple. One point that reinforces the charge of oversimplification is that his books are easy to read because he wrote for the general public and because some of them were compiled from his popular lectures.

A related charge is that Adler's concepts appear to rely heavily on commonsense observations from everyday life. A book reviewer in the *New York Times* noted: "Although [Adler] is one of the most eminent psychologists in the world, when he writes about psychology there is no other who can equal him in simplicity and non-technicality of language" (quoted in Hoffman, 1994, p. 276).

Critics allege that Adler was inconsistent and unsystematic in his thinking and that his theory contains gaps and unanswered questions. Are inferiority feelings the only problem we face in life? Do all people strive primarily for perfection? Can we become reconciled to a degree of inferiority and no longer try to compensate for it? These and

FIGURE 4.1
Adler's books achieved considerable popularity in the United States and spawned the huge genre of self-help books.

"One of those rare books that help you to know yourself . . . an adventure in understanding."

UNDERSTANDING HUMAN NATURE

By ALFRED ADLER
Translated by W. Beran Wolfe, M. D.

DO you have an inferiority complex . . . do you feel insecure . . . are you faint-hearted . . . are you imperious . . . are you submissive . . . do you believe in hard luck . . . do you understand the other fellow . . . do you understand yourself?

Spend the evening with yourself. Try the adventure of looking inside of yourself. Let one of the greatest psychologists of the age help you look in the right places, discover the right things. $3.50

Heywood Broun:
"For wisdom and keener comprehension of social problems I recommend 'Understanding Human Nature' by Alfred Adler."

Joseph Jastrow:
"I regard the book as the best available expression of Dr. Adler's views for the general public."

The Boston Transcript:
"One of the finest things about the whole book is its freedom from academic discussion as such and its very real help to human beings to be what they ought to be and can be."

The Hartford Courant:
"Adler's law, in our opinion, will be ranked by posterity with the fruitful discoveries of Darwin, Dalton, Pasteur, Koch and Priestly. Its alternative is chaos."

Understanding Human Nature

GREENBERG PUBLISHER
112 East 19th St., New York

Source: Hoffman, E. (1994). *The drive for self: Alfred Adler and the founding of individual psychology.* Reading, MA: Addison-Wesley.

other questions cannot all be answered adequately by Adler's system, but as we have seen, most theorists leave us with unanswered questions.

Some psychologists dispute Adler's position on the issue of determinism versus free will. Early in his career, Adler did not oppose the notion of determinism. It was broadly accepted in science at the time, and it characterized Freud's psychoanalytic theory. Later, Adler felt the need to grant more autonomy to the self, and his final formulation rejected determinism.

His concept of the creative self proposes that before the age of 5, we fashion a style of life using material provided by our heredity and our environment. However, it is not clear how a child is able to make such momentous decisions. We know that Adler favored free will and opposed the idea that we are victims of innate forces and childhood events. That position is clear, but the specifics of forming the style of life are not.

Later Recognition and Influence

Although his ideas have been widely accepted, Adler's public recognition declined after his death in 1937, and he has received relatively little subsequent praise or credit for his contributions. Many concepts have been borrowed from his theory without acknowledgment. A typical instance of this lack of recognition can be found in Sigmund Freud's obituary in the *Times* newspaper of London, which named Freud as the originator of the term *inferiority complex*. When Carl Jung died, the *New York Times* said he had coined the term. Neither newspaper mentioned Adler, the originator of the concept. However, Adler did receive one unique honor: A British composer named a string quartet for him.

Adler's followers claim that individual psychology remains popular among psychologists, psychiatrists, social workers, and educators. *Individual Psychology: The Journal of Adlerian Theory, Research and Practice* is published quarterly by the North American Society of Adlerian Psychology. Other Adlerian journals are published in Germany, Italy, and France. Adlerian training institutes have been established in New York, Chicago, and other cities.

Chapter Summary

Adler's childhood was marked by intense efforts to compensate for his feelings of inferiority. His system of individual psychology differs from Freudian psychoanalysis in its focus on the uniqueness of the individual, on consciousness, and on social rather than biological forces. It minimizes the role of sex.

Inferiority feelings are the source of all human striving, which results from our attempts to compensate for these feelings. Inferiority feelings are universal and are determined by the infant's helplessness and dependency on adults.

An inferiority complex (an inability to solve life's problems) results from being unable to compensate for inferiority feelings. An inferiority complex can originate in childhood through organic inferiority, spoiling, or neglect. A superiority complex (an exaggerated opinion of one's abilities and accomplishments) results from overcompensation.

Our ultimate goal is superiority or perfection; that is, making the personality whole or complete. Fictional finalism refers to fictional ideas, such as perfection, that guide our behavior. Style of life refers to unique patterns of characteristics and behaviors by which we strive for perfection. The creative power of the self refers to our ability to create our selves from the materials provided by our heredity and environment. Four basic styles of life are the dominant or ruling type, the getting type, the avoiding type, and the socially useful type. Social interest is innate but the extent to which it is realized depends on early social experiences.

Order of birth is a major social influence in childhood from which one's style of life is created. First-borns are oriented toward the past, pessimistic about the future, and concerned with maintaining order and authority. Second-borns compete with first-borns and are apt to be ambitious. Last-borns, spurred by the need to surpass older siblings, may become high achievers. Only children mature early but are apt to face a shock in school when they are no longer the center of attention.

Adler's image of human nature is more hopeful than Freud's. In Adler's view, people are unique, and they possess free will and the ability to shape their own development. Although childhood experiences are important, we are not victims of them.

Adler's methods of assessment are order of birth, early recollections, and dream analysis. Research has provided support for Adler's views on the following: dreams, early memories, and childhood neglect and pampering; his belief that social interest is related to emotional well-being; the idea that first-borns are high achievers, dependent on others, suggestible, and anxious under stress; and the notion that last-borns are more likely to become alcoholics.

Adler's emphasis on cognitive and social factors in personality, the unity of personality, the creative power of the self, the importance of goals, and cognitive factors has influenced many personality theorists.

Review Questions

1. In what ways did Adler's theory of personality reflect his own childhood experience?
2. On what points did Adler differ with Freud?
3. What is the difference between inferiority feelings and the inferiority complex? How does each develop?
4. How does the superiority complex differ from the idea of striving for superiority? How did Adler define superiority?
5. Describe the concept of fictional finalism and explain how it relates to the notion of striving for superiority.

6. How, according to Adler, does the self develop? Do people play an active or a passive role in the development of the self?

7. What are Adler's four basic styles of life?

8. What parental behaviors may foster a child's development of social interest? Which basic style of life is identified with social interest?

9. How do people who score high in social interest differ from those who score low?

10. Describe the personality characteristics proposed by Adler that may develop in first-born, second-born, and youngest children as a result of their order of birth within the family.

11. According to Adler, what are the advantages and disadvantages of being an only child?

12. If it were possible to choose, which birth-order position would you select for yourself in your family? Why?

13. Summarize the research findings on the personalities of first-born and only-born children. Do the results support Adler's predictions.

14. Discuss the ways in which Adler's image of human nature differs from Freud's.

15. How did Adler assess the personalities of his patients?

16. What is the importance of early recollections in personality assessment? Give an example of how one of Adler's recollections revealed an aspect of his personality.

17. What is the purpose of dreams? Does contemporary research on sleep and dreaming support Adler's views?

18. How do people who score high in social interest differ from people who score low?

19. Discuss the contributions of Adler's system within psychology today.

Suggested Readings

Adler, A. (1930). Individual psychology. In C. Murchison (Ed.), *Psychologies of 1930* (pp. 395–405). Worcester, MA: Clark University Press. A clear exposition of the basic principles of Adler's individual psychology.

Ansbacher, H. L. (1990). Alfred Adler's influence on the three leading cofounders of humanistic psychology. *Journal of Humanistic Psychology, 30*(4), 45–53. Traces Adler's influence, in person and through his writings, on the development of humanistic psychology in the United States, most notably through his contact with Maslow and Rogers.

Ansbacher, R. R. (1997). Alfred Adler, the man, seen by a student and friend. *Individual Psychology, 53,* 270–274. Using Adler's technique of early recollections, the author evaluates her memories of Adler's lectures and therapy sessions in New York and Vienna.

Carlson, J., & Maniacci, M. P. (Eds). (2011). *Alfred Adler revisited.* New York: Routledge/Taylor & Francis Group. A collection of readings by Adler scholars detailing the basic elements of his work and linking many of his ideas to contemporary developments in psychology.

Ellenberger, H. F. (1970). *The discovery of the unconscious: The history and evolution of dynamic psychiatry.* New York: Basic Books. Traces the study of the unconscious from primitive times to Freudian psychoanalysis and its derivatives. See Chapter 8, "Alfred Adler and Individual Psychology."

Fiebert, M. S. (1997). In and out of Freud's shadow: A chronology of Adler's relationship with Freud. *Individual Psychology, 53,* 241–269. Reviews the 7-year correspondence between Adler and Freud describing changes in their personal and professional relationships and their acrimonious breakup.

Grey, L. (1998). *Alfred Adler, the forgotten prophet: A vision for the 21st century.* Westport, CT: Praeger. A biography and an assessment of the continuing influence of Adler's ideas.

Hoffman, E. (1994). *The drive for self: Alfred Adler and the founding of individual psychology.* Reading, MA: Addison-Wesley. Discusses Adler's contributions to personality theory, psychoanalysis, and popular psychology. Recounts events in his life as the basis for familiar concepts such as inferiority complex, overcompensation, and style of life.

Sulloway, F. J. (1996). *Born to rebel: Birth order, family dynamics, and creative lives.* New York: Pantheon. Analyzes revolutions in social, scientific, and political thought dating back to the 16th century to demonstrate the influence of birth order on personality development. Suggests that birth-order effects transcend gender, social class, race, national origin, and time.

chapter 5

Karen Horney: Neurotic Needs and Trends

Fair Use

The basic evil is invariably a lack of genuine warmth and affection.

—*Karen Horney*

Karen Danielsen Horney was another defector from the orthodox Freudian point of view. Although she was never a colleague of Freud's, as Jung and Adler had been, Horney was trained in the official psychoanalytic doctrine. She did not remain long in the Freudian camp, however. Her differences with Freud began when she took issue with his psychological portrayal of women.

An early feminist, she argued that psychoanalysis focused more on men's development than on women's. To counter Freud's contention that women are driven by penis envy, she proposed that men are envious of women for their ability to give birth. "I know just as many men with womb envy as women with penis envy," she said (quoted in Cherry & Cherry, 1973, p. 75). Freud was not happy with that remark, nor were most male analysts.

Horney's theory was strongly influenced by her personal experiences in childhood and adolescence, as well as by social and cultural forces that were different from those that had influenced Freud. Horney developed her theory in the United States, a culture radically different from Freud's Vienna. Also, by the 1930s and 1940s, major changes had occurred in popular attitudes about sex and the roles of men and women. These changes were occurring in Europe as well, but they were considerably more advanced in the United States.

Horney found that her American patients were so unlike her earlier German patients, both in their neuroses and their normal personalities, that she believed only the social forces to which they had been exposed could account for such a difference. She concluded that personality does not depend wholly on biological forces, as Freud proposed. If it did, she said, we would not see such major differences from one culture to another.

Horney, like Adler, placed a much greater emphasis than Freud on social relationships and interactions as significant factors in the formation of personality. She argued that sex is not the governing factor, as Freud claimed, and she questioned his concepts of the Oedipus complex, the libido, and the three-part structure of personality. To Horney, people are motivated not by sexual or aggressive forces but rather by the needs for security and love, which clearly reflected her life experiences.

The Life of Horney (1885–1952)

A Neglected Second-Born

Karen Danielsen grew up in a small village near Hamburg, Germany. She was the second-born child who, from an early age, envied her older brother, Berndt. He was attractive and charming, the adored first-born, but she was smarter and more vivacious. She confided to her diary, "It was always my pride that in school I was better than Berndt, that there were more amusing stories about me than about him" (Horney, 1980, p. 252). She also envied him because he was a boy, and girls were considered inferior. "I know that as a child I wanted for a long time to be a boy, that I envied Berndt because he could stand near a tree and pee" (Horney, 1980, p. 252).

An even stronger influence was her father. At the time of her birth he was a 50-year-old ship's captain of Norwegian background. Her mother was 17 years younger and of vastly different temperament. The father was religious, domineering, imperious, and morose; the mother was attractive, spirited, and freethinking. Horney's father spent long periods away at sea but when he was home, the opposing natures of the parents led to frequent arguments. Her mother made no secret of her wish to see her husband dead, and she told young Karen that she had married him not for love but from fear of becoming a spinster.

A Search for Love

We can see the roots of Horney's personality theory in these and other childhood experiences. For most of her youth she doubted that her parents wanted her and believed they loved Berndt more than they loved her. At 16, she wrote in her diary, "Why is everything beautiful on earth given to me, only not the highest thing, not love!" (Horney, 1980, p. 30). Although she desperately wanted her father's love and attention, he intimidated her with his fierce eyes and stern, demanding manner. She felt belittled and rejected when he often made disparaging comments about her intelligence and appearance.

Rebellion and Hostility

As a way of retaining her mother's affection, she acted the part of the adoring, obedient daughter. Until the age of 8, she was a model child, clinging and compliant. Despite her efforts, however, she did not think she was getting sufficient love and security. Her self-sacrifice and good behavior were not working, so she changed tactics and deliberately became ambitious and rebellious, deciding that if she could not have love and security, she would take revenge for her feelings of unattractiveness and inadequacy. "If I couldn't be beautiful, I decided I would be smart" (Horney quoted in Rubins, 1978, p. 14).

As an adult she realized how much hostility she had developed as a child. Her personality theory describes how a lack of love in childhood fosters anxiety and hostility. A biographer concluded, "In all her psychoanalytic writings Karen Horney was struggling to make sense of herself and to obtain relief from her own difficulties" (Paris, 1994, p. xxii).

Still Searching for Love

At 14, she developed an adolescent crush on a teacher and filled her diary with emotional comments about him. She continued to have infatuations with her male teachers, in the confused and unhappy way of many adolescents (Seiffge-Krenke & Kirsch, 2002). At 17, she awakened to the reality of sex and soon met a man she described as her first real love, but the relationship lasted only two days. Another man came into her life, prompting 76 pages of soul-searching in her diary. Horney decided that being in love eliminated, at least temporarily, her anxiety and insecurity; it offered an escape (Sayers, 1991).

Although Horney's quest for love and security was often thwarted, her search for a career was straightforward and successful. She decided at age 12, after being treated kindly by a physician, that she would become a doctor. Despite the medical establishment's discrimination against women and her father's opposition, she worked hard in school to prepare herself for medical studies. In 1906, she entered the University of Freiburg medical school, only 6 years after the first woman had, reluctantly, been admitted.

Marriage and Career

During her years at medical school, Horney met two men; she fell in love with one and married the other. Oskar Horney was studying for a Ph.D. in political science and after their marriage became a successful businessman. Karen Horney excelled in her medical studies and received her degree from the University of Berlin in 1913.

The early years of her marriage were a time of great personal distress. She gave birth to three daughters but felt overwhelmed by unhappiness and feelings of oppression. She complained of crying spells, stomach pains, chronic fatigue, compulsive behaviors, frigidity, and a longing for sleep, even death. The marriage ended after 17 years.

During and after her marriage, Horney had a number of love affairs. A biographer wrote:

> When she did not have a lover, or a relationship was breaking down, she felt lost, lonely, desperate, and sometimes suicidal. When she was involved in a morbidly dependent relationship,

she hated herself for her inability to break free. She attributed her desperate need for a man to her unhappy childhood. (Paris, 1994, p. 140)

When she realized these attachments were not helping to alleviate her depression and other emotional problems, she decided to undergo psychoanalysis.

Horney's Psychoanalysis

The therapist Horney consulted, Karl Abraham (a Freudian loyalist), attributed her problems to her attraction to forceful men, which he told her was a residue of her childhood Oedipal longings for her powerful father. "Her readiness to abandon herself to such patriarchal figures, said Abraham, was betrayed by her leaving her handbag [in Freud's view, a symbolic representation of the female genitals] in his office on her very first visit" (Sayers, 1991, p. 88). The analysis was not a success. She decided that Freudian psychoanalysis was of only minimal help to her, and she turned instead to self-analysis, a practice she continued for the rest of her life.

During her self-analysis, Horney was strongly influenced by Adler's notion of compensation for inferiority feelings. She was particularly sensitive to Adler's remark that physical unattractiveness was a cause of inferiority feelings. She concluded that she "needed to feel superior because of her lack of beauty and sense of inferiority as a woman, which led her to masculine protest" by excelling in a male-dominated domain, such as medicine was at the time (Paris, 1994, p. 63). Apparently she believed that by studying medicine, and by promiscuous sexual behavior, she was acting more like a man.

Still Searching for Love

Horney's search for love and security continued when she immigrated to the United States. Her most intense love affair was with another analyst, Erich Fromm, who was 15 years younger. When it ended after 20 years, she was deeply hurt. One event that led to the breakdown of the relationship was that she persuaded Fromm to analyze her daughter Marriane. Fromm helped the woman to understand her hostility toward her mother, giving Marriane the confidence to confront Horney for the first time (McLaughlin, 1998).[1]

Horney's relentless search for love continued, with younger and younger men, many of whom were analysts whose training she was supervising. Her attitude toward them could sometimes be detached. She told a friend about one young man, saying that she didn't know whether to marry him or get a cocker spaniel. She chose the dog (Paris, 1994).

From 1932 to 1952, Horney served on the faculty of psychoanalytic institutes in Chicago and New York. She was a founder of the Association for the Advancement of Psychoanalysis and the American Institute for Psychoanalysis. In l941, she began the *American Journal of Psychoanalysis*. For many years she was a popular lecturer, writer, and therapist.

Karen Horney

Various sites provide biographical information, discussions of her theory, research on relevant concepts, and links to other resources.

---

[1]In 2006, in a commemoration of the 120th anniversary of Horney's birth, Marriane described her mother as a private person who "never was a good team player, never a family person" (Eckardt, 2006, p. 3).

The Childhood Need for Safety and Security

Horney agreed with Freud on one major point—the importance of the early years of childhood in shaping the adult personality. However, she differed from him on the specifics of how personality is formed. Horney believed that social forces in childhood, not biological forces, influence personality development. There are neither universal developmental stages nor inevitable childhood conflicts. Instead, the social relationship between children and their parents is the key factor.

Horney believed that childhood was dominated by the **safety need**, by which she meant the need for security and freedom from fear (Horney, 1937). Whether infants experience a feeling of security and an absence of fear is decisive in determining the normality of their personality development. A child's security depends entirely on how the parents treat the child. The major way parents weaken or prevent security is by displaying a lack of warmth and affection.

safety need A higher-level need for security and freedom from fear.

That was Horney's situation in childhood. Her parents provided very little warmth and affection, and she, in turn, later behaved the same way with her three daughters. She believed children could withstand much that is usually considered traumatic, such as abrupt weaning, occasional beatings, or even premature sexual experiences, as long as they feel wanted and loved and, therefore, secure.

Ways of Undermining a Child's Security

Parents can act in various ways to undermine their child's security and thereby induce hostility. These include obvious preference for one sibling over another, unfair punishment, erratic behavior, promises not kept, ridicule, humiliation, and isolation of the child from peers. Horney argued that children know whether their parents' love is

The state of help-lessness in infancy can lead to neurotic behavior.

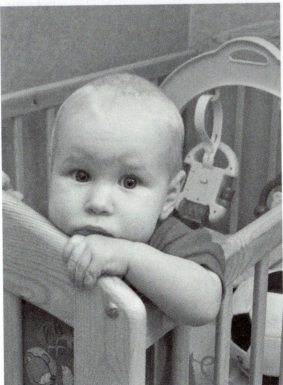

Oleg Kozlov/Shutterstock.com

genuine. False demonstrations and insincere expressions of affection do not easily fool children. The child may feel the need to repress the hostility engendered by the parents' undermining behaviors for reasons of helplessness, fear of the parents, need for genuine love, or guilt feelings.

Repressing Hostility toward Parents

Horney placed great emphasis on the infant's helplessness, which depends totally on their parents' behavior. If children are kept in an excessively dependent state, then their feelings of helplessness will be encouraged. The more helpless children feel, the less they dare to oppose or rebel against the parents. This means that the child will repress the resulting hostility, saying, in effect, "I have to repress my hostility because I need you."

Children can easily be made to feel fearful of their parents through punishment, physical abuse, or more subtle forms of intimidation. The more frightened children become, the more they will repress their hostility. In this instance, the child is saying, "I must repress my hostility because I am afraid of you."

Paradoxically, love can be another reason for repressing hostility toward parents. In this case, parents tell their children how much they love them and how much they are sacrificing for them, but the parents' warmth and affection are not honest. Children recognize that these verbalizations and behaviors are poor substitutes for genuine love and security, but they are all that is available. The child must repress his or her hostility for fear of losing even these unsatisfactory expressions of love.

Guilt is yet another reason why children repress hostility. They are often made to feel guilty about any hostility or rebelliousness. They may be made to feel unworthy, wicked, or sinful for expressing or even harboring resentments toward their parents. The more guilt the child feels, the more deeply repressed will be the hostility. This repressed hostility, resulting from a variety of parental behaviors, undermines the childhood need for safety and is manifested in the condition Horney called basic anxiety.

Basic Anxiety: The Foundation of Neurosis

basic anxiety A pervasive feeling of loneliness and helplessness; the foundation of neurosis.

Horney defined **basic anxiety** as an "insidiously increasing, all-pervading feeling of being lonely and helpless in a hostile world" (Horney, 1937, p. 89). It is the foundation on which all later neuroses develop, and it is inseparably tied to feelings of hostility, helplessness, and fear (see Hjertass, 2009).

Regardless of how we express basic anxiety, the feeling is similar for all of us. In Horney's words, we feel "small, insignificant, helpless, deserted, endangered, in a world that is out to abuse, cheat, attack, humiliate, betray" (1937, p. 92). In childhood we try to protect ourselves against basic anxiety in four quite different ways: securing affection and love, being submissive, attaining power, or withdrawing.

Securing Affection

By securing affection and love from other people, the person is saying, in effect, "If you love me, you will not hurt me." There are several ways by which we may gain affection, such as trying to do whatever the other person wants, trying to bribe others, or threatening others into providing the desired affection.

Being Submissive

Being submissive as a means of self-protection involves complying with the wishes of either one particular person or of everyone in our social environment. Submissive people avoid doing anything that might antagonize others. They dare not criticize or give offense in any way. They must repress their personal desires and cannot defend against abuse for fear that such defensiveness will antagonize the abuser. Most people who act submissive believe they are unselfish and self-sacrificing. Such persons seem to be saying, "If I give in, I will not be hurt." This describes Horney's own childhood behavior until the age of 8 or 9.

Attaining Power

By attaining power over others, a person can compensate for helplessness and achieve security through success or through a sense of superiority. Such people seem to believe that if they have power, no one will harm them. This could describe Horney's childhood once she decided to strive for academic success.

Withdrawing

These three self-protective devices have something in common—by engaging in any of them the person is attempting to cope with basic anxiety by interacting with other people. The fourth way of protecting oneself against basic anxiety involves withdrawing from other people, not physically but psychologically. Such a person attempts to become independent of others, not relying on anyone else for the satisfaction of internal or external needs.

The withdrawn person achieves independence with regard to internal or psychological needs by becoming aloof from others, no longer seeking them out to satisfy emotional needs. The process involves a blunting, or minimizing, of emotional needs. By renouncing these needs, the withdrawn person guards against being hurt by other people.

Characteristics of Self-Protective Mechanisms

The four self-protective mechanisms Horney proposed have a single goal: to defend against basic anxiety. They motivate the person to seek security and reassurance rather than happiness or pleasure. They are a defense against pain, not a pursuit of well-being or happiness. Another characteristic of these self-protective mechanisms is their power and intensity. Horney believed that they could be more compelling than sexual or other physiological needs. These mechanisms may reduce anxiety, but the cost to the individual is usually an impoverished personality.

Often, the neurotic will pursue the search for safety and security by using more than one of these mechanisms, and the incompatibility among them can lay the groundwork for additional problems. For example, a person may be driven by the needs to attain power and to gain affection. A person may want to submit to others while also desiring power over them. Such incompatibilities cannot be resolved and can lead to even more severe conflicts.

Neurotic Needs

neurotic needs Ten irrational defenses against anxiety that become a permanent part of personality and that affect behavior.

Horney believed that any of the self-protective mechanisms could become so permanent a part of the personality that it assumes the characteristics of a drive or need in determining the individual's behavior. She listed 10 such needs, which she termed **neurotic needs** because they are irrational solutions to one's problems. The 10 neurotic needs are:

1. Affection and approval
2. A dominant partner
3. Power
4. Exploitation
5. Prestige
6. Admiration

7. Achievement or ambition
8. Self-sufficiency
9. Perfection
10. Narrow limits to life

The neurotic needs encompass the four ways of protecting ourselves against anxiety. Gaining affection is expressed in the neurotic need for affection and approval. Being submissive includes the neurotic need for a dominant partner. Attaining power relates to the needs for power, exploitation, prestige, admiration, and achievement or ambition. Withdrawing includes the needs for self-sufficiency, perfection, and narrow limits to life.

Horney noted that we all manifest these needs to some degree. For example, at one time or another, everyone seeks affection or pursues achievement. None of the needs is abnormal or neurotic in an everyday, transient sense. What makes them neurotic is the person's intensive and compulsive pursuit of their satisfaction as the "only" way to resolve basic anxiety. When that happens, the neurotic need becomes increasingly severe, then tyrannical, as it overtakes and comes to dominate the personality (Hess & Hess, 2010).

Satisfying these needs will not make us feel safe and secure but will only help us to escape the discomfort caused by our anxiety. They will do nothing for the underlying anxiety. In other words, they will help with the symptoms, but not their cause. Also, when we pursue gratification of these needs solely to cope with anxiety, we tend to focus on only one need and compulsively seek its satisfaction in all situations.

Neurotic Trends

neurotic trends Three categories of behaviors and attitudes toward oneself and others that express a person's needs; Horney's revision of the concept of neurotic needs.

In her later writings, she reformulated the list of needs (Horney, 1945). From her work with patients, she concluded that the needs could be presented in three groups, each indicating a person's attitudes toward the self and others. She called these three categories of directional movement the **neurotic trends** (see Table 5.1).

Because the neurotic trends evolve from and elaborate on the self-protective mechanisms, we can see similarities with our earlier descriptions. The neurotic trends involve compulsive attitudes and behaviors; that is, neurotic persons are compelled to behave in

TABLE 5.1 Horney's neurotic needs and neurotic trends

NEEDS	TRENDS
Components of the compliant personality	
Affection and approval	Movement toward other people (the compliant personality)
A dominant partner	
Components of the aggressive personality	
Power	Movement against other people (the aggressive personality)
Exploitation	
Prestige	
Admiration	
Achievement	
Components of the detached personality	
Self-sufficiency	Movement away from other people (the detached personality)
Perfection	
Narrow limits to life	

accordance with at least one of the neurotic trends. They are also displayed indiscriminately, in any and all situations. The neurotic trends are:

- Movement toward other people—the compliant personality,
- Movement against other people—the aggressive personality, and
- Movement away from other people—the detached personality.

The Compliant Personality

compliant personality
Behaviors and attitudes associated with the neurotic trend of moving toward people, such as a need for affection and approval.

The **compliant personality** displays attitudes and behaviors that reflect a desire to move toward other people. Such a person has an intense and continuous need for affection and approval, an urge to be loved, wanted, and protected. Compliant personalities display these needs toward everyone, although they usually have a need for one dominant person, such as a friend or spouse, who will take charge of their lives and offer protection and guidance.

Compliant personalities manipulate other people, particularly their partners, to achieve their goals. They often behave in ways others find attractive or endearing. For example, they may seem unusually considerate, appreciative, responsive, understanding, and sensitive to the needs of others. Compliant people are concerned with living up to others' ideals and expectations, and they act in ways others perceive as unselfish and generous.

In dealing with other people, compliant personalities are conciliatory. They subordinate their personal desires to those of other people. They are willing to assume blame and defer to others, never being assertive, critical, or demanding. They do whatever the situation requires, as they interpret it, to gain affection, approval, and love. Their attitude toward themselves is consistently one of helplessness and weakness. Horney suggested that compliant people are saying, "Look at me. I am so weak and helpless that you must protect and love me."

Consequently, they regard other people as superior, and even in situations in which they are competent, they see themselves as inferior. Because the security of compliant personalities depends on the attitudes and behavior of other people toward them, they become excessively dependent, needing constant approval and reassurance. Any sign of rejection, whether actual or imagined, is terrifying to them, leading to increased efforts to regain the affection of the person they believe has rejected them.

The source of these behaviors is the person's repressed hostility. Horney found that compliant persons have repressed profound feelings of defiance and vindictiveness. They have a desire to control, exploit, and manipulate others, the opposite of what their behaviors and attitudes express. Because their hostile impulses must be repressed, compliant personalities become subservient, always trying to please and asking nothing for themselves.

The Aggressive Personality

aggressive personality
Behaviors and attitudes associated with the neurotic trend of moving against people, such as a domineering and controlling manner.

Aggressive personalities move against other people. In their world, everyone is hostile, and only the fittest and most cunning survive. Life is a jungle in which supremacy, strength, and ferocity are the paramount virtues. Although their motivation is the same as that of the compliant type, to alleviate basic anxiety, aggressive personalities never display fear of rejection. They act tough and domineering and have no regard for others. To achieve the control and superiority so vital to their lives, they must consistently perform at a high level. By excelling and receiving recognition, they find satisfaction in having their superiority affirmed by others.

Because aggressive personalities are driven to surpass others, they judge everyone in terms of the benefit they will receive from the relationship. They make no effort to appease others but will argue, criticize, demand, and do whatever is necessary to achieve and retain superiority and power. They drive themselves hard to become the best. As a result, they may actually become highly successful in their careers, although the work itself will not provide intrinsic satisfaction. Like everything else in their lives, work is a means to an end, not an end in itself.

Aggressive personalities may appear confident of their abilities and uninhibited in asserting and defending themselves. However, like compliant personalities, aggressive personalities are driven by insecurity, anxiety, and hostility.

The Detached Personality

detached personality
Behaviors and attitudes associated with the neurotic trend of moving away from people, such as an intense need for privacy.

People described as **detached personalities** are driven to move away from other people and to maintain an emotional distance. They must not love, hate, or cooperate with others or become involved in any way. To achieve this total detachment, they strive to become self-sufficient. If they are to function as detached personalities, they must rely on their own resources, which must be well developed.

Detached personalities have an almost desperate desire for privacy. They need to spend as much time as possible alone, and it disturbs them to share even such an experience as listening to music. Their need for independence makes them sensitive to any attempt to influence, coerce, or obligate them. Detached personalities must avoid all constraints, including timetables and schedules, long-term commitments such as marriages or mortgages, and sometimes even the pressure of a belt or necktie.

They need to feel superior, but not in the same way aggressive personalities do. Because detached people cannot actively compete with other people for superiority—that would mean becoming involved with others—they believe their greatness should be recognized automatically, without struggle or effort on their part. One manifestation of this sense of superiority is the feeling that one is unique, that one is different and apart from everyone else.

Detached personalities suppress or deny all feelings toward other people, particularly feelings of love and hate. Intimacy would lead to conflict, and that must be avoided. Because of this constriction of their emotions, detached personalities place great stress on reason, logic, and intelligence.

You have probably noticed the similarity between the three personality types proposed by Horney and the styles of life in Adler's personality theory. Horney's compliant personality is similar to Adler's getting type, the aggressive personality is like the dominant or ruling type, and the detached personality is similar to the avoiding type. This is yet another example of how Adler's ideas influenced later explanations of personality.

The Dominance of One Trend

Horney found that in the neurotic person, one of these three trends is dominant, whereas the other two are present to a lesser degree. For example, the person who is predominantly aggressive also has some need for compliance and detachment. The dominant neurotic trend is the one that determines the person's behaviors and attitudes toward others. This is the mode of acting and thinking that best serves to control basic anxiety, and any deviation from it is threatening to the person. For this reason, the other two trends must actively be repressed, which can lead to additional problems. Any indication that a repressed trend is pushing for expression causes conflict within the individual.

Conflict

conflict To Horney, the basic incompatibility of the neurotic trends.

In Horney's system, **conflict** is defined as the basic incompatibility of the three neurotic trends; this conflict is the core of neurosis. All of us, whether neurotic or normal, suffer some conflict among these basically irreconcilable modes. The difference between the normal person and the neurotic person lies in the intensity of the conflict; it is much more intense in the neurotic. Neurotic people must battle to keep the non-dominant trends from being expressed. They are rigid and inflexible, meeting all situations with the behaviors and attitudes that characterize the dominant trend, regardless of their suitability.

The Expression of All Three Trends

In the person who is not neurotic, all three trends can be expressed as circumstances warrant. A person may sometimes be aggressive, sometimes compliant, and sometimes detached. The trends are not mutually exclusive and can be integrated harmoniously within the personality. The normal person is flexible in behaviors and attitudes and can adapt to changing situations.

The Idealized Self-Image

Horney argued that all of us, normal or neurotic, construct a picture of our selves that may or may not be based on reality. Horney's own search for self was difficult and long-lasting. At age 21, she wrote, "There's still such chaos in me…. Just like my face: a formless mass that only takes on shape through the expression of the moment. The searching for our selves is the most agonizing" (Horney, 1980, p. 174).

In normal people, the self-image is built on a realistic appraisal of our abilities, potentials, weaknesses, goals, and relations with other people. This image provides a sense of unity and integration to the personality and a framework within which to approach others and ourselves. If we are to realize our full potential, a state of self-realization, our self-image must clearly reflect our true self.

Neurotics, who experience conflict between incompatible modes of behavior, have personalities characterized by disunity and disharmony. They construct an **idealized self-image** for the same purpose as normal people do: to unify the personality. But their attempt is doomed to failure because their self-image is not based on a realistic appraisal of their strengths and weaknesses. Instead, it is based on an illusion, an unattainable ideal of absolute perfection.

Tyranny of the Shoulds

In attempting to realize this unattainable ideal, neurotics engage in what Horney called the **tyranny of the shoulds**. They tell themselves they should be the best or most perfect student, spouse, parent, lover, employee, friend, or child. Because they find their real self-image so undesirable, they believe they must live up to their illusory, idealized self-image, in which they see themselves in a highly positive light, for example, being virtuous, honest, generous, considerate, and courageous.

In doing so, they deny their real selves and try to become what they think they should be, or what they need to be to match their idealized self-image. However, their efforts are doomed to failure. They can never achieve their unrealistic self-image and end up in a state of self-hatred with no ability to forgive themselves or others (Kerr, 1984).

The Neurotic's Self-Image

Although the neurotic or idealized self-image does not coincide with reality, it is real and accurate to the person who created it. Other people can easily see through this false picture, but the neurotic cannot. The neurotic person believes that the incomplete and misleading self-picture is real. The idealized self-image is a model of what the neurotic thinks he or she is, can be, or should be.

idealized self-image
For normal people, the self-image is an idealized picture of oneself built on a flexible, realistic assessment of one's abilities. For neurotics, the self-image is based on an inflexible, unrealistic self-appraisal.

tyranny of the shoulds
An attempt to realize an unattainable idealized self-image by denying the true self and behaving in terms of what we think we should be doing.

A realistic self-image, on the other hand, is flexible and dynamic, adapting as the individual develops and changes. It reflects strengths, growth, and self-awareness. The realistic image is a goal, something to strive for, and as such it both reflects and leads the person. By contrast, the neurotic self-image is static, inflexible, and unyielding. It is not a goal but a fixed idea, not an inducement to growth but a hindrance demanding rigid adherence to its proscriptions.

The neurotic's self-image is an unsatisfactory substitute for a reality-based sense of self-worth. The neurotic has little self-confidence because of insecurity and anxiety, and the idealized self-image does not allow for correction of those deficiencies. It provides only an illusory sense of worth and alienates the neurotic from the true self.

Developed to reconcile incompatible modes of behavior, the idealized self-image becomes just one more element in that conflict. Far from resolving the problem, it adds to a growing sense of futility. The slightest crack in the neurotic's idealized self-picture threatens the false sense of superiority and security the whole edifice was constructed to provide, and little is needed to destroy it. Horney suggested that the neurotic self-image is like a house filled with dynamite, with the always-ready potential for self-destruction.

Externalization

externalization A way to defend against the conflict caused by the discrepancy between an idealized and a real self-image by projecting the conflict onto the outside world.

One way in which neurotics attempt to defend themselves against the inner conflicts caused by the discrepancy between idealized and real self-images is by **externalization**, projecting the conflicts onto the outside world. This process may temporarily alleviate the anxiety caused by the conflict but will do nothing to reduce the gap between the idealized self-image and reality.

Externalization involves the tendency to experience conflicts as though they were occurring outside of one. It also entails depicting external forces as the source of the conflicts. For example, neurotics who experience self-hatred because of the discrepancy between real and idealized selves may project that hatred onto other people or institutions and come to believe that the hatred is emanating from these external sources and not from themselves.

Feminine Psychology

feminine psychology To Horney, a revision of psychoanalysis to encompass the psychological conflicts inherent in the traditional ideal of womanhood and women's roles.

Early in her career, Horney expressed her disagreement with Freud's views on women. She began work on her version of **feminine psychology** in 1922, the year she became the first woman to present a paper on the topic at an international psychoanalytic congress. That meeting, held in Berlin, was chaired by Sigmund Freud.

Horney was especially critical of Freud's notion of penis envy, which she believed was derived from inadequate evidence (that is, from Freud's clinical interviews with neurotic women). Freud described and interpreted this alleged phenomenon from a strictly male point of view in a place and time when women were considered second-class citizens.

He suggested that women were victims of their anatomy, forever envious and resentful of men for possessing a penis. Freud also concluded that women had poorly developed superegos (a result of inadequately resolved Oedipal conflicts), and inferior body images, because women believed they were really castrated men.

Womb Envy

womb envy The envy a male feels toward a female because she can bear children and he cannot. Womb envy was Horney's response to Freud's concept of penis envy in females.

Horney countered these ideas by arguing that men envied women because of their capacity for motherhood. Her position on this issue was based on the pleasure she said she had experienced in childbirth. She uncovered in her male patients what she called **womb envy**. "When one begins to analyze men only after a fairly long experience of analyzing women, one receives a most surprising impression of the intensity of this envy of pregnancy, childbirth, and motherhood" (Horney, 1967, pp. 60–61).

Men have such a small part to play in the act of creating new life that they must sublimate their womb envy and overcompensate for it by seeking achievement in their work (Gilman, 2001). Womb envy and the resentment that accompanies it are manifested unconsciously in behaviors designed to disparage and belittle women and to reinforce their inferior status. By denying women equal rights, minimizing their opportunities to contribute to society, and downgrading their efforts to achieve, men retain their so-called natural superiority. Underlying such typical male behavior is a sense of inferiority deriving from their womb envy.

Horney did not deny that many women believed themselves to be inferior to men. What she questioned was Freud's claim of a biological basis for these feelings. If women feel themselves to be unworthy, she argued, it is because they have been treated that way in male-dominated cultures. After generations of social, economic, and cultural discrimination, it is understandable that many women saw themselves in that light.

The Flight from Womanhood

As a result of these feelings of inferiority, women may choose to deny their femininity and to wish, unconsciously, that they were men. Horney referred to this as the flight from womanhood, a condition that can lead to sexual inhibitions (Horney, 1926). Part of the sexual fear associated with this condition arises from childhood fantasies about the difference in size between the adult penis and the female child's vagina. The fantasies focus on vaginal injury and the pain of forcible penetration. This produces a conflict between the unconscious desire to have a child and the fear of intercourse. If the conflict is sufficiently strong, it can lead to emotional disturbances that manifest themselves in relations with men. These women distrust and resent men and reject their sexual advances.

Horney disputed Freud's views on the accepted sex stereotypes of men and women.

Matthias Tunger/The Image Bank/Getty Images

The Oedipus Complex

Horney also disagreed with Freud about the nature of the Oedipus complex. She did not deny the existence of conflicts between children and their parents, but she did not believe they had a sexual origin. By removing sex from the Oedipus complex, she reinterpreted the situation as a conflict between dependence on one's parents and hostility toward them.

We discussed parental behaviors that undermine the satisfaction of the childhood need for safety and security and lead to the development of hostility. At the same time, the child remains dependent on the parents so that expressing hostility is unacceptable. The child is saying, in effect, "I have to repress my hostility because I need you."

As we noted, the hostile impulses remain and create basic anxiety. To Horney, "The resulting picture may look exactly like what Freud describes as the Oedipus complex: passionate clinging to one parent and jealousy toward the other" (Horney, 1939, p. 83). Thus, her explanation for Oedipal feelings lies in neurotic conflicts that evolve from parent–child interactions. These feelings are not based on sex or other biological forces, nor are they universal. They develop only when parents act to undermine their child's security.

What Did Freud Say about Horney?

Freud did not respond directly to Horney's challenge to his views on women, nor did he alter his concept of the Oedipus complex. However, in a thinly veiled allusion to Horney's work, he wrote, "We shall not be very greatly surprised if a woman analyst, who has not been sufficiently convinced of the intensity of her own wish for a penis, also fails to attach proper importance to that factor in her patients" (Freud, 1940). Of Horney herself, Freud remarked, "She is able but malicious" (quoted in Blanton, 1971, p. 65). Horney was bitter about Freud's failure to recognize the legitimacy of her views.

Motherhood or Career?

As an early feminist, Horney expressed concern about the psychological conflicts in defining women's roles and pointed out the differences between the traditional ideal of womanhood with the more modern view (Horney, 1967). In the traditional scheme, promoted and endorsed by most men, the woman's role was to love, admire, and serve her man. Her identity was solely a reflection of her husband's.

Horney argued that women must seek their own identity, as she did, by developing their abilities and pursuing careers. These contrasting traditional and more modern roles create conflicts that some women to this day have difficulty resolving. Drawing on Horney's work, a feminist at the height of the women's movement in the 1980s wrote that:

> modern women are caught between wanting to make themselves desirable to men and pursuing their own goals. The competing purposes elicit conflicting behaviors: seductive versus aggressive, deferential versus ambitious. Modern women are torn between love and work and are consequently dissatisfied in both. (Westkott, 1986, p. 14)

It remains as troublesome for some women in the 21st century to combine marriage, motherhood, and career as it was for Karen Horney in the 1930s. Her decision to develop her abilities and focus on her work brought her enormous satisfaction, but she continued throughout her life to search for security and love.

Cultural Influences on Feminine Psychology

Horney recognized the impact of social and cultural forces on the development of personality. She also noted that different cultures and social groups view women's roles in different ways. Thus, there can be many different feminine psychologies. "The American woman is different from the German woman;" she wrote, "both are different from certain Pueblo Indian women. The New York society woman is different from the farmer's wife in Idaho … Specific cultural conditions engender specific qualities and faculties, in women as in men" (Horney, 1939, p. 119).

One example of the power of culture to shape women's lives and expectations can be found in what was once considered traditional Chinese society. As far back as the first millennium B.C., women were subordinate to men. Society was governed by the belief that the universe contained two contrasting yet interacting elements, *yin* and *yang*. *Yang* represents the male element and contains all that is vital, positive, strong, and active. *Yin* represents the female element and contains all that is dark, weak, and passive. Over time, these elements came to form a hierarchy in which men were considered superior and women inferior.

This idea became part of the teaching of the Chinese philosopher Confucius (551–479 B.C.), whose work was the ruling ideology of China for centuries. Strict rules of conduct were established for women. They were expected to be submissive, obedient, respectful, chaste, and unselfish. The Chinese word for woman literally meant "inside person," denoting her status as restricted to the confines of the home.

> A respectable Chinese woman was not to be seen or heard. She was expected never to be freed from male domination, as her duty was to obey her father at home, her husband after marriage, and her eldest son when widowed. Men were counseled against listening to women for fear that disaster would result. The exercise of willfulness and ambition, considered heroic in a man, was considered wicked and depraved in a woman. (Loo, 1998, p. 180)

When we contrast this attitude with the widely accepted views of a woman's place in contemporary American society, and in the rapidly changing Chinese society as well, we can easily accept Horney's position that the feminine psyche is influenced, even determined, by cultural forces.

Questions about Human Nature

Horney's image of human nature is considerably more optimistic than Freud's. One reason for her optimism was her belief that biological forces do not condemn us to conflict, anxiety, neurosis, or universality in personality. To Horney, each person is unique. Neurotic behavior, when it occurs, results from social forces in childhood. Parent–child relationships will either satisfy or frustrate the child's need for safety. If that need is frustrated, the outcome is neurotic behavior. Neuroses and conflicts can be avoided if children are raised with love, acceptance, and trust.

Each of us has the innate potential for self-realization, and this is our ultimate and necessary goal in life. Our intrinsic abilities and potential will blossom as inevitably and naturally as an acorn grows into an oak tree. The only thing that can obstruct our development is the thwarting in childhood of our need for safety and security.

Horney also believed that we have the capacity to consciously shape and change our personality. Because human nature is flexible, it is not formed into immutable shapes in childhood. Each of us possesses the capacity to grow. Therefore, adult experiences may be as important as those of childhood.

So confident was Horney of our capacity for self-growth that she emphasized self-analysis in her therapeutic work as well as in her own life. In her book entitled *Self-Analysis* (Horney, 1942), she noted our ability to help resolve our own problems. On the issue of free will versus determinism, then, Horney argued in favor of the former. We can all shape our lives and achieve self-realization.

Assessment in Horney's Theory

The methods Horney used to assess the functioning of the human personality were essentially those favored by Freud—free association and dream analysis—but with some modification. The most basic difference in technique between Horney and Freud was in the relationship between analyst and patient. Horney believed that Freud played too passive a role and was too distant and intellectual. She suggested that analysis should be an "exquisitely cooperative enterprise" between patient and therapist (Horney quoted in Cherry & Cherry, 1973, p. 84).

Although Horney kept a couch in her office, she did not use it with every patient. She adopted an attitude she called constructive friendliness, and wrote that: "This is something one needs to try through trial and error, asking if the patient operates better lying on the couch or sitting upright. It is particularly helpful to encourage a patient so he feels free to sit up, lie down, walk around, or whatever he wants" (Horney, 1987, p. 43).

Free Association

With free association, Horney did not follow Freud's lead in trying to probe the unconscious mind. She believed that patients could easily distort or hide aspects of their inner lives or falsify feelings about events that they remembered. Instead, Horney focused on her patients' visible emotional reactions toward her, believing that these could explain her patients' attitudes toward other people. She did not delve into presumed infantile sexual fantasies but inquired about the early years of patients' life only after evaluating their present attitudes, defenses, and conflicts.

Horney believed that each attitude or feeling resulted from a deeper, pre-existing attitude, which in turn had resulted from a deeper one, and so on. Through free association, the analyst gradually uncovered the patient's early experiences and emotions, similar to peeling the layers of an onion.

Dream Analysis

Horney believed that dream analysis could reveal a person's true self, and that dreams represented attempts to solve problems, in either a constructive or a neurotic way. Dreams can show us a set of attitudes that may differ from those of our self-image. She did not offer a list of universal dream symbols but insisted that each dream be explained within the context of the patient's conflict. Focusing on a dream's emotional content, she concluded that the "safest clue to the understanding of a dream is in the feelings of the patient as he has them in the dream" (Horney, 1987, p. 61).

Self-Report Inventories

Although Horney did not use psychological tests, later researchers developed several based on portions of Horney's theory.

A 35-item self-report inventory, the CAD, was devised to measure Horney's three neurotic trends, the Compliant, Aggressive, and Detached personality types (Cohen, 1967). The Horney-Coolidge Type Indicator (HCTI), a 57-item self-report inventory, is another measure of Horney's three neurotic trends. Research with children and with college students confirmed the HCTI as a valid measure of the compliant, aggressive, and detached personality types (Coolidge, Moor, Yamazaki, Stewart, & Segal, 2001; Coolidge, Segal, & Estey, 2010).

Other studies using college student responses on the HCTI found that men tended to score higher on the aggressive and detached scales, whereas women scored higher in compliance. The research also showed a relationship between Horney's three neurotic types and various personality disorders. For example, aggression and detachment correlated highly with psychoticism; compliance was associated with neuroticism (Coolidge et al., 2001; Shatz, 2004; for additional research support see Coolidge, Segal, Benight, & Danielian, 2004). More recently, a new version of the HCTI, the Horney-Coolidge Tridimensional Inventory, was developed for use with children and adolescents ages 5 to 17 (Coolidge, Segal, Estey, & Neuzil, 2011).

Research on Horney's Theory

Horney used the case study method. Therefore, her approach, data, and interpretations are subject to the same criticisms made earlier of the work of Freud, Jung, and Adler. The weaknesses inherent in the case study method apply to her work no less than to theirs.

Horney was opposed to taking verbatim notes of her patients' recollections. "I don't see how anybody can employ a wholehearted receptivity and productivity of attention at the same time that he is anxiously scribbling everything down" (Horney, 1987, p. 30). As with Freud, Jung, and Adler, then, we do not have complete records of her analytic sessions and the data she collected during them. However, she tried to be rigorous and scientific in her clinical observations, formulating hypotheses, testing them in therapeutic situations, and maintaining that her data were tested the same way scientists in other fields test theirs.

Neurotic Trends

Researchers have studied Horney's three proposed neurotic trends, redefining them as follows (Caspi, Elder, & Bem, 1987, 1988):

- moving against people (ill-tempered),
- moving away from people (shy), and
- moving toward people (dependent).

The behavior of people belonging to each of these types in late childhood was compared with their behavior 30 years later to discover whatever continuities might exist. Ill-tempered children, both boys and girls, tended to become ill-tempered adults, prone to divorce and downward occupational mobility. Gender differences were found in the shy and dependent types. Shy boys became aloof adults who experienced marital and job instability. On the other hand, shy girls manifested no such problems later in life. Dependent boys became agreeable, socially poised, warm, and giving adults with stable marriages and careers; the opposite was found for dependent girls (Caspi, Bem, & Elder, 1989).

A study dealing with the neurotic trends of moving against people (aggressive) and moving away from people (detached) compared measures from aggressive and detached children at ages 7 to 13 with their behavior 5 to 7 years later (Moskowitz & Schwartzman, 1989). Those high in aggressiveness were found to be low in school achievement and to have psychiatric problems. Those who were detached or withdrawn were found to have inaccurate and negative self-images. The researchers concluded that Horney's proposed personality types had predictive value for later behavior.

Research using the CAD inventory found that college students preparing for careers in helping professions such as nursing and social work scored higher in compliance than did students considering careers in business or science. The business students, on a more competitive career path, scored higher on aggression. Science students scored highest on the detached scale. These results appear to be consistent with Horney's descriptions of the three neurotic trends (Cohen, 1967; Rendon, 1987).

A study conducted in Iran found, perhaps not surprisingly, that people who scored high in aggression had significantly more automobile accidents than people who scored low on aggression (Haghayegh & Oreyzia, 2009).

Feminine Psychology

Some research applies indirectly to Horney's ideas on feminine psychology. In our discussion of research on the Oedipus complex, we mentioned a classic study on dreams that provided support for the Freudian concept of penis envy (Hall & Van de Castle, 1965). This study fails to support Horney's questioning of the concept of penis envy. However, research that refutes Freud's notion that women have inadequately developed superegos and inferior body images can be taken to support Horney's views.

The Tyranny of the Shoulds

Research with college students asked them to recall three things they did during the week prior to the study. They were also asked to indicate whether they did those things because they felt they should or ought to do them, or whether they had really wanted to do them. Students who had done more things because they genuinely wanted to, rather than because they felt they should, scored significantly higher on general life satisfaction than those whose behavior was directed primarily by what they believed they ought to do (Berg, Janoff-Bulman, & Cotter, 2001).

Neurotic Competitiveness

neurotic competitiveness An indiscriminate need to win at all costs.

Horney spoke of **neurotic competitiveness** as a major aspect of contemporary culture. She defined it as an indiscriminate need to win at all costs. The attitude of the person manifesting this need can be "compared to that of a jockey in a race, for whom only one thing matters—whether he is ahead of the others" (Horney, 1937, p. 189).

Self-report inventories, such as the Hyper-competitive Attitude Scale (HCA) and the Neurotic Competitiveness Inventory (NCI), were developed to measure the concept of neurotic competitiveness (Deneui, 2001; Ryckman, Thornton, & Butler, 1994). The tests contain such items as "Winning in competition makes me feel more powerful as a person." Subjects evaluate the items on a five-point scale ranging from "never true of me" to "always true of me."

People who scored high on competitiveness were also high in narcissism, neuroticism, authoritarianism, dogmatism, and mistrust, and low in self-esteem and psychological health. Those who deliberately avoided competitiveness showed higher levels of neuroticism and a lower drive to prove themselves in competitive situations (Ryckman, Thornton, & Gold, 2009). Hyper-competitive men were also found to be hyper-masculine or macho, who believe that women are sex objects who deserved neither respect nor consideration.

A comparison of college students in the United States and the Netherlands found that the Americans scored higher in hyper-competitiveness, suggesting cultural differences in this aspect of their personality (Dru, 2003; Ryckman, Hammer, Kaczor, & Gold, 1990; Ryckman, Thornton, & Butler, 1994; Ryckman, Thornton, Gold, & Burckle, 2002). These findings support Horney's description of the neurotic competitive personality.

Two Types of Competitiveness

Researchers identified two types of competitiveness: competing to win (CW) in order to dominate others, and competing to excel (CE) to surpass one's personal goals. CE competing was linked to high self-esteem and low depression among high school

HIGHLIGHTS: Research on Horney's Ideas

People who score high in the aggressive neurotic trend:

- May not do well in school
- May have mental health issues
- Are more likely to major in business than in the helping professions

People who score high in neurotic competitiveness tend to be:

- Neurotic
- Narcissistic
- Authoritarian
- Low in self-esteem

students. In general, teen boys scored higher on CW than teen girls. However, girls who did score high on CW showed greater depression and loneliness and had fewer close friends than girls who scored low on this drive to compete in order to win (Hibbard & Buhrmester, 2010).

Reflections on Horney's Theory

Contributions of Horney's Theory

Horney's contributions, although impressive, are not as well known or recognized within psychology as those of Freud, Jung, and Adler. However, her work drew a large public following, partly because of her personal qualities. A student recalled:

> There was about her an air of wholeness, of certainty, of total dedication and commitment, of a conviction that her ideas were valuable, that they were worth sharing with colleagues and students, because knowing them would make a difference to helping those in need. (Clemmens, 1987, p. 108)

These characteristics are also evident in her books, which were written in a style readily understood by people who do not have professional analytical training. Her theory has a commonsense appeal and for many people it seems applicable to their own personality or to that of a relative or friend.

Horney's ideas may be more relevant to problems inherent in American culture today than the ideas of Freud, Jung, or Adler were. Many personality researchers see Horney's conception of the neurotic trends as a valuable way to categorize deviant behavior. Others accept Horney's emphasis on self-esteem, the need for safety and security, the role of basic anxiety, and the importance of the idealized self-image.

Her work had a significant impact on the personality theories developed by Erik Erikson and Abraham Maslow, as we will see later. Maslow used her concept of the real self and self-realization, and her notion of basic anxiety is similar to Erikson's concept of basic mistrust.

Criticisms of Horney's Theory

Although Horney was trained in orthodox Freudian theory and paid tribute to Freud for providing the foundation and tools for her work, her theory deviated from psychoanalysis in several ways. Not surprisingly, she received a great deal of criticism from those who continued to adhere to Freud's position. To the Freudians, Horney's denial of the importance of biological instincts and her reduced emphasis on sexuality and the unconscious were obvious weaknesses.

Horney's personality theory has also been criticized on the grounds that it is not as completely or consistently developed as Freud's. It has been suggested that because Freud's model was constructed so elegantly and precisely, it would have been better for Horney to reject it and start anew rather than attempt to refashion it along different lines.

Another criticism is that her observations and interpretations were too greatly influenced by the middle-class American culture in which she developed so much of her theory. Of course, as we have seen, and will continue to see throughout the book, all personality theorists are affected by the class, culture, and time in which they worked.

Renewed Interest in Horney's Ideas?

Primarily due to the women's movement that began in the 1960s, Horney's books again attracted attention. Her writings on feminine psychology and sexuality may constitute the most influential of her contributions, of value to scholars on the role of women in society well more than 50 years after Horney's death (see Gilman, 2001; Miletic, 2002). "Had she written nothing else," a biographer stated, "these papers would have earned Horney a place of importance in the history of psychoanalysis" (Quinn, 1987, p. 211).

The work of the Karen Horney Clinic and the Karen Horney Psychoanalytic Institute (a training center for analysts), both in New York City, attests to the lasting impact of her work. The clinic, established in 1945, continues to treat people with mild to moderate neurotic problems at a moderate cost (Paul, 2010). A loyal, albeit small, group of disciples carries on her work, much of which is published in the *American Journal of Psychoanalysis*.

Chapter Summary

Karen Horney differed from Freud in her views on feminine psychology and her emphasis on social rather than biological forces as shapers of personality. Her childhood experiences helped shape her lifelong quest for love and security as well as her theory of personality.

The need for safety refers to security and freedom from fear. It depends on being loved and wanted as a child. When security is undermined, hostility is induced. The child may repress this hostility out of a sense of helplessness, fear of the parents, the need to receive parental affection, or guilt about expressing hostility. Repressing hostility leads to basic anxiety, defined as a feeling of being lonely and helpless in a hostile world.

Four ways to protect oneself against basic anxiety are by gaining affection, being submissive, attaining power, and withdrawing. Any of these protective devices may become a neurotic need or drive. Horney proposed 10 neurotic needs, which she later grouped into three neurotic trends: moving toward people (the

compliant personality), moving against people (the aggressive personality), and moving away from people (the detached personality). Compliant types need affection and approval and will do what other people want. Aggressive types are hostile toward others and seek to achieve control and superiority. Detached types keep an emotional distance from others and have a deep need for privacy.

In the normal person, the idealized self-image is built on a realistic appraisal of one's abilities and goals. It helps the person achieve self-realization—the maximum development and use of one's potential. The idealized self-image in the neurotic person is based on an unrealistic, misleading appraisal of one's abilities.

Horney argued against Freud's contention that women have penis envy, poorly developed superegos, and inferior body images. She believed that men envy women because of their capacity for motherhood and, consequently, experience womb envy, which they sublimate through achievement. She rejected the sexual basis for the Oedipus complex, suggesting that it involved a conflict between dependence on and hostility toward parents.

Horney's image of human nature is more optimistic than Freud's. She believed that each person is unique and is not doomed to conflict. Although childhood influences are important, later experiences also shape personality. The ultimate goal of life is self-realization, an innate urge to grow, which can be helped or hindered by social forces. According to Horney, we can consciously shape and change our personalities.

Horney's methods of assessment were free association and dream analysis, and her research method was the case study. Some psychologists see value in her concepts of neurotic trends, the need for safety, the role of anxiety, and the idealized self-image. Research supports certain aspects of her theory, namely, the neurotic trends, feminine psychology, the tyranny of the shoulds, and neurotic competitiveness. The theory has been criticized for not being developed as fully as Freud's and for being heavily influenced by middle-class American culture.

Review Questions

1. In what ways did Horney's childhood experiences influence her personality theory?
2. Describe the childhood need for safety and the kinds of parental behaviors necessary to assure a child's security.
3. What is basic anxiety and how does it originate?
4. Describe the four basic types of behavior people use in childhood to try to protect themselves from basic anxiety.
5. Discuss the three neurotic trends and the behaviors associated with each one.
6. How do people labeled "compliant personalities" deal with other people? Why do they behave that way?
7. In what ways do aggressive personalities differ from detached personalities? Which type is more likely to be successful in their career?
8. How are the neurotic trends related to the self-protective defenses against anxiety?
9. Explain the difference between normal and neurotic people in terms of the neurotic trends.

10. How does the idealized self-image of the normal, realistic person differ from the idealized self-image of the neurotic person?
11. Contrast the tyranny of the shoulds with the process of externalization.
12. How did Horney account for women in earlier times who experienced feelings of inadequacy?
13. How did Horney reinterpret Freud's notion of the Oedipus complex?
14. Discuss the impact of cultural forces on women's roles in society. Give examples.
15. In what ways does Horney's image of human nature differ from Freud's?
16. How did Horney's use of free association as a method of assessment differ from Freud's?
17. Describe the results of research conducted on neurotic trends, on neurotic competitiveness, and on the tyranny of the shoulds.
18. What criticisms have been directed against Horney's theory of personality?
19. In your opinion, what is Horney's major contribution to the study of personality?

Suggested Readings

Berger, M. M. (Ed.). (1991, September). Special issue commemorating the 50th anniversary of the founding by Karen Horney, M.D. (1885–1952), of the Association for the Advancement of Psychoanalysis; the American Institute for Psychoanalysis; and the *American Journal of Psychoanalysis. American Journal of Psychoanalysis, 51*(3). Includes tributes to and personal recollections of Karen Horney, along with an overview and evaluations of her work.

Gilman, S. L. (2001). Karen Horney, M.D., 1885–1952. *American Journal of Psychiatry, 158*, 1205. Discusses Horney's life and work and assesses the impact of her ideas on the beginnings of feminist theory.

Horney, K. (1937). *The neurotic personality of our time.* New York: Norton. Describes the development of conflict and anxiety within the personality and relates neuroses to past experiences and to the sociocultural climate.

Horney, K. (1980). *The adolescent diaries of Karen Horney*. New York: Basic Books. A publication of diary entries Horney wrote between the ages of 13 and 25; the entries are characterized by intense emotion and intellectual honesty.

Horney, K. (1987). *Final lectures*. New York: Norton. Contains lectures Horney delivered during the last year of her life. Presents refinements of her views on psychoanalytic techniques, such as free association and dream analysis.

Mitchell, J. (2014). *Individualism and the moral character: Karen Horney's depth psychology*. Piscataway, NJ: Transaction Publishers. An analysis of how Horney's approach to personality differed from Freud's. Includes her views on how people establish their own identities instead of being victims of childhood experiences.

Paris, B. J. (1994). *Karen Horney: A psychoanalyst's search for self-understanding*. New Haven, CT: Yale University Press. A study of Horney's life and work, exploring the relationship between her struggle for self-understanding and the evolution of her ideas. Assesses her later work as a contribution to psychology, psychoanalysis, and the study of gender and culture.

Quinn, S. (1987). *A mind of her own: The life of Karen Horney*. New York: Summit Books. Discusses Horney's life, her work on feminine psychology, and her conflicts with the orthodox Freudian establishment.

Sayers, J. (1991). *Mothers of psychoanalysis: Helene Deutsch, Karen Horney, Anna Freud, Melanie Klein*. New York: Norton. Describes the post-Freudian modification of psychoanalytic theory from patriarchal to matriarchal. Shows how the experiences of these influential women psychoanalysts changed the focus from sex, repression, and castration anxiety to identification, projection, and separation anxiety.

The Life-Span Approach

Most personality theorists devote some attention to the way our personalities develop over time. They differ, however, about the time period during which they believe personality continues to grow and change. For example, Freud wrote that personality evolved only up to the age of 5. Jung, in contrast, argued that middle age was the most important time of change. Adler and Horney agreed that personality may keep on changing well beyond childhood.

The life-span approach to understanding personality, represented here by the work of Erik Erikson, focuses on its development over the entire life span. His theory attempts to explain human behavior and growth through eight stages from birth to death. Erikson believed that all aspects of personality could be explained in terms of individual crises or turning points we must face and resolve at each of these stages of development.

chapter 6

Erik Erikson: Identity Theory

Fair Use

The personality is engaged with the hazards of existence continuously, even as the body's metabolism copes with decay.

—*Erik Erikson*

The work of Erik Erikson has had a profound influence on psychoanalysis as well as the general culture. His books were bestsellers, and his picture appeared on the covers of *Newsweek* and the *New York Times Magazine*, unusual recognition for a personality theorist. And he achieved this high level of prominence without ever earning a university degree in any subject.

Trained in the Freudian tradition by Freud's daughter Anna, Erikson developed an approach to personality that broadened the scope of Freud's work while maintaining its core. Although he offered significant innovations, his ties to the Freudian position were strong. "Psychoanalysis is always the starting point," he said (quoted in Keniston, 1983, p. 29). Erikson "publicly defined himself as a loyal

Freudian, even as he departed substantially from orthodox psychoanalytic theory" (Anderson & Friedman, 1997, p. 1063).

Erikson extended Freud's theory in three ways:

1. He elaborated on Freud's stages of development, suggesting that personality continues to develop over the entire life span.
2. He placed greater emphasis on the ego than on the id. In Erikson's view, the ego is an independent part of the personality. It is not dependent on or subservient to the id, as Freud had said.
3. He recognized the impact on personality of cultural and historical forces. He argued that we are not governed entirely by innate biological factors at work in childhood. Although they are important, they do not provide a complete explanation of personality.

The Life of Erikson (1902–1994)

Personal Identity Crises

It is not surprising that the theorist who gave us the concept of the identity crisis experienced several of the same kind of crises of his own which "he was never able, over his lifetime to resolve" (Wallerstein, 2014, p. 657). Erikson was born in Frankfurt, Germany. His Danish mother, from a wealthy Jewish family, had married several years earlier but her husband disappeared within hours of the wedding. She became pregnant by another man and was sent to Germany to give birth in order to avoid the social disgrace of having a child out of wedlock. Despite his pleading to her for years, she never told her son who his father was.

She remained in Germany after the baby was born and married Dr. Theodore Homburger, the infant's pediatrician. Erik did not know for some years that Homburger was not his biological father and said that he grew up unsure of his name and psychological identity. He kept the surname Homburger until age 37 when he became a U.S. citizen and changed his name to Erik Homburger Erikson.

Another crisis of identity occurred when Erik started school. Despite his Danish parentage he considered himself German, but his German classmates rejected him because his mother and stepfather were Jewish. His Jewish classmates rejected him because he was tall and blond and had Aryan facial features. He earned only mediocre grades, but he showed some talent for art. After graduating from high school, he used that ability to try to establish an identity.

Dropping Out of Society

Erikson dropped out of conventional society and traveled extensively in Europe, reading, recording his thoughts in a notebook, and observing life around him. He described himself as morbidly sensitive and neurotic, even close to psychotic. Many years later one of his daughters wrote:

> My father suffered terribly from the sense that his real father had abandoned him and had never cared to know him. He struggled with a depressive tendency all his life. His childhood experience of abandonment and rejection had left him plagued with self-doubt. He felt deeply insecure and unsure of his footing. He craved constant support, guidance, and reassurance from others. (Bloland, 2005, pp. 52, 71)

Erikson studied at two art schools and had his work exhibited at an art gallery in Munich, but each time he left formal training to continue his wandering, his search for an identity. Later, when discussing his concept of the identity crisis he wrote, "No doubt, my best friends will insist that I needed to name this crisis and to see it in everybody else in order to really come to terms with it in myself" (Erikson, 1975, pp. 25–26).

As with many personality theorists we can see a close correspondence between Erikson's life experiences, particularly in childhood and adolescence, and the personality theory he developed as an adult. A biographer noted that what Erikson "saw and felt happening to himself (as with Freud's examination of his own dreams, memories, fantasies) became the 'research' that enabled a flow of ideas, articles, books" (Friedman, 1999, p. 16).

Becoming a Freudian

At the age of 25, Erikson received an offer to teach at a small school in Vienna that had been established for the children of Sigmund Freud's patients and friends. Freud was attracting patients from all over the world. Being wealthy, they moved to Vienna with their families for the duration of their psychoanalysis. Erikson later confessed that he was drawn to Freud in part because of his search for a father. It was then that Erikson's professional career began and that he felt he had finally found an identity.

He trained in psychoanalysis and was analyzed by Anna Freud. The analytic sessions were held almost daily for 3 years, for a fee of $7 a month. Anna Freud, unlike her father, was interested in the psychoanalysis of children. Her influence, plus Erikson's own classroom teaching experiences, made him aware of the importance of social influences on personality and led him to also focus on child development. After he completed his program of study, he became a member of the Vienna Psychoanalytic Institute.

Three Marriages and a Stable Foundation

In 1929, at a masquerade ball in Vienna, Erikson met Joan Serson, a Canadian-born artist and dancer who had been analyzed by one of Freud's disciples. They fell in love, but when she became pregnant, Erikson refused to marry her. He told her that he was afraid to make a permanent commitment and that his mother and stepfather would not approve of a daughter-in-law who was not Jewish. Only the intercession of friends persuaded him that if he did not marry Joan, he would be repeating the behavior pattern of the man who had fathered him, and condemning his child to the stigma of illegitimacy, which Erikson himself felt so keenly.

When he finally decided to marry Joan, he did so three times, in separate Jewish, Protestant, and civil ceremonies. Joan arrived at the synagogue for the Jewish ceremony carrying a bag that reeked of pork and bacon, strongly forbidden foods, while Erik forgot the wedding ring. A biographer remarked that the wedding was both a comedy of errors and a mockery of the strict Jewish customs followed by his mother and stepfather (Friedman, 1999). Joan abandoned her own career to become Erikson's lifelong intellectual partner and editor. She provided a stable social and emotional foundation for his life and helped him develop his approach to personality. Erikson's half-sister commented that "he would have been nothing without Joan" (quoted in Friedman, 1999, p. 86). Erikson agreed.

Coming to America

In 1933, recognizing the growing Nazi menace, the Eriksons immigrated to Denmark and then to the United States, settling in Boston. Erikson established a private psychoanalytic practice specializing in the treatment of children. He also worked at a guidance center for emotionally disturbed delinquents and served on the staff of Massachusetts General Hospital.

Erikson began graduate work at Harvard, intending to get a Ph.D. in psychology, but he failed his first course and dropped out of school. In 1936, with no academic degree, he was invited to the Institute of Human Relations at Yale, where he taught in the medical school and continued his psychoanalytic work with children. Erikson and a Yale anthropologist collaborated on a study of the child-rearing practices of South Dakota's Sioux Indians.

This research reinforced his belief in the influence of culture on childhood. Erikson continued to expand on his ideas at the Institute of Human Development of the University of California at Berkeley. Unlike many psychoanalysts, Erikson wanted his clinical experience to be as broad as possible, so he looked for patients from diverse cultures and saw those he considered normal as well as those who were emotionally disturbed.

Honors and Accolades—but No Identity

In his observations of American Indians in South Dakota and in California, Erikson noted certain psychological symptoms that could not be explained by orthodox Freudian theory. The symptoms appeared to be related to a sense of alienation from cultural traditions and resulted in the lack of a clear self-image or self-identity. This phenomenon, which Erikson initially called identity confusion, was similar to the condition he had observed among emotionally disturbed veterans after World War II.

Erikson suggested that those men were not suffering from repressed conflicts but rather from confusion brought about by traumatic war experiences and by being temporarily uprooted from their culture. He had described the veterans' situation as a confusion of identity about whom and what they were.

In 1950, Erikson joined the Austen Riggs Center in Stockbridge, Massachusetts, which was a treatment facility for emotionally disturbed adolescents. Ten years later he returned to Harvard to teach a graduate seminar and a popular undergraduate course on the human life cycle, retiring in 1970.

At the age of 84, Erikson published a book about old age. Even after a lifetime of accomplishments, honors, and accolades, however, his daughter wrote that he still felt disappointed with what he had achieved. "It was still a source of shame to this celebrated man that he had been an illegitimate child" (Bloland, 2005, p. 51).

Erik Erikson

Various sites provide biographical information, discussions of his theory, research on relevant concepts, and links to other resources.

Psychosocial Stages of Personality Development

psychosocial stages of development To Erikson, eight successive stages encompassing the life span. At each stage, we must cope with a crisis in either an adaptive or a maladaptive way.

Erikson divided the growth of the personality into eight **psychosocial stages**. The first four are similar to Freud's oral, anal, phallic, and latency stages. The major difference between their theories is that Erikson emphasized psychosocial correlates, whereas Freud focused on biological factors.

The Role of Genetics and the Environment

Erikson suggested that the developmental process was governed by what he called the **epigenetic principle of maturation**. By this he meant that inherited forces are the determining characteristics of the developmental stages. The prefix *epi* means "upon"; therefore, development depends on genetic factors.

However, it is the social and environmental forces to which we are exposed that control the ways in which the genetically predetermined stages of development are realized. Thus, our personality development is affected by both biological and social factors.

Conflicts and Crises

In Erikson's theory, human development involves a series of personal conflicts. The potential for these conflicts exists at birth as innate predispositions, each of which will become prominent at different stages when our environment demands certain adaptations. Each confrontation with our environment is called a **crisis**. The crisis involves a shift in perspective, requiring us to refocus our instinctual energy in accordance with the needs of each stage of the life cycle.

Each developmental stage has its particular crisis or turning point that necessitates some change in our behavior and personality. We may respond to the crisis in one of two ways: a maladaptive (negative) way or an adaptive (positive) way. Only when we have resolved each conflict can the personality continue its normal developmental sequence and acquire the strength to confront the next stage's crisis. If the conflict at any stage remains unresolved, we are less likely to be able to adapt to later problems. A successful outcome is still possible, but it will be more difficult to achieve.

Adaptive Coping

Erikson believed that the ego must incorporate both maladaptive as well as adaptive ways of coping. For example, in infancy, the first stage of psychosocial development, we can respond to the crisis of helplessness and dependency by developing a sense of trust or a sense of mistrust.

Trust, the more adaptive, desirable way of coping, is obviously the healthier psychological attitude. Yet each of us must also develop some degree of mistrust as a form of protection. If we are totally trusting and gullible, we will be vulnerable to other people's attempts to deceive, mislead, or manipulate us.

Ideally, at every stage of development the ego will consist primarily of the positive or adaptive attitude but will be balanced by some portion of the negative attitude. Only then can the crisis be considered satisfactorily resolved.

Basic Strengths

Erikson also proposed that each of the eight psychosocial stages provides an opportunity to develop our **basic strengths**. These strengths, or virtues, emerge once the crisis has been resolved satisfactorily. He suggested that basic strengths are interdependent in that one strength cannot develop until the strength associated with the previous stage has been confirmed (see Table 6.1).

Trust versus Mistrust

Erikson's oral-sensory stage of psychosocial development, paralleling Freud's oral stage, occurs during our first year of life, the time of our greatest helplessness. The infant is totally dependent on the mother or primary caregiver for survival, security, and affection.

epigenetic principle of maturation The idea that human development is governed by a sequence of stages that depend on genetic or hereditary factors.

crisis To Erikson, the turning point faced at each developmental stage.

basic strengths To Erikson, motivating characteristics and beliefs that derive from the satisfactory resolution of the crisis at each developmental stage.

TABLE 6.1 Erikson's stages of psychosocial development and basic strengths

STAGE	AGES	ADAPTIVE VS. MALADAPTIVE WAYS OF COPING	BASIC STRENGTH
Oral-sensory	Birth–1	Trust vs. mistrust	Hope
Muscular-anal	1–3	Autonomy vs. doubt, shame	Will
Locomotor-genital	3–5	Initiative vs. guilt	Purpose
Latency	6–11	Industriousness vs. inferiority	Competence
Adolescence	12–18	Identity cohesion vs. role confusion	Fidelity
Young adulthood	18–35	Intimacy vs. isolation	Love
Adulthood	35–55	Generativity vs. stagnation	Care
Maturity—old age	55+ years	Ego integrity vs. despair	Wisdom

During this stage, the mouth is of vital importance. Erikson wrote that the infant "lives through, and loves with, [the] mouth" (1959, p. 57). However, the relationship between the infant and the world is not exclusively biological. It is also social. The baby's interaction with the mother determines whether an attitude of trust or mistrust for future dealings with the environment will be incorporated into his or her personality.

It's up to the Mother If the mother responds appropriately to the baby's physical needs and provides ample affection, love, and security, then infants will develop a sense of trust, an attitude that will characterize the growing child's view of themselves and others. In this way, we learn to expect "consistency, continuity, and sameness" from other people and situations in our environment (Erikson, 1950, p. 247). Erikson said that this expectation provides the beginning of our ego identity.

On the other hand, if the mother is rejecting, inattentive, or inconsistent in her behavior, infants may develop an attitude of mistrust and will become suspicious, fearful, and anxious. According to Erikson, mistrust can also occur if the mother does not display an exclusive focus on the child. Erikson argued that a new mother who resumes a job outside the home and leaves her infant in the care of relatives or in a day care center risks promoting mistrust in the child.

Trust Can Be Lost Later in Life Although the pattern of trust or mistrust as a dimension of personality is set in infancy, the problem may reappear at a later developmental stage. For example, an ideal infant–mother relationship produces a high level of trust, but this can be destroyed if the mother dies or leaves home. If that occurs, mistrust may overtake the personality. Childhood mistrust can be altered later in life through the companionship of a loving and patient teacher or friend.

Hope The basic strength of *hope* is associated with the successful resolution of the crisis during the oral-sensory stage. Erikson described this strength as the belief that our desires will be satisfied. Hope involves a persistent feeling of confidence, a feeling we will maintain despite temporary setbacks or reverses.

Autonomy versus Doubt and Shame

During the muscular-anal stage at the second and third years of life, corresponding to Freud's anal stage, children rapidly develop a variety of physical and mental abilities and are able to do many things for themselves. They learn to communicate more effectively and to walk, climb, push, pull, and hold on to an object or let it go. Children take pride in these skills and usually want to do as much as possible for themselves.

Of all these abilities, Erikson believed the most important involved holding on and letting go. He considered these to be prototypes for reacting to later conflicts in behaviors and attitudes. For example, holding on can be displayed in a loving way or in a hostile way. Letting go can become a venting of destructive rage or a relaxed passivity.

Choice   The most important point about this stage is that for the first time children are able to exercise some choice, to experience the power of their autonomous will. Although still dependent on their parents, they begin to see themselves as persons in their own right and want to exercise their newfound strengths. The key question becomes how much will society, in the form of parents, allow children to express themselves and do all they are capable of doing?

The Toilet Training Crisis   The major crisis between parent and child at this stage typically involves toilet training, seen as the first instance when society attempts to regulate an instinctual need. The child is taught to hold on and let go only at appropriate times and places. Parents may permit the child to proceed with toilet training at his or her own pace or may become annoyed. In the latter case, parents may deny the child's free will by forcing the training, showing impatience and anger when the child does not behave correctly. When parents thus frustrate their child's attempt to exercise independence, the child develops feelings of self-doubt and a sense of shame in dealing with others. Although the anal region is the focus of this stage because of the toilet training crisis, you can see that the expression of the conflict is more psychosocial than biological.

Will   The basic strength that develops from autonomy is *will*, which involves a determination to exercise freedom of choice and self-restraint in the face of society's demands.

Initiative versus Guilt

The locomotor-genital stage, which occurs between ages 3 and 5, is similar to the phallic stage in Freud's system. Motor and mental abilities are continuing to develop, and children can accomplish more on their own. They express a strong desire to take the initiative in many activities.

The Oedipal Relationship   One initiative that may develop is in the form of fantasies, manifested in the desire to possess the parent of the opposite sex and establish a rivalry with the parent of the same sex. How will the parents react to these self-initiated activities and fantasies? If they punish the child and otherwise inhibit these displays of initiative, the child will develop persistent guilt feelings that will affect self-directed activities throughout the person's life.

In the Oedipal relationship, the child inevitably fails, but if the parents guide this situation with love and understanding, then the child will acquire an awareness of what is permissible behavior and what is not. The child's initiative can be channeled toward realistic and socially sanctioned goals in preparation for the development of adult responsibility and morality. In Freudian terms, we would call this the superego.

Purpose   The basic strength called *purpose* arises from initiative. Purpose involves the courage to envision and pursue goals.

Industriousness versus Inferiority

Erikson's latency stage of psychosocial development, which occurs from ages 6 to 11, corresponds to Freud's latency period. The child begins school and is exposed to new social influences. Ideally, both at home and at school, the child learns good work and study habits, which Erikson referred to as industriousness, primarily as a means of getting praise and satisfaction from successfully completing a task.

Developing New Skills The child's growing powers of deductive reasoning and the ability to play by rules lead to the deliberate refinement of the skills displayed in building things. Here Erikson's ideas reflected the sex stereotypes of the period in which he proposed his theory. In his view, boys will build tree houses and model airplanes, whereas girls will cook and sew.

Whatever the activities associated with this age, however, the children are making serious attempts to complete a task by applying concentrated attention, diligence, and persistence. In Erikson's words, "The basic skills of technology are developed as the child becomes ready to handle the utensils, the tools, and the weapons used by the big people" (1959, p. 83).

The attitudes and behaviors of parents and teachers largely determine how well children perceive themselves to be developing and using their skills. If children are scolded, ridiculed, or rejected, they are likely to develop feelings of inferiority and inadequacy. Praise and reinforcement foster feelings of competence and encourage continued striving.

Competence The basic strength that emerges from industriousness during the latency stage is *competence*. It involves the exertion of skill and intelligence in pursuing and completing tasks.

The Final Four Developmental Stages The outcome of the crisis at each of the first four childhood stages depends on other people. The resolution is a function more of what is done to children than of what they can do for themselves. Although children

Children take pride in developing new skills and abilities.

experience increasing independence from birth to age 11, their development remains mostly under the influence of parents and teachers, who are typically the most significant people in their lives at this time.

In the last four stages of psychosocial development, we have increasing control over our environment. We consciously and deliberately choose our friends, colleges, careers, spouses, and leisure activities. However, these deliberate choices are obviously affected by the personality characteristics that have developed during the stages from birth to adolescence. Whether our ego at that point shows primarily trust, autonomy, initiative, and industriousness, or mistrust, doubt, guilt, and inferiority, will determine the course of the rest of our lives.

Identity Cohesion versus Role Confusion

ego identity The self-image formed during adolescence that integrates our ideas of what we are and what we want to be.

Adolescence, between ages 12 and 18, is the stage at which we must meet and resolve the crisis of our basic **ego identity**. This is when we form our self-image, the integration of our ideas about ourselves and about what others think of us. If this process is resolved satisfactorily, the result is a consistent and congruent picture.

Shaping an identity and accepting it are difficult tasks, often filled with anxiety. Adolescents experiment with different roles and ideologies, trying to determine the most compatible fit. Erikson suggested that adolescence was a hiatus between childhood and adulthood, a necessary psychological moratorium to give the person time and energy to play different roles and live with different self-images.

identity crisis The failure to achieve ego identity during adolescence.

The Identity Crisis   People who emerge from this stage with a strong sense of self-identity are equipped to face adulthood with certainty and confidence. Those who fail to achieve a cohesive identity—who experience what Erikson called an **identity crisis**—will exhibit a confusion of roles. They do not know who or what they are, where they belong, or where they want to go.

They may withdraw from the normal life sequence (education, job, marriage) as Erikson did for a time or seek a negative identity in crime or drugs. Even a negative identity, as society defines it, is preferable to no identity at all, although it is not as satisfactory as a positive identity.

Erikson noted the strong impact of peer groups on the development of ego identity in adolescence. He noted that excessive association with fanatical groups and cults, or obsessive identification with icons of popular culture, could restrict the developing ego.

Fidelity   The basic strength that should develop during adolescence is *fidelity*, which emerges from a cohesive ego identity. Fidelity encompasses sincerity, genuineness, and a sense of duty in our relationships with other people.

Intimacy versus Isolation

Erikson considered young adulthood to be a longer stage than the previous ones, extending from the end of adolescence to about the age of 35. During this period we establish our independence from our parents and quasi-parental institutions, such as college, and begin to function more autonomously as mature, responsible adults. We undertake some form of productive work and establish intimate relationships, typically close friendships and sexual unions.

Caring and Commitment   In Erikson's view, intimacy was not restricted to sexual relationships but also encompassed feelings of caring and commitment. These emotions could be displayed openly without resorting to self-protective or defensive mechanisms

Adolescents who experience an identity crisis do not seem to know where they belong or what they want to become.

Anthony Redpath/Comet/Corbis

and without fear of losing our sense of self-identity. We can merge our identity with someone else's without submerging or losing it in the process.

People who are unable to establish such intimacies in young adulthood will develop feelings of isolation. They avoid social contacts, reject other people, and may even become aggressive toward them. They prefer to be alone because they fear intimacy as a threat to their ego identity.

Love   The basic strength that emerges from the intimacy of the young adult years is *love*, which Erikson considered to be the greatest of all human virtues. He described it as a mutual devotion in a shared identity, the fusing of oneself with another person.

Generativity versus Stagnation

Adulthood, approximately ages 35–55, is a stage of maturity in which we need to be actively involved in teaching and guiding the next generation. This need extends beyond our immediate family. In Erikson's view, our concern becomes broader and more long-range, involving future generations and the kind of society in which they will live. One need not be a parent in order to be able to display generativity, nor does having children automatically satisfy this urge.

Erikson believed that all institutions—whether business, government, social service, or academic—provide opportunities for us to express generativity. Thus, in whatever organizations or activities we are involved, we can usually find a way to become a mentor, teacher, or guide to younger people for the betterment of society at large.

When middle-aged people cannot or will not find an outlet for generativity, they may become overwhelmed by "stagnation, boredom, and interpersonal impoverishment" (Erikson, 1968, p. 138). Erikson's depiction of these emotional difficulties in middle age is similar to Jung's description of the midlife crisis. These people may regress to a stage of pseudo-intimacy, indulging themselves in childlike ways. And they may become physical or psychological invalids because of their absorption with their own needs and comforts.

Care   *Care* is the basic strength that emerges from generativity in adulthood. Erikson defined care as a broad concern for others and believed it was manifested in the need to teach, not only to help others but also to fulfill one's identity.

Ego Integrity versus Despair

During the final stage of psychosocial development, maturity and old age, we are confronted with a choice between ego integrity and despair. These attitudes govern the way we evaluate our whole life. Our major endeavors are at or nearing completion. We examine and reflect on life, taking its final measure. If we look back with a sense of fulfillment and satisfaction, believing we have coped with life's victories and failures, then we are said to possess ego integrity

Simply stated, ego integrity involves accepting one's place and one's past. If we review our life with a sense of frustration, angry about missed opportunities and regretful of mistakes that cannot be rectified, then we will feel despair. We become disgusted with ourselves, contemptuous of others, and bitter over what might have been.

Erikson's Own Final Stage   At 84, Erikson reported the results of a long-term study of 29 people in their 80s on whom life-history data had been collected since 1928. The book, *Vital Involvement in Old Age*, indicates in its title Erikson's prescription for achieving ego integrity (Erikson, Erikson, & Kivnick, 1986).

Older people must do more than reflect on the past. They must remain active, vital participants in life, seeking challenge and stimulation from their environment. They must involve themselves in such activities as grandparenting, returning to school, and developing new skills and interests. As an older person himself, Erikson said that generativity (the focus of mature adulthood) was even more important than he had thought when he was first developing his theory. "Much of the despair [of older people] is in fact a continuing sense of stagnation" (quoted in Cheng, 2009, p. 45). Generativity, developed in the seventh stage of life, may be the most important factor contributing to ego integrity in the eighth and final stage.

Wisdom   The basic strength associated with this final developmental stage is *wisdom*. Deriving from ego integrity, wisdom is expressed in a detached concern with the whole of life. It is conveyed to succeeding generations in an integration of experience best described by the word *heritage*.

Basic Weaknesses

basic weaknesses
Motivating characteristics that derive from the unsatisfactory resolution of developmental crises.

Similar to the way basic strengths arise at each stage of psychosocial development, so may **basic weaknesses**. We saw earlier that the adaptive and maladaptive ways of coping with the crisis at each stage of life are incorporated into the ego identity in a kind of creative balance. Although the ego should consist primarily of the adaptive attitude, it will also contain a share of the negative attitude.

Maladaptive and Malignant Conditions

maldevelopment A condition that occurs when the ego consists solely of a single way of coping with conflict.

In an unbalanced development, the ego consists solely of one attitude, either the adaptive or the maladaptive one. Erikson labeled this condition **maldevelopment**. When only the positive, adaptive, tendency is present in the ego, the condition is said to be "maladaptive." When only the negative tendency is present, the condition is called "malignant." Maladaptions can lead to neuroses; malignancies can lead to psychoses.

Erikson believed that both conditions could be corrected through psychotherapy. Maladaptions, which are the less severe disturbances, can also be relieved through a process of re-adaptation, aided by environmental changes, supportive social relationships, or successful adaptation at a later developmental stage. Table 6.2 lists the maldevelopmental characteristics for each of the eight stages.

Questions about Human Nature

A personality theorist who delineates basic human strengths presents an optimistic view of human nature. Erikson believed that although not everyone is successful in attaining hope, purpose, wisdom, and the other virtues, we all have the potential to do so. Nothing in our nature prevents it. Nor must we inevitably suffer conflict, anxiety, and neurosis because of instinctual biological forces.

Erikson's theory allows for optimism because each stage of psychosocial growth, although centered on a crisis, offers the possibility of a positive outcome. We are capable of resolving each situation in a way that is both adaptive and strengthening. Even if we fail at one stage and develop a maladaptive response or a basic weakness, there is hope for change at a later stage.

He believed that we have the potential to consciously direct and shape our growth throughout our lives. We are not exclusively products of childhood experiences. Although we have little control over life during the first four developmental stages, we gain increasing independence and the ability to choose ways of responding to crises and society's demands. Childhood influences are important, but events at later stages can counteract unfortunate early experiences.

Erikson's theory is only partially deterministic. During the first four stages, the experiences to which we are exposed through parents, teachers, peer groups, and various opportunities are largely beyond our control. We have more chance to exercise free will during the last four stages, although the attitudes and strengths we have formed during the earlier stages will affect our choices.

In general, Erikson believed that personality is affected more by learning and experience than by heredity. Psychosocial experiences, not instinctual biological forces, are the greater determinant. Our ultimate, overriding goal is to develop a positive ego identity that incorporates all the basic strengths.

TABLE 6.2 Erikson's maldevelopmental tendencies

STAGE	WAY OF COPING	MALDEVELOPMENT
Oral-sensory	Trust	Sensory maladjustment
	Mistrust	Withdrawal
Muscular-anal	Autonomy	Shameless willfulness
	Doubt, shame	Compulsion
Locomotor-genital	Initiative	Ruthlessness
	Guilt	Inhibition
Latency	Industriousness	Narrow virtuosity
	Inferiority	Inertia
Adolescence	Identity cohesion	Fanaticism
	Role confusion	Repudiation
Young adulthood	Intimacy	Promiscuity
	Isolation	Exclusivity
Adulthood	Generativity	Overextension
	Stagnation	Rejectivity
Maturity and old age	Ego integrity	Presumption
	Despair	Disdain

Source: Adapted from *Vital Involvement in Old Age*, by Erik H. Erikson, Joan M. Erikson, and Helen Q. Kivnick by permission of W. W. Norton & Company, Inc. Copyright © 1986 by Joan M. Erikson, Erik H. Erikson, and Helen Kivnick.

Assessment in Erikson's Theory

Erikson agreed with certain of Freud's theoretical formulations, but he differed from Freud in his methods of assessing personality. Erikson questioned the usefulness and even the safety of some Freudian techniques, beginning with the psychoanalytic couch.

To Erikson, asking patients to lie on a couch could lead to sadistic exploitation, creating an illusion of objectivity, overemphasizing unconscious material, and engendering impersonality and aloofness on the part of the therapist. To promote a more personal relationship between therapist and patient and to ensure that they viewed each other as equals, Erikson preferred that patients and therapists face one another while seated in comfortable chairs.

In dealing with his patients, Erikson relied less on formal assessment techniques than Freud. Erikson occasionally used free association but rarely attempted to analyze dreams, a technique he called wasteful and harmful. He believed that assessment techniques should be selected and modified to fit the unique requirements of the individual patient.

Play Therapy

For work with emotionally disturbed children and in research on normal children and adolescents, Erikson chose play therapy. He provided a variety of toys and observed how children interacted with them. The form and intensity of play revealed aspects of personality that might not be manifested verbally because of a child's limited powers of verbal expression.

In developing his personality theory, Erikson used data obtained primarily from play therapy, anthropological studies, and psychohistorical analysis.

Psychohistorical Analysis

psychohistorical analysis The application of Erikson's life-span theory, along with psychoanalytic principles, to the study of historical figures.

Erikson's most unusual assessment technique is **psychohistorical analysis**. These analyses are essentially biographical studies. Erikson used the framework of his life-span theory of personality to describe the crises and the ways of coping of significant political, religious, and literary figures, such as Gandhi, Martin Luther, and George Bernard Shaw.

Erikson's psychohistories typically focus on a significant crisis, an episode that represents a major life theme uniting past, present, and future activities. Using what he called "disciplined subjectivity," Erikson adopted the subject's viewpoint as his own to assess life events through that person's eyes.

Psychological Tests

Although Erikson did not use psychological tests for personality assessment, several instruments were developed later based on his formulations. The Ego-Identity Scale is designed to measure the development of ego identity during adolescence (Dignan, 1965). The Ego Identity Process Questionnaire, also for adolescents, contains 32 items to measure the dimensions of exploration and commitment (Balistreri, Busch-Rossnagel, & Geisinger, 1995). The Loyola Generativity Scale (see Table 6.3) is a 20-item self-report inventory to measure the level of generativity or stagnation in adulthood (McAdams & de St. Aubin, 1992).

Research on Erikson's Theory

Erikson's primary research method was the case study. By now you are familiar with the weaknesses of this method—the difficulty of duplicating and verifying case material—but you also know that much useful information can be obtained through this technique. Erikson argued that case histories yield many insights into personality development and can help resolve a patient's problems.

Play Constructions

play constructions A personality assessment technique for children in which structures assembled from dolls, blocks, and other toys are analyzed.

Erikson used play therapy to conduct research on his theory, focusing on what he called **play constructions**. In one study, boys and girls, ages 10 to 12, were asked to construct a scene from an imaginary movie using dolls, toy animals, toy cars, and wooden blocks. The girls tended to build static, peaceful scenes that contained low, enclosed structures. Intruders (animal figures or male figures, never female figures) tried to force their way into the interiors. By contrast, the boys focused on exteriors, action, and height. Their creations tended to be actionoriented, with tall towering structures and cars and people in motion (see Figure 6.1).

Trained as an orthodox Freudian, Erikson interpreted these play constructions along standard psychoanalytic lines. He wrote:

> Sexual differences in the organization of a play space seem to parallel the morphology of genital differentiation itself: in the male, an external organ, erectable and intrusive in character ... in the female, internal organs, with vestibular access, leading to a statically expectant ova. (Erikson, 1968, p. 271)

TABLE 6.3 Examples of items from a scale to measure generativity

Do these apply to any middle-aged people you know?

1. I try to pass along to others the knowledge I have gained through my experiences.
2. I do not believe that other people need me.
3. I believe I have made a difference in the lives of other people.
4. Other people say I am a productive person.
5. I believe I have done nothing that will survive after I die.
6. People come to me for advice.
7. I believe that society cannot be responsible for providing sustenance and shelter for all homeless people.
8. I have important skills that I try to teach others.
9. I do not like to do volunteer work for charities.
10. Throughout my life I have made and kept many commitments to people, groups, and activities.

Source: Adapted from D. P. McAdams & E. de St. Aubin. (1992). A theory of generativity and its assessment through self-report, behavioral acts, and narrative themes in autobiography. *Journal of Personality and Social Psychology, 62,* 1003–1015.

In other words, based on the determining effect of biological differences, girls would build low enclosures in which people are walled in, and boys would build towers.

Erikson has been criticized for this view, which suggests that women are victims of their anatomy and that their personalities are determined by the absence of a penis. Erikson admitted that differences in play constructions could also result from societal sex-role training, in which girls are less oriented toward action, aggression, and achievement than boys are.

Gender Preferences for Toys   More than 50 years after Erikson's research on play constructions, traditional gender stereotyping with regard to toys and play behaviors persists. Most children still prefer gender-based toys. Boys typically play with trucks, soldiers, and guns. Girls typically play with dolls, jewelry, and toy kitchen implements.

A study of 2- to 4-year-olds found that boys played more with a toy train than with a doll, whereas girls chose to play with the doll and not the train (Wong & Hines, 2014). Similar results occurred with college students. Men were attracted to a so-called boy's toy, a model fighter jet plane, but only when it was painted blue; they rejected the object when it was painted pink, a traditional "girls" color (Dinella, Devita, & Weisgram, 2013).

The same kind of gender preference was found with a group of 10- to 11-year-olds who were asked to choose software for computer-based problems. Boys chose the software labeled "Pirates," whereas girls chose the one labeled "Princesses" (Joiner, 1998).

The Role of Parents in Determining Gender Preferences for Toys   These patterns of toy preferences are still taught and encouraged by some parents, who purchase most of their young children's toys. Parents praise children for playing with the appropriate gender-typed toy and discourage them from playing with toys intended for the other sex. The message is learned quickly. One psychologist observed a boy who "had been playing with a race car and its driver when the driver's helmet fell off revealing long blond hair. The driver was a woman. The boy dropped the race car like it was a hot potato" (Martin, 1999, p. 49).

Fathers treat boys and girls in a more stereotypical way than mothers do. Therefore, it is primarily the fathers who teach and reinforce gender-based play. They also instruct their sons and daughters in other gender-typed behaviors and attitudes. Fathers tend to

FIGURE 6.1
Play constructions created by boys (top) and girls (bottom).

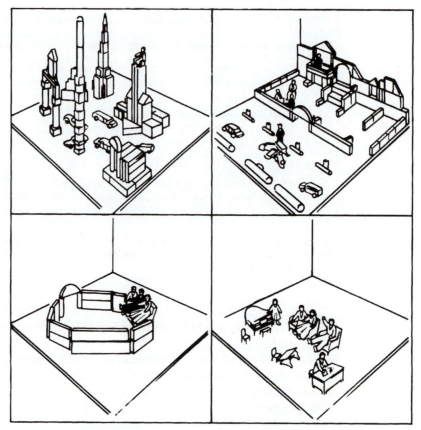

Source: Redrawn from *Childhood and Society*, 2nd ed., by Erik H. Erikson, by permission of W. W. Norton & Company, Inc. Copyright 1950, © 1963 by W. W. Norton & Company, Inc. Copyright renewed 1978, 1991 by Erik H. Erikson, and reprinted by permission of The Random House Group Limited.

encourage and reward passive, compliant behaviors in girls and assertive, aggressive behaviors in boys (Quiery, 1998).

Trust and Security Erikson emphasized the importance of developing an early sense of trust if we are to achieve feelings of security and well-being later in life. This position has received strong research support (see, for example, Jacobson & Wille, 1986; Londerville & Main, 1981; Sroufe, Fox, & Pancake, 1983).

Studies of infants aged 12 to 18 months old showed that those who had a strong emotional bond with their mothers (therefore presumed to be high in trust) functioned, when observed 3 years later, at a higher social and emotional level than infants whose attachment to their mothers was less secure.

Children with a well-developed sense of trust were also more curious, sociable, and popular. They were more likely to be leaders at games and showed greater sensitivity to the needs and feelings of others. Those low in trust were more withdrawn socially and emotionally, reluctant to play with other children, less curious, and less forceful in pursuing goals.

A study of survivors of the Holocaust who were interviewed 30 to 40 years after the end of World War II (1945) showed that they had dealt successfully with all of Erikson's proposed psychosocial stages except the first: trust versus mistrust. Their view of other people included significantly more mistrust than trust (Suedfeld, Soriano, McMurtry, Paterson, Weiszbeck, & Krell, 2005).

However, the fact that they were able to cope with the later developmental crises confirms Erikson's notion that positive events at later stages can counteract or overcome negative early experiences.

The Psychosocial Stages

When children aged 4, 8, and 11 were asked to make up stories based on several test pictures, their stories were analyzed to determine which psychosocial stage they reflected. The results supported the themes proposed in Erikson's theory. For example, the stories of the 4-year-olds concerned autonomy (the stage just completed). Similarly, the stories of the older children reflected their developmental stages (Ciaccio, 1971).

Psychohistorical analysis of the diaries, letters, and novels of Vera Brittain (1893–1970), a well-known British feminist and writer, from age 21 into middle age, showed an initial concern with ego identity. This changed over time to a concern with intimacy and then generativity, exactly as Erikson's theory predicted (Peterson & Stewart, 1990).

Adaptive and Maladaptive Development   A study using the Inventory of Psychosocial Development, a test designed to assess adaptive and maladaptive development in Erikson's first six stages, found a significant relationship between happiness and adaptive development at each stage (Constantinople, 1969). Another study showed a high correlation between maladaptive development in the first six stages and a sense of alienation and uprootedness (Reimanis, 1974).

These findings support Erikson's work as does a study of adults ages 18 to 25 in Canada, which found that the period of emerging adulthood was a time of increased psychological well-being (Galambos, Barker, & Krahn, 2006).

The Effects of Growing Up   Psychologists tested Erikson's belief that positive outcomes in resolving the identity crisis are related to positive outcomes at prior developmental stages (Waterman, Buebel, & Waterman, 1970). Adolescents who developed trust, autonomy, initiative, and industriousness (adaptive ways of coping) in the first four stages of psychosocial development displayed a high level of identity cohesion rather than role confusion. Adolescents who had not resolved their identity crisis and who experienced role confusion had not developed adaptive ways of coping in the earlier stages.

Three groups of men in Canada (ages 19–25, 35–55, and 65–87) were asked to take self-report measures of identity, self-worth, and psychological distress. The results confirmed Erikson's theory. The younger men experienced the highest levels of distress while the older men had the lowest rates of distress. This is in line with Erikson's view that "the older the individual, the better one is able to cope with life's challenges due to exposure and resolution of earlier psychological dilemmas" (Beaumont & Zukanovic, 2005, p. 77).

When adults in Britain ages 62 to 89 were asked to recall memories from earlier times, the results supported the psychosocial developmental stages. Memories of their first decade of life focused on issues of trust, autonomy, initiative, and industry. Memories of their second decade (ages 11–20) dealt with identity issues, whereas memories from young adulthood centered on intimacy. Thus, recollections of each succeeding period centered on those situations Erikson foresaw as crucial to development in those stages (Conway & Holmes, 2004).

Adolescent Development

An extensive research program on the adolescent stage of development identified five psychosocial types, or statuses, for that period (Marcia, 1966, 1980). These are identity achievement, moratorium, foreclosure, identity diffusion, and alienated achievement.

Identity Achievement Identity achievement describes adolescents who are committed to occupational and ideological choices. A study of college students found a positive correlation between achieved identity status and objective measures of commitment (Streitmatter, 1993). These students had developed a strong ego identity.

They were stable, concerned with realistic goals, and able to cope with changing environmental demands. They performed better on difficult tasks than adolescents experiencing role confusion. These stable adolescents majored in more difficult areas in college, attracted to courses in engineering and the physical sciences (Marcia & Friedman, 1970).

Male and female teens who reached the identity status earlier in adolescence were found to be more likely to have a stable intimate romantic relationship in their twenties (Beyers & Seiffge-Krenke, 2010). They were also less likely to engage in binge drinking, illegal drug use, and high-risk sexual behaviors than those who had not achieved identity status (Schwartz et al., 2010).

Studies of American, Chinese, and Turkish high school and college students found that the identity achievement status correlated highly with self-esteem, positive forms of coping, psychological well-being, and a stronger sense of self. It represented the most psychologically and socially mature identity status (Cakir, 2014; Ickes, Park, & Johnson, 2012; Markstrom & Marshall, 2007; Meuss, 2011; Wang, Shi, & Chen, 2010). A large-scale research program including more than 120 studies found that identity achievement status rose over late adolescence and young adulthood, in line with Erikson's theory (Kroger, Martinussen, & Marcia, 2010).

There is also evidence that adolescents who thought seriously about what they wanted to do with their lives, and so were more likely to achieve an identity, had parents who provided direction and control in a loving and caring way, in contrast to parents who were either too permissive or too authoritarian (Berzonsky, 2004). This was also found in a study of Iranian college students. Those least likely to reach identity achievement had parents who were either too authoritarian or too permissive in their child-rearing behavior (Mohammadi, 2013).

Moratorium Moratorium, the second adolescent status, describes people who are still undergoing their identity crisis. Their occupational and ideological commitments are vague. They hold ambivalent views toward authority figures, alternately rebelling and needing guidance from them. Their behavior ranges from indecisive to active and creative, and they score high in anxiety (Blustein, Devenis, & Kidney, 1989; Lillevoll, Kroger, & Martinussen, 2013; Podd, Marcia, & Rubin, 1968). They also tend to daydream, believe in supernatural phenomena, and enjoy behaving childishly (Bilsker & Marcia, 1991).

Foreclosure Foreclosure describes adolescents who have not yet experienced an identity crisis but who express commitment to an occupation and an ideology. However, these commitments often have been determined for them by their parents and do not result from the adolescents' deliberate choice. These teens tend to be rigid and authoritarian and have difficulty coping with change (Marcia, 1967). Those in the foreclosure status tend to be achievement-oriented, but they focus their energy toward external rather than internal goals (Stephen, Fraser, & Marcia, 1992).

Identity Diffusion   The *identity diffusion* status characterizes people who have no occupational or ideological commitments in adolescence and who may not have experienced an identity crisis. Their chosen lifestyle may actively reject any kind of commitments and in the extreme may result in aimless drifting and wandering, as Erikson did in his late teens. These adolescents have distant relationships with their parents, whom they see as indifferent and rejecting (Waterman, 1982).

Studies of adolescents in Greece, Belgium, and the United States in the identity diffusion status showed that they ranked lower in psychological adjustment and subjective well-being and higher in unstable self-image and interpersonal relationships. They were also more likely to engage in impulsive and self-destructive behavior, to show an excessive need for attention, and to have grandiose fantasies (Crawford, Cohen, Johnson, Sneed, & Brook, 2004; Luyckx, Goossens, Soenens, Beyers, & Vansteenkiste, 2005; Vleioras & Bosma, 2005).

Alienated Achievement   The fifth and final status, *alienated achievement*, describes adolescents who have experienced an identity crisis, have no occupational goal, and cling to beliefs that are critical of the social and economic system. Their strong commitment to this rationale precludes any career that would entangle them in the very system they oppose. As students they tend to be cerebral, philosophical, and cynical (Marcia & Friedman, 1970; Orlofsky, Marcia, & Lesser, 1973).

Achieving an Integrated Ego Identity   Four of these statuses, in the following order (identity diffusion, foreclosure, moratorium, and identity achievement), represent increasingly successful resolutions of the identity problem. Erikson predicted that people who have achieved an integrated ego identity will have greater ego strength than those who are farther from resolving their identity dilemma. That prediction was supported by research on college men (Bourne, 1978a, 1978b).

The Effect of Other Activities on Ego Identity   A study of high school students found that those who were more heavily involved in extracurricular and volunteer activities were higher in the ego strength of fidelity than were those not so involved (Markstrom, Li, Blackshire, & Wilfong, 2005). Similar results were found with physical activity and participation in sports and exercise programs with both Japanese and American students. The more time they devoted to those kinds of activities, the stronger was their sense of ego identity (Fukama & Mizuochi, 2011; Jones, Dick, Coyl-Shepherd, & Ogletree, 2014).

Sex Differences in Ego Identity

Sex differences have been found in the resolution of the identity crisis. Men in one study showed a tendency toward separation and detachment from other people, whereas women showed a tendency toward connection and attachment to others (Mellor, 1989). Other studies support and extend that finding, showing that male identity focuses on individual competence and knowledge, whereas female identity is more centered on relating to others.

Therefore, when women establish an identity, they depend heavily on social relationships. Men focus more on self and individual skills and abilities (Curry, 1998). Data from teenagers in the Netherlands also suggest that female adolescents form an identity at an earlier age than male adolescents, but that most males achieve some level of identity by the end of the teen years (Klimstra, Hale, Raaijmakers, Branje, & Meeus, 2010).

A Stressful Time to Search for Identity   As you may well know, adolescence can be a turbulent and stressful period. Three key elements for this developmental stage have been identified.

- Conflict with parents, characterized by a forceful resistance to adult authority;
- Mood disruption, characterized by a volatile emotional life, mood swings, and episodes of depression; and
- Risky behaviors, characterized by reckless, rule-breaking, and antisocial behavior that may harm themselves and others.

A study in which 155 adolescents kept diaries of their daily interactions over a 2-week period showed that 31 percent of their interactions involved conflicts with other people. The teenage subjects reported that conflicts with their parents were more important to them, and more emotionally intense, than were conflicts with their peers (Jensen-Campbell & Graziano, 2000).

Studies tracking individuals from childhood to adolescence found that many of those who experienced depression and other emotional problems during the teen years had also suffered some form of psychological distress as children. This suggests that difficulties reported in adolescence do not necessarily arise because of adolescence (Steinberg & Morris, 2001).

HIGHLIGHTS: Research on Childhood and Adolescence

Children with a well-developed *sense of trust* tend to be:

- Well-developed socially and emotionally
- Popular
- High in curiosity
- Sensitive to the needs and feelings of other people

Adolescence includes the following types or *statuses*:

- Identity achievement
- Moratorium
- Foreclosure
- Identity diffusion
- Alienated achievement

Adolescents high in *identity achievement* tend to:

- Have a strong sense of ego identity
- Be concerned with realistic goals
- Score high in self-esteem
- Establish mature romantic relationships in young adulthood

Virtual Identity   Computer games and social media sites offer adolescents a unique, high-tech opportunity to do precisely what Erikson said was so necessary at that developmental stage: to try different roles to see which offers the best fit. This is exemplified in the role-playing games such as *Second Life (SL)* and *Dungeons and Dragons*, which allowed young people to take on fictional personas to act out complex fantasies.

The word *dungeon* is part of a specialized computer vocabulary to denote a virtual place. Virtual places shared by a number of computer users simultaneously are known as multi-user dungeons or MUDs. MUDs allow a player to interact with others and also to build a personal virtual world whose imaginary characters interact with others.

Building a Persona Online   Participants can play roles as like or unlike their real selves as they choose without revealing their real identity. "You can be whoever you want to be," one writer noted. "You can completely redefine yourself if you want" (Turkle, 1995, p. 184). That is precisely what Erikson urged us to do during adolescence, to experiment with different identities.

A study of MUD players in Germany, average age 25, found that interpersonal attraction among the players increased the longer they played, as did the intensity of their social identification with the virtual community (Utz, 2003). The degree of identification with their virtual world was thought to be as intense and satisfying as identifying with the real world (Calvert, Strouse, Strong, Huffaker, & Lai, 2009).

An online study of *Second Life* users suggested that they may not be creating entirely new "second lives" online as much as they are bringing portions of their own real, offline lives into their online presentations of themselves. In other words, they are not presenting totally fictional or imaginary personas online but projecting at least portions of their real lives into the situation (Linares, Subrahmanyam, Cheng, & Guan, 2011).

Advantages and Disadvantages of an Online Persona   Research has found that disclosing too much personal information online can lead some teenagers to an extended period of adolescence, delaying the construction of a sound ego identity for themselves (Jordan-Conde, Menneckem, & Townsend, 2014).

A study of seventh to ninth graders found that those who had not yet developed a sense of their true selves were prone to greater use of the social media than those who had a stronger sense of self and personal identity (Israelashvili, Kim, & Bukobza, 2012). This can lead to the danger that a person could become so absorbed in a virtual identity that it comes to replace the true developing self. Of course, that can also happen in the real world when adopting a different persona.

Research in Australia demonstrated that children and adolescents who score high in loneliness and social anxiety were far more likely to communicate online with others about personal and intimate matters than children and adolescents who score lower in loneliness and anxiety (Bonetti, Campbell, & Gilmore, 2010).

Other data confirms that one's personal home page plays an important and positive role in identity formation. These researchers concluded: "Children who create personal home pages have strong feelings of mastery and use personal home pages to express who they are in a way that may be more comfortable than telling people face-to-face" (Schmitt, Dayanim, & Matthias, 2008, p. 504).

Gender and Ego Identity

Effects of Social Forces over Time   Erikson believed that social and historical factors affect the formation of ego identity, which in turn affects the nature of the personality. The women's movement of the 1960s and 1970s provided a real-world laboratory in which to test the effects of those changing social forces. Specifically, psychologists asked whether women then at the adolescent stage of psychosocial development, the time of striving for an ego identity, were more influenced by the women's movement than women who were older at that time. It was assumed that the identity of the older women had already been formed.

Two major studies answered "yes." Both studied women who had graduated from college during the 1940s to the mid-1960s. Data were gathered from interviews, questionnaires, and self-report personality tests. Women attending college when the women's movement began were found to have greater aspirations. They valued their independence more than did the older women and eventually attained higher levels of education, job status, and income. They were more assertive and self-confident in middle age than women who had passed through the adolescent stage before the advent of the women's movement (Duncan & Agronick, 1995; Helson, Stewart, & Ostrove, 1995).

Effects of a Career Orientation One legacy of the women's movement was that more adolescent women included a career orientation as part of their ego identity. This viewpoint has been found to affect dating behavior as well as age at the time of marriage. Questionnaire studies of several hundred women college students revealed that those who are career-oriented tended to marry later in life. They dated less while in college and were more wary of committed relationships.

The same study found the opposite situation for men. Questionnaire results for college men revealed that the stronger their career identity, the more committed they were to a dating relationship. Indeed, they were unlikely to become involved in a dating relationship until they felt a definite commitment to an occupation.

Differences in Emotional Life over Time Additional longitudinal research studied women who graduated from college in the 1960s and the men they married. It focused on changes in their emotional life over time, specifically,

* Changes in positive emotionality (PEM), defined as an active, happy involvement in one's work and social environments, and
* Negative emotionality (NEM), characterized by feelings of stress, anxiety, anger, and other negative emotions.

Measures of these two factors, taken at various ages from the late 20s to the middle 50s, showed that in young adulthood women tended to score higher on NEM than did their husbands and to score higher on PEM in late middle age. These findings indicated that women showed greater feelings of social power, accomplishment, and breadth of interest, along with reduced stress and alienation, once the period of child rearing ended. Thus, social factors were seen to influence the affective dimension of ego identity (Helson & Klohnen, 1998).

Adjustment to Changing Demands Erikson defined identity consolidation as the process of dealing successfully with the social realities of adult life. This involves making adjustments to the changing demands of our social world. He believed that identity consolidation usually occurs during the 20s, as people assume adult responsibilities of marriage, family, and career. A study of women college graduates evaluated at ages 21 and 27 found that those who ranked high in ego resiliency and had found an identity in marriage were higher in identity consolidation than those who did not meet these criteria (Pals, 1999).

A study of women ages 22 to 60 found a positive relationship between their readiness and willingness to change, and changes in their identity commitment at different developmental stages. Looking ahead and contemplating life changes was positively linked to the likelihood of exploring a different identity later in life (Anthis & LaVoie, 2006).

Some women must also deal with changing physical realities of adult life, such as body image in breast cancer patients after surgery. A study of these women in Britain found that the alteration of body image led to an identity crisis that was difficult to resolve (Piot-Ziegler, Sassi, Raffoul, & Delaloye, 2010).

The Identity Crisis Erikson suggested that the identity crisis began around age 12 and was resolved, one way or another, by approximately age 18. However, for some people the identity crisis may not occur until later. In one study, up to 30 percent of the people studied were still searching for an identity as late as age 24 (Archer, 1982).

Also, college may delay the resolution of the identity crisis and prolong the period during which young adults experiment with different roles and ideologies (Cote & Levine, 1988). When college students were compared with people of the same age who held full-time jobs, it was found that employed persons had achieved ego identity at an earlier age than students had. The students remained longer in the moratorium status (Adams & Fitch, 1982).

Additional research suggests that the construction of a person's identity may even be a continuing process that occurs over the entire life span (McAdams, 2001). A large-scale study of adolescents in India found that the girls were higher in ego identity than were boys (Janarthanam & Gnanadevan, 2014).

Generativity

Antecedents of Generativity Generativity in middle age appears to be significantly related to having experienced warm, affectionate parenting in childhood (Franz, McClelland, & Weinberger, 1991). Research supports the importance of both the mother and father to a child's emotional well-being. Middle-aged adults who scored high in generativity tended to believe in the goodness and worth of human life and to feel happier and more satisfied with their own life than did people who scored low in generativity (McAdams & de St. Aubin, 1992; Van de Water & McAdams, 1989).

When a group of men and women were asked to describe the major themes of their lives, those who had previously scored high on the Loyola Generativity Scale revealed different issues from those who scored low. Common themes of the high scorers included some event of good fortune in their early lives, sensitivity to the suffering of others, a stable personal belief system, and clear goals for themselves and for society. Low scorers did not record any of these themes (McAdams, Diamond, de St. Aubin, & Mansfield, 1997).

A group of middle-aged adults were asked to write accounts of personally meaningful episodes from their past, including events that were high points, low points, and turning points. Those who scored high in generativity were far more likely to describe scenes in which a negative life experience had been transformed into a positive redemptive experience. Those who scored low in generativity tended to describe the opposite, in which a positive life experience had been transformed into a negative life event (McAdams, Reynolds, Lewis, Patten, & Bowman, 2001).

When a group of college students were studied 20 years later and again 30 years later, it was found that most of those who were slow to reach ego identity in their younger years were able to catch up by middle age and reach the stage of generativity (Whitbourne, Sneed, & Sayer (2009).

Correlates of Generativity Research on the adulthood stage of psychosocial development has shown that generativity in middle age is positively correlated with power and with intimacy motivation (McAdams, Ruetzel, & Foley, 1986). Thus, as Erikson's theory predicts, generativity evokes the needs to feel close to others and to feel strong in relation to them. Another study associated generativity with nurturance (Van de Water & McAdams, 1989). All these are necessary characteristics for teaching and mentoring the next generation, which is the adaptive way of coping in midlife according to Erikson.

The Benefits of Generativity People high in generativity have scored higher on extraversion, self-esteem, conscientiousness, altruism, competence, dutifulness, and openness to new experiences than people low in generativity (Cox, Wilt, Olson, & McAdams, 2010; Peterson, Smirles, & Wentworth, 1997; Van Hiel, Mervielde, & De Fruyt, 2006). Those high in generativity are also more likely to be involved in satisfying social relationships, to feel attached to their community, and to be more emotionally stable (McAdams, Hart, & Maruna, 1998). In addition, those high in generativity are more likely to have successful marriages, greater success at work, and more close friendships. They display more altruistic behavior than those who score low on generativity (Westermeyer, 2004).

A strong positive association has also been found between generativity and psychological well-being. This held for people at midlife who did not have children as well as for those who were parents. This relationship between generativity and well-being was highest among people who reported satisfaction and success from their job and career, however, rather than satisfaction and success as a parent (Clark & Arnold, 2008; Rothrauff & Cooney, 2008).

Generativity in Women Two longitudinal studies of college-educated women tested at intervals from ages 31 to 48 found that those who were high in generativity at midlife scored significantly higher in emotional well-being than those low in generativity (Vandewater, Ostrove, & Stewart, 1997). Another longitudinal study of college-educated women found that those who valued social recognition and achievement had more fully developed identities in their 40s, and were significantly higher in generativity, than those who did not value social recognition and achievement (Helson & Srivastava, 2001).

Additional research on college-educated women in their 40s found that, as Erikson predicted, generativity was higher during that stage of life than it was when the women were in their 20s. However, this study also reported, contrary to Erikson's view, that the level of generativity remained at the same level in these women well into their 60s (Zucker, Ostrove, & Stewart, 2002).

In a related study, college-educated women who scored high in generativity at age 43 maintained that level 10 years later. They also demonstrated a higher level of care-giving to their aging parents and reported a higher level of care for their spouses and children than women scoring low in generativity at age 43 (Peterson, 2002).

The Effect of Technology on Generativity Large-scale technological changes may have a negative impact on the attitude of younger generations toward their elders, which may prevent useful mentoring activities from occurring. Research in Hong Kong found a marked decrease in generativity among those older people who felt out of touch with the developments in modern technology. They felt obsolete with regard to the use of the Internet and social media and so were unable to relate to and mentor younger generations. They came to believe they were not valued or respected, which led to a disengagement from generative goals and behaviors (Cheng, 2009).

Maturity

Reflecting on Our Lives Erikson believed that people in the maturity and old age stage of psychosocial development spend time recalling and examining their lives, accepting or regretting past choices. A study of older psychologists found that most of their memories were of college and early adult years, the period involving the greatest number of critical decisions that affected the course of their lives (Mackavey, Malley, & Stewart, 1991).

Other research found that elderly subjects who scored high in ego integrity devoted far more time to reviewing their lives to resolve troubling issues and come to a better understanding of their circumstances than those who scored low in ego integrity (Taft & Nehrke, 1990). A study of people over the age of 65 in Portugal confirmed that reminiscing about their past lives brought on a feeling of ego integrity as well as psychological well-being (Alfonso, Bueno, Loureiro, & Pereira, 2011).

Studies of adults in their 50s and 60s found that, as Erikson predicted, acknowledging regrets and missed opportunities related directly to their degree of life satisfaction and physical health for both men and women (Torges, Stewart, & Duncan, 2008; Torges, Stewart, & Miner-Rubino, 2005). Other research on people between the ages of 60 and 69 found an increased awareness of mortality, a downsizing of goals and life activities and, for many, a continuing struggle with ego integrity (Robinson & Stell, 2014).

Concern with Ego Integrity   A study in Belgium of adults in their 60s and 70s found that the achievement of ego integrity was linked to high feelings of subjective well-being, positive psychological health, a lower fear of death, and less bitterness and resentment (Van Hiel & VanSteenkiste, 2009).

A comparison of the younger and older stages of the life span in a sample of adults ages 17–82 found that older people were far more concerned with generativity and ego

---

HIGHLIGHTS: Research on Ego Identity

Establishing a *virtual identity* online:

- Allows you to try on different identities
- Can be as satisfying as establishing an identity in the real world
- Can play both a positive and a negative role in identify formation
- May be used more by people who are lonely and socially anxious

Formation of *ego identity in women*:

- Was influenced (for those at the time) by the women's movement of the 1960s and 1970s
- Is more influenced by career concerns
- Is linked to the willingness to change
- May be affected by changes in body image

People high in *generativity* tend to be:

- Happy and satisfied with their lives, and successful in their marriages and careers
- Extraverted, conscientious, and open to new experiences
- High in self-esteem

People high in *ego integrity*:

- Spend quality time examining their past
- Can acknowledge regrets and missed opportunities
- Have few feelings of bitterness and resentment

integrity, and less concerned with ego identity, than were younger people. These findings support Erikson's views. The results also found a significant positive correlation between age and subjective well-being; in general, older people were happier than younger people (Sheldon & Kasser, 2001). A study of men and women in Australia ages 55 to 93 showed that continued involvement in family and community activities led to continued feelings of generativity well into old age (Warburton, McLaughlin, & Pinsker, 2006).

When younger adults (ages 25–35) were compared with older adults (ages 60–85), there were no significant differences between the groups in reported frequency of life reflections. However, the reasons for reflecting on life events did differ. Younger people engaged in reflection to gain self-insight and find solutions to current problems. Older people reflected on their past to evaluate their lives and achieve a sense of ego integrity (Staudinger, 2001a, 2001b).

Gender Differences in Aging   Gender differences in aging may make it more difficult for women than for men to engage in a dispassionate process of reflection, or taking stock of life, such as Erikson described. This was demonstrated in research involving adults in their 60s. Men reported much higher levels of identity, certainty, confidence, and power than women did (Miner-Rubino, Winter, & Stewart, 2004).

The so-called double standard in society considers aging as more negative for women and sees women as "old" at an earlier age than men. For example, whereas a 50-year-old male actor may still be offered powerful movie roles, a 50-year-old female actor is often stereotyped as a widow or grandmother, if she is offered movie roles at all.

In addition, women tend to live longer than men, so they are more likely to have to deal with issues of illness and incapacity, bereavement, loss of social support, and reduced income. This may contribute to the observation that women's retrospective reviews of their lives are often less positive than those of men and more likely to lead to the condition Erikson noted as despair in later years, rather than ego integrity (Rainey, 1998).

Racial and Ethnic Identity

One aspect of ego development not considered by Erikson is the impact of racial identity and its positive benefits.

Benefits of Racial Identity   Research on this topic consistently shows the importance of developing and maintaining a racial or ethnic identity for minority groups. Denying one's racial identity can be stressful (see, for example, Franklin-Jackson & Carter, 2007). Many studies of Latino, Asian, and Black teenagers in the United States, Hong Kong, and Canada show clearly that a strong ethnic identity is related to psychological well-being, high self-esteem, strong social bonds, satisfaction with life, and good academic motivation (Chae & Foley, 2010; Kiang, Witkow, Baldomar, & Fuligni, 2010; Lam & Tam, 2011; Lee & Lee, 2014; Smith & Silva, 2011; Usborne & Taylor, 2010; Whittaker & Neville, 2010; Yap, Settles, & Pratt-Hyatt, 2011).

Research involving Black adolescents showed clear, consistent, and strong relationships between racial identity and psychological health. Those who scored high on racial identity were also high in subjective well-being, life satisfaction, and self-esteem. They were also less likely to have mental health problems, including anxiety and depression (Constantine, Alleyne, Wallace, & Franklin-Jackson, 2006; Cross, Grant, & Ventunaec, 2012; Pillay, 2005).

A study of Black, Asian, and biracial teens found that self-esteem was highest among Blacks and lowest among Asians. The self-esteem of the biracial adolescents was significantly lower than for Blacks and significantly higher than for Asians (Bracey, Bamaca, & Umana-Taylor, 2004). Thus, racial identity appeared to be a stronger and more important factor for self-esteem among Black adolescents than among biracial or Asian adolescents.

Group esteem (that is, how people feel about being members of their racial or ethnic group) has been shown to increase in African-American and Latino-American teenagers during the period of early and middle adolescence. Group esteem among White students remained stable, measuring high at both the beginning and the end of the period studied (French, Seidman, Allen, & Aber, 2006).

Other research found that Black adolescents high in ethnic identity expressed more negative attitudes toward drugs and more positive attitudes toward school, which were related to positive behaviors at school. However, those who scored high on a measure of anti-White attitudes were far more likely to use drugs, have negative attitudes toward school, and misbehave at school (Resnicow, Soler, Braithwaite, Ben Selassie, & Smith, 1999).

Students who experienced more racism reported higher stress and lower psychological functioning than those who experienced little or no racism (Bynum, Burton, & Best, 2007). Another study of Black adolescents found that, in addition to ethnic identity, gender identity also assumes a greater importance as they got older. Those who were high in both racial and gender identity scored high in mental health and adjustment to school (Rogers, 2013).

Research on teenagers in the United States who had been born in Mexico found that those who had a more traditional and easily recognizable Latino appearance were higher in racial identity (Santos & Updegraff, 2014).

Women and Racial Identity A study of Black and Hispanic women found that identity confusion (a conflict in identity between one's minority culture and the majority culture) may lead to eating disorders. Identification with a North American model of beauty that emphasizes extreme thinness created in some women a tendency to exhibit disorders such as anorexia. The researchers suggested that this condition resulted from attempts to emulate the appearance standards of the ideal woman of the majority White culture (Harris & Kuba, 1997).

Racial Identity and Ego Identity Studies of Asian-American and Hispanic-American adolescents confirm that ethnicity is central to forming an ego identity. A strong ethnic identity was associated with high self-esteem and with better peer and family relations (Phinney & Chavira, 1992). A study of Hispanic-American teens found that those who attended predominantly White schools reported significantly higher levels of ethnic identity than those who attended more ethnically balanced schools (Umana-Taylor, 2004). Other research found that a strong ethnic identity commitment among Latinos served as a buffer or protector against stress and also enhanced subjective well-being and academic achievement (Chang & Le, 2010; French & Chavez, 2010; Torres & Ong, 2010).

Young Asian Americans with high ethnic identity showed stronger resistance to drinking alcoholic beverages and smoking marijuana than Asian Americans with a higher degree of assimilation into the majority culture (Suinn, 1999). Similar results were found in young Hispanic adolescents in immigrant families (Schwartz, Mason, Pantin, & Szapocznik, 2008).

In Canada, among those adolescents identified as members of the First Nation (Indians), those who identified more strongly with their own culture scored higher on measures of identity strength than those who considered themselves bicultural (Gfellner & Armstrong, 2012).

Stages of Developing Racial Identity   One model of ethnic identity for African-American adolescents is the Revised Racial Identity Model proposed by William Cross. He published the 64-item Cross Racial Identity Scale to measure the developmental stages of his model. Research has shown the scale to be a valid test of ethnic identity (Vandiver, Cross, Worrell, & Fhagen-Smith, 2002). Cross posits four stages in the development of a psychologically healthy Black identity (Cokley, 2002): Pre-encounter, Encounter, Immersion-Emersion, and Internalization.

The *pre-encounter stage* includes three identity clusters. The pre-encounter assimilation identity contains little racial awareness or racial identity. The pre-encounter miseducation identity internalizes negative stereotypes about being Black. The pre-encounter self-hatred identity involves holding highly negative views about Blacks, resulting in anti-Black and self-hating attitudes.

In the *encounter stage* the person is subjected to racism or discrimination, which causes a shift in the adolescent's worldview.

The *immersion-emersion stage* proposes two identities. The immersion-emersion intense Black involvement identity celebrates everything Black as good and desirable. The immersion-emersion anti-White identity views everything White as evil and wrong.

The *internalization stage* also consists of two identities. One is Black nationalism, which adheres to a pro-Black Afrocentric perspective, whereas the multiculturalist inclusive identity embraces not only a Black identity but also other types of ethnic, racial, and gender identity.

A study of Black men (average age 20) showed that those in the pre-encounter stage of their ethnic identity reported significantly less self-esteem, greater psychological distress, and lower psychological well-being than those in the internalization stage (Pierre & Mahalik, 2005). And a study of Black college students found that as racial identity proceeded from the earliest through the more mature stages of this model, the level of defense mechanisms changed from the least sophisticated and immature defenses to more mature ones. This is what could be predicted as a person's racial identity becomes more fully developed (Nghe & Mahalik, 2001).

The importance of this kind of minority ego identity development model lies in the recognition of ethnic identity as a vital component of ego identity and in the suggestion that ethnic identity develops over a series of stages, similar to the concept of Erikson's psychosocial stages. As we noted, Erikson did not deal directly with the concept of ethnic identity, but this model adheres to the same developmental pattern he proposed.

Gender Preference Identity

Another aspect of ego identity not considered directly by Erikson is gender preference identity, which may affect overall ego identity and vary as a function of ethnic identity. For example, a study of White, Black, and Hispanic children (average age 11) found that the Black and Hispanic children reported far more pressure for gender conformity than did White children (Corby, Hodges, & Perry, 2007).

Stages of Identity   Researchers have proposed that lesbian, gay, bisexual, and transgender (LGBT) identity develops over a series of stages, similar to the way Erikson explained the development of ego identity or ethnic identity. One model lists four stages in the development of gender preference identity (Frable, 1997).

1. Sensitization. This stage, which occurs prior to adolescence, refers to one's initial perception of being different from peers of the same sex.

2. Identity confusion. This adolescent stage is marked by the confusing, perhaps frightening, realization that one's feelings and thoughts could be characterized as homosexual.
3. Identity assumption. During this stage the person comes to believe that he or she is homosexual and begins to accept the beginnings of a gay identity.
4. Commitment. In this stage the person fully accepts the gay identity as a way of life.

Consequences of Gay Identity   Even though there has been greater acceptance of people with transgender identities, they often have to confront significant challenges in their everyday lives. In general, those with nontraditional gender preference identities experience higher levels of stress, depression, suicide, feelings of failure and guilt, and physical and mental health problems (Blosnich, Brown, Shipherd, Kauth, Piegeri, & Bossarte, 2013; Budge, Adelson, & Howard, 2013; Glicksman, 2013; Liu, Rochlen, & Mohr, 2005).

They are also subject to bullying, harassment, and discrimination, particularly in school, which can affect emotional well-being as well as school grades. However, seeing other students intervene to stop such harassment can soften the impact and encourage other students to also intervene. Having strong social support from family and friends can greatly reduce the effects of harassment (Wernick, Kulick, & Inglehart, 2014).

Coming out, or identifying themselves publicly, and expressing pride in their identity with no desire to alter or conceal it results in higher scores on measures of mental and emotional well-being (Bockting, 2014). These people were found to experience higher self-esteem and lower levels of depression than those who had not announced their identity (Frable, 1997; Kosciw, Palmen, & Kull, 2014).

A study of male inmates in a medium-security prison found that those whose personality style included a strong need for personal relationships had less gender role conflict. "This need for others may override their homophobia or fear of appearing feminine" in a culture such as prison, which typically dictates a wariness of forming close relationships with other inmates. Those whose personalities showed less need for personal contact had greater gender role conflict about homosexual tendencies (Schwartz, Buboltz, Seemann, & Flye, 2004, p. 63).

HIGHLIGHTS: Research on Erikson's Ideas

People of ethnic minorities who score high in *ethnic and racial identity* tend to:

- Score high in subjective well-being and self-esteem
- Have less positive attitudes toward illegal drugs
- Get along well with family and peers
- Perform better in school
- Experience less stress

Gender preference research shows that:

- Black and Hispanic children feel great pressure to conform to gender roles
- Conflicts over gender preference are related to low self-esteem, guilt, and stress
- Those high in gay identity show high self-esteem and no desire to change

Reflections on Erikson's Theory

Contributions and Criticisms

Erikson's substantial contributions to psychology include the recognition that personality continues to develop throughout the life span, the concept of the identity crisis in adolescence, and the incorporation in his theory of the impact of cultural, social, and historical forces. However, his system does not lack critics. Some point to ambiguous terms and concepts, conclusions drawn in the absence of supporting data, and an overall lack of precision (Rosenthal, Gurney, & Moore, 1981; Waterman, 1982).

Erikson agreed that these charges were valid and blamed them on his artistic temperament and lack of formal training in science. He wrote, "I came to psychology from art, which may explain, if not justify, the fact that at times the reader will find me painting contexts and backgrounds where he would rather have me point to facts and concepts" (Erikson, 1950, p. 13).

A more specific criticism relates to the incomplete description of the developmental stage of maturity, which Erikson attempted to correct in his 1986 book, *Vital Involvement in Old Age.* (Erikson et al., 1986). Also, some psychologists question whether personality development after age 55 is likely to be as positive as Erikson suggested with his concept of ego integrity. For many people, this stage of life is characterized by pain, loss, and depression, even for people who develop the basic strength of wisdom.

Erikson's position on sex differences, as revealed in his interpretation of the play-constructions research, has also come under attack. What he saw as biologically based differences in personality for boys and girls, emerging from the presence or absence of a penis, could as well be cultural differences or the result of sex-role training. Erikson later admitted these possibilities.

Erikson's developmental stages may not be applicable to women. When social psychologist Carol Tavris read Erikson's description of his so-called stages of *man*, she wrote, "It was worrying. I wasn't having any of my crises in the right order.... My identity was shaky, although I was no longer a teenager, and I hadn't married when I was supposed to, which was putting my intimacy and generativity crises on hold" (Tavris, 1992, p. 37).

Some critics charge that Erikson's personality theory does not apply to people in reduced economic circumstances who cannot afford a moratorium in adolescence to explore different roles and develop an ego identity. This stage may be a luxury available only to those with the means to attend college or take time out to travel, as Erikson did for seven years trying to find himself (Slugoski & Ginsburg, 1989).

Erikson showed little interest in responding to his critics. He recognized that there are many ways of describing personality development and that no single view was adequate. His influence grew through his books and the work of succeeding generations of psychologists, psychiatrists, teachers, and counselors who found in his ideas useful ways to describe personality development from infancy through old age.

Recognition and Influence

Erikson's ideas have been recognized in both professional and popular circles. *Time* magazine called him the "most influential living psychoanalyst" (March 17, 1975), and *Psychology Today* described him as "an authentic intellectual hero" (Hall, 1983, p. 22). His concepts are useful in education, social work, vocational and marriage counseling, and clinical practice with children and adolescents. His work "continues to prove meaningful for contemporary psychology and social thought" (Clark, 2010, p. 59). The Erikson Institute for Early Childhood Education was established for graduate training in 1966 at Chicago's Loyola University.

The field of life-span developmental psychology, which has seen a massive increase in research and theory in recent years, owes much of its spark to Erikson's approach, as does the current interest in developmental problems of middle and old age. In addition, Erikson's method of play therapy has become a standard diagnostic and therapeutic tool for work with emotionally disturbed and abused children. Youngsters who cannot verbalize the details of a physical or sexual attack can express their feelings through play, using dolls to represent themselves and their abusers.

Chapter Summary

Erikson suffered several personal identity crises and developed a personality theory in which the search for identity plays a major role. He built on Freud's theory by elaborating on the developmental stages, emphasizing the ego over the id, and recognizing the impact on personality of culture, society, and history.

The growth of personality is divided into eight stages. A conflict at each stage confronts the person with adaptive and maladaptive ways of coping. Development is governed by the epigenetic principle; each stage depends on genetic forces but the environment helps determine whether they are realized.

The oral-sensory stage (birth to age 1) can result in trust or mistrust. The muscular-anal stage (ages 1–3) leads to an autonomous will or to self-doubt. The locomotor-genital stage (3–5) develops initiative or guilt. The latency stage (6–11) results in industriousness or inferiority.

Adolescence (12–18) is the stage in which the ego identity is formed (the time of the identity crisis), leading to identity cohesion or role confusion. Young adulthood (18–35) results in intimacy or isolation. Adulthood (35–55) leads to generativity or stagnation. Maturity (over 55) is expressed in ego integrity or despair.

Each stage allows for the development of basic strengths that emerge from the adaptive ways of coping with the conflicts. The basic strengths are hope, will, purpose, competence, fidelity, love, care, and wisdom. Maldevelopment can occur if the ego consists solely of either the adaptive or the maladaptive tendency.

Erikson presented a flattering, optimistic image of human nature. We have the ability to achieve basic strengths, to resolve each conflict in a positive way, and to consciously direct our growth. We are not victims of biological forces or childhood experiences and are influenced more by learning and social interactions than by heredity.

Erikson's assessment methods were play therapy, anthropological studies, and psychohistorical analysis. His research relied on case studies. There is considerable research support for the first six stages of psychosocial development and for the concept of ego identity. However, the identity crisis may occur later than Erikson believed, and attending college may delay resolution of the crisis.

Other research confirms the importance of developing a sense of trust early in life and the benefits of generativity in middle age. Among minority group members, the formation of ethnic identity in adolescence may affect the development of ego identity and influence subsequent behavior.

The Cross Racial Identity Model describes four stages in the development of a psychologically healthy adolescent Black identity. Gender preference identity may also affect characteristics of ego identity. People who have conflicts about their gender preference appear to be less psychologically healthy than people who experience no such conflicts.

Criticisms of Erikson's theory focus on ambiguous terminology, incomplete descriptions of the psychosocial stages, and poorly supported claims of male-female personality differences based on biological factors.

Review Questions

1. What identity crises did Erikson experience in his childhood and adolescence? How were they reflected in his theory?
2. In what ways does Erikson's theory differ from Freud's?
3. What did Erikson mean by the concept of identity confusion? What evidence did he find for it among Native Americans and among combat veterans of World War II?

4. How does Erikson's epigenetic principle of maturation account for the effects of both genetic and social factors on personality?

5. Describe the role of conflict in the stages of psychosocial development.

6. What are two ways of responding to the crisis that develops at each stage of growth?

7. Describe the four childhood stages of psychosocial development.

8. Contrast identity cohesion and role confusion as adaptive versus maladaptive ways of coping during adolescence.

9. What is the major difference between the first four developmental stages and the last four developmental stages?

10. What factors affect the development of ego identity? Why do some people fail to achieve an identity at this stage?

11. How can the conflicts of the adult stages of psychosocial development be resolved in positive ways?

12. Describe the concept of generativity and give an example of how it can be achieved.

13. What are the two ways of adapting to maturity and old age? How can a person achieve the positive way of adapting?

14. Describe the basic strengths at each stage of psychosocial development.

15. Distinguish between the two types of maldevelopment. How can these conditions be corrected?

16. How does Erikson's image of human nature differ from Freud's?

17. What methods of assessment did Erikson use in developing his theory?

18. Based on the results of his play-constructions research, what did Erikson conclude about sex differences in personality? Do you agree with his conclusion?

19. Describe research findings on the development of ego identity in adolescence and on generativity in middle age.

20. Discuss how the ethnic identity of ethnic-minority adolescents can affect the formation of ego identity as well as subsequent attitudes and behavior.

21. How can online role-playing games help adolescents establish an ego identity?

22. In what ways do people high in generativity differ from people low in generativity?

23. According to Erikson, what role did generativity play in old age, the last stage of development?

24. What are the proposed stages for the development of gender preference identity?

25. What criticisms have been made of Erikson's approach to personality?

26. What is your opinion of Erikson's theory relative to the others you have studied so far in this course?

Suggested Readings

Erikson, E. H. (1950). *Childhood and society*. New York: Norton. A collection of essays covering child-rearing practices, family life, and social and cultural structures, illustrating their relationship to personality development. The book was an instant success with scholars and the general public.

Erikson, E. H. (1968). *Identity: Youth and crisis*. New York: Norton. Erikson's classic work on the identity crisis and ways of coping with conflict at this stage of development.

Erikson, E. H. (1987). *A way of looking at things: Selected papers from 1930 to 1980*. New York: Norton. A collection of Erikson's writings on children's play constructions, adult dreams, cross-cultural research, and development over the life cycle. Edited by Stephen Schlein.

Erikson, E. H., Erikson, J. M., & Kivnick, H. Q. (1986). *Vital involvement in old age*. New York: Norton.

A sensitive psychosocial analysis of the need for stimulation and challenge in old age and a personal perspective on Erikson as he approached the age of 90.

Evans, R. I. (1967). *Dialogue with Erik Erikson*. New York: Harper & Row. Conversations with Erikson about his life and work.

Friedman, L. J. (1999). *Identity's architect: A biography of Erik H. Erikson*. New York: Simon & Schuster. A sympathetic treatment showing how Erikson's ideas of the identity crisis and the stages of the life cycle grew out of his own complicated life.

Josselson, R. (1996). *Revising herself: The story of women's identity from college to midlife*. New York: Oxford University Press. In an outgrowth of Erikson's theory, this longitudinal account compiled from interviews traces the cultural changes in women's roles and identities in the last third of the 20th century.

The Genetics Approach

A trait is a distinguishing personal characteristic or quality. In our daily lives, we often use trait names to describe the personalities of people we know. We tend to select an outstanding characteristic or feature to summarize what we think a particular person is like. We may say, "Kayla is very self-assured," or "Ian is so competitive," or "Brandi is really compulsive."

Grouping people by traits is easy and has a commonsense appeal to it, which may explain why the trait approach to personality has been popular for so long. Trait classifications date from the time of the Greek physician Hippocrates (460– 377 B.C.), more than 2,000 years before the theories described in this book. Hippocrates distinguished four types of people: happy, unhappy, temperamental, and apathetic. The causes of these different types were internal bodily fluids, or "humors." He believed that these personality traits were constitutionally based, determined by biological functioning rather than by experience or learning.

In the 1940s, an American physician William Sheldon (1899–1977) offered a personality typology based on body build (see Figure 7.1). He proposed three body types, each associated with a different temperament (Sheldon, 1942). Like the approach taken by Hippocrates, Sheldon's work considered personality traits or characteristics to be largely fixed, that is, constant and unvarying regardless of the situations in which we find ourselves.

The trait approach to personality begun by Gordon Allport decades ago has become central to the study of personality today, as we shall see in this and the next chapter.

FIGURE 7.1
The body types and personality characteristics proposed by Sheldon has not been supported by research, but his work shows another attempt to classify personality according to traits.

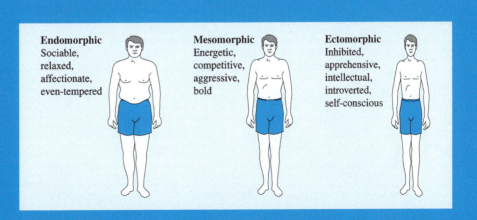

Endomorphic
Sociable, relaxed, affectionate, even-tempered

Mesomorphic
Energetic, competitive, aggressive, bold

Ectomorphic
Inhibited, apprehensive, intellectual, introverted, self-conscious

chapter 7

Gordon Allport: Motivation and Personality

Fair Use

As the individual matures, the bond with the past is broken.

—*Gordon Allport*

Allport Brings Personality into the Classroom and the Psychology Lab

During a career that spanned more than four decades, Gordon Allport made personality an academically respectable topic. Psychoanalysis and the personality theories that derived from it that we have discussed so far were not considered part of mainstream scientific psychology.

The formal and systematic study of personality was not recognized by the psychology establishment until Allport published *Personality: A Psychological Interpretation* in 1937. The book was an immediate success and became a classic in the study of personality. Thus, Allport served two purposes: He helped bring personality into the mainstream, and he formulated a theory of personality development in which traits play a prominent role.

Allport Challenges Freud

Allport challenged Freud's psychoanalysis on several points. First, Allport did not accept the notion that unconscious forces dominate the personality of normal mature adults. He argued that emotionally healthy people function rationally and consciously, aware and in control of many of the forces that motivate them. According to Allport, the unconscious is important only in the behavior of neurotic or disturbed people.

Second, with regard to historical determinism—the importance of the past in determining the present—Allport said that we are not prisoners of childhood conflicts and past experiences, as Freud believed. Instead, we are guided more by the present and by our view of the future. Allport wrote that people are "busy leading their lives into the future, whereas psychology, for the most part, is busy tracing them into the past" (Allport, 1955, p. 51).

Third, Allport opposed collecting data from abnormal personalities. Whereas Freud saw a continuum between the normal and abnormal, Allport saw a clear distinction. To Allport, the abnormal personality functioned at an infantile level.

The only proper way to study personality, he believed, was to collect data from emotionally healthy adults. Other populations, such as neurotics, children, and animals, should not be compared with normal adults. No functional similarity in personality existed between child and adult, abnormal and normal, or animal and human, as far as he was concerned.

Allport Makes Each Person Unique

Another distinguishing feature of Allport's theory is his emphasis on the uniqueness of personality as defined by each person's traits. He opposed the traditional scientific emphasis on forming general constructs or laws to be applied universally. He argued that personality is not general or universal but is particular and specific to the individual.

The Life of Allport (1897–1967)

Restrictions, Morality, and No Bright Colors

Born in Montezuma, Indiana, Allport was the youngest of four sons. His mother was a teacher, and his father was a salesman who decided to become a doctor. They were in such dire financial circumstances while the elder Allport attended medical school in Baltimore that he smuggled drugs from Canada into the United States and sold them to support the family.

When the law came knocking on the front door, he skipped out the back and escaped over a fence. He took the family to Indiana and opened a private practice in which Allport believed his own birth was his father's first case.

The devout religious beliefs and practices of Allport's mother dominated the household. No smoking, drinking, dancing, or card playing were allowed, nor could a family member wear bright colors, distinctive clothing, or jewelry of any kind. Allport wrote that his mother was "on the severe side with a strong sense of right and wrong and quite strict in her moral ideals" (quoted in Nicholson, 2003, p. 17).

Isolation and Rejection

Too young to be a playmate to his older brothers, Allport was isolated from children outside the family as well. "I fashioned my own circle of activities," he wrote later. "It was a select circle, for I never fitted the general boy assembly" (Allport, 1967, p. 4).

"I suffered agonies on the playground. I never really got on with my brothers. They didn't like me and they weren't kind and I couldn't possibly compete with them. They were all a little more masculine in type than I was" (quoted in Nicholson, 2003, p. 25).

He described himself as skillful with words but not good at sports or games and as someone who worked hard to be the center of attention of the few friends he did have.

In Allport's personality theory, one of the major propositions is that psychologically healthy adults are unaffected by childhood events. Perhaps reflecting this belief, Allport revealed very little about his childhood years. What he did tell, however, demonstrates a parallel between his own early experiences and the theory he later developed.

Inferiority

Arising from his childhood conditions of isolation and rejection, Allport developed inferiority feelings for which he attempted to compensate by striving to excel. He wrote about the identity quest that resulted from his inferiority feelings with regard to his brothers and other children. As Allport grew older, he began to identify with his oldest brother, Floyd, envious of his brother's accomplishments. Well into adulthood, Gordon Allport continued to feel inferior compared to Floyd, whose achievements he tried to emulate. He followed Floyd to Harvard and earned a Ph.D. in psychology, just as Floyd had done.

Floyd became a noted social psychologist, and even when Gordon was becoming well known himself in the field, the feelings of being in his brother's shadow persisted. At the age of 31, Gordon wrote that he had "published several articles of no great importance and [was] not to be confused with my more eminent brother" (quoted in Nicholson, 2003, pp. 168–169).

The attempt to emulate Floyd may have threatened Gordon's sense of identity. To assert his individuality, Gordon Allport may have been motivated to refute his identification with Floyd by declaring in his personality theory that his adult motives and interests were independent of his childhood feelings. He later formalized this idea as the concept of functional autonomy.

College Years

Although Allport ranked second in his high school graduating class of 100, he admitted to being uninspired about what to do next. At the end of the summer of 1915, he applied to Harvard and was accepted. He wrote, "Overnight my world was remade." Allport's college years were a great adventure for him as he discovered new frontiers of intellect and culture. But shocked by low grades on his first exams, he doubled his efforts and finished the year with straight A's.

Allport's interest in social ethics and social service, acquired from his parents, was reinforced at Harvard. He did volunteer work for a boy's club, a group of factory workers, and a contingent of foreign students. He also worked as a probation officer. He found these activities satisfying because he genuinely liked to help people. "It gave me a feeling of competence, to offset a generalized inferiority feeling." He believed this kind of service reflected his search for an identity (Allport, 1967, pp. 5–7).

He took several undergraduate courses in psychology but at that time did not intend to pursue a career in the field. He graduated in 1919 with a bachelor's degree, on the same day Floyd received his Ph.D. After graduation, Gordon spent a year on the faculty of Robert College in Istanbul, Turkey, and later accepted the fellowship Harvard offered for graduate study in psychology. His biographer noted, "The thought of becoming a psychologist and perhaps becoming more like his successful brother appealed to Allport" (Nicholson, 2003, p. 67).

Allport Meets Freud

On his return trip to the United States, Allport stopped in Vienna to see one of his brothers. While there, he sent a note to Sigmund Freud and received an invitation to visit the great man. When Allport entered Freud's office, he found Freud waiting patiently, expecting the young American to explain the purpose of his visit.

The awkward period of silence lengthened until an uncomfortable Allport, looking desperately for something to say, blurted out an account of an incident he had seen on the streetcar ride to Freud's office. He told of watching a small boy who had an obvious fear of dirt. Everything seemed dirty to the child. He even changed his seat, telling his mother not to let a dirty man sit beside him.

Freud studied the prim, proper, carefully groomed young man and asked, "Was that little boy you?" By asking this question, Freud was expressing his belief that the story Allport told betrayed his own unconscious fears and conflicts.

Allport appeared to Freud to be "neat, meticulous, orderly and punctual—possessing many of the characteristics [he] associated ... with the compulsive personality" (Pervin, 1984, p. 267). Another psychologist commented that "Freud just hit [Allport] right on the head, right on the nose" (quoted in Anderson, 1990, p. 326).

Allport was shaken by Freud's question. For the rest of his life, Allport denied that he was the super-clean, proper little boy in the story but the incident clearly left a deep impression on him. Years later he wrote, "My single encounter with Freud was traumatic" (Allport, 1967, p. 22). He suspected that psychoanalysis probed the unconscious too deeply, as Freud tried to do with him. Psychology, Allport decided, should pay more attention to conscious or visible motivations. This was the path he chose for his study of personality.

Many years later, two American psychologists used this Freud story in a study, which found that the use of this kind of anecdote made classroom lectures, and presumably textbooks as well, more enjoyable to students. As a result, they found that students learn and remember information better when it is presented in this kind of social and personal context (Kaufman & Bristol, 2001).

Becoming a Success

Allport completed his Ph.D. at Harvard in 1922, after two years of graduate study. His dissertation, "An Experimental Study of the Traits of Personality," foreshadowed his lifelong work and was the first research ever to be conducted on personality traits in the United States. Awarded a traveling fellowship, Allport spent two years studying with noted psychologists in Germany and England. He returned to Harvard as an instructor, offering a course on the psychological and social aspects of personality, which was apparently the first formal American college course on the subject. He spent nearly four decades at Harvard, conducting research on personality and social psychology and instructing several generations of students.

Considered an elder statesman in the field, Allport received many awards, including the American Psychological Foundation's Gold Medal, the American Psychological Association's Distinguished Scientific Contribution Award, and the presidencies of the American Psychological Association and the Society for the Psychological Study of Social Issues.

Gordon Allport

Various sites provide biographical information, discussions of his theory, research on relevant concepts, and links to other resources.

The Nature of Personality

In his book *Pattern and Growth in Personality*, Allport reviewed some 50 definitions of personality before offering his own. "Personality is the dynamic organization within the individual of those psychophysical systems that determine ... characteristic behavior and thought" (Allport, 1961, p. 28).

By *dynamic organization*, Allport means that although personality is constantly changing and growing, the growth is organized, not random. *Psychophysical* means that personality is composed of both mind and body functioning together as a unit. It is neither all mental nor all biological.

By *determine*, Allport means that all facets of personality activate or direct specific behaviors and thoughts. The phrase *characteristic behavior and thought* means that everything we think and do is characteristic, or typical, of us. Thus, each person is unique.

The Roles of Heredity and Environment

To support his emphasis on the uniqueness of the individual personality, Allport stated that we reflect both our heredity and our environment. Heredity provides the personality with raw materials, such as physique, intelligence, and temperament, that may then be shaped, expanded, or limited by the conditions of our environment. In this way, Allport invokes both personal and situational variables to indicate the importance of both genetics and learning.

However, our genetic background is responsible for the major portion of our uniqueness. An infinite number of possible genetic combinations exist, and, except for identical twins, the chance that someone else's genetic endowment will be duplicated in any one of us is too small to consider.

Allport believed that our genetic endowment interacts with our social environment, and no two people, not even siblings brought up in the same house, have precisely the same environment. The inevitable result is a unique personality. Therefore, Allport concluded that to study personality, psychology must deal with the individual case and not with average findings among groups.

Two Distinct Personalities for Two Stages of Life

Allport considered personality to be discrete, or discontinuous. Not only is each person distinct from all others, but each adult is also divorced from his or her past. He found no continuum of personality between childhood and adulthood. Primitive biological urges and reflexes drive infant behavior, whereas adult functioning is more psychological in nature. In a sense there are two personalities: one for childhood and one for adulthood. The adult personality is not constrained by childhood experiences.

This unique view of Allport's emphasizes the conscious rather than the unconscious, and the present and future rather than the past. He recognized the uniqueness of personality rather than proposing generalities or similarities for large groups of people. And he chose to study the normal rather than the abnormal personality.

Personality Traits

traits To Allport, distinguishing characteristics that guide behavior. Traits are measured on a continuum and are subject to social, environmental, and cultural influences.

Allport considered personality **traits** to be predispositions to respond, in the same or a similar manner, to different kinds of stimuli. In other words, traits are consistent and enduring ways of reacting to our environment. He summarized the characteristics of traits as follows (Allport, 1937):

1. Personality traits are real and exist within each of us. They are not theoretical constructs or labels made up to account for behavior.
2. Traits determine or cause behavior. They do not arise only in response to certain stimuli. They motivate us to seek appropriate stimuli, and they interact with the environment to produce behavior.

3. Traits can be demonstrated empirically. By observing behavior over time, we can infer the existence of traits in the consistency of a person's responses to the same or similar stimuli.
4. Traits are interrelated; they may overlap, even though they represent different characteristics. For example, aggressiveness and hostility are distinct but related traits and are frequently observed to occur together in a person's behavior.
5. Traits vary with the situation. For example, a person may display the trait of neatness in one situation and the trait of disorderliness in another situation.

Initially, Allport proposed two types of traits: individual and common. *Individual traits* are unique to a person and define his or her character. *Common traits* are shared by a number of people, such as the members of a culture.

It follows that people in different cultures will have different common traits. Common traits are also likely to change over time as social standards and values change. This demonstrates that common traits are subject to social, environmental, and cultural influences.

Personal Dispositions

personal dispositions Traits that are peculiar to an individual, as opposed to traits shared by a number of people.

cardinal traits The most pervasive and powerful human traits.

central traits The handful of outstanding traits that describe a person's behavior.

secondary traits The least important traits, which a person may display inconspicuously and inconsistently.

Allport later realized that some confusion could result from calling both of these phenomena *traits*, and so he revised his terminology. He relabeled common traits as **traits** and individual traits as **personal dispositions**. Our personal dispositions do not all have the same intensity or significance. They may be cardinal traits, central traits, or secondary traits.

A **cardinal trait** is so pervasive and influential that it touches almost every aspect of a person's life. Allport described it as a ruling passion, a powerful force that dominates behavior. He offered the examples of sadism and chauvinism. Not everyone has a ruling passion, and those who do may not display it in every situation.

Everyone has a few **central traits**, some 5 to 10 themes that best describe our behavior. Allport's examples are aggressiveness, self-pity, and cynicism. These are the kinds of characteristics we would mention when discussing a friend's personality or writing a letter of recommendation.

The least influential individual traits are the **secondary traits**, which appear much less consistently than cardinal and central traits. Secondary traits may be so inconspicuous or weak that only a close friend would notice evidence of them. They may include, for example, a minor preference for a particular type of music or for a certain food.

Motivation: What We Strive for

Allport believed that the central problem for any personality theory is how it treats the concept of motivation. Allport emphasized the influence of a person's present situation not only in his personality theory but also in his view of motivation. It is the individual's current state that is important, not what happened in the past during toilet training, school, or some other childhood crisis. Whatever happened in the past is exactly that: past. It is no longer active and does not explain adult behavior unless it exists as a current motivating force.

Cognitive processes, that is, our conscious plans and intentions, are a vital aspect of our personality. Allport criticized approaches such as Freud's that focused on unconscious, irrational forces at the expense of the conscious and rational. Deliberate intentions are an essential part of our personality. What we want and what we strive for are the keys to understanding our behavior. Thus, Allport attempted to explain the present in terms of the future rather than in terms of the past.

Functional Autonomy

functional autonomy of motives The idea that motives in the normal, mature adult are independent of the childhood experiences in which they originally appeared.

Allport's concept of **functional autonomy** proposes that the motives of mature, emotionally healthy adults are not functionally connected to the prior experiences in which they initially appeared. Forces that motivated us early in life become autonomous, or independent, of their original circumstances.

Allport offered the example of a tree. It is obvious that the tree's development can be traced back to its seed. Yet when the tree is fully grown, the seed is no longer required as a source of nourishment. The tree is now self-determining, no longer functionally related to its seed.

Similarly, when we grow up, we become independent of our parents. Although we remain related to them, we are no longer functionally dependent on them and they (should) no longer control or guide our lives.

Consider the example of new college graduates embarking on a career in business. They may be motivated to work hard in order to achieve financial success and security. Eventually their investment of time and energy may pay off, and they amass enough money to be able to retire. Yet, some continue to work just as hard as they did when they started out.

The retired 55-year-old is no longer striving for the same goals that the 25-year-old did. The goal of financial security has been reached and surpassed. The motivation to work hard, once a means to a specific end (money, for example), has now become an end in itself. The motive has become independent of its original source, transformed into something autonomous. Therefore, adult motives cannot be understood by exploring the person's childhood, as Freud believed. The only way to understand adult motives, Allport stressed, is to investigate why people behave as they do today.

Allport proposed two levels of functional autonomy: perseverative functional autonomy and propriate functional autonomy.

perseverative functional autonomy The level of functional autonomy that relates to low-level and routine behaviors.

Perseverative Functional Autonomy **Perseverative functional autonomy**, the more elementary level, is concerned with such behaviors as addictions and repetitive physical actions such as habitual ways of performing some routine, everyday task. The behaviors continue or persevere on their own without any external reward. The actions once served a purpose but they no longer do and are at too basic and low a level to be considered an integral part of personality.

Allport cited both animal and human examples as evidence for perseverative functional autonomy. When a rat that has been trained to run a maze for food is given more than enough food, it may still run the maze, but obviously for some purpose other than the food. At the human level, he noted our preference for routine, familiar behaviors that we continue to perform even in the absence of external reinforcement.

propriate functional autonomy The level of functional autonomy that relates to our values, self-image, and lifestyle.

proprium Allport's term for the ego or self.

Propriate Functional Autonomy **Propriate functional autonomy** is more important than perseverative functional autonomy and is essential to understanding adult motivation. The word *propriate* derives from **proprium**, Allport's term for the ego or self.

Propriate motives are unique to each individual. The ego determines which motives will be maintained and which will be discarded. We retain motives that enhance our self-esteem or self-image. Thus, a direct relationship exists between our interests and our abilities: We enjoy doing what we do well.

The original motivation for learning a skill such as playing the piano may have nothing to do with our interests. For example, in childhood we may be coerced by our parents into taking piano lessons and to practice. As we become proficient, however, we may become more committed to playing the piano. The original motive (fear of parental displeasure) has disappeared, and the continued behavior of playing the piano becomes necessary to our self-image.

The Organizing of Our Propriate Functioning Our propriate functioning is an organizing process that maintains our sense of self. It determines how we perceive the world, what we remember from our experiences, and how our thoughts are directed. These perceptual and cognitive processes are selective. They choose from the mass of stimuli in our environment only those that are relevant to our interests and values. This organizing process is governed by the following three principles: organizing the energy level, mastery and competence, and propriate patterning.

> The first principle, *organizing the energy level*, explains how we acquire new motives. These motives arise from necessity, to help consume excess energy that we might otherwise express in destructive and harmful ways. For example, when people retire from their jobs, they have extra time and energy that, ideally, they should direct toward new interests and activities.

Mastery and competence, the second principle, refers to the level at which we choose to satisfy motives. It is not enough for us to achieve at an adequate level. Healthy, mature adults are motivated to perform better and more efficiently, to master new skills, and to increase their degree of competence.

The third principle, *propriate patterning*, describes a striving for consistency and integration of the personality. We organize our perceptual and cognitive processes around the self, keeping what enhances our self-image and rejecting the rest. Thus, our propriate motives are dependent on the structure or pattern of the self.

Allport noted that not all behaviors and motives could be explained by these principles of functional autonomy. Some behaviors, such as reflexes, fixations, neuroses, and behaviors arising from biological drives, are not under the control of functionally autonomous motives.

Personality Development in Childhood: The Unique Self

As we noted, Allport chose the term *proprium* for the self or ego. He rejected the words *self* and *ego* because of the diversity of meanings ascribed to them by other theorists. We can best understand the word *proprium* by considering it in the sense of the adjective *appropriate*. The proprium includes those aspects of personality that are distinctive and thus appropriate to our individual emotional life. These aspects are unique to each of us and unite our attitudes, perceptions, and intentions.

Stages of Development

Allport described the nature and development of the proprium over seven stages from infancy through adolescence (see Table 7.1).

Before the proprium begins to emerge, the infant experiences no self-consciousness, no awareness of self. There is not yet a separation of "me" from everything else. Infants receive sensory impressions from the external environment and react to them automatically and reflexively, with no ego to mediate between stimulus and response. Allport described infants as pleasure seeking, destructive, selfish, impatient, and dependent. He called them "unsocialized horrors." They possess little of what could be called a

TABLE 7.1   The development of the proprium

STAGE	DEVELOPMENT
1. *Bodily self*	Stages 1–3 emerge during the first three years. In this stage, infants become aware of their own existence and distinguish their own bodies from objects in the environment.
2. *Self-identity*	Children realize that their identity remains intact despite the many changes that are taking place.
3. *Self-esteem*	Children learn to take pride in their accomplishments.
4. *Extension of self*	Stages 4 and 5 emerge during the fourth through sixth year. In this stage, children come to recognize the objects and people that are part of their own world.
5. *Self-image*	Children develop actual and idealized images of themselves and their behavior and become aware of satisfying (or failing to satisfy) parental expectations.
6. *Self as a rational coper*	Stage 6 develops during ages 6–12. Children begin to apply reason and logic to the solution of everyday problems.
7. *Propriate striving*	Stage 7 develops during adolescence. Young people begin to formulate long-range goals and plans.
Adulthood	Normal, mature adults are functionally autonomous, independent of childhood motives. They function rationally in the present and consciously create their own lifestyles.

"personality." The infant simply is driven by reflexes to reduce tension and maximize pleasure.

The first three stages in the development of the proprium span the years from birth to about age 4. The bodily self develops when infants begin to be aware of what Allport referred to as a "bodily me." For example, infants begin to distinguish between their own fingers and the object they are grasping.

The self-identity stage is marked by a sense of continuity of one's identity. Children realize that they remain the same people despite changes in their bodies and their abilities. Self-identity is enhanced when children learn their names and see themselves as distinct from others.

Self-esteem develops when they discover that they can accomplish things on their own. They are motivated to build, explore, and manipulate objects, behaviors that sometimes can be destructive. If parents frustrate their child's need to explore at this stage, then the emerging sense of self-esteem can be thwarted, replaced by humiliation and anger.

The extension-of-self stage involves the growing awareness of objects and people in the environment and the identification of them as belonging to the child. Children speak of "my house," "my parents," and "my school."

A self-image develops next, incorporating how children see and would like to see themselves. These actual and ideal self-images develop from interaction with the parents, who make the child aware of their expectations and of the extent to which the child is satisfying or failing to satisfy those expectations. The self-extension and self-image stages typically occur between the ages of 4 and 6.

The self-as-a-rational-coper stage occurs between ages 6 and 12, when children realize that reason and logic can be applied to solving everyday problems. The propriate striving stage follows, when adolescents begin to formulate plans and goals for the future. Until they do so, their sense of self (their proprium) will remain incomplete.

Children develop actual and idealized self-images, reflecting how they actually see and would like to see themselves.

Radius Images/Jupiter Images

The Importance of the Infant–Mother Bond

Our social interaction with our parents is vitally important throughout all the stages of development of the proprium. Most important of all, however, is the infant–mother bond as a source of affection and security.

If the mother or primary caregiver provides sufficient affection and security, the proprium will develop gradually and steadily, and the child will achieve positive psychological growth. Childhood motives will be free to be transformed into the autonomous propriate strivings of adulthood. A pattern of personal dispositions will form and the result will be a mature, emotionally healthy adult.

If childhood needs are frustrated, however, the self will not mature properly. The child becomes insecure, aggressive, demanding, jealous, and self-centered. Psychological growth is stunted. The result is a neurotic adult who functions at the level of childhood drives.

Adult motives do not become functionally autonomous but remain tied to their original conditions. Traits and personal dispositions do not develop and the personality remains undifferentiated, as it was in infancy.

The Healthy Adult Personality

In Allport's view, the healthy personality changes and grows from being a biologically dominated organism in infancy to a mature psychological organism in adulthood. Our motivations become separated from childhood and are oriented toward the future. As

Normal, mature adults are functionally autonomous, independent of childhood motives. They function rationally in the present and consciously create their own lifestyles.

Onoky - Fabrice Lerouge/Brand X Pictures/Jupiter Images

we noted, if our childhood needs for affection and security have been met, the proprium will develop satisfactorily. The adult personality grows out of childhood and is no longer dominated or determined by childhood drives.

Allport described six criteria for normal, mature, emotionally healthy adult personalities:

1. Mature adults extend their sense of self to people and activities beyond the self.
2. Mature adults relate warmly to other people, exhibiting intimacy, compassion, and tolerance.
3. Mature adult's high degree of self-acceptance helps them to achieve emotional security.
4. Mature adults hold a realistic perception of life, develop personal skills, and make a commitment to some type of work.
5. Mature adults have a sense of humor and self-objectification (an understanding of or insight into the self).
6. Mature adults subscribe to a unifying philosophy of life, which is responsible for directing the personality toward future goals.

By meeting these six criteria, adults can be described as emotionally healthy and functionally autonomous, independent of childhood motives. As a result, they cope with the present and plan for the future without being victimized by what happened to them in their early years.

Questions about Human Nature

Allport's view of functional autonomy and personality development holds that emotionally healthy adults are not tied to or driven by childhood conflicts. Thus, his theory presents an optimistic view of adults in conscious control of their lives, rationally attending to current situations, planning for the future, and actively fashioning an identity. Always in the process of becoming, we creatively design and implement an appropriate style of life, influenced more by events of the present and plans for the future than by our past.

Allport took a moderate stance on the question of free will versus determinism. He granted free choice in our deliberations about our future, but he also recognized that some behaviors are determined by traits and personal dispositions. Once these behaviors are formed, they are difficult to change.

On the nature–nurture issue, he believed that both heredity and environment influence personality. Our genetic background supplies our basic physique, temperament, and level of intelligence. These raw materials are then shaped by learning and experience. Allport believed in each person's uniqueness. Although common traits show some universality in behavior, individual traits or personal dispositions describe our nature more precisely.

To Allport, the ultimate and necessary goal of life is not to reduce tension, as Freud proposed, but rather to increase tension, impelling us to continually seek new sensations and challenges. When we have met one challenge, we are motivated to seek another. The reward is the process of achieving rather than the specific achievement, striving for the goal rather than reaching it. In essence, he meant that "getting there is more fun than being there." We constantly need new goals to motivate us and to maintain an optimal level of tension in the personality.

Allport's optimistic image of human nature was reflected in his personal liberal stance and his interest in social reform. The humanistic attitude expressed in his work was mirrored in his own personality. His colleagues and students described him as someone who genuinely cared about people and that these feelings were reciprocated.

Assessment in Allport's Theory

Allport wrote more about personality assessment techniques than most other theorists did. In his popular book *Pattern and Growth in Personality* (1961), he noted that, despite the existence of many approaches to assessment, there was no single best technique.

Personality is so complex that to evaluate it we must employ many techniques. He listed 11 major methods:

- Constitutional and physiological diagnosis
- Cultural setting, membership, role
- Personal documents and case studies
- Self-appraisal
- Conduct analysis
- Ratings
- Tests and scales
- Projective techniques
- Depth analysis
- Expressive behavior
- Synoptic procedures (combining information from several sources in a synopsis)

Allport relied heavily on the personal-document technique and the Study of Values. He also observed expressive behavior, which we will discuss in the section on research.

The Personal-Document Technique

personal-document technique The personal-document technique involves the study of a person's written or spoken records.

The **personal-document technique** involves examining diaries, autobiographies, letters, literary compositions, and other samples of a person's written or spoken records to determine the number and kinds of personality traits.

Allport's most famous case is an analysis of a collection of more than 300 letters written over a 12-year period by a middle-aged woman identified as Jenny (Allport, 1965, 1966). It was later revealed that Jenny was the mother of Allport's college roommate and had written the letters to Allport and his wife (Winter, 1993a).

In the personal-document approach, a group of judges read the autobiographical or biographical material on the subject and record the traits they find in it. Given a reasonable degree of agreement among the judges, the assessments can be grouped into a relatively small number of categories. In the research with Jenny's letters, 36 judges listed nearly 200 traits. Because many terms were synonymous, Allport was able to reduce them to eight categories.

One of Allport's students performed a computer analysis on the letters to find categories of words that might indicate the existence of a particular trait (Paige, 1966). For example, words expressing anger, rage, hostility, and aggression were coded as constituting the trait of aggression.

This approach is more sophisticated and quantitative than Allport's original analysis of the letters because it involves fewer subjective judgments. The computer analysis yielded eight prominent traits in Jenny's personality that were similar to the categories Allport had identified. Because of that consistency, he concluded that his subjective approach to personality assessment provided information on traits that was valid and comparable to the more objective computer analysis.

The Study of Values

Allport and two colleagues developed an objective self-report assessment test called the Study of Values (Allport, Vernon, & Lindzey, 1960). They proposed that our personal values are the basis of our unifying philosophy of life, which is one of the six criteria for a mature, healthy personality.

Our values are personality traits and represent strongly held interests and motivations. Allport believed that everyone possesses some degree of each type of value, but one or two of these will be more dominant in the personality. The categories of values are as follows.

1. *Theoretical values* are concerned with the discovery of truth and are characterized by an empirical, intellectual, and rational approach to life.
2. *Economic values* are concerned with the useful and practical.
3. *Aesthetic values* relate to artistic experiences and to form, harmony, and grace.
4. *Social values* reflect human relationships, altruism, and philanthropy.
5. *Political values* deal with personal power, influence, and prestige in all endeavors, not just in political activities.
6. *Religious values* are concerned with the mystical and with understanding the universe as a whole.

Research on Allport's Theory

Allport criticized psychologists who insisted that experimental and correlational methods were the only legitimate ways to study personality. He argued that not every aspect of personality could be tested in those ways, and that psychologists should be more open and eclectic in their research methodology.

He also opposed applying methods used with the emotionally disturbed, such as case studies and projective techniques, to the study of emotionally healthy people. Because case studies focus on the past, Allport considered them to be of no value for understanding normal adults because their personality is divorced from childhood influences.

He also argued that projective techniques, such as the Thematic Apperception Test and the Rorschach inkblot test, may present a distorted picture of the normal personality because they deal with unconscious forces that have little effect on the normal adult personality. Allport suggested that more reliable information could be obtained by simply asking people to describe themselves, a method that reveals their dominant traits.

Allport favored the idiographic approach, that is, the study of the individual case, as indicated by his use of personal documents. However, he did also use some nomothetic methods involving the statistical analysis of differences among large samples of subjects when he believed them to be appropriate. Psychological tests, such as the Study of Values, use the nomothetic approach.

Expressive Behavior

expressive behavior
Spontaneous and seemingly purposeless behavior, usually displayed without our conscious awareness.

coping behavior Consciously planned behavior determined by the needs of a given situation and designed for a specific purpose, usually to bring about a change in one's environment.

Allport conducted considerable research on what he called **expressive behavior**, described as behavior that expresses our personality traits. He also identified **coping behavior**, which is oriented toward a specific purpose and is consciously planned and carried out. Coping behavior is determined by needs inspired by the situation and is ordinarily directed toward bringing about some change in our environment.

The Nature of Expressive Behavior   Expressive behavior is spontaneous and reflects basic aspects of the personality. In contrast to coping behavior, expressive behavior is difficult to change, has no specific purpose, and is usually displayed without our awareness. Allport offered the example of public speaking. The speaker communicates with the audience on two levels.

The formal, planned level (coping behavior) includes the lecture's content. The informal, unplanned level (expressive behavior) consists of the speaker's movements, gestures, and vocal inflections. The speaker may be nervous, or may talk rapidly, pace back and forth, or fidget with an earring. These spontaneous behaviors can express elements of the speaker's personality.

In his landmark study of expressive behavior, Allport gave subjects a variety of tasks to perform and then judged the consistency of their expressive movements over the different situations (Allport & Vernon, 1933). He found a high level of consistency in voice, handwriting, posture, and gestures. From these behaviors, he deduced the existence of such traits as introversion and extraversion.

There has been considerable theoretical and experimental work describing both facial and vocal expressive behavior (see Russell, Bachorowski, & Fernandez-Dols, 2003). This research has shown that personality can be assessed from voice recordings, films, and videotapes. Facial expressions, vocal inflections, and idiosyncratic gestures and mannerisms can reveal personality traits to a trained observer. The expressive behaviors linked to specific traits have even been assessed from still photographs (Allport & Cantril, 1934; Berry, 1990; DePaulo, 1993; Riggio & Friedman, 1986; Riggio, Lippa, & Salinas, 1990).

Researchers have accumulated an impressive body of evidence to show that some people can form reliable impressions of a stranger's personality based solely on facial appearance and expression (Berry & Wero, 1993). For example, observers have accurately assessed personality factors such as anxiety from watching a film of the person for no more than 30 seconds (Ambody & Rosenthal, 1992).

Effects of Gender and Age   It has been found that women and younger people are better at correctly recognizing emotions in facial expressions than men and older people

(Sasson, Pinkham, Richard, Hughett, Gur, & Gur, 2010). The ability of children to read facial expressions accurately can occur as early as the age of 5 and improves rapidly thereafter (Gao & Maurer, 2010).

An analysis of the yearbook photographs of women college graduates found that those who exhibited positive emotional expressions at age 21 scored higher on self-report inventories of feelings of subjective well-being when tested again later at ages 27, 43, and 52. They also reported better marriages and scored higher in affiliation, competence, and achievement orientation than did those who displayed less positive emotions in their yearbook pictures at age 21 (Harker & Keltner, 2001).

Interpreting Facial Expressions   Sometimes our personal experiences influence our ability to recognize emotions in the facial expressions of others. For example, a study of 8- to 10-year-old children who had been physically abused showed that they could more readily identify facial displays of anger in pictures of female adults than could a control group of children who had not been abused (Pollak & Sinha, 2002).

A study of adults demonstrated that emotional state may influence the ability to read the facial expressions of other people. Those diagnosed with major depression needed to see facial expressions of greater intensity in order to identify correctly happiness on the faces of the pictures they were shown. In contrast, to correctly identify sadness they required less intense facial expressions (Joormann & Gotlib, 2006).

Children who scored high on a scale of social anxiety were better at correctly interpreting facial expressions. Adults high in depression were better in recognizing sad facial expressions than adults who were not depressed (Ale, Chorney, Brice, & Morris, 2010; Gollan, McCloskey, Hoxha, & Coccaro, 2010).

A study of Japanese children found that those who spent more time playing video games were better at recognizing facial expressions correctly than those who did not play video games as much (Tamamiya & Jiraki, 2013).

It has also been found that close friends are far more accurate in decoding emotions such as sadness, anger, and happiness than are casual acquaintances (Zhang & Parmley, 2011). These and similar studies provide strong support for Allport's proposition that expressive behavior reflects our personality traits.

Coding Facial Expressions   A long-term research program conducted by Paul Ekman identified facial expressions of seven emotions that can be objectively and consistently distinguished from one another. These emotions are anger, contempt, disgust, fear, sadness, surprise, and happiness (Ekman, Matsumoto, & Friesen, 1997). Ekman, director of the Human Interaction Laboratory at the University of California at San Francisco, and his colleagues, have developed a coding system based on their analysis of 43 facial muscles. The system provides 3,000 different configurations useful in reading the emotional expressions in a person's face.

This Facial Action Coding System (FACS) is used in the United States by police departments, as well as the CIA and the FBI, to detect lying by criminal suspects and by terrorists. According to the FACS, tiny movements of their facial muscles will betray them (Kaufman, 2002). In 2009, Ekman was named by *Time* magazine as one of the world's 100 most influential people (Taylor, 2009).

Other research has also shown that some basic aspects of personality are revealed by facial expressions. For example, neuroticism reveals itself in looks of anger, contempt, and fear. Agreeableness shows in laughter and other expressions of friendly social interaction.

Extraversion appears in smiles, laughter, and other expressions of enjoyment and amusement. Conscientiousness is marked by expressions of embarrassment including a tightly controlled smile, an averted gaze, and head movements down and away from the observer (Keltner, 1997).

We recognize smiles by unconsciously mimicking them. Using the same muscles as the person we are looking at sends the same message to activate the regions of the brain that are active in the person who is smiling at us (Niedenthal, Mermillod, Maringer, & Hess, 2010; Zimmer, 2011).

Emotional States and Facial Expressions Type A behavior, the pattern suggested to be associated with the potential for heart disease, has been distinguished from Type B behavior by expressions of disgust, glaring, grimacing, and scowling (Chesney, Ekman, Friensen, Black, & Hecker, 1997). A study of depressed patients in Switzerland found that facial expressions distinguished those who later attempted suicide from those who did not (Heller & Haynal, 1997).

Research on Japanese college students found that those who scored high on a test of anxiety exhibited different facial expressions, particularly around the mouth and the left side of the face, than did those who scored low on anxiety (Nakamura, 2002). These results confirm Allport's ideas.

Cultural Differences in Facial Expressions

Are facial expressions the same the world over? Or do they differ from one culture to another? Studies of American and Chinese infants and adults found that some basic emotions were revealed by identical facial expressions in both cultures and in both age groups (Albright et al., 1997; Camras, Oster, Campos, Miyake, & Bradshaw, 1998).

However, a study comparing facial expressions of American, Chinese, and Japanese infants reached a different conclusion. Chinese infants showed consistently less variety in facial expressive behavior than American and Japanese infants. American infants differed significantly in facial expressions of emotions from Chinese infants but not so much from Japanese infants (Camras, 1998).

A study comparing facial expressions from a remote tribe in Northwestern Namibia in Africa found that their facial expressions of emotions did not match those of American subjects. The researchers noted that these results suggest that perceptions of emotions are not universal (Gendron, Roberson, van der Vyver, & Barrett, 2014).

Additional research involving 3-year-old girls found that White children smiled more than mainland Chinese or Chinese-American children. The degree of maternal strictness and the number of other children and adults in the home also influenced the intensity of facial expression in those cultures. The depth to which the girls' faces expressed their emotions was found to vary as a function of both cultural and family characteristics (Camras, Bakeman, Chen, Norris, & Cain, 2006).

Research involving adults in the United States and in Japan showed that each group was much better at recognizing the facial expressions of people of their own culture (Dailey et al., 2010). The same cultural differences between East and West in recognizing facial expressions were found when subjects were shown different faces on robots (Trovato, Kishi, Endo, Zecca, Hashimoto, & Takanishi, 2014).

A study in which pictures of faces had been digitized so as to be neutral (not displaying any emotion) found that White faces were judged to have angry expressions more often than Black faces, and Black faces were judged to have happy or surprised expressions more often (Zebrowitz, Kikuchi, & Fellous, 2010).

Consistent differences were found in facial recognition of emotions between Eastern and Western cultures. Even the ways in which faces changed to represent emotions differed. In one study, people in Eastern cultures expressed emotion primarily with the eyes, while those in Western cultures were more likely to use eyebrows and mouth to express their feelings (Jack, Caldara, & Schyns, 2012). Another comparison found that people in Hong Kong, Singapore, and Taiwan showed less intense facial expressions on their Facebook pictures than Americans did (Huang & Park, 2013).

When Caucasian Americans and Asian Americans who scored high in depression were shown a humorous film, the Caucasian Americans exhibited fewer smiles and other facial reactions than did the Asian Americans (Chentsova-Dutton, Tsai, & Gotlib, 2010).

Computer Recognition of Facial Expressions

If some people can accurately interpret the facial expressions of others, can computer recognition be far behind? Apparently not. A computer program has been developed that monitors video images of faces at the rate of 30 frames per second. The computer achieved a high degree of accuracy in recognizing basic emotions including happiness, sadness, fear, disgust, anger, and surprise (Susskind, Littlewort, Bartlett, Movellan, & Anderson, 2007).

And if computers can recognize the emotions expressed in the human face, can they also be used to transmit emotional states? In a study of adolescents in the Netherlands, average age 16, emoticons were used to study the online transmission of personal feelings. In simulated chat rooms the teenagers were found to use more emoticons in their communication in a social context than in a task- or job-oriented context.

They used more positive icons, such as those representing smiles, in positive situations and more negative icons, such as those representing sadness, in negative situations, just the way people do in face-to-face contact. Thus the researchers concluded that people express emotions in computer-mediated communication in a similar way as in face-to-face situations (Derks, Bos, & von Grumbkow, 2007).

HIGHLIGHTS: Research on Expressive Behavior

Research on *expressive behavior* has found that:

- Personality traits can be assessed from facial expressions
- Women and children are better than men and older people at reading facial expressions
- Close friends are better than strangers at decoding facial expressions of emotion
- As many as seven separate emotions can be identified in facial expressions
- We recognize smiles in others by unconsciously mimicking them
- Depressed people are better at recognizing sad expressions
- Computers can recognize and express basic emotions

Reflections on Allport's Theory

Although considerable research has been conducted on expressive behavior, Allport's theory as a whole has stimulated little research to test its propositions. His idiographic research approach ran counter to the main current of thought in contemporary psychology, which accepted nomothetic research instead (the study of large subject groups through sophisticated statistical analysis). Allport's focus on emotionally healthy adults was also at variance with the then prevalent position in clinical psychology, which dealt with the neurotic and psychotic.

Questions and Criticisms

It is difficult to translate Allport's concepts into specific terms and propositions suitable for study by the experimental method. For example, how do we observe functional autonomy or propriate striving in the laboratory? How can we manipulate these concepts to test their effects?

Criticisms have been leveled against the concept of functional autonomy. Allport did not make clear how an original motive is transformed into an autonomous one. For example, once a person is financially secure, by what process is the motive to work hard for financial gain altered to become a motive to continue to work hard for the sake of the task itself? If the mechanism of transformation is not explained, how can we predict which childhood motives will become autonomous in adulthood?

Allport's emphasis on the uniqueness of personality has been challenged because his position focuses so exclusively on the individual that it is impossible to generalize from one person to another. Many psychologists find it difficult to accept Allport's proposed discontinuity between child and adult, animal and human, normal and abnormal. They point out that research on the behavior of children, animals, and emotionally disturbed subjects has yielded considerable knowledge about the functioning of the normal, emotionally healthy adult.

Recognition and Influence

Despite these criticisms, Allport's theory has been well received by a number of psychologists who continue to maintain that Allport's views provide a better basis for understanding personality than the approaches of most other theorists (Piekkola, 2011). His approach to personality development, his emphasis on uniqueness, and his focus on the importance of goals are reflected in the work of the humanistic psychologists Abraham Maslow and Carl Rogers (see Chapters 9 and 10).

Allport is often considered to be one of the first psychologists to bring humanistic values and concerns to the field (Jeshmaridian, 2007). Interest in Allport's work has been revived recently as part of the current focus on personality traits, which is providing empirical support for some of his ideas.

Allport's major work on the expression of emotions has been of vital importance in the development of the field of cognitive neuroscience. There has also been a revival of interest in his personal-document technique for studying personality (Barenbaum, 2008; Zunshine, 2010).

His books are written in a readable style and his concepts have a commonsense appeal. The emphasis on conscious, rational determinants of behavior provides an alternative to the psychoanalytic position that sees people irrationally and unconsciously driven by uncontrollable forces.

Allport's view that people are shaped more by future expectations than by past events is congenial with a hopeful and humanistic philosophy. His most enduring contributions to psychology are making the study of personality academically respectable and emphasizing the role of genetic factors within a trait approach to personality.

Chapter Summary

Gordon Allport focused on the conscious instead of the unconscious. He believed that personality is guided more by the present and future than by the past. He studied normal rather than emotionally disturbed people.

Personality is defined as the dynamic organization within the individual of those psychophysical systems that determine characteristic behavior and thought. It is a product of heredity and environment and divorced from childhood experiences.

Traits are consistent, enduring predispositions to respond in the same or a similar way to different stimuli. Individual traits (personal dispositions) are unique to the person; common traits are shared by many people. Cardinal traits are powerful and pervasive; central traits are less pervasive. Secondary traits are displayed less conspicuously and less consistently than other types of traits.

Functional autonomy means that a motive in the normal adult is not functionally related to the past experiences in which it originally appeared. Two levels of functional autonomy are perseverative (behaviors such as addictions and repeated physical movements) and propriate (interests, values, attitudes, intentions, lifestyle, and self-image related to the core of personality). Three principles of propriate functional autonomy are organizing the energy level, mastery and competence, and propriate patterning.

The proprium (self or ego) develops from infancy to adolescence in seven stages: bodily self, self-identity, self-esteem, extension of self, self-image, self as a rational coper, and propriate striving. An infant is controlled by drives and reflexes and has little personality.

The mature, healthy adult personality is characterized by an extension of self to other people and activities, a warm relating to others, emotional security, a realistic perception, the development of skills, a commitment to work, self-objectification, and a unifying philosophy of life.

Allport presented an optimistic image of human nature and emphasized the uniqueness of the individual. We are not driven by childhood events. In conscious control of our lives, we creatively design a lifestyle and grow through an inherent need for autonomy, individuality, and selfhood. Our ultimate goal is for increases in tension that impel us to seek new sensations and challenges.

The personal-document approach to personality assessment involves the examination of diaries, letters, and other personal records to uncover personality traits. The Study of Values is a psychological test to assess six types of values.

Research on expressive behavior reveals a consistency in expressive facial movements and relates them to a variety of emotions and personality patterns. Some research suggests a consistency of facial expressions from one culture to another and that computer programs can recognize facial expressions and can be used to recognize and to communicate emotions to others.

Allport's theory has been criticized on the grounds that it is difficult to test empirically such concepts as functional autonomy. Allport's focus on the uniqueness of personality and on the discontinuity between childhood and adult personalities has also been questioned.

Review Questions

1. What problems and issues did Allport have to deal with in his childhood and adolescence that may have influenced his approach to personality?
2. In what ways does Allport's personality theory differ from Freud's?
3. Explain Allport's definition of personality. In Allport's system, how do heredity and environment influence personality?
4. Describe four characteristics of traits.
5. How do cardinal traits, central traits, and secondary traits differ from one another? Which type exerts the most powerful influence on the personality?
6. According to Allport, what is the relationship between personality and motivation?
7. What is propriate functional autonomy? Describe three principles that govern propriate functional autonomy.
8. What is the role of cognitive processes in personality development?
9. What is the relationship between adult motives and childhood experiences?

10. According to Allport, what are the first three stages of human development? Describe briefly the changes that occur at each stage.
11. Describe the concept of proprium.
12. What parental behaviors are necessary for a child to achieve positive psychological growth?
13. How does Allport's theory account for emotional disturbances in adulthood?
14. What are the characteristics of the mature, healthy adult personality?
15. What is Allport's proposed ultimate and necessary goal of life. How do we achieve it?
16. Describe the research findings on how expressive behavior can reveal aspects of our personality.
17. Is there a universality of facial expressions over all cultures or do they vary from one culture to another?
18. How are people able to express emotions in computer-mediated communication? How do you express your own emotions online?

Suggested Readings

Allport, G. W. (1937). *Personality: A psychological interpretation*. New York: Holt. Allport's classic book that established the study of personality as an integral part of scientific academic psychology and defined the focus of personality psychology as the unique individual.

Allport, G. W. (1955). *Becoming: Basic considerations for a psychology of personality*. New Haven, CT: Yale University Press. Outlines Allport's approach to personality, emphasizing the human capacity for growth and development.

Allport, G. W. (1967). Autobiography. In E. G. Boring & G. Lindzey (Eds.), *A history of psychology in autobiography* (Vol. 5, pp. 1–25). New York: Appleton-Century-Crofts. Allport's account of his life and career.

Elms, A. C. (1994). *Uncovering lives: The uneasy alliance of biography and psychology*. New York: Oxford University Press. Chapter 5, "Allport meets Freud and the clean little boy" (pp. 71–84), discusses Gordon Allport's 1920 encounter with Sigmund Freud.

Evans, R. I. (1971). *Gordon Allport: The man and his ideas*. New York: Dutton. Interviews with Allport about his life and work.

Nicholson, I. (2003). *Inventing personality: Gordon Allport and the science of selfhood*. Washington, DC: American Psychological Association. Focuses on Allport's early career in developing his theory of personality and relates his work to the social climate of the times in America in the 1920s and 1930s.

Rosenzweig, S., & Fisher, S. L. (1997). "Idiographic" vis-à-vis "idiodynamic" in the historical perspective of personality theory: Remembering Gordon Allport, 1897–1997. *Journal of the History of the Behavioral Sciences, 33*, 405–419. A reappraisal of Allport's focus on the uniqueness of the human personality. Considers the extent to which his personal spirituality and religious views may have affected his image of human nature.

chapter 8

Raymond Cattell, Hans Eysenck, The Five-Factor Theory, HEXACO, and the Dark Triad

Fair Use

Personality is that which permits a prediction of what a person will do in a given situation.

—*Raymond Cattell*

Predicting Behavior

Cattell's goal in his study of personality was to predict how a person will behave in response to a given stimulus situation. Cattell was not interested in changing or modifying behavior from abnormal to normal, which had been the approach of other personality theorists.

Those more clinically oriented theorists based their work on case studies of patients who were unhappy or emotionally disturbed and wanted to change. In contrast, Cattell's subjects were normal people. His aim was to study their personality, not to treat it. He believed it was impossible, or at least unwise, to attempt to change a personality before understanding fully what was to be modified.

A Scientific Approach

Cattell's approach to personality was rigorously scientific, relying on observations of behavior and masses of data. In his research, it was not unusual for more than 50 kinds of measurements to be taken from a single subject. "His theory of personality [was] rivaled by no other in its comprehensiveness and adherence to evidence derived from empirical research" (Horn, 2001, p. 72).

Factor Analysis

factor analysis A statistical technique based on correlations between several measures, which may be explained in terms of underlying factors.

The hallmark of Cattell's approach was his treatment of the data. He submitted them to the statistical procedure called **factor analysis**, which involves assessing the relationship between each possible pair of measurements taken from a group of subjects to determine common factors. For example, scores on two different psychological tests or on two subscales of the same test would be analyzed to determine their correlation.

If the two measures showed a high correlation with one another, Cattell concluded that they measured similar or related aspects of personality. For example, if the anxiety and introversion scales of a personality test yielded a high correlation coefficient, we could conclude that both scales were measuring the same personality characteristic. Thus, two sets of data about a person are combined to form a single dimension, or factor.

Personality Traits

Cattell referred to these factors as *traits*, which he defined as the mental elements of the personality. Only when we know someone's traits can we predict how that person will behave in a given situation. Thus, to be able to understand someone fully, we must be able to describe in precise terms the entire pattern of traits that define that person as an individual.

The Life of Cattell (1905–1998)

An Older Brother and Wounded Soldiers

Cattell was born in Staffordshire, England. His parents had high, exacting standards of behavior for their children but were also permissive about how the children spent their spare time. Cattell, his brothers, and friends spent much time outdoors, sailing and swimming, exploring caves, and fighting mock battles, although they "occasionally drowned or fell over cliffs."

Cattell's life changed dramatically at the age of 9, when England entered World War I. A nearby mansion was converted to a hospital, and he saw trainloads of wounded soldiers returning from the battlefields of France. He wrote that this experience made him unusually serious for a young boy and aware of the "brevity of life and the need to accomplish while one might."

His lifelong, intense dedication to work may have originated from these experiences. He also felt highly competitive with an older brother and wrote of the problems of maintaining his own freedom of development while confronted with this brother who could not be "overcome" (1974a, pp. 62–63).

Psychology: A Bad Choice

At age 16, Cattell enrolled at the University of London to study physics and chemistry, graduating with honors in 3 years. His time in London intensified his interest in social problems, and he came to realize that the physical sciences did not equip him to deal with social ills. He decided that the best solution was to study the human mind.

That was a courageous decision to make in 1924 because the field of psychology in England offered few professional opportunities and only six academic professorships in the entire country. It was regarded as a discipline for eccentrics. Against the advice of friends, Cattell began graduate studies at the University of London, working with the eminent psychologist-statistician Charles E. Spearman, who had developed the technique of factor analysis.

Awarded his Ph.D. in 1929, Cattell found that his friends were right. There were very few jobs for psychologists. He did some lecturing at Exeter University, wrote a book about the English countryside, and set up a psychology clinic for the schools in the city of Leicester, all while pursuing his own research interests. Whereas Spearman had used factor analysis to measure mental abilities, Cattell resolved to apply the method to the structure of personality.

A Time of Hardship

During this period, Cattell developed chronic digestive disorders from overwork, a deficient diet, and being forced to live in a cold basement apartment. His wife left him due to his poor economic prospects and total absorption in his work. However, Cattell did claim some positive benefits from that time of hardship.

The experience forced him to focus on practical problems rather than theoretical or experimental issues, which he might have done given more secure and comfortable circumstances. "Those years made me as canny and distrustful as a squirrel who has known a long winter. It bred asceticism and impatience with irrelevance, to the point of ruthlessness" (1974b, p. 90).

Success in America

Eight years after he earned his doctoral degree, Cattell finally received an opportunity to work full-time in his chosen field. The prominent American psychologist Edward L. Thorndike invited Cattell to spend a year at Thorndike's laboratory at Columbia University in New York. The following year, Cattell accepted a professorship at Clark University in Worcester, Massachusetts, and in 1941 moved to Harvard, where, he said, the "sap of creativity" rose (1974a, p. 71).

His colleagues included Gordon Allport and William Sheldon, who was then developing his theory of personality and body type. Cattell married a mathematician who shared his research interests, and at the age of 40 settled at the University of Illinois as a research professor. He published more than 500 articles, as well as 43 books, a monumental accomplishment that reflected his dedication and perseverance.

> For the next twenty years, my life was that of a humming dynamo—smooth but powerful. I was generally the last out of the parking lot at midnight. There is a story that I arrived at the laboratory one day to find, to my amazement, not a soul there. I phoned [home] and was told, "We are just sitting down to Thanksgiving dinner." All days were the same to me. (Cattell, 1993, p. 105)

In his 70s, Cattell joined the graduate faculty of the University of Hawaii, where he permitted himself the luxury of swimming in the ocean every day. It was said that he worked "as hard as an assistant professor up for tenure and not sure that it will be granted" (Johnson, 1980, p. 300).

He died in Honolulu at the age of 92, one year after he had been awarded the Gold Medal Award for Life Achievement in Psychological Science from the American Psychological Association, for his "prodigious, landmark contributions to psychology, including factor analytic mappings of the domains of personality" (Gold Medal Award, 1997, p. 797).

Raymond Cattell

Various sites provide biographical information, discussions of his theory, research on relevant concepts, and links to other resources.

Raymond Cattell Interview

An informative interview with Raymond Cattell was originally published in The Eugenics Bulletin, Spring–Summer 1984.

16 PF Questionnaire

Several sites provide information on the origins and research results of this significant test to measure personality factors.

Cattell's Approach to Personality Traits

traits To Cattell, reaction tendencies, derived by the method of factor analysis, that are relatively permanent parts of the personality.

Cattell defined **traits** as relatively permanent reaction tendencies that are the basic structural units of the personality. He classified traits in several ways (see Table 8.1).

Common Traits and Unique Traits

common traits Traits possessed in some degree by all persons.

Cattell distinguished between common traits and unique traits. A **common trait** is one that is possessed by everyone to some degree. Intelligence, extraversion, and gregariousness are examples of common traits. Everyone has these traits, but some people have them to a greater extent than others. Cattell's reason for suggesting that common traits are universal is that all people have a similar hereditary potential and are subject to similar social pressures, at least within the same culture.

unique traits Traits possessed by one or a few persons.

People differ, as we said, in that they possess different amounts or degrees of these common traits. They also differ because of their **unique traits**, those aspects of personality shared by few other people. Unique traits are particularly apparent in our interests and attitudes. For example, one person may have a consuming interest in genealogy,

---

TABLE 8.1 Ways of classifying traits

Common traits	Everyone shares common traits to some degree; for example, everyone has some measure of intelligence or of extraversion.
Unique traits	Each of us has unique traits that distinguish us as individuals; for example, a liking for politics or an interest in baseball.
Ability traits	Our skills and abilities determine how well we can work toward our goals.
Temperament traits	Our emotions and feelings (whether we are assertive, fretful, or easygoing, for example) help determine how we react to the people and situations in our environment.
Dynamic traits	The forces that underlie our motivations and drive our behavior.
Surface traits	Characteristics composed of any number of source traits, or behavioral elements; they may be unstable and impermanent, weakening or strengthening in response to different situations.
Source traits	Single, stable, permanent elements of our behavior.
Constitutional traits	Source traits that have biological origins, such as the behaviors that result from drinking too much alcohol.
Environmental-mold traits	Source traits that have environmental origins, such as the behaviors that result from the influence of our friends, work environment, or neighborhood.

---

ability traits Traits that describe our skills and how efficiently we will be able to work toward our goals.

temperament traits Traits that describe our general behavioral style in responding to our environment.

dynamic traits Traits that describe our motivations and interests.

surface traits Traits that show a correlation but do not constitute a factor because they are not determined by a single source.

source traits Stable and permanent traits that are the basic factors of personality, derived by the method of factor analysis.

whereas another may be passionately interested in Civil War battles or baseball or Chinese martial arts.

Ability, Temperament, and Dynamic Traits

A second way to classify traits is to divide them into ability traits, temperament traits, and dynamic traits. **Ability traits** determine how efficiently we will be able to work toward a goal. Intelligence is an ability trait; our level of intelligence will affect the ways in which we strive for our goals.

Temperament traits describe the general style and emotional tone of our behavior; for example, how assertive, easygoing, or irritable we are. These traits affect the ways we act and react to situations.

Dynamic traits are the driving forces of behavior. They define our motivations, interests, and ambitions.

Surface Traits and Source Traits

A third class of traits is surface traits versus source traits according to their stability and permanence. **Surface traits** are personality characteristics that correlate with one another but do not constitute a factor because they are not determined by a single source. For example, several behavioral elements such as anxiety, indecision, and irrational fear combine to form the surface trait labeled neuroticism. Thus, neuroticism does not derive from a single source. Because surface traits are composed of several elements, they are less stable and permanent and, therefore, less important in describing personality.

Of greater importance are **source traits**, which are unitary personality factors that are much more stable and permanent. Each source trait gives rise to some aspect of behavior. Source traits are those individual factors derived from factor analysis that combine to account for surface traits.

Constitutional Traits and Environmental-Mold Traits

constitutional traits Source traits that depend on our physiological characteristics.

Source traits are classified by their origin as either constitutional traits or environmental-mold traits. **Constitutional traits** originate in biological conditions but are not necessarily innate. For example, alcohol or drug use can lead to behaviors such as carelessness, talkativeness, and slurred speech.

environmental-mold traits Source traits that are learned from social and environmental interactions.

Environmental-mold traits derive from influences in our social and physical environments. These traits are learned characteristics and behaviors that impose a pattern on the personality. The behavior of a person reared in an impoverished inner-city neighborhood is molded differently from the behavior of a person reared in upper-class luxury. A career military officer shows a different pattern of behavior from a jazz musician. Thus, we see that Cattell recognized the interaction between personal and situational variables.

Source Traits: The Basic Factors of Personality

After more than two decades of intensive factor-analytic research, Cattell (1965) identified 16 source traits as the basic factors of personality. These factors are best known in the form in which they are most often used, in an objective personality test called the Sixteen Personality Factor (16 PF) Questionnaire (see Table 8.2).

As you can see from Table 8.2, the personality characteristics associated with these traits are expressed in words we use in our everyday conversation when describing our

TABLE 8.2 Cattell's source traits (factors) of personality

FACTOR	LOW SCORERS	HIGH SCORERS
A	Reserved, aloof, detached	Outgoing, warmhearted, easygoing
B	Low in intelligence	High in intelligence
C	Low ego strength, easily upset, less emotionally stable	High ego strength, calm, emotionally stable
E	Submissive, obedient, docile, unsure, meek	Dominant, assertive, forceful
F	Serious, sober, depressed, worrying	Happy-go-lucky, enthusiastic, cheerful
G	Expedient, low in superego	Conscientious, high in superego
H	Timid, shy, aloof, restrained	Bold, adventurous
I	Tough-minded, self-reliant, demanding	Tender-minded, sensitive, dependent
L	Trusting, understanding, accepting	Suspicious, jealous, withdrawn
M	Practical, down-to-earth, concerned with detail	Imaginative, absentminded
N	Forthright, naïve, unpretentious	Shrewd, worldly, insightful
O	Self-assured, secure, complacent	Apprehensive, insecure, self-reproaching
Q_1	Conservative, holds traditional values, dislikes change	Radical, liberal, experimenting, embraces change
Q_2	Group-dependent, prefers to join and follow others	Self-sufficient, resourceful, independent
Q_3	Uncontrolled, lax, impulsive	Controlled, compulsive, exacting
Q_4	Relaxed, tranquil, composed	Tense, driven, fretful

friends and ourselves. No doubt you can tell at a glance whether you score high, low, or somewhere in between on these basic personality factors.

Cattell later identified additional factors he designated as *temperament traits* because they relate to the general style and emotional tone of behavior. He gave as examples excitability, zest, self-discipline, politeness, and self-assurance (Cattell, 1973; Cattell & Kline, 1977).

It is important to remember that in Cattell's system, source traits are the basic elements of personality just as atoms are the basic units of the physical world. He argued that psychologists cannot understand or generate laws about personality without describing precisely the nature of these elements.

Dynamic Traits: The Motivating Forces

Cattell described dynamic traits as the traits concerned with motivation, which is an important issue in many personality theories. Cattell believed that a personality theory that failed to consider the impact of dynamic, or motivating, forces is incomplete, like trying to describe an engine but failing to mention the type of fuel on which it runs.

The Influences of Heredity and Environment

Cattell showed great interest in the relative influences of heredity and environment in shaping personality. He investigated the importance of hereditary and environmental factors by statistically comparing similarities found between twins reared in the same family, twins reared apart, non-twin siblings reared in the same family, and non-twin siblings reared apart. Thus, he was able to estimate the extent to which differences in traits could be attributed to genetic or to environmental influences.

The results of his analyses showed that for some traits, heredity plays a major role. For example, Cattell's data suggest that 80 percent of intelligence (Factor B) and 80 percent of timidity versus boldness (Factor H) can be accounted for by genetic factors. Cattell concluded that overall, one-third of our personality is genetically based, and two-thirds is determined by social and environmental influences.

Stages of Personality Development

Cattell proposed six stages in the development of personality covering the entire life span (see Table 8.3).

TABLE 8.3   Cattell's stages of personality development

STAGE	AGE	DEVELOPMENT
Infancy	Birth to 6	Weaning; toilet training; formation of ego, superego, and social attitudes
Childhood	6–14	Independence from parents and identification with peers
Adolescence	14–23	Conflicts about independence, self-assertion, and sex
Maturity	23–50	Satisfaction with career, marriage, and family
Late maturity	50–65	Personality changes in response to physical and social circumstances
Old age	65+	Adjustment to loss of friends, career, and status

Infancy

The period of infancy, from birth to age 6, is the major formative period for personality. The child is influenced by parents and siblings and by the experiences of weaning and toilet training. Social attitudes develop along with the ego and the superego, feelings of security or insecurity, attitudes toward authority, and a possible tendency to neuroticism. Cattell was not a follower of Freud's, but he incorporated several Freudian ideas into his theory; namely, that the early years of life are crucial in personality formation, and that oral and anal conflicts can affect personality.

Childhood

Between ages 6 and 14, the childhood stage of personality formation, there are few psychological problems. This stage marks the beginning of a move toward independence from parents and an increasing identification with peers.

Adolescence

The childhood stage is followed by a more troublesome and stressful stage, adolescence, ages 14 to 23. Emotional disorders and delinquency may be evident as young people experience conflicts centered on the drives for independence, self-assertion, and sex.

Maturity

The fourth phase of development, maturity, lasts from approximately age 23 to 50. It is generally a productive, satisfying time in terms of career, marriage, and family situations. The personality becomes less flexible, compared with earlier stages, and thus emotional stability increases. Cattell found little change in interests and attitudes during this period.

Adolescence can be a stressful stage of development.

Oliveromg/Shutterstock.com

In late maturity, after one's children have left home, there is often a reexamination of the values of one's life.

Alexander Raths/Shutterstock.com

Late Maturity

Late maturity, ages 50 to 65, involves personality developments in response to physical, social, and psychological changes. Health, vigor, and physical attractiveness may decline and the end of life may be in view. During this phase, people reexamine their values and search for a new self. This period is somewhat similar to Carl Jung's view of the midlife period.

Old Age

The final stage, old age, from 65 onward, involves adjustments to different kinds of losses—the death of spouses, relatives, and friends; a career lost to retirement; loss of status in a culture that worships youth; and a pervasive sense of loneliness and insecurity.

Questions about Human Nature

Cattell's definition of personality gives us clues about his view of human nature. He wrote, "Personality is that which permits a prediction of what a person will do in a given situation" (1950, p. 2). For behavior to be considered predictable, it must be lawful and orderly. Prediction would be difficult without regularity and consistency in the personality.

For example, one spouse can usually predict with considerable accuracy what the other spouse will do in a given situation because that person's past behavior has been consistent and orderly. Therefore, Cattell's view of human nature admits little spontaneity because that would make predictability more difficult. On the free will versus determinism issue, then, Cattell falls more on the side of determinism.

Cattell did not propose any ultimate or necessary goal that dominates behavior, no drive for self-actualization to pull us toward the future, no psychosexual conflicts to push us from the past. Although he noted the impact of early life events, he did not believe that childhood forces determine the personality permanently.

Cattell accepted the influence on personality of both nature and nurture. For example, constitutional traits are innate, whereas environmental-mold traits are learned. On the uniqueness versus universality issue, Cattell took a moderate position, noting the existence of common traits, which apply to everyone in a culture, and unique traits, which describe the individual.

Cattell's personal view of human nature is clearer. In his younger years, he was optimistic about our ability to solve social problems. He predicted that we would gain greater awareness of and control over our environment. He expected to see the level of intelligence rise, along with the development of "a more gracious community life of creatively occupied citizens" (1974b, p. 88). Reality did not live up to his expectations, however, and eventually he came to believe that human nature and society had regressed.

Assessment in Cattell's Theory

Cattell's objective measurements of personality used three primary assessment techniques, which he called L-data (life records), Q-data (questionnaires), and T-data (tests).

Life records (L-data)

L-data Life-record ratings of behaviors observed in real-life situations, such as the classroom or office.

The **L-data** technique involves observers' ratings of specific behaviors exhibited by people in real-life settings such as a classroom or office. For example, observers might record frequency of absence from work, grades at school, conscientiousness in performing job duties, emotional stability on the soccer field, or sociability in the office.

The important point about L-data is that they involve overt behaviors that can be seen by an observer and occur in a naturalistic setting rather than in the artificial situation of a psychology laboratory.

Questionnaires (Q-data)

Q-data Self-report questionnaire ratings of our characteristics, attitudes, and interests.

The **Q-data** technique relies on questionnaires. Whereas the L-data technique calls for observers to rate the subjects, the Q-data technique requires them to rate themselves. Cattell recognized the limitations of Q-data. First, some people may have only superficial self-awareness, so their answers will not reflect the true nature of their personality.

Second, even if they do know themselves well, they may not want researchers to know them. Therefore, they may deliberately falsify their responses. Because of these problems, Cattell warned that Q-data must not automatically be assumed to be accurate.

Personality tests (T-data)

T-data Data derived from personality tests that are resistant to faking.

The **T-data** technique involves the use of what Cattell called "objective" tests, in which a person responds without knowing what aspect of behavior is being evaluated. These tests circumvent the Q-data's shortcomings by making it difficult for a subject to know precisely what a test is measuring.

If you cannot guess what the experimenter is trying to find out, then you cannot distort your responses to conceal your traits. For example, if you were shown an inkblot, you probably would not be able to predict whether the researcher's interpretation of your response revealed that you were conservative, relaxed, adventurous, or apprehensive.

Cattell considered tests such as the Rorschach, the Thematic Apperception Test, and the word-association test to be *objective* because they are resistant to faking. However, it is important to note that to most psychologists, this use of the word *objective* is misleading; such tests are usually called *subjective* because of the biases that affect scoring and interpretation.

FIGURE 8.1

Sample 16 PF Test profile for a hypothetical airline pilot.

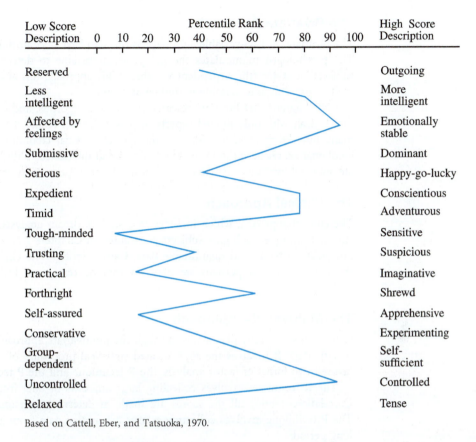

Low Score Description	Percentile Rank	High Score Description

Based on Cattell, Eber, and Tatsuoka, 1970.

The 16 PF (Personality Factor) Test

Cattell developed several tests to assess personality. The most notable is the 16 PF Test, which is based on the 16 major source traits. The test is intended for use with people 16 years of age and older and yields scores on each of the 16 scales. The responses are scored objectively; computerized scoring and interpretation are available. The 16 PF Test is widely used to assess personality for research, clinical diagnosis, and predicting success on a job. It has been translated into some 40 languages.

Consider a sample 16 PF Test profile for a hypothetical airline pilot (see Figure 8.1). By reading the high and low points of the plot of test scores, we can see that this person is emotionally stable, conscientious, adventurous, tough-minded, practical, self-assured, controlled, and relaxed. The pilot is not tense, apprehensive, or timid.

Cattell developed several variations of the 16 PF Test. Scales have been prepared to measure specific aspects of personality—such as anxiety, depression, and neuroticism—and for special purposes such as marriage counseling and performance evaluation of business executives. There are also versions of the test for use with children and with adolescents.

Research on Cattell's Theory

In discussing research methods, Cattell listed three ways to study personality: bivariate, clinical, and multivariate approaches.

The Bivariate Approach

The bivariate, or two-variable, approach is the standard laboratory experimental method. The psychologist manipulates the independent variable to determine its effect on the subjects' behavior (the dependent variable). This approach has also been called *univariate* because only one variable is studied at a time.

Cattell agreed that bivariate research is scientific, rigorous, and quantitative but argued that it dealt with only limited aspects of personality. In reality, personality is affected by many interacting variables. Also, in the typical artificial laboratory situation, significant emotional experiences cannot be manipulated and duplicated. Thus, for Cattell, the bivariate approach was too restrictive to reveal much about personality traits.

The Clinical Approach

The clinical approach, which includes case studies, dream analysis, free association, and similar techniques, is highly subjective, as noted in Chapters 2 and 5. These methods do not yield verifiable and quantifiable data. Cattell wrote, "The clinician has his heart in the right place, but perhaps we may say that he remains a little fuzzy in his head" (1959, p. 45).

The Multivariate Approach

Cattell chose to study personality through the multivariate approach, which yields highly specific data. It involves the sophisticated statistical procedure of factor analysis. Cattell favored two forms of factor analysis: the R technique and the P technique.

The R technique involves collecting large amounts of data from a group of people. Correlations among all the scores are made to determine personality factors or traits. The P technique involves collecting a large amount of data from a single subject over a long period.

A Sample of Research Findings

Let us consider a few of the hundreds of factor-analytic studies Cattell and his associates conducted, as well as more recent examples of research using Cattell's test. We noted that he was interested in the relative effects on personality of heredity and environment.

From a factor analysis of 16 PF Test data from 3,000 male subjects ages 12 to 18, Cattell (1982) concluded that three of the source traits were determined primarily by heredity. These source traits are Factor F (serious versus happy-go-lucky), Factor I (tough-minded versus tender-minded or sensitive), and Factor Q_3 (uncontrolled versus controlled). Three other traits were found to be determined primarily by environmental influences: Factor E (submissive versus dominant), Factor G (expedient versus conscientious), and Factor Q_4 (relaxed versus tense).

Cattell used the 16 PF Test to define the relationship between personality traits and marital stability (Cattell & Nesselroade, 1967). The subjects were married couples identified as having either a stable or an unstable marriage. The criterion for stability was whether a couple had taken steps toward dissolving the marriage.

Factor analysis showed that marital stability could be predicted from the test scores. Partners in stable marriages had similar personality traits, whereas partners in unstable marriages showed highly different personality traits.

It has also been found that the 16 PF Test, like other personality tests, can be distorted or faked. In one study, college students, prisoners, and substance abusers took the test twice. The first time they were asked to answer honestly, whereas the second time they were asked to answer in ways that would present them in a more favorable light. The results showed significant differences in the two sets of responses (Simon, 2007).

A study conducted in South Africa found that translation into the Tshivenda language changed the meanings of the test questions so much that the responses were invalid. As with other personality tests and some languages, a literal translation proved impossible (Van Eeden & Mantsha, 2007).

Research using the Greek version of the 16 PF Test (which had been translated satisfactorily) clearly distinguished the personality characteristics of Greek elementary and preschool teachers from the test norms for the population of Greece as a whole (Roussi-Vergou, Angelosopoulou, & Zafiropoulou, 2009; Roussi-Vergou & Zafiropoulou, 2011). A Turkish translation of the 16 PF Test has also been found to be valid measure of personality differences (Aksu, Sekercioglu, Ehtiyar, Yildiz, & Yimaz, 2010).

HIGHLIGHTS: Research on Cattell's Ideas

Studies have shown that the 16 PF Test:

- Can predict marital stability
- Can be faked if you want to present yourself in a more favorable light
- Can be used in many cultures, but for some languages a literal translation of the test items is not possible
- Yielded results indicating that some source traits are primarily inherited while others are determined primarily by environmental influences
- Can identify 16 source traits of personality
- Can be used for research, clinical diagnosis, and predicting success on the job

Reflections on Cattell's Theory

Despite Cattell's legitimate claim that factor analysis is an objective, precise technique, critics argue that the opportunity exists for subjectivity to affect the outcome. At several stages in the research process, decisions are required that may be influenced by personal preferences.

In the initial step of data collection, researchers must decide which tests to use and what aspects of behavior to measure. They must then determine which factor-analytic technique to apply and what level of statistical significance will be accepted as appropriate.

Once the factors, or traits, have been identified, the researcher labels them. If these names are ambiguous in any way, they may not accurately express the nature of the factors. This criticism does not suggest inherent weaknesses in Cattell's theory but that there is potential for subjective error in the factor-analytic approach. Perhaps it is this very subjectivity that accounts for the difficulty other researchers have in replicating Cattell's findings and confirming his 16 basic source traits.

Cattell understood his failure to persuade other psychologists of the wisdom of his views and defended his approach as the only one of value for studying personality. At the age of 85, he reiterated this point, criticizing contemporary psychologists for failing to master and apply factor analysis and lamenting that his work remained isolated from the mainstream of personality theorizing. He remained convinced that one day his work would allow for the prediction of human behavior with the same degree of accuracy with which astronomers predict the movements of planets (1974a, 1974b, 1990, 1993).

The consensus of current opinion among personality psychologists affirms Cattell's belief in the value of his approach. He is generally considered to be not only the father of the personality trait approach but also one of the 20th century's most influential psychologists (see Denis, 2009; Revelle, 2009; Tucker, 2009). Whatever the eventual outcome of Cattell's specific proposals, it is clear that the trait approach to personality and the investigation of genetic influences, which he initiated, continue to fascinate contemporary researchers, as we shall see throughout the rest of this chapter.

Behavioral Genetics

behavioral genetics
The study of the relationship between genetic or hereditary factors and personality traits.

We have mentioned the growing evidence to support the idea that some traits are influenced by hereditary factors. The area of study focusing on the connection between genetics and personality is often called **behavioral genetics**. Regardless of the method used to evaluate or investigate personality, a significant genetic component must be considered.

Allport and Cattell were among the first to suggest that inherited factors shape personality and that they rank in importance with environmental factors. Let us now consider other researchers who have pursued this causal connection between genetic inheritance and personality.

Hans Eysenck (1916–1997)

Resigned to Psychology

Hans Eysenck was born in Berlin, and immigrated to England in 1934, after Adolf Hitler came to power in Germany. Eysenck wanted to study physics at the University of London, but was told that he lacked the requisite academic background. Greatly discouraged, he asked university officials if there was any other science in which he could major.

Eysenck recalled, "I was told there was always psychology. 'What on earth is that?' I inquired in my ignorance. 'You'll like it,' they said. And so I enrolled in a subject whose scientific status was perhaps a little more questionable than my advisers realized" (1980, p. 156). More than 40 years later, the highly successful and productive Eysenck was asked if he had ever regretted his career choice. Often, he replied, but admitted that he was resigned to it.

A Prolific Record

Over the course of his career, Eysenck published amazing 79 books, including some for the general public, and an equally amazing 1,097 journal articles. At the time of his death, he was the world's most frequently cited psychologist (Farley, 2000). Unfortunately, when he died, his wife destroyed all of his personal and professional papers (Harris, 2011).

He developed several personality assessment devices including the Eysenck Personality Inventory, the Eysenck Personality Profiler, the Maudsley Medical Questionnaire, and the Maudsley Personality Inventory. His work has been pivotal in supporting the role of inheritance in personality and in integrating the scientific study of personality into psychology as a whole (see Corr, 2007; Revelle & Oehlberg, 2008; Rose, 2010).

The Dimensions of Personality

Eysenck spent most of his career at the University of London's Maudsley Hospital and Institute of Psychiatry, conducting research on the measurement of personality. He agreed with Cattell that personality is composed of traits, or factors, derived by the factor-analytic method. However, Eysenck was also a critic of factor analysis and of Cattell's research because of the potential subjectivity in the technique and the difficulty in replicating Cattell's findings. Although Eysenck used factor analysis to uncover personality traits, he supplemented the method with personality tests and experimental studies that considered a wide range of variables.

A Joint Effort

Eysenck and his second wife, Sybil (Ph.D., University of London), together developed many of the questionnaires used in their research (Furnham, Eysenck, & Saklofske, 2010). The Eysenck Personality Inventory (Eysenck & Eysenck, 1963) required 12 years of joint research and 20 factor analyses. Hans Eysenck wrote, "Although published in our joint names, [it] is largely a monument to her skill, patience, and endurance" (1980, p. 172). Few scientists in any discipline have been so straightforward in acknowledging the research contributions of their spouses.

Three Dimensions of Personality

The result of their efforts is a personality theory based on three dimensions, defined as combinations of traits or factors. We might think of the dimensions as *superfactors* (Eysenck, 1990a, 1990b; Eysenck & Eysenck, 1985). The three personality dimensions are:

E—Extraversion versus introversion

N—Neuroticism versus emotional stability

P—Psychoticism versus impulse control (or superego functioning)

Eysenck noted that the dimensions of extraversion and neuroticism have been recognized as basic elements of personality since the time of the ancient Greek philosophers. Eysenck (1997) also suggested that formulations of the same dimensions could be found on nearly every personality assessment device ever developed. The Eysenck Personality Inventory has since been used with great success in translated forms in nearly 40 countries, including those as diverse as Italy and Kuwait (see Abdel-Khalek, 2012; Dazzi, 2011).

Consider the list of personality traits associated with Eysenck's three personality dimensions (see Table 8.4). You can see clearly, for example, that people who score high on the traits of the E dimension would be classified as extraverts, whereas people who score low would be classified as introverts.

TABLE 8.4   Traits of Eysenck's personality dimensions

EXTRAVERSION/ INTROVERSION	NEUROTICISM/EMOTIONAL STABILITY	PSYCHOTICISM/IMPULSE CONTROL
Sociable	Anxious	Aggressive
Lively	Depressed	Cold
Active	Guilt feelings	Egocentric
Assertive	Low self-esteem	Impersonal
Sensation seeking	Tense	Impulsive
Carefree	Irrational	Antisocial
Dominant	Shy	Creative
Venturesome	Moody	Tough-minded

Stability over Time

The traits and dimensions Eysenck proposed tend to remain stable throughout the life span despite our different social and environmental experiences. Our situations may change but the dimensions remain consistent. For instance, the introverted child tends to remain introverted through adolescence and into adulthood (see Ganiban, Saudino, Ulbricht, Neiderhiser, & Reiss, 2008). Other studies in England and the Scandinavian countries confirm the stability over time of Eysenck's dimensions, particularly extraversion and neuroticism (Billstedt et al., 2014; Gale, Booth, Mottus, Kuh, & Deary, 2013).

The Role of Intelligence

Eysenck also conducted considerable research on intelligence. Although he did not list intelligence as a personality dimension, he considered it an important influence on personality. He noted that a person with an IQ of 120, which is high, is likely to have a more complex and multidimensional personality than a person with an IQ of 80. His research also suggested that some 80 percent of our intelligence is inherited, leaving only 20 percent as the product of social and environmental forces (Eysenck & Eysenck, 1985).

Hans Eysenck

Various sites provide biographical information, discussions of his theory, research on relevant concepts, and links to other resources.

Extraversion

Based on your own experience, you can probably describe most extraverts and introverts pretty accurately. Extraverts are oriented toward the outside world, prefer the company of other people, and tend to be sociable, impulsive, adventurous, assertive, and dominant.

In addition, people who score high in extraversion on the Eysenck Personality Inventory have been found to experience more pleasant emotions and to be happier than those who score low in extraversion (Fisher & Francis, 2013; Holder & Klassen, 2010; Lucas & Fujita, 2000). Extraverted businessmen have been shown to be much better at performing difficult tasks than introverted businessmen (Campbell, Alana, Davalos, McCabe, & Troup, 2011).

Eysenck was interested in how extraverts and introverts might differ biologically and genetically. He found that extraverts have a lower base level of cortical arousal than introverts do. Because the cortical arousal levels for extraverts are low, they need, and actively seek, excitement and stimulation. In contrast, introverts shy away from excitement and stimulation because their cortical arousal levels are already high (Eysenck, 1990b).

As a result, introverts react more strongly than extraverts to sensory stimulation. Studies have shown that introverts exhibit greater sensitivity to low-level stimuli and have lower pain thresholds than extraverts. Other research supports differential responses to sensory stimulation but reports less convincing evidence that such differences can be attributed to variations in cortical arousal levels (Bullock & Gilliland, 1993; Hagemann & Naumann, 2009; Stelmack, 1997). Nevertheless, as Eysenck predicted, these differences are genetically based.

Neuroticism

As you can see in Table 8.4, neurotics are characterized as anxious, depressed, tense, irrational, and moody. They may also have low self-esteem and be prone to guilt feelings.

Eysenck suggested that neuroticism is largely inherited, a product of genetics rather than learning or experience.

Research on 16- to 70-year-old Americans conducted over a 2-year period showed that increasing satisfaction gained from work and social relationships was associated with a lower level of neuroticism and a higher level of extraversion (Scollon & Diener, 2006). Studies in Australia found that people who scored high in neuroticism on the Eysenck Personality Inventory outperformed those who scored low when their work environment was fast-paced and stressful. In other words, neurotics seem to function best in busy situations where they were forced to work harder (Smillie, Yeo, Furnham, & Jackson, 2006).

A study in England showed that people high in neuroticism scored lower in verbal abilities than did people low in neuroticism (Chamorro-Premuzic, Furnham, & Petrides, 2006). And research on people in Sweden found that those who scored high in neuroticism in middle age were much more likely to show cognitive impairments when tested again 25 years later (Crowe, Andel, Pedersen, Fratiglioni, & Gatz, 2006).

People high in neuroticism have greater activity in the brain areas that control the sympathetic branch of the autonomic nervous system. This is the body's alarm system, which responds to stressful or dangerous events by increasing breathing rate, heart rate, blood flow to the muscles, and release of adrenaline. Eysenck argued that in neurotics, the sympathetic nervous system overreacts even to mild stressors, resulting in chronic hypersensitivity.

This condition leads to heightened emotionality in response to almost any difficult situation. Indeed, neurotics react emotionally to events other people consider insignificant. According to Eysenck, these differences in biological reactivity on the neuroticism dimension are innate. People are genetically predisposed either toward neuroticism or toward emotional stability.

Psychoticism

People who score high in psychoticism are aggressive, antisocial, tough-minded, cold, and egocentric. Also, they have been found to be cruel, hostile, and insensitive to the needs and feelings of others. In addition, they score low on emotional well-being and have greater problems with alcohol, drug abuse, and violent criminal behavior than people who score low in psychoticism (Boduszek, Shevlin, Adamson, & Hyland, 2013; Ciarrochi & Heaven, 2007; Sher, Bartholow, & Wood, 2000).

Paradoxically, people who score high in psychoticism can also be highly creative. The research evidence tends to suggest a large genetic component. However, it has also been found that those who scored high in psychoticism had more authoritarian and controlling parents than those who scored low, thus supporting the potentially harmful influence of the childhood environment (Heaven & Ciarrochi, 2006).

Men generally tend to score higher on psychoticism than women, which led Eysenck to suggest that psychoticism may be related to male hormones. He also speculated that people who score high on all three dimensions may be apt to display criminal behavior but cited only modest empirical support for this idea (Eysenck & Gudjonsson, 1989). Research conducted in China has demonstrated a significant positive correlation between criminal behavior and high scores on both the psychoticism and neuroticism dimensions (Huo-Liang, 2006).

Eysenck believed that society needs the diversity provided by people characterized by all aspects of these three personality dimensions. An ideal society affords people the opportunity to make the best use of their traits and abilities. However, some people will adapt to the social environment better than others will.

The person high in psychoticism, for example, typified by hostile and aggressive behaviors, may become emotionally disturbed, or exhibit criminal tendencies, or channel the aggressive traits into a socially acceptable enterprise such as coaching college football.

The Primary Role of Heredity

To Eysenck, traits and dimensions are determined primarily by heredity, although the research evidence shows a stronger genetic component for extraversion and neuroticism than for psychoticism. Eysenck did not rule out environmental and situational influences on personality, such as family interactions in childhood, but he believed their effects on personality were limited (Eysenck, 1990a).

His research design involved comparisons of identical (monozygotic) and fraternal (dizygotic) twins. The studies showed that identical twins are more alike in their personalities than are fraternal twins, even when the identical twins were reared by different parents in different environments during childhood. Studies of adopted children demonstrate that their personalities bear a greater similarity to the personalities of their biological parents than of their adoptive parents, even when the children had no contact with their biological parents. This is additional support for Eysenck's idea that personality owes more to our genetic inheritance than to our environment.

Cross-cultural research demonstrates that Eysenck's three personality dimensions have been found consistently in more than 35 nations including the United States, England, Australia, Japan, China, Nigeria, and Sweden (see, for example, Bouchard, 1985; Eaves, Eysenck, & Martin, 1989; Floderus-Myrhed, Pedersen, & Rasmuson, 1980; Hur, 2009; Martin & Jardine, 1986; Tellegen, Lykken, Bouchard, Wilcox, Segal, & Rich, 1988). The confirmation of the same three personality dimensions in diverse cultures is further evidence for the primacy of inherited factors in the shaping of personality.

HIGHLIGHTS: Research on Eysenck's Ideas

Research on Eysenck's three dimensions of personality shows that:

- Extraverts experience more pleasant emotions
- Extraverts have lower base levels of cortical arousal
- Neurotics have low self-esteem and high guilt feelings
- Neurotics function well in fast-paced, stressful jobs
- Neurotics score lower in verbal ability
- Psychotics can be cruel, hostile, and insensitive
- Psychotics have more problems with alcohol and drug abuse
- Psychotics are aggressive, antisocial, and egocentric
- All three personality dimensions are determined primarily by heredity

---

Robert McCrae and Paul Costa: The Five-Factor Model

Using the factor-analytic method, the personality traits Cattell and Eysenck derived varied in number. This does not indicate an inherent weakness in the method but instead reflects the way each theorist chose to measure personality. Some more recent personality researchers have expressed dissatisfaction with both theories, suggesting that Eysenck had too few dimensions (three) and Cattell had too many factors (sixteen).

Working at the Gerontology Research Center of the National Institutes of Health in Baltimore, Maryland, Robert McCrae (1949–) and Paul Costa (1942–) embarked on an extensive research program starting in the 1980s that identified five so-called robust or Big Five factors (McCrae & Costa, 1985b, 1987). These factors are neuroticism, extraversion, openness, agreeableness, and conscientiousness. More than 25 years and hundreds of studies later, one of the originators of the five-factor model accurately described it as marking "a turning point in the history of personality psychology" (McCrae, 2011, p. 210).

Measuring the Five Factors

The factors were confirmed through a variety of assessment techniques including self-ratings, objective tests, and observers' reports. McCrae and Costa then developed a personality test, the NEO Personality Inventory, using an acronym derived from the initials of the first three factors. The test is available in a number of revised forms.

A shorter version has been developed for research use on the Internet (Buchanan, Johnson, & Goldberg, 2005). The consistent finding of the same factors from different assessment procedures suggests that these factors can be relied on as distinguishing aspects of personality. The five factors and their characteristic traits are listed in Table 8.5.

Other researchers, following the lead provided by McCrae and Costa, developed adjective checklists that have proven to be quicker measures of the five factors. Research subjects typically respond to the lists by selecting the words that best describe themselves. One such list uses 100 adjectives to measure the five factors; another uses only 40.

It is important to note that even though other tests have been proposed as ways to measure the Big Five factors, the NEO remains the most frequently used technique. However, research has shown that the results of the NEO, like all self-report inventories, can be distorted by the deliberate behavior of subjects who want to create the impression of positive psychological adjustment.

Origin and Overlap of Factors

Studies of twins have found that four of the five factors show a stronger hereditary component: neuroticism, extraversion, openness, and conscientiousness. Agreeableness was found to have a stronger environmental component (Bergeman et al., 1993; Pedersen, Plomin, McClearn, & Friberg, 1988).

There is a similarity between the extraversion and neuroticism factors of McCrae and Costa and the extraversion and neuroticism dimensions proposed by Eysenck. Further, agreeableness and conscientiousness in the McCraeCosta model may represent the low

TABLE 8.5   McCrae and Costa's Big Five personality factors

FACTOR	DESCRIPTION
Neuroticism	Worried, insecure, nervous, highly strung
Extraversion	Sociable, talkative, fun-loving, affectionate
Openness	Original, independent, creative, daring
Agreeableness	Good-natured, softhearted, trusting, courteous
Conscientiousness	Careful, reliable, hardworking, organized

end of Eysenck's psychoticism dimension (impulse control). Openness shows a high positive correlation with intelligence. Similarly, agreeableness correlates with Adler's concept of social interest, which we discussed in Chapter 4.

Cross-Cultural Consistency

The five factors have been consistently observed in Eastern as well as Western cultures, a finding that also supports a genetic component. McCrae and Costa noted that the Big Five factors and their traits appear to represent a "common human structure of personality" that transcends cultural differences (1997, p. 515).

These five factors and their traits have been found in more than 50 diverse nations including Britain, Germany, Portugal, the Czech Republic, Turkey, Israel, China, Korea, Japan, France, the Philippines, Russia, India, Denmark, Italy, Lebanon, Canada, and Romania, and among both native-born and Hispanic residents of the United States (see Allik, Realo, Mottus, Pullmann, Trifonova, & McCrae, 2009; Heine & Buchtel, 2009; Ispas, Iliescu, Llie, & Johnson, 2014).

It is important to note that those countries in which the five factors have been measured tend to be urban, literate, well-educated societies. No evidence of the five factors was found in an extensive study of a small, isolated, largely illiterate tribal group residing in a remote area of Bolivia (Gurven, von Rueden, Massenkoff, Kaplan, & Lero Vie, 2013).

The Relative Value of the Factors in Different Cultures

Although the same factors are common to virtually all urban cultures, major differences have been recognized in their relative importance and social desirability from one culture to another. For example, Australians consider extraversion and agreeableness to be more desirable to have than the other three factors.

By contrast, Japanese consider conscientiousness to be more important than all other factors. In other words, in Japanese society it is more important for a person to be conscientious than to be extraverted, agreeable, open, or even emotionally stable.

In Hong Kong and in India, agreeableness was found to be the most important factor. In Singapore, emotional stability was more important, whereas in Venezuela, the primary characteristic to praise is extraversion.

No single factor was found to be more significant than others in Chile, Finland, Germany, the Netherlands, Norway, Turkey, and the United States. Overall, Europeans and Americans tended to score higher in extraversion and openness to experience and lower in agreeableness than did Asians and Africans (Allik & McCrae, 2004; McCrae & Terracciano, 2005).

Gender Differences

There seem to be consistent sex differences in the five factors. Research carried out in 55 countries, both Eastern and Western, found that women reported higher levels of neuroticism, extraversion, agreeableness, and conscientiousness than men. These differences were most pronounced in prosperous and egalitarian nations where women had greater opportunity for education and employment (Schmitt, Realo, Voracek, & Allik, 2008).

How People View Themselves and Others

There appears to be a consistency across cultures in how people view their own personalities and those of others. People tend to see themselves as being more neurotic and open to experience than others see them. They also tend to see others as higher in conscientiousness than they believe themselves to be (Allik, Realo, Mottus, Borkenau, Kuppens, & Hrebickova, 2010).

Stability of the Factors over Time

There are a large number of studies dealing with the stability of the five factors over time, some of which may appear to offer contradictory findings. Note carefully how the results may vary by country and, most important, by the range of ages included in these studies. Some cover longer time periods then others.

The five factors have been found in children as well as adults. Longitudinal research studying the same people over a 6-year period demonstrated a high level of stability for all five traits (Costa & McCrae, 1988). Those high in agreeableness as children were likely to remain so as adults. A study in Finland of twins ages 18 to 59 found a high degree of stability for both men and women on extraversion and neuroticism over that 40-year age span (Viken, Rose, Kaprio, & Koskenvuo, 1994).

A study of American men and women from late adolescence into adulthood, found modest but statistically significant stability for the extraversion and neuroticism factors (Carmichael & McGue, 1994). A comparison of American and Belgian adolescents over a 4-year period showed that the factors of extraversion, agreeableness, and conscientiousness remained stable, whereas openness to experience increased for both males and females during those 4 years (McCrae et al., 2002).

Men and women college graduates were tested for extraversion when they were students and again 20 years later. The researchers found a significant positive correlation between the test scores at the two ages, suggesting that those who were extraverted in college remained so at midlife. The study also showed that those who scored high in extraversion were, as expected, more sociable and outgoing than those who scored low (Von Dras & Siegler, 1997).

Another large-scale study comparing measures taken 40 years apart from adults in the United States found that the factors of extraversion and conscientiousness remained the most stable over the duration of the research period (Hampson & Goldberg, 2006).

Changes in personality over a shorter time period, from adolescence to adulthood, as studied in the Czech Republic and in Russia, showed that neuroticism, extraversion, and openness to experience declined during those years, whereas agreeableness and conscientiousness rose (McCrae et al., 2004a, 2004b). Research on adults in Germany in their 40s and then again in their 60s showed that neuroticism declined from the earlier decade to the later one (Allemand, Zimprich, & Hertzog, 2007).

A large-scale research review showed that neuroticism, extraversion, and openness appeared to decrease as people reached their 60s, whereas agreeableness and conscientiousness seem to increase with age (Debast et al., 2014).

Predicting Changes over Time

Preschool teachers were asked to predict what their 3- to 6-year-old students would be like in 20 years. Their expectations, based on observations of the children's behavior, corresponded with the students' scores on the Big Five personality factors. These results suggest that the teachers assumed that preschool behavior would be closely related to adult behavior (Graziano, Jensen-Campbell, & Sullivan-Logan, 1998).

This raises the question of whether such expectations might lead teachers and parents to reinforce certain behaviors to strengthen genetically based personality characteristics. Do parents and teachers treat extraverted children differently from introverted children, for example, in ways that would strengthen each group's differential inherited behavioral tendencies?

> ## HIGHLIGHTS: Research on McCrae and Costa's Ideas
>
> Research on the five factors of personality shows that:
>
> - Neuroticism, extraversion, openness, and conscientiousness have a strong hereditary component
> - The factor of agreeableness has a strong environmental component
> - All five factors have been found in diverse cultures
> - Most of the factors remain stable to some degree over the life span
> - Women report higher levels of neuroticism, extraversion, agreeableness, and conscientiousness than men
> - We tend to see others as being more conscientious and less neurotic than ourselves

Emotional Correlates

Emotional well-being and happiness In a number of studies, extraversion was positively related to emotional well-being (see, for example, Heller, Watson, & Hies, 2004; Lischetzke & Eid, 2006). Neuroticism has been negatively related to emotional well-being. Researchers have concluded that people high in extraversion and low in neuroticism were genetically predisposed to emotional stability (Costa & McCrae, 1984; Watson, Clark, McIntyre, & Hamaker, 1992).

A study of men and women college students found that those scoring high in extraversion were able to cope with everyday life stress better than those scoring low in extraversion. Extraverts were also more likely to seek social support to help them deal with stress (Amirkhan, Risinger, & Swickert, 1995). It has also been found that the depression facet of neuroticism and the positive emotions/cheerfulness facet of extraversion are the most consistent predictors of general life satisfaction and emotional well-being (Schimmack, Oishi, Furr, & Funder, 2004).

Other studies of teenagers conducted in the United States, Brazil, and Italy confirmed that extraversion was related to happiness, optimism, and life satisfaction. Openness to new experiences, conscientiousness, and low scores on neuroticism were also involved in having positive feelings (Bassi, Steca, Monzani, & Fave, 2014; Suldo, Minch, & Hearon, 2014; Zanon, Bastianello, Pacico, & Huiz, 2014).

In another study, persons high in agreeableness and conscientiousness showed greater emotional well-being than persons low in these traits (McCrae & Costa, 1991). People high in the agreeableness factor were also found to be cooperative, helpful, altruistic, honest, and selfless (Digman, 1990; John, 1990). A study of workers in China found that the factors of extraversion, conscientiousness, and low neuroticism were related to subjective well-being (Zhai, Willis, O'Shea, Zhai, & Yang, 2013).

Psychological distress has been associated with high scores on the neuroticism factor (DeRaad, 2000; Larsen & Kasimatis, 1991; Ormel & Wohlfarth, 1991). People high in neuroticism have been found to be prone to depression, anxiety, substance abuse, and self-blame (Jorm, 1987; Kotov, Gamez, Schmidt, & Watson, 2010; Parkes, 1986).

A large-scale study in Germany found that those who scored high on neuroticism and openness had a greater risk for suicide. Those with the lowest risk were high in extraversion and conscientiousness (Bluml, Kapusta, Doering, Brahler, Wagner, & Kersting, 2013).

Popularity and Success   Studies of college students in the United States found that those who scored high in extraversion enjoyed higher status and prominence among their peers than those who scored low in extraversion (Anderson, John, Keltner, & Kring, 2001). Those high in extraversion rated social situations as positive only if the situation was pleasant, indicating the importance of positive emotions in the factor of extraversion (Lucas & Diener, 2001).

A study of fifth- to eighth-grade students showed that those high in conscientiousness were more likely to be accepted by their peers, to have more and better quality friendships, and to be less likely to be the target of aggression than those low in conscientiousness (Jensen-Campbell & Malcolm, 2007).

Other research with college students found that over a 4-year period, extraverts were likely to experience a greater number of positive events, such as a good grade, a pay raise, or marriage. Students scoring high in neuroticism were more predisposed to negative events such as illness, weight gain, traffic tickets, or rejection by graduate school (Magnus, Diener, Fujita, & Pavot, 1993). Research on adults in the United States, ages 25 to 74, found that everyday life stressors had significantly higher negative emotional effects for the people who scored high in neuroticism (Mroczek & Almeida, 2004).

A study in Sweden of identical and fraternal twins reared together and apart confirmed the relationship for women between personality variables and desirable life events. Women who scored high in extraversion and openness to experience were significantly more likely to experience positive life events. Women who scored high in neuroticism were significantly more likely to experience negative life events (Saudino, Pedersen, Lichtenstein, McClearn, & Plomin, 1997).

Teenagers in the Netherlands who scored high in extraversion, emotional stability, and agreeableness were judged by their classmates to be more popular and likeable (Van der Linden, Scholte, Cillessen, Nijenhuis, & Segers, 2010). Research in the United States found that people high in extraversion and agreeableness were rated by others as physically more attractive than those low in extraversion and agreeableness (Meier, Robinson, Carter, & Hinsz, 2010).

Behavioral Correlates

Personal characteristics   People high in openness tend to have a wide range of intellectual interests and to seek challenges. They are more likely to change jobs, try different careers, and expect more varied life experiences than people scoring low in openness (McCrae & Costa, 1985a, 1985b). Those high in both openness and extraversion are more likely to be self-employed. Extraverts are also likely to be more active during their retirement years and more satisfied with retirement (Lockenhoff, Terracciano, & Costa, 2009; Robinson, Demetre, & Corney, 2010; Shane, Nicolaou, Cherkas, & Spector, 2010).

Not surprisingly, people high in conscientiousness tend to be reliable, responsible, punctual, efficient, and dependable, and usually earn better grades in school than people low in conscientiousness (Back, Schmukle, & Egloff, 2006; Chowdhury & Amin, 2006; Wagerman & Funder, 2007). A study of British university students found that those high in conscientiousness were more organized, self-disciplined, and achievement oriented in terms of planning for future goals (Conner & Abraham, 2001).

In other research, the factors of agreeableness, conscientiousness, and openness correlated positively with academic performance in college. Those high in all three got better grades (Poropat, 2009). Other research found that those high in those three factors were also rated as better parents and better at coping with stress (Carver & Connor-Smith, 2010; Prinzie, Stams, Dekovic, Reijntjes, & Belsky, 2009).

In research conducted in the workplace, it was found that people who scored high in conscientiousness were more likely than low scorers to set high goals for themselves and strive to achieve them, to initiate desirable work behaviors, and to receive high performance ratings. The conscientiousness factor was also shown to be a valid predictor of job performance for professional, police, managerial, sales, and skilled labor jobs (Barrick & Mount, 1996; Barrick, Mount, & Strauss, 1993; Stewart, Carson, & Cardy, 1996).

Physical health   Research indicates that high scorers in conscientiousness are likely to be healthier and live longer (Friedman & Martin, 2011). A study of adult smokers showed that those who were more conscientious were less likely to smoke at home than those who were less conscientious. This suggests that the conscientious smokers were more aware of the health risks of smoking indoors (both to themselves and to others living with them) and acted to reduce those risks (Hampson, Andrews, Barckley, Lichtenstein, & Lee, 2000).

American college students high in conscientiousness are more likely to wear seat belts, exercise, get sufficient sleep, and eat more fruits and vegetables than those low in conscientiousness (Raynor & Levine, 2009).

Research on adolescents and young adults who had been diagnosed with diabetes showed that those who scored higher in conscientiousness sought more information about managing their condition and were more diligent about self-care than those who scored lower in conscientiousness (Skinner, Hampson, & Fife-Schau, 2002).

British university students who were more conscientious were far less likely to display hypochondriacal complaints (that is, to believe they were sick) than those who were less conscientious (Ferguson, 2000). And a telephone survey of American adults showed that those who scored higher in conscientiousness took greater responsibility for engaging in healthy behaviors than did those who scored lower in conscientiousness (Tucker, Elliott, & Klein, 2006).

Research on people diagnosed with attention deficit/hyperactivity disorder found that symptoms such as hyperactivity, impulsivity, inattention, and cognitive and behavioral disorganization were significantly lower in those who scored higher in agreeableness than those who scored lower in agreeableness (Nigg et al., 2002).

A study of male and female patients with chronic renal insufficiency (a kidney disorder), conducted over a 4-year period, found that those who scored higher in neuroticism on the NEO had a mortality rate 37.5 percent higher than those who scored lower in neuroticism (Christensen et al., 2002).

More contradictory findings relate to neuroticism. Although high neuroticism predicted reduced physical health and subjective well-being in old age, it was also associated with greater longevity. This suggests that neurotics may live longer but are not happy about it and have more health problems (Eysenck, 2009; Friedman, Kern, & Reynolds, 2010). Those who score high in neuroticism appear to show fewer declines in cognitive functioning of the type associated with dementia in old age (Williams, Suchy, & Kraybill, 2010).

Two large-scale studies of Americans found that higher extraversion was linked to an increased risk for stroke (cerebrovascular accidents). In addition, high conscientiousness was associated with a lower risk of death from both stroke and coronary heart disease. Those scoring high in neuroticism were found to be more likely to have heart disease (Jokela, Pulkki-Raback, Elovainio, & Kivmaki, 2014; Lee, Offidani, Ziegelstein, Bienvenu, Samuels, Eaton, & Nestadt, 2014).

Two characteristics related to health—weight and sleep—may also be affected by personality type. Research in Australia and in Finland showed that those who scored high in extraversion, agreeableness, and conscientiousness got more and better quality sleep, whereas those high in neuroticism reported worse sleep (Hintsanen et al., 2014).

A study in Korea found that men who were classified as overweight to obese scored high on openness to new experiences and low on conscientiousness. Overweight women scored low on neuroticism and openness to new experiences (Shim et al., 2014).

Addictive and criminal behavior   A study of adults showed that those who scored low in conscientiousness and agreeableness were far more likely to be heavy users of alcohol or illegal drugs than were those who scored high in these factors (Walton & Roberts, 2004). Among members of sexual minorities (gays, lesbians, and transgendered persons), those high in extraversion and conscientiousness were likely to show high levels of drug and alcohol use (Livingston, Oost, Heck, & Cochran, 2014).

A study of young adults found that those who scored high in neuroticism and openness to new experiences were more likely to use prescription drugs that had not been prescribed for them (Benotsch, Jefers, Snipes, Martin, & Koester, 2013).

A 25-year study of residents of Finland found that those high in agreeableness reported less alcoholism and lower levels of depression, had lower arrest records, and showed greater career stability than those low in agreeableness (Laursen, Pulkkinen, & Adams, 2002). A study of adolescents in Ireland found that the factors of agreeableness, conscientiousness, neuroticism, and extraversion were linked to criminal behavior (O'Riordan & O'Connell, 2014).

Among college students in Norway, it was found that neuroticism was linked to Internet addiction, exercise addiction, compulsive buying, and study addiction. Extraversion was linked to being addicted to Facebook and smartphone usage as well as exercise addiction and compulsive buying (Andreassen, Griffiths, Gjertsen, Krossbakken, Kvam, & Pallesen, 2013).

Social relationships   An 18-month study of university students in Germany from the beginning of their first year of college found significant effects of three of the Big Five personality factors on the students' social relationships. Students scoring high in extraversion made more friends during the 18-month period and were more likely to fall in love than students scoring low in extraversion. Those high in agreeableness experienced less conflict with acquaintances of the opposite sex, and those high in conscientiousness were more likely to maintain contact with their parents and siblings. The factor of openness showed no significant effect on social relationships (Asendorpf & Wilpers, 1998).

A study of high school graduates in Germany found that those who stayed living with their parents scored low on openness to new experiences. Those who chose to live with roommates showed increases in openness, whereas those who chose to live with a romantic partner showed increases in conscientiousness (Jonkmann, Thoemmes, Ludtke, & Trautwein, 2013).

A study of couples in the Netherlands showed that low scores in neuroticism and high scores in extraversion for both partners was related to marital happiness (Barelds, 2005). Research on newlywed couples in the United States showed that self-ratings of agreeableness and conscientiousness increased significantly and self-ratings in neuroticism decreased significantly over the first two years of the marriage.

Ratings of each person made by their spouses were different, however. Those showed significant decreases in conscientiousness, agreeableness, extraversion, and openness over the 2-year period (Watson & Humrichouse, 2006). In other words, the adults believed they were becoming better people during the two years they had been married but their spouses did not agree.

When American college students were asked to rate the importance they placed on a variety of life goals—for example, marriage, fun-filled activities, and the serious pursuit of a career—it was found that those who desired higher economic, social, and political status scored high in extraversion and low in agreeableness (Roberts & Robins, 2000).

The five-factor model pinpointed differences between so-called dog people and cat people. Those who prefer dogs score higher in extraversion, agreeableness, and conscientiousness but lower in neuroticism and openness than those who prefer cats (Gosling, Sandy, & Potter, 2010).

Comment   The evidence is clear from studies of a wide range of emotions and behaviors that the five-factor model of personality has a high predictive value. Most research uses the five factors as self-contained entities and not the individual traits of which they are composed (see Table 8.5).

Research comparing the predictive value of the five factors and of the traits found that higher level factors and lower level traits have high predictive validities but that validities of the traits were higher than those of the factors (Paunonen, 1998; Paunonen & Ashton, 2001).

McCrae and Costa's findings have been replicated and continue to inspire considerable research. They provided an intriguing and well-supported approach to personality and to our understanding of the relative importance of heredity and environment. However, as you might suspect, not all psychologists agree that these are the only factors that make up our personalities.

HIGHLIGHTS: Research on the Five Factors

People who score high in extraversion tend to:

- Be high in emotional stability and life satisfaction
- Be better able to cope with everyday stress
- Get high grades
- Enjoy high status and prominence in college

People who score high in conscientiousness are likely to:

- Be reliable, efficient, and punctual
- Get better grades
- Be well-organized and disciplined
- Set high personal goals
- Be accepted by their peers and have more friends
- Be healthier and live longer
- Wear seat belts, exercise, get enough sleep, and eat more fruits and vegetables

People who score high in conscientiousness, agreeableness, openness, and extraversion are likely to:

- Be popular and judged more attractive
- Get good grades
- Cope well with stress
- Be good parents
- Prefer dogs over cats

Michael Ashton and Kibeom Lee: HEXACO: The Six-Factor Model

Michael Ashton, of the Psychology Department at Brock University in St. Catherine's, Ontario, Canada, and Kibeom Lee, of the Psychology Department at the University of Calgary, Alberta, Canada, have proposed a six-factor model of personality (2007, 2009). Two of the factors—extraversion and conscientiousness—are similar to those found in the five-factor model; the other four differ in various degrees from the earlier work and are unique to this model of personality (Ashton & Lee, 2008; Shepherd & Belicki, 2008). The six factors or dimensions of the HEXACO (an acronym derived from the factors) model are listed in Table 8.6.

Assessing the Six Factors

The dimensions of this six-factor model can be assessed by two self-report inventories: the 100-item HEXACO Personality Inventory, Revised, or the 60-item HEXACO-60. Both have been shown to be valid and reliable tests (Ashton & Lee, 2009). The factors have been documented in several different cultures including Dutch, French, German, Hungarian, Italian, Korean, Polish, Greek, Croatian, Turkish, and Filipino (Ashton et al., 2006; Ashton et al., 2004; DeRaad & Barelds, 2008).

Research is ongoing to determine the behavioral and emotional correlates of the six-factor model. For example, in a study of adults in Italy, a high score on the HEXACO factor of conscientiousness was linked to the tendency to vote for right-wing political parties, whereas people who tended to vote for left-wing political parties scored higher in honesty, agreeableness, and openness (Chirumbolo & Leone, 2010).

Research with college students in New Zealand found that those low in openness to experience and emotionality scored high in right-wing authoritarianism and prejudice toward dissident groups (Sibley, Harding, Perry, Asbrock, & Duckitt, 2010).

A study of employed Americans found that those who scored high in honesty/humility received higher job performance ratings than those who scored low (Johnson, Rowatt, & Petrini, 2011). Research in Egypt found that high scores on the honesty/humility factor correlated with stronger religious feelings but not with happiness (Aghababaei, 2012;

TABLE 8.6   Six personality factors of the HEXACO model

FACTOR	DESCRIPTION
Honesty/humility	Sincere, honest, faithful VERSUS greedy, pretentious, hypocritical, boastful
Emotionality	Emotional, oversensitive, faithful, anxious VERSUS brave, tough, self-assured, stable
Extraversion	Outgoing, lively, sociable, cheerful VERSUS shy, passive, withdrawn, reserved
Agreeableness	Tolerant, peaceful, gentle, agreeable VERSUS quarrelsome, stubborn, and ill-tempered
Conscientiousness	Disciplined, diligent, thorough, precise VERSUS reckless, lazy, irresponsible, absent-minded
Openness to experience	Creative, innovative, unconventional VERSUS shallow, conventional, unimaginative

Source: Hexaco Personality Inventory—Revised. © 2007. Used by kind permission of Michael C. Ashton and Kibeom Lee.

Aghababaei & Arji, 2014). Among college students in Portugal, the honesty/humility factor did correlate with happiness (Oliveira, 2013). Adult delinquents in England and those convicted of crimes in Australia scored low on honesty/humility and high on Eysenck's psychoticism dimension (Dunlop, Morrison, Loenig, & Silcox, 2012; Rollison, Hanoch, & Gummerum, 2013).

Delroy Paulhus and Kevin Williams: The Dark Triad of Personality

Paulhus and Williams, of the University of British Columbia, Vancouver, Canada, introduced a three-factor approach to understanding the darker side of personality, which includes the following traits (2002):

- Narcissism: extreme selfishness, an inflated sense of one's abilities and talents, and the constant need for admiration and attention.
- Machiavellianism: the need to manipulate others, characterized by cunning, deceit, and unscrupulous behaviors.
- Psychopathy: callous, insensitive, egocentric, antisocial, takes advantage of other people, using great charm and often violence.

Assessing the Dark Triad

You can get a better idea of what people exhibiting these characteristics are like by considering the items in the so-called Dirty Dozen Scale, a self-rating test developed as a quick way of assessing the Dark Triad (Jonason & Webster, 2010, p. 429). How would you rate yourself on these items?

- I tend to manipulate others to get my way.
- I have used deceit or lied to get my way.
- I have used flattery to get my way.
- I tend to exploit others toward my own end.
- I tend to lack remorse.
- I tend to be unconcerned with the morality of my actions.
- I tend to be callous or insensitive.
- I tend to be cynical.
- I tend to want others to admire me.
- I want others to pay attention to me.
- I tend to seek prestige or status.
- I tend to expect special favors from others.

Behavioral Correlates

Studies have found that those who scored high on all three traits engaged in more antisocial activities than those who scored low. They also derived greater satisfaction from the misfortune of others (James, Kavanagh, Jonason, Chonody, & Scrutton, 2014; Porter, Bhanwer, Woodworth, & Black, 2014).

They were given to strong acts of self-promotion and tended to be cold, duplicitous, and aggressive (Paulhus & Webster, 2010). Another study found that the verbal content of subjects' Facebook updates was a valid predictor of their levels of psychopathy and narcissism. Their updates tended to be emotionally cold, aggressive, and highly self-promoting (Garcia & Silkstrom, 2014).

Those who scored high in machiavellianism and psychopathy also scored low on the Big Five factors on conscientiousness, agreeableness, and openness. In addition, they showed little empathy or consideration for others, a high level of aggression, a vengeful and unforgiving attitude, and low scores on emotional stability (Giammarco & Vernon, 2014; Muris, Meesters, & Timmermans, 2013; Oliveira, 2013).

The Dark Triad is also associated with short-term exploitative sexual relationships. Psychopathy is linked to a high sex drive with strong sexual and sadomasochistic themes and fantasies. People who scored high in psychopathy and narcissism engaged in a number of short-term sexual relationships with no intention of commitment (Adams, Luevano, & Jonason, 2014; Baughman, Jonason, Veselka, & Vernon, 2014).

Personality Traits and the Internet

We saw in Chapter 1 that the Internet, particularly social networking sites, can influence as well as reflect our personality. Much research is being done to determine how the traits discussed in this chapter influence Internet use.

Eysenck's Personality Dimensions

A study of college students in Germany found that becoming addicted to Internet use is greater among those who score high in neuroticism and are excessively focused on themselves (Montag, Jurkiewicz, & Reuter, 2010). Research on college students in Turkey found that those scoring high on Eysenck's trait of psychoticism relied on the Internet as a substitute for face-to-face social interaction. Often their friendships were only maintained via the Internet (Tosun & Lajunen, 2010).

Five-Factor Model

- In Israel, people who scored high in conscientiousness had more Facebook friends than those who scored low. Those in the highly neurotic group posted more of their photos on Facebook than those who scored low in neuroticism (Amichai-Hamburger & Vinitzky, 2010).
- In Finland, those who scored high in extraversion had more Facebook friends than those who scored low (Lonnqvist, Itkonen, Verkasaio, & Poutvaara, 2014).
- In the Netherlands, high Internet use bordering on the compulsive and addictive was greatest among introverted, disagreeable, and emotionally less stable and lonely adolescents (Van der Aa, Overbeek, Engels, Scholte, Meerkerk, & Van den Eijnden, 2009).
- In Germany, addiction to video gaming was highest among those high in neuroticism and low in conscientiousness and extraversion (Muller, Beutel, Egloff, & Wolfling, 2014).
- In the United States and in Germany, college students high in conscientiousness, agreeableness, and emotional stability were far less likely to post on Facebook about personal matters such as substance abuse or sexual behavior. Overall, however, more American students were inclined to post such content than German students, independent of personality traits (Karl, Peluchette, & Schlaegel, 2010).
- American adults high in extraversion were more likely to use social media than those low in extraversion (Mark & Ganzach, 2014). American men high in emotional instability were even more likely to use these sites (Correa, Hinsley, & deZuniga, 2010).
- In Taiwan, research on college students showed that those high in conscientiousness shopped online for convenience; those high in openness shopped online to have a new adventure; those high in neuroticism shopped online in order to avoid other people (Huang & Yang, 2010).
- In Australia, adults who scored high in extraversion, low in conscientiousness, and reported being socially lonely were more likely to use Facebook (Ryan & Xenos, 2011).

- A study of 11- to 16-year-old Americans who scored high in openness to new experiences spent more time using computers and playing video games than those who scored low in openness to experience (Witt, Massman, & Jackson, 2011).
- Among American college students, those more likely to engage in sexting by sending suggestive and sexy photos were found to be high in neuroticism and low in agreeableness (Delevi & Weisskirch, 2013).

Reflections on the Trait Approach

The theories presented in this chapter, together with their supporting research, indicate that inheritance may account for as much as 50 percent of personality (Brody, 1997; Buss, 1988; Stelmack, 1997). The evidence is greatest for the factors of extraversion, neuroticism, and psychoticism, but virtually every other dimension investigated by personality researchers displays a strong biological component.

In many cases, a shared family environment has only a minor influence. Some researchers hold a more uncompromising view, arguing that twins, whether reared together or apart, will be alike in all facets of their personality regardless of the family situation in which they were raised, suggesting that the genetic effect far outweighs the environmental effect.

This area of research has practical and theoretical implications for personality psychologists, who in the past tended to concentrate on the family and social interactions in early childhood. Findings from behavioral genetics may require a restructuring of research efforts in the future if we are to account fully for the development of personality.

However, we must not conclude prematurely that family and other environmental factors can be completely discounted as shapers of personality. The various components of personality remain products of both our genetic makeup and the experiences of our life. The task for psychologists remains to determine the relative importance of each.

Chapter Summary

According to Cattell, factors, or traits, are the basic structural units of personality. We all possess the common traits to some degree; unique traits typify one or a few persons. Ability traits determine how efficiently we work toward a goal. Temperament traits define emotional style of behavior. Dynamic traits are concerned with motivation.

Surface traits are personality characteristics that correlate with one another but do not constitute a factor because they are not determined by a single source. The 16 source traits Cattell identified are single factors, and each is the sole source of some aspect of behavior. Source traits may be constitutional traits, which originate in internal bodily conditions, or environmental-mold traits, which derive from environmental influences.

Cattell's research suggests that one-third of personality is genetically determined, with the rest determined by environmental influences. Thus, Cattell holds a deterministic view of personality. He does not suggest any ultimate life goals. Childhood influences are important in personality development, as are heredity and environment.

Cattell's three major assessment techniques are L-data (ratings made by observers), Q-data (self-ratings made through questionnaires, personality inventories, and attitude scales), and T-data (data from tests that are resistant to faking).

Cattell developed the 16 PF Test. He used two forms of factor analysis: the R technique, which gathers large amounts of data from groups of research participants, and the P technique, which collects a large amount of data from a single subject over time. Cattell's work is highly technical, and the amount of supporting data is massive. Factor analysis has been criticized for its potential subjectivity.

Research on behavioral genetics shows a significant influence of genetic factors on personality. Eysenck demonstrated a genetic influence on the personality dimensions of extraversion, neuroticism, and psychoticism.

McCrae and Costa proposed five biologically based factors: neuroticism, extraversion, openness, agreeableness, and conscientiousness. The factors are stable over the lifetime, appear in many cultures, are valid predictors of emotions and behaviors in many situations, and can influence many aspects of our behavior.

HEXACO, a six-factor model of personality, adds the dimension of Honesty/humility to the five-factor model. That factor has been documented in more than a dozen different cultures.

The Dark Triad of personality includes narcissism, machiavellianism, and psychopathy, which can lead to antisocial, duplicitous, and aggressive behavior.

Personality traits influence our Internet behavior, including how we interact with others on social networking sites, to becoming addicted to the Internet, and to our online shopping habits.

Review Questions

1. How does Cattell's concept of personality traits differ from Allport's view of traits?
2. Explain how traits can be identified through the use of factor analysis.
3. Describe three ways to categorize traits.
4. Define surface traits and source traits. Give examples of each.
5. What is the difference between source traits and environmental-mold traits?
6. According to Cattell's research, which source traits are determined primarily by heredity?
7. Describe how Cattell's image of human nature differs from Freud's.
8. What is self-sentiment? What is its role in personality?
9. What Freudian ideas did Cattell incorporate into his stages of personality development?
10. Identify the three types of data collected by Cattell. Give an example of each.
11. Describe the three personality types proposed by Eysenck. Does Eysenck suggest that personality traits are determined largely by genetic factors or by environmental factors?
12. In what ways do people who score high in extraversion on Eysenck's personality test differ from people who score low?

13. Describe the behavior of people who score high in psychoticism on Eysenck's personality test.
14. How does Eysenck's research on identical and fraternal twins and on adopted children support his conclusion about the role of genetic factors in personality?
15. Describe McCrae and Costa's five factors of personality. What is the role of heredity and of environment in each of these factors?
16. In what ways do people who score high in extraversion and in conscientiousness differ from people who score low in these factors?
17. What are the emotional and behavioral correlates of high scores in neuroticism?
18. What are the dimensions of personality in the HEXACO model? How do they differ from those of the five-factor model?
19. What traits constitute the Dark Triad of personality? Give examples of ways in which they can affect our behavior.
20. In what ways do our personality traits influence our behavior online? Give examples from your own online behavior.

Suggested Readings

Buchanan, R. (2010). *Playing with fire. The controversial career of Hans Eysenck.* New York: Oxford University Press. A thoughtful discussion of Eysenck's long and distinguished career and his work on the dimensions of personality.

Cattell, R. B. (1974). Autobiography. In G. Lindzey (Ed.), *A history of psychology in autobiography* (Vol. 6, pp. 59–100). Englewood Cliffs, NJ: Prentice-Hall; Travels in psychological hyperspace. In T. S. Krawiec (Ed.), *The psychologists* (Vol. 2, pp. 85–133). New York: Oxford University Press. Two essays by Cattell about his life and work.

Cattell, R. B. (1993). Planning basic clinical research. In E. C. Walker (Ed.), *The history of clinical psychology in autobiography* (Vol. 2, pp. 101–111). Pacific Grove, CA: Brooks/Cole. Cattell's evaluation of his life's work, concluding that his approach to the measurement of personality structures and processes was the only correct one to pursue.

Eysenck, H. J. (1976). H. J. Eysenck. In R. I. Evans (Ed.), *The making of psychology: Discussions with creative contributors* (pp. 255–265). New York: Alfred A. Knopf. Interviews with Eysenck about his work, especially his criticisms of psychoanalysis and his controversial views on the genetic basis of intelligence.

Eysenck, H. J. (1990). Genetic and environmental contributions to individual differences: The three major dimensions of personality. *Journal of Personality, 58,* 245–261. Describes the relative impact of heredity and environment on Eysenck's proposed dimensions of personality (extraversion, neuroticism, and psychoticism) and emphasizes the importance to psychology of the study of behavioral genetics.

Eysenck, H. J. (1997). *Rebel with a cause: The autobiography of Hans Eysenck.* London: Transaction Publishers. Eysenck's reflections on his life and work. Notes how some of his ideas on personality dimensions have stood the test of time, and suggests the relative importance of heredity versus environment in his own personality.

Farley, F. (2000). Hans J. Eysenck (1916–1997). *American Psychologist, 55,* 674–675. An obituary article describing Eysenck's contributions to psychology.

Horn, J. (2001). Raymond Bernard Cattell (1905–1998). *American Psychologist, 56,* 71–72. An obituary article describing Cattell's contributions to psychology.

Lee, K., & Ashton, M. (2012). *The H factor of personality: Why some people are manipulative, self-entitled, materialistic, and exploitive—and why it matters for everyone.* Waterloo, Canada: Wilfred Laurier University Press. Covers the H Factor (honesty/humility) in the HEXACO model of personality and how it influences people in ways both good and bad, desirable and undesirable.

Tucker, W. (2009). *The Cattell controversy: Race, science, and ideology.* Chicago: University of Illinois Press. Examines Cattell's career, his use of the factor-analytic method, and his personal philosophy.

The Humanistic Approach

The humanistic approach to personality flourished in the 1960s and 1970s and still continues to influence psychology today. The goal of this movement was to radically change psychology's methods and subject matter. Humanistic psychologists objected to psychoanalysis and to behaviorism, which were then the two major forces in American psychology, arguing that they presented too limited and demeaning an image of human nature.

Humanistic psychologists criticized Freud and other psychoanalysts for studying only the emotionally disturbed side of human nature. They questioned how we could ever learn about positive human characteristics and qualities if we limited our focus to neuroses and psychoses. Instead, humanistic psychologists proposed to study our strengths and virtues; the best of human behavior, not its worst.

The humanistic psychologists believed that behavioral psychologists were too narrow and sterile in their outlook because they disavowed conscious and unconscious forces, dealing instead only with the objective observation of overt behavior.

But a psychology based on conditioned responses to stimuli depicts people as little more than mechanized robots, reacting to events in predetermined ways. Humanistic psychologists insisted that people were not just big laboratory rats or slow computers. Human behavior is too complex to be explained solely by the behaviorists' methods.

The humanistic approach to personality is represented here by the works of Abraham Maslow and Carl Rogers. Their theories emphasize human strengths and aspirations, conscious free will, and the fulfillment of human potential. They present a flattering and optimistic image of human nature and describe us as active, creative beings concerned with growth and self-actualization.

chapter 9

Abraham Maslow: Needs-Hierarchy Theory

Fair Use

What humans can be, they must be. They must be true to their own nature.

—*Abraham Maslow*

Abraham Maslow is considered the founder and spiritual leader of the humanistic psychology movement. He objected to both behaviorism and psychoanalysis, particularly Freud's approach to personality. According to Maslow, when psychologists study only abnormal or emotionally disturbed examples of humanity, they ignore all the positive human qualities such as happiness, contentment, and peace of mind.

We underestimate human nature, Maslow charged, when we fail to examine the best in people, that is, the most creative, healthy, and mature individuals. Therefore, Maslow decided that his approach to personality would assess society's outstanding representatives. When you want to determine how fast people can run, he reasoned, you study not the average runner but the fastest runner you can find.

Only in this way is it possible to determine the full range of human potential. His theory does not derive from case histories of clinical patients but from research on creative, independent, self-sufficient, fulfilled adults. He concluded that each person is born with the same set of instinctive needs that enable us to grow, develop, and fulfill our potential.

The Life of Maslow (1908–1970)

A Miserable Childhood

The oldest of seven children, Maslow was born in 1908 in Brooklyn, New York. His parents were immigrants with little education and few prospects of rising above their desperately poor circumstances. Maslow's childhood was not pleasant. He told an interviewer, "with my childhood, it's a wonder I'm not psychotic" (quoted in Hall, 1968, p. 37). In a statement found in his unpublished papers years after his death, Maslow had written, "My family was a miserable family and my mother was a horrible creature" (quoted in Hoffman, 1996, p. 2).

Isolated and unhappy, he grew up without close friends or loving parents. His father was aloof and periodically abandoned his wife and children. Maslow said that his father "loved whiskey and women and fighting" (quoted in Wilson, 1972, p. 131). Eventually Maslow reconciled with his father but as a child and adolescent he felt anger and hostility toward him.

Maslow's relationship with his mother was even worse. A biographer reported that Maslow "grew to maturity with an unrelieved hatred toward [her] and he never achieved the slightest reconciliation" (Hoffman, 1988, p. 7). She openly favored his younger siblings, never showed the slightest sign of affection for him, and constantly punished him for the slightest wrongdoing. She told him that God would retaliate for his misbehavior.

When Maslow once brought home two stray kittens, his mother killed them in front of him by bashing their heads against a wall. Maslow never forgave her, and when she died many years later he refused to go to her funeral. The experience affected not only his emotional life but also his work in psychology. "The whole thrust of my life-philosophy, and all my research and theorizing … has its roots in a hatred for and revulsion against everything she stood for" (quoted in Hoffman, 1988, p. 9).

Alone in the World

As if his mother was not difficult enough, Maslow faced other problems. Convinced he was ugly because of his prominent nose, he also felt inferior because of his scrawny build. His parents taunted him about his appearance and often told him how unattractive and awkward he was. At a large family gathering, his father pointed to the boy and said, "Isn't Abe the ugliest kid you've ever seen?" (quoted in Hoffman, 1996, p. 6).

He remembered his teenage years as marked by a huge inferiority complex. "I was all alone in the world," Maslow told an interviewer. "I felt peculiar. This was really in my blood, a very profound feeling that somehow I was wrong. Never any feelings that I was superior. Just one big aching inferiority complex" (quoted in Milton, 2002, p. 42). Elsewhere he wrote, "I tried to compensate for what I felt was a great [physical] lack by forcing my development in the direction of athletic achievements" (quoted in Hoffman, 1988, p. 13). Thus, the man who would later become interested in Alfred Adler's work was a living example of Adler's concept of compensation for inferiority feelings.

Finding a New Style of Life

When Maslow's early attempts at compensation to achieve recognition and acceptance as an athlete did not succeed, he turned to books. The library became the playground of his childhood and adolescence, and reading and education marked the road out of his ghetto of poverty and loneliness.

Maslow's early memories are significant because they indicate the style of life, the life of scholarship, he would fashion for himself. He recalled going to the neighborhood library early in the morning and waiting on the steps until the doors opened. He typically arrived at school an hour before classes began, and his teacher would let him sit in an empty classroom reading books she loaned him.

Although his grades remained mediocre, they were good enough to be accepted at City College of New York. He failed a course during his first semester and by the end of his freshman year was on academic probation, but with persistence his grades improved. He began to study law at his father's request, but decided after two weeks that he did not like it. What he really wanted to do was study "everything."

Becoming a Behaviorist

Maslow's desire for learning was matched by his great passion for his cousin Bertha. He soon left home, first for Cornell and then for the University of Wisconsin, where she joined him. He was 20 and she was 19 when they married. The union provided Maslow with a feeling of belonging and a sense of direction. He later said that his life had little meaning until he married Bertha and began his studies at Wisconsin. At Cornell, he had enrolled in a psychology course and pronounced it "awful and bloodless." It had "nothing to do with people, so I shuddered and turned away from it" (quoted in Hoffman, 1988, p. 26).

At Wisconsin, however, he found the behavioral psychology of John B. Watson, leader of the revolution to make psychology a science of behavior. Like many people in the early 1930s, Maslow became enraptured, believing that behaviorism could solve all the world's problems. His training in experimental psychology included work on dominance and sexual behavior in primates. It was a giant step from this type of research in the behaviorist framework to developing the ideas of humanistic psychology—from monkeys to self-actualization.

From Monkeys to Self-Actualization

Several influences brought about this profound shift in his thinking. He was deeply affected by the onset of World War II and by the birth of his first child. About the baby he said, "I was stunned by the mystery and by the sense of not really being in control. I felt small and weak and feeble before all this. I'd say anyone who had a baby couldn't be a behaviorist" (quoted in Hall, 1968, p. 56).

Maslow received his Ph.D. from the University of Wisconsin in 1934 and returned to New York for a postdoctoral fellowship under E. L. Thorndike at Columbia University, and later to teach at Brooklyn College where he remained until 1951. Maslow took several intelligence and scholastic aptitude tests, scoring an IQ of 195, which Thorndike described as within the genius range. At first Maslow was surprised, but soon he accepted the revelation and thereafter considered it a triumph. He often managed to work the information about his high IQ into social conversations.

A Parade Changes His Life Teaching in New York in the late 1930s and early 1940s, Maslow had the opportunity to meet the wave of emigrant intellectuals fleeing Nazi Germany, including Karen Horney and Alfred Adler. Maslow "talked about Adler all the time and was tremendously excited by his theories" recalled Bertha Maslow (quoted in Hoffman, 1988, p. 304). He also met the Gestalt psychologist Max Wertheimer and the American anthropologist Ruth Benedict. His admiration for Wertheimer and Benedict later kindled his ideas about self-actualization.

In 1941, Maslow witnessed a parade shortly after Japan's surprise attack on the American naval base at Pearl Harbor in Hawaii, precipitating U.S. involvement in World War II. The experience changed his thinking and he resolved to devote himself to developing a psychology that would deal with the highest human ideals. He would work to improve the human personality and to demonstrate that people are capable of displaying better behavior than prejudice, hatred, and aggression.

Becoming Famous From 1951 to 1969, Maslow taught at Brandeis University in Massachusetts. A foundation grant enabled him to move to California to work on his philosophy of politics, economics, and ethics based on a humanistic psychology. He became an immensely popular figure in psychology and among the general public. He received many awards and honors and was elected president of the American Psychological Association in 1967.

At the peak of his fame, Maslow developed a variety of ailments including stomach disorders, insomnia, depression, and heart disease. In the face of these growing physical limitations, he pushed himself to work even harder to accomplish his goal of humanizing psychology. "I find myself getting narrow," he said in a 1968 interview. "I've given up plays and poetry and making new friends.... I love my work so much, and am so absorbed with it, that everything else starts to look smaller and smaller" (quoted in Frick, 2000, p. 135).

Maslow died in 1970 of a massive heart attack while jogging around his swimming pool, an exercise recommended by his cardiologist.

Abraham Maslow

Various sites provide biographical information, discussions of his theory, research on relevant concepts, and links to other resources.

Personality Development: The Hierarchy of Needs

hierarchy of five innate needs An arrangement of innate needs, from strongest to weakest, that activates and directs behavior.

instinctoid needs Maslow's term for the innate needs in his needs-hierarchy theory.

Maslow proposed a **hierarchy of five innate needs** that activate and direct human behavior (1968, 1970b). They are the physiological, safety, belongingness and love, esteem, and self-actualization needs, as shown in Figure 9.1. Maslow described these needs as **instinctoid**, by which he meant that they have a hereditary component. Although we come equipped with these needs at birth, however, the behaviors we use to satisfy them are learned and, therefore, subject to variation from one person to another.

The needs are arranged in order from strongest at the bottom to the weakest at the top. Lower needs must be at least partially satisfied before higher needs become influential. For example, hungry people feel no urge to satisfy the higher need for esteem. They are preoccupied with satisfying the physiological need for food, not with obtaining approval and esteem from other people. It is only when people have adequate food and shelter, and when the rest of the lower needs are satisfied, that they are motivated by needs that rank higher in the hierarchy.

Thus, we are not driven by all the needs at the same time. In general, only one need will dominate our personality at any one point in time. Which one it will be depends on

FIGURE 9.1

Maslow's hierarchy of needs

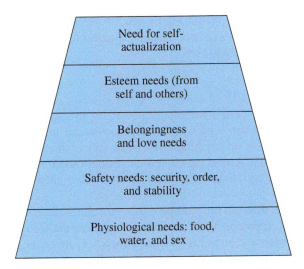

which of the others have been satisfied. For example, people who are successful in their careers are no longer driven by their physiological and safety needs. Those needs have been amply taken care of. Successful people are more likely to be motivated by the needs for esteem or self-actualization.

However, the order of the needs can be changed. If an economic recession causes some people to lose their jobs, then the safety and physiological needs may reassume priority. Being able to pay the mortgage becomes more prized than popularity with colleagues or an award from a civic organization.

Characteristics of Needs

- The lower the need is in the hierarchy, the greater is its strength, potency, and priority. The higher needs are weaker needs.
- Higher needs appear later in life. Physiological and safety needs arise in infancy. Belongingness and esteem needs arise in adolescence. The need for self-actualization does not arise until midlife.
- Because higher needs are less necessary for actual survival, their gratification can be postponed. Failure to satisfy a higher need does not produce a crisis. Failure to satisfy a lower need, on the other hand, does produce a crisis. For this reason, Maslow called lower needs **deficit, or deficiency, needs**; failure to satisfy them produces a deficit or lack in the individual.
- Although higher needs are less necessary for survival, they can contribute to our personal growth. Satisfaction of higher needs leads to improved health, happiness, contentment, fulfillment, and longevity. For this reason, Maslow called higher needs **growth or being needs**.
- Gratification of higher needs requires better external social, economic, and political circumstances than does gratification of lower needs. For example, pursuing self-actualization requires greater freedom of expression and opportunity than pursuing safety needs.
- A need does not have to be satisfied fully before the next need in the hierarchy becomes important. Maslow proposed a declining percentage of satisfaction for each need. Offering a hypothetical example, he described a person who satisfied, in turn,

deficit (deficiency) needs The lower needs; failure to satisfy them produces a deficiency in the body.

growth (being) needs The higher needs; although growth needs are less necessary than deficit needs for survival, they involve the realization and fulfillment of human potential.

85 percent of the physiological needs, 70 percent of the safety needs, 50 percent of the belongingness and love needs, 40 percent of the esteem needs, and 10 percent of the self-actualization need.

Physiological Needs

If you have ever been swimming and had to struggle for air while under water, or if you have gone too long without eating, you can understand how trivial the needs for love or esteem or anything else can be when your body is experiencing a physiological deficiency. A starving person craves only food. But once that need is satisfied, the person is no longer driven by it. The need then ceases to direct or control behavior.

That is the situation for most people in an affluent, industrialized culture. It is rare for middle-class Americans to be concerned with satisfying their basic survival needs. Physiological needs have a greater personal impact as motivating forces in cultures where basic survival remains an everyday concern. Because a need that has been gratified no longer serves to motivate behavior, the physiological needs play a minimal role for most of us.

Safety Needs

Maslow believed that the needs for safety and security are important drives for infants and neurotic adults. Emotionally healthy adults have usually satisfied their safety needs, a condition that requires stability, security, and freedom from fear and anxiety. For infants and children, the safety needs can be seen clearly in their behavior because youngsters react visibly and immediately to any threat to their security. Adults have learned ways to inhibit their reactions to dangerous situations.

Another visible indication of children's safety needs is their preference for a structure or routine, for an orderly and predictable world. Too much freedom and permissiveness

When the basic needs for food and shelter are unsatisfied, the higher needs, such as esteem and self-actualization, are of less importance.

Visions of America, LLC/Alamy

leads to an absence of structure and order. This situation is likely to produce anxiety and insecurity in children because it threatens their security. Some measure of freedom must be granted to children, but only within the limits of their capacity to cope. This freedom must be offered with guidance because children are not yet capable of directing their own behavior and realizing the consequences.

Neurotic and insecure adults also need structure and order because their safety needs still dominate their personality. Neurotics compulsively avoid new experiences. They arrange their world to make it predictable, budgeting their time and organizing their possessions. Pencils must be kept in orderly neat rows with none out of line, and shirts hung in the closet facing the same direction.

Maslow pointed out that although most normal adults have satisfied the safety needs, those needs may still have an impact on behavior. Many of us choose the predictable over the unknown and prefer order to chaos. That is why we save for the future, buy insurance, and opt to remain in a secure job rather than risk a new venture. However, the safety needs are not as overwhelming a driving force for normal adults as they are for children or neurotics.

Belongingness and Love Needs

Once our physiological and safety needs have been reasonably well satisfied, we attend to the needs for belongingness and love. These needs can be expressed through a close relationship with a friend, lover, or mate, or through social relationships formed within a group. They can also be developed and maintained through the various forms of social media that allow us to keep in touch with others at a moment's notice anywhere and anytime.

The need to give and receive love can be satisfied in an intimate relationship with another person. Maslow did not equate love with sex, which is a physiological need, but he recognized that sex is one way of expressing the love need. He suggested that the failure to satisfy the need for love is a fundamental cause of emotional maladjustment.

Esteem Needs

Once we feel loved and have a sense of belonging, we may find ourselves driven by two forms of the need for esteem. We require esteem and respect from ourselves, in the form of feelings of self-worth, and from other people, in the form of status, recognition, or social success. Satisfaction of the need for self-esteem allows us to feel confident of our strength, worth, and adequacy, which will help us become more competent and productive in all aspects of our life. When we lack self-esteem, we feel inferior, helpless, and discouraged with little confidence in our ability to cope.

The Self-Actualization Need

self-actualization The fullest development of the self.

The highest need in Maslow's hierarchy, **self-actualization**, involves the maximum realization and fulfillment of our potentials, talents, and abilities. Although a person may satisfy all the other needs in the hierarchy, if that person is not self-actualizing, he or she will be restless, frustrated, and discontent. Maslow wrote, "A musician must make music, an artist must paint, a poet must write … to be ultimately at peace" (1970b, p. 46).

The self-actualizing process may take many forms, but Maslow believed that everyone, regardless of occupation or interests, is capable of maximizing personal abilities and reaching the fullest personality development. Self-actualization is not limited to creative and intellectual superstars such as musicians, artists, and writers. What is important is to fulfill one's own potentials, whatever they are, at the highest level possible. Maslow put it this way, "A first-rate soup is more creative than a second-rate painting … cooking or parenthood or making a home could be creative, while poetry need not be" (1987, p. 159).

Belongingness and love needs can be satisfied through a relationship with a friend.

Nancy Honey/Cultura/Riser/Getty Images

Conditions for Achieving Self-Actualization

The following conditions are necessary in order for us to satisfy the self-actualization need:

- We must be free of constraints imposed by society and by ourselves.
- We must not be distracted by the lower-order needs.
- We must be secure in our self-image and in our relationships with other people, and we must be able to love and be loved in return.
- We must have a realistic knowledge of our strengths and weaknesses, virtues and vices.

Achieving Self-Actualization in Non-Traditional Ways

Although the hierarchy of needs Maslow proposed applies to most of us, there can be exceptions. Some people dedicate their lives to an ideal and willingly sacrifice everything for their cause. People have been known to fast until death in the service of their beliefs, thus denying their physiological and safety needs. Religious figures may abandon all worldly goods to fulfill a vow of poverty, thus satisfying the self-actualization need while frustrating the lower-order needs. Artists throughout history have imperiled their health and security for the sake of their work. A more common reversal in the hierarchy occurs when people place a greater importance on esteem than on love, believing that the belongingness and love needs can be satisfied only if they first feel self-confident.

Cognitive Needs

cognitive needs Innate
needs to know and to
understand.

Maslow later proposed a second set of innate needs, the **cognitive needs**—to know and
to understand, which exist outside the hierarchy we have described. The need to know is
stronger than the need to understand, and must therefore be at least partially satisfied
before the need to understand can emerge.

Evidence for the Cognitive Needs   Several points of evidence support the existence
of cognitive needs (Maslow, 1970b).

- Laboratory studies show that animals explore and manipulate their environment for
  no apparent reason other than curiosity, that is, a desire to know and to understand.
- Historical evidence shows that people often have sought knowledge at the risk of
  their lives, thus placing the needs to know and to understand above the safety needs.
- Studies suggest that emotionally healthy adults are attracted to mysterious and
  unexplained events and are motivated to improve their knowledge about them.
- Emotionally healthy adults in Maslow's own clinical practice complained of boredom and a lack of zest and excitement in their lives. He described them as "intelligent people leading stupid lives in stupid jobs" and found that they improved when
  they took steps to fulfill the needs to know and to understand by becoming involved
  in more challenging activities.

How the Cognitive Needs Affect Personality   The needs to know and to understand appear in late infancy and early childhood and are expressed by children as a natural curiosity. Because the needs are innate, they do not have to be taught, but the
actions of parents and teachers can serve to inhibit a child's spontaneous curiosity. Failure to satisfy the cognitive needs is harmful and hampers the full development and functioning of the personality.

The hierarchy of these two needs overlaps the original five-need hierarchy. Knowing
and understanding—essentially, finding meaning in our environment—are basic to interacting with that environment in an emotionally healthy, mature way to satisfy physiological, safety, belongingness and love, esteem, and self-actualization needs. It is impossible
to become self-actualizing if we fail to meet the needs to know and to understand.

The Study of Self-Actualizers

According to Maslow's theory, self-actualizers differ from others in terms of their basic
motivation. Maslow proposed a distinct type of motivation for self-actualizers which he
called **metamotivation** (sometimes called B-motivation or Being). The prefix *meta*-
means after or beyond. Metamotivation, then, indicates that it goes beyond psychology's
traditional idea of motivation.

metamotivation The
motivation of self-
actualizers, which
involves maximizing
personal potential
rather than striving for
a particular goal
object.

Metamotivation

Metamotivation implies a condition in which motivation, as we know it, plays no role.
Self-actualizers are not motivated to strive for a particular goal. Instead, they are said to
be developing from within. Maslow described the motivation of people who are not self-
actualizers as a condition of D-motivation or Deficiency. D-motivation involves striving
for something specific to make up for something that is lacking within us. For example,
failure to eat produces a deficiency in the body that we feel as discomfort. This feeling
motivates us to take some action to reduce the resulting tension.

Thus, a specific physiological need (hunger) that requires a specific goal object (food) produces a motivation to act to attain something we lack (we search for food). Maslow's (1971) writing about the development of B-motivation and D-motivation is incomplete, but apparently D-motivation applies not only to physiological needs, as in this example, but also to safety, belongingness and love, andesteem needs.

Fulfilling Potential   In contrast, self-actualizers are concerned with fulfilling their potential and with knowing and understanding their environment. In their state of meta-motivation, they are not seeking to reduce tension, satisfy a deficiency, or strive for a specific object. Their goal is to enrich their lives by acting to increase tension so as to experience a variety of stimulating and challenging events. Because their lower-order deficiency needs have been met, self-actualizers function at a level beyond striving for specific goal objects to satisfy a deficit. Thus, they are in a state of "being," spontaneously, naturally, and joyfully expressing their full humanity.

metaneeds States of growth or being toward which self-actualizers evolve.

Metaneeds   Having explained that self-actualizers are thus, in a sense, unmotivated, Maslow proposed a list of **metaneeds** toward which self-actualizers evolve (see Table 9.1). Metaneeds are states of being—such as goodness, uniqueness, and perfection—rather than specific goal objects.

metapathology A thwarting of self-development related to failure to satisfy the metaneeds.

Failure to satisfy metaneeds is harmful and produces a kind of **metapathology**, which thwarts the full development of the personality. Metapathology prevents self-actualizers from expressing, using, and fulfilling their potential. They may come to feel helpless and depressed, unable to pinpoint a source for these feelings or identify a goal that might alleviate the distress.

Characteristics of Self-Actualizers

Maslow's research on emotionally healthy people formed the basis of his personality theory (1970b, 1971). He did not find many examples of self-actualizers and estimated that they constitute 1 percent or less of the population. However, he concluded that they share certain characteristics (see Table 9.2).

- *An efficient perception of reality.* Self-actualizers perceive their world, including other people, clearly and objectively, unbiased by prejudgments or preconceptions.
- *An acceptance of themselves, others, and nature.* Self-actualizers accept their strengths and weaknesses. They do not try to distort or falsify their self-image, and they do not feel guilty about their failings. They also accept the weaknesses of other people and of society in general.
- *A spontaneity, simplicity, and naturalness.* The behavior of self-actualizers is open, direct, and natural. They rarely hide their feelings or emotions or play a role to satisfy society, although they may do so to avoid hurting other people. Self-actualizers are individualistic in their ideas and ideals but not necessarily unconventional in their behavior. They feel secure enough to be themselves without being overly assertive.
- *A focus on problems outside themselves.* Self-actualizers have a sense of mission, a commitment, to which they devote their energy. This dedication to a cause or vocation is a requirement for self-actualization. Self-actualizers find pleasure and excitement in their hard work. Through their intense dedication, self-actualizers are able to satisfy the metaneeds. Their commitment challenges and develops their abilities and helps define their sense of self.

TABLE 9.1   Maslow's metaneeds and metapathologies

METANEEDS	METAPATHOLOGIES
Truth	Mistrust, cynicism, skepticism
Goodness	Hatred, repulsion, disgust, reliance only upon self and for self
Beauty	Vulgarity, restlessness, loss of taste, bleakness
Unity, wholeness	Disintegration
Dichotomy-transcendence	Black/white thinking, either/or thinking, simplistic view of life
Aliveness, process	Deadness, robotizing, feeling oneself to be totally determined, loss of emotion and zest in life, experiential emptiness
Uniqueness	Loss of feeling of self and individuality, feeling oneself to be interchangeable or anonymous
Perfection	Hopelessness, nothing to work for
Necessity	Chaos, unpredictability
Completion, finality	Incompleteness, hopelessness, cessation of striving and coping
Justice	Anger, cynicism, mistrust, lawlessness, total selfishness
Order	Insecurity, wariness, loss of safety and predictability, necessity for being on guard
Simplicity	Over-complexity, confusion, bewilderment, loss of orientation
Richness, totality, comprehensiveness	Depression, uneasiness, loss of interest in the world
Effortlessness	Fatigue, strain, clumsiness, awkwardness, stiffness
Playfulness	Grimness, depression, paranoid humorlessness, loss of zest in life, cheerlessness
Self-sufficiency	Responsibility given to others
Meaningfulness	Meaninglessness, despair, senselessness of life

Source: Adapted from *The Farther Reaches of Human Nature*, by A. H. Maslow. Copyright © 1971 by Bertha G. Maslow.

- *A sense of detachment and the need for privacy.* Self-actualizers can experience isolation without harmful effects and seem to need solitude more than persons who are not self-actualizing. Self-actualizers depend on themselves, not on others, for their satisfactions. This independence may make them seem aloof or unfriendly, but that is not their intent. They are simply more autonomous than most people and do not crave social support.

- *A freshness of appreciation.* Self-actualizers have the ability to perceive and experience the world around them with freshness, wonder, and awe. An experience may grow stale for someone who is not self-actualizing, but self-actualizers will enjoy each recurrence as though it was the first. Whether it is a sunset, a painting, a symphony, a baseball game, or a birthday gift—all of these experiences can be viewed with delight. Self-actualizers appreciate what they have and take little for granted.

- *Mystical or peak experiences.* Self-actualizers know moments of intense ecstasy, not unlike deep religious experiences, that can occur with virtually any activity. Maslow called these events **peak experiences**, during which the self is transcended and the person feels supremely powerful, confident, and decisive.

peak experience
A moment of intense ecstasy, similar to a religious or mystical experience, during which the self is transcended.

TABLE 9.2 Characteristics of self-actualizing people

Clear perception of reality

Acceptance of self, others, and nature

Spontaneity, simplicity, and naturalness

Dedication to a cause

Independence and need for privacy

Freshness of appreciation

Peak experiences

Social interest

Deep interpersonal relationships

Tolerance and acceptance of others

Creativeness and originality

Resistance to social pressures

- *Social interest.* Maslow adopted Alfred Adler's concept of social interest to indicate the sympathy and empathy self-actualizing persons have for all humanity. Although often irritated by the behavior of other people, self-actualizers feel a kinship with and an understanding of others as well as a desire to help them.
- *Profound interpersonal relations.* Although their circle of friends is not large, self-actualizers have deep, lasting friendships. They tend to select as friends those with personal qualities similar to their own, just as we all choose as friends the people we find compatible. Self-actualizers often attract admirers or disciples. These relationships are usually one-sided; the admirer asks more of the self-actualizer than the self-actualizer is able or willing to give.
- *Creativeness.* Self-actualizing people are highly creative and exhibit inventiveness and originality in their work and other facets of their lives. They are flexible, spontaneous, and willing to make mistakes and learn from them. They are open and humble, in the way children are before society teaches them to be embarrassed or shy about possibly doing something foolish.
- *Resistance to enculturation.* Self-actualizers are autonomous, independent, and self-sufficient. They feel free to resist social and cultural pressures to think or behave in a certain way. They do not openly rebel against cultural norms or social codes, but they are governed by their own nature rather than the strictures of society.

This is quite an amazing set of attributes. According to Maslow's research, self-actualizers seem almost perfect. But they do have human flaws and imperfections. On occasion they can be rude, even ruthless, and they experience doubts, conflicts, and tension. Nevertheless, such incidents are rare and less intense than for the person who is not self-actualizing.

Failure to Become Self-Actualizing

If the need for self-actualization is innate and, therefore, does not have to be taught and learned, then why isn't everyone self-actualizing? Why does less than 1 percent of the population reach this state of being? One reason is that the higher the need in Maslow's proposed hierarchy, the weaker it is. As the highest need, self-actualization is the weakest of all; it can easily be inhibited. For example, hostile or rejecting parents make it difficult

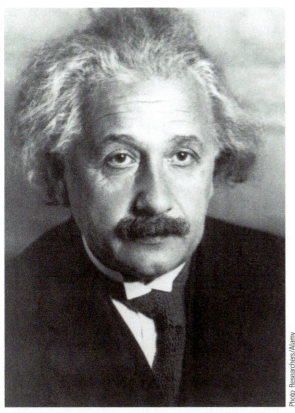

Among the self-actualizers Maslow studied by analyzing biographies and other written records were the noted physicist Albert Einstein and Harriet Tubman, a leader of the antislavery movement at the time of the American Civil War.

for a person to satisfy love and esteem needs. In this case, the self-actualization need may not emerge at all. At a lower level, poor economic conditions can make it difficult to satisfy physiological and safety needs, so self-actualization assumes less importance.

The Importance of Childhood in Self-Actualization   Inadequate education and improper child-rearing practices can thwart the drive for self-actualization in adulthood. Maslow cited the typical sex-role training for boys, who are taught to inhibit qualities such as tenderness and sentimentality. Thus, this aspect of their nature is not encouraged to fully develop. If children are overprotected and not permitted to try new behaviors, explore new ideas, or practice new skills, then they are likely to be inhibited as adults, unable to express themselves fully in activities vital to self-actualization.

The opposite behavior, excessive parental permissiveness, can also be harmful. Too much freedom in childhood can lead to anxiety and insecurity, thus undermining the safety needs. To Maslow, the ideal situation in childhood is a balance of permissiveness and regulation.

Sufficient love in childhood is a prerequisite for self-actualization, as well as for satisfaction of physiological and safety needs within the first two years of life. If children feel secure and confident in the early years, they will remain so as adults. This position is similar to Erik Erikson's emphasis on the development of trust in early childhood and to Karen Horney's ideas on the childhood need for security. Without adequate parental love, security, and esteem in childhood, it is difficult to strive for self-actualization in adulthood.

Jonah complex The fear that maximizing our potential will lead to a situation with which we will be unable to cope.

The Jonah Complex   Another reason for the failure to self-actualize is what Maslow called the **Jonah complex**. This idea is based on the biblical tale of Jonah, described by Maslow as "called by God to prophesy, but [Jonah] was afraid of the task. He tried to run away from it. But no matter where Jonah ran, he could find no hiding place. Finally, he understood that he had to accept his fate" (quoted in Hoffman, 1996, p. 50).

Thus, the Jonah complex refers to our doubts about our own abilities. We may fear that taking action to maximize our potential will lead to new situations with which we may be unable to cope. Simultaneously, we are afraid of and thrilled by the possibilities but too often the fear takes precedence.

It Takes Courage!   Self-actualization requires courage. Even when the lower needs have been satisfied, we cannot simply sit back and wait to be swept along some flower-strewn path to ecstasy and fulfillment. The self-actualizing process takes effort, discipline, and self-control. For many people it may seem easier and safer to accept life as it is rather than seek new challenges. Self-actualizers will constantly test themselves by abandoning secure routines and familiar behaviors and attitudes.

Association for Humanistic Psychology

The Web site for the Association for Humanistic Psychology includes access to its online bookstore, a list of college programs in humanistic studies, a history of the humanistic psychology movement, and links to related sites.

American Psychological Association: Society for Humanistic Psychology

The Web site for the Society for Humanistic Psychology of the American Psychological Association provides the history and goals of the division as well as access to its journal, programs of study, student awards, and more.

Questions about Human Nature

Maslow's view of personality is humanistic and optimistic. He focused on psychological health rather than illness, growth rather than stagnation, virtues and potentials rather than weaknesses and limitations. He had a strong sense of confidence in our ability to shape our lives and our society.

We have the free will to choose how best to satisfy our needs and to actualize our potential. We can either create an actualizing self or refrain from pursuing that supreme state of achievement. Thus, we are ultimately responsible for the level of personality development we reach, or fail to reach.

Although the needs in Maslow's hierarchies are innate, the behaviors by which we satisfy them are learned. Therefore, personality is determined by the interaction of heredity and environment, of personal and situational variables. Although not explicit in his writings, Maslow seemed to favor the uniqueness of personality.

Our motivations and needs are universal, but the ways in which the needs are satisfied will vary from one person to another because these ways of behaving are learned. Even among self-actualizers, although they share certain qualities, their behaviors are not identical.

Maslow recognized the importance of early childhood experiences in fostering or inhibiting adult development, but he did not believe that we are victims of these experiences. We have more potential than we may realize to manage our lives and our society and would be happier and more productive if we would learn to do so.

Self-actualization as the ultimate and necessary goal reflects Maslow's belief that, given the proper conditions, we are capable of reaching the highest level of human functioning.

Maslow argued that human nature is basically good, decent, and kind, but he did not deny the existence of evil. He believed some people were evil beyond reclamation and wrote in his journal that "nothing will work ultimately [with them] but shooting" (1979, p. 631).

He suggested that wickedness was not an inherited trait but rather the result of an inappropriate environment. Maslow's compassion for humanity is clear in his writings, and his optimism is expressed in the belief that each of us is capable of fulfilling our vast human potential.

Assessment in Maslow's Theory

Maslow's work on self-actualization did not begin as a formal program of personality assessment and research. He started his investigation simply to satisfy his own curiosity about two well-known people who impressed him, the anthropologist Ruth Benedict and the Gestalt psychologist Max Wertheimer. Maslow admired them greatly and wanted to understand what made them so outstandingly different from other people. After much careful observation, he concluded that they shared certain qualities that set them apart from the average person.

Maslow attempted to assess those qualities in other people. His first research subjects were college students, but he found only 1 out of 3,000 he could describe as self-actualizing. He decided that the characteristics for the self-actualizing personality, those qualities he had identified in Benedict and Wertheimer, were not yet developed in young people. His next step was to study people who were middle-aged and older. However, even among this group Maslow found less than 1 percent of the population capable of meeting his criteria for self-actualization.

The self-actualizers he finally identified included several dozen whom he designated as certain or highly probable cases, partial cases, or potential cases. Some were Maslow's contemporaries. Others were historical figures such as Thomas Jefferson, Albert Einstein, George Washington Carver (an African-American scientist in the early 20th century), Harriet Tubman (an African-American former slave who became an abolitionist before the Civil War), and Eleanor Roosevelt (wife of the president and a prominent social activist).

Maslow used a variety of techniques to assess their personalities. For historical figures, he worked with biographical material, analyzing written records for similarities in personal characteristics. For the living subjects he relied on interviews, free association, and projective tests. He found that many of these people were self-conscious when questioned, so often he was forced to study them indirectly, although he did not explain precisely how that was done.

The Personal Orientation Inventory

The Personal Orientation Inventory (POI), a self-report questionnaire consisting of 150 pairs of statements, was developed by psychologist Everett Shostrom (1964, 1974) to measure self-actualization. People taking the test must indicate which of each pair is more applicable to them (see Table 9.3).

TABLE 9.3 Sample items from the Personal Orientation Inventory. Respondents select the item in each pair that is more descriptive of them.

I do what others expect of me.
I feel free to not do what others expect of me.
I must justify my actions in the pursuit of my own interests.
I need not justify my actions in the pursuit of my own interests.
I live by the rules and standards of society.
I do not always need to live by the rules and standards of society.
Reasons are needed to justify my feelings.
Reasons are not needed to justify my feelings.
I only feel free to express warm feelings to my friends.
I feel free to express both warm and hostile feelings to my friends.
I will continue to grow only by setting my sights on a high-level, socially approved goal.
I will continue to grow best by being myself.
People should always control their anger.
People should express honestly felt anger.

Source: From "An Inventory for the Measurement of Self-Actualization," by E. L. Shostrom, 1964, *Educational and Psychological Measurement, 24*, pp. 207–218.

The POI is scored for 2 major scales and 10 subscales. The major scales are *time competence*, which measures the degree to which we live in the present, and *inner directedness*, which assesses how much we depend on ourselves rather than on others for judgments and values.

The Smartphone Basic Needs Scale

The Smartphone Basic Needs Scale is a 20-item self-report inventory designed to assess the degree to which smartphone use can satisfy the needs in Maslow's system. It was developed using college students in the United States and in South Korea as subjects, and the developers reported high levels of validity and reliability (Kang & Jung, 2014). For example, the following items were used to measure Maslow's belongingness need—respondents were instructed to select the statement or statements that applied to them:

By using my Smartphone, I can….

1. Get closer to important people around me
2. Can meet nice people
3. Develop relationships with others
4. Get along with people well
5. Work and communicate together

Research on Maslow's Theory

Maslow did not use case studies or the experimental or correlational methods in his research. Critics have charged that Maslow's methods for studying self-actualizers were not rigorous or controlled. Maslow agreed; he knew his investigations failed to adhere to the requirements of scientific research. He wrote, "By ordinary standards of laboratory research, this simply was not research at all" (1971, p. 42). But he believed that because self-actualization could not be studied by accepted scientific procedures, the alternative was to wait until appropriate techniques were developed—or not to study the issue at all. Maslow was too impatient to postpone his research, too committed to the conviction that he could help humanity. He wrote that he did not have enough time to perform careful experiments. "They take too long in view of the years I have left and the extent of what I want to do" (1979, p. 694).

He referred to his program as consisting of pilot studies only. Convinced that his results were valid, he expected other researchers to eventually confirm his theory. Maslow also believed that to support and justify his conclusions, which he was convinced were correct, he somehow needed to collect less data than did other theorists.

The Hierarchy of Needs

In support of Maslow's theory, a study of male and female college students found that satisfaction of the needs for safety, belongingness, and esteem was negatively related to neuroticism and depression (Williams & Page, 1989). This research also showed that esteem needs were stronger than belongingness needs. The subjects expressed less concern with safety needs, as expected among people able to afford to go to college.

A study using the Need Satisfaction Inventory, a self-report questionnaire designed to measure how well a person satisfies Maslow's needs, correlated test scores of college students with their scores on the Eysenck Personality Inventory. Again, the results showed that those who were higher in need satisfaction were lower in neuroticism (Lester, 1990).

An elaborate test of the hierarchy using a sample representative of the general population supported the order of the five needs (Graham & Balloun, 1973). The study also demonstrated that the amount of concern people expressed about each need increased from the lowest to the highest need. Physiological needs, presumably well satisfied in these subjects, were of little concern to them. The self-actualization need was of the greatest interest, presumably because it was not so easily satisfied.

Research on economically disadvantaged youth in Midwestern United States found that they were primarily focused on trying to satisfy the safety needs and showed little concern for higher needs (Noltemeyer, Bush, Patton, & Bergen, 2012). This is in line with Maslow's theory. A study of more than 40,000 people in 123 countries supported his view that the basic physiological and safety needs must be satisfied before people can achieve fulfillment and happiness (Tay & Diener, 2011).

Other studies have found that the more the basic needs are satisfied, the greater the chances that the higher needs will also be satisfied, and that people older than 36 are far more likely to achieve self-actualization than those who are younger (Taormina & Gao, 2013; Ivtzan, Gardner, Bernard, Sekhon, & Hart, 2013).

The Belongingness Need

Maslow's proposed need for belongingness can only be satisfied through association with, and, more important, acceptance by, other people. Some psychologists consider the need to belong to be as powerful a drive as the physiological needs for food and water.

In one study, American college students who were led to believe they were interacting with others in an Internet chat room were then excluded and rejected by those other perceived participants. No one responded to their messages; no one replied to their comments and questions. All the other participants seemed to be engaged in convivial online conversation. But the participants in the study had been made social isolates.

Following that experience, they were asked to read a diary, allegedly written by a college student. They were then instructed to write down as many of the activities mentioned in the diary as they could remember. Those students whose need to belong had been thwarted by the online experience recalled significantly more social events from the diary than did students whose need to belong had been satisfied in the simulated chat room.

The researchers concluded that failure to satisfy the need to belong can influence a cognitive activity such as memory and affect the type of events a person will recall (Gardner, Pickett, & Brewer, 2000).

When another group of college students were led to believe that they had been excluded or rejected by members of an Internet chat room, they reported lower levels of self-esteem, control, and belongingness than students who had not been told they had been ostracized (Smith & Williams, 2004). These negative feelings developed within only 8 minutes of being informed of their exclusion.

It has also been found that people in the Netherlands and the United States who were high in the need to belong perceived that other people must also be high in the belongingness need, and that the need to belong triggers a feeling of nostalgia for the past where, in their memories at least, they had a greater sense of belonging (Collisson, 2013; Seehusen et al., 2013).

American teenagers who felt a sense of belonging were found to be physically healthier than those who did not express a sense of belonging (Begen & Turner-Cobb, 2012). Thus, it seems that satisfying the need to belong can have important consequences on our behavior and feelings.

Self-Esteem

Numerous studies have been conducted on many aspects of Maslow's need for self-esteem, a characteristic we all possess to some degree or another.

High Self-Esteem   Research supports Maslow's position that people high in self-esteem have greater self-worth and self-confidence. They also feel more competent and productive than those low in self-esteem. People high in self-esteem function better in many situations. Among college students applying for jobs, those with high self-esteem received more job offers and were rated more favorably by recruiters than were students with low self-esteem (Ellis & Taylor, 1983).

People with high self-esteem are able to cope more effectively with the difficulties of job loss than those with low self-esteem (Shamir, 1986). In addition, people high in self-esteem perceive themselves to be significantly higher in intellectual skills, agreeableness, and morality, and to be more extraverted, than those low in self-esteem (Campbell, Rudich, & Sedikides, 2002).

Young adults in the United States and in Canada who measured high in self-esteem were much more likely to participate in school sports and to have lower levels of anxiety and defensive behaviors than those who scored low (Bowker, 2006; Pyszczynski, Greenberg, Solomon, Arndt, & Schimel, 2004).

A study of women college students whose self-esteem levels were unstable (shifting between high and low self-esteem) exhibited a much stronger desire to become famous than those who had more stable levels of self-esteem (Noser & Zeigler-Hill, 2014).

Low Self-Esteem   Large-scale research programs in several countries including the United States, Iceland, Canada, China, Norway, and New Zealand found that low self-esteem was related to anxiety, depression, smoking addiction, school dropout rates, criminal convictions, financial problems, strong emotional reactions to negative outcomes, and difficulties at work (Brown, 2010; Cai, Wu, & Brown, 2009; Donnellan,

Trzesniewski, Robins, Moffitt, & Caspi, 2005; Jonsdottir, Arnarson, & Smari, 2008; Moksnes, Moljord, Espnes, & Byrne, 2010; Trzesniewski, Donnellan, Moffitt, Robins, Poulton, & Caspi , 2006).

Research in Canada and in China showed that people with low self-esteem suffer more physical health problems and more anxiety about death than those with high self-esteem (Routledge, Ostafin, Juhl, Sedikides, Cathey, & Jiangqun, 2010; Stinson et al., 2008). College students who rated low in self-esteem experienced significantly more social problems of adjustment and getting along with other people than those rated high in self-esteem (Crocker & Luhtanen, 2003).

A study of adolescents in Canada in the 7th, 9th, and 11th grades of school found that more than one-third reported that their perceived physical appearance (how attractive they thought they were) determined their level of self-esteem. The results also showed that teenagers who were more concerned with their appearance reported lower self-esteem than those who were less concerned with their appearance. No differences were found between boys and girls on these variables (Seidah & Bouffard, 2007).

People who measured low in self-esteem and who had been led to believe they had been deliberately excluded from a laboratory group by the other members reported a significantly greater feeling of rejection than did people who measured high in self-esteem (Nezlek, Kowalski, Leary, Blevins, & Holgate, 1997).

Failure to achieve self-esteem goals, such as high grades in school or success on the job, can lead to increased anger, shame, sadness, and feelings of worthlessness (Crocker & Park, 2004). Thus, one's level of self-esteem can have enduring effects. People with low self-esteem may think and act in self-defeating ways that "diminish their quality of life" (Swann, Chang-Schneider, & McClarty, 2007, p. 92).

College students who reported lower self-esteem spent more time on Facebook and other social networking sites than those who had higher self-esteem (Kalpidou, Costin, & Morris, 2011; Mehdizadeh, 2010; Vogel, Rose, Roberts, & Eckles, 2014). And college students placed a far greater value on activities that boosted their self-esteem, such as praise or high grades, than they did on eating a favorite food, drinking alcohol, spending time with a friend, getting a paycheck, or having sex (Bushman, Moeller, & Crocker, 2011; Salamon, 2011).

Effects of Self-Esteem on Other Behaviors   Self-esteem can affect our political views and voting behavior. Studies in Belgium and the United States found that among older people (average age 71), conservative political beliefs were related to high self-esteem. In other words, with age, people became more conservative and also felt better about themselves (Van Hiel & Brebels, 2011).

In the U.S. 2008 presidential primaries and election, people were much more likely to vote for candidates they believed had greater self-esteem (Ziegler-Hill & Myers, 2009).

Stability of Self-Esteem over Time   Our self-esteem tends to change over the life span, increasing during adolescence and adulthood, peaking at approximately age 60, and then declining (Gentile, Twenge, & Campbell, 2010; Orth & Robins, 2014; Orth, Trzesniewski, & Robins, 2010). Research in Taiwan, however, found that self-esteem increased throughout childhood, adolescence, and early adulthood but changed very little after age 30 (Huang, 2010b).

Among subjects in Germany it was found that being married, which does not usually occur until the post-adolescent years, and scoring high in subjective well-being, were linked to high self-esteem (Wagner, Lang, Neyer, & Wagner, 2014).

Ethnic and Cultural Differences in Self-Esteem   Studies have found that Black teenagers report higher self-esteem than White teenagers. Self-esteem has been shown to increase for Blacks throughout adulthood but to decline more steeply than for Whites after age 60 (Shaw, Liang, & Krause, 2010).

Self-esteem among Black women college students seems to be much higher among those who identify strongly with Black culture (Eaton, Livingston, & McAdoo, 2010). However, Black college students who feel they are incompetent or inadequate, despite evidence to the contrary, score high in stress and low in self-esteem (Peteet, Brown, Lige, & Lanaway, 2014).

Cultural and ethnic differences have also been documented in self-esteem in comparative studies across more than 50 countries. College students in Japan consistently scored the lowest in self-esteem among all the nations surveyed (Schmitt & Allik, 2005; Tafarodi, Shaughnessy, Yamaguchi, & Murakoshi, 2011; Yamaguchi et al., 2007).

Among college students in the United States, Asian Americans generally reported lower self-esteem than European Americans. However, those Asian-American students who felt they had greater social connections in their dorms or residence halls scored higher in self-esteem than those who did not (Fong & Mashek, 2014).

High self-esteem also appears to correlate with delinquency rates, as documented in a sample of Mexican-American teenage boys (Caldwell, Beutler, Ross, & Silver, 2006; Swenson & Prelow, 2005). Among first-generation Mexican immigrants to the United States, those who felt the greatest pressure to adopt the practices of American culture experienced lower self-esteem than those who did not feel such pressure (Kim, Hogge, & Salvisberg, 2014).

A study in the Netherlands found that among immigrants from Turkey and from Morocco, people who identified more strongly with their ethnic background had greater self-esteem than those who did not (Verkuyten, 2009). Similar results were found among U.S. immigrants from Puerto Rico; the stronger the ethnic identity, the greater the self-esteem (Lopez, 2008).

Self-Actualization   Scores indicating higher self-actualization on the POI have been positively related to several factors: emotional health, creativity, well-being following therapy, academic achievement, autonomy, and racial tolerance. Other studies report negative correlations between high self-actualization scores and alcoholism, institutionalization for mental disturbances, neuroticism, depression, and hypochondriasis.

These results are in the expected directions based on Maslow's description of self-actualizers. POI research on women, ages 19 to 55, confirmed Maslow's view that self-actualization occurs gradually over the life span.

Peak Experiences   Research on Americans between the ages of 40 and 65 found that the three most frequently reported peak experiences involved joyful experiences with other people, a sense of achievement, and personal growth (Hoffman, Kaneshiro, & Compton, 2012).

Cross-cultural comparisons found that mainland Chinese reported more experiences involving serenity, whereas Chinese residents of Hong Kong reported more peak experiences involving interpersonal joy and external achievement. People in Brazil and Portugal reported that their most frequent peak experiences involved achieving some developmental landmark, such as finishing college, getting married, or finding their first job (Ho, Chen, & Hoffman, 2012; Ho, Chen, Hoffman, Guan, & Iversen, 2013).

Self-Determination Theory

A contemporary outgrowth of the essence of Maslow's self-actualization theory is the self-determination theory, which suggests that people have an innate tendency to express their interests, to exercise and develop their capabilities and potentials, and to overcome challenges (Deci & Ryan, 2009; Ryan & Deci, 2000; Deci & Ryan, 2012).

Research supporting the notion of self-determination has come from diverse groups such as football players in Australia, teenagers in India and Nigeria, and older women in the United States. Those who scored highest in self-determination showed the greatest improvement in overall behavior and subjective well-being (Deci, 2011; Podlog & Eklund, 2010; Sheldon, Abad, & Omoile, 2009; Stephan, Boiche, & LeScanff, 2010).

More recent research studying people in the United States, Belgium, China, Peru, Australia, Mexico, Venezuela, the Philippines, Malaysia, and Japan have provided further support for the role of self-determination in facilitating positive growth needs and self-actualization (Chen et al., 2014; Church et al., 2013).

Intrinsic Motivation

Self-determination is facilitated by a person's focus on *intrinsic motivation*, such as engaging in an activity solely because of the interest and challenge of the activity itself. *Extrinsic motivation*, on the other hand, involves engaging in some activity only for the sake of some external reward such as praise, a promotion or pay raise, or a higher grade.

There is a basic similarity between the notions of intrinsic motivation and self-determination, and Maslow's description of self-actualization. Both are concerned with

---

HIGHLIGHTS: Research on Maslow's Ideas

People high in *self-esteem*:

- Feel competent and productive
- Receive more job offers and cope better with job loss
- Are less likely to have anxiety or depression or to drop out of school
- Get along well with others
- Are emotionally healthy and creative
- Are likely to have strong ethnic identities
- Have a greater sense of self-worth and confidence
- May spend less time on Facebook and other social networking sites

People low in *self-esteem* tend to

- Become depressed
- Drop out of school and get criminal convictions
- Experience social problems and poor health
- Have a lower quality of life and psychological well-being
- Spend more time on social media

People high in *self-determination* tend to:

- Have satisfied the needs for competence, autonomy, and relatedness
- Be high in self-esteem and self-actualization
- Possess an innate tendency to overcome challenges and develop their capabilities

fulfilling or realizing one's talents and abilities for the goal of inner satisfaction rather than any kind of external reward.

Three Basic Needs   Self-determination theory specifies three basic needs; it is through the satisfaction of these needs that a person can reach a state of well-being.

1. Competence—the need to feel that one can master difficult tasks
2. Autonomy—the freedom to base one's course of action on one's own interests, needs, and values
3. Relatedness—the need to feel a close connection with other people

Satisfaction of these needs among both the young and the elderly in cultures as diverse as the United States, France, and Russia was positively associated with high self-esteem, self-actualization, and psychological well-being (Ferrand, Martinent, & Dumaz, 2014; Milyavskaya & Koestner, 2011; Ryan & Deci, 2000, Strizhitskaya & Davedyuk, 2014).

Reflections on Maslow's Theory

Criticisms of Maslow's theory center on his research methods and lack of experimentally generated supporting data. The sample of self-actualizing people from which the data were derived, fewer than half of whom were interviewed in person, is too small for generalization to the population at large. Critics also charge that the ways in which Maslow amassed information about his original self-actualizing subjects are inconsistent and vague. He did not describe how he interpreted test results or analyzed biographical materials, nor did he indicate precisely what led him to identify those particular people as self-actualizing. However, as we have seen with other theorists, weakness in scientific methodology is not unique to Maslow.

For his subjects Maslow selected people he admired, according to his own personal criteria for self-actualization. These criteria were not specified at the time, and he later admitted that self-actualization was difficult to describe accurately. His list of characteristics of self-actualizers derives solely from his clinical interpretations of the data and may easily have been influenced by his personal philosophy and moral values. Thus, the descriptions may actually reflect Maslow's own ideal of the worthy and emotionally healthy individual.

Other criticisms have been directed at Maslow's definitions of various concepts such as metaneeds, metapathology, peak experiences, and self-actualization. His use of these terms could be inconsistent and ambiguous. Critics also have asked on what basis self-actualization is presumed to be innate. Why could it not be learned behavior, the result of some unique combination of childhood experiences?

Maslow's defense against these charges was that although his theory was not widely supported by laboratory research, it was successful in social, clinical, and personal terms. He wrote, "It has fitted very well with the personal experience of most people, and has often given them a structured theory that has helped them to make better sense of their inner lives" (1970b, p. xii).

Partly because of Maslow's optimism and compassion, his theory, and the humanistic approach to psychology in general, became extremely popular in the 1960s and 1970s. The trappings of a formal school of thought were then set in place. Journals and organizations were founded, and a division of humanistic psychology was formed within the American Psychological Association. The concerns of humanistic psychologists experienced a rebirth in the positive psychology movement (Chapter 14). Leaders of that movement credit humanistic psychology as a forerunner of positive psychology.

Thus, Maslow's legacy still flourishes today, influencing personality, social psychology, developmental psychology, and organizational behavior (Kenrick, Griskevicius, Neuberg, & Schaller, 2010). Few theories have had such a broad impact beyond the discipline. Teachers and counselors, business and government leaders, health care professionals, and many ordinary people trying to cope with the hassles of everyday life have found Maslow's views compatible with their needs and useful in solving their problems.

Chapter Summary

Maslow argued that each person is born with instinctoid needs that lead to growth, development, and actualization. The hierarchy of needs includes physiological needs (for food, water, air, sleep, and sex) and the needs for safety, belongingness and love, esteem, and self-actualization.

The lower needs must be satisfied before the higher needs emerge. The lower the need, the greater its strength. Lower needs are called deficit needs because failure to satisfy them produces a deficit in the body. Higher needs (growth or being needs) are less necessary for survival but enhance physical and emotional well-being.

Safety needs (for security, stability, order, and freedom from fear and anxiety) are most important in infants and neurotic adults. Belongingness and love needs can be satisfied through association with a group or affectionate relations with one person or with people in general. Esteem needs include self-esteem and esteem from others. Self-actualization involves the realization of one's potential and requires a realistic knowledge of one's strengths and weaknesses. The needs to know and to understand form a hierarchy of cognitive needs that emerges in late infancy and early childhood.

Motivation in self-actualizers (metamotivation) serves not to make up for deficits or reduce tension but to enrich life and increase tension. Metaneeds are states of growth toward which self-actualizers move. Frustration of metaneeds produces metapathology, a formless illness for which no specific cause can be identified.

Self-actualizers constitute less than 1 percent of the population. They share the following characteristics: efficient perception of reality; acceptance of themselves and others; spontaneity and simplicity; focus on problems rather than self in which metaneeds are satisfied through commitment to work; privacy and independence; freshness of appreciation; peak experiences; social interest; intense interpersonal relationships; creativeness;

democratic character structure; and resistance to enculturation. Not everyone becomes self-actualizing because self-actualization is the weakest need in the hierarchy and easily interfered with. Too much freedom or lack of security in childhood inhibits self-actualization. Also, some people fear realizing their highest potential, what Maslow termed the Jonah complex.

Maslow's image of human nature is optimistic, emphasizing free will, conscious choice, uniqueness, the ability to overcome childhood experiences, and innate goodness. Personality is influenced both by heredity and by environment. Our ultimate goal is self-actualization.

Maslow used interviews, free association, projective techniques, and biographical material to assess personality. The POI is a self-report test to measure self-actualization. The Smartphone Basics Needs Scale is an attempt to measure how the use of smartphones might satisfy Maslow's hierarchy of needs. Some research supports the characteristics of self-actualizers, the relationship between self-esteem and self-competence and self-liking, the order of the needs in the hierarchy, and the greater concern with higher than lower needs. People high in self-esteem feel better about themselves, work harder at tasks, and see themselves as more intelligent, agreeable, and moral than people low in self-esteem. Self-esteem levels are reported to be high in childhood and low in adolescence, rising in adulthood and falling in middle age and old age. A contemporary outgrowth of Maslow's work is self-determination theory, which posits three needs: competence, autonomy, and relatedness.

Maslow has been criticized for using too small a sample as the basis for his theory and for not making explicit his criteria for selecting self-actualizing subjects. His theory has had a broad impact on education, counseling, health care, business, and government. It has proven to be a stimulus for the positive psychology movement, which focuses on subjective well-being.

Review Questions

1. What criticisms did the humanistic psychologists make of behaviorism and psychoanalysis?
2. In what ways was Maslow's childhood an example of Adler's theory of personality?
3. How did Maslow's childhood influence the theory he developed as an adult?
4. Describe the hierarchy of needs Maslow proposed.
5. What are the differences between the higher needs and the lower needs?
6. Distinguish between deficiency needs and growth needs. Which type was Maslow more concerned with?
7. Describe Maslow's characteristics of needs. Do we always seek to satisfy these needs in a particular order of importance? Why or why not?
8. Describe the differences between the safety needs and the belongingness and love needs.
9. What conditions are necessary in order to satisfy the self-actualization need?
10. At what age do we develop the needs to know and to understand? Which of these needs is the strongest?
11. Define metaneeds and metapathology.
12. Describe the characteristics of self-actualizing people.
13. What are peak experiences? Are they necessary for self-actualization?
14. Why do so few people satisfy the need for self-actualization?
15. What child-rearing practices can thwart the drive for self-actualization?
16. How does Maslow's image of human nature differ from Freud's?
17. What does correlational research reveal about the relationship between self-actualization and certain personality characteristics?
18. What cultural and ethnic differences have been found with regard to self-esteem?
19. How do people who are high in self-esteem differ from people who are low in self-esteem?
20. Describe the developmental changes in self-esteem from childhood to old age. Has your own self-esteem changed as you have matured?
21. Describe the nature of self-determination theory. Identify the three needs proposed by the theory.
22. On what grounds has Maslow's work on self-actualization been criticized? How did he respond to his critics?

Suggested Readings

Frick, W. B. (2000). Remembering Maslow: Reflections on a 1968 interview. *Journal of Humanistic Psychology, 40*, 128–147. Excerpts from an interview with Maslow and commentary on his personal difficulties with his work, his ideas about self-actualization, and the future of third-force psychology.

Hall, M. H. (1968, July). A conversation with Abraham H. Maslow. *Psychology Today*, pp. 35–37, 54–57. An interview with Maslow about the scope of his work.

Hoffman, E. (1988). *The right to be human: A biography of Abraham Maslow*. Los Angeles: Jeremy Tarcher. A biography based on published and unpublished material describing Maslow's difficult childhood and tracing his career from his early work with primates to his involvement with the human potential movement.

Maslow, A. H. (1968). *Toward a psychology of being* (2nd ed.). New York: Van Nostrand Reinhold. States Maslow's view that humans can be loving, noble, and creative and are capable of pursuing the highest values and aspirations. Also acknowledges the importance of Freud's concept of the unconscious.

Maslow, A. H. (1970). *Motivation and personality* (2nd ed.). New York: Harper & Row. Presents Maslow's theory of motivation and personality, emphasizing psychological health and self-actualization. A third edition (Harper & Row, 1987), revised and edited by Robert Frager and James Fadiman, includes material on Maslow's life, the historical significance of his work, and applications of self-actualization to management, medicine, and education.

Maslow, A. H. (1996). *The unpublished papers of Abraham Maslow*. Edited by E. Hoffman. Thousand Oaks, CA: Sage. Includes previously unpublished essays, articles, and papers with annotations and a biographical sketch.

Milton, J. (2002). *The road to malpsychia: Humanistic psychology and our discontents*. San Francisco, CA: Encounter Books. A biography of Maslow in the context of a cultural history of the rise and fall of the humanistic psychology movement.

chapter 10

Carl Rogers:
Self-Actualization
Theory

Fair Use

The organism has one basic tendency and striving—to actualize, maintain, and enhance the experiencing organism.

—*Carl Rogers*

Carl Rogers originated a popular approach to psychotherapy known initially as non-directive or client-centered therapy, which later came to be called person-centered therapy. This form of psychotherapy has generated an enormous amount of research and is widely used today in counseling situations (see, for example, Cain, 2014; Kirschenbaum, 2009).

Rogers's personality theory, like Maslow's, is rooted in humanistic psychology, which Rogers made the framework for the patient–therapist relationship. Rogers did not develop his theory from experimental research conducted in laboratories, but rather from his experiences working with patients, or clients as he preferred to call them. Rogers's view of the therapeutic situation tells us much about his view of human nature.

Consider the phrase *person-centered therapy*. It tells us that the ability to change and improve personality is centered within the person. In other words, it is the person and not the therapist who directs such change. The therapist's role is to assist or facilitate the change (see Bozarth, 2012).

Rogers believed that we are rational beings ruled by a conscious perception of our selves and our experiential world. He gave very little importance to unconscious forces or other Freudian explanations. He also rejected the notion that events from our past exert a controlling influence on our present behavior. Although he recognized that childhood experiences affect the way we perceive our environment, and ourselves, Rogers insisted that current feelings and emotions have a greater impact on personality.

Because of this emphasis on the conscious and the present, Rogers believed that personality could only be understood from our own viewpoint, based on our subjective experiences. Rogers dealt with reality as consciously perceived by each of us, and he noted that this perception did not always coincide with objective reality.

Rogers proposed one single, innate, overriding motivation: the inborn tendency to actualize, to develop our abilities and potentials to the fullest. This ultimate goal is to actualize the self, to become what Rogers called a *fully functioning person*. His approach to therapy and theory, and the optimistic and humanistic picture he painted, received enthusiastic acceptance in psychology, education, and family-life research.

The Life of Rogers (1902–1987)

Relying on His Own Experience

The fourth child in a family of six, Rogers was born in 1902 in Oak Park, Illinois, a suburb of Chicago. His parents held extremely strict religious views and emphasized moral behavior, suppressing all displays of emotion, and the virtue of hard work. Rogers later wrote that their fundamentalist teachings gripped him like a vise throughout his childhood and adolescence. His parents' beliefs forced him to live by their view of the world rather than his own. His parents promoted their influence in subtle and loving ways, as Rogers later did in his nondirective approach to counseling. It was understood by all the children that they must never "dance, play cards, attend movies, smoke, drink, or show any sexual interest" (Rogers, 1967, p. 344). He would soon make their beliefs a target for revolt.

An Older Brother and a Lonely Childhood   Rogers had little social life outside his family, and he came to believe that his parents favored an older brother. As a result, there was considerable competitiveness between them. Rogers described himself as shy, solitary, dreamy, and often lost in fantasy. A biographer noted that Rogers grew up with "bitter memories of being the inevitable butt of his brother's jokes, even as he was starved of joy by his mother" (Milton, 2002, p. 128).

In an attempt to escape his loneliness, he read incessantly, any book he could find, even dictionaries and encyclopedias. His solitude led him to depend on his own resources and experiences, his personal view of the world. That characteristic remained with him throughout his life and became the foundation of his personality theory. In later years, he realized how strongly his loneliness had influenced his theory as well as his own personality.

> As I look back, I realize that my interest in interviewing and in therapy certainly grew out of my early loneliness. Here was a socially approved way of getting really close to individuals and thus filling some of the hunger I had undoubtedly felt. (Rogers, 1980, p. 34)

Moths and Bizarre Fantasies   When Rogers was 12, the family moved to a farm 30 miles from Chicago where rural life awakened his interest in science. First, he became fascinated by a species of moth he discovered in the woods. He observed, captured, and bred them over many months. Second, he became interested in farming, which his father pursued with modern, scientific methods.

Rogers read about agricultural experiments and came to appreciate the value of the scientific approach with its use of control groups, isolation of a variable for study, and statistical analysis of data. It was an unusual undertaking for an adolescent. At the same time, his emotional life continued in turmoil, the nature of which he never fully explained. He wrote, "My fantasies during this period were definitely bizarre, and probably would be classified as schizoid by a diagnostician, but fortunately, I never came in contact with a psychologist" (1980, p. 30).

Finding Freedom in China   Rogers decided to study agriculture at the University of Wisconsin, the college his parents, two older brothers, and a sister had attended. But following his sophomore year, he gave up the scientific study of agriculture to prepare for the ministry. In his junior year at Wisconsin, Rogers was selected to attend an international Christian student conference in Beijing, China. During his 6 months of travel, he wrote to his parents that his philosophy of life was changing. His religious views had swung from fundamentalist to liberal.

Freeing himself of his parents' ways grieved them, but brought him emotional and intellectual independence. He realized, he later wrote, that he could "think my own thoughts, come to my own conclusions, and take the stands I believed in" (1967, p. 351). This liberation, and the confidence and direction it gave him, reinforced his opinion that all human beings must learn to rely on their own experiences, ideas, and beliefs. But reaching that conclusion was a difficult process, and he paid a high emotional price. After being hospitalized for 5 weeks for ulcers, which may have been induced by stress, he remained at the family farm for a year to recuperate before returning to college.

A Unique Approach to Counseling

In 1924, Rogers graduated from the University of Wisconsin, married a childhood friend, and enrolled at Union Theological Seminary in New York to become a clergyman. After two years, however, he transferred to Teachers College of Columbia University across the street to study clinical and educational psychology. He received his Ph.D. in 1931 and joined the staff of the Child Study Department of the Society for the Prevention of Cruelty to Children in Rochester, New York. His job involved diagnosing and treating delinquent and underprivileged children.

In 1940, he moved from a clinical to an academic setting with an appointment as professor of psychology at Ohio State University. There, Rogers began to formulate his person-centered views on counseling for the emotionally disturbed. He also worked to bring clinical psychology into the mainstream of contemporary psychological thought. He spent the years 1945 to 1957 at the University of Chicago, teaching and developing the Counseling Center.

A Breakdown and Therapy Finding himself unable to help a severely disturbed client, he became so upset that he fell ill himself, suffering what was then called a nervous breakdown. His self-confidence was shattered. He wrote that he felt "deeply certain of my complete inadequacy as a therapist, my worthlessness as a person, and my lack of any future in the field of psychology" (1967, p. 367).

He and his wife left Chicago and set out for their cabin in upstate New York, where Rogers remained secluded for the next 6 months. When he felt well enough to return to the university, he also began undergoing therapy for himself, becoming aware of just how deep his feelings of insecurity were. He said he believed that "no one could ever love *me*, even though they might like what I did" (quoted in Milton, 2002, p. 131).

Finally Finding Himself Rogers's therapy was apparently successful, and he emerged with a newfound ability to give and receive love and to form deep emotional relationships with other people, including his clients.

He taught at the University of Wisconsin from 1957 to 1963. During those years, he published many articles and books that brought his personality theory and person-centered therapy to a wide audience. His clinical experience while in academia was mostly with college students in the counseling centers. Thus, the kind of person he treated during that time—young, intelligent, highly verbal, and, in general, facing adjustment problems rather than severe emotional disorders—was vastly different from the kind of person treated by the Freudians or by clinical psychologists in private practice.

In 1964, Rogers became a resident fellow at the Western Behavioral Sciences Institute in California, working to apply his person-centered philosophy to international problems such as the reduction of tension between Protestants and Catholics in Northern Ireland, and Jews and Arabs in the Middle East. He served as president of the American Psychological Association in 1946 and received that organization's Distinguished Scientific Contribution Award and Distinguished Professional Contribution Award.

Carl Rogers

Various sites provide biographical information, discussions of his theory, research on relevant concepts, and links to other resources.

Person-Centered Therapy

Several sites provide information on the development and applications of Rogers's unique approach to psychotherapy.

The Self and the Tendency toward Actualization

During his trip to China, Rogers came to recognize the importance of an autonomous self as a factor in his own development. His early research reinforced the importance of the self in the formation of the personality. In the 1930s, he developed a method for determining whether a child's behavior was healthy and constructive or unhealthy and destructive. He investigated the child's background and had the child rated on factors he believed would influence behavior. These factors included the family environment, health, intellectual development, economic circumstances, cultural influences, social interactions, and level of education. All of these factors are external, that is, part of the child's environment.

Rogers also investigated a potential internal influence, the child's self-understanding or self-insight. Rogers described self-insight as an acceptance of self and reality, and a sense of responsibility for the self. But he continued to believe that the external factors were of greater importance in shaping one's personality.

Self-Insight

Ten years later, William Kell, one of Rogers's students, attempted to predict the behavior of delinquent children. Rogers predicted that the factors of family environment and social interactions (external factors) would correlate most strongly with delinquent behavior, but he was wrong. The factor that most accurately predicted later behavior was self-insight.

Surprised to learn that family environment did not relate highly to later delinquent behavior, Rogers wrote, "I was simply not prepared to accept this finding, and the study was put on the shelf" (1987, p. 119). Two years later, Helen McNeil replicated the study using a different group of subjects and got results similar to those of Kell. A person's level of self-insight was the single most important predictor of behavior.

This time, faced with such an accumulation of data, Rogers accepted the findings and, on reflection, came to appreciate their significance. If one's attitude toward the self was more important in predicting behavior than the external factors widely thought to be so influential in childhood, then counselors and social workers were emphasizing the wrong things in trying to treat delinquent children and adolescents!

Counselors traditionally focus on external factors such as a poor family environment and alter the circumstances by removing children from a threatening home situation and placing them in foster care. Instead, they should be trying to modify the children's self-insight. That realization was important to Rogers personally.

> This experience helped me decide to focus my career on the development of a psychotherapy that would bring about greater awareness of self-understanding, self-direction, and personal responsibility, rather than focusing on changes in the social environment. It led me to place greater emphasis on the study of the self and how it changes. (Rogers, 1987, p. 119)

Thus, the idea of the self became the core of Rogers's theory of personality, as it had become the core of his own life.

Actualizing Tendency

actualization tendency
The basic human motivation to actualize, maintain, and enhance the self.

Rogers believed people are motivated by an innate tendency to actualize, maintain, and enhance the self. This drive toward self-actualization is part of a larger **actualization tendency**, which encompasses all of our physiological and psychological needs. By attending to basic requirements, such as the needs for food, water, and safety, the actualization tendency serves to maintain the organism, providing for sustenance and survival.

Rogers believed that the actualization tendency begins in the womb, facilitating human growth by providing for the differentiation of the physical organs and the development of physiological functioning. It is responsible for maturation—the genetically determined development of the body's parts and processes—ranging from the growth of the fetus to the appearance of the secondary sex characteristics at puberty. These changes, programmed into our genetic makeup, are all brought to fruition by the actualization tendency.

Even though such changes are genetically determined, progress toward full human development is neither automatic nor effortless. To Rogers, the process involves struggle and pain. For example, when children take their first steps, they may fall and hurt themselves. Although it would be less painful to remain in the crawling stage, most children persist. They may fall again and cry, but they persevere despite the pain because the tendency to actualize is stronger than the urge to regress simply because the growth process is difficult.

Organismic Valuing Process

organismic valuing process The process by which we judge experiences in terms of their value for fostering or hindering our actualization and growth.

The governing process throughout the life span, in Rogers's view, is the **organismic valuing process**. Through this process, we evaluate all life experiences by how well they serve the actualization tendency. Experiences that we perceive as promoting actualization are evaluated as good and desirable; we assign them a positive value. Experiences perceived as hindering actualization are undesirable and, thus, earn a negative value. These perceptions influence behavior because we prefer to avoid undesirable experiences and repeat desirable experiences.

The Experiential World

In developing his theory, Rogers weighed the impact of the experiential world in which we operate daily. This provides a frame of reference or context that influences our growth. We are exposed to countless sources of stimulation every day. Some are trivial and some important, some threatening and others rewarding. He wanted to know how we perceive and react to this multifaceted world of experiences to which we are constantly exposed.

Rogers answered the question by saying that the reality of our environment depends on our perception of it, which may not always coincide with reality. We may react to an experience far differently from the way our best friend does. You may judge the behavior of your roommate in a dramatically different way than does someone decades older. Our perceptions change with time and circumstances. Your own opinion of what you consider to be acceptable behavior for college students will probably change by the time you are 70.

As the actualization tendency in infancy leads us to grow and develop, our experiential world broadens. Infants are exposed to more and more sources of stimulation and respond to them as they are subjectively perceived. Our experiences become the only basis for our judgments and behaviors. Rogers wrote, "Experience is, for me, the highest authority. The touchstone of validity is my own experience" (1961, p. 23). Higher levels of development sharpen our experiential world and ultimately lead to the development of the self.

The Development of the Self in Childhood

As infants gradually develop a more complex experiential field from widening social encounters, one part of their experience becomes differentiated from the rest. This separate part, defined by the words *I*, *me*, and *myself*, is the self or self-concept. The formation of the self-concept involves distinguishing what is directly and immediately a part of the self from the people, objects, and events that are external to the self. The self-concept is also our image of what we are, what we should be, and what we would like to be.

Ideally, the self is a consistent pattern, an organized whole. All aspects of the self strive for consistency. For example, people who are disturbed about having aggressive feelings and choose to deny them dare not express any obvious aggressive behaviors. To do so would mean behaving in ways that are inconsistent with their self-concept, because they believe they should not be aggressive.

Positive Regard

positive regard
Acceptance, love, and approval from others.

As the self emerges, infants develop a need for what Rogers called **positive regard**. It includes acceptance, love, and approval from other people, most notably from the mother during infancy. This need is probably learned, although Rogers said the source was not important. The need for positive regard is universal and persistent.

Infants find it satisfying to receive positive regard and frustrating not to receive it or to have it withdrawn. Because positive regard is crucial to personality development, infant behavior is guided by the amount of affection and love bestowed. If the mother does not offer positive regard, then the infant's innate tendency toward actualization and development of the self-concept will be hampered.

Infants perceive parental disapproval of their behavior as disapproval of their newly developing self. If this occurs frequently, infants will cease to strive for actualization and development. Instead, they will act in ways that will bring positive regard from others, even if these actions are inconsistent with their self-concept.

unconditional positive regard Approval granted regardless of a person's behavior. In Rogers's person-centered therapy, the therapist offers the client unconditional positive regard.

Unconditional Positive Regard   Even though infants may receive sufficient acceptance, love, and approval, some specific behaviors may bring punishment. However, if positive regard for the infant persists despite the infant's undesirable behaviors, the condition is called **unconditional positive regard**. By this, Rogers meant that the mother's love for the child is granted freely and fully; it is not conditional or dependent on the child's behavior.

An important aspect of the need for positive regard is its reciprocal nature. When people perceive themselves to be satisfying someone else's need for positive regard, they in turn experience satisfaction of that need themselves. Therefore, it is rewarding to satisfy someone else's need for positive regard.

Because of the importance of satisfying the need for positive regard, particularly in infancy, we become sensitive to the attitudes and behaviors of other people. By interpreting the feedback we receive from them (either approval or disapproval), we refine our self-concept. Thus, in forming the self-concept we internalize the attitudes of other people.

positive self-regard
The condition under which we grant ourselves acceptance and approval.

Positive Self-Regard   In time, positive regard will come more from within us than from other people, a condition Rogers called **positive self-regard**. Positive self-regard becomes as strong as our need for positive regard from others, and it may be satisfied in the same way. For example, children who are rewarded with affection, approval, and love when they are happy will come to generate positive self-regard whenever they behave in a happy way. Thus, in a sense, we learn to reward ourselves.

Positive self-regard can be defined as a feeling of contentment with oneself and is related to positive mental health (Leising, Borkenau, Zimmermann, Roski, Leonhardt, & Schutz, 2013). Like positive regard, positive self-regard is reciprocal. When people receive positive regard and develop positive self-regard, in turn they may provide positive regard to others.

Ideally, a parent provides unconditional positive regard.

Shawn Gearhart/iStockphoto.com

Conditions of Worth

conditions of worth To Rogers, a belief that we are worthy of approval only when we express desirable behaviors and attitudes and refrain from expressing those that bring disapproval from others; similar to the Freudian superego.

conditional positive regard Approval, love, or acceptance granted only when a person expresses desirable behaviors and attitudes.

Conditions of worth evolve from this developmental sequence of positive regard leading to positive self-regard. Positive self-regard is Rogers's version of the Freudian superego, and it derives from **conditional positive regard**. We noted that *unconditional* positive regard involves the parents' love and acceptance of the infant without conditions, independent of the child's behavior.

Conditional positive regard is the opposite. Parents may not react to everything their infant does with positive regard. Some behaviors annoy, frighten, or bore them and for those behaviors they may not provide affection or approval. Thus, infants learn that parental affection has a price; it depends on behaving in certain acceptable ways. They come to understand that sometimes they are prized, and sometimes they are not.

If a parent expresses annoyance every time the infant drops an object out of the crib, the child learns to disapprove of himself or herself for behaving that way. External standards of judgment become internal and personal. In a sense, then, children come to punish themselves as their parents did. Children develop self-regard only in situations that have brought parental approval, and in time the self-concept, thus formed, comes to function as a parental surrogate.

As a result, children develop conditions of worth. They come to believe they are worthy only under certain conditions, the ones that brought parental positive regard and then personal positive self-regard. Having internalized their parents' norms and standards, they view themselves as worthy or unworthy, good or bad, according to the terms their parents defined.

A study of adolescents found that when their mothers used conditional positive self-regard to reward them for academic achievement, and punish them for non-achievement, their feelings of self-worth became erratic. When they got good grades, for example, they behaved in self-aggrandizing ways. But when they did not get good grades, they felt shame and tend to downplay or devalue their sense of self-worth (Assor & Tai, 2012).

Children thus learn to avoid certain behaviors and no longer function freely. Because they feel the need to evaluate their behaviors and attitudes so carefully, and refrain from taking certain actions, they are prevented from fully developing or actualizing the self. They inhibit their development by living within the confines of their conditions of worth.

Incongruence

Not only do children learn, ideally, to inhibit unacceptable behaviors, but they also may come to deny or distort unacceptable ways of perceiving their experiential world. By holding an inaccurate perception of certain experiences, they risk becoming estranged from their true self. We learn to evaluate experiences, and to accept or reject them, not in terms of how they contribute to our overall actualization tendency, but in terms of whether they bring positive regard from others. This leads to **incongruence** between the self-concept and the experiential world, the environment as we perceive it.

incongruence A discrepancy between a person's self-concept and aspects of his or her experience.

Experiences that are incongruent or incompatible with our self-concept become threatening and are manifested as anxiety. For example, if our self-concept includes the belief that we love all humanity, once we meet someone toward whom we feel hatred, we are likely to develop anxiety.

Hating is not congruent with our image of us as loving persons. To maintain our self-concept, we must deny the hatred. We defend ourselves against the anxiety that accompanies the threat by distorting it, thus closing off a portion of our experiential field. The result is a rigidity of some of our perceptions.

Congruence and Emotional Health

Our level of psychological adjustment and emotional health is a function of the degree of congruence or compatibility between our self-concept and our experiences. Psychologically healthy people are able to perceive themselves, other people, and events in their world much as they really are. They are open to new experiences because nothing threatens their self-concept. They have no need to deny or distort their perceptions because as children they received unconditional positive regard and did not have to internalize any conditions of worth.

They feel worthy under all conditions and situations and are able to use all their experiences. They can develop and actualize all facets of the self, proceeding toward the goal of becoming a fully functioning person and leading what Rogers called "the good life."

Characteristics of Fully Functioning Persons

fully functioning person Rogers's term for self-actualization, for developing all facets of the self.

To Rogers, the **fully functioning person** is the most desirable end result of psychological development and social evolution (Rogers, 1961). He described several characteristics of fully functioning (self-actualizing) people (see Table 10.1).

Fully functioning persons are aware of all experiences   No experience is distorted or denied; all of it filters through to the self. There is no defensiveness because there is nothing to defend against, nothing to threaten the self-concept. Fully functioning persons are open to positive feelings such as courage and tenderness, and to negative feelings

TABLE 10.1 Characteristics of fully functioning persons

Awareness of all experience; open to positive as well as negative feelings

Freshness of appreciation for all experiences

Trust in one's own behavior and feelings

Freedom of choice, without inhibitions

Creativity and spontaneity

Continual need to grow, to strive to maximize one's potential
In a state of actualizing

such as fear and pain. They are more emotional in the sense that they accept a wider range of positive and negative emotions and feel them more intensely.

Fully functioning persons live fully and richly in every moment All experiences are potentially fresh and new. Experiences cannot be predicted or anticipated but are participated in fully rather than merely observed.

Fully functioning persons trust in their own organism By this phrase Rogers meant that fully functioning persons trust their own reactions rather than being guided by the opinions of others, by a social code, or by their intellectual judgments. Behaving in a way that feels right is a good guide to behaving in a way that is satisfying. Rogers did not suggest that fully functioning persons ignore information from their own intellect or from other people. Rather, he meant that all data are accepted as congruent with the fully functioning person's self-concept.

Nothing is threatening; all information can be perceived, evaluated, and weighed accurately. Thus, the decision about how to behave in a particular situation results from a consideration of all experiential data. Fully functioning persons are unaware of making such considerations, however, because of the congruence between their self-concept and experience, so their decisions appear to be more intuitive and emotional than intellectual.

Fully functioning persons feel free to make choices without constraints or inhibitions This brings a sense of power because they know their future depends on their own actions and not present circumstances, past events, or other people. They do not feel compelled, either by themselves or by others, to behave in only one way.

Fully functioning persons are creative and live constructively and adaptively as environmental conditions change Allied with creativity is spontaneity. Fully functioning persons are flexible and seek new experiences and challenges. They do not require predictability, security, or freedom from tension.

Fully Functioning Persons are in a State of Actualizing Rogers used the word *actualizing*, not *actualized*, to characterize the fully functioning person. The latter term implies a finished or static personality, which was not Rogers's intent. Self-development is always in progress. Rogers wrote that being fully functioning is "a direction, not a destination" (1961, p. 186). If striving and growing cease, then the person loses spontaneity, flexibility, and openness. Rogers's emphasis on change and growth is neatly captured in the word *becoming* in the title of his book, *On Becoming a Person* (1961).

Fully functioning persons feel a sense of freedom and have the ability to live richly and creatively in every moment.

Being fully functioning is not always easy   Being fully functioning involves continually testing, growing, striving, and using all of one's potential, a way of life that brings complexity and challenge. Rogers did not describe fully functioning persons as happy, blissful, or contented, although at times they may be. More appropriately, their personality may be described as enriching, exciting, and meaningful.

Questions about Human Nature

On the issue of free will versus determinism, Rogers's position is clear. Fully functioning persons have free choice in creating their selves. In other words, no aspect of personality is predetermined for them. On the nature–nurture issue, Rogers gave prominence to the role of the environment. Although the actualization tendency is innate, the actualizing process itself is influenced more by social than by biological forces.

Childhood experiences have some impact on personality development, but experiences later in life have a greater influence. Our present feelings are more vital to our personality than the events of our childhood.

Rogers recognized a universal quality in personality when he noted that fully functioning persons share certain characteristics. However, we may infer from his writings that there is opportunity for uniqueness in the ways these characteristics are expressed. The ultimate and necessary goal of life is to become a fully functioning person.

A personality theorist who credits people with the ability, motivation, and responsibility to understand and improve themselves obviously views people in an optimistic and positive light. Rogers believed we have a basically healthy nature and an innate tendency to grow and fulfill our potential. Rogers never lost this optimism. In an interview at the age of 85, he said, "in working with individuals and working with groups my positive view of human nature is continually reinforced" (1987, p. 118).

In Rogers's opinion, we are not doomed to conflict with our selves or with our society. We are not ruled by instinctive biological forces or controlled by events of the first 5 years of life. Our outlook is progressive rather than regressive, toward growth rather than stagnation. We experience our world openly, not defensively, and we seek challenge and stimulation instead of the security of the familiar. Emotional disturbances may occur, but these are uncommon.

Through Rogers's person-centered therapy, people are able to overcome difficulties by using their inner resources, the innate drive for actualization.

> I am quite aware that out of defensiveness and inner fear individuals can and do behave in ways which are incredibly cruel, horribly destructive, immature, regressive, antisocial, hurtful. Yet one of the most refreshing and invigorating parts of my experience is to work with such individuals and to discover the strongly positive directional tendencies which exist in them, as in all of us. (Rogers, 1961, p. 27)

The urge to become a fully functioning person benefits society as well. As more people in a given culture become self-actualizing, the improvement of society will naturally follow.

Assessment in Rogers's Theory

To Rogers, the only way to assess personality is in terms of the person's subjective experiences, the events in the person's life as he or she perceives them and accepts them as real. Rogers maintained that his clients (he never called them "patients") had the ability to examine the roots of their problems and to redirect the personality growth that had been impeded by some incongruence between their self-concept and their experiences.

Person-Centered Therapy

person-centered therapy Rogers's approach to therapy in which the client is assumed to be responsible for changing his or her personality.

In **person-centered therapy**, Rogers explored the client's feelings and attitudes toward the self and toward other people. He listened without any preconceptions, trying to understand the client's experiential world as the client viewed it. Although Rogers considered person-centered therapy the only worthwhile approach to personality assessment, he realized that it was not infallible. By focusing on subjective experiences, the therapist learns only about those events the client consciously expresses.

Experiences that are not in conscious awareness remain hidden. The danger in trying to infer too much about these *non-conscious* experiences is that the inferences the therapist draws may represent the therapist's own projections more than the client's actual experiences.

Also, what the therapist learns about a client depends on the client's ability to communicate. Because all forms of communication are imperfect, the therapist necessarily will see the client's world of experience imperfectly and incompletely.

Within these limits, Rogers argued that person-centered therapy provides a clearer view of a person's experiential world than all other forms of assessment and therapy. One advantage Rogers claimed for his approach is that it does not rely on a predetermined theoretical structure, such as Freudian psychoanalysis, into which the therapist must fit the patient's problem.

The only predetermined belief of the person-centered therapist is the client's inherent value and worth. Clients are accepted as they are. The therapist gives them unconditional positive regard and offers no judgments about their behavior or advice on how to behave. Everything centers on the client, including the responsibility for changing behavior and reevaluating relationships.

Rogers opposed assessment techniques such as free association, dream analysis, and case histories. He believed they made clients dependent on the therapist, who then assumed an aura of expertise and authority. These techniques removed personal responsibility from the clients by giving them the impression that the therapist knew all about them. Clients could conclude that the therapist would then solve their problems and all they needed to do was sit back and follow the expert's instructions.

Encounter Groups

encounter groups A group therapy technique in which people learn about their feelings and about how they relate to (or encounter) one another.

Rogers demonstrated that person-centered therapy could help individuals who were out of touch with their feelings and closed to life's experiences. He then wanted to bring this state of enhanced psychological health and functioning to a greater number of people, and so he developed a group technique in which people could learn more about themselves and how they related to, or encountered, one another. He called his approach the **encounter group** (Rogers, 1970).

Group sizes ranged from 8 to 15 people. They typically met 20 to 60 hours over several sessions. They began with no formal structure or agenda. The group facilitators who conducted the sessions were not leaders in the usual sense. They established an atmosphere in which group members could express themselves and focus on how others perceived them. The job of the facilitator was to make it easier for members to achieve self-insight and become more fully functioning. Rogers believed that most (though not all) participants would become more fully functioning.

Not all psychologists agreed. A large-scale analysis of studies on encounter groups revealed that the results were comparable to traditional psychotherapies (Faith, Wong, & Carpenter, 1995). The analysis also showed that larger groups that met more frequently produced more favorable outcomes than smaller groups that met less often.

Encounter groups are no longer as popular today as when Rogers himself was promoting them, but they are still conducted by some of his followers as a way of inducing people to enhance their potentials and become more fully functioning.

Psychological Tests

Rogers did not use psychological tests to assess personality, nor did he develop any tests. However, other psychologists have devised tests to measure aspects of the experiential world. The Experience Inventory (Coan, 1972), a self-report questionnaire, attempts to assess openness or receptivity to experience, a characteristic of the fully functioning person. The Experiencing Scale (Gendlin & Tomlinson, 1967) measures our level of self-trust.

Persons being assessed by this test do not respond directly. They may talk about whatever they choose, and their recorded comments are later rated for degree of self-trust; for example, how much they claim their feelings are an important source of information on which to base behavior, or how much they deny that personal feelings influence their decisions.

The Experiencing Scale has been used with person-centered therapy. For example, one study found that people who made the greatest improvement during therapy revealed an increase in self-trust from before therapy to after therapy. Those who showed little improvement during therapy showed a small or no increase in self-trust over the period. Those with less severe emotional disorders showed greater self-trust than those with more severe emotional disorders (Klein, Malthieu, Gendlin, & Kiesler, 1969).

Research on Rogers's Theory

Rogers believed that person-centered interviews, which rely on clients' self-reports, were of greater value than experimental methods. In his view, the more orthodox scientific approaches yielded less information on the nature of personality than did his clinical approach. He said, "I never learned anything from research. Most of my research has been to confirm what I already felt to be true" (quoted in Bergin & Strupp, 1972, p. 314).

Although Rogers did not use laboratory methods to collect data about personality, he did use them to attempt to verify and confirm his clinical observations. He was enthusiastic about research on the nature of the therapy sessions, an idea resisted by many clinicians who saw it as a violation of privacy.

What Rogers did was to introduce what was then a radical procedure (Goldfried, 2007). He recorded and filmed therapy sessions to enable researchers to study the client–therapist interaction. Before Rogers's innovation, the only data available from therapy sessions were the therapist's after-the-fact reconstructions—the notes made on the therapy session some time after it was over. In addition to distortions of memory with the passage of time, a written record misses the client's emotional state and body language. Sometimes a facial expression or tone of voice might reveal more than words. With recorded therapy sessions, everything became available for study.

Rogers referred to it as a microscope with which to examine the "molecules of personality change" (1974, p. 120). He always obtained the client's permission to record the sessions and he found that the presence of the equipment did not impede the course of therapy.

Evaluating Person-Centered Therapy

Rogers and his associates also studied how the self-concept changes during a course of therapy. Using qualitative and quantitative techniques in the scientific tradition (despite Rogers's claim of not being a scientist), they analyzed the therapy sessions. By applying rating scales and content analyses of a client's verbalizations, they investigated changes in the self-concept.

Q-sort technique A self-report technique for assessing aspects of the self-concept.

Much of the research used the **Q-sort technique**, a procedure developed by William Stephenson (1953). In this technique, clients sort a large number of statements about the self-concept into categories that range from most descriptive to least descriptive. Thus, the Q sort is a way of empirically defining the client's self-image.

Typical Q-sort statements include the following:

- I enjoy being alone.
- I feel helpless.
- I am emotionally mature.

The Q-sort can be used in several ways. For example, after sorting the statements in terms of the perceived self, clients can be asked to sort the same statements in terms of an ideal self, that is, the person they would most like to be. Applying the correlational method, Rogers used Q-sort responses to determine how closely a client's self-image or perceived self corresponded to the ideal self.

He also noted how greatly the self-concept changed from the period before therapy to the period following therapy. For one client, identified as "Mrs. Oak," the data yielded an initial correlation coefficient of +.36 between perceived self and ideal self. A year after therapy, the correlation coefficient had shown an increase to +.79, indicating to Rogers that Mrs. Oak's perceived self had become much more congruent with her ideal or desired self (Rogers, 1954). He concluded that this dramatic change reflected an increase in emotional health.

Mrs. Oak chose different Q-sort phrases to describe herself before and after therapy. Prior to her sessions with Rogers, she saw her self-image as dependent and passive. She also felt rejected by other people. After the course of therapy, Mrs. Oak believed she was more like the self she really wanted to be. She felt more secure, less fearful, and better able to relate to other people (see Table 10.2).

TABLE 10.2   Mrs. Oak's Q-sort statements of perceived self before and after therapy

SELF BEFORE THERAPY	SELF 12 MONTHS AFTER THERAPY
I usually feel driven.	I express my emotions freely.
I am responsible for my troubles.	I feel emotionally mature.
I am really self-centered.	I am self-reliant.
I am disorganized.	I understand myself.
I feel insecure within myself.	I feel adequate.
I have to protect myself with excuses, with rationalizing.	I have a warm emotional relationship with others.

Source: From Rogers, C. R. (1954). The case of Mrs. Oak: A research analysis. In C. R. Rogers & R. F. Dymond (Eds.), *Psychotherapy and personality change*. Chicago: University of Chicago Press.

A study by Rogers's associates measured the discrepancy between perceived self and ideal self in 25 clients (Butler & Haigh, 1954). The researchers found that the discrepancy decreased over time during and following therapy. Before therapy, the average correlation coefficient between perceived self and ideal self was −.01. After therapy, it was +.31.

More recent research has shown that person-centered therapy is more likely to be successful when clients perceive their therapists to:

1. Be empathic and understanding
2. Demonstrate unconditional positive regard for them
3. Show congruence by demonstrating that they are being genuine in the therapeutic relationship (Cain, 2013).

More recently, a Sexual Satisfaction Q-Sort technique has been developed in which people sort 63 statements concerning their behaviors, feelings, and experiences during sexual satisfaction. Initial findings suggest that most people taking the test sort their sexual experiences into one or more of four categories: emotional and masculine, relational and feminine, partner focused, or orgasm focused (McClelland, 2014a, 2014b).

Conditional Positive Regard   Research conducted on three generations of women and on college students demonstrated that the use of conditional positive regard by parents had successfully brought about the behaviors they desired in their children. However, self-reports from children whose parents used conditional regard showed poor coping skills, fluctuating levels of self-esteem, low self-worth, feelings that their parents disapproved of them, and resentment toward their parents. No such negative consequences were reported by children whose parents did not use conditional regard (Assor, Roth, & Deci, 2004).

Organismic Valuing Process   There is some evidence to support Rogers's concept of the organismic valuing process. Studies have also suggested that positive self-regard may not be as prevalent in a collectivist culture such as Japan as it is in a more individualistic culture such as the United States (Heine, Lehman, Markus, & Kitayama, 1999; Joseph & Linley, 2005; Sheldon, Arndt, & Houser-Marko, 2003).

Openness to Experience

In a classic study, college students completed the Q-sort list to test Rogers's proposition that fully functioning persons are open to all experiences, whereas psychologically unhealthy people erect defenses to protect themselves against experiences that threaten their self-image (Chodorkoff, 1954). A separate Q-sort description of each subject was prepared by clinicians who based their reports on a variety of data, including responses to the Thematic Apperception Test and the Rorschach inkblot test. Based on these clinical measurements, the students were divided into good- and poor-adjustment groups.

Measures of perceptual defense against material perceived to be threatening were obtained from the subjects' reactions to neutral words such as *table* and to allegedly threatening words such as *penis*. The results showed that all subjects were slower to perceive threatening words than neutral words, but this response was more marked in the defensive subjects of the poorly adjusted group. Significantly less perceptual defense was shown by people in the good-adjustment group, presumed to be psychologically healthier. With regard to agreement between the students' self-descriptions and the clinicians' descriptions, researchers found that the closer the two sets of Q-sort statements, the better adjusted that person was found to be.

Acceptance of Self

A study of 56 mothers explored the relationship between their self-acceptance and the extent to which they accepted their children as they were rather than as they wished them to be (Medinnus & Curtis, 1963). This early research was based on Rogers's idea that people who accept their own nature realistically (whose perceived and ideal selves are congruent) are more likely to accept others as they really are.

The results revealed significant differences between self-accepting mothers and those who were not self-accepting. Self-accepting mothers were more accepting of their children's nature. Also, the child's degree of self-acceptance depended to some extent on the mother's degree of self-acceptance.

Racial identity A study of multiracial adults in the United States found that people who showed a high degree of self-acceptance about their racial identities had stronger positive growth than those who showed a lesser degree of self-acceptance about their racial identities (Pedrotti & Edwards, 2010).

Parental behavior Parents who accept their children unconditionally and display democratic child-rearing practices were found to have children with higher self-esteem and greater emotional security than parents who failed to accept their children and who displayed authoritarian behavior (Baldwin, 1949).

Parents of children with high self-esteem displayed their affection and used reward rather than punishment to guide their child's behavior. Parents of children with low self-esteem were more aloof, less loving, and more likely to use punishment (Coopersmith, 1967).

Adolescents whose parents provided unconditional positive regard and allowed them to express themselves without restraint developed greater creative potential than did adolescents whose parents did not provide those conditions (Harrington, Block, & Block, 1987).

It has also been found that adolescents who received unconditional positive regard from their parents were more confident and hopeful about their ability to receive support from others in the future. They also engaged in more behaviors that were consistent with their perception of their interests and talents.

Teens who received conditional positive regard from their parents lacked such confidence and hope. They took more actions that were inconsistent with their true selves in an effort to obtain support and approval from their parents (Harter, Marold, Whitesell, & Cobbs, 1996). High school students who received unconditional positive regard from their teachers were found to score higher in positive self-esteem than those who did not receive unconditional positive regard from their teachers (Nolan, 2008).

Age Growing older has been found to increase the level of self-adjustment, as well as to decrease feelings of anger and anxiety (Shallcross, Ford, Floerke, & Mauss, 2013).

Emotional Adjustment

Several studies provide support for Rogers's suggestion that incongruence between perceived self and ideal self indicates poor emotional adjustment. Researchers have concluded that the greater the discrepancy, the higher the anxiety, insecurity, self-doubt, depression, social incompetence, and other psychological disorders.

Also, high inconsistency between perceived and ideal self correlates with low levels of self-actualization and self-esteem (Achenbach & Zigler, 1963; Gough, Fioravanti, & Lazzari, 1983; Mahoney & Hartnett, 1973; Moretti & Higgins, 1990; Straumann, Vookles, Berenstein, Chaiken, & Higgins, 1991). Persons with a great discrepancy between perceived and ideal selves were rated by others as awkward, confused, and unfriendly (Gough, Lazzari, & Fioravanti, 1978).

Rogers believed that failure to realize our innate actualization tendency can lead to maladjustment. To test this idea, one researcher studied the inherited temperaments proposed by Buss and Plomin (Emotionality, Activity, and Sociability, or EAS) in male and female college students (Ford, 1991). Using the EAS Temperament Survey to assess behavior, the college students' parents were asked to recall their children's temperaments when very young.

These temperament profiles were compared with the college students' current self-perceptions on the three temperaments. The results supported Rogers's views. The greater the discrepancy in temperament between childhood potential and adult realization, the greater was the level of maladjustment.

HIGHLIGHTS: Research on Rogers's Ideas

Research on Rogers's approach has found that:

- Positive self-regard may be more important in individualistic cultures
- Fully functioning persons are open to all experiences
- A child's self-acceptance depends in part on the mother's degree of self-acceptance
- Children whose parents accept them unconditionally have high self-esteem
- Those who possess incongruence between perceived self and ideal self are poorly adjusted emotionally and have low self-esteem and self-actualization
- Failing to realize our innate potential can lead to maladjustment

Reflections on Rogers's Theory

Criticisms

Rogers insisted that the only way to explore personality is through person-centered therapy to examine a person's subjective experiences. He did this by listening to a client's self-reports. Critics charge that he ignored those factors of which the client was not consciously aware but which could influence behavior. People may distort reports of their subjective experiences, repressing some events and elaborating on or inventing others, to conceal their true nature and present an idealized self-image.

The Influence of World War II on Person-Centered Therapy

Rogers's person-centered psychotherapy quickly became popular. Its rapid acceptance was fostered in part by social circumstances in the United States at the end of World War II (1945). Veterans returning from service overseas needed help readjusting to civilian life. The result was a demand for psychologists and for a counseling technique they could master and put into practice quickly.

Training in traditional psychoanalysis required a medical degree and a lengthy period of specialization. However, "person-centered psychotherapy," wrote one analyst, "was simple, informal, and brief, and it required little training" (DeCarvalho, 1999, p. 142).

More than 400 college counseling centers based on Rogers's teachings were established after World War II under the auspices of the Veterans Administration to help returning veterans adjust to civilian life. Client-centered therapy received an enormous boost and hundreds more colleges established their own counseling centers.

Rogers later acknowledged that the stresses of post–World War II America had catapulted his method and his name to prominence and worldwide fame as a leader in a new approach to understanding and treating personality (see Barrett-Lennard, 2012; McCarthy, 2014).

Acceptance of Rogers's Therapy

Rogers's therapy has since found broad application not only as a treatment for emotional disturbances but also as a means of enhancing the self-image. In the business world, it has been used as a training method for managers. In the helping professions, it is used to train clinical psychologists, social workers, and counselors.

In addition, psychotherapists of many different orientations have accepted some of Rogers's core concepts in their therapeutic work with clients. Thus, the person-centered approach remains influential in counseling and psychotherapy (see Bohart, 2014; Hazler, 2011; Kirschenbaum & Jourdan, 2005; Patterson & Joseph, 2007).

More than 200 training centers, mostly in Europe, promote Rogers's form of therapy. In addition, several dozen journals are devoted to research and application of Rogers's ideas (Murdock, 2008). The journal *Person-Centered & Experiential Psychotherapies* began publication in 2002 and remains influential today.

Rogers's Personality Theory

Rogers's personality theory, although less influential than his psychotherapy, has also received wide recognition, particularly for its emphasis on the self-concept. However, Rogers did not believe he had influenced academic or scientific psychology. Nonetheless, his theory and therapy have stimulated research on the nature of psychotherapy, the client–therapist interaction, and the self-concept. His ideas have had a significant impact on psychology's theoretical and empirical definitions of the self.

Rogers's background was a unique combination of clinic, lecture hall, and laboratory. He drew on his considerable experience with emotionally disturbed clients and on the intellectual stimulation of colleagues and students. He attracted large numbers of followers who continue to test his ideas in the clinic and in the laboratory.

Chapter Summary

Rogers's person-centered theory proposes that we are conscious, rational beings not controlled by unconscious forces or past experiences. Personality can only be understood by a phenomenological approach, that is, from an individual's own viewpoint based on his or her subjective experiences (one's experiential field).

Our goal in life is self-actualization, an innate tendency toward growth and development. The organismic valuing process evaluates life experiences in terms of how well they serve the actualizing tendency. Experiences that promote actualization will be sought; experiences that hinder it will be avoided.

Positive regard is a need for acceptance, love, and approval from others, particularly from the mother, during infancy. In unconditional positive regard, the mother's love and approval are granted freely and are not conditional on the child's behavior. When love and approval are conditional, a state of conditional positive regard exists. Once we internalize the attitudes of others, positive regard comes from ourselves (positive self-regard).

Conditions of worth (similar to the Freudian superego) involve seeing ourselves as worthy only under conditions acceptable to our parents. We avoid behaviors and perceptions that oppose our parents' conditions of worth.

Incongruence develops between the self-concept and behaviors that threaten the self-image. We defend against anxiety by denying threatening aspects of the experiential field.

The fully functioning person represents the peak of psychological development. Characteristics of the fully functioning person are an awareness of all experiences, no conditions to defend against, the ability to live fully in each moment, trust in one's self, a sense of freedom and personal power, creativity, and spontaneity.

Rogers's optimistic image of human nature encompassed a belief in free will, the prominence of environment over heredity, and some universality in personality. Individuals and societies can grow unhampered by past events.

Personality can be assessed in terms of subjective experiences as revealed in self-reports. In this person-centered approach, the therapist gives the client unconditional positive regard. Rogers opposed free association and dream analysis because they make the client dependent on the therapist. By recording therapy sessions, Rogers enabled researchers to investigate the nature of the client–therapist interaction.

The Q-sort technique, in which clients sort statements about their self-concept into categories ranging from most to least descriptive, is a way of quantifying the self-image. Q-sort research has revealed a greater correspondence between perceived self and ideal self after therapy. The better adjusted a person is, the greater the agreement between self-descriptions and descriptions made by others. Discrepancies between perceived self and ideal self indicate poor psychological adjustment.

Rogers's work has been criticized for ignoring the impact of unconscious forces, and for accepting the possible distortion of a client's subjective experiences in self-reports. Nevertheless, his person-centered approach to therapy remains influential in the fields of counseling and psychotherapy.

Review Questions

1. How Rogers's childhood led to his interest in interviewing and in therapy?
2. In what ways did Carl Rogers's clinical experience differ from Sigmund Freud's?
3. Describe the research on delinquent children that influenced Rogers's view of the role of the self in personality.
4. Explain how the need to actualize promotes biological and psychological growth?
5. What is the organismic valuing process? How does it influence behavior?
6. What is the experiential field? How does our experiential field change with age?
7. Explain the differences between positive regard and positive self-regard.
8. What parental behaviors affect a child's development of positive self-regard?
9. Compare Rogers's concept of conditions of worth with Freud's concept of the superego.
10. Describe Rogers's concept of incongruence. How is incongruence related to anxiety?
11. Describe the roles of (a) the intellect, (b) positive and negative feelings, and (c) spontaneity in becoming a fully functioning person.
12. What are the characteristics of the fully functioning person? Can we say that a fully functioning person is self-actualized?
13. How does Rogers's image of human nature differ from that of Freud?

14. Would you describe Rogers as an optimist or a pessimist in his view of human nature?
15. How does the clinical interview in Rogers's system differ from the psychoanalytic clinical interview?
16. What did Rogers call his approach? Why?
17. How does the Q-sort technique measure a person's self-image?
18. What has Q-sort research shown about the self-concept before and after therapy?
19. What do studies show to be the results of parental use of conditional positive regard?
20. Describe the ways in which parents' behavior can affect the behavior of their children, according to Rogers.
21. What was Rogers's position on the importance of childhood experiences and adult experiences in personality development?
22. What criticisms have been made of Rogers's personality theory?
23. Why was his person-centered therapy accepted so quickly?

Suggested Readings

Barrett-Lennard, G. (2013). Origins and evolution of the person-centered innovation in Carl Rogers' lifetime. In Cooper, M., O'Hara, M., Schmid, P., Bohart, A. (Eds.), *Handbook of person-centered psychotherapy and counseling* (2nd ed.). New York: Palgrave Macmillan, pp. 32–45. An overview of Roger's early life and family background, including his travels and the World War II era that influenced his outlook and the acceptance of his form of therapy.

Cornelius-White, J. (2013). *Carl Rogers: The China diary.* Las Vegas: CreateSpace Independent Publishing. A replica of the diary Rogers kept at age 20 in China (including his unique spelling and grammar!). A foreword by his daughter provides her views.

Evans, R. I. (1975). *Carl Rogers: The man and his ideas.* New York: Dutton. Interviews with Rogers on the evolution of the self, techniques of person-centered therapy, and applications of his theory to education. Contrasts Rogers's humanistic views with B. F. Skinner's behaviorist views.

Kirschenbaum, H. (1979). *On becoming Carl Rogers.* New York: Delacorte Press. (2009). *The life and work of Carl Rogers.* Alexandria, VA: American Counseling Association. Biographies of Rogers and his contributions to humanistic psychology and psychotherapy.

Milton, J. (2002). *The road to Malpsychia: Humanistic psychology and our discontents.* San Francisco: Encounter Books. A cultural and social history of the humanistic psychology movement including an assessment of the contributions of Carl Rogers.

Rogers, C. R. (1961). *On becoming a person: A therapist's view of psychotherapy.* Boston: Houghton Mifflin. Summarizes Rogers's views on psychotherapy, especially problems in communication and interpersonal relations. Discusses the effects of enhanced personal growth on personal and family life.

Rogers, C. R. (1967). Autobiography. In E. G. Boring & G. Lindzey (Eds.), *A history of psychology in autobiography* (Vol. 5, pp. 341–384). New York: Appleton-Century-Crofts. Rogers's assessment of his work and the influence of his early experiences.

Rogers, C. R. (1974). In retrospect: Forty-six years. *American Psychologist, 29,* 115–123. Rogers evaluates the impact of his work on the fields of counseling, psychotherapy, education, leadership, and international relations and on the empirical investigation of subjective phenomena.

Rogers, C. R. (1980). *A way of being.* Boston: Houghton Mifflin. Presents the work of Rogers's later years concerning individual and group psychotherapy, the helping professions, scientific progress, and personal growth.

Rogers, C. R. (1989). *The Carl Rogers reader.* Boston: Houghton Mifflin. A selection of Rogers's writings over 60 years, edited by Howard Kirschenbaum and Valerie Henderson. Includes personal recollections, case studies, and essays on personality change, psychotherapy, education, marriage, aging, international relations, and world peace.

The Cognitive Approach

The word *cognition* means the act or process of knowing. The cognitive approach to personality focuses on the ways in which people come to know their environments and themselves. It deals with the question of how we perceive, evaluate, learn, think, make decisions, and solve problems.

This is a truly *psychological* approach to personality because it focuses exclusively on conscious mental activities. In the cognitive approach, we will not find needs, drives, or emotions as separate activities of the personality. Instead, they are aspects of personality under the control of the cognitive processes.

Contemporary psychoanalysts acknowledge the importance of cognitive processes. So did Erikson, who, as we saw, granted greater autonomy to the ego and to cognitive functioning. Humanistic psychologists Maslow and Rogers also dealt with perceptions, how we evaluate and mentally process our experiences. Allport wrote about human reasoning, and Adler proposed a creative self, which results from our perception or interpretation of experience. Social-learning theorists (Chapter 13) also invoke cognitive processes.

The difference between these approaches and George Kelly's cognitive theory of personality is that Kelly attempted to describe *all* aspects of personality, including its emotional components, strictly in terms of cognitive processes.

chapter 11

George Kelly: Personal Construct Theory

Fair Use.

It occurred to me that what seemed true of myself was probably no less true of others. If I initiated my actions, so did they.

—George Kelly

personal construct theory Kelly's description of personality in terms of cognitive processes: We are capable of interpreting behaviors and events and of using this understanding to guide our behavior and to predict the behavior of other people.

The Cognitive Movement in Psychology

Kelly's **personal construct theory** of personality differs substantially from every other approach discussed in this book. Kelly warned us that we would not find in his system such familiar concepts as the unconscious, the ego, needs, drives, stimuli and responses, and reinforcement—not even motivation and emotion. The obvious question is how can we understand the human personality without considering these ideas, especially motivation and emotion?

Kelly's answer was that each person creates a set of cognitive constructs about the environment. By that he meant that we interpret and organize the events and social relationships of our lives in a system or pattern. On the basis of this pattern, we make predictions about ourselves and about other people and events, and we use these predictions to formulate our responses and guide our actions. Therefore, in order to understand personality, we must first understand our patterns, the ways we organize or construct our world. According to Kelly, our interpretation of events is more important than the events themselves.

Like Maslow, Kelly was opposed to the behavioral and the psychoanalytic approaches to the study of personality. He viewed them both as denying the human ability to take charge of our own lives, to make our own decisions, and to pursue our chosen course of action.

He argued that behaviorism viewed people as merely passive responders to stimuli in their environment, and that psychoanalysis viewed people as passive responders to their unconscious forces. In contrast, "for Kelly, [people] are forms of motion and we propel ourselves. No one or no thing does it to us" (Fransella & Neimeyer, 2003, p. 25).

An Experiential-Based Theory

The personality theory Kelly offered derived from his experience as a clinician. For several reasons, he interpreted his clinical experience differently from Freud and other theorists who treated patients. The model of human nature Kelly developed from his clinical work is unusual. He concluded that people function in the same way scientists do.

Scientists construct theories and hypotheses and test them against reality by performing experiments in the laboratory. If the results of their experiments support the theory, the theory is retained. If the data do not support the theory, the theory must be rejected or modified and retested.

As we have seen, this is how psychologists who study personality typically proceed. Yet Kelly believed that psychologists do not attribute to their subjects the same intellectual and rational abilities they ascribe to themselves. It is as if psychologists have two theories about human nature, one that applies to scientists and their way of looking at the world, and another that applies to everybody else.

The logical assumption, then, is that psychologists consider their subjects to be incapable of rational functioning, as being motivated by all sorts of conflicting drives, or as victims of rampant unconscious forces. Thus, human beings are believed to function largely on an emotional level, unlikely to use their cognitive processes to learn, think, evaluate experiences, or solve problems. Surely this is quite unlike the way psychologists function.

Are Psychologists Superior Beings?

Are psychologists really superior beings? You know the answer to that as well as Kelly did. He said they are no different from the people they study. What works for one works for the other; what explains one explains the other. Both are concerned with predicting and controlling the events in their lives, and both are capable of doing so rationally.

Like scientists, all of us construct theories, which Kelly called *personal constructs*, by which we try to predict and control the events in our lives. He proposed that the way to understand someone's personality is to examine his or her personal constructs.

Kelly and the Cognitive Movement

How does Kelly's cognitive theory fit with the cognitive movement that began around 1960 and now dominates mainstream experimental psychology? Despite the similarity in terminology, the cognitive movement has not embraced Kelly's work because the theory is not consistent with the movement's subject matter and methods.

Kelly's approach is that of a clinician dealing with the conscious constructs by which people arrange their lives. In contrast, cognitive psychologists are interested in both cognitive variables and overt behavior, which they study primarily in an experimental, not a clinical, setting. Also, cognitive psychologists do not limit their focus to personality. They study overt behavior and learning in social situations. They believe that cognitive processes such as learning influence a person's response to a given stimulus situation.

Although cognitive psychology took hold some time after Kelly proposed his explanation of personality, his theory had little influence on it. At best, Kelly's theory could be considered a precursor to contemporary cognitive psychology. The two approaches share the term *cognitive*, with its implied interest in conscious activities, but little else. Kelly's recognition of the importance of cognitive processes is noteworthy, but we must place it in perspective. It is not part of mainstream American psychology as defined by experimental psychologists, but that does not detract from its usefulness for studying personality.

The Life of Kelly (1905–1967)

Kelly was born on a farm in Kansas. An only child, he received a great deal of attention and affection from his parents, who were fundamentalist in their religious beliefs and committed to helping the less fortunate. They opposed every form of frivolous entertainment such as dancing and card playing. When Kelly was 4 years old, the family traveled by covered wagon to Colorado to try farming but soon returned to Kansas.

An Erratic Education

Kelly's early education was erratic and conducted as much by his parents as by schoolteachers. At 13, he went to high school in Wichita and seldom lived at home after that. In 1926, he earned a bachelor's degree in physics and mathematics from Park College in Parkville, Missouri. But his interests had shifted from science to social problems. Kelly's future was uncertain.

He worked briefly as an engineer, and then took a teaching job at a labor college in Minneapolis. Next, he became an instructor in speech for the American Banking Association and also taught citizenship courses to immigrants. He then enrolled in graduate school and received a master's degree in educational sociology from the University of Kansas in Lawrence. Accepting a job offer from a junior college in Iowa, Kelly taught various courses and coached the drama program.

No Interest in Psychology

His career certainly showed no inclination toward psychology. In college, he had not been impressed by the coursework in the field.

> In the first course in psychology, I sat in the back row of a very large class, tilted my chair against the wall, made myself as comfortable as possible, and kept one ear cocked for anything interesting that might turn up. One day the professor, a very nice person who seemed to be trying hard to convince himself that psychology was something to be taken seriously, turned to the blackboard and wrote an "S," an arrow, and an "R." Thereupon I straightened up in my chair and listened, thinking to myself that now, after two or three weeks of preliminaries, we might be getting to the meat of the matter. (Kelly, 1969, p. 46)

Kelly paid attention for several more class meetings and then gave up. He said he could not understand what the arrow connecting the stimulus (S) and the response (R) stood for. He never did figure it out. The traditional behaviorist, experimental approach to psychology had failed to spark his interest. He also explored psychoanalysis, which was not successful either. He wrote, "I don't remember which one of Freud's books I was trying to read, but I do remember the mounting feeling of incredulity that anyone could write such nonsense, much less publish it" (1969, p. 47).

Finding Himself and Psychology

Kelly's professional training took a different turn in 1929 when he was awarded a fellowship at the University of Edinburgh, Scotland. During his year there, he earned a Bachelor of Education degree and finally developed an interest in psychology. He returned to the United States for doctoral studies at the State University of Iowa and received his Ph.D. in 1931.

Finding an Intellectual Approach to Counseling

Kelly began his academic career at Fort Hays Kansas State College in the midst of the economic depression of the 1930s. There was no money to conduct research in physiological psychology, the specialty in which he had trained, so he switched to clinical psychology for which there was a need. He developed a clinical psychology service for the local public school system and for the students at his college. He established traveling clinics, going from school to school, which gave him the opportunity to deal with a variety of problems and to try different approaches to treatment.

Kelly was not committed to any particular therapeutic technique or to a specific theory about the nature of personality. He felt free to use traditional methods of assessment and treatment as well as those of his own design. He pretty much taught himself how to do therapy by assuming that each new patient was just as much a scientist as himself (Routh, 2011).

His clinical experiences strongly influenced the nature of his personal construct theory. The people he treated were not severely disturbed psychotics in mental hospitals or neurotics with troublesome emotional problems. His patients were students who had been referred by their teachers for counseling.

Thus, unlike the emotionally maladjusted patients in a psychiatric ward or a psychoanalyst's office, Kelly's clients were much more capable of discussing their concerns rationally, of expressing their problems in intellectual terms, the level of functioning expected in an academic setting.

In the classroom, we are taught to analyze, to think and process information logically. This intellectual attitude carried over from the classroom to the counseling situation. Had circumstances placed Kelly during his formative professional years at work with schizophrenics in a mental institution, his theory might not have depended so heavily on cognitive information-processing abilities.

Becoming a Major Force

World War II interrupted Kelly's academic career. He joined the U.S. Navy and served as a psychologist in the Bureau of Medicine and Surgery in Washington DC. When the war ended in 1945, he taught for a year at the University of Maryland before joining the faculty of Ohio State University replacing Carl Rogers.

There he spent 19 years teaching, refining his personality theory, and conducting research. Kelly also lectured at universities throughout the world about how his personal construct theory of personality could be used to resolve international tensions. In 1965, he accepted an invitation from Abraham Maslow for an appointment to an endowed chair at Brandeis University but Kelly died shortly thereafter.

Kelly was a major force in the development of the clinical psychology profession during its rapid growth following World War II. He held several honored positions in the field, including the presidencies of the Clinical and Consulting divisions of the American Psychological Association and the American Board of Examiners in Professional Psychology.

George Kelly

Various sites provide biographical information, discussions of his theory, research on relevant concepts, and links to other resources

Personal Construct Theory

Kelly suggested that people perceive and organize their world of experiences the same way scientists do, by formulating hypotheses about the environment and testing them against the reality of daily life. In other words, we observe the events of our life—the facts or data of our experience—and interpret them in our own way. This personal interpreting, explaining, or *construing* of experience is our unique view of events (Winter & Proctor, 2014). It is the pattern within which we place them. Kelly said that we look at the world through "transparent patterns that fit over the realities of which the world is composed" (Kelly, 1955, pp. 8–9).

We might compare these patterns to sunglasses that add a particular tint or color to everything we see around us. One person's glasses may have a bluish tint, whereas another's may have a greenish tint. As a result, several people can look at the same scene and perceive it differently, depending on the tint of the lenses that frame their point of view. So it is with the hypotheses or patterns we construct to make sense of our world. This special view, the unique pattern created by each individual, is what Kelly called our *construct system*.

Life Is a Construct

construct An intellectual hypothesis that we devise and use to interpret or explain life events. Constructs are bipolar, or dichotomous, such as tall versus short or honest versus dishonest.

A **construct** is a person's unique way of looking at life, an intellectual hypothesis devised to explain or interpret events. We behave in accordance with the expectation that our constructs will predict and explain the reality of our world. Like scientists, we constantly test these hypotheses. We base our behavior on our constructs, and we evaluate the effects.

Consider a student who is in danger of failing an introductory psychology course and is trying to persuade the professor to give a passing grade. After observing the professor for most of the semester, the student concludes that the professor behaves in a superior and authoritarian manner in class and has an inflated sense of personal importance. From this observation, the student forms the hypothesis, or construct, that acting to reinforce the professor's exaggerated self-image will bring a favorable response.

The student tests this idea against reality by reading an article the professor has written and praising it to the professor. If the professor feels flattered and gives the student a good grade, then the student's construct has been confirmed. It has been found to be useful and can be applied the next time the student takes a course with that professor or with any other professor who behaves similarly. However, if the student receives a failing grade, then the construct was found to be inappropriate. A new one will be required for dealing with that professor.

Constructive Alternativism: Adapting to the World

Over the course of our lives, we develop many constructs, one for almost every type of person or situation we encounter. We expand our inventory of constructs as we meet new people and face new situations. Further, we may alter or discard constructs periodically as situations change. Revising our constructs is a necessary and continuous process; we must always have an alternative construct to apply to a situation.

If our constructs were inflexible and incapable of being revised (which is what would happen if personality was totally determined by childhood influences), then we would not be able to cope with new situations. Kelly called this adaptability **constructive alternativism** to express the view that we are not controlled by our constructs but we are free to revise or replace them with other alternatives.

constructive alternativism The idea that we are free to revise or replace our constructs with alternatives as needed.

Ways of Anticipating Life Events

Kelly's personal construct theory is presented in a scientific format, organized into a fundamental postulate and 11 corollaries (see Table 11.1). The fundamental postulate states that *our psychological processes are directed by the ways in which we anticipate events*.

By using the word *processes*, Kelly was suggesting that personality was a continually flowing, moving process. Our psychological processes are directed by our constructs, by the way each of us construes our world. Another key word in the fundamental postulate is *anticipate*. Kelly's notion of constructs is anticipatory. We use constructs to predict the future so that we have some idea of the consequences of our actions, of what is likely to occur if we behave in a certain way.

TABLE 11-1	Corollaries of personal construct theory
Construction	Because repeated events are similar, we can predict or anticipate how we will experience such an event in the future.
Individuality	People perceive events in different ways.
Organization	We arrange our constructs in patterns, according to our view of their similarities and differences.
Dichotomy	Constructs are bipolar; for example, if we have an opinion about honesty, that idea must also include the concept of dishonesty.
Choice	We choose the alternative for each construct that works best for us, the one that allows us to predict the outcome of anticipated events.
Range	Our constructs may apply to many situations or people, or they may be limited to a single person or situation.
Experience	We continually test our constructs against life's experiences to make sure they remain useful.
Modulation	We may modify our constructs as a function of new experiences.
Fragmentation	We may sometimes have contradictory or inconsistent subordinate constructs within our overall construct system.
Commonality	Although our individual constructs are unique to us, people in compatible groups or cultures may hold similar constructs.
Sociality	We try to understand how other people think and predict what they will do, and we modify our behavior accordingly.

The Construction Corollary

Similarities among repeated events   Kelly believed no life event or experience could be reproduced exactly as it occurred the first time. An event can be repeated, but it will not be experienced in precisely the same way. For example, if you watch a movie today that you first saw last month, your experience of it may be different the second time.

Your mood may not be the same, and during the elapsed month you were exposed to events that affected your attitudes and emotions. Maybe you read something unpleasant about an actor in the film. Or you may feel more content because your grades are improving.

However, although such repeated events are not experienced identically, recurrent features or themes will emerge. Some aspects of a situation will be similar to those experienced earlier. It is on the basis of these similarities that we are able to predict or establish anticipations about how we will deal with that type of event in the future. Our predictions rest on the idea that future events, though they are not exact duplicates of past events, will nevertheless be similar.

For example, some scenes in the movie probably affect you the same way every time. If you liked the car chase scenes the first time, you will probably like them again. You base your behavior on your anticipation of liking the chases, so that explains why you choose to watch the film again. Themes of the past reappear in the future, and we formulate our constructs on the basis of these recurring themes.

The Individuality Corollary

Individual differences in interpreting events   With this corollary, Kelly introduced the notion of individual differences. He pointed out that people differ from one another in how they perceive or interpret an event, and because people construe events differently, they thus form different constructs. Our constructs do not so much reflect the objective reality of an event as they constitute the unique interpretation each of us places on it.

The Organization Corollary

Relationships among constructs   We organize individual constructs into a pattern according to our view of their interrelationships, their similarities and differences. People who hold similar constructs may still differ from one another if they organize those constructs in different patterns.

Typically, we organize our constructs into a hierarchy, with some constructs subordinate to others. A construct can include one or more subordinate constructs. For example, the construct *good* may include among its subordinates the constructs *intelligent* and *moral*. Thus, if we meet someone who fits our idea of a good person, we anticipate that he or she will also have the attributes of intelligence and high moral standards.

The relationships among constructs are usually more enduring than the specific constructs themselves, but they, too, are open to change. A person who feels insulted by someone who appears more intelligent may switch the construct *intelligent* from a subordinate place under the construct *good* to a place under the construct *bad*. The only valid test for a construct system is its predictive efficiency. If the organization of our constructs no longer provides a useful way to predict events, we will modify it.

The Dichotomy Corollary

Two mutually exclusive alternatives   All constructs are bipolar or dichotomous. This is necessary if we are to anticipate future events correctly. Just as we note similarities among people or events, we must also account for dissimilarities. For example, it is not enough to have a construct about a friend that describes the personal characteristic of *honesty*. We must also consider the opposite, *dishonesty*, to explain how the honest person differs from someone who is not honest.

If we did not make this distinction—if we assumed that all people are honest—then forming a construct about honesty would not help us anticipate or predict anything about people we might meet in the future. A person can be expected to be honest only in contrast to someone who is expected to be dishonest. The appropriate personal construct in this example, then, is *honest versus dishonest*. Our constructs must always be framed in terms of a pair of mutually exclusive alternatives.

The Choice Corollary

Freedom of choice   The notion that people have freedom of choice is found throughout Kelly's writings. According to the dichotomy corollary described previously, each construct has two opposing poles. For every situation we must choose the alternative that works best for us, the one that allows us to anticipate or predict the outcome of future events.

Kelly suggested that we have some latitude in deciding between the alternatives, and he described it as a choice between security and adventure. Suppose you have to decide which of two courses to take next semester. One is easy because it is not much different from a course you've already taken and is taught by a professor known to give high grades for little work.

There is virtually no risk involved in choosing that course, but there may not be much reward either. You know the professor is dull, and you have already studied much of the course material. However, it is the secure choice, because you can make a highly accurate prediction about the consequences of deciding to take it.

The other course is more of a gamble. The professor is new and rumored to be tough, and you don't know much about the subject, but it would expose you to a field of study you've been curious about. In this case, you cannot make an accurate prediction about

People differ from one another in the ways they perceive and interpret the same event.

Comstock Images/Stockbyte/Getty Images

the outcome of your choice. This more adventurous alternative means more risk, but the potential reward and satisfaction are greater.

Low Risk versus High Risk   You must choose between the low-risk, minimal-reward secure option and the high-risk, high-reward adventurous option. The first has a high predictive efficiency, the second a lower predictive efficiency. Kelly believed we face such choices throughout our lives, choices between defining or extending our personal construct system. The secure choice, which is similar to past choices, further defines and limits our construct system by repeating experiences and events. The more adventurous choice extends our construct system by encompassing new experiences and events.

The popular tendency to opt for the secure, low-risk alternative may explain why some people persist in behaving in an unrewarding way. For example, why do some people act aggressively toward others even when they are continually rebuffed? Kelly's answer was that they are making the low-risk choice because they have come to know what to expect from others in response to aggressive behavior. These hostile people do not know how others will react to friendliness because they have rarely tried it. The potential rewards may be greater for friendly behavior but so is the uncertainty.

Remember that our choices are made in terms of how well they allow us to anticipate or predict events, not necessarily in terms of what is best for us. And it is Kelly's contention that each of us, in the best scientific tradition, desires to predict the future with the highest possible degree of certainty.

The Range Corollary

The range of convenience   Few personal constructs are appropriate or relevant for all situations. Consider the construct *tall versus short*, which obviously has a limited **range of convenience** or applicability. It can be useful with respect to buildings, trees, or basketball players, but it is of no value in describing a pizza or the weather.

range of convenience The spectrum of events to which a construct can be applied. Some constructs are relevant to a limited number of people or situations; other constructs are broader.

Some constructs can be applied to many situations or people, whereas others are more limited, perhaps appropriate for one person or situation. The range of convenience or relevance for a construct is a matter of personal choice. For example, we may believe that the construct *loyal versus disloyal* applies to everyone we meet or only to our family members or to our pet dog. According to Kelly, if we are to understand personality fully, it is just as important to know what is excluded from a construct's range of convenience as it is to know what is included.

The Experience Corollary

Exposure to new experiences   We have seen that each construct is a hypothesis generated on the basis of past experience to predict or anticipate future events. Each construct is then tested against reality by determining how well it predicts a given event. Most of us are exposed to new experiences daily, so the process of testing the fit of a construct to see how well it predicted the event is ongoing. If a construct is not a valid predictor of the outcome of the situation, then it must be reformulated or replaced.

As a result, we evaluate and reinterpret our constructs as our environment changes. Constructs that worked for us at age 16 may be useless, or even harmful, at age 40. In the intervening years, our experiences will have led us to revise our construct system. If you never have any new experiences, then your construct system would never have to change. But for most of us, life involves meeting new people and coping with new challenges. Therefore, we must re-construe our experiences and constructs accordingly.

The Modulation Corollary

permeability The idea that constructs can be revised and extended in light of new experiences.

Adapting to new experiences   Constructs differ in their **permeability**. To permeate means to penetrate or pass through something. A permeable construct is one that allows new elements to penetrate or be admitted to the range of convenience. Such a construct is open to new events and experiences and is capable of being revised or extended by them.

How much our construct system can be modulated, or adjusted, as a function of new experience and learning depends on the permeability of the individual constructs. An impermeable or rigid construct is not capable of being changed, no matter what our experiences tell us.

For example, if a bigoted person applies the construct *high intelligence versus low intelligence* in a fixed or impermeable way to people of a certain ethnic minority group, believing that all members of this group have low intelligence, then new experiences will not penetrate or alter this belief. The prejudiced person will not modify that construct, no matter how many highly intelligent people of that ethnic group he or she meets. The construct is a barrier to learning and to new ideas because it is incapable of being changed or revised.

The Fragmentation Corollary

Competition among constructs.   Kelly believed that within our construct system some constructs might be incompatible even though they coexist within the overall pattern. Recall that our construct system may change as we evaluate new experiences. However, new constructs do not necessarily derive from old ones. A new construct may be compatible or consistent with an old one in a given situation, but if the situation changes, these constructs can become inconsistent.

Consider the following situation. A man meets a woman in a psychology class and decides that he is attracted to her. She is also a psychology major, and her interests seem similar to his. She fits the *friend* alternative of the construct *friend versus enemy*.

People may accept one another as friends in one situation, such as playing a board game, but may act as adversaries in another situation, such as a political debate.

Fuse/Jupiter Images

Thus, she is someone to be liked and respected. He sees her the next day at a political rally and is disappointed to find her loudly expressing conservative views that are the opposite of his own liberal opinions. Now she also fits the opposite alternative of the construct. In that situation she has become the *enemy*.

This inconsistency in the man's construct about this woman is at a subordinate level in his overall construct system. In one situation she is a friend, and in another situation she is an enemy. However, his broader construct, that liberals are friends and conservatives are enemies, remains undisturbed. According to Kelly, this is the process by which we tolerate subordinate inconsistencies without damaging our overall construct system.

The Commonality Corollary

Similarities among people in interpreting events   Because people differ in the ways they construe events, each person develops unique constructs. However, people also show similarities in their ways of construing events. Kelly suggested that if several people construe an experience similarly, we can conclude that their cognitive processes are similar.

Consider a group of people with the same cultural norms and ideals. Their anticipations and expectations of one another will have much in common and they will construe many of their experiences in the same way. People from the same culture may show a resemblance in their behaviors and characteristics even though they are exposed to different individual life events.

The Sociality Corollary

Interpersonal relationships   As already noted, people in the same culture tend to construe events similarly. Although this accounts for some commonalities among people, it does not in itself bring about positive social relationships. It is not enough for one person to construe or interpret experiences in the same way as another person. The first person must also construe the other person's constructs. In other words, we must understand how another person thinks if we are to anticipate how that person will predict events.

Construing another person's constructs is something we do routinely. Think about driving a car. We stake our lives on being able to anticipate what other drivers on the road will do. We anticipate that they will stop at a red light and move ahead at a green light. It is only when we can predict with some certainty what drivers, friends, bosses, or teachers will do that we can adjust our behaviors to theirs. And while we are adapting to them, they are doing the same to us.

Each person assumes a role with respect to others. We play one role with a partner, another with a child, another with our supervisor at work. Each role is a behavior pattern that evolves from understanding how the other person construes events. In a sense, then, we fit ourselves into the other person's constructs.

Personal Construct Theory

Several sites provide information on the development and applications of Kelly's approach to personality.

Centre for Personal Construct Psychology, England

Offers courses and workshops on the theory and practice of George Kelly's personal construct psychology.

Questions about Human Nature

Kelly's personality theory presents an optimistic, even flattering, image of human nature (Kelly, 1969). He treated people as rational beings capable of forming a framework of constructs through which to view the world. He believed we are the authors, not the victims, of our destiny.

His view endows us with free will, the ability to choose the direction our lives will take, and we are able to change when necessary by revising old constructs and forming new ones. We are not committed to a path laid down in childhood or adolescence. Our direction is clearly toward the future because we formulate constructs to predict or anticipate events.

Thus, Kelly did not accept the notion of determinism. He did not consider past events to be the determinants of our present behavior. We are not prisoners of toilet training, early sex experiences, or parental rejection, nor are we bound by biological instincts or unconscious forces. We need no push from internal drives or needs because we are motivated by the fact of being alive. Kelly saw no reason to invoke any other explanation.

Although Kelly did not discuss the role of heredity in personality, he noted that we are not totally determined by environmental influences. We live by constructs based on our interpretation of events. Therefore, it is the operation of our rational mental processes and not the specific events that influence the formation of personality.

Kelly did not posit an ultimate and necessary life goal, but we may infer that our goal is to establish a construct system that enables us to predict events.

On the question of uniqueness versus universality, Kelly took a moderate position. The commonality corollary states that people in the same culture develop similar constructs, whereas the individuality corollary emphasizes the uniqueness of many of our constructs and therefore of the self.

Assessment in Kelly's Theory

The Interview

Kelly's primary assessment technique was the interview. As he put it, "If you don't know what is going on in a person's mind, ask him; he may tell you!" (1958, p. 330). Adopting what he called a "credulous attitude," Kelly accepted the client's words at face value, believing this was the best way to determine the person's constructs. He also recognized that a person might deliberately lie or distort the reported version of events. However, what the client said must be respected, even if not always fully believed.

Self-Characterization Sketches

self-characterization sketch A technique designed to assess a person's construct system; that is, how a person perceives himself or herself in relation to other people.

Another technique used to assess a construct system is to have the person write a **self-characterization sketch**. Kelly's instructions to the client were as follows. "I want you to write a character sketch of [client's name] just as if he were the principal character in a play. Write it as it might be written by a friend who knew him very intimately and very sympathetically, perhaps better than anyone ever really could know him" (1955, p. 323). Kelly found this technique useful for learning how clients perceive themselves in relation to other people.

The Role Construct Repertory Test

Kelly devised the Role Construct Repertory (REP) Test to uncover the constructs we apply to the important people in our lives. The client is asked to list by name the people who have played a significant role in his or her life such as mother, father, spouse, closest friend, and the most intelligent or interesting person he or she knows (see Table 11.2).

TABLE 11-2 Role title list from the Role Construct Repertory Test

1. A teacher you liked.
2. A teacher you disliked.
3. Your wife/husband or present boyfriend/girlfriend.
4. An employer, supervisor, or officer under whom you worked or served and whom you found hard to get along with.
5. An employer, supervisor, or officer under whom you worked or served and whom you liked.
6. Your mother or the person who has played the part of a mother in your life.
7. Your father or the person who has played the part of a father in your life.
8. Your brother nearest your age or the person who has been most like a brother.
9. Your sister nearest your age or the person who has been most like a sister.
10. A person with whom you have worked who was easy to get along with.
11. A person with whom you have worked who was hard to understand.
12. A neighbor with whom you get along well.
13. A neighbor whom you find hard to understand.
14. A boy you got along well with when you were in high school.
15. A girl you got along well with when you were in high school.
16. A boy you did not like when you were in high school.
17. A girl you did not like when you were in high school.
18. A person of your own sex whom you would enjoy having as a companion on a trip.
19. A person of your own sex whom you would dislike having as a companion on a trip.
20. A person with whom you have been closely associated recently who appears to dislike you.
21. The person whom you would most like to be of help to or whom you feel most sorry for.
22. The most intelligent person whom you know personally.
23. The most successful person whom you know personally.
24. The most interesting person whom you know personally.

Source: Reprinted from *The Psychology of Personal Constructs*, by George A. Kelly. Copyright © 1991 by Routledge, Chapman & Hall, Inc. Reproduced by permission of Taylor & Francis Books UK.

The names are sorted, three at a time, and clients are asked to select from each group of three the two people who are most alike, noting how they differ from the third. For example, the client may be given the names of most threatening person, successful person, and attractive person and must describe how any two of them are similar in some aspect of behavior or character and how they differ from the other.

The Repertory Grid This information is presented in a diagram called a repertory grid. For each row the client judges the three people indicated by circles and formulates a construct about them, such as *happy versus sad*. The client writes a word or phrase that describes two of them in the column labeled *Emergent Pole*. The client writes the opposite word (*sad*) to describe the third person in the group in the column labeled *Implicit Pole*. The client places a check mark in the squares of anyone else in the grid who shares the *Emergent Pole* characteristics—anyone significant in the client's life who could be described as happy.

The Role of Dichotomies

The assumption underlying the REP Test is that people construe events in dichotomies, according to the dichotomy corollary, in terms of like versus unlike or similar versus dissimilar. By forcing clients to make repeated judgments about their social relationships, Kelly believed he could uncover their anticipations and expectations. The dichotomies or alternatives by which we guide our life will show the pattern of our personal constructs.

Interpreting the REP Test   Interpretation of the REP Test depends on the skill and training of the psychologist who administers it. Kelly did not intend the test to be a standardized, objective self-report inventory. He designed it as a way to assess constructs as a necessary stage in psychotherapy, to induce clients to reveal the constructs by which they organize their world. However, computer programs have since been developed to analyze individual repertory grids in more objective terms (Grice, 2002).

Fixed Role Therapy

After assessing a client's system of personal constructs, Kelly attempted to bring about a change in undesirable or ineffective constructs. He promoted a form of psychotherapy he called **fixed role therapy**. To help clients formulate new constructs and discard old ones, he asked them to write a self-characterization sketch describing them as the lead character in a play.

fixed role therapy A psychotherapeutic technique in which the client acts out constructs appropriate for a fictitious person. This shows the client how the new constructs can be more effective than the old ones he or she has been using.

Playing a Role   In fixed role therapy, the therapist prepares a fixed role sketch containing constructs that differ from the client's negative self-perceptions as revealed in the self-characterization sketch. The client is told that the fixed role sketch is about a fictitious character and is asked to act out that character in the therapist's office and later in everyday life. Through this role-playing, the client is expected to project personal needs and values onto the fictitious character.

The therapist expects the client to discover that the new constructs in the fixed role sketch work better in anticipating events than do the old constructs by which the client was living. Once the client realizes this, he or she can incorporate the new constructs into the overall construct system and function in a more satisfying and effective way.

Kelly developed fixed role therapy from observing a friend who began to live the role he was performing in a college play. The friend was so strongly influenced by the part that his behavior offstage gradually became more and more like the character. The goal of fixed role therapy, then, is to first play a role and then come to live it.

A Sample Fixed Role Therapy   Based on interviews with a male client named Roy Taylor, his written self-characterization sketch, and his REP Test results, a therapist concluded that the client was overly concerned with finding a female companion. His attempts to do so were having a negative impact on his other social relationships.

The client had difficulty being open and assertive because in his construct system assertiveness and extraversion were negative personality characteristics. Yet, in dealing with other people, he was convinced that his opinions were the correct ones and that everybody else was wrong. At work, he felt isolated, believing he belonged to a higher social class than his colleagues.

The therapist's fixed role sketch for this client made no mention of the client's desire to have an intimate relationship with a woman. Instead, taking as a framework the client's skill at tennis, the therapist encouraged the client, through the fictitious character, to be more curious about and tolerant of different kinds of people and their views (Winter, 1992, pp. 270–271).

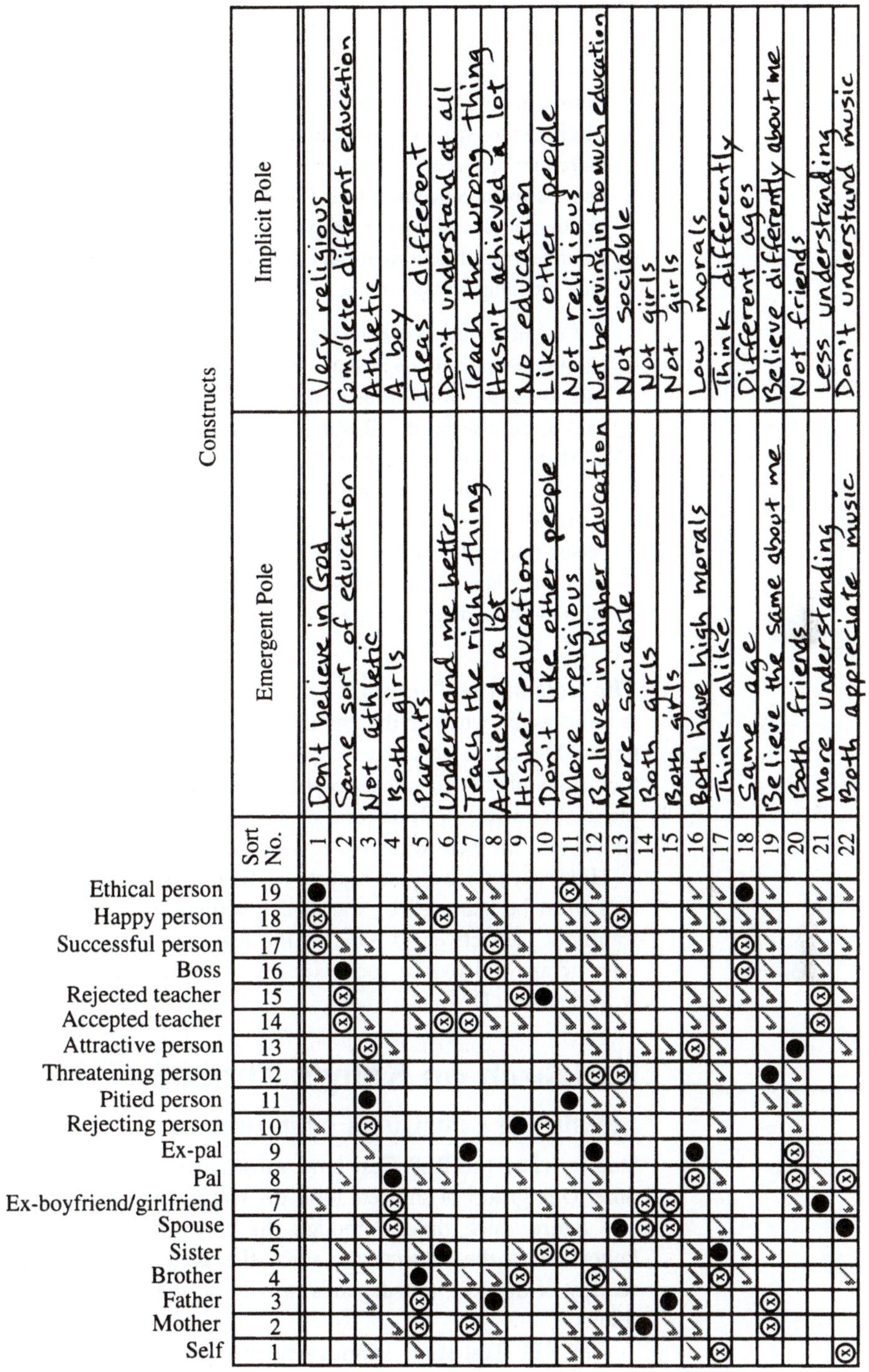

FIGURE 11.1

A grid for the Role Construct Repertory Test.

Constructs

Implicit Pole

Emergent Pole	Implicit Pole
Don't believe in God	Very religious
Same sort of education	Complete different education
Not athletic	Athletic
Both girls	A boy
Parents	Ideas different
Understand me better	Don't understand at all
Teach the right thing	Teach the wrong thing
Achieved a lot	Hasn't achieved a lot
Higher education	No education
Don't like other people	Like other people
More religious	Not religious
Believe in higher education	Not believing in too much education
More sociable	Not sociable
Both girls	Not girls
Both girls	Not girls
Both have high morals	Low morals
Think alike	Think differently
Same age	Different ages
Believe the same about me	Believe differently about me
Both friends	Not friends
More understanding	Less understanding
Both appreciate music	Don't understand music

Rows (Sort No.):

- Ethical person — 19
- Happy person — 18
- Successful person — 17
- Boss — 16
- Rejected teacher — 15
- Accepted teacher — 14
- Attractive person — 13
- Threatening person — 12
- Pitied person — 11
- Rejecting person — 10
- Ex-pal — 9
- Pal — 8
- Ex-boyfriend/girlfriend — 7
- Spouse — 6
- Sister — 5
- Brother — 4
- Father — 3
- Mother — 2
- Self — 1

Source: Reprinted from *The Psychology of Personal Constructs*, by George A. Kelly. Copyright © 1991 by Routledge, Chapman & Hall, Inc. Reproduced by permission of Taylor & Francis Books UK.

Roy Taylor's philosophy of life very much reflects his approach to his favorite sport, tennis: It's not whether a player wins or loses that's important but whether they've played the game to the best of their ability. Whether at work or at play, he believes that if a job is worth doing it's worth doing well, and he brings to everything that he does a certain passion and conviction, which cannot fail to earn your respect. Although you might perhaps think that this would make him appear a little too serious and intense, once you get to know him you soon realize that his main concern is to live life to the full and that this includes having fun as well as working hard. Life doesn't always run smoothly for him, of course, but when he has a disappointment he always seems able to learn something from it, and to look to the future rather than brooding on his present or past misfortunes.

One of his greatest strengths at tennis is his ability to anticipate the moves of the other players, be they his opponents or doubles partners. In other areas of his life, he also always tries to see the world through the eyes of the people with whom he comes into contact, perhaps because he has mixed with people from so many different walks of life. His lively curiosity in what makes other people tick is usually reciprocated and leads him, almost before he knows it, into some very rewarding relationships. He also, of course, has his fair share of disagreements with others, but when this happens he always makes an effort to understand the other person's point of view, even though he might not accept it. Because of this, he has a reputation both for commitment to those causes that are close to his heart and tolerance of the right of others to hold different opinions.

The Role of the Therapist   The therapist reviewed the fixed role sketch with the client and asked whether the character seemed like someone that the client might want to know. The client agreed to try behaving like the character in the sketch while in the therapist's office. He was asked to try acting, thinking, and talking like the character for the next two weeks. Behavioral changes instilled by fixed role therapy are reported to last far beyond the two-week role-playing period.

However, positive case reports on treatment outcomes such as this for individual clients must be balanced by the fact that there has been little controlled research on the technique's effectiveness. One of the few studies to be conducted found that the fixed role therapy did reduce social anxiety in a small sample of clients in Japan (Abe, Imai, & Nedate, 2011).

Research on Kelly's Theory

Stability of Constructs over Time

Studies using the REP Test have shown that a person's constructs remain stable over time. One group of subjects took the test twice, using the names of different people as role figures each time. Although the role models changed, the constructs that were important to the subjects remained the same. However, research has shown that the validity of the REP test depends heavily on the skill of the psychologist interpreting the results.

One REP Test study investigated the complexity of a person's construct system. The results showed that the pattern becomes increasingly differentiated and integrated over the life span and can process more information as it is able to function in more abstract terms (Crockett, 1982). Another study suggested that forming friendships depends on a similarity of personal constructs.

A group of students took the REP Test during their first week at college and again six months later. The results showed that the similarity in constructs or attitudes among friends did not develop during the six-month period but had existed before the relationships were formed.

The researchers concluded that we seek as friends those whose constructs are already similar to ours (Duck & Spencer, 1972). Also, for married subjects, spouses whose constructs were more alike reported greater happiness with their marriage than did couples whose constructs were more unlike (Neimeyer, 1984).

Effects of Emotional State

Other research showed a correspondence between one's personal characteristics and the ways of construing other people. For example, among a group of student nurses, those identified as highly anxious tended to use *anxious versus non-anxious* as a construct for evaluating others. Those who were judged by peers as friendly tended to view others in terms of a *friendly versus unfriendly* construct (Sechrest, 1968).

The REP Test has been used to study schizophrenics, neurotics, depressives, and persons with organic brain damage. Compared with normal subjects, schizophrenics were found to be unstable and inconsistent in construing other people. However, their construing of objects was stable and consistent, suggesting that their thought disorders applied only to social situations. Their thought processes were also characterized by paranoid delusions and irrational links between constructs (see, for example, Bannister, Fransella, & Agnew, 1971; Bannister & Salmon, 1966; Winter, 1992).

A study using a modified version of the REP Test compared the personal construct systems of repeat patients in psychiatric hospitals with those hospitalized for the first time. The repeat patients construed their social network as small, limited to a few people on whom they believed they could depend. First-time patients construed their social network as significantly larger (Smith, Stefan, Kovaleski, & Johnson, 1991).

REP Test research with juvenile and adult offenders revealed that delinquents tended to identify with action-oriented television heroes rather than with real adults. Newly released prisoners showed poor self-esteem and lowered aspirations for the future. Rapists felt inadequate, immature, and preoccupied with personal failure (Needs, 1988).

Real-World Applications

The REP Test has been used in market research to assess the criteria consumers use to evaluate products. Industrial-organizational psychologists have used the REP Test for vocational counseling, employee selection, evaluation of performance on the job, and evaluation of training programs (Benjafield, 2008).

Research on Personal Constructs

Studies in nontherapeutic situations have dealt with a variety of behaviors that might be affected by one's personal constructs. A study in Australia found that the degree of automobile drivers' reckless behavior on the road could be related to the constructs they held (McNally & Bradley, 2014). An American professor teaching in Paris was able to coach his beginning statistics students not only to understand statistics, but also to get them enthusiastic about the subject, by relating the methods to their personal constructs (Clayson, 2013).

A groundbreaking study by British psychologists on the personal constructs developed by convicted Islamic terrorists in India found that those who were unable to re-construe their future lives in ways not linked to terrorism were the least likely to disengage themselves from future terrorist acts (Canter, Sarangi, & Youngs, 2014).

Cognitive Complexity and Cognitive Simplicity

An outgrowth of Kelly's work on personal constructs relates to cognitive styles, that is, differences in how we perceive or construe the persons, objects, and situations in our environment. Research on cognitive styles was derived from the REP Test and focuses on the concept of **cognitive complexity**.

cognitive complexity A cognitive style or way of construing the environment characterized by the ability to perceive differences among people.

Cognitive complexity is defined as the ability to discriminate in the process of applying personal constructs to other people. People high in cognitive complexity are able to see variety among people and can easily place a person in many categories.

The other extreme, **cognitive simplicity**, refers to being less capable of perceiving differences when judging other people. People high in cognitive simplicity are likely to place others in only one or two categories, unable to see much variety.

cognitive simplicity A cognitive style or way of construing the environment characterized by a relative inability to perceive differences among people.

Effects on Personality and Behavior   Research has found personality differences in terms of cognitive style. Those high in cognitive complexity are better able to make predictions about other people's behavior. They more readily recognize differences between themselves and others, display more empathy toward others, and deal better with inconsistent information in construing others than do people high in cognitive simplicity (Crockett, 1982).

Studies of college students in the United States and Canada have found that those high in cognitive complexity are lower in anxiety and instability, adjust better to the stresses of college life, and tend to possess more than the traditional five factors of personality. People with lower cognitive complexity display fewer than the five factors of personality, suggesting that they are less complex emotionally (Bowler, Bowler, & Phillips, 2009; Lester, 2009; Pancer, Hunsberger, Pratt, & Alisat, 2000).

Studies of politicians in the United States and England found that conservatives were high in cognitive simplicity, whereas moderates and liberals displayed higher levels of cognitive complexity (Tetlock, 1983, 1984). Mental health counselors and therapists with more training and experience demonstrated greater cognitive complexity than those with less training and fewer years of experience (Granello, 2010; Owen & Lindley, 2010).

In Kelly's theory, cognitive complexity is the more desirable and useful cognitive style. Our goal in developing a construct system is to reduce uncertainty by being able to predict or anticipate what people will do. This gives us a guide for our own behavior. People with a more complex cognitive style will be more successful at this task than will people with a simpler cognitive style. Therefore, cognitive style is an important dimension of personality.

Changes over Time   Cognitive complexity has been shown to increase with age with adults generally displaying greater cognitive complexity than children. However, age is not a complete explanation for cognitive complexity. Many adults still possess cognitive simplicity. Much depends on the level of complexity of our childhood experiences.

Those adults high in cognitive complexity typically had more diverse experiences in childhood. In addition, their parents were less authoritarian and more likely to grant autonomy than parents of adults high in cognitive simplicity (Sechrest & Jackson, 1961).

Becoming Alike or Being Alike?   A study of 40 couples found that although the women scored significantly higher in cognitive complexity than the men did, there was a high correlation in cognitive complexity between men and women who were partners. The researcher suggested that these partners may have chosen each other because of their similar pre-existing levels of cognitive complexity, or else they developed this similarity as a result of living together. Either way, these partners tended to construe their worlds in a similar manner (Adams-Webber, 2001).

Cultural Factors　Comparisons were made of monocultural Anglo-American and bicultural Chinese-American college students. The Chinese-American students had been born in China and lived at least five years in the United States. The results showed that the bicultural students scored higher in cognitive complexity than the monocultural students (Benet-Martinez, Lee, & Leu, 2006).

Attributional Complexity　A variant of cognitive complexity is *attributional complexity*, which is defined as the extent to which people prefer complex rather than simple explanations for social behavior. In other words, they attribute the behavior of other people to complicated, multifaceted, and more sophisticated causes.

People who measure high in attributional complexity have been shown to be more sensitive to and perceptive of subtle signs of racism. They also show greater empathy toward and greater understanding of other people (Foels & Reid, 2010; Reid & Foels, 2010). Business leaders high in attributional complexity are more effective in their management behavior than those low in attributional complexity (Sun & Anderson, 2012).

HIGHLIGHTS: Research on Kelly's Ideas

Research using the *REP Test* has found that:

- Our personal constructs remain stable over time
- We chose friends whose constructs are like ours
- Spouses whose constructs were alike were happier
- Schizophrenics formed stable constructs of objects but not of people
- Delinquents identified with action heroes rather than real people

People who score high in *cognitive complexity* tend to:

- Score low in anxiety
- Have more than the traditional five factors of personality
- Be good at predicting how others will behave
- Have moderate to liberal political views
- Had more diverse experiences in childhood
- Adjust better to the stresses of college

People high in *attributional complexity:*

- Attribute the behavior of others to complex causes
- Have greater empathy and understanding of others
- Are sensitive to subtle signs of racism

Reflections on Kelly's Theory

Kelly developed a unique and radical personality theory that did not derive from or build on other theories. It emerged from his interpretation, his own construct system, of data provided by his clinical practice. It is a personal view, and its originality parallels its message, that we are capable of developing the framework for our own lives.

Kelly's system has been criticized on several points. It focuses on intellectual and rational aspects of human functioning to the exclusion of emotional aspects. Kelly's image of a person rationally constructing the present and future, forming and testing hypotheses, and making predictions as the basis for behavior does not coincide with the everyday experiences of clinical psychologists who see more extreme examples of human behavior. To them, Kelly's rational being seems to be an ideal that exists in the abstract but not in reality. Although Kelly did not deal explicitly with emotions, he recognized them as personal constructs, similar in their formation to other constructs.

We saw that Sigmund Freud's view of personality derived from his exposure to neurotic, middle-class Viennese patients, who presented him with a distorted, unrepresentative sample of human nature. Other theorists have been similarly criticized. Kelly's viewpoint was also unrepresentative, limited largely to Midwestern young adults in the process of defining a construct system that would help them cope with college life.

Kelly's theory, like many others, leaves unanswered questions. Each of us is able to construe events in a unique way, but why does one person construe an event in one way while another person construes the same event in a different way? What process or mechanism accounts for the difference? A person makes choices about defining or extending the construct system. What determines whether to opt for security or for adventure, for the safer or the riskier alternative?

Personal construct theory continues to enjoy a large and growing base of support, although this is much broader in Europe, Canada, and Australia than in the United States. In the mid-1980s, the Centre for Personal Construct Psychology was established in England to train clinicians in Kelly's psychotherapeutic techniques and to promote applications of the theory. The *International Journal of Personal Construct Psychology* and the *Journal of Constructivist Psychology* began publication in the late 1980s, and in 1990 the first volume of the series *Advances in Personal Construct Psychology* appeared.

Kelly's work is not as popular in the United States for several reasons. First, many psychologists see it as too different from prevailing ideas. Personality psychologists typically think in terms of the familiar concepts of motivation and emotion, unconscious forces, drives, and needs, which form no part of Kelly's system. Second, Kelly published few books, articles, or case studies, devoting most of his time to clinical work and to training graduate students. The writing style of his two major books is scholarly, not intended for the public or for the therapist looking for explanations of human passions and emotions, loves and hatreds, fears and dreams. Such was not the style of the man or his theory.

Kelly recognized the limitations of his program and made no pretense of setting forth a finished theory. Just as an individual's constructs change in light of new experiences, so Kelly expected the personal construct theory to change with further research and application. His contributions have been recognized with honors from the profession and from former students.

His theory is one of the most unusual to appear in a century of theorizing about the nature of the human personality. Adherents continue to apply it to problems in clinical psychology, industrial psychology, anthropology, criminology, and urban planning as a way of modifying and predicting behavior in many walks of life (Butt, 2008; Walker & Winter, 2007).

Chapter Summary

Kelly viewed people as similar to scientists who construct hypotheses and test them against reality. A personal construct is a unique way of looking at events in our lives to try to explain and predict future events. Kelly's fundamental postulate states that psychological processes are directed by the ways we anticipate events and construe our world. The theory includes 11 corollaries.

Kelly presented an optimistic image of human nature that depicts us as rational beings with free will, capable of directing our destiny. We are not bound by constructs developed at one stage of life or by past experiences, unconscious conflicts, and biological instincts. Our goal is to define a set of constructs that enables us to predict events.

Kelly assessed personality by accepting a person's words at face value, by having the person write a self-characterization sketch, and by the Role Construct Repertory (REP) Test. The REP Test uncovers dichotomies important in a person's life, revealing the pattern of personal constructs.

People high in cognitive complexity are better able to predict the behavior of others. They more readily recognize differences between themselves and others. They are more empathic, less anxious and unstable, deal better with inconsistent information in construing others, and experience greater complexity in childhood than people high in cognitive simplicity.

Those high in attributional complexity view the behavior of other people as being more complex and multifaceted than do those low in attributional complexity.

Kelly's work has been criticized for omitting familiar concepts such as motivation and emotion, for focusing on the rational aspects of human functioning to the exclusion of emotional aspects, and for relying on an unrepresentative sample of subjects.

Review Questions

1. What did Kelly mean when he suggested that we all function like scientists in trying to predict and control the events in our lives?
2. How does Kelly's approach to personality differ from the other approaches we have discussed?
3. What is the relationship between Kelly's cognitive theory and modern cognitive psychology?
4. How might Kelly's theory have been influenced by the kinds of clients he treated?
5. What is Kelly's definition of the term *construct*? Why must constructs be dichotomous?
6. Why did Kelly believe that we must always be revising our constructs?
7. What factors influence the ways we anticipate those events that are similar to past events?
8. How do we choose between the two alternatives offered by a construct?
9. How does our anticipation of events, and of how other people will behave, influence our personality?
10. Explain how the individuality corollary differs from the organization corollary.
11. What is a construct's range of convenience?
12. In your construct system, what is the range of convenience for the construct *cheerful versus sad*?
13. What mechanism did Kelly propose to account for changes in a construct's range of convenience?
14. How is it possible to hold incompatible or inconsistent constructs?
15. Why is it important to construe the constructs of other people in our daily lives?
16. What is Kelly's position on the issue of free will versus determinism?
17. What is a self-characterization sketch? How is it used in therapy?
18. Describe how the Role Construct Repertory Test works with clients.
19. What is fixed role therapy? How does it relate to role-playing?
20. How do people high in cognitive complexity differ from people high in cognitive simplicity?
21. How do people who are high in attributional complexity view the behavior of those around them, compared to people who are low in attributional complexity?
22. Discuss some of the criticisms that have been made of Kelly's approach to personality.

Suggested Readings

Butler, R. (Ed.). (2009). *Reflections in personal construct theory.* New York: Wiley. Essays by leading practitioners of Kelly's approach to therapy from a variety of countries, offering advice on how to conduct therapeutic relationships with patients using personal construct psychology.

Butt, T. (2008). *George Kelly and the psychology of personal constructs (mind shapers).* New York: Palgrave Macmillan. Explores Kelly's idea that personality is not caused by what happens to us but rather by our widely differing interpretations of what happens. Sets the theory in its historical and philosophical context.

Caputo, P., Viney, l., Walker, B., & Crittenden, N. (Eds.). (2012). Articles by followers of Kelly's approach detailing techniques for gathering and analyzing data along with descriptions and examples of applications of personal construct psychology in clinical and nonclinical settings.

Epting, F. R. (1984). *Personal construct counseling and psychotherapy.* New York: Wiley. The first major textbook on the principles of Kelly's personality theory and their clinical applications.

Fransella, F. (1995). *George Kelly.* London: Sage. Describes Kelly's life and the development and applications of personal construct theory. Reviews the concept of constructive alternativism using Kelly's personality as an example.

Jancowicz, A. D. (1987). *Whatever became of George Kelly? Applications and implications.* American Psychologist, *42*, 481–487. Published on the 20th anniversary of Kelly's death, this article reviews and assesses the impact of Kelly's work.

Kelly, G. A. (1969). *Clinical psychology and personality: The selected papers of George Kelly.* New York: Wiley. Selections from Kelly's writings, edited by Brendan Maher. See Chapter 2, "The Autobiography of a Theory," for Kelly's description of the impact of his personal experiences on the development of his theory.

Thompson, G. G. (1968). George Alexander Kelly: 1905–1967. *Journal of General Psychology, 79,* 19–24. Reviews and assesses Kelly's life and work.

The Behavioral Approach

You already know of John B. Watson, the founder of behaviorism, from your other courses in psychology. His behaviorist psychology focused solely on overt behavior, on how people respond to external stimuli. This natural-science approach to psychology, based on careful experimental research and the precise quantification of stimulus and response variables, became immensely popular in the 1920s and remained a dominant force in psychology for more than 60 years.

Watson's behaviorism had no place for conscious or unconscious forces because they could not be seen, manipulated, or measured under laboratory conditions. Watson believed that whatever might be happening inside an organism, be it a person or an animal, between the presentation of the stimulus and the elicitation of the response had no role to play in science. Why? Because scientists could not perform experiments on internal, unobservable conditions.

In the behavioral approach to psychology, therefore, we find no reference to anxiety, drives, motives, needs, or defense mechanisms—the kinds of internal processes invoked by most other personality theorists. To behaviorists, personality is merely an accumulation of learned responses to various stimuli. Personality refers only to what can be objectively observed and manipulated.

The behavioral approach to personality is represented here by the work of B. F. Skinner, who, continuing with Watson's approach, rejected as irrelevant any alleged internal forces or processes. His sole concern was with overt behavior and the external stimuli that shape it.

Skinner attempted to understand what we call "personality" through laboratory research with rats and pigeons rather than clinical work with patients. His ideas turned out, however, to become immensely useful in the clinical setting, through the application of behavior-modification techniques.

Fair Use

chapter 12

B. F. Skinner: Reinforcement Theory

It is the environment which must be changed.

—*B. F. Skinner*

Rats, Pigeons, and an Empty Organism

Skinner did not offer a personality theory that can easily be contrasted and compared with others discussed in this book. In fact, he did not offer a personality theory at all, nor did his research deal specifically with personality. His work attempted to account for *all* behavior, not just personality, in factual, descriptive terms. Skinner argued that psychologists must restrict their investigations to facts, to only what they can see, manipulate, and measure in the laboratory. That meant an exclusive emphasis on the overt responses a subject makes and nothing more. Skinner's contention was that psychology is the science of behavior, of what an organism does. His study of behavior was the antithesis of the psychoanalytic, trait, life-span, cognitive, and humanistic approaches, differing not only in subject matter but in methodology and aims.

In explaining personality, most other theorists look inside the person for clues. The causes, motives, and drives—the forces that direct our development and behavior—originate within each of us. In contrast, Skinner made no reference to internal, subjective states to account for behavior. Unconscious influences, defense mechanisms, traits, and other driving forces cannot be seen, he argued, and therefore they have no place in a scientific psychology.

They have no more value for science than the old theological concept of the soul. Skinner did not deny the existence of internal forces, only their usefulness for science. Skinner applied similar reasoning to physiological processes, which are not overtly observable and so have no relevance for science. He said, "The inside of the organism is irrelevant either as the site of physiological processes or as the locus of mentalistic activities" (quoted in Evans, 1968, p. 22). He saw no need to look inside the organism for some form of inner activity. To Skinner, human beings are "empty organisms," by which he meant that there is nothing inside us that can explain behavior in scientific terms.

Where Are the People?

Another way Skinner differed from other theorists is in his choice of experimental subject. Some personality theorists focus on emotionally disturbed persons, others on normal or average individuals. At least one, Abraham Maslow, based his theory on the best and brightest people. Although Skinner's ideas about behavior have been applied to people, the research for his behavioral approach used rats and pigeons. What can we learn from pigeons about the human personality? Remember that Skinner's interest was in behavioral responses to stimuli, not in childhood experiences or adult feelings.

Responding to stimuli is something animals do well, sometimes better than people do. Skinner admitted that human behavior is more complex than animal behavior but suggested that the differences are in degree, not in kind. He believed that the fundamental processes are similar. And because a science must proceed from simple to complex, the more elemental processes should be studied first. Thus, he chose animal behavior because it is simpler than human behavior.

Despite Skinner's focus on studying animal behavior, his work has had wide practical applications for changing human behavior. Techniques such as behavior therapy derived from his research are used in clinical settings to treat a variety of disorders including psychoses, mental retardation, and autism. His behavior-modification techniques are also widely used in schools, businesses, correctional institutions, and hospitals.

The Life of Skinner (1904–1990)

A Strict Childhood

B. F. Skinner was born in Susquehanna, Pennsylvania, the older of two sons, but his brother died at the age of 16. His parents were hardworking people who constantly dictated to him clear rules of proper behavior. "I was taught to fear God, the police, and what people will think" (Skinner, 1967, p. 407). His mother never deviated from her strict standards. Her method of control was to say "tut tut."

Skinner's grandmother made certain that he understood the punishments of Hell by pointing out the red-hot coals in the parlor stove. Skinner's father contributed to his son's moral education by teaching him what happens to criminals. He showed Skinner the county jail and took him to a lecture about what life was like in a notorious New York state prison.

In his autobiography, Skinner made many references to the impact of these childhood warnings on his adult behavior. He wrote of visiting a cathedral as an adult and taking care to avoid stepping on the gravestones set in the floor. As a child he had been told time and time again that such behavior wasn't proper.

Those kinds of experiences made it clear to Skinner that his adult behaviors had been determined by the rewards and punishments (the "reinforcements") he had received as a child. Thus, his system of psychology and his view of people as "complex system[s] behaving in lawful ways" clearly reflected his own early life experiences (Skinner, 1971, p. 202).

Machines and Animals

Also prophetic of his view of people as machines that operate predictably were the many hours he spent as a child constructing mechanical devices such as wagons, seesaws, carousels, slingshots, model airplanes, and a steam cannon that shot potato and carrot plugs over neighboring houses. Skinner also worked on a perpetual-motion machine, which perpetually failed. His interest in animal behavior also derived from childhood.

He made pets of turtles, snakes, toads, lizards, and chipmunks. A flock of performing pigeons at a county fair fascinated him. He watched the pigeons race onstage, pull a toy fire engine up to a burning building, and shove a ladder against the wall. One pigeon, wearing a fireman's hat, climbed up the ladder to an upper-story window and rescued a stranded pigeon. Skinner would later train pigeons to play Ping-Pong and guide a missile to its target. He also taught his daughters' cat to play the piano and his pet Beagle how to play hide and seek.

A Dark Year

Skinner majored in English at Hamilton College in upstate New York and after graduation expected to become a novelist. He built a study in the attic of his parents' home in Scranton, Pennsylvania, and sat down to write. The results were disastrous. He read, listened to the radio, played the piano, and built ship models while waiting for inspiration, which never came. He considered seeing a psychiatrist, but his father told him it would be a waste of money. Skinner was 22 years old and a failure at the only thing he wanted to do.

He later referred to that time as his dark year, what Erikson would call an identity crisis. Skinner's occupational identity as a writer, which he had so carefully constructed during his college years, had collapsed and took with it his sense of self-worth. He left Scranton for New York City's Greenwich Village but found he could not write there either. Worse, in his view, was that several women spurned his proclaimed love for them, leaving him so upset that he branded one woman's initial on his arm, where it remained for years (Skinner, 1983).

A New Identity

Just when Skinner thought he had lost all hope, he discovered a new identity that suited him, to which he would cling for the rest of his life. He decided that since writing had failed him (rather than the other way around), he would study human behavior by the methods of science rather than the methods of fiction. He read Pavlov and Watson and committed himself to behaviorism in thought and deed. Finally, his self-image and identity were secure, at least for a while.

He entered Harvard in 1928 to study psychology. He had never taken a course in the field before, but he earned his Ph.D. in three years. His choice of behaviorism led him to reject all the feelings and emotions he had tried to draw on as a writer. As one historian of psychology noted:

> [There are] essential differences between a career devoted to writing poetry and fiction and one devoted to promoting the cause of behaviorism. The former requires commitment to such intra-psychic processes as inspiration, intuition, free association, the stream of consciousness, and the participation of the unconscious, as well as considering fantasies and feelings important parts of one's being. The latter denies it all—makes fantasies and feelings, indeed the entire intra-psychic domain, recede into a background of (to use Skinner's favorite term) "pre-scientific" notions, while attention is focused on observable behavior and the operations necessary to record, predict, and control it effectively. (Mindess, 1988, p. 105)

Psychic processes appeared in Skinner's work only as objects of derision.

A Period of Depression

With postdoctoral fellowships, Skinner stayed at Harvard until 1936. He then taught at the University of Minnesota and Indiana University, returning to Harvard in 1947. In his 40s, Skinner experienced a period of depression, which he resolved by returning to his failed identity as a writer. He projected all of his emotional and intellectual discontent onto the protagonist of a novel, *Walden Two*, letting the character vent his personal and professional frustrations (Skinner, 1948).

The book, which is still in print, has sold more than two million copies. It describes a society in which all aspects of life are controlled by positive reinforcement, which is the basic principle of Skinner's system of psychology (Altus & Morris, 2009). It has been suggested that *Walden Two* can be seen as a precursor to the major themes in the more recent positive psychology (Adams, 2012) (Chapter 14).

Quirky, Conscientious, and Somewhat Neurotic

Early on in his career, Skinner allowed himself to be tested using both the Rorschach and the Thematic Apperception Test. In 2012, a group of psychologists in Norway examined his test results and drew several conclusions about Skinner's personality (Gronerod, Overskeid, & Hartmann, 2013; Koren, 2013; Overskeid, Gronnerod, & Simonton, 2012).

They rated him high in conscientiousness and openness to new experiences, somewhat extraverted, and neurotic. He was also characterized as quirky and driven in his work, with strained social relationships and a lack of liveliness. One of his daughters said he was a wonderful father who spent a great deal of time with his children (Freeman, 2013).

Well into his 80s, Skinner continued to work with enthusiasm and dedication. He regulated his habits, recording his daily work output and the average time spent per published word (2 minutes). Thus, he became a living example of his definition of humans as complex systems behaving in lawful ways.

He once commented to a friend that he was cited in the psychology literature more frequently than Freud was. When asked if that had been his goal, Skinner said, "I thought I might make it" (quoted in Bjork, 1993, p. 214).

B. F. Skinner

Various sites provide biographical information, discussions of his theory, research on relevant concepts, and links to other resources.

B. F. Skinner Foundation

Provides biographical information, publications, and videos, as well as *Operants*, which are free reports to download.

Reinforcement: The Basis of Behavior

Skinner's approach to behavior, simple in concept, is based on thousands of hours of well-controlled research. His fundamental idea is that behavior can be controlled by its consequences, that is, by what follows the behavior. Skinner believed that an animal or a human could be trained to perform virtually any act and that the type of reinforcement that followed the behavior would be responsible for determining it. This means that whoever controls the reinforcers has the power to control human behavior, in the same way an experimenter can control the behavior of a laboratory rat.

Respondent Behavior

respondent behavior
Responses made to or elicited by specific environmental stimuli.

Skinner distinguished between two kinds of behavior: respondent behavior and operant behavior. **Respondent behavior** involves a response made to or elicited by a specific stimulus. A reflexive behavior such as a knee jerk is an example of respondent behavior. A stimulus is applied (a tap on the knee) and the response occurs (the leg jerks). This behavior is unlearned. It occurs automatically and involuntarily. We do not have to be trained or conditioned to make the appropriate response.

Conditioning   At a higher level is respondent behavior that is learned. This learning, called *conditioning*, involves the substitution of one stimulus for another. The concept originated in the work of the Russian physiologist Ivan Pavlov in the early 1900s. Later, Pavlov's ideas on conditioning were adopted by John B. Watson as the basic research method for behaviorism.

Working with dogs, Pavlov discovered that they would salivate to neutral stimuli such as the sound of their keeper's footsteps. Previously, the salivation response had been elicited by only one stimulus, the sight of food. Intrigued by this observation, Pavlov studied the phenomenon systematically.

He sounded a bell shortly before feeding a dog. At first, the dog salivated only in response to the food and not to the bell because the bell had no meaning. However, after a number of pairings of the bell followed by the food, the dog began to salivate at the sound of the bell. Thus, the dog had been conditioned, or trained, to respond to the bell. The dog's response shifted from the food to what previously had been a neutral stimulus.

reinforcement The act of strengthening a response by adding a reward, thus increasing the likelihood that the response will be repeated.

Reinforcement   This classic experiment by Pavlov demonstrated the importance of **reinforcement**. The dogs would not learn to respond to the bell unless they were rewarded for doing so. In this example, the reward was food. Pavlov then formulated a fundamental law of learning: A conditioned response cannot be established in the absence of reinforcement. The act of reinforcing a response strengthens it and increases the likelihood that the response will be repeated.

Extinction   However, an established conditioned response will not be maintained in the absence of reinforcement. Consider a dog conditioned to respond to the sound of a bell. Every time the bell rings, the dog salivates. Then the experimenter stops presenting food after sounding the bell. The dog hears the bell and nothing happens—no more food, no more reinforcement or reward. With successive ringing of the bell, the dog's salivary response decreases in frequency and intensity until no response occurs at all.

extinction The process of eliminating a behavior by withholding reinforcement.

This process is called **extinction**. The response has been wiped out or extinguished because reinforcers or rewards for it were no longer provided. A great deal of research has demonstrated that the greater the reinforcement given during training, the more resistant the conditioned response will be to extinction (Shull & Grimes, 2006). Eventually, however, extinction will occur.

Operant Behavior

operant behavior Behavior emitted spontaneously or voluntarily that operates on the environment to change it.

Respondent behavior depends on reinforcement and is related directly to a physical stimulus. Every response is elicited by a specific stimulus. To Skinner, respondent behavior was less important than **operant behavior**. We are conditioned to respond directly to many stimuli in our environment, but not all behavior can be accounted for in this way. Much human behavior appears to be spontaneous and cannot be traced directly to a specific stimulus. Such behavior is emitted rather than elicited by a stimulus. It involves

Animals can be conditioned by reinforcing them with food when they exhibit desired behaviors.

Luis Marden/National Geographic Vintage Premium/Corbis

FIGURE 12.1
A simple operant-conditioning apparatus

acting in a way that appears to be voluntary rather than reacting involuntarily to a stimulus to which we have been conditioned.

The nature and frequency of operant behavior will be determined or modified by the reinforcement that follows the behavior. Respondent behavior has no effect on the environment. In Pavlov's experiment, the dog's salivary response to the ringing bell did nothing to change the bell or the reinforcer (the food) that followed. In contrast, operant behavior operates on the environment and, as a result, changes it.

Operant Conditioning and the Skinner Box

operant conditioning
The procedure by which a change in the consequences of a response will affect the rate at which the response occurs.

To illustrate the **operant-conditioning** process, let us follow the progress of a rat in Skinner's operant-conditioning apparatus, also known as the Skinner box (Figure 12.1). When a food-deprived rat is placed in the box, its behavior at first is spontaneous and random. The rat is active, sniffing, poking, and exploring its environment. These behaviors are emitted, not elicited; in other words, the rat is not responding to any specific stimulus in its environment.

At some time during this random activity, the rat will depress a lever or bar located on one wall of the Skinner box, causing a food pellet to drop into a trough. The rat's behavior (pressing the lever) has operated on the environment and, as a result, has changed it. How? The environment now includes a food pellet. The food is a reinforcer for the behavior of depressing the bar.

The rat now begins to press the bar more often. What happens? It gets more food—more reinforcement—and so presses the bar even more frequently. The rat's behavior is now under the control of the reinforcers. Its actions in the box are less random and spontaneous because it is spending most of its time pressing the bar, and eating.

If we put the rat back in the box the next day, we can predict its behavior and we can control its bar-pressing actions by presenting or withholding the reinforcers or by presenting them at a different rate. Withholding the food extinguishes operant behavior in the same way that it extinguishes respondent behavior. If the unreinforced behavior no longer works, in that it no longer brings a reward, after a while it will stop. Thus, the person who controls the reinforcers controls the subjects' behavior.

From the Skinner Box to the Real World

A variety of animals have been taught to perform a great many behaviors through operant conditioning. Dogs have been conditioned to sniff out drugs or explosives, giant African rats in Mozambique have been trained to detect buried land mines, lobsters have been taught to grasp a bar with their claws to receive food, whales and dolphins have been taught how to perform a variety of tricks in places like SeaWorld, and calves have been taught to urinate only in designated places (Gillaspy, Brinegar, & Bailey, 2014; Poling, Weetjens, Cox, Beyene, Bach, & Sully, 2010; Tomina & Takahata, 2010; Vaughan, de Passille, Stookey, & Rushen, 2014).

Operating on the Environment

Skinner believed that most human and animal behavior is learned through operant conditioning. Consider how babies learn. An infant initially displays random, spontaneous behaviors, only some of which are reinforced (rewarded with food or hugs or toys, for example) by parents, siblings, or caregivers. As the infant grows, the positively reinforced behaviors, those of which the parents approve, will persist, whereas those of which the parents disapprove will be extinguished or discontinued.

The concept is the same with the rat in the Skinner box. Behaviors that work (like pressing the bar to obtain food) are displayed frequently, and behaviors that do not work are not repeated. Thus, the organism's behavior operates on the environment. And in turn, the environment, in the form of reinforcement, operates on the organism's behavior.

You can see how powerful reinforcement can be in determining and controlling behavior. Skinner wrote, "Operant conditioning shapes behavior as a sculptor shapes a lump of clay" (1953, p. 91). If that lump of clay, that organism, needs the reinforcer badly enough, there is virtually no limit to how its behavior can be shaped—by an experimenter with a food pellet, a puppy owner with a dog biscuit, a mother with a smile, a boss with a pat on the back, or a government with a promise.

Personality: A Collection of Operant Behaviors

From infancy on, we display many behaviors, and those that are reinforced will strengthen and form patterns. This is how Skinner conceived of personality, as a pattern or collection of operant behaviors. What other psychologists called neurotic or abnormal behavior was nothing more mysterious to Skinner than the continued performance of undesirable behaviors that somehow have been reinforced.

Having demonstrated how behavior could be modified by continuous reinforcement, that is, by presenting a reinforcer after every response, Skinner decided to consider how behavior would change if he varied the rate at which the behavior was reinforced.

Operant Conditioning

Various sites provide descriptions and examples of operant conditioning experiments, including videos.

Schedules of Reinforcement

Skinner pointed out that in everyday life outside the psychology laboratory, our behavior is rarely reinforced every time it occurs. Babies are not picked up and cuddled every time they cry. Baseball superstars do not hit a home run every time at bat. The bagger in the

reinforcement schedules Patterns or rates of providing or withholding reinforcers.

supermarket does not receive a tip for each bag packed. And your favorite singing group doesn't win a Grammy for every new song. You can think of many more examples of behaviors that persist even though they are reinforced only occasionally.

After observing that his rats continued to press the bar at a fairly constant rate even when they were not being reinforced for each response, Skinner decided to investigate different **reinforcement schedules** to determine their effectiveness in controlling behavior. Among the rates of reinforcement he tested are the following.

- Fixed interval
- Fixed ratio
- Variable interval
- Variable ratio

Fixed Interval

A *fixed-interval schedule of reinforcement* means that the reinforcer is presented following the first response that occurs after a fixed time interval has elapsed. That interval might be 1 minute, 3 minutes, or any other fixed period of time. The timing of the reinforcement has nothing to do with the number of responses. Whether the rat responds 3 times or 20 times per minute during the fixed time interval, the reinforcer still arrives only after the passage of a given time period and the emission of the correct response.

Many situations operate in accordance with the fixed-interval reinforcement schedule. A job in which your salary is paid once a week or once a month operates on the fixed-interval schedule. You are not paid according to the number of items you produce or the number of sales you make (the number of responses) but by the number of hours, days, or weeks that elapse.

Skinner's research showed that the shorter the interval between presentations of the reinforcer, the greater the frequency of response. The response rate declined as the interval between reinforcements lengthened. How frequently reinforcers appeared also affected how quickly the response could be extinguished.

A parent's smile of approval can reinforce a child's behavior.

The response stopped sooner if the rat had been reinforced continuously and the reinforcement was then stopped if the rat had been reinforced intermittently. The fixed-interval schedule has been found to be highly effective in real-world situations, including special education classrooms where disruptive behavior can be reduced by its use (Tomlin & Reed, 2012).

Fixed Ratio

In the *fixed-ratio schedule of reinforcement*, reinforcers are given only after a specified number of responses have been made. For example, the experimenter could reinforce after every 10th or 20th response. In this schedule, unlike the fixed-interval schedule, the presentation of reinforcers depends on how often the subject responds. The rat will not get a food pellet until it performs the required number of responses. This reinforcement schedule brings about a faster rate of responding than does the fixed-interval schedule.

The higher response rate for the fixed-ratio reinforcement schedule also applies to humans. In a job in which your pay is determined on a piece-rate basis, how much you earn depends on how much you produce. The more items you produce, the higher your pay. Your reward is based directly on your response rate. The same is true for a salesperson working on commission. Income depends on the number of products sold; the more sold, the more earned. In contrast, a salesperson on a weekly salary (a fixed-interval schedule) earns the same amount each week regardless of the number of items sold.

Variable Interval

Everyday life doesn't always permit a fixed-interval or fixed-ratio reinforcement schedule. Sometimes reinforcers are presented on a variable basis. In the *variable-interval schedule of reinforcement*, the reinforcer might appear after 2 hours the first time, after 1 hour 30 minutes the next time, and after 2 hours and 15 minutes the third time. A person who spends the day fishing might be rewarded, if at all, on a variable-interval basis. The reinforcement schedule is determined by the random appearance of fish nibbling at the bait.

Variable Ratio

A *variable-ratio schedule of reinforcement* is based on an average number of responses between reinforcers, but there is great variability around that average. Skinner found that the variable-ratio schedule is effective in bringing about high and stable response rates, as the people who operate gambling casinos can happily attest.

Slot machines, roulette wheels, horse races, and state lottery games pay on a variable-ratio reinforcement schedule, an extremely effective means of controlling behavior. Variable reinforcement schedules result in enduring response behaviors that tend to resist extinction. Most everyday learning occurs as a result of variable-interval or variable-ratio reinforcement schedules.

Skinner's research on reinforcement schedules shows that they are effective for controlling, modifying, and shaping behavior. If you are in charge of rats, salespeople, or assembly-line workers, or are trying to train your pet or your child, these operant-conditioning techniques can bring about the behaviors you want.

The Shaping of Behavior

In Skinner's original operant-conditioning experiment, the operant behavior (pressing the lever) is a simple behavior that a laboratory rat would be expected to display eventually in the course of randomly exploring its environment. Thus, the chance is high that such a behavior will occur, assuming the experimenter has sufficient patience.

It is obvious, however, that animals and humans demonstrate many more complex operant behaviors that have a much lower probability of occurring in the normal course of events. How are these complex behaviors learned? How can an experimenter or a parent reinforce and condition a pigeon or a child to perform behaviors that are not likely to occur spontaneously?

Successive Approximation

successive approximation An explanation for the acquisition of complex behavior. Behavior such as learning to speak will be reinforced only as it comes to approximate or approach the final desired behavior.

Skinner answered these questions with the method of **successive approximation**, or *shaping* (Skinner, 1953). He trained a pigeon in a very short time to peck at a specific spot in its cage. The probability that the pigeon on its own would peck at that exact spot was low. At first, the pigeon was reinforced with food when it merely turned toward the designated spot. Then reinforcement was withheld until the pigeon made some movement, however slight, toward the spot.

Next, reinforcement was given only for movements that brought the pigeon closer to the spot. After that, the pigeon was reinforced only when it thrust its head toward the spot. Finally, the pigeon was reinforced only when its beak touched the spot. Although this sounds like a time-consuming process, Skinner conditioned pigeons in less than 3 minutes.

The experimental procedure itself explains the term *successive approximation*. The organism is reinforced as its behavior comes in successive, or consecutive, stages to approximate the final behavior desired. Skinner suggested that this is how children

Parents teach their children acceptable behaviors by reinforcing those activities that approximate the final desired behaviors.

Brand X Pictures/Stockbyte/Getty Images Plus/Jupiter Images

learn the complex behavior of speaking. Infants spontaneously emit meaningless sounds, which parents reinforce by smiling, laughing, and talking.

After a while, parents reinforce this babbling in different ways, providing stronger reinforcers for sounds that approximate real words. As the process continues, parental reinforcement becomes more restricted, given only for appropriate usage and proper pronunciation. Thus, the complex behavior of acquiring language skills in infancy is shaped by providing differential reinforcement in stages.

Shaping the Behavior of a Person in Five Minutes

Skinner once shaped the behavior of a noted psychoanalyst, Erich Fromm, whose comments during a lecture annoyed him.

> Fromm proved to have something to say about almost everything, but with little enlightenment. When he began to argue that people were not pigeons, I decided that something had to be done. On a scrap of paper I wrote [to a colleague] "Watch Fromm's left hand. I am going to shape a chopping motion" … [Fromm] gesticulated a great deal as he talked, and whenever his left hand came up, I looked straight at him. If he brought the hand down, I nodded and smiled. Within five minutes he was chopping the air so vigorously that his wristwatch kept slipping out over his hand. (Skinner, 1983, pp. 150–151)

Superstitious Behavior

We know that life is not always as orderly or well controlled as events in a psychology laboratory. Sometimes we are reinforced accidentally after we have displayed some behavior. As a result, that behavior, which did not lead to or cause the reinforcement in any way, may be repeated in a similar situation.

Consider two examples from football. An offensive lineman for the Tampa Bay (FL) Buccaneers was having a terrible season early in his career. He asked his roommate to switch beds so that he could sleep closer to the bathroom. Immediately thereafter, his playing improved. For the rest of his career, he insisted on the bed nearest the bathroom door in every motel in which the team stayed.

Then there was an NFL kicker who hugged the goal posts before each game. He had done it once just before making a successful kick, and so because it had worked then, he continued the practice. He told a reporter that he wanted the goal posts to know he loved them and to implore them to stay still when he kicked.

How to Shape Superstitious Behavior

superstitious behavior
Persistent behavior that has a coincidental and not a functional relationship to the reinforcement received.

Skinner called this phenomenon **superstitious behavior** and demonstrated it in the laboratory. A hungry pigeon was placed in the operant-conditioning apparatus and reinforced every 15 seconds on a fixed-interval schedule. It is highly likely that the pigeon would be doing something, displaying some behavior or activity, when the reinforcing food pellet was presented. It might be turning, raising its head, strutting, hopping, or standing still. Whatever behavior was being emitted at the moment of reward would be reinforced.

Skinner found that a single reinforcement was powerful enough to lead the pigeon to repeat the accidentally reinforced behavior more frequently for a while, which increased the probability that another food pellet would appear while the same behavior was being shown. And with short intervals between reinforcers, superstitious behaviors are learned quickly.

Like the football players in the examples mentioned previously, the superstitious behaviors displayed by the pigeon have no functional relationship to the reinforcers.

The connection is unintentional. In humans, such behaviors may persist throughout life and require only occasional reinforcement to sustain them.

A study of major league baseball players in the United States and Japan found that 74 percent of the players admitted engaging in superstitious behavior. It was also found that American players were more superstitious than Japanese players, suggesting that cultural differences may influence the extent of these actions (Burger & Lynn, 2005).

The Self-Control of Behavior

According to Skinner, behavior is controlled and modified by variables that are external to the organism. There is nothing inside us—no process, drive, or other internal activity—that determines behavior. However, although these external stimuli and reinforcers are responsible for shaping and controlling behavior, we do have the ability to use what Skinner called **self-control**, which he described as acting to alter the impact of external events. Skinner did not mean acting under the control of some mysterious "self."

He suggested that to some extent we can control the external variables that determine our behavior through four self-control techniques:

self-control The ability to exert control over the variables that determine our behavior.

- Stimulus avoidance
- Self-administered satiation
- Aversive stimulation
- Self-reinforcement

Stimulus Avoidance

In *stimulus avoidance*, for example, if your roommate is too noisy and interferes with your studying for an exam in the morning, you could leave the room and go to the library, removing yourself from an external variable that is affecting your behavior. By avoiding a person or situation that makes you angry, you reduce the control that person or situation has over your behavior. Similarly, alcoholics can act to avoid a stimulus that controls their behavior by not allowing liquor to be kept in their homes.

Self-Administered Satiation

Through the technique of *self-administered satiation*, we exert control to cure ourselves of some bad habit by overdoing the behavior. Smokers who want to quit can chain-smoke for a period of time, inhaling until they become so disgusted, uncomfortable, or sick that they quit. This technique has been successful in formal therapeutic programs designed to eliminate smoking.

Aversive Stimulation

The *aversive stimulation* technique of self-control involves unpleasant or repugnant consequences. Obese people who want to lose weight declare their intention to their friends in person or to a larger audience through Facebook or other social networking sites. If they do not keep their resolution, they face the unpleasant consequences of personal failure, embarrassment, and criticism.

Self-Reinforcement

In *self-reinforcement*, we reward ourselves for displaying good or desirable behaviors. A teenager who agrees to strive for a certain grade point average or to take care of a younger brother or sister might reward himself or herself by buying concert tickets or new clothes. To Skinner, then, the crucial point is that external variables shape and control behavior. But sometimes, through our own actions, we can modify the effects of these external forces.

Benefits of Self-Control

A large-scale study of American college students found that that those who scored high on a measure of self-control had better grades, higher psychological adjustment scores, and greater self-acceptance and self-esteem. They also had better interpersonal skills and family relationships, as well as lower levels of anger compared to those who scored low on self-control (Tangney, Baumeister, & Boone, 2004). A high level of self-control is also related to satisfaction with life, happiness, and the avoidance of frequent conflict (Hofmann, Luhmann, Fisher, Vohs, & Baumeister, 2014).

A study of African-American children (average age of 11.2 years) found that those whose parents were more nurturing and involved in their upbringing had higher levels of self-control than those whose parents were less nurturing and involved (Wills et al., 2007).

Recently, a researcher noted that self-control had become a "hot topic," and that "most of the problems that plague modern individuals in our society—addiction, over-eating, crime, domestic violence, sexually transmitted diseases, prejudice, debt, unwanted pregnancy, underperformance at school and work, lack of savings, failure to exercise—have some degree of self-control failure as a central aspect" (Baumeister, quoted in Weir, 2012, p. 36).

Applications of Operant Conditioning

Psychologists have applied Skinner's operant-conditioning techniques to modify human behavior in clinical, business, and educational settings. **Behavior modification** has been used successfully with children and adults, with the mentally healthy and the mentally disturbed, and with individual as well as group behaviors.

Token Economy Programs

behavior modification A form of therapy that applies the principles of reinforcement to bring about desired behavioral changes.

token economy A behavior-modification technique in which tokens, which can be exchanged for valued objects or privileges, are awarded for desirable behaviors.

The classic application of behavior modification is the **token economy**. In the pioneering study, a ward of female psychotic patients in a state mental institution was treated as a giant Skinner box (Ayllon & Azrin, 1968). The patients could no longer be helped by conventional treatments. They had been institutionalized for a long time and were unable to care for themselves.

In this setting of utter hopelessness, the patients were offered opportunities to work at jobs, usually performed by paid hospital attendants, for which they would receive tokens. The tokens functioned like money, hence the term *token economy*. Like people outside the institution, the patients could buy goods and privileges to improve the quality of life.

With a certain number of tokens, they could purchase candy, cigarettes, lipstick, gloves, and newspapers, or go to a movie on the ward, walk around the hospital grounds, or upgrade to a better room. The most expensive privileges, requiring 100 tokens, were an escorted trip into town and a private meeting with a social worker. A private meeting with a psychologist was worth only 20 tokens.

What kinds of behaviors did the patients have to emit to be reinforced and receive tokens? If they took baths at the designated time, brushed their teeth, made their beds, combed their hair, and dressed properly, they earned a token for each activity. They would be paid up to 10 tokens for each period of work in the hospital kitchen or laundry, or for helping to clean the ward, run errands, or take other patients for walks.

The tasks may seem simple to us, but before the token economy program began, these patients were considered helpless, aimless, and incapable of doing almost anything for themselves.

The conditioning worked dramatically. Not only did the patients groom themselves and clean their surroundings, but they also busied themselves at a variety of tasks. They began interacting socially with one another and with the staff and even assumed some responsibility for patient care. Their self-esteem improved markedly, and they became less dependent.

Token economy programs have worked in a variety of institutional settings as a way of reducing problem behaviors. For example, aggressive behaviors among cognitively impaired patients in a psychiatric hospital were reduced by 79 percent following a nine-month token economy program (DePhilippis, Quintieri, Noble, Reyes, & Akundi, 2008). The use of the token-economy approach also proved highly effective in changing the behavior of autistic children in Japan (Ogasahara, Hirono, & Kato, 2013).

The Token Economy Online   This token-economy approach to changing behavior has also worked online, as shown in a study of heavy smokers. Over a four-week period the smokers made video recordings of themselves at home twice a day. They also used a web camera to provide a carbon monoxide sample, which was sent electronically to the smoking clinic.

The subjects could earn vouchers by reducing their carbon monoxide level over a four-day period and by maintaining a level consistent with that of a non-smoker. The vouchers could be exchanged for various items purchased over the Internet. The technique proved effective. Subjects showed significant decreases in carbon monoxide levels and sustained abstinence throughout the period of the study (Dallery, Glenn, & Raiff, 2007).

What Happens When the Tokens Stop?   A note of caution about these impressive results. Reinforcement must be continued if the desired behavior changes are to persist. When tokens are no longer provided, reinforced behaviors usually revert to their original state (Kazdin & Bootzin, 1972; Repucci & Saunders, 1974). However, if caregivers are trained to reward desirable behaviors with reinforcers such as smiles, praise, hugs, and other signs of affection, then behaviors conditioned in the institutional token-economy situation are more likely to be continued in the home setting (Kazdin, 1989).

Behavior Modification Programs

Behavior modification programs have been successfully applied to education, where it has improved academic performance and social behavior in classrooms, and reduced behavioral, emotional, and developmental behavioral problems (Lang & Rispoli, 2015). Operant-conditioning techniques have also been applied to problems in business and industry. Behavior modification programs at major manufacturers, financial institutions, and government agencies have been shown to reduce absenteeism, lateness, and abuse of sick-leave privileges, and to lead to improvements in job performance and safety.

The techniques can also be used to teach low-level job skills. Reinforcers used in business include pay, job security, recognition from supervisors, perks and status within the company, and the opportunity for personal growth. No attempt is made to deal with any alleged anxieties, repressed traumas, or unconscious motivating forces. The focus is on changing overt behavior, defining the nature of the appropriate reinforcers, and determining their optimal rate of presentation to modify behavior.

Punishment and Negative Reinforcement

punishment The application of an aversive stimulus following a response in an effort to decrease the likelihood that the response will recur.

Most operant-conditioning applications involve positive reinforcement rather than **punishment**. The token-economy patients were not punished for failing to behave appropriately. Instead, they were reinforced when their behavior changed in positive ways. Skinner said that punishment was ineffective in changing behavior from undesirable to desirable or from abnormal to normal. Positive reinforcement administered for desirable behaviors is much more effective than punishment.

> What's wrong with punishments is that they work immediately, but give no long-term results. The responses to punishment are either the urge to escape, to counterattack, or a stubborn apathy. These are the bad effects you get in prisons or schools, or wherever punishments are used. (Skinner quoted in Goleman, 1987)

negative reinforcement The strengthening of a response by the removal of an aversive stimulus.

Negative reinforcement is not the same as punishment. A negative reinforcer is an aversive or noxious stimulus, the removal of which is rewarding. In the laboratory or classroom, an operant-conditioning situation can be established in which the unpleasant stimulus (such as a loud noise or an electric shock) will continue until the subject emits the desired response. As with positive reinforcement, the environment changes as a consequence of the behavior; in this case, the noxious stimulus will disappear.

We can see examples of negative reinforcement in everyday situations. A person may stop smoking to avoid the aversive stimulus of a nagging spouse or colleague. The aversive stimulus (the nagging) should cease when the desirable behavior (not lighting a cigarette in the home or office) is displayed. Skinner opposed using noxious stimuli to modify behavior, noting that the consequences were not as predictable as with positive reinforcement. Also, negative reinforcement does not always work, whereas positive reinforcement is more consistently effective.

Questions about Human Nature

Skinner's position is clear on the nature–nurture issue. People are primarily products of learning, shaped more by external variables than genetic factors. We may infer that childhood experiences are more important in Skinner's view than are later experiences because our basic behaviors are formed in childhood. However, this does not mean that behavior cannot change in adulthood.

What is learned in childhood can be modified, and new behavior patterns can be acquired at any age. The success of behavior modification programs verifies that assertion. Skinner's belief that behavior is shaped by learning also leads us to conclude that each person is unique. Because we are shaped by experience—and we all have different experiences, particularly in childhood—no two people will behave in precisely the same way.

Skinner did not address the issue of an ultimate and necessary goal. He made no reference to overcoming inferiority, reducing anxiety, or striving for self-actualization. Such motives assume internal, subjective states, which Skinner did not accept.

Any indication of a life goal in Skinner's work seems to be societal, not individual. In his novel *Walden Two* and in other writings, he discussed his notion of the ideal human society. He stated that individual behavior must be directed toward the type of society that has the greatest chance of survival.

On the issue of free will versus determinism, Skinner believed people function like machines, in lawful, orderly, predetermined ways. He rejected all suggestions of an inner being or autonomous self that determines a course of action or chooses to act freely and spontaneously.

From Skinner's scholarly writings to his popular novel about a utopian society based on operant conditioning his message is the same: Behavior is controlled by reinforcers. In a sense, this means that it is pointless to blame or punish people for their actions. In this view, a dictator who orders the mass killing of thousands of people, or a serial killer who murders a dozen, can no more be held responsible for their actions than can a driverless car that plunges down a hill. Both operate in lawful, predictable ways, controlled by external variables.

Are we left, then, with a pessimistic conception of people as helpless and passive robots, unable to play any active role in determining their behavior? That is not Skinner's complete view. Despite his belief that behavior is controlled by external stimuli and reinforcers, we are certainly not victims. Although controlled by our environment, we are responsible for designing that environment.

Our buildings, cities, consumer goods, factories, media, and government institutions are the result of human fabrication. So, too, are our social systems, languages, laws, customs, and recreations. We constantly change our environment, often to our advantage. When we do so, we are acting as both controller and controlled. We design the controlling culture, and we are products of that culture. "We may not be free agents," he wrote, "but we can do something about our lives, if we would only rearrange the controls that influence our behavior.... I am not trying to change people. All I want to do is change the world in which they live" (quoted in Bjork, 1993, pp. 16, 233).

Assessment in Skinner's Theory

Skinner did not use the typical assessment techniques favored by other theorists. There was no place in his work for free association, dream analysis, or projective techniques. Because he was not dealing directly with personality, he really had no interest in assessing it. He did, however, assess behavior.

In the application of his behavior-modification techniques, it is necessary to first assess specific behaviors, both desirable and undesirable. Also to be assessed are the environmental factors that serve as reinforcers and that can be manipulated to alter behavior. No behavior can be modified appropriately without such prior assessment. Skinner's approach to assessing behavior is called **functional analysis** and it involves three aspects of behavior.

functional analysis An approach to the study of behavior that involves assessing the frequency of a behavior, the situation in which it occurs, and the reinforcers associated with it.

1. The frequency of the behavior
2. The situation in which the behavior occurs
3. The reinforcement associated with the behavior

Unless these factors have been evaluated, it is not possible to plan and implement a behavior modification program.

Consider a functional analysis for cigarette smokers who want to break the smoking habit. The smokers are asked to keep an accurate record of the number of cigarettes they smoke each day and the situations in which they smoke. Does smoking occur in a particular place or at a certain time? In the presence of others or when alone? After meals or while driving? And what are the reinforcers? Most smokers smoke more frequently in the presence of certain stimuli. Identifying these stimuli is necessary because modifying the stimuli should lead to a change in the smoking behavior.

Direct Observation of Behavior

Three approaches to assessing behavior are direct observation, self-reports, and physiological measurements. Many behaviors can be assessed through direct observation. Usually, two or more people conduct the observation to assure accuracy and reliability. For example, in a classic report of a behavior modification situation, a woman sought treatment for her 4-year-old son whose behavior was considered unruly (Hawkins, Peterson, Schweid, & Bijou, 1966). Two psychologists observed the mother and child in their home to evaluate the nature and frequency of the child's undesirable behaviors, when and where they occurred, and the reinforcers the child received for the behaviors.

Nine undesirable behaviors were identified, including kicking, throwing things, biting, and pushing a sibling. The psychologists observed that the mother reinforced the child by giving him toys or food when he behaved badly. Her intention was to get him to stop misbehaving. Instead, she was rewarding him and thus reinforcing the misbehavior. The direct observation assessment lasted 16 hours, but without it the psychologists would not have known exactly which undesirable behaviors to try to eliminate or what reinforcers the child expected.

With a comprehensive direct-observation program, it is possible to plan a course of behavior modification. In this case, the psychologists instructed the mother to use attention and approval as reinforcers when the child behaved in positive ways and never to reward him when he displayed one of the nine observed undesirable behaviors. The frequency of the undesirable behaviors, as determined in the direct observation assessment, provided a baseline against which to compare behavior during and after treatment.

Self-Reports of Behavior

Another approach to assessing behavior is the self-report technique carried out through interviews and questionnaires. The person observes his or her own behavior and reports on it. For example, a questionnaire may assess the extent of a person's fear in situations such as driving a car, going to the dentist, or speaking in public. Questionnaires for assessing behavior are similar in format to self-report inventories that assess personality.

Physiological Measurements of Behavior

Physiological assessments of behavior include heart rate, muscle tension, and brain waves. By recording such measurements, it is possible to evaluate the physiological effects of various stimuli. The measures can also be used to confirm the accuracy of information obtained by other assessment methods. For example, a person who is too embarrassed to reveal in an interview or on a questionnaire a fear of being in an elevator might exhibit a change in heart rate or muscle tension when asked about elevators.

Whatever assessment technique is chosen to assess behavior in different stimulus situations, the focus remains on what people do, not on what might have motivated them to do it. The ultimate goal is to modify behavior, not to change personality.

Research on Skinner's Theory

As you can see, Skinner's assessment methods differ radically from those used by other theorists we have discussed. His research methods also diverged from mainstream experimental psychology. The usual procedure is to study large groups of animal or human subjects and to statistically compare their average responses. In contrast, Skinner preferred the intensive study of a single subject. He argued that data on the average performance of groups is of little value in dealing with a particular case. A science that deals with averages provides little information to help in understanding the unique individual.

Skinner believed that valid and replicable results could be obtained without statistical analysis as long as sufficient data were collected from a single subject under well-controlled experimental conditions. The use of large groups of subjects forced the experimenter to deal with average behavior. The resulting data could not reflect individual response behavior and individual differences in behavior.

Skinner and his followers conducted thousands of operant-conditioning experiments on topics such as reinforcement schedules, language acquisition, behavior shaping, superstitious behavior, and behavior modification. The results have been highly supportive of Skinner's ideas.

Reflections on Skinner's Theory

Skinner's approach has been criticized on several points. Those who oppose determinism find much to dislike in Skinner's views. The humanistic psychologists, who believe that people are more complex than machines or rats or pigeons, object to Skinner's image of human nature. They argue that the exclusive emphasis on overt behavior ignores uniquely human qualities such as conscious free will.

There has been criticism of the type of subject and the simplicity of the situations in Skinner's experiments. He made broad assertions and predictions about human behavior and society—about social, economic, religious, and cultural issues—with considerable confidence. But, some critics ask, can we extrapolate from a pigeon pecking at a disc to a person functioning in the real world? The gap seems too vast to permit broad generalizations. Many aspects of human behavior cannot be reduced meaningfully to the level at which Skinner conducted his research.

Skinner's belief that all behaviors are learned was challenged by two of his former students who conditioned more than 6,000 animals of 38 different species to perform for television commercials and tourist attractions. The animals included pigs, raccoons, chickens, hamsters, porpoises, whales, and cows. The animals displayed a tendency toward **instinctive drift** by substituting instinctive behaviors for the behaviors that had been reinforced, even when the instinctive behaviors interfered with receiving food.

instinctive drift The substitution of instinctive behaviors for behaviors that had been reinforced.

In one example, pigs and raccoons were conditioned to pick up a coin, carry it some distance, and deposit it in a toy bank (a piggy bank, of course). When the animals had deposited a certain number of coins, they were given food as a reinforcer. They learned the desired behaviors quickly,

> but after having performed the sequence nicely for some time, they began to engage in undesirable behaviors, at least from the viewpoint of the trainers. Pigs would stop on their way [to the bank], bury the coin in the sand, and take it out with their snout; raccoons would spend a lot of time handling the coin, with their well-known washing-like movements. This was at first amusing, but eventually it became time-consuming and would make the whole show appear very imperfect to the spectator. Commercially, it was a disaster. (Richelle, 1993, p. 68)

What had happened was that instinctive behavior, such as the pigs' rooting in the dirt and the raccoons' rubbing their paws as if washing their hands, came to take precedence over the learned behavior, even though it meant a delay in receiving the reinforcement (the food). The trainers published an article on the phenomenon called "The Misbehavior of Organisms" (Breland & Breland, 1961). This was a parody of the title of Skinner's groundbreaking book, *The Behavior of Organisms* (1938), and it reportedly left Skinner feeling displeased (Gillaspy, 2009).

Skinner ignored most of the criticisms of his work. He told an interviewer about one critic's book review, "I read a bit of it and saw that he missed the point.... There are better things to do with my time than clear up their misunderstandings" (quoted in Rice, 1968). When asked how he dealt with being misunderstood so frequently, he said, "I find that I need to be understood only three or four times a year" (quoted in Blackman, 1995, p. 126).

Skinner was a potent force in 20th-century American psychology. He shaped the field perhaps more than any other individual. The *Journal of the Experimental Analysis of*

Behavior, begun in 1958, publishes research on the behavior of individual subjects. In 1968, the *Journal of Applied Behavior Analysis* was established as an outlet for work on behavior-modification techniques.

The American Psychological Foundation awarded Skinner its Gold Medal, and the American Psychological Association gave him the Distinguished Scientific Contribution Award (1958). The citation reads: "Few American psychologists have had so profound an impact on the development of psychology and on promising younger psychologists."

Skinner's first book on behaviorism, *The Behavior of Organisms: An Experimental Analysis* (Skinner, 1938), was described as one of the few books to truly change the nature of the field (Thompson, 1988). Skinner also received the U.S. National Medal of Science and appeared on the cover of *Time*, headlined as the world's most famous American psychologist. His controversial 1971 book, *Beyond Freedom and Dignity*, became a best seller and made him a celebrity.

> Skinner was, for a short period, the hottest item on national and big-city talk shows.... Within a month, millions of Americans had read or heard about B. F. Skinner and *Beyond Freedom and* Dignity. He was "completely swamped" by mail, telephone calls, and visits.... Strangers often asked to shake his hand in restaurants. He had, as one writer noted, "acquired the celebrity of a movie or TV star." (Bjork, 1993, p. 192)

Current Status

Although Skinner's radical behaviorist position continues to be applied in laboratory, clinical, and organizational settings, its dominance has been challenged by the cognitive movement in psychology, which began in the 1960s. Skinner conceded that his form of psychology lost ground to the cognitive approach. Other psychologists agreed, noting that Skinnerian behaviorism had "fallen from favor among the majority of active workers in the field [and was] often referred to in the past tense" (Baars, 1986, pp. viii, 1).

Despite the inroads of cognitive psychology, however, Skinner's position remains influential in many areas, from classrooms to assembly lines, from Skinner boxes to treatment programs for behavior disorders. Skinner believed that with operant conditioning he offered a technique to improve human nature and the societies people design.

HIGHLIGHTS: Research on Skinner's behaviorism has found that

- The greater the reinforcement given during training, the more resistant is the conditioned response to extinction
- Operant conditioning can shape most forms of behavior in humans and animals
- Even a lobster can be conditioned
- American major league baseball players engage in more superstitious behaviors than Japanese players do
- College students who measure high in self-control get better grades, are better adjusted psychologically, and have higher self-esteem
- Token economy programs have reduced aggressive acts by cognitively impaired patients by as much as 79 percent

Chapter Summary

Skinner denied the existence of an entity called personality and did not seek causes of behavior within the organism. Mental and physiological processes are not overtly observable, so they have no relevance for science. The causes of behavior are external to the organism. Behavior can be controlled by its consequences, by the reinforcer that follows the behavior. Respondent behavior involves a response elicited by specific environmental stimuli. Conditioning (respondent behavior that is learned) involves substituting one stimulus for another.

Conditioning will not occur without reinforcement. Operant behavior is emitted and is determined and modified by the reinforcer that follows it. Operant behavior operates on the environment and changes it. Personality is simply a pattern of operant behaviors. Reinforcement schedules include fixed interval, fixed ratio, variable interval, and variable ratio. Shaping (successive approximation) involves reinforcing the organism only as its behavior comes to approximate the behavior desired. Superstitious behavior results when reinforcement is presented on a fixed- or variable-interval schedule. Whatever behavior is occurring at the moment of reinforcement will come to be displayed more frequently.

Self-control of behavior refers to altering or avoiding certain external stimuli and reinforcers. Other self-control techniques are satiation, aversive stimulation, and self-reinforcement for displaying desirable behaviors.

Behavior modification applies operant-conditioning techniques to real-world problems. Desirable behaviors are positively reinforced; undesirable behaviors are ignored. The token-economy approach rewards desirable behaviors with tokens that can be used to acquire objects of value. Behavior modification deals only with overt behavior and uses positive reinforcement, not punishment. Negative reinforcement involves removing an aversive or noxious stimulus. It is less effective than positive reinforcement.

Skinner's image of human nature emphasizes determinism, uniqueness, the importance of the environment, and the design of a society that maximizes the opportunity for survival. Although people are controlled by the environment, they can exert control by designing that environment properly.

Skinner assessed behavior (not personality) using functional analyses to determine the frequency of the behavior, the situation in which the behavior occurred, and the reinforcers associated with the behavior. Three ways to assess behavior are direct observation, self-report, and physiological measures.

Skinner's system has considerable empirical support but has been criticized for its deterministic view, the simplicity of the experimental situations, the lack of interest in behavior other than response rate, and the failure to consider human qualities that set us apart from rats and pigeons. Skinner's techniques for the modification of behavior using operant conditioning remain popular, but his behavioristic position has been overtaken by the cognitive movement within psychology.

Review Questions

1. In what ways does Skinner's approach to personality differ from other approaches we have discussed?
2. How did Skinner justify the use of rats and pigeons instead of humans as subjects in the study of behavior?
3. How did Skinner's childhood experiences influence his later approach to studying behavior?
4. Distinguish between operant behavior and respondent behavior. Give an example of each.
5. Describe Pavlov's classical-conditioning experiment with dogs. How did Pavlov extinguish conditioned responses?
6. Distinguish between positive reinforcement, negative reinforcement, and punishment.
7. In Skinner's view, why is positive reinforcement more effective than punishment in changing behavior?
8. Explain the difference between the fixed-interval and variable-interval schedules of reinforcement.
9. Which reinforcement schedule applies to the person who sells computer software on commission? Which schedule applies to the child who is allowed to have an ice-cream cone for good behavior only occasionally?

10. Explain how a complex behavior such as learning to speak is acquired through successive approximation.
11. Describe how you would use the method of successive approximation to train a dog to walk in a circle.
12. How does the notion of reinforcement account for the acquisition of superstitious behaviors?
13. Explain the use of self-administered satiation in getting rid of bad habits.
14. What are the techniques for the self-control of behavior?
15. Describe the token-economy approach to behavior modification. Give an example.
16. Why did Skinner prefer to study the individual case rather than groups of subjects?
17. What was Skinner's position on the nature–nurture issue? On free will versus determinism?
18. What techniques do Skinner's followers use to assess human behavior?
19. Discuss the impact of cognitive psychology on Skinnerian behaviorism.
20. In your opinion, what is the value of Skinnerian behaviorism compared to the other approaches we have discussed so far?

Suggested Readings

Antony, M., & Roemer, L. (2011). *Behavior therapy.* Washington, DC: American Psychological Association. A readable and concise overview of the history and nature of behavior therapy, focusing on both the theoretical and practical aspects.

Baumeister, R., & Tierney, J. (2012). *Willpower: Rediscovery of the greatest human strength.* New York: Penguin. Covers the current status of self-control in psychology and in daily life—how to achieve and strengthen it; reviews the extensive research on the topic as well as real-world applications.

Miltenberger, R. (2015). *Behavior modification: Principles and procedures* (6th ed.). San Francisco: Cengage. A textbook on behavior modification and the wide range of applications in everyday situations; everything you might need to know about behavior modification and how to use it!

Nye, R. D. (1992). *The legacy of B. F. Skinner: Concepts and perspectives, controversies and misunderstandings.* Pacific Grove, CA: Brooks/Cole. A primer on Skinner's basic concepts and their relevance for behavior in today's world. Examines controversies and misunderstandings surrounding Skinner's views and compares his system with those of Freud and Rogers.

O'Donohue, W., & Ferguson, K. E. (2001). *The psychology of B. F. Skinner.* Thousand Oaks, CA: Sage. Presents a clearly written and balanced look at the controversies surrounding Skinner's work on behaviorism, cognition, verbal behavior, and applied behavior analysis. Includes Skinner's ideas for improving society as a whole, as well as a brief biography.

Pryor, K. (2006). *Don't shoot the dog: The new art of teaching and training.* (3rd ed.). Lydney, England: Ringpress Books. Shows the practical value of behavior-modification techniques in teaching dogs, children, students, and employees.

Skinner, B. F. (1948). *Walden Two.* New York: Macmillan. Skinner's novel about human values and conduct in a utopian society based on behaviorist principles.

Skinner, B. F. (1976). *Particulars of my life; (1979). The shaping of a behaviorist; (1983). A matter of consequences.* New York: Alfred A. Knopf. Skinner's three-volume autobiography.

Skinner, B. F. (1987). *Upon further reflection.* Englewood Cliffs, NJ: Prentice-Hall. Essays on cognitive psychology, verbal behavior, education, and self-management in old age.

The Social-Learning Approach

The social-learning approach to personality, represented here by the work of Albert Bandura, is an outgrowth of, and rebellion against, Skinner's behaviorist approach. Like Skinner, Bandura focused on overt behavior rather than on inner needs, traits, drives, or defense mechanisms. Unlike Skinner, Bandura allowed for internal cognitive variables that mediate between stimulus and response. For Bandura, the organism is not empty.

Bandura investigated cognitive variables with a high degree of experimental sophistication and rigor, drawing inferences from careful observations of behavior in the laboratory. He observed the behavior of human subjects in social settings, whereas Skinner dealt with animal subjects in individual settings. Bandura agreed with Skinner that behavior is learned and that reinforcement is vital to learning, but he differed from Skinner in his interpretation of the nature of reinforcement.

Bandura and Skinner both attempted to understand personality through laboratory research rather than clinical work, but their principles have been widely applied in the clinical setting through behavior-modification techniques. Because Bandura used cognitive variables, his work reflected and reinforced the cognitive movement in psychology. His approach has also been called *cognitive-behavioral* in recognition of this emphasis.

chapter 13

Albert Bandura: Modeling Theory

Fair Use

Virtually every phenomenon that occurs by direct experience can occur vicariously as well— by observing other people and the consequences for them.

—*Albert Bandura*

Bandura agreed with Skinner that behavior is learned, but with that point their similarity ends. Bandura criticized Skinner's emphasis on individual animal subjects rather than on human subjects interacting with one another. Bandura's approach is a social-learning theory that investigates behavior as it is formed and modified in a social context. He argued that we cannot expect data from experiments that involve no social interaction to be relevant to the everyday, real world, because very few people live in social isolation.

Vicarious Reinforcement

observational learning
Learning new responses by observing the behavior of other people.

Although Bandura agreed with Skinner that much learning takes place as a result of reinforcement, he also stressed that virtually all forms of behavior can be learned without directly experiencing any reinforcement. Bandura's approach is also called **observational learning**, indicating the importance in the learning process of observing other people's behavior.

Rather than experiencing reinforcement ourselves for each of our actions, we learn through **vicarious reinforcement** by observing the behavior of other people and the consequences of that behavior. This focus on learning by observation or example, rather than always by direct reinforcement, is a distinctive feature of Bandura's theory.

vicarious reinforcement Learning or strengthening a behavior by observing the behavior of others, and the consequences of that behavior, rather than experiencing the reinforcement or consequences directly.

The Role of Cognitive Processes

Another feature of Bandura's observational-learning approach is its treatment of internal cognitive or thought processes. Unlike Skinner, Bandura believed that cognitive processes can influence observational learning. We do not automatically imitate the behaviors we see other people displaying. Rather, we make a deliberate, conscious decision to behave in the same way. To learn through example and vicarious reinforcement we must be capable of anticipating and appreciating the consequences of the behaviors we observe.

We can regulate and guide our behavior by visualizing or imagining those consequences, even though we have not experienced them ourselves. No direct link exists between stimulus and response or between behavior and reinforcer, as Skinner proposed. Instead, our cognitive processes mediate between the two.

A Less Extreme Form of Behaviorism

Bandura presented a less extreme form of behaviorism than Skinner. He emphasized the observation of others as a means of learning, and he considered learning to be mediated by cognitive processes. His theory is based on rigorous laboratory research with normal people in social interaction rather than a rat in a cage or a neurotic person on a couch.

The Life of Bandura (1925–)

Get Drunk or Go to School

Bandura was born in the province of Alberta, Canada, in a town so small that his high school had only two teachers and 20 students. His parents were immigrants from Poland who emphasized the value of education. "You have a choice," his mother told him when he was young. "You can work in the field and get drunk in the beer parlor, or you might get an education" (quoted in Foster, 2007, p. 3). He chose an education.

During the summer following his graduation from high school, he took a construction job in the wilderness of the Yukon Territory, filling holes in the Alaska Highway. It was a unique experience for a bright, inquisitive young person.

> Finding himself in the midst of a curious collection of characters, most of whom had fled creditors, alimony, and probation officers, Bandura quickly developed a keen appreciation for the psychopathology of everyday life, which seemed to blossom in the austere tundra. (Distinguished Scientific Contribution Award, 1981, p. 28)

Finding Psychology

He went to the University of British Columbia in Vancouver as an undergraduate and took a course in psychology out of expediency. The carpool in which he commuted to the campus every day included engineering and pre-med students, all of whom had early-morning classes. Psychology was also offered in that time period, and so Bandura enrolled in the course, not out of any real interest, but simply because it was a convenient time. He quickly found the material fascinating and went on to earn his Ph.D. in 1952 from the University of Iowa.

After a year at the Wichita, Kansas, Guidance Center, he joined the faculty of Stanford University, where he began his new approach to psychology. Challenging the leading position in the field (Skinner's behaviorism) was a risky undertaking for a young unknown psychologist. "When I began my career, more than half a century ago," he wrote in 2011, "behaviorism had a stranglehold on the field of psychology. . . . It was in this inhospitable conceptual climate that I launched a program of research on the determinants of observational learning" (Bandura, 2011).

He quickly became very successful and compiled an extensive record of publications. In 1973, only 21 years after getting his Ph.D., he was elected president of the American Psychological Association. In 1980, he received its Distinguished Scientific Contribution Award and in 2006 was presented with the American Psychological Foundation's Gold Medal Award for Life Achievement.

Bandura's sense of humor has often been directed at himself. When he was once asked whether he walked to his office every day or drove his car, he said, "Both, sometimes in the same day." Having driven to work, he would become so absorbed in his ideas that he would absentmindedly walk home, leaving his car in the university parking lot.

LOG ON

Albert Bandura

Various sites provide biographical information, discussions of his theory, research on relevant concepts, and links to other resources.

Modeling: The Basis of Observational Learning

Bandura's basic idea is that learning can occur through observation or example rather than solely by direct reinforcement. Bandura did not deny the importance of direct reinforcement as a way to influence behavior, but he challenged the notion that behavior can be learned or changed *only* through direct reinforcement. He argued that operant conditioning, in which trial-and-error behavior continues until the person happens upon the correct response, is an inefficient and potentially dangerous way to learn certain skills such as swimming or driving.

A person could drown or crash before finding the correct sequence of behaviors that brings positive reinforcement. To Bandura, most human behavior is learned through example, either intentionally or accidentally. We learn a wide and varied range of behaviors in our daily lives by simply observing other people and patterning our behavior after theirs (see Gaskins & Paradise, 2010; Oates, 2012).

modeling A behavior-modification technique that involves observing the behavior of others (the models) and participating with them in performing the desired behavior.

Bobo the Inflatable Doll

Through **modeling**, by observing the behavior of a model and repeating the behavior ourselves, it is possible to acquire responses that we have never performed or displayed

Courtesy of Dr. Albert Bandura, Stanford University

In the Bobo doll studies, children exhibited aggressive behavior after observing an aggressive model.

before and to strengthen or weaken existing responses. Bandura's now-classic demonstration of modeling involves the Bobo doll, an inflatable plastic figure about 4 feet tall (Bandura, Ross, & Ross, 1963).

In Bandura's studies, preschool children watched an adult hit and kick Bobo. While attacking the doll, the adult model shouted, "Sock him in the nose!" and "Throw him in the air!" When the children were left alone with the doll, they modeled their behavior after the example they had just witnessed. Their behavior was compared with that of a control group of children who had not seen the model attack the Bobo doll. The experimental group was found to be twice as aggressive as the control group.

The intensity of the aggressive behavior remained the same in the experimental subjects whether the model was seen live, on television, or as a cartoon character. The effect of the model in all three media was to elicit aggressive behavior that was not displayed with the same strength by children who had not seen the models.

Other Modeling Studies

In his early research on the impact of modeling on learning, Bandura compared the behavior of parents of two groups of children (Bandura & Walters, 1963). One group consisted of highly aggressive children, the other of more inhibited children. According to Bandura's theory, the children's behavior should reflect their parents' behavior. The research showed that the parents of the inhibited children were inhibited, and the parents of the aggressive children were aggressive. The children had modeled their behavior on the examples provided by their parents.

Verbal modeling can induce certain behaviors, as long as the activities involved are fully and adequately explained. Verbal modeling is often used to provide instructions, a technique applicable to teaching such skills as driving a car. Verbal instructions are usually supplemented by behavioral demonstrations, such as when a driving instructor serves as a model performing the behaviors involved in driving.

Disinhibition

disinhibition The weakening of inhibitions or constraints by observing the behavior of a model.

Research has shown that behaviors a person usually suppresses or inhibits may be performed more readily under the influence of a model (Bandura, 1973, 1986). This phenomenon, called **disinhibition**, refers to the weakening of an inhibition or restraint through exposure to a model. For example, people in a crowd may start a riot, breaking windows and shouting, exhibiting physical and verbal behaviors they would never perform when alone. They are more likely to discard their inhibitions against aggressive behavior if they see other people around them doing so.

The disinhibition phenomenon can influence sexual behavior. In an experiment that demonstrated how sexual responses could be disinhibited by models, a group of male undergraduate college students was shown a film that contained erotic pictures of nude males and females (Walters, Bowen, & Parke, 1963). The students were told that a spot of light would move over the film, indicating the eye movements of a previous subject, to show what parts of the pictures that subject looked at. Those alleged eye movements of the previous subject represented the model. For half the subjects, the spot of light concentrated on breasts and genitals. For the other half, the light stayed in the background, as though the model had avoided looking at the naked bodies.

After watching the film, the students were shown stills from the movie while their eye movements were recorded. Those subjects whose model was considered uninhibited (who had looked directly at the erotic parts of the bodies) behaved in the same way. Those whose model had avoided looking at the nudes spent significantly more time examining the background of the pictures. The researchers concluded that modeling affected the subjects' perceptual responses to the stimuli. In other words, modeling determined not only what the subjects did but also what they looked at and perceived.

Trolling   Posting comments online following the example or model of others offers the same anonymity as being in a large crowd. This can lead to an online form of disinhibition known as trolling—the posting of inflammatory, derogatory, or hateful messages about a person or a group. Some adolescents have been driven to suicide by the cruel and widespread comments directed at them by name (Zhuo, 2010).

Research on frequent video gamers found that those most into trolling were younger and male. The reasons they gave for trolling were varied. Some did it for deliberate revenge on someone else, while others trolled simply because they were bored, and others out of amusement with no other purpose in mind (Thacker & Griffiths, 2012).

The good news is that the disinhibition effect seems to decline with age. A study of young Americans ages 18 to 25 showed that disinhibition was strong among the 18- to 19-year-olds but greatly reduced among the 22- to 25-year-olds (Vaidya, Latzman, Markon, & Watson, 2010).

The Effects of Society's Models

On the basis of his extensive research, Bandura concluded that much of our behavior—good and bad, normal and abnormal—is learned by imitating the behavior of other people. From infancy on, we develop responses to the models our society offers us. Beginning with parents as models, we learn their language and become socialized by the culture's customs and acceptable behaviors. People who deviate from cultural norms have learned their behavior the same way as everyone else. The difference is that deviant individuals have followed models the rest of society considers undesirable.

Bad Models   Bandura was an outspoken critic of the type of society that provides the wrong models for its children, particularly the examples of violent behavior that are standard fare on television and in movies and video games. His research clearly shows the effect of models on behavior. If what we see is what we become, then the distance between watching an aggressive animated character and committing a violent act ourselves is not very great.

Among the many behaviors children acquire through modeling are non-rational fears. A child who sees that his or her parents are fearful during thunderstorms or are nervous around strangers will easily adopt these anxieties and carry them into adulthood with little awareness of their origin. Of course, positive behaviors such as strength, courage, and optimism will also be learned from parents and other models. In Skinner's system, reinforcers control behavior; for Bandura, it is the models who control behavior.

Characteristics of the Modeling Situation

Bandura and his associates (Bandura, 1977, 1986) investigated three factors found to influence modeling:

- the characteristics of the models
- the characteristics of the observers
- the reward consequences associated with the behaviors

Characteristics of the models

Models Who Are Like Us   The characteristics of the models affect our tendency to imitate them. In real life, we may be more influenced by someone who appears to be similar to us than by someone who differs from us in obvious and significant ways. In the laboratory, Bandura found that although children imitated the behavior of a child model in the same room, a child in a film, and a filmed cartoon character, the extent of the modeling decreased as the similarity between the model and the subject decreased.

The children showed greater imitation of a live model than an animated character, but even in the latter instance the modeled behavior was significantly greater than that of the control group that observed no models.

Age and Sex of Models   Other characteristics of the model that affect imitation are age and sex. We are more likely to model our behavior after a person of the same sex than a person of the opposite sex. Also, we are more likely to be influenced by models our own age. Peers who appear to have successfully solved the problems we are facing are highly influential models.

Status of Models   Status and prestige are also important factors. For example, pedestrians are much more likely to cross a street against a red light if they see a well-dressed person crossing than if they see a poorly dressed person crossing. Television commercials make effective use of high-status, high-prestige models with athletes or celebrities who claim to use a particular product. The expectation is that consumers will imitate their behavior and buy the advertised product.

Type of Behavior Displayed by Models   The type of behavior the model performs affects the extent of imitation. Highly complex behaviors are not imitated as quickly and readily as simpler behaviors. Hostile and aggressive behaviors tend to be strongly imitated, especially by children.

In one study, infants as young as 16 months learned to imitate the behavior of a model using a tool, but only if they had been previously shown the object or purpose of using the tool. They successfully imitated the behavior of a model using a rake after they had been shown the use of the rake in retrieving a toy that was out of their reach (Esseilly, Rat-Fischer, O'Regan, & Fagard, 2013).

Research on American college students found that those who had observed a positive relationship between a caregiver and a child successfully modeled that behavior in their ongoing romantic relationships (Kuhn & Kinsky, 2013).

Size and Weight of Models   The size and weight of a model can also influence behavior. A study of 9th- and 10th-grade students in Canada found that those who attended a school where the older students tended to be overweight, even obese, gained more weight than students who attended a school where the older students were not overweight (Leatherdale & Papadakis, 2011).

Characteristics of the observers

Age of Observers   In infancy, modeling is limited to immediate imitation. Infants have not yet developed the cognitive capacities (the imaginal and verbal representational systems) needed to imitate a model's behavior some period of time after observing it. In infancy, it is necessary for the modeled behavior to be repeated several times after the infant's initial attempt to duplicate it. Also, the modeled behavior must be within the infant's range of sensorimotor development. By about age 2, children have developed sufficient attentional, retention, and production processes to begin imitating behavior some time after the observation rather than immediately.

Children tend to imitate the behavior of an adult model of the same sex who is considered high in status.

selimaksan/iStockphoto.com

The behaviors we find reinforcing, and thus choose to imitate, will change with age. Younger children are reinforced primarily by physical stimuli such as food, affection, or punishment. Older children associate positive physical reinforcers with signs of approval from significant models and unpleasant reinforcers with signs of disapproval. Eventually these rewards or punishments become self-administered.

Attributes of the Observers The attributes of the observers also determine the effectiveness of observational learning. People who are low in self-confidence and self-esteem are much more likely to imitate a model's behavior than are people high in self-confidence and self-esteem. A person who has been reinforced for imitating a behavior—for example, a child rewarded for behaving like an older sibling—is more susceptible to the influence of models than a child who has not been so reinforced.

The reward consequences associated with the behaviors The reward consequences linked to a particular behavior can affect the extent of the modeling and even override the impact of the characteristics of the models and the observers. A high-status model may lead us to imitate a certain behavior, but if the rewards are not meaningful to us, we will discontinue the behavior and be less likely to be influenced by that model in the future.

Seeing a model being rewarded or punished for displaying a particular behavior affects imitation. In a Bobo doll study, some of the children watched as the model who hit the Bobo doll was given praise and a soda and candy. Another group of children saw the model receive verbal and physical punishment for the same aggressive behavior. The children who observed the punishment displayed significantly less aggression toward the Bobo doll than did the children who saw the model being reinforced (Bandura, 1965).

The Processes of Observational Learning

Bandura analyzed the nature of observational learning and found it to be governed by four related mechanisms: attentional processes, retention processes, production processes, and incentive and motivational processes (see Table 13.1).

Attentional Processes

Observational learning or modeling will not occur unless the subject pays attention to the model. Merely exposing the subject to the model does not guarantee that the subject will be attentive to the relevant cues and stimulus events or even perceive the situation accurately. The subject must perceive the model accurately enough to acquire the information necessary to imitate the model's behavior.

Several variables influence attentional processes. In the real world, as in the laboratory, we are more attentive and responsive to some people and situations than to others. Thus, the more closely we pay attention to a model's behavior, the more likely we are to imitate it.

We mentioned such characteristics as age, status, sex, and the degree of similarity between model and subject. These factors help determine how closely a subject attends to the model. It has also been found that celebrity models, experts, and those who appear confident and attractive command greater attention and imitation than models who lack these attributes. Some of the most effective models in American culture today appear on television, YouTube, and other online sites. Viewers often focus on them even in the absence of reinforcement.

Attention to modeled behavior varies as a function of the observers' cognitive and perceptual skills and the value of the behavior being modeled. The more highly developed are our cognitive abilities and the more knowledge we have about the behavior being modeled, the more carefully we will attend to the model and perceive the behavior.

TABLE 13.1   Observational learning processes

Attentional processes	Developing our cognitive processes and perceptual skills so that we can pay sufficient attention to a model, and perceiving the model accurately enough, to imitate displayed behavior. Example: Staying awake during driver's education class.
Retention processes	Retaining or remembering the model's behavior so that we can imitate or repeat it at a later time; for this, we use our cognitive processes to form mental images and verbal descriptions of the model's behavior. Example: Taking notes on the lecture material or the video of a person driving a car.
Production processes	Translating the mental images or verbal symbolic representations of the model's behavior into our own overt behavior by physically producing the responses and receiving feedback on the accuracy of our continued practice. Example: Getting in a car with an instructor to practice shifting gears and dodging the traffic cones in the school parking lot.
Incentive and moti-vational processes	Perceiving that the model's behavior leads to a reward and thus expecting that our learning—and successful performance—of the same behavior will lead to similar consequences. Example: Expecting that when we have mastered driving skills, we will pass the state test and receive a driver's license.

When observers watch a model doing something they expect to do themselves, they pay greater attention than when the modeled behavior has no personal relevance. Observers also pay closer attention to modeled behavior that produces positive or negative consequences rather than neutral outcomes.

Retention Processes

We must be able to remember significant aspects of the model's behavior in order to repeat it later. To retain what has been attended to, we must encode it and represent it symbolically. We can retain information about a model's behavior in two ways: through an imaginal internal representational system or through a verbal system. In the imaginal system, we form vivid, easily retrievable images while we are observing the model.

This common phenomenon accounts for your being able to summon up a picture of the person you dated last week or the place you visited last summer. In observational learning, we form a mental picture of the model's behavior and use it as a basis for imitation at some future time.

The verbal representational system operates similarly and involves a verbal coding of some behavior we have observed. For example, during observation we might describe to ourselves what the model is doing. These descriptions or codes can be rehearsed silently, without overtly displaying the behavior.

For example, we might talk ourselves through the steps in a complicated skill, mentally rehearsing the sequence of behaviors we will perform later. When we wish to perform the action, the verbal code will provide hints, reminders, and cues. Together, these images and verbal symbols offer the means by which we store observed situations and rehearse them for later performance.

Production Processes

Translating imaginal and verbal symbolic representations into overt behavior requires the production processes, described more simply as practice. Although we may have attended to, retained, and rehearsed symbolic representations of a model's behavior, we still may not be able to perform the behavior correctly. This is most likely to occur with highly skilled actions that require the mastery of many component behaviors.

Consider learning how to drive a car. We learn fundamental motions from watching a model drive. We may consider the symbolic representations of the model's behavior many times, but at first our translation of these symbols into actual driving behavior will be clumsy. We may apply the brakes too soon or too late, or overcorrect the steering. Our observations may not have been sufficient to ensure immediate and skilled performance of the actions. Practice of the proper physical movements, and feedback on their accuracy, is needed to produce the smooth performance of the behavior.

Incentive and Motivational Processes

No matter how well we attend to and retain behaviors we observe or how much ability we have to perform them, we will not do so without the incentive or motivation processes. When incentives are available, observation is more quickly translated into action. Incentives also influence the attentional and retention processes. We may not pay as much attention without an incentive to do so, and when less attention is paid, there is less to retain.

Anticipation of Reinforcement   Our incentive to learn is influenced by our anticipation of the reinforcement or punishment for doing so. Seeing that a model's behavior produces a reward or avoids a punishment can be a strong incentive for us to pay attention to, remember, and perform that same behavior correctly. The reinforcement is experienced vicariously during our observation of the model, after which we expect our performance of the same behavior to lead to the consequences we saw.

Reinforcement Is Not Always Necessary   Bandura also pointed out that although reinforcement can facilitate learning, reinforcement is not always required for learning to occur. Many factors other than the reward consequences of the behavior determine what we attend to, retain, and rehearse. For example, loud sounds, bright lights, and exciting videos may capture our interest even though we may not have received any reinforcement for paying attention to them.

Bandura's research showed that children watching a model on television or in a video game imitate the model's behavior regardless of whether they have been promised a reward. Therefore, reinforcement can assist in modeling but is not vital to it. When reinforcement does occur, it can be given by another person, experienced vicariously, or administered by oneself.

Self-Reinforcement and Self-Efficacy

In Bandura's approach to personality, the self is not some psychic agent that determines or causes behavior. Rather, the self is a set of cognitive processes and structures concerned with thought and perception. Two important aspects of the self are self-reinforcement and self-efficacy.

Self-Reinforcement

self-reinforcement
Administering rewards or punishments to oneself for meeting, exceeding, or falling short of one's own expectations or standards.

Self-reinforcement is as important as reinforcement administered by others, particularly for older children and adults. We set personal standards of behavior and achievement. We reward ourselves for meeting or exceeding these expectations and standards, and we punish ourselves for our failures. Self-administered reinforcement can be tangible such as buying yourself a new pair of gym shoes or a car, or it can be emotional such as pride or satisfaction from a job well done.

Self-administered punishment can be expressed in feelings of shame, guilt, or depression about not behaving the way we wanted to. Self-reinforcement appears conceptually similar to what other theorists call *conscience* or superego, but Bandura denies that it is the same.

A continuing process of self-reinforcement regulates much of our behavior. It requires internal standards of performance, subjective criteria or reference points against which we evaluate our behavior. Our past behavior may become a reference point for evaluating present behavior and an incentive for better performance in the future. When we reach a certain level of achievement, it may no longer challenge, motivate, or satisfy us, so we raise the standard and require more of ourselves. Failure to achieve may result in lowering the standard to a more realistic level.

Unrealistic Performance Standards People who set unrealistic performance standards—who observed and learned behavioral expectations from unusually talented and successful models, for example—may continue to try to meet those excessively high expectations despite repeated failures. Emotionally, they may punish themselves with feelings of worthlessness and depression. These self-produced feelings can lead to self-destructive behaviors such as alcohol and drug abuse or a retreat into a fantasy world.

We learn our initial set of internal standards, whether realistic or not, from the behavior of models, typically our parents and teachers. Increasingly, however, we are learning performance standards from online sources such as celebrity blogs and social media sites. Once we adopt a given style of behavior, we begin a lifelong process of comparing our behavior with theirs.

Self-Efficacy, or "Believing You Can"

self-efficacy Our feeling of adequacy, efficiency, and competence in coping with life.

How well we meet our behavioral standards determines our **self-efficacy**. In Bandura's system, *self-efficacy* refers to feelings of adequacy, efficiency, and competence in coping with life. Meeting and maintaining our performance standards enhances self-efficacy; failure to meet and maintain them reduces it (Bandura, 2012, 2013).

Another way Bandura described self-efficacy was in terms of our perception of the control we have over our lives.

> People strive to exercise control over events that affect their lives. By exerting influence in spheres over which they can command some control, they are better able to realize desired futures and to forestall undesired ones. The striving for control over life circumstances permeates almost everything people do. (Bandura, 1995, p. 1)

Another psychologist defined self-efficacy quite simply and effectively as the "power of believing you can," and added that "believing that you can accomplish what you want to accomplish is one of the most important ingredients … in the recipe for success" (Maddux, 2002, p. 277). Thus, believing that you have the ability to be successful becomes a powerful asset as you strive for achievement.

Low and High Self-Efficacy People low in self-efficacy feel helpless, unable to exercise control over life events. They believe any effort they make is futile. When they encounter obstacles, they quickly give up if their initial attempt to deal with a problem did not work. People who are extremely low in self-efficacy will not even attempt to cope because they are convinced that nothing they do will make a difference. Why, they ask, should they even try? Low self-efficacy can destroy motivation, lower aspirations, interfere with cognitive abilities, and adversely affect physical health.

People high in self-efficacy believe they can deal effectively with events and situations. Because they expect to succeed in overcoming obstacles, they persevere at tasks and often perform at a high level. These people have greater confidence in their abilities than do those who are low in self-efficacy, and they express little self-doubt. They view difficulties as challenges instead of threats and actively seek novel situations. High self-efficacy reduces fear of failure, raises aspirations, and improves problem solving and analytical thinking abilities.

Sources of information about self-efficacy   Our judgment about our self-efficacy is based on the following four sources of information:

- performance attainment
- vicarious experiences
- verbal persuasion
- physiological and emotional arousal

Performance Attainment   The most influential source of efficacy judgments is *performance attainment*. Previous success experiences provide direct indications of our level of mastery and competence. Prior achievements demonstrate our capabilities and strengthen our feelings of self-efficacy. Prior failures, particularly repeated failures in childhood, lower self-efficacy.

An important indicator of performance attainment is getting feedback on one's performance on a task, such as a work assignment or a classroom quiz. One study of college students performing complicated puzzles found that those who received positive feedback on their performance reported higher levels of perceived competence at that task than did those who received negative feedback (Elliot, Faler, McGregor, Campbell, Sedikides, & Harackiewicz, 2000). Older adults who completed a six-month training program in the Chinese art of Tai Chi reported significant increases in feelings of self-efficacy as compared to those who did not undertake the training (Li, McAuley, Harmer, Duncan, & Chaumeton, 2001).

Female college students who completed a 16-hour physical self-defense training course showed significantly higher levels of self-efficacy in a variety of areas including physical competence, general coping skills, and interpersonal assertiveness. A control group that had not taken the self-defense course showed no change in self-efficacy (Weitlauf, Cervone, Smith, & Wright, 2001). Thus, put simply, the more we achieve, the more we believe we can achieve, and the more competent and in control we feel.

Vicarious Experiences   *Vicarious experiences*—seeing other people perform successfully—strengthen self-efficacy, particularly if the people we observe are similar to us in their abilities. In effect, we are saying, "If they can do it, so can I." In contrast, seeing others fail can lower self-efficacy: "If they can't do it, neither can I." Therefore, effective models are vital in influencing our feelings of adequacy and competence. These models also show us appropriate strategies for dealing with difficult situations.

Verbal Persuasion   *Verbal persuasion*, which involves simply reminding people that they have the ability to achieve whatever they want to achieve, can enhance self-efficacy. This may be the most common of the four informational sources and one frequently used by parents, teachers, spouses, coaches, friends, and therapists who say, in effect, "You can do it." To be effective, verbal persuasion must be realistic. It is probably not the best advice to encourage someone 5 feet tall to play professional basketball when other sports, such as martial arts, might be more appropriate.

Physiological and Emotional Arousal   The fourth and final source of information about self-efficacy is *physiological and emotional arousal*. How fearful or calm do we feel in a stressful situation? We often use this type of information as a basis for judging our ability to cope. We are more likely to believe we will master a problem successfully if we are not agitated, tense, or bothered by headaches. The more calm and composed we feel, the greater our self-efficacy. The higher our level of physiological and emotional arousal, the lower our self-efficacy. The more fear, anxiety, or tension we experience in a given situation, the less we feel able to cope.

Ways of Increasing Self-Efficacy Bandura concluded that certain conditions increase self-efficacy:

1. Exposing people to success experiences by arranging reachable goals increases performance attainment.
2. Exposing people to appropriate models who perform successfully enhances vicarious success experiences.
3. Providing verbal persuasion encourages people to believe they have the ability to perform successfully.
4. Strengthening physiological arousal through proper diet, stress reduction, and exercise programs increases strength, stamina, and the ability to cope.

Bandura applied these conditions to enhance self-efficacy in a variety of situations. He has helped subjects learn to play musical instruments, relate better to people of the opposite sex, master computer skills, give up cigarette smoking, and conquer phobias and physical pain.

Self Efficacy

Various sites provide definitions, discussions of research results, and self-tests to determine your level of self-efficacy.

Developmental Stages of Self-Efficacy

Childhood

Self-efficacy develops gradually over time. Infants begin to develop self-efficacy as they try to exercise greater influence over their physical and social environments. They learn about the consequences of their own abilities such as their physical prowess, social skills, and language competence. These abilities are in almost constant use acting on the environment, primarily through their effects on parents. Ideally, parents are responsive to their growing child's activities and attempts to communicate, and will provide stimulating surroundings that permit the child the freedom to grow and explore.

These early efficacy-building experiences are centered on the parents. Parental behaviors that lead to high self-efficacy in children differ for boys and girls. High self-efficacy men tend to have had, when they were children, warm relationships with their fathers. Mothers were more demanding than fathers, expecting higher levels of performance and achievement. In contrast, high self-efficacy women experienced, as children, pressure from their fathers for high achievement (Schneewind, 1995).

Reduction of Parental Influence The significance of parental influence diminishes as the child's world expands and admits additional models such as siblings, peers, and other adults. Like Adler, Bandura considered birth order within the family to be important. He argued that first-born children and only children have different bases for judging their own abilities than do later-born children.

Also, siblings of the same sex are likely to be more competitive than are siblings of the opposite sex, a factor also related to the development of self-efficacy. Among playmates, children who are the most experienced and successful at tasks and games serve as high-efficacy models for other children. Peers provide comparative reference points for appraising one's own level of achievement.

Teachers influence self-efficacy judgments through their impact on the development of cognitive abilities and problem-solving skills, which are vital to efficient adult functioning. Children often rate their own competence in terms of their teachers' evaluations of them. In Bandura's view, schools that use ability groupings undermine self-efficacy and self-confidence in students who are assigned to the lower groups. Competitive practices such as grading on a curve also doom poor achievers to average or low grades.

Adolescence

The transitional experiences of adolescence involve coping with new demands and pressures, from a growing awareness of sex to the choice of college and career. Adolescents must establish new competencies and appraisals of their abilities. Bandura noted that the success of this stage typically depends on the level of self-efficacy established during the childhood years.

Adulthood

Bandura divided adulthood into two periods: young adulthood and the middle years. Young adulthood involves new adjustments such as marriage, parenthood, and trying to establish a career. High self-efficacy is necessary for successful outcomes of these experiences. People low in self-efficacy will not be able to deal adequately with these situations and are likely to fail to adjust.

Women who feel high in self-efficacy about their parenting skills are likely to promote self-efficacy in their children. Women who believe they are good parents are less subject to despondency and emotional strain in their role as a parent than are women low in self-efficacy (Olioff & Aboud, 1991; Teti & Gelfand, 1991). High self-efficacy mothers who worked outside the home experienced significantly less physical and emotional strain from work–family conflicts than did women low in self-efficacy (Bandura, 1995).

The middle years of adulthood are also stressful as people reevaluate their careers and their family and social lives. As we confront our limitations and redefine our goals, we must reassess our skills and find new opportunities for enhancing our self-efficacy.

Old Age

Self-efficacy reassessments in old age are difficult. Declining mental and physical abilities, retirement from active work, and withdrawal from social life may force a new round of self-appraisal. A lowering of self-efficacy can further affect physical and mental functioning in a kind of self-fulfilling prophecy. For example, reduced self-confidence about sexual performance can lead to a reduction in sexual activity.

Lower physical efficacy can lead to fatigue and a curtailing of physical activities. If we no longer believe we can do something we used to enjoy and do well, then we may no longer even try to do it as we get older. To Bandura, self-efficacy is the single most important factor in determining success or failure throughout the entire life span.

Behavior Modification

Bandura's goal in developing his social-cognitive theory was to modify or change those learned behaviors that society considers undesirable or abnormal. Like Skinner's approach to therapy, Bandura focused on external aspects, those inappropriate or destructive behaviors, in the belief that they are learned, just as all behaviors are learned. Bandura did not attempt to deal with any supposed underlying unconscious conflicts. It is the behavior or symptom, rather than any presumed internal neurosis that is the target of the social-learning approach.

Bandura developed three forms of behavior therapy: modeling, guided participation, and covert modeling. We shall see examples of these approaches in dealing with fears, phobias, and anxieties.

Fears and Phobias

If modeling is the way we learn our behaviors originally, then it should also be an effective way to relearn or change behavior. Bandura applied modeling techniques to eliminate fears and other intense emotional reactions. In one early study, children who were afraid of dogs observed a child of the same age playing with a dog (Bandura, Grusec, & Menlove, 1967). While the subjects watched from a safe distance, the model made progressively bolder movements toward the dog. The model petted the dog through the bars of a playpen, then went inside the pen and played with the dog. The observers' fear of dogs was considerably reduced as a result of this observational learning situation.

In a classic study of snake phobia, Bandura and his associates eliminated an intense fear of snakes in adults (Bandura, Blanchard, & Ritter, 1969). The subjects watched a film in which children, adolescents, and adults made progressively closer contact with a snake. At first, the filmed models handled plastic snakes, then touched live snakes, and finally let a large snake crawl over their body. The phobic subjects were allowed to stop the film whenever the scenes became too threatening. Gradually, their fear of snakes was overcome.

The technique called *guided participation* involves watching a live model and then participating with the model. For example, to treat a snake phobia, subjects watch through an observation window while a live model handles a snake. The subjects then enter the room with the model and observe the handling of the snake at close range. Wearing gloves, subjects are coaxed into touching the middle of the snake while the model holds the head and tail. Subjects eventually come to touch the snake without gloves.

Modeling has been shown to be effective even in the absence of an observable model. In *covert modeling*, subjects are instructed to imagine a model coping with a feared or threatening situation; they do not actually see a model. Covert modeling has been used to successfully treat snake phobias and social inhibitions.

You may not think that a fear of snakes is so terrible, but overcoming this fear has brought about significant changes in many people's lives, even for those who never encounter snakes. In addition to bolstering self-esteem and self-efficacy, eliminating a snake phobia can alter personal and work habits. A woman was able to wear a necklace for the first time after modeling therapy. Previously she had not been able to do so because necklaces reminded her of snakes. A realtor treated successfully for snake phobia was able to increase his income because he no longer feared visiting properties in rural areas. Many other phobics treated by modeling therapy were freed from nightmares about snakes.

Phobias restrict our daily lives. For example, many people who fear spiders react with rapid heartbeat, shortness of breath, and vomiting just from seeing a picture of a spider. Phobics doubt their self-efficacy in these fear-provoking situations and have little confidence in their ability to deal with the source of the phobia. To relieve people of these fears greatly expands their environment and increases their self-efficacy.

Advantages of Modeling Therapy

Modeling therapy, particularly using online video techniques, offers several practical advantages. Complex behaviors can be seen as a whole. Extraneous behaviors can be edited out so that the subject's time is spent viewing only relevant behaviors. The same videos can be repeated with many patients and used by a number of therapists simultaneously. Modeling techniques can also be used with groups, saving time and money in treating people with the same problem.

This approach has been effective with phobias, obsessive-compulsive disorders, and sexual dysfunction. The positive effects have been reported to last for years. Considerable research has been conducted on self-efficacy during and after behavior modification therapy. The results have shown that as the subjects' self-efficacy improved during treatment, they were increasingly able to deal with the source of the fear. It was the therapeutic procedure itself that enhanced self-efficacy.

Anxiety

We noted that many behaviors can be modified through the modeling approach. We will consider two instances: fear of medical treatment and test anxiety.

Fear of medical treatment   Some people have such an intense fear of medical situations that they are prevented from seeking treatment. One early study dealt with children who were scheduled for surgery and had never been in a hospital before. They were divided into two groups: an experimental group that watched a film about a boy's experience in the hospital and a control group that saw a film about a boy taking a trip (Melamed & Siegel, 1975).

The child in the hospital film was an exemplary model. Despite some initial anxiety, he coped well with the doctors and the medical procedures. The modeling film was effective in reducing anxiety. In addition, those who had seen the hospital film had fewer behavior problems after hospitalization than did those in the control group.

Similar procedures have been used to reduce fear of hospitalization in adults as well as fear of dental treatment. One study involved a medical procedure considered so stressful that more than 80 percent of patients initially refused to undergo it or quit it prematurely (Allen, Danforth, & Drabman, 1989). Those who watched a video of a model having the procedure and describing how he coped with his distress were more likely to complete the treatment with less anxiety and a shorter hospital stay.

Test anxiety   For some college students, test anxiety is so serious a problem that their exam scores do not accurately reflect their knowledge of the material being tested. In a classic research study, a sample of college students was divided into groups based on their personality test scores: those high in test anxiety and those low in test anxiety (Sarason, 1975).

Some of the students saw a filmed model talking about her anxiety when taking tests and her ways of dealing with it. Other students saw a film of the same model who talked about test anxiety but not about coping mechanisms. Under a third condition, students watched the filmed model talking about other college activities.

Then the subjects were given a list of nonsense syllables to memorize and were tested on their ability to recall them. The results showed that subjects high in test anxiety were most strongly affected by the model who talked about coping mechanisms. They performed significantly better on the recall test than did high-anxiety subjects who had been exposed to the other two conditions.

Ethical Issues in Behavior Modification

Although the results of behavior modification are impressive, the techniques have drawn criticism from some educators, politicians, and even psychologists. They suggest that behavior modification exploits people, manipulating and controlling them against their will. Bandura argued that these charges are misleading. Behavior modification does not occur without the client's awareness. Indeed, self-awareness and self-regulation are vital for the effectiveness of any program to change or relearn behaviors. In other words, behavior-modification techniques will not be successful unless the person is able to understand what behaviors are being reinforced. They are not being treated against their will.

Further, the clients themselves decide what they want to change. They are not being controlled by anyone else. People come to a therapist to eliminate specific fears and anxieties that inhibit their ability to function or to cope with daily life. Bandura noted that the client–therapist relationship is a contract between two consenting individuals, not a relationship between a sinister master-controller and a spineless puppet.

Bandura also explained that far from manipulating or enslaving, modeling techniques actually increase personal freedom. People who are afraid to leave the house or who have a compulsion to wash their hands continually are not truly free. They are living within the constraints imposed by their phobic or compulsive behavior. Those constraints allow little choice. Removing the constraints through behavior-modification techniques can increase our feelings of freedom and the opportunity for personal growth.

Many such techniques have derived from Bandura's work and are popular alternatives to psychoanalysis and other therapeutic approaches.

Questions about Human Nature

reciprocal determinism The idea that behavior is controlled or determined by the individual, through cognitive processes, and by the environment, through external social stimulus events.

Bandura's position is clear on the issue of free will versus determinism. Behavior is controlled by the person through the cognitive processes, and by the environment through external social situations. Bandura calls this view **reciprocal determinism**. He noted that people are neither "powerless objects controlled by environmental forces nor free agents who can become whatever they choose. Both people and their environments are reciprocal determinants of each other" (1977, p. vii).

Assessment in Bandura's Theory

Like Skinner, Bandura focused on overt behavior rather than on internal motivating variables. He did not use assessment measures such as free association, dream analysis, or projective techniques. Unlike Skinner, Bandura accepted the operation of cognitive variables. It is these cognitive variables, as well as behavior, that can be assessed.

For example, in the modeling study we described involving children about to undergo surgery, assessment techniques included direct observation of their behavior, self-report inventories, and physiological measurements. In studies of self-efficacy, behavioral and cognitive variables were assessed quantitatively. Self-efficacy with regard to phobias was assessed by the subjects' self-ratings of the number of tasks on a behavioral-avoidance test they expected they could complete. College students' test anxiety was assessed by personality inventories. Thus, the assessment of behavioral and cognitive variables is important in the social-learning approach to personality.

Research on Bandura's Theory

Bandura favored well-controlled laboratory investigations in the rigorous tradition of experimental psychology. We noted his use of experimental and control groups and the precise measurement of independent and dependent variables. He studied large subject groups and compared their average performance by statistical analysis. To illustrate further the kind of research that has proceeded from Bandura's theory, we consider representative studies on self-efficacy, collective efficacy, and the effect of televised models on aggressive behavior.

Self-Efficacy

Age and gender differences Self-efficacy differs as a function of gender and age. On the average, men score higher than women in self-efficacy. These gender differences peak during the 20s and then decline in later years. For both men and women, self-efficacy increases through childhood and early adulthood, peaks in middle age, and then declines after age 60 (Gecas, 1989; Lachman, 1985).

However, even though self-efficacy appears to decline with age, there exists a wide range of individual differences in our beliefs about our capabilities. For example, in a study of adults in the Netherlands, average age 66, the people who believed that their memory was getting worse performed significantly less well on tests of memory functioning six years later than did those whose sense of self-efficacy included the belief that their memory capabilities were high (Valentijn et al., 2006). A large-scale analysis of more than 100 studies confirms this finding that low memory self-efficacy, that is, the level of our belief about how good our memory is, can affect performance on tests of memory (Beaudoin & Desrichard, 2011). This research provides further support for the proposition that our belief in our own abilities may, indeed, affect those abilities. The more we believe we can do something, the more likely we will do it.

The role of parental self-efficacy We noted earlier the influence of parents, siblings, peers, and others in affecting self-efficacy. Research in Italy showed that adolescents whose parents scored high in parental self-efficacy (who believed they were effective parents) also scored higher in their own self-efficacy beliefs than those whose parents scored low in parental self-efficacy. And those teens with high self-efficacy parents also had fewer behavioral problems, less anxiety, performed better in school, and were more open and honest in communicating with their parents than those with low self-efficacy parents (Steca, Bassi, Caprara, & Fave, 2011).

A study of African-American teenage boys in a public housing project found that those with higher levels of parental support, control, and self-efficacy had higher levels of self-efficacy themselves. Lack of parental support and guidance as well as low parental self-efficacy led to greater substance abuse and other delinquent behavior (Nebbitt, 2009).

Research on teenagers in Chicago found that having supportive parents was positively related to the students' sense of self-efficacy. The more supportive the parents, the higher their children's self-efficacy (McCoy & Bowen, 2014). A study of Mexican-American families showed that high parental self-efficacy was related to higher self-efficacy and fewer behavioral problems among both male and female adolescents (Dumka, Gonzales, Wheeler, & Millsap, 2010).

American young adults whose parents had exercised tight control over their upbringing showed lower self-efficacy than those whose parents were less controlling (Givertz & Segrin, 2014). A study of teenagers in Malaysia showed that involvement in their upbringing on the part of their fathers was just as important as involvement by their mothers in their development of self-efficacy and overall happiness (Yap & Baharudin, 2015).

Physical appearance We noted Bandura's suggestion that physical appearance can influence the reinforcers people receive from others and, thus, how they feel about themselves. A study of adult men and women aged 25 to 76 showed that physical appearance had a greater effect on their feelings of being in control of their lives than did their level of self-esteem or their health (Andreoletti, Zebrowitz, & Lachman, 2001).

For example, having a round face, large eyes, small nose bridge, and small chin ("baby-faceness") was found to be strongly related to low control beliefs in young and middle adulthood. Older baby-faced adults reported stronger feelings of control, perhaps because people reacted to them differently since they looked younger than thin-faced people of the same age. The findings were stronger for women. A more youthful appearance later in life was shown to have definite advantages both socially and in the workplace.

Another major finding in this study was the significant effect of physical attractiveness on control beliefs. People who were rated less attractive reported lower feelings of control in both job and social situations. In addition, shorter people reported lower feelings of control in young adulthood than did taller people or those of average height.

Academic performance   There is a significant positive relationship between self-efficacy and academic performance. Teachers with a high degree of self-efficacy or confidence in their teaching abilities create more opportunities for their students to achieve at a high level. Self-efficacy in students has also been positively related to motivation, level of effort, level of aspiration, and persistence in classroom situations (see, for example, Bassi, Steca, Fave, & Caprara, 2007; Gibson & Dembo, 1984; Multon, Brown, & Lent, 1991; Zimmerman, 1995).

Classroom teachers in Germany who were high in self-efficacy were rated by their students as being more effective teachers than those low in self-efficacy. In addition, those whose students rated them high in quality of classroom instruction developed higher levels of self-efficacy. In other words, the positive feedback from their students' ratings made them feel even surer of themselves (Holzberger, Philipp, & Kunter, 2013).

Bandura also found differences in the ways schools inculcate self-efficacy in their students. In high-achieving schools, principals were more concerned with education than with implementing policies and regulations, and teachers set high expectations and standards for their students. In low-achieving schools principals functioned more as administrators and disciplinarians than as educators, and teachers expected little in the way of academic performance from their students (Bandura, 1997).

Cultural differences have been shown to influence self-efficacy in children. A study was conducted with elementary school students in grades two to six in East and West Germany, before those nations were reunified in 1990. Students in the East German communist-collectivist culture scored lower in self-efficacy than children in the West German capitalist-individualist culture. The East German children had less confidence in their ability to perform well in school and considered themselves less intelligent than West German students (Oettingen & Maier, 1999). High school students in Iran who had a higher sense of ethnic identity had a higher level of self-efficacy than did those with a poor sense of ethnic identity (Hejazi & Hasany, 2014).

Career choice and job performance   Gender differences in self-efficacy can influence our choice of career. Research has shown that men perceive themselves to be high in self-efficacy for so-called traditional "male" as well as traditional "female" occupations. In contrast, women perceive themselves high in self-efficacy for so-called female occupations but low in self-efficacy for traditional male occupations.

The male and female subjects in this research performed at comparable levels on standardized tests of verbal and quantitative skills. Thus, they possessed similar measurable abilities but perceived these abilities differently. Their feelings about their own competence for various careers differed as a function of gender (Hackett, 1995).

Self-efficacy can affect the amount of time spent job hunting as well as future job success. Employees high in self-efficacy set higher personal goals and are more committed to them than employees low in self-efficacy. Those high in self-efficacy tend to focus on analyzing and solving problems on the job. Those low in self-efficacy focus on personal deficiencies and the fear of failure, which can undermine their productivity (Locke & Latham, 1990). In addition, failure in performing a computer-based task was shown to reduce a person's level of self-efficacy (Hardy, 2014).

The significant positive relationship between self-efficacy and job performance was supported by a meta-analysis of 114 research studies involving more than 21,600 subjects. The higher the level of self-efficacy, the better was the performance on the job (Stajkovic & Luthans, 1998). An update of this research found that self-efficacy was a better predictor of performance for jobs of low complexity than it was for jobs of medium or high complexity (Judge, Jackson, Shaw, Scott, & Rich, 2007). Also, those high in self-efficacy are much more likely to be more fully engaged in their work and to experience less burnout from their jobs (Ventura, Salanova, & Llorens, 2015).

Those high in self-efficacy perform better when they receive greater feedback about their job performance. They often do not perform well in situations that provide little or no feedback. In other words, not knowing how well they are doing can be a negative factor for people who score high in self-efficacy (Schmidt & DeShon, 2010). Other research has demonstrated that people high in self-efficacy are more successful in job training programs and report higher levels of job satisfaction, organizational commitment, and job performance than do people who are low in self-efficacy (Gupta, Ganster, & Kepes 2013; Salas & Cannon-Bowers, 2001).

Physical health Self-efficacy also affects several aspects of physical well-being, including pain tolerance, living a healthy lifestyle, and recovering from illness.

Pain Tolerance In one study, pregnant women who had been taught relaxation and breathing exercises to reduce pain during childbirth believed they had greater control over that pain than did women who had not been taught relaxation techniques. The higher the women's self-efficacy and feeling of control, the longer they were able to tolerate the discomfort experienced during delivery before requesting pain medication. In addition, the higher their perceived self-efficacy, the less pain medication they required (Manning & Wright, 1983).

Other research supports the positive relationship between self-efficacy and pain tolerance. One study of more than 15,000 patients in China found that those higher in self-efficacy suffered less impairment, emotional distress, and severity of pain than those who were lower in self-efficacy (Jackson, Wang, Wang, & Fan, 2014).

Coping techniques that improve self-efficacy produce substantial increases in endorphins, which are the body's natural painkillers. In a study on chronic pain, patients suffering from low back pain were given a pain-rating scale and a self-efficacy rating scale. Their progress in a three-week rehabilitation program was monitored. After six months it was found that patients higher in self-efficacy reported better physical functioning and less back pain than did patients lower in self-efficacy (Altmaier, Russell, Kao, Lehmann, & Weinstein, 1993).

Maintaining a Healthy Lifestyle Self-efficacy is also related to the maintenance of healthy behaviors. Bandura wrote that:

> Life-style habits can enhance or impair health. This enables people to exert some behavioral control over their vitality and quality of health. Efficacy beliefs affect every phase of personal change—whether people even consider changing their health habits; whether they enlist the motivation and perseverance needed to succeed should they choose to do so; and how well they maintain the habit changes they have achieved. (Bandura, 1995, p. 28)

It has been found, for example, that the use of techniques for enhancing feelings of self-efficacy among adults 60 years and older led to increased levels of physical activity. Those whose self-efficacy remained lower led more sedentary, unhealthy lives (French, Olander, Chrisholm, & McSharry, 2014).

A study of Native American and native Alaskan adults showed a clear relationship between self-efficacy and alcohol use. The lower the level of self-efficacy, the greater the alcohol consumption (Taylor, 2000). In the case of cigarette smoking, studies of adolescents show that the higher their self-efficacy, the more resistant they are to peer pressure to start smoking (Schwarzer & Fuchs, 1995; Stacy, Sussman, Dent, Burton, & Floy, 1992).

Recovering from Illness Self-efficacy can affect recovery from physical illness. For example, one study found that people high in self-efficacy responded better to cognitive and behavioral treatment for pulmonary disease than did patients low in self-efficacy. Men who suffered heart attacks showed a higher rate of return to normal activities and less fear and depression when both they and their spouses believed in their cardiac fitness.

The higher the patients' self-efficacy, the more likely they were to follow prescribed exercise programs and the more they improved (Kaplan, Atkins, & Reinsch, 1984; McLeod, 1986). These findings were confirmed in a large-scale study of heart patients in Italy. Higher levels of self-efficacy eased the impact of their illness and led to higher overall feelings of health satisfaction (Greco, Steca, Monzani, Malfatto, & Parati, 2015).

Research in Israel on patients with diabetes found that those high in self-efficacy were far more likely to persist in their self-care treatment programs than were those low in self-efficacy (Mishali, Omer, & Heymann, 2011).

Adult patients recovering from orthopedic surgery (hip or knee replacement) who scored high in self-efficacy performed significantly better in rehabilitation therapy programs than did those low in self-efficacy (Waldrop, Lightsey, Ethington, Woemmel, & Coke, 2001). And a study of breast cancer patients found that the higher the expectation of remaining cancer-free in the future, the better the emotional adjustment to the disease (Carver et al., 2000).

Mental health Self-efficacy has been found to affect several aspects of our mental health, including depression and anxiety, as well as social interest and self-esteem.

Depression and Anxiety In Italy, a study of boys and girls, average age 11.5 years, found that children who rated themselves low in social and academic efficacy were significantly more likely to experience depression than were children who rated themselves high in efficacy. Low social efficacy has also been significantly related to depression in a sample of adolescents in the United States (Bandura, Pastorelli, Barbarelli, & Caprara, 1999).

Research on adolescents in the Netherlands found that low social efficacy was related to high levels of anxiety, neuroticism, and symptoms of depression (Muris, 2002). Studies in such diverse cultures as China and Nigeria showed that those high in self-efficacy experienced less on-the-job stress and less test anxiety than those low in self-efficacy (Li, 2010; Onyeizugbo, 2010).

A similar relationship was documented with adults. Low social efficacy was found to contribute to feelings of depression, partly because a lack of coping skills inhibited the development of a social support network (Holahan & Holahan, 1987). These findings may indicate a circular relationship rather than simple cause-and-effect.

Low self-efficacy can lead to depression, and depression can further reduce self-efficacy. People who are depressed believe that they are far less capable than others of performing effectively in many areas of life and that they have little control over their situations (Bandura, 1997).

Social Interest and Self-Esteem   A study of American college students related self-efficacy to several of the characteristics of mental health proposed by Alfred Adler. Students who scored high in self-efficacy also scored higher in social interest, the desire to strive for perfection, and a sense of belonging than did students who scored low in self-efficacy (Dinter, 2000).

Research in Canada, Iran, and the United States showed that high school students and adults who scored high on a measure of self-efficacy were likely also to score high in self-esteem. They were less likely to procrastinate or to give up trying when dealing with an obstacle than were subjects low in self-efficacy (Hoseinzadah, Azizi, & Tavakoli, 2014; Lightsey, Burke, Ervin, Henderson, & Yee, 2006; Steel, 2007).

Coping with stress   Enhanced self-efficacy and a sense of control over life events are positively related to the ability to cope with stress and to minimize its harmful effects on biological functioning. Bandura wrote, "A strong sense of coping efficacy reduces vulnerability to stress and depression in taxing situations and strengthens resiliency to adversity" (Bandura, 2001, p. 10). High self-efficacy has been associated with strengthening the body's immune system, lowering the release of stress-related hormones, and reducing susceptibility to respiratory infections.

High self-efficacy has been shown to help women cope with the stress of abortion. Subjects higher in self-efficacy adjusted more satisfactorily with significantly less depression and higher mood states than did those lower in self-efficacy (Cozzarelli, 1993). Another study dealt with stress experienced following the birth of one's first child. Women higher in self-efficacy coped better with the demands than did those lower in self-efficacy (Ozer, 1995).

A study of refugees migrating from East to West Germany after the destruction of the Berlin Wall in 1990 showed that people higher in self-efficacy adapted significantly better to the change from an economically disadvantaged lifestyle under a communist system to an affluent lifestyle under a capitalist system.

> Perceived self-efficacy proved to be a powerful personal resource regarding the impact of migration stress on cognitive appraisals as well as on psychological and physical wellbeing.... Highly self-efficacious migrants perceived the demands in their new life more as challenges and less as threats. They experienced lower anxiety, better health, and fewer health complaints than low self-efficacious migrants. (Jerusalem & Mittag, 1995, p. 195)

Among adults in the Netherlands who had suffered facial disfigurement as a result of treatment for cancers of the head or neck, those who measured lower in self-efficacy experienced higher levels of stress in response to unpleasant or rejecting behaviors of other people. Those who scored higher in self-efficacy experienced less stress because they believed they could exercise some control over how other people reacted to them (Hagedoorn & Molleman, 2006).

Collective Efficacy

Just as an individual may develop a sense of self-efficacy, a group of people working together in a common enterprise to achieve specific goals may develop a sense of collective efficacy (Dithurbide & Feltz, 2012). For example, a sports team, a department within a large organization, a military combat unit, or a group of neighbors uniting to fight drug dealers can engender the strong feeling that they will be able to overcome obstacles and achieve their goals.

The value of collective efficacy has been studied in college basketball teams. It was demonstrated that a high sense of collective efficacy arose in teams that had highly

HIGHLIGHTS: Research on Self-Efficacy

Studies on *self-efficacy* have shown that:

- Men score higher than women in self-efficacy when younger
- Self-efficacy increases into adulthood, peaks in middle age, and declines after age 60
- Those whose parents scored high in parental self-efficacy were high in personal self-efficacy
- Those whose parents were high in self-efficacy did better in school and had less anxiety and fewer behavior problems
- Self-efficacy is higher in individualistic cultures

People high in *self-efficacy*:

- Earn better grades in school
- Set higher career goals, are more committed to attaining those goals, and perform better on the job
- Are in better health, are better able to tolerate pain, and recover faster from illness
- Are less likely to drink alcohol and smoke cigarettes
- Are less likely to experience depression, test anxiety, on-the-job stress, or become neurotic
- Score higher in self-esteem; they feel good about themselves.

competent leaders early in the season and that had won most of their games in the previous season. Teams with the highest collective efficacy at the beginning of the new season placed better in end-of-season standings than did teams that scored low in collective efficacy (Watson, Chemers, & Preiser, 2001).

Collective Efficacy in Family and Schools   High levels of collective efficacy in families have been shown to result in more open family communications, more truthful disclosures by teenagers to their parents, and a greater sense of satisfaction with family life by both parents and children (Bandura, Caprara, Barbaranelli, Regalia, & Scabini, 2011).

High collective efficacy among teachers in the Netherlands led to higher student achievements and better grades (Moolenaar, Sleegers, & Daly, 2012). Higher collective efficacy among a large group of 5th-, 8th-, and 11th-grade students in the United States led to a reduction of bullying (Williams & Guerra, 2011). Among 11- to 14-year-olds in Greece enrolled in classes shown to be high in collective efficacy displayed and received far less bullying from classmates than those in classes with low collective efficacy (Sapouna, 2010).

Collective Efficacy in Neighborhoods and Organizations   The feeling of high collective efficacy in a neighborhood, even a tough inner city one, has been related to decreases in alcoholism, drug use, violence, and criminal behavior (including murder) (Ahern, Cerda, Lippnnan, Tardiff, Vlahov, & Galea, 2013; Fagan, Wright, & Pinchevsky, 2014; Maxwell, Garner, & Skogan, 2011).

The collective efficacy of employing organizations has been shown to increase on-the-job performance and helping behavior among employees, and to reduce stress in the workplace. These findings have been found in Western cultures and in China (Du, Shin, & Choi, 2015; Esnard & Roques, 2014).

In Italy, air force military personnel who showed higher collective efficacy scored higher in commitment to their organization and satisfaction with their job than those in units with low collective efficacy (Borgogni, Petitta, & Mastrorilla, 2010).

Self-Efficacy and the Internet

Research on Internet self-efficacy (our feelings of confidence in our ability to effectively use the Internet) conducted on 8th-grade students in Taiwan found no gender differences. However, girls ranked higher than boys in level of confidence in communicating online, whereas boys were higher in level of confidence in exploring online (Tsai & Tsai, 2010). A study of American college students found that men ranked higher in computer self-efficacy than women (Buse, 2010).

Research with college students in Turkey found that those high in social self-efficacy (confidence in their ability to initiate social contact and make new friends easily) had greater self-esteem and emotional well-being, but were far more likely to become addicted to Internet use than those who scored low in social self-efficacy (Iskender & Akin, 2010).

Adults in Germany who scored high in self-efficacy regarding their ability to make a favorable impression on other people tended to post more informal personal photos (such as at a party) and to present themselves as relaxed, funny, and cool on their Facebook pages than those low in that aspect of personal self-efficacy (Kramer & Winter, 2008).

The Relationship between Aggressive Behavior and Televised and Online Violence

Bandura and researchers in many countries have demonstrated convincingly that in laboratory situations and in the real world, seeing violence begets violence whether on a television or computer screen, movies, video games, or in homes, streets, and schools (Elson & Ferguson, 2014). The evidence on the effects of the exposure to violence in the media or in person is so strong that the U.S. Surgeon General, the National Institute of Mental health, the American Psychological Association, the American Medical Association, and the American Psychiatric Association agree that exposure to violence is a significant risk factor in producing violence in those who witness it (Pozios, Kamban, & Bender, 2013).

Television   A large-scale literature review confirms the relationship between the viewing of violent television programs in childhood and later aggressive behavior (Rogoff, Paradise, Arauz, Correa-Chavez, & Angelillo, 2003). A study of people in their early and mid-20s found a strong positive correlation between the amount of violence they had watched on television between the ages of 6 and 10 and their aggressive behavior as adults.

In other words, the more TV violence to which they had been exposed as children, the more aggressive they were in their 20s (Huesmann, Moise-Titus, Podolski, & Eron, 2003). Research on teenagers in Germany also found that exposure to violence in the media was highly related to aggressive behavior (Krahe, Busching, & Moller, 2012).

In a different approach to the relationship between observed violence and aggressive behavior, researchers investigated the incidence of aggressive acts shortly after people viewed televised models committing violent acts. One analysis found a brief but sharp rise in violent actions peaking three to four days following highly publicized riots (Phillips, 1985).

Murder rates in the United States were found to increase by more than 12 percent over the expected rate for the three-day period following a televised championship boxing match, a phenomenon that was maintained over a 15-year period (Phillips, 1983). Self-directed violence also appears to increase following exposure to similar violence widely reported in the news media. The incidence of suicide tends to climb following the suicide of a movie star or other celebrity (Phillips, 1974).

Video Games Research on large samples of children, teenagers, and college students in the United States, Japan, and several other countries showed that playing violent video games resulted in increases in aggressive and hostile behaviors and greater drinking and drug use than among people who did not play violent video games. Those who played violent games were more likely to get into fights, argue with teachers, do poorly in school, and also were less likely to help others. In addition, they were found to have higher levels of cardiovascular arousal. In general, the more violent the games, the more violent the resulting behavior (Anderson, et al., 2010; Bartholow, Sestir, & Davis, 2005; Gentile, Lynch, Linder, & Walsh, 2004; Holtz & Appel, 2011; Huesmann, 2010; Krahe & Moller, 2004; Padilla-Walker, Nelson, Carroll, & Jensen, 2010; Uhlmann & Swanson, 2004).

Cyberbullying Studies in the United States, Canada, and Spain concluded that having a computer without parental control or monitoring can lead to a high level of online aggression, including cyberbullying, among boys and girls ages 12 to 17 (Calvete, Orue, Estevez, Villardon, & Padilla, 2010; Law, Shapka, & Olson, 2010; Werner & Bumpus, 2010).

People high in self-efficacy and self-esteem are much less bothered by being targets of cyberbullying than those who are low on those characteristics (Raskauskas, Rubiano, Offen, & Wayland, 2015). Those who are high in disinhibition, whose moral constraints are weakened by watching a model performing a harmful act, are much more given to cyberbullying (Bussey, Fitzpatrick, & Raman, 2015; Udris, 2014).

HIGHLIGHTS: Research on Bandura's Ideas

Groups that score high in *collective efficacy*:

- Win more basketball games and get better grades in school
- Show a higher level of commitment to their organization
- Score high in job satisfaction and job performance
- Engage in less bullying in the classroom
- Experience greater openness and satisfaction with their family

Research on *Internet self-efficacy* has found that:

- Male college students in the United States score higher than females
- In Taiwan, girls in the 8th grade score higher than boys
- Those high in social self-efficacy (confident in their ability to make new friends) are more likely to become addicted to the Internet

- Those who feel sure of their ability to make a good impression on others use more informal photos such as selfies on their Facebook page

Studies show that *aggressive behavior* is related to:

- Watching violent behavior on television and online in childhood
- Playing violent video games in childhood, adolescence, and young adulthood

Cyberbullying

- Is more likely to be practiced by those who are high in disinhibition
- Has fewer effects on those who are high in self-efficacy

Reflections on Bandura's Theory

Social-learning theory focuses on overt behavior. Critics charge that this emphasis ignores distinctly human inner aspects of personality such as motivation and emotion. They draw an analogy with a physician whose patients have stomach pains. The physician who deals only with overt behavior may treat such patients by asking them to stop groaning and complaining and clutching their stomachs. What may be required instead is medication or surgery. The physician must diagnose and treat the afflicted internal organ, the underlying cause of the pain. If just the symptom is treated and not the cause, critics say, substitute symptoms may appear.

The social-learning approach has several distinct advantages. First, it is objective and amenable to laboratory methods of investigation, making it compatible with the emphasis in experimental psychology. Most experimental psychologists reject theoretical work in personality that posits unconscious or other internal driving forces that cannot be manipulated or measured under laboratory conditions. Therefore, Bandura's approach boasts a great amount of empirical support. This is particularly true for his concept of self-efficacy. Research continues to confirm its usefulness in the laboratory and in real-world situations.

Second, observational learning and behavior modification are compatible with the functional, pragmatic spirit of American psychology. More readily than other approaches, observational-learning techniques can be taken from the laboratory and applied to practical problems. The techniques also provide more immediate reinforcement for the practitioner than do other approaches. For example, in clinical situations, dramatic changes can be seen in client behavior within weeks or even days.

The Widespread Use of Role Models

Behavioral changes on a larger scale in some 60 nations have also been demonstrated. Bandura's central idea, that people learn behaviors from role models whom they wish to emulate, has been used in radio and television programs in less well-developed nations to promote such social issues as population control, improving the status of women, and decreasing the spread of AIDS (Kaufman, Cornish, Zimmerman, & Johnson, 2014).

The stories presented in these media revolve around characters who modeled behaviors designed to achieve public health goals not only for themselves but for society as a whole. Studies have demonstrated significant changes in safe sex practices and family planning among millions of people following exposure to these models, reinforcing the notion that Bandura's ideas can be applied to national as well as individual problems (Smith, 2002). It is not surprising, then, that many researchers and clinicians continue to study and promote Bandura's social-learning theory. The great number of books, articles, and research studies still deriving from it attests to its continuing popularity as a way to study behavior in the laboratory and to modify behavior in the real world.

Chapter Summary

Behavior can be learned through vicarious reinforcement by observing the behavior of others and anticipating the rewards for behaving in the same way. Cognitive processes are the mediating mechanisms between stimulus and response and bring about control of behavior through self-regulation and self-reinforcement.

In the classic Bobo doll study, children patterned their behavior on the model's aggressive behavior whether the model was observed live, on television, or in a cartoon. Disinhibition involves weakening an inhibition through exposure to a model. Three factors that influence modeling are the model's characteristics, the observer's characteristics, and the behavior's reward consequences. Watching violence on television and online has been shown to lead to aggressive and violent behavior in children, teenagers, college students, and young adults. Playing violent video games also can result in aggressive behavior toward others.

Observational learning is governed by attentional, retention, production, and incentive and motivational processes. The self is a set of cognitive processes concerned with thought and perception. Self-reinforcement requires internal performance standards against which to evaluate behavior. Self-efficacy refers to the ability to control life events. People low in self-efficacy feel helpless and give up quickly when faced with obstacles. People who score high in self-efficacy persevere at tasks and perform at a high level. Judgments of self-efficacy are based on performance attainment, vicarious experiences, verbal persuasion, and physiological arousal. Using these information sources, it is possible to increase self-efficacy. Infants and children are reinforced primarily by physical stimuli. Older children are reinforced more by others' approval or disapproval; this is internalized so that reinforcement becomes self-administered.

In behavior therapy, models are used to demonstrate ways of coping with threatening situations.

Behavior can be modified through observation and guided participation. In covert modeling, subjects imagine how a model copes with a feared situation. Bandura's approach to behavior modification deals with overt behavior and cognitive variables, particularly self-efficacy. As self-efficacy improves during treatment, the client is increasingly able to deal with threatening situations. Behavior modification has been criticized for manipulating people against their will, but Bandura argues that with self-awareness and self-regulation, people undergoing behavior modification understand what is being reinforced.

Behavior is controlled by internal cognitive processes and external stimuli; a position Bandura calls reciprocal determinism. Most behavior is learned and genetic factors play only a minor role. Learning in childhood may be more influential than learning in adulthood but adults are not victims of childhood experiences.

Our ultimate goal is to set realistic performance standards to maintain an optimal level of self-efficacy. Self-efficacy varies with age and gender and can influence career choice, school performance, job performance, physical and mental health, and the ability to cope with stress. In addition, groups have been shown to develop collective efficacy. Computer self-efficacy strongly influences our online behavior.

Bandura assesses behavior and cognitive variables through direct observation, self-report inventories, and physiological measures. He favors controlled laboratory investigations using large groups of subjects and statistical analysis of data. Criticisms of Bandura's theory relate to his focus on overt behavior to the exclusion of emotions and conflicts, his treatment of symptoms rather than possible internal causes, and his failure to state precisely how cognitive variables affect behavior. Social-learning theory and the successful use of modeling to change behavior remain extremely popular.

Review Questions

1. In what ways does the observational-learning approach to personality differ from the other approaches we have discussed?
2. How does Bandura deal with internal cognitive, or thought, processes, and with the unconscious?
3. What is Bandura's position on the role of reinforcement in learning?
4. Describe a typical experiment in which modeling is used to change behavior.
5. Explain disinhibition. How can the same phenomenon of disinhibition explain both the behavior of people in a mob and the behavior of people trolling online?
6. How does modeling vary as a function of the characteristics of the models, the characteristics of the observers, and the reward consequences of the behavior?
7. What are the four processes of observational learning? How are they related?
8. Explain how the production processes can be used to teach a person to play tennis.
9. How do the types of behaviors we acquire through modeling change with age?
10. What is the *self* in Bandura's view? How does self-reinforcement operate to change behavior?
11. What does Bandura mean by self-efficacy? Give an example of how we can use self-efficacy to exert control over our lives.
12. How do people high in self-efficacy differ from people low in self-efficacy in terms of their ability to cope with life?
13. On what sources of information do we base our judgment about our own level of efficacy?
14. Describe the developmental changes that occur in self-efficacy from infancy to old age. How can self-efficacy be increased?
15. Describe the guided participation and the covert modeling approaches to behavior modification.
16. Give an example of how modeling can be used to reduce anxiety.
17. What is the relationship between self-efficacy and physical health and mental health?
18. What is Bandura's position on the issue of free will versus determinism? On the relative influences of heredity and environment?
19. How does self-efficacy differ as a function of gender, age, and physical attractiveness?
20. In what ways does self-efficacy influence performance in school and on the job? How does self-efficacy affect our ability to cope with stress?
21. Describe how exposure to televised violence and video-game violence affects behavior.
22. In what ways can collective efficacy influence the behavior of members of a group?
23. What is computer self-efficacy? How might it influence our behavior online?

Suggested Readings

Bandura, A. (Ed.). (1995). *Self-efficacy in changing societies*. New York: Cambridge University Press. Discusses various ways in which self-efficacy beliefs shape lifestyles and goals. Considers these issues from life-span and social-cultural perspectives.

Bandura, A. (1997). *Self-efficacy: The exercise of control*. New York: Freeman. Describes 20 years of research on the idea that we can accomplish what we truly want to accomplish; we are capable of consciously directing our actions to achieve success. Extends the concept of efficacy to society at large—to political beliefs, social practices, and collective action.

Bandura, A. (2001). Social cognitive theory: An agentic perspective. *Annual Review of Psychology, 52,* 1–26. Discusses the basis of social-cognitive theory as the capacity to exercise control over the nature and quality of one's life.

Bandura, A. (2013). The role of self-efficacy in goal-based motivation. In E. Locke & G. Latham (Eds.), *New developments in goal setting and task performance* (pp. 147–157). New York: Routledge/Taylor & Francis. Bandura's views, at age 88, of the role of self-efficacy in determining life goals and the standards we set for ourselves.

Evans, R. (1989). *Albert Bandura: The man and his ideas: A dialogue.* New York: Praeger. A detailed interview about many aspects of Bandura's life and work.

The Limited-Domain Approach

Personality theorists have generally attempted to deal with all aspects of personality. However, an increasing number of contemporary personality psychologists have concluded that no single theory can provide a comprehensive explanation for all aspects of personality 2and behavior.

This has given rise to a newer, limited-domain approach to personality that is more restricted in scope, focusing on more circumscribed personality factors. These factors can be experimentally tested more easily than a global theory that attempts to explain the total personality.

It is easy to see why the global theory approach to personality characterized the field for so long. The early theorists—such as Freud, Jung, and Adler—treated individual patients in their clinical practices in an attempt to cure abnormal behavior in order to help people function in the real world. Of necessity, then, these theorists focused on the total person, not just one or two traits or characteristics.

The focus began to shift away from the whole person when the study of personality was brought out of the clinic and into the research laboratory. Experimental psychologists typically study only one variable at a time, controlling or holding constant all others. In this way, they concentrate on a limited area of investigation.

They collect large amounts of data from their research on the ways in which an experimental variable relates to its antecedents and its behavioral consequences. Thus, the newer, more limited-domain theories are distinguished by supporting data that are different from the data generated in the clinical approach.

Proponents of these limited-domain theories place less emphasis on the therapeutic value of their ideas. Typically they are researchers, not clinicians, and, as a result, are more interested in investigating personality than in changing it. This does not mean that this limited-domain approach offers no treatment applications. Rather, it says that the theories were not developed specifically for use with patients, as was the case with many of the earlier personality theories.

In this chapter, we describe some personality variables currently being investigated: locus of control, sensation seeking, learned helplessness, optimism–pessimism, and the happy personality. They represent two approaches we discussed earlier—the trait approach and the social-learning (social-cognitive) approach.

Sensation seeking is one of the traits in Eysenck's personality dimension E (extraversion versus introversion). It is primarily an inherited attribute and reflects the impact of behavioral genetics on personality. Locus of control and learned helplessness are learned behaviors. They have a strong cognitive component, reflecting the influence of the behaviorist, social learning, and cognitive movements in personality. The happy personality is an outgrowth of the positive psychology movement.

These facets of personality are presented as examples of the limited-domain approach. They are not comprehensive systems, nor are they the only theories that focus on limited facets of personality. Our aim here is to give you the flavor of each and acquaint you with the idea of studying personality in this way.

Julian Rotter

Marvin Zuckerman

Martin E. P. Seligman

chapter 14

Facets of Personality: Taking Control, Taking Chances, and Finding Happiness

Julian Rotter: Locus of Control

Rotter (1916–2014) was born in Brooklyn, New York, the youngest of three brothers. He said they "fit quite well into Adler's descriptions of the oldest, the middle, and the 'fighting' youngest child" (1993, p. 273). The family lived comfortably until the 1929 economic depression when Rotter's father lost his business.

This dramatic change in circumstances was a pivotal event for the teenage boy. "It began in me a lifelong concern with social injustice and provided me with a powerful lesson on how personality and behavior were affected by situational conditions" (1993, p. 274).

In high school, Rotter discovered books about psychoanalysis by Freud and Adler. As a game, he began trying to interpret the dreams of his friends, and decided he wanted to become a psychologist. Disappointed to learn that there were not many jobs for psychologists, however, he chose to major in chemistry at Brooklyn College. Once there, he happened to meet Alfred Adler and switched his major to psychology after all, even though he knew it was impractical.

He wanted to pursue an academic career but found out about the widespread prejudice against hiring Jewish faculty in American colleges and universities at the time. "At Brooklyn College and again in graduate school," he wrote, "I had been warned that Jews simply could not get academic jobs, regardless of their credentials. The warnings seemed justified" (Rotter, 1982, p. 346).

After Rotter received his Ph.D. from Indiana University in 1951, he went to work at a state mental hospital in Connecticut. He served as a psychologist with the U.S. Army during World War II and then accepted a teaching position at Ohio State University, where George Kelly was director of the clinical psychology program.

At Ohio State, Rotter advanced his social-learning approach to personality. His research program attracted many outstanding graduate students who went on to productive careers. One of them later referred to that time at Ohio State as the "glory days," with "Rotter and Kelly right in the midst of refining their theoretical positions and writing their magnum opuses" (Sechrest, 1984, p. 228).

In 1963 Rotter left Ohio State for the University of Connecticut at Storrs. In 1988 he received the Distinguished Scientific Contribution Award from the American Psychological Association. Well into his 80s, he kept up his vigorous tennis and squash games and his weekly poker sessions (Strickland, 2014). By the time of his death in 2014, he had become "one of the most eminent psychologists of the 20th century" (Rotter, 2014, p. 1).

Internal versus External Control of Reinforcement

Rotter tried to explain personality and behavior by looking both outside and inside the organism, considering external reinforcements as well as internal cognitive processes. In the course of an extensive research program, he found that some people believe that their reinforcers depend on their own actions, whereas others believe their reinforcers are controlled by other people and by outside forces. He called this concept *locus of control*.

People who have an **internal locus of control** believe that the reinforcement they receive is under the control of their own behaviors and abilities. Those with an **external locus of control** believe that other people, fate, or luck control the rewards they receive. They are convinced that they are powerless with respect to outside forces.

You can see how the source of our locus of control can have a considerable influence on our behavior. External locus-of-control people, who believe that their own behaviors

internal locus of control A belief that reinforcement is brought about by our own behavior.

external locus of control A belief that reinforcement is under the control of other people, fate, or luck.

and abilities make no difference in the reinforcers they receive, see little value in exerting any effort to improve their situation. Why should they even try when they have no expectation of being able to control present or future events?

In contrast, internal locus-of-control people believe they have a firm grip on their own lives and behave accordingly. They perform at a higher level on their jobs than do external locus-of-control people. In addition, internals are less susceptible to attempts to influence them, place a higher value on their skills, and are more alert to environmental cues that they use to guide behavior. They report lower anxiety, higher self-esteem, and greater happiness. They enjoy greater mental and physical health than those who are high in external control (Saric & Pahic, 2013).

Assessment of Locus of Control

Rotter developed self-report inventories to assess locus of control. The Internal-External (I-E) Scale (Rotter, 1966) consists of 23 forced-choice alternatives. From each pair of items, subjects select the one that best describes their beliefs (see Table 14.1). It is not difficult to determine which of each pair of alternatives represents an internal or an external locus of control.

Another scale to assess locus of control is the Children's Nowicki-Strickland Internal-External Scale, a widely used 40-item test that has been translated into two dozen languages (Nowicki & Strickland, 1973; Strickland, 1989). An adult form of the scale is available, as well as a cartoon version for use with preschool children (Nowicki & Duke, 1983). Variants of the I-E Scale measure specific behaviors such as the relationship between locus of control and factors relating to successful dieting and weight loss as well as performance in a variety of situations.

Age and Gender Differences

Attempts to control our external environment begin in infancy, becoming more pronounced between ages 8 and 14. A study of 14- and 15-year-olds in Norway found that

---

TABLE 14-1   Sample items from the I-E Scale

1. a. Many of the unhappy things in people's lives are partly due to bad luck.
   b. People's misfortunes result from the mistakes they make.

2. a. One of the major reasons why we have wars is because people don't take enough interest in politics.
   b. There will always be wars, no matter how hard people try to prevent them.

3. a. In the long run people get the respect they deserve in this world.
   b. Unfortunately, an individual's worth often passes unrecognized no matter how hard he or she tries.

4. a. The idea that teachers are unfair to students is nonsense.
   b. Most students don't realize the extent to which their grades are influenced by accidental happenings.

5. a. Without the right breaks one cannot be an effective leader.
   b. Capable people who fail to become leaders have not taken advantage of their opportunities.

6. a. No matter how hard you try some people just don't like you.
   b. People who can't get others to like them don't understand how to get along with others.

Source: Rotter, J. B. (1966). Generalized expectancies for internal versus external control of reinforcement. *Psychological Monographs, 80,* 11.

girls scored significantly higher than boys did on internal locus of control (Manger & Ekeland, 2000). College students generally have been found to show an internal rather than an external orientation.

People apparently become more internally oriented as they grow older, reaching a peak in middle age (Heckhausen & Schulz, 1995). Also, a study of men and women in the United States, ages 60 to 75, found that their internal locus of control was significantly improved by cognitive training (Wolinsky et al., 2009).

In terms of overall scores on the I-E Scale, no significant differences between adult men and women in the United States were found (DeBrabander & Boone, 1990). However, a more recent study of men and women in England, ages 18 to 29, found that women had more external control than men (Holland, Geraghty, & Shah, 2010). In China, men have been found to score higher than women in internal control (Tong & Wang, 2006).

Cultural Differences

Ethnic Group Comparisons Studies conducted in Africa found that native Africans, like American-born Blacks in general, scored higher in external locus of control than did American-born Whites (Okeke, Draguns, Sheku, & Allen, 1999). In the African nation of Botswana, Black male and female adolescents scored higher in external locus of control than did White adolescents in the United States. In both countries, however, teens who were higher in socioeconomic status scored higher in internal control than did teens lower in socioeconomic status (Maqsud & Rouhani, 1991).

A comparison of adolescent Caucasian, Hispanic, Asian, and African-American teenagers found that having a more internal locus of control was considered to be more important for the Caucasians but less so for the other groups (Kang, Chang, Chen, & Greenberger, 2015). A comparison between native-born people in the Netherlands and immigrants to that country found that the immigrants (in this case from Morocco and Turkey) scored much higher on external locus of control than the natives (van Dijk, Dijkshoorn, van Dijk, Cremer, & Agyemang, 2013).

Research on Hispanic immigrants to the United States showed that those with a higher internal locus of control were more effective in adapting to the demands of their new culture and in dealing with the effects of discrimination or being marginalized (Llamas & Consoli, 2014).

Collectivist versus Individualistic Cultural Differences In general, Asians have been shown to be more externally oriented than Americans, a finding that may be explained in terms of different cultural beliefs. Whereas American culture traditionally prizes self-reliance and individualism, Asian culture emphasizes collectivism, community reliance, and interdependence.

Therefore, for Asians, success is viewed more as a product of external than internal factors. The more contact Asians have with Americans, however, the more internally oriented they become. For example, Chinese residents of Hong Kong measured higher in external locus of control than did Americans of Chinese heritage, and Americans of Chinese heritage were more externally oriented than Americans of European heritage (Uba, 1994).

A large-scale comparison of 18 cultures confirmed that people in collectivist cultures such as China scored higher in external control than those in Westernized countries who placed a greater value on having an internal locus of control (Cheng, Cheung, Chio, & Chan, 2013).

A study of college students in South Africa and in Lebanon found that the South African students scored significantly higher in internal locus of control than the Lebanese students. This provides another example of the difference in locus of control between an individualistic culture such as South Africa and the more collectivist, structured culture of Lebanon (Nasser & Abouchedid, 2006).

Behavioral Differences

Studies of workers in China and of athletes in Sweden found that those who measured high in internal locus of control were more able to adapt and commit to change; they also scored higher on tests of mental skills than those with a more external locus of control (Chen & Wang, 2007; Fallby, Hassmen, Kentta, & Durand-Burand, 2006). Other research concluded that high internal locus of control at work was positively related to job satisfaction, job commitment, and general satisfaction with life (Wang, Bowling, & Eschleman, 2010).

Research in Korea found that people high in internal academic locus of control (believing they would do well in school) were more likely to persist in an online college program than those who scored low in internal academic locus of control (Joo, Joung, & Sim, 2011). A study of college students in Turkey found that those high in internal academic locus of control were far less likely to become addicted to Internet use than those who scored low in internal academic locus of control (Iskender & Akin, 2010).

Similar to the idea of a collective self-efficacy, there may be a kind of collective locus of control that defines groups that work or study together. This was demonstrated in research in Austria on entrepreneurial work teams. The results showed that teams showing the highest internal locus of control performed at a far more efficient and effective level than teams lower in internal control (Khan, Breitenecker, & Schwarz, 2014).

Mental Health Differences

People high in internal locus of control are less likely to have emotional problems or to become alcoholics. They also cope better with stress, as was demonstrated in a study of nurses in Germany. Those who reported higher levels of work-related stress and burnout scored higher in external locus of control than those less bothered by stress and burnout (Owen, 2006; Schmitz, Neumann, & Oppermann, 2000).

Other research among diverse populations—including pregnant women, female prisoners, and police officers—found that those high in external control are more prone to fantasies, anxiety, depression, fear of death on the job (police), psychotic episodes, and hopelessness. They were also more likely to become victims of cyberbullying than those high in internal control (Ariso & Reyero, 2014; Asberg & Renk, 2014; Hutcheson, Fleming, & Martin, 2014; Marcano, Michaels, & Pierce, 2014; Ryon & Gleason, 2014; Samreen & Zubair, 2013).

College students in Greece, a family-oriented and highly protective culture, were followed as they dealt with the social and emotional challenges of leaving home, many for the first time. Students who scored high in internal control adjusted more readily than those high in external control (Leontopoulou, 2006). A study of first-year college students in Turkey found that those high in external locus of control were far more indecisive in new situations than those high in internal locus of control (Bacanli, 2006).

High external locus of control has been associated with compulsive hoarding behavior (Benson-Townsend & Silver, 2014). People suffering from various kinds of addiction have been found to benefit from therapy when they are able to develop a greater internal locus of control (Amram & Benbenishty, 2014). People high in internal control experience less anxiety and depression, are less likely to be lonely or attempt suicide, and find greater meaning in life (Castro, Echavarria, & Velasquez, 2010; Keltikangas-Jaruinen & Raikkonen, 1990; Kulshrestha & Sen, 2006; O'Neal, Vosvick, Catalano, & Logan, 2010; Petrosky & Birkhimer, 1991; Spann, Molock, Barksdale, Matlin, & Puri, 2006).

A study of teenagers in Israel during the 1990 Persian Gulf War, when frequent explosions of Scud missiles caused widespread injury and destruction, found that the adolescents who scored higher on perceived control experienced significantly less anxiety and fewer stress-related symptoms during the fighting than adolescents who scored lower in perceived control (Zeidner, 1993). Similarly, people high in internal control show higher levels of mental health, experience more meaningful lives, and score higher on measures of subjective well-being than those high in external control (Shojaee & French, 2014; Singh & Choudhri, 2014).

Physical Health Differences

Internally oriented people tend to be physically healthier than externally oriented people and to have lower blood pressure and fewer heart attacks. When they do develop cardiac problems, they cooperate better with the hospital staff and are released earlier than patients who are externally oriented. A study in Norway found that they also tend to go back to work sooner than those with a high external locus of control (Bergvik, Sorlie, & Wynn, 2012).

Research on patients recovering from coronary artery bypass surgery found that those high in internal control had achieved a higher level of physical functioning at six weeks and six months after surgery than those low in internal control (Barry, Kasl, Lichtman, Vaccarino, & Krumholz, 2006). Among older cancer patients in the Netherlands, those high in internal control experienced less depression than those high in external control (Aarts, Deckx, Abbema, Tjan-Heijnen, Akker, & Buntinx, 2015).

Some studies show that internals tend to be more cautious about their health and are more likely to wear seat belts, eat well, exercise regularly, and quit smoking (Cobb-Clark, Kassenboehmer, & Schurer, 2014; Phares, 1993; Seeman, Seeman, & Sayles, 1985; Segall & Wynd, 1990). Research in Nigeria found that those high in internal control were more likely to undergo screening for cervical and breast cancers (Adebimpe & Oladimeji, 2014). Cancer patients in the Netherlands who were high in external control had more trust in their oncologists than those low in external control (Hillen et al., 2014).

However, studies in France, Germany, and South Africa found that people high in internal health locus of control took less care of their health in general, but had fewer eating disorders and undertook fewer behaviors that put them at risk for HIV (Grotz, Hapke, Lampert, & Baumeister, 2011; Gwandure & Mayekiso, 2010; Scoffier, Paquet, & d'Arripe-Longueville, 2010).

Research in Sweden found that up to one-third of older people, those with little formal education, and immigrant groups all scored low in internal health locus of control (Lindstrom, 2011).

Developing Locus of Control in Childhood

Evidence suggests that locus of control is learned in childhood and is directly related to parental behavior (Ahlin & Lobo Antunes, 2015). External control beliefs are likely to be expressed by children reared in homes without an adult male role model. Also, external control beliefs tend to increase with the number of siblings. Children in large single-parent families headed by women were found to be more likely to develop an external locus of control (Schneewind, 1995). Later research shows that children whose mothers are depressed and have little formal education or income are likely to develop an external locus of control (Freed & Tompson, 2011). Children raised in low-income families have a lower sense of control in all aspects of their lives than children from higher-income families (Mittal & Griskevicius, 2014).

Parents of children who possess an internal locus of control were found to be highly supportive, to offer praise (positive reinforcement) for achievements, and to be consistent in their discipline; they were not authoritarian. As their children grew older, these parents continued to foster an internal orientation by encouraging independence.

HIGHLIGHTS: Research on Rotter's Ideas

People with *high internal locus of control* tend to:

- Live in wealthy individualistic cultures
- Perform well in school
- Not become addicted to Internet use
- Score high in job satisfaction and life satisfaction
- Score low in anxiety and depression
- Cope better with stress
- Be physically healthy
- Have parents who score high in internal control

Reflections on Locus of Control

A large-scale research program using both college students and sales representatives as subjects reported a strong relationship between Rotter's concept of locus of control and Bandura's concept of self-efficacy (Judge, Erez, Bono, & Thoresen, 2002). Some researchers have suggested that both ideas deal with our perception or belief about the degree of control we have over events in our life and our ability to cope with them. A major difference between the two concepts is that locus of control can be generalized over many situations, whereas self-efficacy tends to be specific to a particular situation. However, Bandura insisted there was little overlap between the concepts of self-efficacy and locus of control. He wrote,

> Beliefs about whether one can produce certain actions (perceived self-efficacy) cannot, by any stretch of the imagination, be considered the same as beliefs about whether actions affect outcomes (locus of control). (1997, p. 20)

Nevertheless, Rotter's research has been highly rigorous and well controlled, and he used objective measures wherever possible. Studies have provided considerable empirical support. The I-E Scale has generated a wealth of research and has been applied in clinical and educational settings. Rotter noted that locus of control has become "one of the most studied variables in psychology" (1990, p. 489). Well into the second decade of the 21st century, locus of control continues to be the subject of research.

Julian Rotter

Various sites provide biographical information, discussions of his theory, research on relevant concepts, and links to other resources.

Marvin Zuckerman: Sensation Seeking

Beginning in the 1970s, psychologist Marvin Zuckerman (1928–), at the University of Delaware, has conducted research on a limited-domain aspect of personality he calls **sensation seeking**. This trait has a large hereditary component initially noted by Eysenck. Zuckerman describes sensation seeking as a desire for "varied, novel, complex, and intense sensations and experience, and the willingness to take physical, social, legal, and financial risks for the sake of such experience" (Zuckerman, 1994a, p. 27). We might call it simply "taking chances."

sensation seeking The need for varied, novel, and complex sensations and experiences.

Assessing Sensation Seeking

To measure sensation seeking Zuckerman constructed the Sensation Seeking Scale (SSS), a 40-item paper-and-pencil questionnaire. When developing this test, he administered it to many people whose behavior corresponded to his definition of sensation seeking. These included people who volunteered for psychological experiments that exposed them to novel experiences, people whose jobs involved physical danger (police officers and race-car drivers), and people who admitted to experimenting with drugs or varied sexual experiences.

Their SSS scores were compared with the scores of people who deliberately avoided novel or risky activities. Those who deliberately sought unusual activities scored high on the SSS, and those who preferred less venturesome activities scored low. Sample items from the test are shown in Table 14.2. Over the years, the test has been revised and is now in its fifth version; there is also a scale developed for use with children.

TABLE 14-2   Sample items from the Sensation Seeking Scale, Form V
Choose the statement in each pair that you prefer

1. a. I like wild uninhibited parties.
   b. I prefer quiet parties with good conversation.

2. a. I get bored seeing the same old faces.
   b. I like the comfortable familiarity of everyday friends.

3. a. A sensible person avoids activities that are dangerous.
   b. I sometimes like to do things that are a little frightening.

4. a. I would like to take off on a trip with no preplanned or definite routes or timetables.
   b. When I go on a trip I like to plan my route and timetable fairly carefully.

5. a. I would like to try parachute jumping.
   b. I would never want to try jumping out of a plane with or without a parachute.

6. a. There is altogether too much portrayal of sex in movies.
   b. I enjoy watching many of the sexy scenes in movies.

7. a. I am not interested in experience for its own sake.
   b. I like new, exciting experiences and sensations even if they are a bit frightening, unconventional, or illegal.

8. a. People should dress according to some standard of taste, neatness, and style.
   b. People should dress in individual ways, even if the effects are sometimes strange.

Source: Zuckerman, M. (1994). *Behavioral expressions and biosocial bases of sensation seeking* (pp. 389–392). Cambridge, England: Cambridge University Press.

Components of Sensation Seeking   Using the method of factor analysis, Zuckerman (1983; Zuckerman & Aluja, 2015) identified four components of sensation seeking.

- Thrill and adventure seeking: A desire to engage in physical activities involving speed, danger, novelty, and defiance of gravity such as parachuting, scuba diving, or bungee jumping.
- Experience seeking: The search for novel experiences through travel, music, art, or a nonconformist lifestyle with similarly inclined people.
- Disinhibition: The need to seek release in uninhibited social activities such as risky sex, impulsiveness, aggressiveness, and antisocial behaviors.
- Boredom susceptibility: An aversion to repetitive experiences, routine work, and predictable people, and a reaction of restless discontent when exposed to such situations.

Good and Bad Sensation Seeking   Zuckerman later noted a distinction between so-called good and bad sensation seeking:

- The good type, or *non-impulsive socialized sensation seeking*, involves the thrill- and adventure-seeking component.
- The bad type, *impulsive unsocialized sensation seeking*, consists of high scores on the disinhibition, experience seeking, and boredom susceptibility components, as well as high scores on Eysenck's psychoticism scale (Roberti, 2004; Zuckerman, 1994b).

Other scales for assessing sensation seeking have been developed in the United States and in other countries. German psychologists published the "Need Inventory of Sensation Seeking" in both German and English languages (Roth & Hammelstein, 2012). Later research suggested that it might be an even more reliable and valid test for measuring sensation seeking than the original Zuckerman scale (Marker & Schneider, 2015).

Another sensation seeking scale for use in China is the Brief Sensation Seeking Scale, which has been proven to be reliable and valid in that culture for predicting reckless behavior in motorcycle riding, excessive use of alcohol and cigarettes, and risky sexual behaviors (Chen et al., 2013; Fan, Lin, Bai, Huang, Chiang, & Chiu, 2014).

Sensation Seeking Scale

Various sites offer definitions, research results, and examples of tests to measure the concept of sensation seeking.

Characteristics of Sensation Seekers

Age Differences   Zuckerman found that differences in sensation seeking occur at a very young age. A study of second-grade schoolchildren in the United States showed that those who scored high in sensation seeking chose to watch a video about scary sharks, whereas those who scored low selected a video about a funny bunny instead (Trice, 2010).

In general, younger people are more inclined to seek adventure, risk, and novel experiences than older people. Among high school and college students in the United States and in Canada, those who scored high in sensation seeking were more likely to engage in reckless and risky behaviors and uncontrolled gambling than those who scored low (Collado, Felton, MacPherson, & Lejuez, 2014; George, Baechtold, Frost, & Campbell, 2006; Gupta, Derevensky, & Ellenbogen, 2006).

Test scores on subjects ranging from adolescents to 60-year-olds showed that sensation seeking begins to increase during the middle school years and decrease in one's twenties (Lynne-Landsman, Graber, Nichols, & Botvin, 2011). No significant differences were reported as a function of educational level. College students did not score significantly higher or lower on the SSS than those who did not attend college.

Zuckerman's Sensation-Seeking Experiences

The research results on the effects of age on sensation seeking were confirmed by Zuckerman's own life experiences. He said that when he was a college student he "reached my full sensation-seeking potential through drinking, sex, and hitch-hiking around the country." At age 74, he wrote,

> When I was a young sensation seeker I imagined that after I retired I would do all kinds of adventurous things like hang gliding, parachute jumping, and learning to fly an airplane. But whereas thrill and adventure seeking and disinhibition fall rapidly with age, experience seeking does not change. (Zuckerman, 2004, pp. 13, 21)

Zuckerman reports that he continues to seek new experiences, but they are less physically adventurous than when he was younger.

Gender Differences

In countries as diverse as the United States and Iran, men consistently scored higher in sensation seeking and lower in impulse control than women (Khodarahimi, 2014; Shulman, Harden, Chein, & Steinberg, 2015). Significant gender differences were also found in the four individual components of sensation seeking. Men scored higher on thrill and adventure seeking, disinhibition, and boredom susceptibility. Women scored higher on experience seeking. Similar results were obtained from subjects in the United States, England, Scotland, Japan, and Thailand.

Racial and Cultural Differences

Researchers found significant racial and cultural differences in SSS scores. Asians scored lower on the SSS than people in Western countries, and white subjects scored higher in sensation seeking than non-Whites.

The need for sensation seeking manifests itself in the desire for varied, novel, and sometimes dangerous experiences.

Mayo5/iStockphoto.com

Behavioral Differences between High and Low Sensation Seekers

Physical Risk Taking   Physical risk-taking behavior has been related to sensation seeking. Skydivers, firefighters, riot-control police officers, bungee jumpers, and race-car drivers score higher on the SSS than groups not engaged in these activities. A study of American Motocross drivers found that the most experienced (those who participated in the most races) had the highest scores on a measure of sensation seeking (Smith, Bissett, & Russo, 2014). Research on male college undergraduates in Israel found that high sensation seekers were more likely than low sensation seekers to participate in risky sports and to volunteer for military combat units (Hobfoll, Rom, & Segal, 1989).

Different Types of Risk Taking   Research has identified three types of risk takers: antisocial risk takers, adventurous risk takers, and pro-social risk takers. Those identified as antisocial (such as drug addicts and criminals) or as adventurous (mountain climbers and sky divers) showed significantly higher SSS scores than pro-social risk takers (police officers and firefighters). The motives of the pro-social group are related to factors other than thrill and adventure seeking (Levenson, 1990). High sensation seekers also appear more willing than low sensation seekers to relocate from familiar to unfamiliar surroundings and to travel to exotic places, even when the journey involves physical hazards.

Drugs, Drinking, Crime, Fast Cars, and Online Poker!   High sensation seekers are more likely than low sensation seekers to use and sell illicit drugs (and to do so at an earlier age), to drink alcoholic beverages, to shoplift, and to commit delinquent behavior. The subjects in these studies included Blacks in the United States (9 to 15 years old), university students in South Africa (16 to 49 years old), high school students and adults in the United States, and teens in Norway (12 to 16 years old) (see Bacon, Burak, & Rann, 2014; Hampson, Tildesley, Andrews, Barckley, & Peterson, 2013; Hansen & Breivik, 2001; Mahoney, Thompson-Lake, Cooper, Verrico, Newton, & De la Garza, 2015; Peltzer, Malaka, & Phaswana, 2001; Stanton, Li, Cottrell, & Kaljee, 2001).

Studies of American high school and college students found that high sensation seekers were more likely to smoke, use alcohol and drugs, drive fast, have more car accidents and convictions for reckless or drunk driving, and engage in frequent sex (McAdams & Donnellan, 2009; Ortin, Kleinman, & Gould, 2012; Ravert, Schwartz, Zamboanga, Kim, Weisskirch, & Bersamin, 2009). Research in Spain and in France confirmed the link between high sensation seeking and speeding and drunk driving (Delhomme, Chaurand, & Paran, 2012; Gonzales-Iglesias, Gomez-Fraguela, & Luengo, 2014).

Online poker players in France tended to score higher in sensation seeking and to experience strong feelings of arousal while doing so than those who did not play poker online (Barrault & Varesconi, 2013).

Risky Sexual Behaviors   A study of young Black women in the United States (ages 15–21) found that those who scored high on a measure of sexual sensation seeking reported greater sexual risk-taking behaviors—such as more instances of intercourse with more partners and less use of condoms—than those who scored low (Spitalnick et al., 2007).

In Zuckerman's research, 16 percent of the high sensation seekers reported risky homosexual encounters, as compared with 7 percent of low sensation seekers. Among college men, high sensation-seeking scores correlated positively with risky sexual behavior which the men knew could expose them to AIDS (Zuckerman, 1994b). These findings were confirmed by research on older subjects.

The correlation between sensation-seeking scores and risky sexual behavior among gay men (both Blacks and Whites) was so strong that the researchers concluded that high-sensation-seeking males constitute a high-risk group for AIDS (Fisher & Misovich, 1990; Kalichman, Johnson, Adair, Rompa, Multhauf, & Kelly, 1994).

Cheating, Color Choices, and Tattoos   There are several other ways in which high sensation seekers have been found to differ from low sensation seekers. Studies in Israel showed that high sensation seekers are more likely to cross a street on foot against a red light. They show a preference for so-called hot colors such as red and orange, rather than pastels such as light blue (Rosenbloom, 2006a, 2006b).

A study of young people in Germany (ages 14–24) found that significantly more high sensation seekers had tattoos and body piercings than low sensation seekers (Stirn, Hinz, & Braehler, 2006). American college students who scored high in sensation seeking were more likely to cheat on academic tests than those who scored low (DeAndrea, Carpenter, Shulman, & Levine, 2009).

Computer Use   High school and college students in China who scored high in sensation seeking were more likely to become obsessed with computer games and Internet use (Qing-Xin, Rong-Gang, & Yan, 2005; Zheng, Ming-Yi, Chun-Li, Jing, Jing, & Xiao-Yun, 2006). Research on workers in the United States showed that high sensation seekers frequently used their workplace computers for personal reasons such as sending emails, playing computer games, and viewing Web sites with sexual content (Everton, Mastrangelo, & Jolton, 2005). However, research with American college students did not support such a relationship (Velezmoro, Lacefield, & Roberti, 2010).

Job Performance   A study of 233 low-level employees in the United States found that high sensation seekers scored lower on job performance than low sensations seekers. High sensation seekers were also less likely to establish social relationships at their place of employment or try to obtain information from co-workers or supervisors. The researchers suggested that such lower level jobs might not be sufficiently stimulating for high sensation seekers (Reio & Sanders-Reio, 2006).

Personality Differences

Zuckerman and other researchers correlated sensation-seeking scores with a number of distinct personality factors. They found that SSS scores, particularly on disinhibition, were related to Eysenck's factor of extraversion and to the asocial tendencies associated with psychoticism. As a result of this finding, Zuckerman suggested that high sensation seekers are egocentrically extraverted, which means they are concerned with other people only as an audience or a source of stimulation. They do not relate to other people in a dependent or nurturing way.

High sensation-seeking scores also correlated positively with extraversion as described by Carl Jung and measured by the Myers-Briggs Type Indicator (Morehouse, Farley, & Youngquist, 1990). However, investigations of sensation seeking and neuroticism showed no correlation. Zuckerman suggested that SSS scores did not point to abnormal or neurotic behavior but that neuroses such as phobias and obsessive-compulsive behaviors might be related to low sensation seeking.

Research on college students and adults in the Netherlands found that high sensation seekers also scored high on the personality factors of openness to experience, extraversion, and conscientiousness (three of the factors of the five-factor model). They also scored high on two factors of the HEXACO model: emotionality and honesty-humility (de Vries, de Vries, & Feij, 2009).

High scores on the SSS correlated with a high degree of autonomy. High scorers openly express their emotions. They are assertive in relating to others, nonconforming, and confirmed risk takers. They act independently of social conventions and of other people's needs and attitudes. Governed primarily by their own needs, they order their lives to maximize opportunities for self-fulfillment. High scores on the SSS were also positively correlated with the openness to experience and the agreeableness dimensions of the five-factor model of personality (Roberti, 2004).

Cognitive Processes

Correlations between sensation seeking and intelligence test scores are generally positive but not high. A study of children in the Republic of Mauritius, an island nation in the Indian Ocean off the coast of Africa, found that those who scored high in sensation seeking at age 3 scored 12 points higher on intelligence tests at age 11 than children who scored low in sensation seeking at age 3. The results were similar for boys and girls and were not affected by the parents' occupation or level of education (Raine, Reynolds, Venables, & Mednick, 2002).

It has also been found that high sensation seekers did not earn better grades in school. Zuckerman suggested that because high sensation seekers were more involved in active recreational pursuits, they used less time for study. Tests of creativity and originality revealed that high sensation seekers have a greater capacity for original thinking but do not always express it in their schoolwork. High SSS scorers seem to be attracted to speculative, bizarre, even pseudoscientific ideas.

They also tend to engage in what Sigmund Freud called primary-process thought. They may have images, dreams, and daydreams so vivid that the distinction blurs between these internal stimuli and the real world. Zuckerman suggested that because high sensation seekers continually search for novel experiences, if they cannot find them in external situations they may look inward and create a fantasy world.

Occupational Preferences

Because high sensation seekers have a greater need for stimulating and varied experiences, they tend to choose different jobs than low sensation seekers. On tests of vocational interests, such as the Kuder Occupational Interest Survey, high and low sensation seekers showed significant differences. High SSS scores correlated positively with scientific interests and negatively with clerical interests. Men with high SSS scores also scored high on the Strong Interest Inventory scales showing interest in the helping professions such as psychologist, physician, psychiatrist, social worker, and minister.

Their scores correlated negatively with business sector jobs such as accountant, purchasing agent, and banker. Women with high SSS scores had high interest test scores for the profession of lawyer and low interest test scores for elementary school teacher. High sensation seekers of both sexes who were interested in the helping professions expressed a preference for risky, cutting-edge jobs such as crisis intervention work or paramedic duty on emergency response teams.

Attitudes

High sensation seekers tend to be more liberal in their political and religious attitudes than low sensation seekers. Those with high SSS scores are more likely to express atheistic views rather than belief in any conventional religion. High scorers on the SSS also express more permissive attitudes toward sexual behavior, whether their own or that of other people. Low sensation seekers are more likely to be frequent churchgoers. They scored high on measures of authoritarianism, a personality style typically characterized by rigid opinions and prejudiced attitudes. Low sensation seekers also show a low tolerance for ambiguity. They believe that ambiguous ideas and situations are threats rather than challenges (Zuckerman, 1994a).

Heredity versus Environment

A large amount of research consistently shows a strong hereditary basis for the sensation-seeking personality factor (Zuckerman, 2013). A study by Eysenck suggested that 58 percent of this trait could be accounted for by genetic factors (Eysenck, 1983). A twin study conducted jointly by Zuckerman and Sybil Eysenck found an even greater genetic component (Zuckerman, 1993). However, research comparing 14- to 20-year-olds in Turkey and in Wales on their motivation to undertake risky behaviors found small but significant differences between the two cultures, which suggest the importance of learning (an environmental factor) (Kloep, Guney, Cok, & Simsek, 2009).

Zuckerman also recognized the influence of other situational or environmental factors, such as parental sensation seeking. Low-sensation-seeking parents may be overly fearful, protective, and inhibiting of their children, forbidding them to engage in adventurous behaviors. High-sensation-seeking parents may encourage and reinforce their children for engaging in unusual activities, thus providing an environment that promotes additional sensation-seeking behaviors.

Ongoing research suggests that other environmental factors in childhood and adolescence that may affect the level of sensation seeking. A study of teenagers in Sweden found that those who scored high in impulsivity and sensation seeking and who attended more privileged schools committed fewer crimes than those with equally high levels of sensation seeking and impulsivity who went to less privileged schools (Eklund & Fritzell, 2014).

It has also been found that children who were raised in orphanages or other types of institutionalized care and who scored high in sensation seeking were much less likely to get into trouble than those with equally high sensation-seeking scores brought up in private homes (Loman, Johnson, Quevedo, Lafavor, & Gunnar, 2014).

Scores on the SSS in early studies supported the idea that first-borns and only-borns (both boys and girls) were higher in sensation seeking than later-borns. Because first-borns and only-borns receive more stimulation and attention from their parents at an early age, they are likely to be exposed to a greater optimal level of stimulation, predisposing them to sensation-seeking behavior as adults (Zuckerman, 1979). However, later research conducted in England failed to find any correlation between birth order and sensation seeking (Crozier & Birdsea, 2003).

HIGHLIGHTS: Research on Zuckerman's Ideas

People who score *high in sensation seeking* tend to:

- Score high in adventure-seeking, disinhibition, and susceptibility to boredom
- Live in Westernized cultures
- Takes risks, do drugs and alcohol, drive fast, and engage in frequent sex
- Spend a lot of time playing computer games
- Be extraverted, open to new experiences, conscientious, and emotional
- Be interested in the helping professions (such as psychologist or social worker) rather than in business
- Have liberal political and religious views
- Be the only child or the first-born child in their family
- Have more body piercings and tattoos

Reflections on Sensation Seeking

Zuckerman's focus on the sensation-seeking personality trait continues to stimulate research. Sensation seeking has been related to a wide range of behavioral, cognitive, personality, and physiological variables. His emphasis on the heritability of sensation seeking places his work in a different category from the behavioral and social-learning approaches to personality, which focus on the influences of situational factors and of learning.

Sensation-seeking theory has a commonsense appeal. It is easy to accept the idea that people differ in their need for excitement and risk, change and adventure. We are usually aware of our own level of sensation seeking and make fairly accurate judgments about the levels of our friends and relatives by considering the activities they enjoy or avoid. Zuckerman asked high and low sensation seekers to choose from a list of adjectives those that best described themselves. The results are shown in Table 14.3. Which ones would you choose?

Martin E. P. Seligman: Learned Helplessness and the Optimistic/Pessimistic Explanatory Style

learned helplessness
A condition resulting from the perception that we have no control over our environment.

In the mid-1960s, psychologist Martin Seligman (1942–) at the University of Pennsylvania, who would later lead the happiness and positive psychology trend in psychology, began research on a limited-domain facet of personality called **learned helplessness**. He first saw this phenomenon in an experiment on dogs on his first day as a graduate student. It marked the beginning of the direction of his future in psychology, and the future of psychology itself.

The dogs were being conditioned to associate a high-pitched sound with an electric shock. This was a simple Pavlovian classical conditioning situation involving respondent behavior (the pairing of the tone with the shock). But that was only the first part of the study.

In the second part, the dogs were placed one at a time in a large box that contained two compartments divided by a low wall. A shock was delivered through the floor of the compartment in which the dog had been placed. To escape the shock, the dog had to show the appropriate operant behavior, that is, to simply jump over the low barrier into the other compartment where there was no electric shock. Once the dogs learned to jump over the

TABLE 14-3   Self-descriptions of high and low sensation seekers

HIGH SENSATION SEEKERS	LOW SENSATION SEEKERS
Enthusiastic	Frightened
Playful	Panicky
Adventurous	Tense
Elated	Nervous
Imaginative	Shaky
Daring	Fearful
Zany	Worried
Mischievous	Upset

Source: From Zuckerman, M. (1978). Sensation seeking. In H. London and J. E. Exner, Jr. (Eds.), *Dimensions of Personality*. New York: Wiley.

wall—something dogs can be expected to do quickly—they would be tested to see if the high-pitched tone without the electric shock would bring about the same response.

A Shocking Finding

The research did not work out the way it was supposed to. The dogs did not jump over the barrier to escape the shock. Instead, when the shock was administered through the floor of their compartment they lay down, whimpered, and made no effort to escape.

The experimenters were baffled, but Seligman thought he had a clue. He suggested that perhaps during the first part of the experiment the dogs had learned that they were helpless to change their situation. When the tone sounded, there was nothing they could do to avoid the paired shock. Why even try? This learned reaction apparently generalized to the second part of the experiment, even though a means of escape was available. Seligman wrote,

> I was stunned by the implications. If dogs could learn something as complex as the futility of their actions, here was an analogy to human helplessness, one that could be studied in the laboratory. Helplessness was all around us—from the urban poor to the newborn child to the despondent patient with his face to the wall. Was this a laboratory model of human helplessness, one that could be used to understand how it comes about, how to cure it, how to prevent it, what drugs worked on it, and who was particularly vulnerable to it? (1990, p. 20)

Determined to find the answers, Seligman launched a research program to study learned helplessness, a condition he described as resulting from the perception that we have no control over our environment, that there is nothing we can do to change our situation. He expanded his research interests to include the issue of optimism versus pessimism and, later, the issue of happiness.

Early Research

Studies with Dogs In Seligman's initial experiments, dogs were harnessed and exposed to painful, though not physically harmful, electric shock. There was no action the dogs could take to escape or avoid the shock. After a series of shocks, the dogs were placed in a two-compartment shuttle box. As in the first experiment Seligman witnessed, a shock was administered through the floor of the compartment. The behavior of these dogs was compared with that of a control group of dogs that had not been exposed to the first electric shocks.

When the dogs in the control group were placed in the box and given the shock through the floor, they raced about the compartment until they accidentally leaped the barrier into the safe compartment. On succeeding trials, they jumped the barrier more quickly each time, having learned that this was the way to escape. The dogs in the experimental group, who had received electric shocks before being placed in the shuttle box, behaved differently. After getting the shock through the compartment floor, they raced around for about 30 seconds and then gave up, dropping to the floor and whimpering. They never learned to escape, not even when experimenters tried to entice them over the barrier with food. These dogs had given up; they had become passive and helpless and would make no attempt to change their situation (Overmier & Seligman, 1967; Seligman & Maier, 1967).

Studies with Humans Learned helplessness has been demonstrated in many studies using human subjects. For example, people in an experimental group were exposed to a loud, irritating noise and told they could turn it off if they pressed a series of buttons in the correct sequence. However, the conditions were arranged so that there was no correct sequence. No matter what action the subjects took, the noise continued. In the control group, people could turn off the noise by pressing the buttons in a sequence that was relatively easy to learn.

In the next step, the experimental subjects were placed in a situation in which all they had to do to stop the noise was move their hand from one side of a box to the other in response to a light signal. Control-group subjects rapidly learned this behavior but experimental-group subjects could not. They sat passively, making no effort to deal with the irritating noise (Hiroto, 1974).

Additional research confirmed and extended these findings. Learned helplessness was found to occur after human subjects simply observed helpless models, especially when the subjects recognized similarities between themselves and the models (Chamber & Hammonds, 2014). The experimenters in these and many other studies suggested that the subjects were saying, in effect, "If the models can't do anything about this, then neither can I."

A meta-analysis of 132 studies involving several thousand people found that the effects of inescapable shock were even stronger in human than in animal subjects. Learned helplessness effects were documented in adult men and women, college students, adolescents, children, elderly persons, unemployed women, and patients in psychiatric hospitals (Li, Mardhekar, & Wadkar, 2012; Villanova & Peterson, 1991).

Learned helplessness can occur in everyday situations where we are subjected to continuous intrusive stimuli over which we have no control, such as noise from a neighbor or outdoors, or being cyberbullied on social media sites on the Internet (Evans & Stecker, 2004; Rabinowitz, 2005; Zucchi, Bacheller, & Muscarella, 2012).

Learned Helplessness as Torture

The same techniques used in human and animal experiments have been applied by the Central Intelligence Agency (CIA) and other organizations committed to fighting terrorism. Prisoners have been placed in situations where no escape from painful stimuli is possible. For example, one was placed inside a coffin for days, another was waterboarded 83 times over 17 days, and others have been stripped and left in solitary confinement for days while constant ear-splitting rock music was piped in.

After exposure to such conditions, the prisoners exhibited the same symptoms of learned helplessness as subjects in the laboratory experiments. They became compliant and no longer tried to do anything about their conditions. When Seligman learned about this years later, he was "grieved and horrified" at the use to which his experiments had been put (McCoy, 2014).

Learned Helplessness and Emotional Health

The beneficial effects on psychological health of having control over one's life have been widely documented. Among cancer patients (ages 29–80), those with the highest perception of control were better adjusted than patients who believed they had little control over their situation. This finding held even for patients who were severely debilitated by their physical condition. Those who believed they could exert some influence over their illness and recovery, and their emotions, showed greater psychological adjustment than people in better physical condition but with a low perception of control (Thompson, Sobolew-Shubin, Galbraith, Schwankovsky, & Cruzen, 1993).

It has also been shown that people can learn to increase their feeling of control. A sample of men and women (average age 55) scheduled for extensive dental work were assessed prior to treatment for their level of anxiety and their desire for control in a dental setting. Half the patients were shown a stress inoculation training video; the other half (the control group) was shown a video about the local sights. Patients with low control in a dental setting but with a strong desire for greater control benefited the most from seeing the stress training video. They believed they felt more control and less pain during the actual treatment than control-group patients who had received no stress training (Law, Logan, & Baron, 1994).

Animal Research on Learned Helplessness and Physical Health

To investigate whether learned helplessness could affect physical health, Seligman and his associates designed a study in which rats were injected with malignant tumor cells. The rats were exposed to one of three conditions: an electric shock from which they could escape, a shock from which they could not escape, and no shock (Visintainer, Volpicelli, & Seligman, 1982). Under normal circumstances, based on the number of cells injected, half the rats would be expected to reject the cells and survive.

In the control group (no electric shock), 50 percent rejected the tumor as expected. Among the rats that received a shock but could escape—thus having some control over their situation—70 percent rejected the tumor and survived. But in the learned helplessness group—the group that could not escape the shock—only 27 percent of the rats rejected the malignant cells and survived.

These results were supported in a similar study of young rats. When the rats reached adulthood, they received injections of malignant cells and were exposed to the same three experimental conditions. The majority of the rats who had learned to be helpless when young failed as adults to reject the tumors. In contrast, the majority of the rats who had learned control when young rejected the tumors as adults (Seligman & Visintainer, 1985). Seligman concluded: "Childhood experiences proved to be crucial in tumor rejection by adults. Childhood mastery immunized, and early helplessness put adult rats at risk for cancer" (1990, p. 170).

Learned helplessness was shown to weaken the immune systems of rats (Maier, Laudenslager, & Ryan, 1985). The immune system forms a major part of the body's defense against illness. It contains several kinds of cells, including T-cells and NK (natural killer) cells, which resist viruses, bacteria, and tumor cells. In rats subjected to inescapable shock, T-cells no longer multiplied rapidly in response to specific invaders, and NK cells lost their ability to destroy other infections. These findings may provide a physiological explanation for the result that the helpless rats were unable to reject their tumors.

Later research with rats demonstrated that most male rats exposed to uncontrollable stress never learn how to escape, whereas most female rats do learn to escape. Thus, the condition of learned helplessness was easier to establish in males than in females, suggesting that females are less subject to the kind of dangerous physiological changes found in the earlier study (Dalla, Edgecomb, Whetstone, & Shors, 2008).

Explanatory Style: Optimism and Pessimism

explanatory style A way of explaining to ourselves our relative lack of control over our environment. An **optimistic explanatory style** can prevent learned helplessness; a **pessimistic explanatory style** spreads helplessness to all facets of life.

Seligman expanded his work on learned helplessness to encompass the factor of optimism versus pessimism. It is not only the lack of control under conditions of learned helplessness that affects our health but how we explain this lack of control to ourselves. He proposed the concept of explanatory style to account for this factor. An **optimistic explanatory style** prevents helplessness; a **pessimistic explanatory style** spreads helplessness to all facets of life.

You may know from your own experience the basic difference between optimists and pessimists. Put simply, "optimists are people who expect good things to happen to them; pessimists are people who expect bad things to happen to them" (Carver & Scheier, 2002, p. 231). Tending toward optimism or pessimism may determine many aspects of our life. For example, it has been found that optimists build better social networks and connections, and are also better able to cope with physical pain (Carver & Scheier, 2014; Ramirez-Maestre, Esteve, & Lopez, 2012). Both are desirable and useful qualities for coping with life situations.

Physical Health   According to Seligman, people with an optimistic explanatory style tend to be healthier than people with a pessimistic explanatory style. Pessimists tend to believe that their actions are of little consequence and, as a result, are unlikely to try to prevent illness by changing their behavior with regard to smoking, diet and exercise, or timely medical attention.

A study of young adults found that optimists were less likely than pessimists to get sick. However, when optimists did get sick, they were far more likely to take responsibility for their care, such as resting, consulting a physician, or drinking appropriate fluids (Peterson, Maier, & Seligman, 1993). In a study of college undergraduates, pessimists had twice as many infectious illnesses over a one-year period than did optimists.

Research in Finland found that optimists recovered a positive attitude more quickly following the severe illness or death of a family member than did pessimists (Kivimaki, Vahtera, Elovainio, Helenius, Singh-Manoux, & Pentti, 2005). Optimists are also much more likely to cope better with health problems, to recover faster from certain medical procedures, and to manage stress better (Aspinwall & Tedeschi, 2010).

Among breast cancer patients experiencing a recurrence, optimists lived longer over a five-year period of study, independent of the severity of their illness. Among a group of women in Norway diagnosed with breast cancer, those who scored high on pessimism were far more likely to be anxious and depressed one year following treatment than those who scored low on pessimism (Schou, Ekeberg, Ruland, Sandvik, & Karesen, 2004). Another study of these same women found that their levels of optimism and pessimism remained stable for the year following treatment regardless of whether their prognosis was favorable or unfavorable (Schou, Ekeberg, Sandvik, & Ruland, 2005). Breast cancer patients who score high on optimism have also been found to function better socially and mentally and to report a higher quality of life than those who score high in pessimism (Colby & Shifren, 2013).

Optimists seem to develop stronger immune systems and are more likely to recover from heart attacks and to experience less pain and fewer symptoms following heart surgery than pessimists (Peterson & Seligman, 1987; Peterson, Maier, & Seligman, 1993; Ronaldson, Poole, Kidd, Leigh, Jahangiri, & Steptoe, 2014).

A study of first-semester law school students found that those who scored high for an optimistic explanatory style had a significantly greater number of T-cells and NK cells, which protect against infections, than those who scored low on optimism (Segerstrom & Taylor, 1998). Research on men and women (ages 30–45) found that those who scored high on pessimism held more negative beliefs about their lives and had higher blood pressure readings than those who scored low on pessimism (Räikkönen, Matthews, Flory, Owens, & Gump, 1999).

Optimism can be beneficial in coping with AIDS. In a study of homosexual and bisexual men, some had been diagnosed as HIV-negative and others as HIV-positive (likely to develop AIDS). Those who scored high on optimism scored lower on psychological distress, had fewer worries about illness, believed they were at lower risk for developing AIDS, and thought they would have a higher degree of control over the disease than those who scored low on optimism. Those who were already HIV-positive were found to be more optimistic about not developing AIDS than those who were HIV-negative (Taylor, Kemeny, Aspinwall, Schneider, Rodriguez, & Herbert, 1992).

Although such beliefs may be illusory, they helped the subjects cope with a serious health threat and minimized the depression that often accompanies a major illness. In addition, the men highest in optimism were no more likely to engage in high-risk sexual behaviors than those lowest in optimism. In general, those highest in optimism took better care of their health.

Longevity   Optimists may live longer than pessimists. A long-range study of nuns in the United States found that those who displayed optimism in the life stories they were asked to write in their early 20s had a significantly lower death rate when surveyed 60 years later than those who displayed pessimism in their early writings (Danner, Snowdon, & Friesen, 2001).

A study of patients under treatment for a variety of medical conditions showed that optimists had 19 percent greater longevity than pessimists when both groups were surveyed 30 years later (Maruta, Colligan, Malinchoc, & Offord, 2002). A study of elderly men and women in England found that those who scored high in optimism were in far better physical health than those who scored low (Steptoe, Wright, Kunz-Ebrecht, & Lliffe, 2006).

Age   People over age 65 tend to have a more optimistic explanatory style and to score higher in subjective well-being than those who are younger. Research on elderly people in China and in the United States showed that those who were more optimistic reported greater subjective well-being and less depression than younger people (Hirsh, Walker, Wilkinson, & Lyness, 2014; Isaacowitz, 2005a; Leung, Moneta, & McBride-Chang, 2005; Olson, Fanning, Awick, & Chung, 2014). Elderly optimists also tended to underreport their weight, whereas pessimists claimed they weighed more than they actually did (Sutin, 2013).

Culture   Studies of Black and Latina grandmothers who were the primary caregivers for their grandchildren, and of Muslim college students in Kuwait and Oman, showed that those who scored high in optimism were happier; suffered less depression, anxiety, and hostility; and reported fewer sleep disorders than people high in pessimism (Abdel-Khalek & Lester, 2010; Alansari & Kazem, 2008; Conway, Magai, Springer, & Jones, 2008).

Cultural differences in explanatory style have been well documented. Optimism-pessimism measures were taken from college students in the United States and in China, as well as college students of Chinese-American heritage. It was found that the American subjects were more optimistic than the Chinese Americans, and that the Chinese Americans were more optimistic than the mainland Chinese (Lee & Seligman, 1997). College students in Kuwait scored significantly lower on optimism than college students in the United States (Abdel-Khalek & Lester, 2006). Among college students in Italy, men demonstrated more optimism than women (Colombo, Balbo, & Baruffi, 2006).

A comparison of college students in the United States and Japan found that Japanese students were more pessimistic than American students. The American students were far more likely to predict that positive events would happen to them rather than to other people. In contrast, Japanese students believed that positive events were much more likely to happen to other people (Chang, Asakawa, & Sanna, 2001).

Stress   Not surprisingly, stressful life experiences can affect one's level of optimism. A group of adults who were primary caregivers for relatives with Alzheimer's disease were compared on measures of optimism-pessimism with a group of adults who were not acting as caregivers. The caregivers grew increasingly pessimistic over a four-year period and experienced greater anxiety, stress, and physical health complaints (Robinson-Whelen, Kim, MacCallum, & Kiecolt-Glaser, 1997).

College students who scored higher on optimism at the beginning of their first semester experienced significantly less stress and depression during that semester than those who scored lower on optimism (Brissette, Scheier, & Carver, 2002). Similarly, middle-aged adults who scored high in optimism reported fewer symptoms of depression than those who scored high in pessimism (Chang & Sanna, 2001). Research on children from third to sixth grade found that those highest in optimism had fewer symptoms of depression and fewer behavioral problems than children low in optimism (Ey et al., 2005).

Performance   A study of American college students found that optimists typically earned better grades than pessimists. This finding also held for a study of college students in Kuwait; optimists earned higher grades (El-Anzi, 2005). In addition, when pessimists received lower grades than their peers, they reported being more depressed about it than did optimists who received lower grades than their peers (Gibbons, Blanton, Gerrard, Buunk, & Eggleston, 2000).

Optimism in playing sports was studied in France and was shown to affect how well an athlete can dribble a basketball. When 14- to 16-year-old boys and girls were led to believe that they had failed a dribbling contest, those who scored high in optimism were less anxious, more confident, and performed better in a second test than those high in pessimism (Martin-Krumm, Sarrazin, Peterson, & Famose, 2003).

Cognitive Functioning   Optimism and pessimism can influence cognitive functioning. This was demonstrated in research on college student responses to positive and negative stimuli. Students who scored high on pessimism were more likely to pay attention to negative stimuli; students who scored high on optimism attended to both positive and negative stimuli (Segerstrom, 2001).

People who are severely depressed believe they are helpless. They generalize their failure in one situation, such as a poor grade in one course, to all other aspects of life.

© Wavebreakmedia ltd/Shutterstock.com

A study of college students in Germany found that optimists were flexible and adaptable in their cognitive activities, whereas pessimists were more often inflexible, rigid, and likely to give up pursuing their goals (Weber, Vollmann, & Renner, 2007).

The Downside of Optimism   An optimistic explanatory style may not always be of value (Schneider, 2001). For example, some optimists may hold unrealistic views about their vulnerability to the effects of their behavior. As a result, they may drink or use drugs to excess, telling themselves that such behaviors cannot hurt them because their attitude is so positive, despite evidence to the contrary. Highly optimistic college students who expected to perform well on an exam experienced greater disappointment after receiving their scores than did those who had been less optimistic about their exam performance (Sweeny & Shepperd, 2010).

Among college students gambling at a casino near their university, the optimists were far more likely to continue gambling in the face of consistent losses, whereas the pessimists were more likely to stop. Apparently, the optimists maintained their positive expectations about winning even during a losing streak (Gibson & Sanbonmatsu, 2004). This type of unrealistic optimism—the belief that good things are much more likely to happen to oneself than to others—is more widespread in individualistic cultures such as the United States than in collectivist cultures such as China, and is more prevalent among men than women (Lin & Raghubir, 2005).

On the other hand, unrealistic pessimism in the face of adversity, such as a serious illness, may also be harmful. Telling yourself that you will never be able to cope or overcome the situation (thus also exhibiting low self-efficacy) may lead to a lack of effort and, consequently, a lack of success (Blanton, Axsom, McClive, & Price, 2001).

Pessimism and Depression   Seligman found a strong association between learned helplessness and depression. A major symptom of depression is the feeling of being unable to control life events. Seligman referred to depression as the "ultimate pessimism." People who are severely depressed believe they are helpless. They see little point in trying to do anything because they do not expect anything to work out well for them. Seligman observed several similarities between the symptoms of depression and the characteristics of learned helplessness (Seligman, 1990).

All of us experience occasional feelings of helplessness when we fail in some situation or when family or job pressures seem overwhelming. No matter how unhappy or angry

---

HIGHLIGHTS: Research on Seligman's Concept of Optimism

People who score high in *optimism* tend to:

- Get sick less often and experience less stress and depression
- Live longer
- Recover faster from the death of a family member
- Live in individualistic cultures such as the United States rather than in collectivistic cultures
- Earn better grades
- Be more flexible and adaptable in their cognitive activities
- Dribble a basketball better

TABLE 14-4   Similarity of symptoms of learned helplessness and depression

LEARNED HELPLESSNESS	DEPRESSION
Passivity	Passivity
Difficulty learning that responses produce relief	Difficulty learning that responses produce outcomes
Lack of aggression	Introjected hostility
Weight loss and anorexia	Loss of libido
Norepinephrine depletion[1]	Norepinephrine depletion
Ulcers and stress	Ulcers and stress, feelings of helplessness

[1]Norepinephrine acts as a neurotransmitter; severe depression is associated with norepinephrine deficiency.

Source: Adapted from Learned Helplessness and Depression in Animals and Men, by M. E. P. Seligman.

we may feel at the moment, however, most of us usually recover after a period of time. But some people do not recover quickly or easily. They may generalize their failure in one activity (say, earning a poor grade or failing to get a promotion) to other areas of life and to their personal sense of self-worth. As a result, they start to feel helpless and depressed in all situations and lose their impetus to strive.

As you can see from Table 14.4, depression is associated with symptoms of poor health such as ulcers, stress, and norepinephrine deficiency, which can cause low levels of energy and increased depression. Depression also puts people at risk for physical illness by reducing the effectiveness of the immune system, suppressing NK cell activity and altering white blood cell count, findings confirmed by more than 40 studies over a 10-year period (Herbert & Cohen, 1993; Weisse, 1992).

According to Seligman, the important difference between people who recover from temporary depression and those who do not is their explanatory style. "A pessimistic explanatory style changes learned helplessness from brief and local to long-lasting and general," he wrote. "Learned helplessness becomes full-blown depression when the person who fails is a pessimist. In optimists, a failure produces only brief demoralization" (1990, p. 76). Pessimists formulate explanations about negative situations in personal and pervasive terms, saying, for example, "It's all my fault," "It's always going to be this way," or "It's going to affect every aspect of my life."

Seligman's research on undergraduate students supports the hypothesis that learned helplessness leads to depression in people with a pessimistic explanatory style. At the beginning of the semester, students were tested to determine their explanatory style and were asked to state the course grade they believed would represent a personal failure on their part. After the midterm exam, the students took a personality test to measure their level of depression. The results showed that 30 percent of those with an optimistic explanatory style and who received grades they considered a personal failure showed symptoms of depression. Among those with a pessimistic explanatory style who received disappointing grades, 70 percent became depressed. Similar results were found in other research with college students and in studies of third-grade elementary school students. In both cases, explanatory style predicted the incidence of depression (Nolen-Hoeksema, Girgus, & Seligman, 1987; Zullow & Seligman, 1985).

Research conducted in the United States and in Finland found that those high in pessimism were more likely to take antidepressant medication and to be at risk for suicide than those who scored high on optimism (Chang, Yu, Lee, Hirsh, Kupfermann, & Kahle, 2013; Kronstrom et al., 2014).

The Development of Learned Helplessness in Childhood

Although learned helplessness can occur throughout life, Seligman suggested that we are particularly vulnerable to developing those feelings in infancy and early childhood. During these formative years the experience of learned helplessness can predispose us to the pessimistic explanatory style (Seligman, 1975).

Infants begin life in a state of total helplessness, with no control over their environment. As they mature, they become increasingly able to exercise control. They can cry, which brings parents or caregivers to tend to their needs. They can crawl, walk, and speak, and the mastery of each skill brings greater possibilities for control, and also for failure. Through these early interactions with the physical and social environments, a child's sense of helplessness, or of mastery and control, will be determined.

When infants make a response, that activity may lead to some change in their environment, such as food, a toy, or a hug, or it may have no effect whatever. At a primitive level, infants form associations between responses and outcomes. If the responses do not lead to successful outcomes, the result is learned helplessness. Infants learn that particular responses don't work, and they may generalize this idea to other responses, believing that none of them will work.

This generalized learned helplessness accompanies a sense of having no control over life. In contrast, a high correlation between responses and outcomes provides positive feedback that leads to feelings of mastery and control. A consistent explanatory style develops by about age 8 and is strongly affected by the parents' explanatory style. Seligman wrote: "pessimistic parents also have pessimistic children" (Peterson, Maier, & Seligman, 1993, p. 293). Studies in India found that the childhood level of pessimism or optimism can be strongly influenced by the parents' level of education. The greater the parents' formal education, the greater the optimism of their children (Daraei & Ghaderi, 2012).

However, it is important to note that research with adolescents in the Netherlands and in other nations also found evidence that their attributional style was influenced by learning as well as by genetic factors (Lau, Rijsdijk, & Eley, 2006; Mavioglu, Boomsma, & Bartels, 2015).

Learned helplessness may develop later in childhood in response to factors such as bullying from peers, a harsh school environment, or other negative experiences. Race and poverty are also related to the development of learned helplessness. Students who have frequent conflicts with peers and who are treated by schoolmates and by teachers as though they are less intelligent or skilled may develop learned helplessness (Orejudo, Puyuelo, Fernandez-Turrado, & Ramos, 2012). Low levels of social support from parents and other family members can lead to high levels of pessimism in children (Ciarrochi & Heaven, 2008).

Reflections on Learned Helplessness

The concepts of learned helplessness and optimism versus pessimism have generated hundreds of research studies. Seligman and his associates have applied the concepts to sports, politics, religion, child rearing, and job performance. Overall, a large and impressive body of data supports the learned helplessness concept. Seligman proposed a program of exercises to teach optimism to adults and to children, thus applying his findings beyond the laboratory to the home and the workplace. He has since extended his ideas to positive psychology and the factors that influence subjective well-being. In other words, "What makes us happy?"

Martin Seligman: Positive Psychology

Positive psychology was advanced by Seligman in the late 1990s during his term as president of the American Psychological Association. He thought psychology should deal with the best of human functioning—happiness, excellence, and optimal human growth. But before we discuss this idea, let's examine Seligman's own life, to see if it meets his own criteria for happiness, or subjective well-being.

The Life of Seligman (1942–)

His writings suggest that he is not particularly happy himself. Despite all his success and even celebrity status, he admitted that he is rarely happy, in the sense of feeling joyful. In 2010, he ranked himself among the lowest 30 percent of people in terms of positive feelings and emotions. "A life can be perfectly good and perfectly satisfactory," he told a reporter, "with no positive feeling. My life is largely run around meaning and purpose now" (quoted in Burling, 2010, p. 14). In an earlier study of college students who scored in the upper 10 percent of happiness, Seligman said that he was not a good candidate for that upper 10 percent (Diener & Seligman, 2002).

However, he added that there are different kinds of happiness and that he is one of those who find their deepest satisfaction in being fully engaged in work. (His wife agreed that Seligman is happiest at those times.)

When Seligman was 13, his father suffered a severe stroke that disabled him and rendered him almost helpless. The episode left the boy with his emotions completely "frozen over" as he put it. He later said that the ordeal was a "real important shadow" over his life (quoted in Burling, 2010, p. 7).

Seligman attended to a private prep school in Albany, New York; most of the students came from wealthy upper-class families and Seligman felt like an outsider. He was keenly aware of the differences between him and the other boys, and as a result felt isolated and alone. A close friend said that Seligman never lost that feeling. The friend said, "I think he still might inwardly struggle with being accepted" (quoted in Burling, 2010, p. 6). But Seligman was sufficiently intelligent and hardworking to be accepted at Princeton and to earn his Ph.D. at the University of Pennsylvania in 1967; he is currently director of the university's Positive Psychology Center. He is also a champion bridge player and has won a number of tournaments.

Characteristics and Causes of Happiness

What does positive psychology tell us about the happy personality? How do happy people differ from people you would not describe as happy? Psychologists have variously labeled the happy personality in terms such as *subjective well-being* or *life satisfaction* and define it as encompassing a cognitive evaluation of the quality of one's life experience and the possession of positive moods and emotions. Thus, happiness has both rational and emotional aspects. As you might expect, research has uncovered a variety of factors that can influence happiness.

Money

Is money the first factor you thought of? It turns out that the old adage is true: "Money does not buy happiness." However, the absence of money can lead to unhappiness. A level of income adequate to pay for our basic needs is a necessary, though not sufficient, prerequisite for happiness. Studies in Sweden, Turkey, and other European countries found that the lowest level of happiness was reported in low-income households and that a major source of satisfaction is having a cash reserve available to handle minor emergencies (Berlin & Kaunitz, 2014; Drakopoulos & Grimani, 2013).

A survey conducted in 123 nations confirmed that life satisfaction varies with income level. People who earn more money report being more satisfied, though not necessarily happier, than people who earn less (Diener, Ng, Harter, & Arora, 2010). Some research suggests that money may be mentioned as an important factor in happiness more frequently by people in the United States than by people in Europe (Mogilner, 2010).

Surveys also show that people who lack the money to provide for essentials are unhappy, but having money significantly beyond what is actually needed has little measurable effect on happiness. Even winning a huge amount in a lottery usually results in only a temporary increase in subjective well-being (DeNeve & Cooper, 1998; Diener, Suh, Lucas, & Smith, 1999; King & Napa, 1998; Pappas, 2010).

So, if you believe all you need to be happy is a bigger house or more expensive car, think again. More and costlier possessions do not guarantee happiness. One researcher concluded: "The more people endorse materialistic goals, the less happy and satisfied they are with life" (Van Boven, 2005, p. 133). Other research has shown that high-income people tend to experience greater stress and to devote less time to relaxation and leisure activities than those with lower incomes (Kahneman, Krueger, Schkade, Schwartz, & Stone, 2006).

Physical Attractiveness

Are attractive or beautiful people happier than people who are less attractive? Research in the United States, Canada, England, and Germany says "yes." Personal attractiveness does seem to increase happiness, but that may be because physical attractiveness generally improves marriage prospects, job opportunities, and income potential (Anderson, Adams, & Plaut, 2008; Bennett, 2011; Hamermesh & Abrevaya, 2011). The relationship between physical attractiveness and happiness was found to be stronger for people who lived in cities rather than rural areas. It was also observed that people in Finland who appear obese are less happy than those who are not obese (Bockerman, Johansson, Saarni, & Saarni, 2014).

Health

The absence of good health can diminish happiness but being healthy is no guarantee of happiness. Thus, health appears to be a necessary but not sufficient condition for subjective well-being. But if being healthy does not necessarily make you happy, being happy can contribute to your health and increase your life span. A review of more than 160 studies confirms that scoring high in subjective well-being contributes to greater longevity and better health (Diener & Chan, 2011). A survey of 25 countries found that those who actively engage in exercise report a higher level of life satisfaction than those who don't exercise (Dolan, Kavetsos, & Vlaev, 2014).

Age

A survey of more than 300,000 Americans (ages 18–85) found that subjective well-being and life satisfaction were high at 18, declined until around age 50, and then increased to the point where 85-year-olds reported greater life satisfaction than 18-year-olds (Stone, Schwartz, Broderick, & Deaton, 2010). However, those findings have not been duplicated in other countries. A large-scale survey conducted by the worldwide Gallup Poll organization found that in English-speaking, developed nations of Western Europe, subjective well-being dropped between the ages of 45 and 54. In less developed nations of Eastern Europe and the former Soviet Union, as well as Latin America, happiness declined overall with increasing age (Steptoe, Deaton, & Stone, 2015).

Adolescence

American adolescents who score high in subjective well-being are far more likely to have parents who value them, show interest in them, and express concern about their future than those who score low. This relationship appears to be stronger for girls than boys (Rayle, 2005). The happier American adolescents had more positive relationships with peers, reported lower anxiety and depression, and had greater hopes for the future. They expressed a feeling of greater personal control over their life than adolescents who scored low in life satisfaction (Gilman & Huebner, 2006).

Teenagers in China who scored high in subjective well-being had better educated parents who rarely quarreled with each other, compared to teenagers who scored low (Guo-Xing & Hai, 2006). Adolescents in Israel who felt they had a high degree of social support from the community and from friends were happier than those who felt they had little such support (Ronen, Hamama, Rosenbaum, & Mishely-Yarlap, 2014).

Older People

Studies of older people suggest that happiness does not necessarily decline with advancing age. The results are not consistent; however, some research shows an increase in happiness with advancing age, whereas others suggest that happiness peaks at 65 and decreases thereafter (Lacey, Smith, & Ubel, 2006; Mroczek & Spiro, 2005).

Research on older adults in Germany (ages 70–103) found that those who experienced health problems and physical limitations in old age suffered a decline in subjective well-being (Kunzmann, Little, & Smith, 2000). Another study on older Germans hospitalized with various disabilities found that it was not the physical impairments that decreased subjective well-being as much as the person's attitude toward the infirmity. People with more positive attitudes scored higher in subjective well-being than those who expressed negative attitudes (Schneider, Driesch, Kruse, Nehen, & Heuft, 2006).

Research with elderly subjects in Slovakia also demonstrated the relationship between attitude and happiness. Those who scored high in what the researchers called "a belief in a just world" reported greater happiness than those who did not subscribe to such a belief (Dzuka & Dalbert, 2006).

Physical exercise is an important component of subjective well-being in older people. Both aerobic exercise and resistance or strength training in the elderly show a strong positive correlation with happiness (Netz, Wu, Becker, & Tenanbaum, 2005). Older people who have stronger social networks and supportive friends report greater happiness than those who are more socially isolated (Pinquart & Soerensen, 2000).

Studies of 70- to 100-year-old people in the United States, England, and Germany found that impending death contributes to a decline in subjective well-being. The last three to five years of life are often marked by a rapid decline in reported happiness (Gerstorf, Ram, Estabrook, Schupp, Wagner, & Lindenberger, 2008; Gerstorf, Ram, Goebel, Schupp, Lindenberger, & Wagner, 2010).

Marriage and Social Support

If social support is important for subjective well-being as people age, does it follow that older persons who are married are happier than those who are not? Yes. The evidence is clear from research conducted in more than 40 countries involving some 60,000 people; married people report higher levels of happiness than people who are divorced, separated, widowed, or who have never married (Carr, Freedman, Cornman, & Schwarz, 2014; Diener, Gohm, Suh, & Oishi, 2000).

Married women of all ages have been found to be happier than unmarried women, and married men are happier than unmarried men (Batanowska-Ratij, Matysiak, & Mynarska, 2014; Mastekaasa, 1995). These findings held true in many countries including the United States and Poland. Happiness has been shown to decline for husbands and for wives following the birth of their first child. In general, people who do not have children report greater happiness than people with children; those with very young children express the least happiness (Munsey, 2010). The lowest level of happiness has been noted among unmarried mothers as a group (Ifcher & Zarghamee, 2014).

A longitudinal study of married couples followed over a 35-year period concluded that happiness will vary in relation to the happiness of one's spouse. The unhappiness of one member of a couple often leads to the unhappiness of the other; the converse is also true (Hoppmann, Gerstorf, Willis, & Schaie, 2011). Research in Germany led to the finding that people who go through more than one divorce score higher in life satisfaction after the second divorce than after the first one (Luhmann & Eid, 2009).

Social support correlates highly with subjective well-being in most countries. Research in Israel found that life satisfaction was higher in people with strong social support networks, and that this was particularly important for new immigrants (Litwin, 2005). Studies in Finland showed that among recent immigrants, active social support was critical to their psychological well-being (Jasinskaja-Lahti, Liebkind, Jaakkola, & Reuter, 2006).

Culture

In all major international surveys of happiness, Denmark consistently ranks highest (Hussain, 2014). Happiness varies across cultures, with a nation's relative wealth being of major importance. Countries marked by such poverty that satisfying basic needs is difficult have much lower levels of happiness than more economically advanced countries (Diener, Diener, & Diener, 1995; Veenhoven, 2005). Those who live in wealthier countries rate themselves as happier than people in impoverished countries (Delhey & Dragolov, 2015; Diener, Ng, Harter, & Arora, 2010; Doherty & Kelly, 2010; Howell & Howell, 2008; Minkov, 2009).

Studies conducted in collectivist Eastern cultures such as China and Turkey revealed little relationship between social support and subjective well-being (Dan, Jun, & Ji-Liang, 2006; Turkum, 2005). Research with college students in Turkey found that the chance to provide social support to other people was significantly related to psychological well-being, but receiving social support from others had no effect on psychological well-being (Gencoz & Ozlale, 2004). Subjective well-being is markedly higher in individualistic cultures such as the United States than in collectivist or group-oriented cultures such as China (Diener, Suh, Smith, & Shao, 1995; Park & Huebner, 2005; Wirtz, Chie, Diener, & Oishi, 2009).

Descendants of immigrants from other cultures tend to reflect the subjective well-being characteristic of those cultures, even in the absence of continued direct contact. For example, people in Denmark and in Sweden report high subjective well-being, as do Americans whose ancestors came from these countries. Americans whose ancestors came from cultures with lower levels of subjective well-being, such as Hungary and Lithuania, have similarly lower levels of subjective well-being (Rice & Steele, 2004).

Geography: Where You Live Is Important

A nationwide survey of Americans (ages 25–75) found different criteria for happiness in various parts of the country (Plaut, Markus, & Lachman, 2002). People in the New England states considered physical well-being, autonomy, and not feeling constrained as necessary for subjective well-being. People in western south-central states (Texas, Oklahoma, Arkansas, and Louisiana) showed a greater concern with personal growth and feelings of cheerfulness and happiness as criteria for subjective well-being. Those in eastern south-central states (Kentucky, Tennessee, Mississippi, and Alabama) focused more on social responsibility and contributing to the welfare and well-being of others as necessary for their own feelings of happiness.

Other research found that subjective well-being was highest in the west coast and mountain states, moderately high in the east coast states, and lowest in the midwestern and southern states. Overall, happiness was significantly related to higher income, higher level of education, and greater tolerance for the views of other people (Rentfrow, Mellander, & Florida, 2009).

A study conducted in regions of Germany over a 24-year period found that as people aged, the life satisfaction of those living in affluent areas remained higher than those living in less affluent regions (Gerstorf, Ram, Goebel, Schupp, Lindenberger, & Wagner, 2010).

Race and Ethnicity

In multicultural societies, people with a stronger sense of ethnic identity rated higher in subjective well-being than people with low levels of identifying with their ethnic heritage (Le, Lai, & Wallen, 2009). Research on African-American college students found that those who felt a greater sense of identification with and acceptance by the Black community at their college or university reported higher levels of psychological well-being than those who felt less of an identification with and acceptance by fellow African Americans (Postmes & Branscombe, 2002).

When African-American adults were asked to rate their life satisfaction, those who had experienced discrimination reported lower levels than those who had experienced no discrimination. Those who attended predominantly White schools reported higher life satisfaction levels than those who went to predominantly Black or mixed-race schools, although this may have changed in the decades since this research was conducted (Broman, 1997).

A study of older African-American adults (ages 55–93) found lower levels of life satisfaction among those who reported the stresses of racial discrimination (Utsey, Payne, Jackson, & Jones, 2002). Similar results were found in studies of Black college students. Those who reported higher levels of perceived racial discrimination had lower levels of life satisfaction as well as greater symptoms of depression (Prelow, Mosher, & Bowman, 2006; Seaton & Yip, 2009).

Personality

Considerable research has been conducted on the personality correlates of the happy personality, particularly facets of the five-factor model (see Chapter 8). People who score low on neuroticism and high on extraversion, agreeableness, and conscientiousness report high levels of subjective well-being (DeNeve & Cooper, 1998; Hayes & Joseph, 2003; Keyes, Shmotkin, & Ryff, 2002; Marrero, Quevedo, & Abella, 2011; Siegler & Brummett, 2000; Solo, 2015). Research in China found that extraversion was one of the most important predictors of subjective well-being (Zhang & He, 2010).

A study in 39 nations of Eysenck's three personality factors, and a study in 26 nations of the Big Five factors, found that low neuroticism and high extraversion correlated significantly with national levels of subjective well-being (Steel & Ones, 2002). A comparison of adult subjects in the United States and in Germany found that low neuroticism was the strongest predictor of subjective well-being (Staudinger, Fleeson, & Baltes, 1999). Other research in more than 30 countries confirmed that low neuroticism and high extraversion were major correlates of subjective well-being (Gomez, Krings, Bangerter, & Grob, 2009; Libran & Howard, 2006; Lynn & Steel, 2006). Similar results were found in apes! The happiest orangutans in zoos in the United States, Canada, and Australia were those rated by zoo employees as being high in extraversion, low in neuroticism, and high in agreeableness (Weiss, King, & Perkins, 2006).

Overall, the importance of the primarily inherited factors of neuroticism, extraversion, and agreeableness as influences on subjective well-being in so many different cultures suggests that life satisfaction and happiness have a strong genetic component.

Additional personality variables contribute to subjective well-being. A study of college students in the United States and in South Korea identified four factors contributing to happiness: autonomy, competence, relatedness, and self-esteem (Sheldon, Elliot, Kim, & Kasser, 2001). Research in England with university students showed that gratitude was strongly related to subjective well-being. The more grateful people were for their personal circumstances, the happier they were (Wood, Joseph, & Maltby, 2009).

A study in Germany on nearly 10,000 adults demonstrated a possible negative effect of being highly conscientious. Among those who had lost their jobs, those highest in conscientiousness suffered a far greater drop in life satisfaction than those low in conscientiousness (Boyce, Wood, & Brown, 2010).

Self-Efficacy and Internal Locus of Control

Both self-efficacy and internal locus of control are positively related to life satisfaction. In general, we are happiest when we feel competent in coping with life and in control of the reinforcers that are important to us. Studies in Germany and in Australia confirmed that the feelings of self-mastery and being in control of one's life were strongly related to subjective well-being (Lang & Heckhausen, 2001; Windsor & Anstey, 2010). Autonomy (having a strong sense of self-determination) is a significant contributor to happiness (Schmutte & Ryff, 1997; Sheldon, Kasser, Houser-Marko, Jones, & Turban, 2005). Trust, emotional stability, self-esteem, and the ability to deal positively with stress all correlate with high subjective well-being (DeNeve & Cooper, 1998).

Thinking Positively

Having positive emotions such as joy, interest, love, and enthusiasm is linked to subjective well-being (Frederickson, 2001). Similarly, negative emotions detract from a sense of well-being. Among eighth-graders and ninth-graders in Finland, having opportunities for self-fulfillment and social relationships in and out of the school environment correlated highly with subjective well-being (Konu, Lintonen, & Rimpelae, 2002).

Among college students, it was found that the factor of vengefulness (the desire to seek revenge or to hurt others) led to lower life satisfaction (McCullough, Bellah, Kilpatrick, & Johnson, 2001). Research on Holocaust survivors living in Israel found that even 60 years after the tragedy the traumatic effects lingered in the form of negative emotions and low levels of subjective well-being (Ben-Zur & Zimmerman, 2005).

Goals

People high in subjective well-being differ from people low in subjective well-being in terms of their motivations and goals. One research review concluded that life satisfaction was enhanced when the goals people set for themselves were concerned with personal growth and community contributions and were considered realistic and of value to the culture. People rated high in life satisfaction were intensely committed to achieving their goals and believed they were making progress toward those ends (Klug & Maier, 2015; Lyubomirsky, 2001).

Research on more than 3,000 managers in the United States (ages 25–74) found a strong positive relationship between life satisfaction and an orientation toward the future, which included actively planning for the future. The relationship was greater for older managers than younger managers (Prenda & Lachman, 2001).

In Germany, research showed that the most important choices among life goals relating to happiness included the characteristics of one's partner, a healthy lifestyle, a proper balance between work and leisure, and social involvement (Headey, Muffels, & Wagner, 2010).

Two studies—one of more than 13,000 college students from 31 countries, and the other of more than 7,000 students from 41 countries—found significant differences in the ways happy and unhappy people perceive, judge, or construe events in their lives. "In assessing their life satisfaction, unhappy individuals appear to give greater weight than happy individuals to what might be wrong in their lives.... In contrast, happy individuals see through the proverbial rose-colored glasses and weigh the positive aspects of their lives more heavily than do unhappy individuals" (Diener, Lucas, Oishi, & Suh, 2002, p. 444).

HIGHLIGHTS: Research on Seligman's Concept of Happiness

People who are *happy* tend to:

- Have more money and live in a wealthy country
- Be more attractive
- Exercise more as they get older
- Be married and without children
- Have a strong sense of ethnic identity
- Be extraverted, conscientious, and high in self-efficacy and locus of control
- Not be neurotic
- Be enthusiastic, optimistic, and grateful
- Have goals, a healthy lifestyle, and a high degree of social involvement
- Have a proper balance between personal life and work
- Spend time on the Internet—or maybe not

Happiness and Success

Which comes first: happiness and success? Are some people happy because they are successful, or are they successful because they are happy? Research tends to show that happiness, or subjective well-being, leads to the kinds of behaviors that bring about success (Boehm & Lyubomirsky, 2008). People high in subjective well-being "are more likely to secure job interviews, to be evaluated more positively by supervisors once they obtain a job, [and] to show superior performance and productivity" (Lyubomirsky, King, & Diener, 2005, p. 8).

Internet Use

Does the use of online social media affect happiness? A study of adolescents in China found no significant effects on happiness of participation in online social interactions. However, college students in Italy showed an increase in subjective well-being and a greater feeling of closeness to their own social group and to society in general after forming social relationships online (Biao-Bin, Man-Na, Bi-Qun, & Yong-Hong, 2006; Contarello & Sarrica, 2007).

Research in Taiwan found that use of the Internet had a slightly negative effect on subjective well-being (Huang, 2010a). A large-scale study of Americans found a stronger negative effect. The more time people spent online—whether browsing, texting, checking the news, or joining a chat room—the lonelier and less happy they said they felt (Stepanikova, Nie, & He, 2010).

When American college students were assigned a classroom task, those students who engaged in personal social media use performed more poorly on the task. They also experienced higher levels of stress and lower levels of happiness than those who did not engage in social media use during the task (Brooks, 2015).

Overall, research on a large sample of people from a variety of rich and poor nations found that Internet communication made people happier, although some benefited more than others (Penard, Poussing, & Suire, 2013). Those with lower incomes or who lived in developing nations reported greater life satisfaction as a result of the Internet. Also, more women than men reported feelings of empowerment from Internet use (Kelly, 2010). We can conclude from this research that the Internet works better for some people than others in contributing to subjective well-being.

Martin Seligman

Various sites provide biographical information, discussions of his theory, research on relevant concepts, and links to other resources.

Pursuit of Happiness

This web site describes research and resources related to Seligman's concepts. It includes a blog and a happiness quiz.

Different Kinds of Happiness: Meaning and Flourishing

As the field of positive psychology advanced, Seligman distinguished different kinds of happiness, or finding satisfaction in life, and he proposed three distinct types:

- Positive emotion: the pleasant life
- Engagement: the engaged life
- Meaning: the meaningful life

The pleasant life consists of a great deal of positive emotion such as satisfaction, job contentment, serenity, and optimism. The engaged life consists of engagement, involvement, purpose, commitment, and absorption in work. As Seligman noted, "time passes quickly" for this type of person. "Attention is completely focused on the activity. The sense of self is lost" (Seligman, Rashid, & Parks, 2006, p. *777*). Research indicates that having a purpose in life is related not only to finding meaning in life but also to healthy aging and longevity (Hill & Turiano, 2014).

The meaningful life involves using one's talents, abilities, and strengths to belong to, serve, or commit to some enterprise larger than the self. This could be a religion, organization, political party, ideal, or anything else that transcends the self. Living a meaningful life, Seligman wrote, "produces a sense of satisfaction and the belief that one has lived well" (Seligman, Rashid, & Parks, 2006, p. *777)*. His research has shown that the pursuit of meaning and engagement are much more strongly correlated with happiness than the pursuit of pleasure (Schueller & Seligman, 2010).

In 2012, Seligman published a book titled *Flourish: A Visionary New Understanding of Happiness and Well-Being*. He argued that "flourishing" is a better term than happiness or well-being to describe those who stand at the top of the happiness scale. This group—approximately 10 to 18 percent of the world's population—includes those who not only feel happy but who also excel in their relationships and accomplishments.

Seligman has concluded that happiness alone is not enough to give one's life full and deep meaning. To reach this higher level of flourishing, we must cultivate our talents and abilities, establish deep and meaningful relationships with others, and contribute in a positive and constructive way to the world around us. Happiness, which he now calls "positive emotion," is but one of five pillars of the flourishing personality. These include: positive emotion (of which happiness and life satisfaction are part), engagement, relationships, meaning, and achievement (Seligman, 2011).

Comment

Seligman's original call for a positive psychology received an enthusiastic response. In 2000, only two years after he introduced the topic, the *Journal of Happiness Studies,* the first such journal in the field, began publication. In 2002, he published a popular book titled *Authentic Happiness: Using the New Positive Psychology to Realize Your Potential for Lasting Fulfillment.* The book was highly praised in reviews; *Newsweek* described the positive psychology movement as a new age for psychology. *Time* magazine put Seligman's picture on the cover and published a 40-page special issue. At Harvard the most popular undergraduate course, with enrollments exceeding 800, was on positive psychology. In 2006, the *Journal of Positive Psychology* began publication. Positive psychology as a distinct branch of psychology has become phenomenally successful and widespread.

In 2012, the Girl Scouts of America instituted a Science of Happiness Badge, which members earn by undergoing a month-long course in strategies and techniques for achieving happiness (Wojcik, 2012). By 2014, more than 10,000 journal articles were being published annually; seminars were held, books written, and popular magazines and talk shows were praising its goals. By 2015, a Google search for "happiness" generated almost 350 million hits.

Chapter Summary

Rotter described those who believe that the reinforcement they receive is under their control as having an internal locus of control; those who believe they have no control over the reinforcements they receive have an external locus of control. Internals feel a stronger sense of personal choice, are in better physical and mental health, are less bothered by stress, earn higher grades in school, score higher in job satisfaction and in life satisfaction, and have higher self-esteem than externals.

People become more internally oriented as they grow older, reaching a peak in middle age. People in lower socioeconomic classes, in some minority groups, and in some cultural groups tend to be externals. Parents of internally oriented children tend to be supportive and consistent in their discipline, encouraging their child's independence.

According to Zuckerman, sensation seeking is an inherited trait concerned with the need for novel and complex sensations and experiences. Four components of sensation seeking are thrill and adventure seeking, experience seeking, disinhibition, and boredom susceptibility. Zuckerman later distinguished between good sensation seeking, which is socialized and non-impulsive, and bad sensation seeking, which is unsocialized, impulsive, and characterized by high scores on measures of psychoticism.

Higher levels of sensation seeking are found among White subjects, males, people from Western cultures, and young people from adolescence to their early 20s. High sensation seekers are more likely to use drugs, smoke, drink alcohol, drive fast, engage in frequent sex, gamble, take physical risks, and travel to dangerous places. In terms of personality, high sensation seekers tend to be extraverted, conscientious, open to experience, autonomous, assertive, nonconforming, and uninhibited in expressing emotions. In cognitive functioning, high sensation seekers recognize symbols and figures more quickly and prefer complexity in visual stimulation.

Vocational interests of high-sensation-seeking males are oriented toward science and the helping professions. Low-sensation-seeking males are more oriented toward clerical and business concerns. High sensation seekers tend to hold more liberal religious and political attitudes. They are higher in tolerance for ambiguity, more permissive in sexual attitudes, and lower in authoritarianism. They display stronger physiological responses to novel stimuli. Sensation seeking is primarily inherited but can be influenced by environmental factors such as birth order and parental level of sensation seeking.

Learned helplessness, investigated by Seligman, results from our perception that we have no control over our environment. An optimistic explanatory style can prevent learned helplessness; a pessimistic style spreads helplessness to all facets of life and can lead to physical illness and depression. Pessimists make personal, permanent, and pervasive explanations to themselves about negative events. Thus, helplessness changes from brief and localized to long lasting and generalized.

The attribution model of learned helplessness involves attributing a failure to some cause. Pessimists attribute their failures to internal, stable, and global causes. Optimists attribute their failures to external, unstable, and specific causes. Optimists tend to live longer, enjoy better health, and experience less stress and depression than do pessimists.

Although learned helplessness can occur at any age, infants and young children are particularly vulnerable. Infants learn that a correspondence exists between their responses and outcomes when responses bring changes in their environment. They learn helplessness when these responses do not bring about desired changes. The major causes of learned helplessness are maternal deprivation and an environment that provides a low level of stimulation and feedback.

Positive psychology focuses on characteristics of the happy personality—people who score high on measures of subjective well-being or life satisfaction. High subjective well-being is associated with social support and positive relations with others, a positive attitude, physical activity, not being a member of a minority group that experiences discrimination, and living in an economically advanced individualistic society. Characteristics of the happy personality include low neuroticism, high extraversion, autonomy, self-esteem, self-efficacy, an internal locus of control, and a sense of being in control of one's life. These people also tend to be successful in their careers, to be in better health, and to live longer.

Seligman posited three types of happiness: the pleasant life consisting of a great deal of positive emotion; the engaged life consisting of engagement, commitment, and absorption in work; and the meaningful life consisting of committing one's talents and abilities in the service of a cause or purpose larger than oneself. Seligman's latest concept, flourishing, refers to those who are not only happy but who also score high in relationships and accomplishments.

Review Questions

1. Describe how the global and the limited-domain approaches to personality differ from one another.
2. How do internal and external locus-of-control people differ in terms of their views of the source of the reinforcements they receive?
3. Give examples of how internal locus-of-control people behave differently from external locus-of-control people.
4. If external locus-of-control people learned that a tornado was approaching, would they be likely to

believe there was nothing they could do about their situation, or would they be likely to take some action to protect themselves, their family, and their property? Why?

5. What parental behaviors foster a child's internal locus of control?

6. Describe the racial, social class, and cultural differences found in research on internal versus external locus of control.

7. Discuss the differences in physical health between internal locus-of-control and external locus-of-control people.

8. How do the concepts of locus of control and self-efficacy differ? In what ways are they similar?

9. Define sensation seeking and describe its four components.

10. How does Zuckerman distinguish between good and bad sensation seeking? Which type are you?

11. What does research show about differences in sensation seeking as a function of age, gender, culture, and race?

12. How do people high in sensation seeking differ from people low in sensation seeking in terms of personality and cognitive functioning?

13. Give examples of ways in which high sensation seekers behave differently from low sensation seekers.

14. Describe the occupational interests and political attitudes of high sensation seekers.

15. Discuss the relative importance of heredity and environment in determining sensation seeking.

16. Define learned helplessness and describe Seligman's early research with dogs.

17. How can learned helplessness affect physical health? How does it relate to depression?

18. Distinguish between optimistic and pessimistic explanatory styles. How can they affect health?

19. Explain how learned helplessness can develop in childhood.

20. Discuss the similarities and differences between Seligman's contemporary version of positive psychology and the earlier humanistic psychology of Maslow and Rogers.

21. Describe the effect on subjective well-being of each of these factors: financial status, attractiveness, health, race, and culture.

22. In what ways do the personalities of people who score high in subjective well-being differ from those who score low?

23. Give examples of how geography, motivations and goals, and Internet use can affect subjective well-being.

24. Describe the three components or types of happiness, according to Seligman. Which one corresponds most closely to Maslow's concept of self-actualization?

25. How does Seligman's concept of flourishing differ from his earlier concept of subjective well-being?

Suggested Readings

Locus of Control

Rotter, J. B. (1993). "Expectancies." In C. E. Walker (Ed.), *The history of clinical psychology in autobiography* (Vol. 2, pp. 273–284). Pacific Grove, CA: Brooks/Cole. Covers Rotter's graduate training, academic experience, and the early work on locus of control. Also describes the growth of academic clinical psychology programs and related political controversies.

Sensation Seeking

Brannigan, G. G, & Merrens, M. R. (Eds.). (1993). *The undaunted psychologist: Adventures in research*. Philadelphia: Temple University Press. Essays by a diverse group of academic psychologists about the origins of their research interests. Includes a chapter by Zuckerman about personal and intellectual approaches to research.

Zuckerman, M. (1991). *Psychobiology of personality.* New York: Cambridge University Press. Outlines a behavioral genetics approach to personality and summarizes relevant research from neuropsychology, psychopharmacology, psychophysiology, and abnormal psychology.

Zuckerman, M. (2007). *Sensation seeking and risky behavior.* Washington, DC, American Psychological Association. A comprehensive overview of the research of Zuckerman and many others on the different kinds of behaviors of those who score high in sensation seeking, ranging from sex and crime to hang gliding.

Learned Helplessness

Seligman, M. E. P. (1975). *Helplessness: On depression, development, and death.* San Francisco: W. H. Freeman. Describes the early research on learned helplessness, its development in childhood, and its impact on depression and physical health.

Seligman, M. E. P. (2006). *Learned optimism: How to change your mind and your life.* New York: Vintage. Describes differences in explanatory style between optimists and pessimists and relates these styles to physical and mental health. Offers techniques for changing pessimism to optimism and tests to check on your own levels of optimism or pessimism.

Positive Psychology

Comptom, W., & Hoffman, E. (2012). *Positive psychology: The science of happiness and flourishing* (2nd ed.). Belmont CA: Cengage. An overview of positive psychology, its significant research, and its applications to problems of everyday life.

Fave, A. (Ed.). *The exploration of happiness: Present and future perspectives* (2nd ed.). New York: Springer Science and Business Media. A collection of articles from the *Journal of Happiness Studies* covering major findings, issues, and challenges for future research.

Seligman, M. E. P. (2002). *Authentic happiness: Using the new positive psychology to realize your potential for lasting fulfillment.* New York: Free Press. A guide to developing positive emotions, positive character, and personal satisfaction.

Seligman, M. E. P. *Martin Seligman: Journey from learned helplessness to learned happiness.* A personal and professional account of how Seligman changed psychology and himself, http://www.upenn.edu/gazette/0199/hirtz.html

Seligman, M. E. P. (2011). *Flourish: A visionary new understanding of happiness and well-being.* New York: Free Press. Seligman's latest offering on positive psychology and his theory of well-being along with exercises that can be used to increase happiness.

chapter 15

Personality in Perspective

In Chapter 1, we said that our purpose in this book was to explore the forces and ideas that shape personality, to try to find out what makes us the way we are. We have discussed nearly two dozen theories, ranging from Sigmund Freud's work at the turn of the 20th century to contemporary developments in the 21st century. Because we have covered so many diverse approaches, you might be tempted to conclude that the field of personality is marked more by chaos than certainty, more by differences than agreements.

Which theory is correct? Which one solves the puzzle of personality? The most complete answer we can suggest is that each of the theories discusses factors that are influential, to some degree, in shaping our personality. Each theorist has contributed vital pieces to the puzzle. Now it is time to examine those pieces to try to see the whole picture.

We will summarize these diverse viewpoints in a brief and broad overview of the themes, or factors, that have emerged from the work of the various theorists.

- The genetic factor
- The environmental factor
- The learning factor
- The parental factor
- The developmental factor
- The consciousness factor
- The unconscious factor

The Genetic Factor

There is increasingly strong evidence that many personality traits or dimensions are inherited. These include:

- Eysenck's dimensions of psychoticism, neuroticism, and extraversion (the latter derived from the work of Jung)

- McCrae and Costa's five-factor model of personality including neuroticism, extraversion, openness to experience, agreeableness, and conscientiousness
- Buss and Plomin's three temperaments of emotionality, activity, and sociability.

In addition, Zuckerman's trait of sensation seeking is primarily influenced by genetic factors. Thus, the trait approach, with its emphasis on the impact of heredity, remains a necessary and useful area of personality research. What remains to be determined is precisely how many inherited factors, traits, or temperaments there are. Would it be Cattell's sixteen, Eysenck's three, McCrae and Costa's five, Buss and Plomin's three, or some as yet undiscovered number?

Research involving twins from Canada, Germany, and Japan provides support for the genetic basis of the five-factor model. The principal author of that study suggested that this may "represent the common heritage of the human species" (Yamagata et al., 2006, p. 96). Additional research has confirmed that the Big Five personality traits were increasingly stable over a period of 20 years from childhood into adulthood (Shiner, 2014).

Other studies in Germany and Belgium on twins and non-twin siblings found a high stability in traits during childhood and adolescence and into young adulthood, which also reinforces the importance of genetic factors in personality (DeFruyt, Bartels, Van Leeuwen, DeClercq, Decuyper, & Mervielde, 2006; Kandler, Bleidorn, Reimann, Spinath, Thiel, & Angleitner, 2010).

A large-scale research program ranging over 50 cultures as diverse as Israel, Korea, and Turkey found that the Big Five personality factors were displayed consistently in the majority of the nations studied. It was mostly in developing countries such as Ethiopia, Lebanon, Malaysia, and Uganda that the traits of the five-factor model were found less consistently (Allik, Realo, & McCrae, 2013; Heine & Buchtel, 2009; Ispas, Illiescu, Ilie, & Johnson, 2014).

A study of adolescent twins (both fraternal and identical) in Sweden found a strong genetic component of the psychopathic personality prone to violent antisocial behavior (Larsson, Andershed, & Lichtenstein, 2006). Other twin research showed that the degree of heritability of the trait of anxiety increased between the ages of 14 and 18 (Garcia, Tully, Tarantino, South, Iacono, & McGue, 2013).

In addition to finding genetic components in major dimensions of personality, researchers have also noted some common, everyday behaviors that are influenced by genetics. Studies in the United States, Finland, the French-speaking portion of Canada, and Sweden have found evidence of genetic influences on sexual attitudes, on eating behaviors in 2-year-olds, on depression in children who are victims of bullying, and on attitudes toward practicing playing a musical instrument. And with regard to gun ownership, identical twins were more likely to own guns than fraternal twins (Barnes, Boutwell, & Beaver, 2014; Butkovic, Ullen, & Mosing, 2015; Dubois et al., 2013; Iyer, Dougall, & Jensen-Campbell, 2013; Westerlund, Santtila, Johansson, Jern, & Sandnabba, 2012). Additional research in behavior genetics will no doubt yield even more facets of personality that are shaped by inherited factors.

No matter how many inherited traits there may be, however, not even the most ardent proponent of the genetics approach argues that personality can be completely explained by heredity. What we inherit are predispositions, not destinies; tendencies, not certainties. Whether our genetic predispositions are realized depends on social and environmental conditions, particularly those of childhood.

The Environmental Factor

Much research indicates that genetic effects are most important in infancy and the very early years, whereas environmental effects on personality become increasingly important as we advance from childhood to adulthood. Environmental influences continue to affect our behavior and personality throughout our life (Briley & Tucker-Drob, 2014; Kandler, 2012).

Every personality theorist we have discussed acknowledged the importance of our social environment in influencing personality. Adler spoke of the impact of birth order, arguing that personality is influenced by our position in the family relative to our siblings. We are exposed to different parental and social problems and challenges as a function of the age difference between our siblings, or whether we have siblings at all. In Adler's view, these different home environments can result in different personalities.

Horney believed that the culture in which we grow up can produce different effects, such as those she found in the different kinds of neuroses exhibited by her German and her American patients. She also pointed out the vastly different social environments to which boys and girls are exposed as children. She spoke of female inferiority developing from the way girls are treated in a male-dominated culture. She suggested that women raised in a matriarchal culture might have higher self-esteem and different personality characteristics.

Even Allport and Cattell, who inaugurated the trait approach to personality, agreed on the importance of the environment. Allport noted that although genetics supplies the raw material of personality, it is the social environment that shapes the material into the finished product. Cattell argued that heredity is more important for some of his 16 personality factors than for others, but environmental influences will ultimately affect every factor to some extent.

Erikson's eight stages of psychosocial development are innate, but the environment determines the ways in which those genetically based stages are realized. He believed that social and historical forces influence the formation of ego identity. Maslow and Rogers contended that self-actualization was innate but recognized that environmental factors could either inhibit or promote the self-actualization need.

Large-scale societal events such as wars and economic recessions can restrict our life choices and influence the formation of self-identity. More ordinary life changes, such as becoming parents, getting a divorce, or changing jobs, can also affect our personality.

Even the time period in which you were born and reared can influence your personality. Societal standards and attitudes, likes and dislikes, as well as the nature of external threats, are different for each generation and can have a substantial influence on personality. This was supported by a major study comparing personality data of more than 50,000 college students and young people. These two birth cohort groups, one from the 1950s and one from the 1980s, showed highly significant differences on two personality dimensions: anxiety and neuroticism. The 1980s group demonstrated substantially higher anxiety and neuroticism. These differences were attributed to decreases in social connectedness from the 1950s to the 1980s, as evidenced by a higher divorce rate, lower birth rate, later age at first marriage, and more people living alone during the 1980s (Twenge, 2000).

Research in Finland found that having children can bring about personality changes. Becoming a parent is associated with increased levels of stress and anxiety as well as lower levels of marital and life satisfaction. The study also showed that emotionality increased in adults once they became parents; the more children they had, the greater the increase in level of emotionality (Jokela, Kivimaki, Elovainio, & Keltikangas-Jarvinen, 2009). Research in the United States, England, and Turkey also found that the status of parenthood lowers marital satisfaction. The more children a couple had, the lower the level of marital satisfaction (Wendorf, Lucas, Imamoglu, Weisfeld, & Weisfeld, 2011).

Our jobs can also influence our personality. This was shown in a study of young adults aged 18 to 26 living in New Zealand. Personality measures given at 18, and again at 26, showed that those who had satisfying, high-status jobs at 26 had increased in positive emotionality (well-being, social closeness, and feelings of achievement) and decreased in negative emotionality (aggressiveness, alienation, and stress) since age 18.

The researchers concluded that the nature of the workplace has the potential to affect our innate personality traits (Roberts, Caspi, & Moffitt, 2003).

Stressful life events, such as the death of a spouse or the loss of a job, may influence personality. Adults in the United States were studied in their mid-40s and again 10 years later. Those who scored high in neuroticism came to believe that the stressful life event was a turning point in their lives. Those high in extraversion felt they would learn a lesson from the stressful event. Those who experienced these stressful events as negative turning points became more neurotic over time, whereas those who saw them as an opportunity to learn became even more extraverted (Sutin, Costa, Wethington, & Eaton, 2010).

Ethnic background and whether we are part of a minority or majority culture can also help to determine personality. We saw examples of ethnic differences in such variables as sensation seeking, locus of control, and the need for achievement. We also learned that members of minority groups develop an ethnic identity as well as an ego identity and have to adapt to both cultures. The success of this adaptation affects personality and psychological health. Among people in Canada who identified themselves as members of minority groups, those with the strongest ethnic identities were highest in self-esteem and subjective well-being (Usborne & Taylor, 2010).

We also saw that culture is an important aspect of the environment that can shape personality. Western cultures tend to be more individualistic than Eastern cultures. People in Western cultures tend to score higher on extraversion, sensation-seeking, and subjective well-being. People in Eastern cultures tend to score lower on these personality characteristics.

We noted in Chapter 14 the differences in subjective well-being that have been documented from one geographical region to another. There are also differences in other aspects of personality depending on where we live. For example, neuroticism is higher in northeastern and southeastern states of the United States. Agreeableness is higher in the southern states. Extraversion was found to be higher in the northeast and lower in the west (Rentfrow, 2010).

Personality can even vary by neighborhood. Children who grow up in economically disadvantaged neighborhoods are more likely to show maladaptive personality tendencies characterized by low resiliency and problem behaviors that can lead to social and emotional problems as they get older (Hart, Atkins, & Matsuba, 2008). A major study in the city of London found that the level of life satisfaction, agreeableness, conscientiousness, and openness to experience varied in different neighborhoods throughout the city (Jokela, Bleidorn, Lamb, Gosling, & Rentfrow, 2015).

For all these reasons, then, it is impossible to deny the impact of diverse environmental and social forces on personality. The most significant way in which that impact is exerted is through learning.

The Learning Factor

Evidence is overwhelming that learning plays a major role in influencing virtually every aspect of our behavior, not only personality but our major life goals as well (Bleidorn, Kandler, Hulsheger, Reimann, Angleitner, & Spinath, 2010). All of the social and environmental forces that shape personality do so by the methods of learning.

Even inherited facets of personality can be modified, disrupted, prevented, or allowed to flourish by the process of learning. Skinner taught us the value of positive reinforcement, successive approximation, superstitious behavior, and other learning variables in shaping what others call personality, but which he described as simply an accumulation of learned responses.

Bandura introduced the idea that we learn from watching models (observational learning) and through vicarious reinforcement. Bandura agreed with Skinner that most behaviors are learned and that genetics plays only a limited role.

We discussed many aspects of personality that have scientific evidence to show that they are learned, such as self-efficacy (Bandura), locus of control (Rotter), learned helplessness, and optimism versus pessimism (Seligman). These concepts appear to be related to the broader notion of level of control. People who believe they have control over their lives are high in self-efficacy, have an internal locus of control, and are not characterized by learned helplessness (which involves lack of control). In Seligman's terms, people who believe they are in control are optimistic rather than pessimistic.

Control is beneficial to many aspects of life. A high degree of control has been related to better coping mechanisms, fewer stress effects, greater mental and physical health, perseverance, higher aspirations and self-esteem, lower anxiety, higher grades, and greater social skills and popularity.

By whatever name—self-efficacy, internal locus of control, or optimism—control is determined by social and environmental factors. It is learned in infancy and childhood, though it can change later in life. We saw that specific parental behaviors can foster a child's feeling of being in control. Thus, the notion of control is one of a number of learned dimensions of personality for which parental behavior is paramount.

The Parental Factor

Although Freud was the first theorist to emphasize parental influences on the formation of personality, virtually every theorist thereafter has echoed his views to some degree. Recall Adler's focus on the consequences for children who feel unwanted or rejected by their parents. Such parental rejection can lead to insecurity, leaving the person angry and deficient in self-esteem. Horney wrote from her own experience about how lack of parental warmth and affection can undermine a child's security and result in feelings of helplessness.

Allport and Cattell, whose work was based on the importance of traits, also recognized the parental factor in personality formation. Allport considered the infant's relationship with the mother to be the primary source of affection and security, conditions crucial to later personality development. Cattell saw infancy as the major formative period, with the behavior of parents and siblings shaping the child's character.

Erikson held that the child's relationship with the mother in the first year of life was vital in promoting a trusting attitude. Maslow commented on how necessary it was for parents to satisfy their child's physiological and safety needs in the first two years of life. This was a prerequisite for the emergence of higher-order needs. Rogers spoke of the parents' responsibility for supplying unconditional positive regard to their children.

We have also seen examples of how parental behaviors can determine, or undermine, specific aspects of personality, such as self-efficacy, locus of control, learned helplessness or optimism, and subjective well-being. Parental behaviors can influence primarily inherited traits such as sensation seeking. You can easily imagine how uncaring and punitive parents could stifle the emergence of inherited traits such as extraversion, sociability, agreeableness, and openness to experience.

There is a great deal of evidence showing that children of parents who are described as authoritative (that is, warm but firm in their child-rearing practices) are more competent and mature than children of parents described as permissive, harsh, or indifferent. Researchers have noted that

Authoritative parenting is associated with a wide range of psychological and social advantages in adolescence, just as it is in early and middle childhood ... the combination of parental responsiveness and demandingness is consistently related to adolescent adjustment, school performance, and psychosocial maturity. (Steinberg & Morris, 2001, p. 88)

A study of adolescents in Singapore found that those whose parents were authoritative had greater confidence in their abilities and were better adjusted socially than those whose parents were authoritarian (strict, harsh, and demanding obedience) (Ang, 2006). A large-scale analysis of parent–child relationships found clear evidence that parents who were high in extraversion, agreeableness, conscientiousness, and openness to new experience behaved in more warm and consistent ways toward their children than parents who scored low on those factors.

Parents higher in agreeableness and lower in neuroticism were also much more supportive of their children's independence (Prinzie, Stams, Dekovic, Reijntjes, & Belsky, 2009). Other research has found that parents play a major role in teaching their children to be kind, caring, and helpful to others in need (Fortuna & Knafo, 2014).

We also discussed cultural differences in parental style. Parents in Arab cultures tend to be more authoritarian than authoritative. A study of mothers who had immigrated with their children to Canada showed that the women from collectivist cultures such as Egypt, Iran, India, and Pakistan were more authoritarian than women from individualistic countries in Western Europe (Rudy & Grusec, 2006).

Considerable research also suggests that praise from parents can promote a child's sense of autonomy, realistic standards and expectations, competence, and self-efficacy, and can enhance intrinsic motivation to achieve. And just as positive parental behaviors have positive effects on children, negative parental behaviors have detrimental effects.

A review of research on the relationship between early childhood experiences and adult psychopathology showed consistently that the childhoods of depressed and anxious adults were related to inadequate parenting. The parents were found to be more rejecting and abusive, and less caring and affectionate, than parents of less troubled adults (Brewin, Andrews, & Gotlib, 1993).

Another study found that mothers characterized by negative emotions and disagreeableness had children who scored higher in defiance, anger, disobedience, and other behavior problems than did mothers who did not exhibit negative emotional qualities (Kochanska, Clark, & Goldman, 1997).

A 12-year study of children in Finland found that when mothers had hostile attitudes toward child rearing (attitudes measured when their children were 3 and 6 years old), their children were highly likely to have hostile attitudes by the time they became 15. Thus, hostile mothers were found to rear children who also became hostile (Raikkonen, Katainen, Keskivaara, & Keltikangas-Jarvinen, 2000). A longitudinal study in the United States comparing subjects at ages 5 and 31 found that restrictive, cold, and strict parenting of the 5-year-olds produced adults who scored high in conformity and low in self-direction (Kasser, Koestner, & Lekes, 2002).

A related question is what determines how parents behave. For a long time, it was assumed that parents' behavior reflected the way they had been raised by their own parents. In other words, parents learn how to behave from the way their own parents had behaved in raising them. A study of more than 20,000 families in a variety of countries from Australia to Japan to the United States found that genetic factors accounted for as much as 40 percent of parental behavior. It also found that some parental behavior is influenced by how their child behaves (Klahr & Burt, 2014). That finding leads to the notion that parents can both influence and reflect the behavior of their children.

What happens in situations when parents are not the primary caregivers, that is, when parents share child-rearing responsibilities with day care workers, friends, or family members while they work outside the home? In a national longitudinal survey of children ages 3 to 12, no significant problems with behavior or self-esteem were found when the mothers had jobs outside the home. The researcher concluded that care-giving by someone other than the child's mother had no negative impact on the variables studied (Harvey, 1999).

A unique real-world laboratory in which to explore the issue of surrogate caregivers is the collective child-care arrangement in kibbutzim (communal settlements) in Israel. In that situation, mothers attend to their infants' needs only for the first few months of life. Then the primary responsibility for child care is assigned to professional caregivers. Children typically spend more time with these surrogate mothers and fathers than they do with their parents.

Overall, kibbutz children were found to function and adapt well, assuming they established a secure relationship with their parents during infancy. Indeed, the strength of that bond was the strongest predictor of children who became dominant, independent, and achievement oriented. However, the barracks style sleeping arrangements (like summer camp or boarding school) in early childhood could lead to a more anxious, restrained, and emotionally flat personality. Adults reared on a kibbutz who failed to bond with their parents or caregivers showed introversion, diminished capacity for friendship, and reduced emotional intensity in interpersonal relations (Aviezer, Van Ijzendoorn, Sagi, & Schuegel, 1994).

A major controversy erupted in the late 1990s when it was suggested that parental behaviors have no long-term effects on their child's personality outside the home. According to this idea, peers influence a child's personality much more than do parents. Children adopt the behaviors, attitudes, values, and characteristics of their classmates and friends in an effort to win their acceptance and approval. Proponents of this view do not completely deny the influence of parents on their child's personality. What they do dispute is the idea that parental influence is maintained outside the home environment.

> Parents do influence their children's behavior. Of course they do. But the influence is in context, specific to the home. When children go out, they leave behind the behavior they acquired at home. They cast it off like the dorky sweater their mother made them wear. (Harris, quoted in Sleek, 1998, p. 9)

Modest support for this proposal was provided by a study of twins in late adolescence. The results showed that twins who had more friends in common were more alike in personality than were twins who had fewer friends in common. This suggests that friends, rather than the home environment, had a greater impact on their personality (Loehlin, 1997).

Researchers who subscribe to the primacy of genetic factors in personality also tend to reject or minimize the parental effect, suggesting that the family environment contributes little to personality. However, this controversy may eventually be resolved—whether personality is determined by parents, peers, genes, or some combination of factors—it leads us to another question. Is personality fixed in early life by these influences or can it be changed in later years? And that brings us to the developmental factor.

The Developmental Factor

Freud believed that personality was shaped and fixed by the age of 5 and that it was difficult after that to change any aspect of it. While it does seem clear that the childhood years are indeed crucial to personality formation, research also indicates that personality continues to develop well beyond childhood, perhaps throughout the entire life span.

Theorists such as Cattell, Allport, and Erikson viewed childhood as important but agreed that personality could be modified in later years. Some theorists suggested that personality development is ongoing in adolescence, whereas Jung, Maslow, Erikson, and Cattell viewed middle age as a time of major personality change.

The question is how long does our personality continue to change and grow? Does your personality at age 20 indicate what you will be like at 40? As with many questions about personality, this one is highly complex. Perhaps it is not even the right question to ask.

It may not surprise you to learn that empirical evidence supports diverse viewpoints. Does personality change? Well, yes. Does personality also remain stable? Uh, probably, yes. But if we were to refine the question and ask whether *some* personality characteristics remain stable over a lifetime while other characteristics change, then we would be able to answer with an unqualified yes.

What has emerged from research is the suggestion that our basic foundation of enduring personality dispositions—such as the traits described in McCrae and Costa's five-factor model as well as other aspects of personality—remains stable over many years. According to the evidence, these basic traits and capacities appear to be enduring from age 30 on (Nave, Sherman, Funder, Hampson, & Goldberg, 2010; Terracciano, McCrae, & Costa, 2010).

Some research shows that the factors of neuroticism, extraversion, and openness decline from college age to middle age, whereas the factors of agreeableness and conscientiousness increase with age. Cross-cultural comparisons have demonstrated this consistency in such diverse countries as the United States, Germany, Italy, Portugal, Croatia, the Netherlands, Australia, and South Korea (Allemand, Zimprich, & Hendriks, 2008; McCrae & Costa, 1997; Lucas & Donnellan, 2009; McCrae et al., 1999).

Other research has led to different results. For example, a 40-year study of several hundred people found that scores on dominance and independence peaked in middle age, and that personality did not stop evolving and changing after age 20 (Helson, Jones, & Kwan, 2002). A meta-analysis of 152 longitudinal studies involving more than 55,000 people showed a high level of consistency in personality traits at all ages. The highest level of consistency was found in adulthood (Roberts & Delvecchio, 2000). According to these findings, traits are consistent over the life span, reaching the highest level after age 50.

Additional research has focused on personality change in childhood and adolescence. A study of teenagers in Estonia ages 12 to 18 showed that their personalities, as measured by the five-factor model, remained stable over the two-year period of the research (Pullmann, Raudsepp, & Allik, 2006). Research with American college students over 30 months showed that they became more open, agreeable, and conscientious during that time (Vaidya, Gray, Haig, & Watson, 2002).

Other longitudinal research has shown that both normal and abnormal personality factors may reach a peak of stability around age 30 and remain fairly stable for the remainder of the life span (Ferguson, 2010). However, a study in Switzerland found that people in their 60s tend to become less neurotic and less extraverted as they age, and less open to new experiences (Allemand, Zimprich, & Martin, 2008).

Studies of twins ranging in age from 64 to 98 found decreases with advancing age in extraversion, conscientiousness, and perceived control, and some indication of increases in neuroticism. Overall, however, there was no significant change in feelings of well-being with advancing age (Berg & Johansson, 2014; Kandler, Kornadt, Hagemeyer, & Neyer, 2014).

A study of more than 32,000 people ages 21 to 60 conducted over the Internet showed that conscientiousness and agreeableness increased through early and middle adulthood. Conscientiousness increased most strongly in the 20s; agreeableness increased most strongly during the 30s (Srivastava, John, Gosling, & Potter, 2003).

Other research suggests that people tend to become more dominant in social situations and more conscientious and emotionally stable, as they grow from young adulthood to middle age (Roberts, Walton, & Viechtbauer, 2006). Large-scale studies also support the notion that personality remains generally stable after age 30 and into late adulthood (Johnson, McGue, & Krueger, 2005; Terracciano, Costa, & McCrae, 2006).

A study of people in New Zealand ages 18 to 26 showed that personality changes during that period showed an increasing level of psychological maturity. The subjects became more self-controlled and confident in social situations, and less angry and alienated. Women showed a higher level of psychological maturity overall than men (Roberts, Caspi, & Moffitt, 2001).

In a study of children ages 8 to 12, who were surveyed again 10 years later, personality changes between the ages of 18 and 22 could be predicted to a significant extent by their personality characteristics in childhood (Shiner, Masten, & Tellegen, 2002). What all these studies confirm is that personality changes as we grow into adolescence and early adulthood, a finding you have probably already observed in yourself.

What brings about personality change in adulthood? Many psychologists believe that the answer is rooted in social and environmental influences and in the adaptations we make to them. Changes in economic circumstances, leaving college, marriage and parenthood, divorce, job loss or advancement, midlife crises, aging parents—all create problems to which adults must adjust (McAdams & Olson, 2010).

A 3-year study in the Netherlands of men and women in their 40s found that those who had adapted to their expected social roles, such as success in a career and family life, scored higher on the five-factor personality dimensions than those who had not adapted successfully. Thus, personality change was found to be associated with the successful adaptation to typical midlife concerns (Van Aken, Denisson, Branje, Dubas, & Goossens, 2006).

In other instances of adjustment, people who have lost their jobs have shown significant increases in neuroticism and decreases in conscientiousness and extraversion. Adults who were actively dating and maintaining social relationships scored lower in neuroticism and higher in extraversion, conscientiousness, and self-esteem than people who were not dating (Costa, Herbst, McCrae, & Siegler, 2000; Neyer & Asendorpf, 2001).

These kinds of cultural and personal challenges leave their impact on the personality. One theorist suggested that personality continues to develop over time on three levels: dispositional traits, personal concerns, and life narrative (McAdams, 1994). *Dispositional traits* are inherited traits of the kind discussed by McCrae and Costa, those characteristics found to remain stable and relatively unchanging from age 30 on.

Personal concerns refer to conscious feelings, plans, and goals; what we want, how we try to achieve it, and how we feel about the people in our lives. These may change often over the life span as a result of the diverse situations and influences to which we are exposed. Although these situations can alter our feelings and intentions, our underlying dispositional traits (such as our basic level of neuroticism or extraversion) with which we confront these life situations may remain relatively stable.

Life narrative implies shaping the self, attaining an identity, and finding a unified purpose in life. We are constantly writing our life story, creating who we are and how we fit into the world. Like personal concerns, the life narrative changes in response to social and environmental situations. As adults we may adjust our narrative to adapt to each stage of life and its needs, challenges, and opportunities.

In sum, then, this view holds that the underlying dispositional traits of personality remain largely constant, while our conscious judgments about who we are and who we would like to be are subject to change. That idea leads to another factor personality theorists have considered: consciousness.

The Consciousness Factor

Almost every personality theory we have described deals explicitly or implicitly with conscious (cognitive) processes. Even Freud and Jung, who focused on the unconscious, wrote of an ego or conscious mind that perceives, thinks, feels, and remembers, enabling us to interact with the real world.

Through the ego we are able to perceive stimuli and later recall an image of them. Jung wrote about rational functioning, making conscious judgments and evaluations of our experiences. Adler described humans as conscious, rational beings capable of planning and directing the course of our lives. We formulate hopes, plans, and dreams and delay gratification, and we consciously anticipate future events.

Allport believed that people who are not neurotic will function in a conscious, rational way, aware of and in control of the forces that motivate them. Rogers thought people were primarily rational beings, governed by a conscious perception of themselves and their world of experience. Maslow also recognized the role of consciousness when he proposed cognitive needs to know and to understand.

Kelly offered the most complete theory based on cognitive factors. He argued persuasively that we form constructs about our environment and other people and that we make predictions (anticipations) about them based on these constructs. We formulate hypotheses about our social world and test them against the reality of our experience. Based on everyday evidence, it is difficult to deny that people construe, predict, and anticipate how others will behave and then modify or adapt their behavior accordingly.

Bandura credited people with the ability to learn through example and vicarious reinforcement. To do so, we must be able to anticipate and appreciate the consequences of the actions we observe in others. We visualize or imagine the results of our reinforcements for behaving the same way a model does, even though we may never have experienced those consequences personally.

Thus, there is widespread agreement that consciousness exists and is an influence on personality. However, there is less agreement on the role or even the existence of another influence, that of the unconscious.

The Unconscious Factor

Sigmund Freud introduced us to the world of the unconscious, that murky repository of our darkest fears, conflicts, and forces that affect our conscious thoughts and behaviors. Psychologists have found some evidence to support Freud's notion that thoughts and memories are repressed in the unconscious, and that repression (as well as other defense mechanisms) may operate at the unconscious level.

The cognitive movement in psychology has led to not only an interest in conscious processes but also a renewed interest in the unconscious. Recent research confirms that the unconscious is a powerful force, perhaps even more pervasive in its influence than Freud suggested. However, the modern depiction of the unconscious is not the same as Freud's view. Contemporary researchers focus on unconscious cognitive processes and describe them as more rational than emotional.

The rational unconscious is often referred to as the non-conscious, to distinguish it from Freud's unconscious, his so-called dark cauldron of repressed wishes and desires. One method for studying the non-conscious involves subliminal activation, in which various stimuli are presented to subjects below their level of conscious awareness. Despite the subjects' inability to perceive the stimuli, their conscious processes and behaviors can be activated by those stimuli.

The obvious conclusion to be drawn from such research is that people can be influenced by stimuli they can neither see nor hear. We also discussed the "Mommy and I are one" study about how subliminal presentation of certain stimuli influenced cognitive as well as emotional responses (Silverman & Weinberger, 1985). The subliminal stimuli had therapeutic value even though the subjects had no conscious awareness of the actual messages. Thus, the unconscious may have both a rational and an emotional component.

Although the unconscious is an ongoing research topic in psychology today, many of the personality theorists who followed Freud ignored it. We might suggest that the emotional unconscious as Freud envisioned it—the startling idea that signaled the formal beginning of the study of personality—remains the least understood factor and still very much what it was in Freud's time, mysterious and inaccessible.

Final Comment

As you have seen throughout this course, most aspects of personality also remain mysterious and some are still not fully accessible. We have gone through diverse ways of defining and describing personality, and each theory we have discussed has contributed another part of the answer to that vital question of what is personality.

We have gone from the viewpoints of Sigmund Freud and his emphasis on anxiety, the unconscious, and a life of fear and repression to positive psychology and the characteristics of the happy personality. And we have covered many other ideas in between, all of which have added to our understanding. But there are more possibilities to consider, more to be learned, and no doubt new approaches will be presented, new theories as yet unimagined.

Your formal course work in this field may be ending, but the attempt to understand personality is not. Although it is true that enormous progress has been made in charting personality and detailing the factors that shape it, the challenges of the field remain active and dynamic. Perhaps the question, "What is personality?" is the most important question of all for psychology, for it reflects the attempt to understand ourselves.

Review Questions

1. Think about the similarities and differences between your personality and the personalities of your mother, father, or siblings. What factors do you see in common, or have you turned out to be totally different from them?

2. As you matured, do you think your personality was still influenced as much by your parents, or did your peers and the outside world, particularly as you interacted through social media, become more dominant influences?

3. Think back to your early adolescence. Who do you believe influenced you more at that time, your parents or your peers? Now that you are older, is your answer to that question the same?

4. Which of the approaches to personality discussed in this text did you find most helpful in understanding yourself? Which was of the least value to you?

5. What changes have you seen in your personality from childhood to the present? Have there been periods in your life when you deliberately tried to alter your personality? Were you successful? If so, what techniques did you use?

6. Do you think it is possible to evaluate personality accurately enough to predict whether certain people will be happy, emotionally stable, or perform well on the job?

7. Have you learned anything useful or surprising about your own personality from this course?

8. Did this book leave you wanting to learn more about the study of personality, or have you had enough?

glossary

A

ability traits   Traits that describe our skills and how efficiently we will be able to work toward our goals.

actualization tendency   The basic human motivation to actualize, maintain, and enhance the self.

aggressive drive   The compulsion to destroy, conquer, and kill.

aggressive personality   Behaviors and attitudes associated with the neurotic trend of moving against people, such as a domineering and controlling manner.

analytical psychology   Jung's theory of personality.

anima archetype; animus archetype   Feminine aspects of the male psyche; masculine aspects of the female psyche.

anxiety   To Freud, a feeling of fear and dread without an obvious cause: reality anxiety is a fear of tangible dangers; neurotic anxiety involves a conflict between id and ego; moral anxiety involves a conflict between id and superego.

archetypes   Images of universal experiences contained in the collective unconscious.

B

basic anxiety   A pervasive feeling of loneliness and helplessness; the foundation of neurosis.

basic strengths   To Erikson, motivating characteristics and beliefs that derive from the satisfactory resolution of the crisis at each developmental stage.

basic weaknesses   Motivating characteristics that derive from the unsatisfactory resolution of developmental crises.

behavior modification   A form of therapy that applies the principles of reinforcement to bring about desired behavioral changes.

behavioral genetics   The study of the relationship between genetic or hereditary factors and personality traits.

C

cardinal traits   The most pervasive and powerful human traits.

case study   A detailed history of an individual that contains data from a variety of sources.

castration anxiety   A boy's fear during the Oedipal period that his penis will be cut off.

catharsis   The expression of emotions that is expected to lead to the reduction of disturbing symptoms.

cathexis   An investment of psychic energy in an object or person.

central traits   The handful of outstanding traits that describe a person's behavior.

cognitive complexity   A cognitive style or way of construing the environment characterized by the ability to perceive differences among people.

cognitive needs   Innate needs to know and to understand.

cognitive simplicity   A cognitive style or way of construing the environment characterized by a relative inability to perceive differences among people.

collective unconscious   The deepest level of the psyche containing the accumulation of inherited experiences of human and pre-human species.

common traits   Traits possessed in some degree by all persons.

compensation   A motivation to overcome inferiority, to strive for higher levels of development.

complex   To Jung, a core or pattern of emotions, memories, perceptions, and wishes in the personal unconscious organized around a common theme, such as power or status.

compliant personality   Behaviors and attitudes associated with the neurotic trend of moving toward people, such as a need for affection and approval.

conditional positive regard   Approval, love, or acceptance granted only when a person expresses desirable behaviors and attitudes.

conditions of worth   To Rogers, a belief that we are worthy of approval only when we express desirable behaviors and attitudes and refrain from expressing those that bring disapproval from others; similar to the Freudian superego.

conflict   To Horney, the basic incompatibility of the neurotic trends.

conscience   A component of the superego that contains behaviors for which the child has been punished.

constitutional traits   Source traits that depend on our physiological characteristics.

construct   An intellectual hypothesis that we devise and use to interpret or explain life events. Constructs are bipolar, or dichotomous, such as tall versus short or honest versus dishonest.

constructive alternativism   The idea that we are free to revise or replace our constructs with alternatives as needed.

control group   In an experiment, the group that does not receive the experimental treatment.

coping behavior   Consciously planned behavior determined by the needs of a given situation and designed for a specific purpose, usually to bring about a change in one's environment.

correlational method   A statistical technique that measures the degree of the relationship between two variables, expressed by the correlation coefficient.

creative power of the self   The ability to create an appropriate style of life.

crisis   To Erikson, the turning point faced at each developmental stage.

D

death instincts   The unconscious drive toward decay, destruction, and aggression.

defense mechanisms   Strategies the ego uses to defend itself against the anxiety provoked by conflicts of everyday life. Defense mechanisms involve denials or distortions of reality.

deficit (deficiency) needs   The lower needs; failure to satisfy them produces a deficiency in the body.

denial   A defense mechanism that involves denying the existence of an external threat or traumatic event.

dependent variable   In an experiment, the variable the experimenter desires to measure, typically the subjects' behavior or response to manipulation of the independent variable.

detached personality   Behaviors and attitudes associated with the neurotic trend of moving away from people, such as an intense need for privacy.

disinhibition   The weakening of inhibitions or constraints by observing the behavior of a model.

displacement   A defense mechanism that involves shifting id impulses from a threatening object or from one that is unavailable to an object that is available; for example, replacing hostility toward one's boss with hostility toward one's child.

dream analysis   A technique involving the interpretation of dreams to uncover unconscious conflicts. Dreams have a manifest content (the actual events in the dream) and a latent content (the symbolic meaning of the dream events).

dynamic traits   Traits that describe our motivations and interests.

E

early recollections   A personality assessment technique in which our earliest memories, whether of real events or fantasies, are assumed to reveal the primary interest of our life.

ego   To Freud, the rational aspect of the personality, responsible for directing and controlling the instincts according to the reality principle. To Jung, the conscious aspect of personality.

ego identity   The self-image formed during adolescence that integrates our ideas of what we are and what we want to be.

ego-ideal   A component of the superego that contains the moral or ideal behaviors for which a person should strive.

Electra complex   During the phallic stage (ages 4-5), the unconscious desire of a girl for her father, accompanied by a desire to replace or destroy her mother.

encounter groups   A group therapy technique in which people learn about their feelings and about how they relate to (or encounter) one another.

entropy principle   A tendency toward balance or equilibrium within the personality; the ideal is an equal distribution of psychic energy over all structures of the personality.

environmental-mold traits   Source traits that are learned from social and environmental interactions.

epigenetic principle of maturation   The idea that human development is governed by a sequence of stages that depend on genetic or hereditary factors.

equivalence principle   The continuing redistribution of energy within a personality; if the energy expended on certain conditions or activities weakens or disappears, that energy is transferred elsewhere in the personality.

experimental group   In an experiment, the group that is exposed to the experimental treatment.

expressive behavior   Spontaneous and seemingly purposeless behavior, usually displayed without our conscious awareness.

explanatory style   A way of explaining to ourselves our relative lack of control over our environment. An optimistic explanatory style can prevent learned helplessness; a pessimistic explanatory style spreads helplessness to all facets of life.

external locus of control   A belief that reinforcement is under the control of other people, fate, or luck.

externalization   A way to defend against the conflict caused by the discrepancy between an idealized and a real self-image by projecting the conflict onto the outside world.

extinction   The process of eliminating a behavior by withholding reinforcement.

extraversion   An attitude of the psyche characterized by an orientation toward the external world and other people.

F

factor analysis   A statistical technique based on correlations between several measures, which may be explained in terms of underlying factors.

feminine psychology   To Horney, a revision of psychoanalysis to encompass the psychological conflicts inherent in the traditional ideal of womanhood and women's roles.

fictional finalism   The idea that there is an imagined or potential goal that guides our behavior.

fixation   A condition in which a portion of libido remains invested in one of the psychosexual stages because of excessive frustration or gratification.

fixed role therapy   A psychotherapeutic technique in which the client acts out constructs appropriate for a fictitious person. This shows the client how the new constructs can be more effective than the old ones he or she has been using.

free association   A technique in which the patient says whatever comes to mind. In other words, it is a kind of daydreaming out loud.

fully functioning person   Rogers's term for self-actualization, for developing all facets of the self.

functional analysis   An approach to the study of behavior that involves assessing the frequency of a behavior, the situation in which it occurs, and the reinforcers associated with it.

functional autonomy of motives   The idea that motives in the normal, mature adult are independent of the childhood experiences in which they originally appeared.

G

growth (being) needs   The higher needs; although growth needs are less necessary than deficit needs for survival, they involve the realization and fulfillment of human potential.

H

hierarchy of five innate needs   An arrangement of innate needs, from strongest to weakest, that activates and directs behavior.

historical determinism   The view that personality is basically fixed in the early years of life and subject to little change thereafter.

I

id   To Freud, the aspect of personality allied with the instincts; the source of psychic energy, the id operates according to the pleasure principle.

idealized self-image   For normal people, the self-image is an idealized picture of oneself built on a flexible, realistic assessment of one's abilities. For neurotics, the self-image is based on an inflexible, unrealistic self-appraisal.

identity crisis   The failure to achieve ego identity during adolescence.

incongruence   A discrepancy between a person's self-concept and aspects of his or her experience.

independent variable   In an experiment, the stimulus variable or condition the experimenter manipulates to learn its effect on the dependent variable.

individual psychology   Adler's theory of personality.

individuation   A condition of psychological health resulting from the integration of all conscious and unconscious facets of the personality.

inferiority complex   A condition that develops when a person is unable to compensate for normal inferiority feelings.

inferiority feelings   The normal condition of all people; the source of all human striving.

instinctive drift   The substitution of instinctive behaviors for behaviors that had been reinforced.

instinctoid needs   Maslow's term for the innate needs in his needs-hierarchy theory.

instincts   In Freud's system, mental representations of internal stimuli, such as hunger, that drive a person to take certain actions.

internal locus of control   A belief that reinforcement is brought about by our own behavior.

introversion   An attitude of the psyche characterized by an orientation toward one's own thoughts and feelings.

J

Jonah complex   The fear that maximizing our potential will lead to a situation with which we will be unable to cope.

L

latency period   To Freud, the period from approximately age 5 to puberty, during which the sex instinct is dormant, sublimated in school activities, sports, and hobbies, and in developing friendships with members of the same sex.

L-data   Life-record ratings of behaviors observed in real-life situations, such as the classroom or office.

learned helplessness   A condition resulting from the perception that we have no control over our environment.

libido   To Freud, the form of psychic energy, manifested by the life instincts, that drives a person toward pleasurable behaviors and thoughts. To Jung, a broader and more generalized form of psychic energy.

life instincts   The drive for ensuring survival of the individual and the species by satisfying the needs for food, water, air, and sex.

life-history reconstruction   Jung's type of case study that involves examining a person's past experiences to identify developmental patterns that may explain present neuroses.

M

maldevelopment   A condition that occurs when the ego consists solely of a single way of coping with conflict.

metamotivation   The motivation of self-actualizers, which involves maximizing personal potential rather than striving for a particular goal object.

metaneeds   States of growth or being toward which self-actualizers evolve.

metapathology   A thwarting of self-development related to failure to satisfy the metaneeds.

modeling   A behavior modification technique that involves observing the behavior of others (the models) and participating with them in performing the desired behavior.

Myers-Briggs Type Indicator (MBTI)   An assessment test based on Jung's psychological types and the attitudes of introversion and extraversion.

N

negative reinforcement   The strengthening of a response by the removal of an aversive stimulus.

neurotic competitiveness   An indiscriminate need to win at all costs.

neurotic needs   Ten irrational defenses against anxiety that become a permanent part of personality and that affect behavior.

neurotic trends   Three categories of behaviors and attitudes toward oneself and others that express a person's needs; Horney's revision of the concept of neurotic needs.

O

observational learning   Learning new responses by observing the behavior of other people.

Oedipus complex   During the phallic stage (ages 4-5), the unconscious desire of a boy for his mother, accompanied by a desire to replace or destroy his father.

operant behavior   Behavior emitted spontaneously or voluntarily that operates on the environment to change it.

operant conditioning   The procedure by which a change in the consequences of a response will affect the rate at which the response occurs.

opposition principle   Jung's idea that conflict between opposing processes or tendencies is necessary to generate psychic energy.

organismic valuing process   The process by which we judge experiences in terms of their value for fostering or hindering our actualization and growth.

P

peak experience   A moment of intense ecstasy, similar to a religious or mystical experience, during which the self is transcended.

penis envy   The envy the female feels toward the male because the male possesses a penis; this is accompanied by a sense of loss because the female does not have a penis.

permeability   The idea that constructs can be revised and extended in light of new experiences.

perseverative functional autonomy   The level of functional autonomy that relates to low-level and routine behaviors.

persona archetype   The public face or role a person presents to others.

personal construct theory   Kelly's description of personality in terms of cognitive processes: We are capable of interpreting behaviors and events and of using this understanding to guide our behavior and to predict the behavior of other people.

personal dispositions   Traits that are peculiar to an individual, as opposed to traits shared by a number of people.

personal unconscious   The reservoir of material that was once conscious but has been forgotten or suppressed. Personal-document technique.

personal-document technique   involves the study of a person's written or spoken records.

personality   The unique, relatively enduring internal and external aspects of a person's character that influence behavior in different situations.

person-centered therapy   Rogers's approach to therapy in which the client (not the "patient") is assumed to be responsible for changing his or her personality.

play constructions   A personality assessment technique for children in which structures assembled from dolls, blocks, and other toys are analyzed.

pleasure principle   The principle by which the id functions to avoid pain and maximize pleasure.

positive regard   Acceptance, love, and approval from others.

positive self-regard   The condition under which we grant ourselves acceptance and approval.

primary-process thought   Childlike thinking by which the id attempts to satisfy the instinctual drives.

projection   A defense mechanism that involves attributing a disturbing impulse to someone else.

projective test   A personality assessment device in which subjects are presumed to project personal needs, fears, and values onto their interpretation or description of an ambiguous stimulus.

propriate functional autonomy   The level of functional autonomy that relates to our values, self-image, and lifestyle.

proprium   Allport's term for the ego or self.

psyche   Jung's term for personality.

psychoanalysis   Sigmund Freud's theory of personality and system of therapy for treating mental disorders.

psychohistorical analysis   The application of Erikson's lifespan theory, along with psychoanalytic principles, to the study of historical figures.

psychological types   To Jung, eight personality types based on interactions of the attitudes (introversion and extraversion) and the functions (thinking, feeling, sensing, and intuiting).

psychosexual stages of development   To Freud, the oral, anal, phallic, and genital stages through which all children pass. In these stages, gratification of the id instincts depends on the stimulation of corresponding areas of the body.

psychosocial stages of development   To Erikson, eight successive stages encompassing the life span. At each stage, we must cope with a crisis in either an adaptive or a maladaptive way.

punishment   The application of an aversive stimulus following a response in an effort to decrease the likelihood that the response will recur.

Q

Q-data   Self-report questionnaire ratings of our characteristics, attitudes, and interests.

Q-sort technique   A self-report technique for assessing aspects of the self-concept.

R

range of convenience   The spectrum of events to which a construct can be applied. Some constructs are relevant to a limited number of people or situations; other constructs are broader.

rationalization   A defense mechanism that involves reinterpreting our behavior to make it more acceptable and less threatening to us.

reaction formation   A defense mechanism that involves expressing an id impulse that is the opposite of the one that is truly driving the person.

reality principle   The principle by which the ego functions to provide appropriate constraints on the expression of the id instincts.

reciprocal determinism   The idea that behavior is controlled or determined by the individual, through cognitive processes, and by the environment, through external social stimulus events.

regression   A defense mechanism that involves retreating to an earlier, less frustrating period of life and displaying the usually childish behaviors characteristic of that more secure time.

reinforcement   The act of strengthening a response by adding a reward, thus increasing the likelihood that the response will be repeated.

reinforcement schedules   Patterns or rates of providing or withholding reinforcers.

reliability   The consistency of response to a psychological assessment device.

repression   A defense mechanism that involves unconscious denial of the existence of something that causes anxiety.

resistance   In free association, a blockage or refusal to disclose painful memories.

respondent behavior   Responses made to or elicited by specific environmental stimuli.

S

safety need   A higher-level need for security and freedom from fear.

secondary traits   The least important traits, which a person may display inconspicuously and inconsistently.

secondary-process thought   Mature thought processes needed to deal rationally with the external world.

self archetype   To Jung, the archetype that represents the unity, integration, and harmony of the total personality.

self-actualization   The fullest development of the self.

self-characterization sketch   A technique designed to assess a person's construct system; that is, how a person perceives himself or herself in relation to other people.

self-control   The ability to exert control over the variables that determine our behavior.

self-efficacy   Our feeling of adequacy, efficiency, and competence in coping with life.

self-reinforcement   Administering rewards or punishments to oneself for meeting, exceeding, or falling short of one's own expectations or standards.

self-report inventory   A personality assessment technique in which subjects answer questions about their behaviors and feelings.

sensation seeking   The need for varied, novel, and complex sensations and experiences.

sentiments   To Cattell, environmental-mold source traits that motivate behavior.

shadow archetype   The dark side of the personality; the archetype that contains primitive animal instincts.

social interest   Our innate potential to cooperate with other people to achieve personal and societal goals.

source traits   Stable and permanent traits that are the basic factors of personality, derived by the method of factor analysis.

striving for superiority   The urge toward perfection or completion that motivates each of us.

style of life   A unique character structure or pattern of personal behaviors and characteristics by which each of us strives for perfection. Basic styles of life include the dominant, getting, avoiding, and socially useful types.

sublimation   A defense mechanism that involves altering or displacing id impulses by diverting instinctual energy into socially acceptable behaviors.

subliminal perception   Perception below the threshold of conscious awareness.

successive approximation   An explanation for the acquisition of complex behavior. Behavior such as learning to speak will be reinforced only as it comes to approximate or approach the final desired behavior.

superego   To Freud, the moral aspect of personality; the internalization of parental and societal values and standards.

superiority complex   A condition that develops when a person overcompensates for normal inferiority feelings.

superstitious behavior   Persistent behavior that has a coincidental and not a functional relationship to the reinforcement received.

surface traits   Traits that show a correlation but do not constitute a factor because they are not determined by a single source.

symptom analysis   Similar to catharsis, the symptom analysis technique focuses on the symptoms reported by the patient and attempts to interpret the patient's free associations to those symptoms.

T

T-data   Data derived from personality tests that are resistant to faking.

temperament traits   Traits that describe our general behavioral style in responding to our environment.

token economy   A behavior-modification technique in which tokens, which can be exchanged for valued objects or privileges, are awarded for desirable behaviors.

traits   To Allport, distinguishing characteristics that guide behavior. Traits are measured on a continuum and are subject to social, environmental, and cultural influences. To Cattell, reaction tendencies, derived by the method of factor analysis, that are relatively permanent parts of the personality.

tyranny of the shoulds   An attempt to realize an unattainable idealized self-image by denying the true self and behaving in terms of what we think we should be doing.

U

unconditional positive regard   Approval granted regardless of a person's behavior. In Rogers's person-centered therapy, the therapist offers the client unconditional positive regard.

unique traits   Traits possessed by one or a few persons.

V

validity   The extent to which an assessment device measures what it is intended to measure.

vicarious reinforcement   Learning or strengthening a behavior by observing the behavior of others, and the consequences of that behavior, rather than experiencing the reinforcement or consequences directly.

W

womb envy   The envy a male feels toward a female because she can bear children and he cannot. Womb envy was Horney's response to Freud's concept of penis envy in females.

word association test   A projective technique in which a person responds to a stimulus word with whatever word comes to mind.

references

Aarts, J., Deckx, L., Abbema, D., Tjan-Heijnen, V., Akker, M., & Buntinx, F. (2015, January 25). The relation between depression, coping and health locus of control: Differences between older and yonger patients, with and without cancer. *Psycho-Oncology*. http://onlinelibrary.wiley.com/doi/10.1002/pon.3748/abstract

Abdallah, T. M. (1989). Self-esteem and locus of control of college men in Saudi Arabia. *Psychological Reports, 65*(3, Pt. 2), 1323–1326.

Abdel-Khalek, A. (2012). Personality and mental health: Arabic scale of mental health: Eysenck personality questionnaire, and NEO five factor inventory. *Psychological Reports, 111,* 75–82.

Abdel-Khalek, A., & Lester, D. (2006). Optimism and pessimism in Kuwaiti and American college students. *International Journal of Social Psychiatry, 52,* 110–126.

Abdel-Khalek, A., & Lester, D. (2010). Personal and psychological correlates of happiness among a sample of Kuwaiti Muslim students. *Journal of Muslim Mental Health, 5*(2), 194–209.

Abe, H., Imai, S., & Nedate, L. (2011). Effects of fixed-role therapy applying decision-making theory on social anxiety. *Japanese Journal of Counseling Science, 44,* 1–9.

Abma, R. (2004). Madness and mental health. In J. Janz & P. Van Drunnen (Eds.), *A social history of psychology* (pp. 93–128). Malden, MA: Blackwell.

Achenbach, T., & Zigler, E. (1963). Social competence and self-image disparity in psychiatric and nonpsychiatric patients. *Journal of Abnormal and Social Psychology, 67,* 197–205.

Adams, D. (1954). *The anatomy of personality.* Garden City, NY: Doubleday.

Adams, G. R., & Fitch, S. A. (1982). Ego stage and identity status development: A cross-sequential analysis. *Journal of Personality and Social Psychology, 43,* 574–583.

Adams, H., Luevano, V., & Jonason, P. (2014). Ricky business: Willingness to be caught in an extra-pair relationship, relationship experiences, and the Dark Triad. *Personality and Individual Differences, 66,* 204–207.

Adams, N. (2012). Skinner's *Walden Two*: An anticipation of positive psychology? *Review of General Psychology, 16,* 1–9.

Adams-Webber, J. R. (2001). Cognitive complexity and role relationships. *Journal of Constructivist Psychology, 14*(1), 43–50.

Adebimpe, O., & Oladimeji, B. (2014). Health beliefs and locus of control as predictors of cancer screening behavior among women in Obafemi Awolowo University community. *Gender & Behavior, 12,* 6457–6464.

Adler, A. (1924). *The practice and theory of individual psychology.* Boston: Littlefield Adams.

Adler, A. (1930). Individual psychology. In C. Murchison (Ed.), *Psychologies of 1930* (pp. 395–405). Worcester, MA: Clark University Press.

Adler, A. (1939). *Social interest: A challenge to mankind.* J. Linton & R. Vaughan (Trans.). New York: Putnam. (Original work published 1933).

Adler, A. (1963). *The practice and theory of individual psychology.* P. Radin (Trans.). Paterson, NJ: Littlefield, Adams. (Original work published 1924).

Adler, J. (2006, March 27). Freud in our midst. *Newsweek,* pp. 43–49.

Ahern, J., Cerda, M., Lippnnan, S., Tardiff, K., Vlahov, D., & Galea, S. (2013). Navigating non-positivity in neighbourhood studies: An analysis of collective efficacy and violence. *Journal of Epidemiology and Community Health, 67,* 159–165.

Ahlin, E., & Lobo Antunes, M. (2015, January 24). Locus of control orientation: Parents, peers, and place. *Journal of Youth and Adolescence.* http://psycnet.apa.org/index.cfm?fa=main.doiEventRedirect &uid=&pc=&nextURL=http%3A%2F%2Fdx%2Fdoi%2Eorg%2F10%2E1007%2Fs10964%252D015%252D0253%252D9

Aksu, A., Sekercioglu, G., Ehtiyar, V., Yildiz, S., & Yilmaz, Y. (2012). The relationship between personality, gender and departments: Application of 16 personality factor questionnaire in the Antalya region of Turkey. *Quality & Quantity: International Journal of Methodology, 44,* 1113–1127.

Alansari, B., & Kazem, A. (2008). Optimism and pessimism in Kuwaiti and Omani undergraduates. *Social Behavior and Personality, 36*(4), 503–518.

Alansari, B. M. (2006). Gender differences in anxiety among undergraduates from 16 Islamic countries. *Social Behavior and Personality, 34,* 651–660.

425

Albright, L., Malloy, T. E., Dong, Q., Kenny, D. A., Fang, X., Winquist, L., et al. (1997). Cross-cultural consensus in personality judgments. *Journal of Personality and Social Psychology, 72,* 558–569.

Ale, C., Chorney, D., Brice, C., & Morris, T. (2010). Facial affect recognition and social anxiety in preschool children. *Early Child Development and Care, 180*(10), 1349–1359.

Alessandri, G., Vecchione, M., Caprara, G., & Letzring, T. (2012). The Ego Resiliency Scale revised: A crosscultural study in Italy, Spain and the United States. *European Journal of Psychological Assessment, 28,* 139–146.

Alexandre, P., Martins, S., Silvia, S., & Richard, P. (2009). Disparities in adequate mental health care for the past-year major depressive episodes among Caucasian and Hispanic youth. *Psychiatric Services, 60*(10), 1365–1371.

Allemand, M., Zimprich, D., & Hendriks, A. (2008). Age differences in five personality domains across the life span. *Developmental Psychology, 44*(3), 758–770.

Allemand, M., Zimprich, D., & Hertzog, C. (2007). Cross-sectional age differences and longitudinal age changes of personality in middle adulthood and old age. *Journal of Personality, 75,* 323–328.

Allemand, M., Zimprich, D., & Martin, M. (2008). Long-term correlated change in personality traits in old age. *Psychology and Aging, 23*(3), 545–557.

Allen, J., & Dana, R. (2004). Methodological issues in cross-cultural and multicultural Rorschach research. *Journal of Personality Assessment, 82,* 189–206.

Allen, K. D., Danforth, J. S., & Drabman, R. C. (1989). Video-taped modeling and film distraction for fear reduction in adults undergoing hyperbaric oxygen therapy. *Journal of Consulting and Clinical Psychology, 57,* 554–558.

Allik, J., & McCrae, R. (2004). Toward a geography of personality traits: Patterns of profiles across 36 cultures. *Journal of Cross-Cultural Psychology, 35,* 13–28.

Allik, J., Realo, A., & McCrae, R. (2013). Universality of the five-factor model of personality. In T. Widiger (Ed.), *Personality disorders and the five-factor model* (pp. 61–74). Washington, DC: American Psychological Association.

Allik, J., Realo, A., Mottus, R., Borkenau, P., Kuppens, P., & Hrebickova, M. (2010). How people see others is different from how people see themselves: A replicable pattern across cultures. *Journal of Personality and Social Psychology, 99*(5), 870–882.

Allik, J., Realo, A., Mottus, R., Pullmann, H., Trifonova, A., & McCrae, R. (2009). Personality traits of Russians from the observer's perspective. *European Journal of Personality, 23*(7), 567–588.

Allport, G. W. (1937). *Personality: A psychological interpretation.* New York: Holt.

Allport, G. W. (1955). *Becoming: Basic considerations for a psychology of personality.* New Haven, CT: Yale University Press.

Allport, G. W. (1961). *Pattern and growth in personality.* New York: Holt.

Allport, G. W. (Ed.). (1965). *Letters from Jenny.* New York: Harcourt, Brace & World.

Allport, G. W. (1966). Traits revisited. *American Psychologist, 21,* 1–10.

Allport, G. W. (1967). Autobiography. In E. G. Boring & G. Lindzey (Eds.), *A history of psychology in autobiography* (Vol. 5, pp. 1–25). New York: Appleton-Century-Crofts.

Allport, G. W., & Cantril, H. (1934). Judging personality from voice. *Journal of Social Psychology, 5,* 37–55.

Allport, G. W., & Vernon, P. (1933). *Studies in expressive movement.* New York: Macmillan.

Allport, G. W., Vernon, P., & Lindzey, G. (1960). *A study of values* (3rd ed.). Boston: Houghton Mifflin.

Alfonso, R., Bueno, B., Loureiro, B., & Pereira, H. (2011). Reminiscence, psychological well-being, and ego integrity in Portuguese elderly people. *Educational Gerontology, 37,* 1063–1080.

Aghababaei, N. (2012). Religious, honest and humble: Looking for the religious person within the HEXACO model of personality structure. *Personality and Individual Differences, 53,* 880–883.

Aghababaei, N., & Arji, A. (2014). Well-being and the HEXACO model of personality. *Personality and Individual Differences, 56,* 139–142.

Altmaier, E. M., Russell, D. W., Kao, C. F., Lehmann, T. R., & Weinstein, J. N. (1993). Role of self-efficacy in rehabilitation outcomes among chronic low back pain patients. *Journal of Counseling Psychology, 40,* 335–339.

Altus, D., & Morris, E. (2009). B. F. Skinner's utopian vision: Behind and beyond *Walden Two. Behavior Analyst, 32*(2), 319–335.

Ambody, N., & Rosenthal, R. (1992). Thin slices of expressive behavior as predictors of interpersonal consequences: A meta-analysis. *Psychological Bulletin, 111,* 256–274.

Amichai-Hamburger, Y., & Vinitzky, G. (2010). Social network use and personality. *Computers in Human Behavior, 26*(6), 1289–1295.

Amirkhan, J. H., Risinger, R. T., & Swickert, R. J. (1995). Extra-version: A "hidden" personality factor in coping? *Journal of Personality, 63,* 189–212.

Amram, Y., & Benbenishty, R. (2014). The impact of therapeutic factors on locus of control of addicts in therapeutic communities. *Journal of Groups in Addiction Recovery, 9,* 313–325.

Anderson, C. (2004). An update on the effects of playing violent video games. *Journal of Adolescence, 27,* 113–122.

Anderson, C., John, O., Keltner, D., & Kring, A. (2001). Who attains social status? Effects of personality and physical attractiveness in social groups. *Journal of Personality and Social Psychology, 81,* 116–132.

Anderson, C. A., Shibuya, A., Ihori, N., Swing, E. L., Bushman, B. J., Sakamoto, A., et al. (2010). Violent video game effects on aggression, empathy, and prosocial behavior in Eastern and Western countries: A meta-analytic review. *Psychological Bulletin, 136,* 151–173.

Anderson, D. C., & Friedman, L. J. (1997). Erik Erikson on revolutionary leadership [Retrospective review of four books by Erikson]. *Contemporary Psychology, 42,* 1063–1067.

Anderson, J. W. (1988). Henry A. Murray's early career: A psychobiographical exploration. *Journal of Personality, 56,* 139–171.

Anderson, J. W. (1990). The life of Henry A. Murray: 1893–1988. In A. I. Rabin, R. A. Zucker, R. A. Emmons, & S. Frank (Eds.), *Studying persons and lives.* New York: Springer.

Anderson, S., Adams, G., & Plaut, V. (2008). The cultural grounding of personal relationships: The important of attractiveness in everyday life. *Journal of Personality and Social Psychology, 95*(2), 352–368.

Andreassen, C., Griffiths, M., Gjertsen, S., Krossbakken, E., Kvam, S., & Pallesen, S. (2013). The relationships between behavioral addictions and the five-factor model of personality. *Journal of Behavioral Addictions, 2,* 90–99.

Andreoletti, C., Zebrowitz, L. A., & Lachman, M. E. (2001). Physical appearance and control beliefs in young, middle-aged, and older adults. *Personality and Social Psychology Bulletin, 27,* 969–981.

Ang, R. (2006). Effects of parenting style on personal and social variables for Asian adolescents. *American Journal of Orthopsychiatry, 76,* 503–511.

Anthis, K., & LaVoie, J. (2006). Readiness to change: A longitudinal study of changes in adult identity. *Journal of Research in Personality, 40,* 209–219.

Apostal, R. A. (1991). College students' career interests and sensing-intuition personality. *Journal of College Student Development, 32,* 4–7.

Appignanesi, L., & Forrester, J. (1992). *Freud's women.* New York: Basic Books.

Arbisi, P., Ben-Porath, Y., & McNulty, J. (2002). A comparison of MMPI-2 validity in African-American and Caucasian psychiatric inpatients. *Psychological Assessment, 14*(1), 3–15.

Archer, S. L. (1982). The lower age boundaries of identity development. *Child Development, 53,* 1551–1556.

Aries, E., & Moorehead, K. (1989). The importance of ethnicity in the development of identity of black adolescents. *Psychological Reports, 65,* 75–82.

Ariso, J., & Reyero, D. (2014). Reconsidering the scenario of cyberbullying: Promoting the internalization of the locus of control in adolescents through cognitive restructuring. *Adolescent Psychiatry, 4,* 98–103.

Armstrong, A., & Dienes, Z. (2014). Subliminal understanding of active versus passive sentences. *Psychology of Consciousness: Theory, Research, and Practice, 1*(1), 32–50.

Arnett, J. J. (1999). Adolescent storm and stress, reconsidered. *American Psychologist, 54,* 317–326.

Arnold, E. (2005). A voice of their own: Women moving into their fifties. *Health Care for Women International, 26,* 630–651.

Arokach, A. (2006). Alienation and domestic abuse: How abused women cope with loneliness. *Social Indicators Research, 78,* 327–340.

Asberg, K., & Renk, K. (2014). Perceived stress, external locus of control, and social support as predictors of psychological adjustment among female inmates with or without a history of sexual abuse. *International Journal of Offender Therapy & Comparative Criminology, 58,* 59–84.

Asendorpf, J. B., & Wilpers, S. (1998). Personality effects on social relationships. *Journal of Personality and Social Psychology, 74,* 1531–1544.

Ashton, M. C., Lee, K., de Vries, R. E., Szarota, P., Marcu, B., Wasti, S. A., et al. (2006, July). *Lexical studies of personality structure.* Paper presented at the 13th European Conference on Personality, Athens, Greece.

Ashton, M. C., Lee, K., Perugini, M., Szarota, P., de Vries, R. E., Di Blas, L., et al. (2004). A six-factor structure of personality-descriptive adjectives: Solutions from psycholexical studies in seven languages. *Journal of Personality and Social Psychology, 86,* 356–366.

Ashton, M. C., & Lee, K. (2001). A theoretical basis for the major dimensions of personality. *European Journal of Personality, 15,* 327–333.

Ashton, M. C., & Lee, K. (2002). Six independent factors of personality variation. *European Journal of Personality, 16,* 63–75.

Ashton, M., & Lee, K. (2007). Empirical, theoretical, and practical advantages of the HEXACO model of personality structure. *Personality and Social Psychology Review, 11*(2), 150–166.

Ashton, M., & Lee, K. (2008). The HEXACO model of personality structure. In G. Boyle, G. Matthews, & D. Saklofske (Eds.), *The SAGE handbook of personality theory and assessment: Vol. 2. Personality measurement and testing* (pp. 239–260). Thousand Oaks, CA: Sage Publications.

Ashton, M., & Lee, K. (2009). The HEXACO-60: A short measure of the major dimensions of personality. *Journal of Personality Assessment, 91*(4), 340–345.

Ashton, M., Lee, K., & Paunonen, S. (2002). What is the central feature of extraversion? Social attention versus reward sensitivity. *Journal of Personality and Social Psychology, 83,* 245–252.

Aspinwall, L., & Tedeschi, R. (2010). The value of positive psychology for health psychology: Progress and pitfalls in examining the relation of positive phenomena to health. *Annals of Behavioral Medicine, 39,* 4–15.

Assor, A., Roth, G., & Deci, E. (2004). The emotional costs of parents' conditional regard: A self-determination theory analysis. *Journal of Personality, 72,* 47–87.

Assor, A., & Tai, K. (2012). When parents' affection depends on child's achievement: Parental conditional positive regard, self-aggrandizement, shame and coping in adolescents. *Journal of Adolescence, 36,* 249–260.

Atay, S. (2012). The standardization of the Myers-Briggs Type Indicator into Turkish: An application on students. *Journal of Instructional Psychology, 39,* 74–79.

Atkinson, J. W., Lens, W., & O'Malley, P. M. (1976). Motivation and ability: Interactive psychological determinants of intellectual performance, educational achievement, and each other. In W. H. Sewell, R. H. Hanser, & D. L. Featherman (Eds.), *Schooling and achievement in American society.* New York: Academic Press.

Ayllon, T., & Azrin, N. (1968). *The token economy.* New York: Appleton-Century-Crofts.

Ayoubui, R., & Ustwani, B. (2014). The relationship between students' MBTI preferences and academic performance at a Syrian university. *Education & Training, 56,* 78–90.

Azar, B. (2010). Your brain on culture: The burgeoning field of cultural neuroscience is finding that culture influences brain development, and perhaps vice versa. *Monitor on Psychology, 41*(10), 44–47.

Azar, B. (2011). Positive psychology advances, with growing pains. *Monitor on Psychology, 42*(4), 32–36.

Baars, B. J. (1986). *The cognitive revolution in psychology.* New York: Guilford Press.

Bacanli, F. (2006). Personality characteristics as predictors of personal indecisiveness. *Journal of Career Development, 32,* 320–332.

Back, M., Schmukle, S., & Egloff, B. (2006). Who is late and who is early? Big Five personality factors and punctuality in attending psychological experiments. *Journal of Research in Personality, 40,* 841–848.

Back, M., Stopfer, J., Vazire, S., Gaddiss, S., Schmuckle, S., Egloff, B., et al. (2010). Facebook profiles reflect actual personality, not self-idealization. *Psychological Science, 21*(3), 372–374.

Bacon, A., Burak, H., & Rann, J. (2014). Sex differences in the relationship between sensation seeking, trait emotional intelligence and delinquent behavior. *Journal of Forensic Psychiatry & Psychology, 25,* 673–683.

Badger, J., & Reddy, P. (2009). The effects of birth order on personality traits and feelings of academic sibling rivalry. *Psychology Teaching Review, 15,* 45–54.

Baek, Y., Bae, Y., & Jang, H. (2013). Social and parasocial relationships on social network sites and their differential relationships with users' psychological well-being. *Cyberpsychology: Behavior and Social Networking, 16*(7), 512–517.

Bair, D. (2003). *Jung: A biography.* Boston: Little Brown.

Bakalar, N. (2011, October 11). First mention: Sigmund Freud, 1909. *New York Times.*

Baldwin, A. L. (1949). The effect of home environment on nursery school behavior. *Child Development, 20,* 49–61.

Balistreri, E., Busch-Rossnagel, N. A., & Geisinger, K. F. (1995). Development and preliminary validation of the Ego Identity Process Questionnaire. *Journal of Adolescence, 18,* 179–182.

Ball, S. A., Carroll, K. M., & Rounsaville, B. J. (1994). Sensation seeking, substance abuse, and psychopathology in treatment-seeking and community cocaine abusers. *Journal of Consulting and Clinical Psychology, 62,* 1053–1057.

Ball, S. A., & Zuckerman, M. (1992). Sensation seeking and selective attention: Focused and divided attention on a dichotic listening task. *Journal of Personality and Social Psychology, 63,* 825–831.

Baltes, M. M., & Bates, P. B. (1986). *Psychology of control and aging.* Hillsdale, NJ: Erlbaum.

Bandura, A. (1965). Influence of models' reinforcement contingencies on the acquisition of imitative responses. *Journal of Personality and Social Psychology, 1,* 589–595.

Bandura, A. (1973). *Aggression: A social learning analysis.* Englewood Cliffs, NJ: Prentice-Hall.

Bandura, A. (1977). *Social learning theory.* Englewood Cliffs, NJ: Prentice-Hall.

Bandura, A. (1981). Distinguished scientific contribution award. *American Psychologist, 36,* 27–42.

Bandura, A. (1986). *Social foundations of thought and action: A social cognitive theory.* Englewood Cliffs, NJ: Prentice-Hall.

Bandura, A. (1995). Exercise of personal and collective efficacy in changing societies. In A. Bandura (Ed.), *Self-efficacy in changing societies* (pp. 1–45). Cambridge, England: Cambridge University Press.

Bandura, A. (1997). *Self-efficacy: The exercise of control.* New York: W. H. Freeman.

Bandura, A. (2001). Social cognitive theory: An agentic perspective. *Annual Review of Psychology, 52,* 1–26.

Bandura, A. (2011). But what about that gigantic elephant in the room? In R. Arkin (Ed.), *Most underappreciated: 50 prominent social psychologists describe their most unloved work* (pp. 51–59). New York: Oxford University Press.

Bandura, A. (2012). On the functional properties of perceived self-efficacy revisited. *Journal of Management, 38,* 9–44.

Bandura, A. (2013). The role of self-efficacy in goal-based motivation. In E. Locke & G. Latham (Eds.), *New developments in goal setting and task performance* (pp. 147–157). New York: Routledge/Taylor & Francis.

Bandura, A., Blanchard, E. B., & Ritter, B. (1969). The relative efficacy of desensitization and modeling approaches for inducing behavioral, affective, and attitudinal changes. *Journal of Personality and Social Psychology, 13,* 173–199.

Bandura, A., Caprara, G., Barbaranelli, C., Regalia, C., & Scabini, E. (2011). Impact of family efficacy beliefs on quality of family functioning and satisfaction with family life. *Applied Psychology: An International Review, 60,* 421–448.

Bandura, A., Grusec, J. E., & Menlove, F. L. (1967). Vicarious extinction of avoidance behavior through symbolic modeling. *Journal of Personality and Social Psychology, 5,* 16–22.

Bandura, A., Pastorelli, C., Barbaranelli, C., & Caprara, G. V. (1999). Self-efficacy pathways to childhood depression. *Journal of Personality and Social Psychology, 76,* 258–269.

Bandura, A., Ross, D., & Ross, S. A. (1963). Imitation of film-mediated aggressive models. *Journal of Abnormal and Social Psychology, 66,* 3–11.

Bandura, A., & Walters, R. (1963). *Social learning and personality development.* New York: Holt, Rinehart & Winston.

Bannister, D., Fransella, F., & Agnew, J. (1971). Characteristics and validity of the grid test on thought disorder. *British Journal of Social and Clinical Psychology, 10,* 144–151.

Bannister, D., & Salmon, P. (1966). Schizophrenic thought disorder: Specific or diffuse? *British Journal of Medical Psychology, 39,* 215–219.

Bardi, A., & Brady, M. (2010). Why shy people use instant messaging: Loneliness and other motives. *Computers in Human Behavior, 26,* 1722–1726.

Bardi, C., & Brady, M. (2010). Why shy people use instant messaging: Loneliness and other motives. *Computers in Human Behavior, 28,* 1722–1726.

Barelds, D. (2005). Self and partner personality in intimate relationships. *European Journal of Personality, 19,* 501–518.

Barenbaum, N. (2008). Allport's use of personal documents in psychological science: The case study book that wasn't. *General Psychologist, 43*(2), 53–55.

Barger, S. D., Kircher, J. C., & Croyle, R. T. (1997). The effects of social context and defensiveness on the physiological responses of repressive copers. *Journal of Personality and Social Psychology, 73,* 1118–1128.

Bargh, J. A., & Chartrand, T. L. (1999). The unbearable automaticity of being. *American Psychologist, 54,* 462–479.

Bargh, J. A., Gollwitzer, P., Lee-Chai, A., Barndollar, K., & Troetschel, R. (2001). The automated will: Nonconscious activation and pursuit of behavioral goals. *Journal of Personality and Social Psychology, 81,* 1014–1027.

Barlow, P., Tobin, D., & Schmidt, M. (2009). Social interest and positive psychology: Positively aligned. *Journal of Individual Psychology, 65*(3), 191–202.

Barnes, J., Boutwell, B., & Beaver, K. (2014). Genetic and non-shared environmental factors predict handgun ownership in early adulthood. *Death Studies, 38,* 156–164.

Barongan, C., & Hall, G. (1995). The influence of misogynous rap [music] on sexual aggression against women. *Psychology of Women Quarterly, 19,* 195–207.

Baroun, K., & Al-Ansari, B. (2005). The impact of anxiety and gender on perceiving the Mueller-Lyer illusion. *Social Behavior and Personality, 33,* 33–42.

Barrault, S., & Varesconi, I. (2013). Impulsive sensation seeking and gambling practice among a sample of online poker players: Comparison between nonpathological, problem and pathological gamblers. *Personality and Individual Differences, 55,* 502–507.

Barrett, A. (2005). Gendered experiences in midlife: Implications for age identity. *Journal of Aging Studies, 19,* 163–183.

Barrett, D., Sogolow, Z., Oh, A., Panton, J., Grayson, M., & Justiniano, M. (2014). Contents of dreams from WWII POWs. *Imagination, Cognition and Personality, 33,* 193–204.

Barrett, L., Lane, R., Sechrest, L., & Schwartz, G. (2000). Sex differences in emotional awareness. *Personality and Social Psychology Bulletin, 26,* 1027–1035.

Barrett-Lennard, G. (2012). The Roosevelt years: Crucial milieu for Carl Rogers' innovation. *History of Psychology, 15*(1), 19–32.

Barrick, M. R., & Mount, M. K. (1996). Effects of impression management and self-deception on the predictive validity of personality constructs. *Journal of Applied Psychology, 81,* 261–272.

Barrick, M. R., Mount, M. K., & Strauss, J. P. (1993). Conscientiousness and performance of sales representatives. Test of the mediating effects of goal setting. *Journal of Applied Psychology, 78,* 715–722.

Barrineau, P. (2005). Personality types among undergraduates who withdraw from liberal arts college. *Journal of Psychological Type, 65,* 27–32.

Barron, K., & Harackiewicz, J. (2001). Achievement goals and optimal motivation: Testing multiple goal models. *Journal of Personality and Social Psychology, 80,* 706–722.

Barry, L., Kasl, S., Lichtman, J., Vaccarino, V., & Krumholz, H. (2006). Perceived control and change in physical functioning after coronary artery bypass grafting. *International Journal of Behavioral Medicine, 13,* 229–236.

Bartholow, B., Sestir, M., & Davis, E. (2005). Correlates and consequences of exposure to videogame violence: Hostile personality, empathy, and aggressive behavior. *Personality and Social Psychology Bulletin, 31,* 1573–1586.

Bassi, M., Steca, P., Fave, A., & Caprara, G. (2007). Academic self-efficacy and quality of experience in learning. *Journal of Youth and Adolescence, 36,* 301–312.

Bassi, M., Steca, P., Monzani, D., Greco, A., & Fave, A. D. (2014). Personality and optimal experience in adolescence: Implication for well-being and development. *Journal of Happiness Studies, 15,* 829–843.

Batanowska-Ratij, A., Matysiak, A., & Mynarska, M. (2014). Does lone motherhood decrease women's happiness? Evidence from qualitative and quantitative research. *Journal of Happiness Studies, 15,* 1457–1477.

Battle, E., & Rotter, J. B. (1963). Children's feelings of personal control as related to social class and ethnic group. *Journal of Personality, 31,* 482–490.

Baughman, H., Jonason, P., Veselka, L., & Vernon, P. (2014). Four shades of sexual fantasies linked to the Dark Triad. *Personality and Individual Differences, 67,* 47–51.

Beaudoin, M., & Desrichard, O. (2011). Are memory self-efficacy and memory performance related? A meta-analysis. *Psychological Bulletin, 137*(2), 211–241.

Beaumont, S., & Zukanovic, R. (2005). Identity development in men and its relation to psychosocial distress and self-worth. *Canadian Journal of Behavioral Science, 37,* 70–81.

Beck, E., Burnet, K., & Vosper, J. (2006). Birth order effects on facets of extraversion. *Personality and Individual Differences, 40,* 953–959.

Becona, E., Frojan, M. J., & Lista, M. J. (1988). Comparison between two self-efficacy scales in maintenance of smoking cessation. *Psychological Reports, 62,* 359–362.

Begen, F., & Turner-Cobb, J. (2012). The need to belong and symptoms of acute physical health in early adolescence. *Journal of Health Psychology, 17,* 907–916.

Begue, L., & Roche, S. (2005). Birth order and youth delinquent behavior: Testing the differential parental control hypothesis in a French representative sample. *Psychology, Crime and Law, 11,* 73–85.

Belmont, L., & Marolla, F. A. (1973). Birth order, family size and intelligence. *Science, 182,* 1096–1101.

Benassi, V. A., Sweeney, P. D., & Dufour, C. L. (1988). Is there a relationship between locus of control orientation and depression? *Journal of Abnormal Psychology, 97,* 357–367.

Benet-Martinez, V., Lee, F., & Leu, J. (2006). Biculturalism and cultural complexity: Expertise in cultural representations. *Journal of Cross-Cultural Psychology, 37,* 386–407.

Benjafield, J. (2008). George Kelly: Cognitive psychologist, humanistic psychologist, or something else entirely? *History of Psychology, 11*(4), 239–262.

Bennett, D., Sullivan, M., & Lewis, M. (2010). Neglected children, shame-proneness, and depressive symptoms. *Child Maltreatment, 15*(4), 305–314.

Bennett, J. (2011, March 30). Does beauty buy happiness? *Yahoo! News.*

Benotsch, E., Jeffers, A., Snipes, D., Martin, A., & Koester, S. (2013). The five factor model of personality and the non-medical use of prescription drugs: Associations in a young adult sample. *Personality and Individual Differences, 55,* 852–855.

Benson-Townsend, B., & Silver, N. (2014, May 23). *Compulsive hoarding and consumer locus of control differences.* American Psychological Association Convention Presentation. http://aps.psychologicalscience.org/convention/program_2014/search/viewProgram.cfm?Abstract_ID=31662&AbType=&AbAuthor=271225&Subject_ID=&Day_ID= all&keyword=

Ben-Zur, H., & Zimmerman, M. (2005). Aging holocaust survivors' well-being and adjustment: Association with ambivalence over emotional expression. *Psychology and Aging, 20,* 710–713.

Berg, A., & Johansson, B. (2014). Personality change in the oldest-old: Is it a matter of compromised health and functioning? *Journal of Personality, 82,* 25–31.

Berg, M. B., Janoff-Bulman, P., & Cotter, J. (2001). Perceiving value in obligations and goals: Wanting to do what should be done. *Personality and Social Psychology Bulletin, 27,* 982–995.

Bergeman, C. S., Chipeur, H. M., Plomin, R., Pedersen, N. L., McClearn, G. E., Nesselroade, J. R., et al. (1993). Genetic and environmental effects on openness to experience, agreeableness, and conscientiousness: An adoption-twin study. *Journal of Personality, 61,* 159–179.

Bergin, A. E., & Strupp, H. H. (1972). *Changing frontiers in the science of psychotherapy.* New York: Aldine-Atherton.

Bergvik, S., Sorlie, T., & Wynn, R. (2012). Coronary patients who returned to work had stronger internal locus of control beliefs than those who did not return to work. *British Journal of Health Psychology, 17,* 596–608.

Berlin, M., & Kaunitz, N. (2014, September 20). Beyond income: The importance for life satisfaction of having access to a cash margin. *Journal of Happiness Studies.* http://link.springer.com/article/10.1007%2Fs10902-014-9575-7#page-2

Berry, D. S. (1990). Taking people at face value: Evidence for the kernel of truth hypothesis. *Social Cognition, 8,* 343–361.

Berry, D. S., & Wero, J. L. F. (1993). Accuracy in face perception: A view from ecological psychology. *Journal of Personality, 61,* 497–520.

Berzonsky, M. (2004). Identity style, parental authority, and identity commitment. *Journal of Youth and Adolescence, 33,* 213–220.

Bettelheim, B. (1984). *Freud and man's soul.* New York: Vintage Books.

Beyers, W., & Seiffge-Krenke, I. (2010). Does identity precede intimacy? Testing Erikson's theory on romantic development in emerging adults of the 21st century. *Journal of Adolescent Research, 25*(3), 387–415.

Biao-Bin, V., Man-Na, H., Bi-Qun, Q., & Yong-Hong, H. (2006). Relationship between Internet behavior and subjective well-being of teenagers. *Chinese Journal of Clinical Psychology, 14,* 68–69.

Billstedt, E., Skoog, I., Duberstein, T., Hallstrom, T., Andre, M., Lissner, L., et al. (2014). A 37-year prospective study of neuroticism and extraversion in women followed from mid-life to late life. *Acta Scandinavica, 129,* 35–43.

Bilsker, D., & Marcia, J. E. (1991). Adaptive regression and ego identity. *Journal of Adolescence, 14,* 75–84.

Birnbaum, M. (2004). Human research on data collection via the Internet. *Annual Review of Psychology, 55,* 803–832.

Bjork, D. W. (1993). *B. F. Skinner: A life.* New York: Basic Books.

Blackhart, G., Fitzpatrick, J., & Williamson, J. (2014). Dispositional factors predicting use of online dating sites and behaviors related to online dating. *Computers in Human Behavior, 33,* 113–118.

Blackman, D. E. (1995). B. F. Skinner (1904–1990). In R. Fuller (Ed.), *Seven pioneers of psychology: Behavior and mind* (pp. 107–129). London: Routledge.

Blais, J., Craig, W., Pepler, D., & Connolly, J. (2008). Adolescents online: The importance of Internet activity choices to salient relationships. *Journal of Youth & Adolescence, 37,* 522–536.

Blanton, H., Axsom, D., McClive, K., & Price, S. (2001). Pessimistic bias in comparative evaluations: A case of perceived vulnerability to the effects of negative life events. *Personality and Social Psychology Bulletin, 27,* 1627–1636.

Blanton, S. (1971). *Diary of my analysis with Sigmund Freud.* New York: Hawthorn Books.

Bleidorn, W., Kandler, C., Hulsheger, U., Reimann, R., Angleitner, A., & Spinath, F. (2010). Nature and nurture of the interplay between personality traits and major life goals. *Journal of Personality and Social Psychology, 99*(2), 366–379.

Block, J., & Block, J. (1980). The role of ego-control and ego-resiliency in the organization of behavior. In W. A. Collins (Ed.), *The Minnesota symposium on child psychology* (Vol. 13, pp. 39–101). Hillsdale, NJ: Erlbaum.

Block, J., & Block, J. (2006). Venturing a 30-year longitudinal study. *American Psychologist, 61,* 315–327.

Bloland, S. (2005). *In the shadow of fame: A memoir by the daughter of Erik H. Erikson.* New York: Viking Press.

Blosnich, J., Brown, G., Shipherd, J., Kauth, M., Piegeri, I., & Bossarte, R. (2013). Prevalence of gender identity disorder and suicide risk among transgender veterans utilizing Veterans Health Administration care. *American Journal of Public Health, 103,* 27–32.

Blume-Marcovici, A. (2010). Gender differences in dreams: Applications to dream work with male clients. *Dreaming, 20* (3), 199–210.

Blumer, T., & Doring, N. (2012). Are we the same online? The expression of the five factor personality traits on the computer and the Internet. *Cyberpsychology: Journal of Psychosocial Research on Cyberspace, 6*(3). http://www.cyberpsychology.eu/view.php?cisloclanku=2012121201

Bluml, V., Kapusta, N., Doering, S., Brahler, E., Wagner, B., & Kersting, A. (2013, October 4). Personality factors and suicide risk in a representative sample of the German general population. *PLoS ONE, 8,* Article e76646.

Blustein, D. L., Devenis, L. E., & Kidney, B. A. (1989). Relationship between the identity formation process and career development. *Journal of Counseling Psychology, 36,* 196–202.

Bockerman, P., Johansson, E., Saarni, S., & Saarni, S. (2014). The negative association of obesity with subjective well-being: Is it all about health? *Journal of Happiness Studies, 15,* 857–867.

Bockting, W. (2014). The impact of stigma on transgender identity development and mental health. In B. Kreukels, T. Steensma, & A. de Vries (Eds.), *Gender dysphoria and disorders of sex development: Progress in care and knowledge* (pp. 319–330). New York: US Springer Science.

Boden, J., & Baumeister, R. (1997). Repressive coping: Distraction using pleasant thoughts and memories. *Journal of Personality and Social Psychology, 73,* 45–62.

Bodin, M., & Romelsjo, A. (2006). Predictors of abstinence and nonproblem drinking after 12-step treatment in Sweden. *Journal of Studies on Alcohol, 67,* 139–146.

Boduszek, D., Shevlin, M., Adamson, G., & Hyland, P. (2013). Etsenck's personality model and criminal thinking within a violent and nonviolent offender sample: Application of propensity score analysis. *Deviant Behavior, 34,* 483–493.

Boehm, J., & Lyubomirsky, S. (2008). Does happiness promote career success? *Journal of Career Assessment, 16*(1), 101–116.

Bogaert, A. (2003). Number of older brothers and social orientation: New tests and the attraction/behavior distinction in two national probability samples. *Journal of Personality and Social Psychology, 84,* 644–652.

Bohart, A. (2014). *A deeper understanding of person-centered principles can enhance practiced.* American Psychological Association Convention Program. http://psycnet.apa.org/psycextra/538772014-001.pdf

Bonetti, L., Campbell, M., & Gilmore, L. (2010). The relationship of loneliness and social anxiety with children's and adolescents' online communication. *Cyberpsychology, Behavior, and Social Networking, 13*(3), 279–285.

Booth-Kewley, S., & Vickers, R. R., Jr. (1994). Associations between major domains of personality and health behavior. *Journal of Personality, 62,* 281–298.

Bores-Rangel, E., Church, A. T., Szendre, D., & Reeves, C. (1990). Self-efficacy in relation to occupational consideration and academic performance in high school equivalency students. *Journal of Counseling Psychology, 37,* 407–418.

Borgogni, L., Petitta, L., & Mastrorilli, A. (2010). Correlates of collective efficacy in the Italian Air Force. *Applied Psychology: An International Review, 59*(3), 515–537.

Borkenau, P., Riemann, R., Angleitner, A., & Spinath, F. (2001). Genetic and environmental influences on observed personality: Evidence from the German observational study of adult twins. *Journal of Personality and Social Psychology, 80,* 655–668.

Bornstein, R. F. (2001). The impending death of psychoanalysis. *Psychoanalytic Psychology, 18,* 2–20.

Bornstein, R. F. (2002). The impending death of psychoanalysis: From destructive obfuscation to constructive dialogue. *Psychoanalytic Psychology, 19,* 580–590.

Bornstein, R. F., & Masling, J. M. (1998). Introduction: The psychoanalytic unconscious. In R. F. Bornstein & J. M. Masling (Eds.), *Empirical perspectives on the psychoanalytic unconscious* (pp. xiii–xxviii). Washington, DC: American Psychological Association.

Bottome, P. (1939). *Alfred Adler: A biography.* New York: Putnam.

Bouchard, T. J. (1985). Twins reared together and apart: What they tell us about human diversity. In S. W. Fox (Ed.), *Individuality and determinism: Chemical and biological bases* (pp. 147–184). New York: Plenum Press.

Boucher, H. (2010). Understanding Western-East Asian differences and similarities in self-enhancement. *Social and Personality Psychology Compass, 4*(5), 304–317.

Bourne, E. (1978a). The state of research on ego identity: A review and appraisal. Part I. *Journal of Youth and Adolescence, 7,* 223–257.

Bourne, E. (1978b). The state of research on ego identity: A review and appraisal. Part II. *Journal of Youth and Adolescence, 7,* 371–392.

Bowker, A. (2006). The relationship between sports participation and self-esteem during early adolescence. *Canadian Journal of Behavioral Science, 38,* 214–229.

Bowler, M., Bowler, J., & Phillips, B. (2009). The Big- 5 ± 2? The impact of cognitive complexity on the factor structure of the five-factor model. *Personality and Individual Differences, 47,* 979–984.

Boyce, C., Wood, A., & Brown, G. (2010). The dark side of conscientiousness: Conscientious people experience greater drops in life satisfaction following unemployment. *Journal of Research in Personality, 44,* 535–539.

Bozarth, J. (2012). "Nondirectivity" in the theory of Carl R. Rogers: An unprecedented premise. *Person-Centered and Experiential Psychotherapies, 11,* 262–276.

Bozarth, J. (2013). Unconditional positive regard. In M. Cooper, M. O'Hara, P. Schmid, & A. Bohart (Eds.), *The handbook of person-centered psychotherapy and counselling*(2nd ed., pp. 180–192). New York: Palgrave Macmillan.

Bracey, J., Bamaca, M., & Umana-Taylor, A. (2004). Examining ethnic identity and self-esteem among biracial and monoracial adolescents. *Journal of Youth and Adolescence, 33,* 123–132.

Brannigan, G. G., Hauk, P. A., & Guay, J. A. (1991). Locus of control and daydreaming. *Journal of Genetic Psychology, 152,* 29–33.

Breger, L. (2000). *Freud: Darkness in the midst of vision.* New York: Wiley.

Breger, L., Hunter, I., & Lane, R. W. (1971). *The effect of stress on dreams.* New York: International Universities Press.

Breland, H. M. (1974). Birth order, family configuration and verbal achievement. *Child Development, 45,* 1011–1019.

Breland, K., & Breland, M. (1961). The misbehavior of organisms. *American Psychologist, 16,* 681–684.

Bridges, A., de Arellano, M., Rheingold, A., Danielson, C., & Silcott, L. (2010). Trauma exposure, mental health, and service utilization rates among immigrant and United States-born Hispanic youth: Results from the Hispanic family study. *Psychological Trauma: Theory, Research, Practice, & Policy, 2*(1), 40–48.

Briggs, K. C., & Myers, I. B. (1943, 1976). *Myers-Briggs type indicator.* Palo Alto, CA: Consulting Psychologists Press.

Briley, D., & Tucker-Drob, E. (2014). Genetic and environmental continuity in personality development: A meta-analysis. *Psychological Bulletin, 140,* 1303–1331.

Brissette, I., Scheier, M., & Carver, C. (2002). The role of optimism in social network development, coping, and psychological adjustment during a life transition. *Journal of Personality and Social Psychology, 82,* 102–111.

Brody, L. R., Rozek, M. K., & Muten, E. O. (1985). Age, sex, and individual differences in children's defensive styles. *Journal of Clinical Child Psychology, 14,* 132–138.

Brody, N. (1997). Dispositional paradigms: Comment on Eysenck (1997) and the biosocial science of individual differences. *Journal of Personality and Social Psychology, 73,* 1242–1245.

Broman, C. L. (1997). Race-related factors and life satisfaction among African Americans. *Journal of Black Psychology, 23,* 36–49.

Brome, V. (1981). *Jung: Man and myth.* New York: Atheneum.

Bronstein, P. (1988). Personality from a sociocultural perspective. In P. Bronstein & K. Quina (Eds.), *Teaching a psychology of people: Resources for gender and sociocultural awareness* (pp. 60–68). Washington, DC: American Psychological Association.

Brooks, S. (2015). Does personal social media usage affect efficiency and well-being? *Computers in Human Behavior, 46,* 26–37.

Brown, C., Matthews, K., & Bromberger, J. (2005). How do African-American and Caucasian women view themselves at midlife? *Journal of Applied Social Psychology, 35,* 2057–2075.

Brown, J. (2010). High self-esteem buffers negative feedback: Once more with feeling. *Cognition and Emotion, 24*(8), 1389–1404.

Brown, L. L., Tomarkin, A., Orth, D., Loosen, P., Kalin, N., & Davidson, R. (1996). Individual differences in repressive-defensiveness predict basal salivary cortisol levels. *Journal of Personality and Social Psychology, 70,* 362–371.

Brown, M., Brown, J., & Kovatch, A. (2013). *Self-enhancement bias in partner choice: My ideal mate is me—only.* Paper presented at the American Psychological Association Convention.

Bruhn, A. R. (1992a). The early memories procedure: A projective test of autobiographical memory. Part 1. *Journal of Personality Assessment, 58,* 1–15.

Bruhn, A. R. (1992b). The early memories procedure: A projective test of autobiographical memory. Part 2. *Journal of Personality Assessment, 58,* 326–346.

Bryant, B. L. (1987). Birth order as a factor in the development of vocational preferences. *Individual Psychology, 43,* 36–41.

Buchanan, L. P., Kern, R., & Bell-Dumas, J. (1991). Comparison of content in created versus actual early recollections. *Individual Psychology, 47,* 348–355.

Buchanan, T., Johnson, J., & Goldberg, L. (2005). Implementing a five-factor personality inventory for use on the Internet. *European Journal of Psychological Assessment, 21,* 115–127.

Buckels, E., Trapnell, P., & Paulhus, D. (2014). Trolls just want to have fun. *Personality and Individual Differences, 67,* 97–102.

Budge, S., Adelson, J., & Howard, K. (2013). Anxiety and depression in transgender individuals: The roles of transition, loss, social support and coping. *Journal of Consulting and Clinical Psychology, 81,* 545–557.

Buhrmester, M., Kwang, T., & Gosling, S. (2011). Amazon's Mechanical Turk: A new source of inexpensive, yet high-quality data? *Perspectives on Psychological Science, 6*(1), 3–5.

Bullard, A. (2005). The critical impact of Franz Fanon and Henri Collomb: Race, gender, and personality testing of North and West Africans. *Journal of the History of the Behavioral Sciences, 41,* 225–248.

Bullock, W. A., & Gilliland, K. (1993). Eysenck's arousal theory of introversion-extraversion: A converging measures investigation. *Journal of Personality and Social Psychology, 64,* 113–123.

Burger, J., & Lynn, A. (2005). Superstitious behavior among American and Japanese professional baseball players. *Basic and Applied Social Psychology, 27,* 71–76.

Burling, S. (2010, May 30). The power of a positive thinker. *Philadelphia Inquirer.*

Busch, F. N., Shear, M. K., Cooper, A. M., Shapiro, T., & Leon, A. (1995). An empirical study of defense mechanisms in panic disorder. *Journal of Nervous and Mental Disease, 183,* 299–303.

Buse, A. (2010). Video game play and computer self-efficacy: College students in computer related and noncomputer related disciplines. *Dissertation Abstracts International. Section A: Humanities and Social Sciences,* 851.

Bushman, B., & Whitaker, J. (2010). Like a magnet: Catharsis beliefs attract angry people to violent video games. *Psychological Science, 21*(6), 790–792.

Bushman, B. J. (2002). Does venting anger feed or extinguish the flame? Catharsis, rumination, distraction, anger, and aggressive responding. *Personality and Social Psychology Bulletin, 28,* 724–731.

Bushman, B. J., Baumeister, R. F., & Stack, A. D. (1999). Catharsis, aggression, and persuasive influence: Self-fulfilling or self-defeating prophecies? *Journal of Personality and Social Psychology, 76,* 367–376.

Bushman, B., Bonacci, A., Pedersen, W., Vasquez, E., & Miller, N. (2005). Chewing on it can chew you up: Effects of rumination on triggered displaced aggression. *Journal of Personality and Social Psychology, 88,* 969–983.

Bushman, B., Moeller, S., & Crocker, J. (2011). Sweets, sex, or self-esteem? Comparing the value of self-esteem boosts with other pleasant rewards. *Journal of Personality, 79,* 993–1012.

Buss, A. H. (1988). *Personality: Evolutionary heritage and human distinctiveness.* Hillsdale, NJ: Erlbaum.

Buss, A. H., & Plomin, R. (1975). *A temperament theory of personality development.* New York: Wiley.

Buss, A. H., & Plomin, R. (1984). *Temperament: Early developing personality traits.* Hillsdale, NJ: Erlbaum.

Buss, A. H., & Plomin, R. (1986). The EAS approach to temperament. In R. Plomin & J. Dunn (Eds.), *The study of temperament: Changes, continuities and challenges* (pp. 67–79). Hillsdale, NJ: Erlbaum.

Bussey, K., Fitzpatrick, S., & Raman, A. (2015). The role of moral disengagement and self-efficacy in cyberbullying. *Journal of School Violence, 14,* 30–46.

Butcher, J. (2004). Personality assessment without borders: Adaptation of the MMPI-2 across cultures. *Journal of Personality Assessment, 83,* 90–104.

Butcher, J. (2010). Personality assessment from the nineteenth to the early twenty-first century: Past achievement and contemporary challenges. *Annual Review of Clinical Psychology, 6,* 1–20.

Butkovic, A., Ullen, F., & Mosing, M. (2015). Personality related traits as predictors of music practice: Underlying environmental and genetic influences. *Personality and Individual Differences, 74,* 133–138.

Butler, J. M., & Haigh, G. V. (1954). Changes in the relationship between self-concepts and ideal concepts consequent upon client-centered counseling. In C. R. Rogers & R. F. Dymond (Eds.), *Psychotherapy and Personality Change.* Chicago, IL: University of Chicago Press.

Butt, T. (2008). *George Kelly and the psychology of personal constructs (mind shapers).* New York: Palgrave Macmillan.

Butts, S., & Phillips, J. (2008). Personality and self reported mobile phone use. *Computers in Human Behavior, 24,* 346–360.

Bynum, M., Burton, E., & Best, C. (2007). Racism experiences and psychological functioning in African-American college freshmen: Is racial socialization a buffer? *Cultural Diversity and Ethnic Minority Psychology, 13,* 64–71.

Cai, H., Wu, Q., & Brown, J. D. (2009). Is self-esteem a universal need? Evidence of People's Republic of China. *Asian Journal of Social Psychology, 12,* 104–120.

Cain, D. (2013). Person-centered therapy. In J. Frew & D. Spiegler (Eds.), *Contemporary psychotherapies for a diverse world* (1st rev. ed., pp. 165–213). New York: Routledge Taylor & Francis.

Cain, D. (2014). Person-centered therapy. In G. VandenBlos, E. Meidenbauer, & N. K. Frank (Eds.), *Psychotherapy techniques: A reader* (pp. 251–259). Washington, DC: American Psychological Association.

Cakir, S. (2014). Ego identity status and psychological well-being among Turkish emerging adults. *Identity: An International Journal of Theory and Research, 14,* 230–239.

Caldwell, R., Beutler, L., Ross, S., & Silver, N. (2006). An examination of the relationships between parental monitoring, self-esteem and delinquency among Mexican-American adolescents. *Journal of Adolescence, 29,* 459–464.

Calvert, S., Strouse, G., Strong, B., Huffaker, D., & Lai, S. (2009). Preadolescent girls' and boys' virtual MUD play. *Journal of Applied Developmental Psychology, 30*(3), 250–264.

Calvete, E., Orue, I., Estevez, A., Villardon, L., & Padilla, P. (2010). Cyberbullying in adolescents: Modalities and aggressors' profile. *Computer in Human Behavior, 26*(5), 1128–1135.

Campbell, A., Alana, M., Davalos, D., McCabe, D., & Troup, L. (2011). Executive functions and extraversion. *Personality and Individual Differences, 51,* 720–725.

Campbell, W. K., Rudich, E. A., & Sedikides, C. (2002). Narcissism, self-esteem, and the positivity of self-views: Two portraits of self-love. *Personality and Social Psychology Bulletin, 28,* 358–368.

Camras, L. (1998). Production of emotional facial expressions in European American, Japanese, and Chinese infants. *Developmental Psychology, 34,* 616–628.

Camras, L., Bakeman, R., Chen, Y., Norris, K., & Cain, T. (2006). Culture, ethnicity, and children's facial expressions: A study of European, American, Mainland Chinese, Chinese American, and adopted Chinese girls. *Emotion, 6,* 103–114.

Camras, L., Oster, H., Campos, J. J., Miyake, K., & Bradshaw, D. (1998). Japanese and American infants' responses to arm restraint. In P. Ekman & E. L. Rosenberg (Eds.), *What the face reveals* (pp. 289–301). New York: Oxford University Press.

Cann, D. R., & Donderi, D. C. (1986). Jungian personality typology and the recall of everyday and archetypal dreams. *Journal of Personality and Social Psychology, 50,* 1021–1030.

Canter, D., Sarangi, S., & Youngs, D. (2014). Terrorists' personal constructs and their roles: A comparison of three Islamic terrorists. *Legal and Criminological Psychology, 19,* 160–178.

Caplan, P. J. (1979). Erikson's concept of inner space: A data-based reevaluation. *American Journal of Orthopsychiatry, 49,* 100–108.

Capron, E. (2004). Types of pampering and the narcissistic personality trait. *Journal of Individual Psychology, 60,* 76–83.

Carlson, R. (1980). Studies of Jungian typology: II. Representations of the personal world. *Journal of Personality and Social Psychology, 38,* 801–810.

Carlson, R., & Levy, N. (1973). Studies of Jungian typology: I. Memory, social perception, and social action. *Journal of Personality, 41,* 559–576.

Carmichael, C. M., & McGue, M. (1994). A longitudinal family study of personality change and stability. *Journal of Personality, 62,* 1–20.

Carr, D. (2004). "My daughter has a career; I just raised babies." The psychological consequences of women's intergenerational social comparison. *Social Psychology Quarterly, 67,* 132–154.

Carr, D., Freedman, V., Cornman, J., & Schwarz, N. (2014). Happy marriage, happy life? Marital quality and subjective well-being in later life. *Journal of Marriage and Family, 76,* 930–948.

Carskadon, T. G. (1978). Use of the Myers-Briggs Type Indicator in psychology courses and discussion groups. *Teaching of Psychology, 5,* 140–142.

Carver, C., & Connor-Smith, J. (2010). Personality and coping. In S. Fiske, R. Schacter, & R. Sternberg (Eds.), *Annual review of psychology, 61,* 679–704.

Carver, C. S., Harris, S. D., Lehman, J. H., Durel, L. A., Anton, M. H., Spencer, S. M., & Pozo-Kaderman, C. (2000). How important is the perception of personal control? Studies of early stage breast cancer patients. *Personality and Social Psychology Bulletin, 26,* 139–149.

Carver, C. S., & Scheier, M. (2002). Optimism. In C. Snyder & S. Lopez (Eds.), *Handbook of positive psychology* (pp. 231–243). New York: Oxford University Press.

Carver, C., & Scheier, M. (2014). Dispositional optimism. *Trends in Cognitive Science, 18,* 293–299.

Caspi, A., Bem, D. J., & Elder, G. H. (1989). Continuities and consequences of interactional styles across the life course. *Journal of Personality, 57,* 375–406.

Caspi, A., Elder, G. H., & Bem, D. J. (1987). Moving against the world: Life course patterns of explosive children. *Developmental Psychology, 23,* 308–313.

Caspi, A., Elder, G. H., & Bem, D. J. (1988). Moving away from the world: Life course patterns of shy children. *Developmental Psychology, 24,* 824–831.

Caspi, A., Roberts, B., & Shiner, R. (2005). Personality development: Stability and change. *Annual Review of Psychology, 56,* 453–484.

Caspi, A., & Silva, P. (1994). Temperamental qualities at age 3 predict personality traits in young adulthood: Longitudinal evidence from a birth cohort. *Child Development, 66,* 486–498.

Castro, A., Echavarria, A., & Velasquez, R. (2010). *Locus of control and depression in culturally diverse psychiatric patients.* American Psychological Association Convention Presentation.

Cattell, R. B. (1950). *Personality: A systematic theoretical and factual study.* New York: McGraw-Hill.

Cattell, R. B. (1959). Foundations of personality measurement theory in multivariate expression. In B. M. Bass & I. A. Berg (Eds.), *Objective approaches to personality assessment* (pp. 42–65). Princeton, NJ: Van Nostrand.

Cattell, R. B. (1965, 1970). *The scientific analysis of personality.* Baltimore, MD: Penguin Books.

Cattell, R. B. (1973). *Personality and mood by questionnaire.* San Francisco: Jossey-Bass.

Cattell, R. B. (1974a). Autobiography. In G. Lindzey (Ed.), *A history of psychology in autobiography* (Vol. 6, pp. 59–100). Englewood Cliffs, NJ: Prentice-Hall.

Cattell, R. B. (1974b). Travels in psychological hyperspace. In T. S. Krawiec (Ed.), *The psychologists* (Vol. 2, pp. 85–133). New York: Oxford University Press.

Cattell, R. B. (1982). *The inheritance of personality and ability: Research methods.* New York: Academic Press.

Cattell, R. B. (1990). Advances in Cattellian personality theory. In (Ed.), *Handbook of personality: Theory and research* (pp. 101–110). New York: Guilford Press.

Cattell, R. B. (1993). Planning basic clinical research. In C. E. Walker (Ed.), *The history of clinical psychology in autobiography* (Vol. 2, pp. 101–111). Pacific Grove, CA: Brooks/Cole.

Cattell, R. B. (1997). Gold medal award for life achievement in psychological science. *American Psychologist, 52,* 797–799.

Cattell, R. B., Eber, H. W., & Tatsuoka, M. M. (1970). *Handbook for the sixteen personality factor questionnare.* Champaign, IL: Institute for Personality and Ability Testing.

Cattell, R. B., & Kline, P. (1977). *The scientific analysis of personality and motivation.* New York: Academic Press.

Cattell, R. B., & Nesselroade, J. R. (1967). Likeness and completeness theories examined by sixteen personality factor measures by stably and unstably married couples. *Journal of Personality and Social Psychology, 7,* 351–361.

Ceci, S. J., & Bruck, M. (1993). Suggestibility of the child witness: A historical review and synthesis. *Psychological Bulletin, 113,* 403–439.

Chae, M., & Foley, P. (2010). Relationship of ethnic identity, acculturation, and psychological well-being among Chinese, Japanese, and Korean Americans. *Journal of Counseling and Development, 88,* 466–476.

Chamber, S., & Hammonds, F. (2014). Vicariously learned helplessness: The role of perceived dominance and prestige of a model. *Journal of General Psychology, 141,* 280–295.

Chamorro-Premuzic, T., Furnham, A., & Petrides, K. (2006). Personality and intelligence: The relationship of Eysenck's giant three with verbal and numerical ability. *Journal of Individual Differences, 27,* 147–150.

Chang, E., Asakawa, K., & Sanna, L. (2001). Cultural variations in optimistic and pessimistic bias: Do Easterners really expect the worst and Westerners really expect the best when predicting future life events? *Journal of Personality and Social Psychology, 81,* 476–491.

Chang, E., & Sanna, L. (2001). Optimism, pessimism, and positive and negative affectivity in middle-aged adults: A test of a cognitive-affective model of psychological adjustment. *Psychology and Aging, 16*, 524–531.

Chang, E., Yu, E., Lee, J., Hirsh, J., Kupfermann, Y., & Kahle, E. (2013). An examination of optimism/pessimism and suicide risk in primary care patients: Does belief in a changeable future make a difference? *Cognitive Therapy and Research, 37*, 796–804.

Chang, J., & Le, T. (2010). Multiculturalism as a dimension of school climate: The impact on the academic achievement of Asian American and Hispanic youth. *Cultural Diversity and Ethnic Minority Psychology, 16*, 485–492.

Chen, B., Vensteenkiste, M., Beyers, W., Boone, L., Deci, E., Kaap-Deeder, J., et al. (2014, November 12). Basic psychological need satisfaction, need frustration, and need strength across four cultures. *Motivation and Emotion.* http://psycnet.apa.org/index.cfm?fa=search.displayRecord&id=FE589B10-CBC6-0020-31B0-7A5C7433870E&resultID=1&page=1&dbTab=all&search=true

Chen, J., & Wang, L. (2007). Locus of control and the three components of commitment to change. *Personality and Individual Differences, 42*, 503–512.

Chen, X., Li, F., Nydegger, L., Gong, J., Ren, Y., Dinaj-Koci, V., et al. (2013). Brief sensation seeking scale for Chinese: Cultural adaptation and psychometric assessment. *Personality and Individual Differences, 54*, 604–609.

Cheng, C., Cheung, S., Chio, J., & Chan, M. (2013). Cultural meaning of perceived control: A meta-analysis of locus of control and psychological symptoms across 18 cultural regions. *Psychological Bulletin, 139*, 152–188.

Cheng, S. (2009). Generativity in later life: Perceived respect from younger generations as a determinant of goal disengagement and psychological well-being. *Journals of Gerontology: Series B: Psychological Sciences and Social Sciences, 64B*(1), 45–54.

Chentsova-Dutton, Y., Tsai, J., & Gotlib, I. (2010). Further evidence for the cultural norm hypothesis: Positive emotion in depressed and control European American and Asian American women. *Cultural Diversity and Ethnic Minority Psychology, 16*, 284–295.

Cherry, R., & Cherry, L. (1973, August 26). The horney heresy. *New York Times Magazine*, p. 12ff.

Chesney, M. A., Ekman, P., Friesen, W. V., Black, G. W., & Hecker, M. H. L. (1997). Type A behavior pattern: Facial behavior and speech components. In P. Ekman & E. L. Rosenberg (Eds.), *What the face reveals* (pp. 456–466). New York: Oxford University Press.

Cheung, F. (2009). The cultural perspectives in personality assessment. In J. Butcher (Ed.), *Oxford handbook of personality assessment* (pp. 44–56). New York: Oxford University Press.

Chiao, J., & Blizinsky, K. (2010). Culture–gene coevolution of individualism–collectivism and the serotonin transporter gene. *Proceedings of the Royal Society of Biological Science, 277*, 529–537.

Chiesa, M. (2010). Research and psychoanalysis: Still time to bridge the great divide? *Psychoanalytic Psychology, 27*(2), 99–114.

Chirumbolo, A., & Leone, L. (2010). Personality and politics: The role of the HEXACO model of personality in predicting ideology and voting. *Personality and Individual Differences, 49*(1), 43–48.

Chodorkoff, B. (1954). Self-perception, perceptual defense, and adjustment. *Journal of Abnormal and Social Psychology, 49*, 508–512.

Chowdhury, M., & Amin, M. (2006). Personality and students' academic achievement: Interactive effects of conscientiousness and agreeableness on students' performance in principles of economics. *Social Behavior and Personality, 34*, 381–388.

Christensen, A., Ehlers, S., Wiebe, J., Moran, P., Raichle, K., Ferneyhough, K., et al. (2002). Patient personality and mortality: A 4-year prospective study of chronic renal insufficiency. *Health Psychology, 21*, 315–320.

Chuah, S., Drasgow, F., & Roberts, B. (2006). Personality assessment: Does the medium matter? No. *Journal of Research in Personality, 40*, 359–376.

Chuang, S., Lamb, M., & Hwang, C. (2006). Personality development from childhood to adolescence: A longitudinal study of ego-control and ego-resiliency in Sweden. *International Journal of Behavioral Development, 30*(4), 338–343.

Chung, H. (2008). Resiliency and character strengths among college students. *Dissertation Abstracts International. Section B: Sciences and Engineering, 2664.*

Church, A., Katigbak, M., Mazuera, A., Rina, R., Brigida, C., Vargas-Flores, J., et al. (2014). A four-culture study of self-enhancement and adjustment using the social relations model: Do alternative conceptualizations and indices make a difference? *Journal of Personality and Social Psychology, 106*, 997–1014.

Church, A., Kayigbak, M., Locke, K., Zhang, H., Shen, J., Vargas-Flores, J., et al. (2013). Need satisfaction and well-being: Testing self-determination theory in eight cultures. *Journal of Cross-Cultural Psychology, 44*, 507–534.

Church, A., & Lonner, W. J. (1998). The cross-cultural perspective in the study of personality. *Journal of Cross-Cultural Psychology, 29*, 32–62.

Ciaccio, N. (1971). A test of Erikson's theory of ego epigenesis. *Developmental Psychology, 4*, 306–311.

Ciarrochi, J., & Heaven, P. (2007). Longitudinal examination of the impact of Eysenck's psychoticism dimension on emotional well-being in teenagers. *Personality and Individual Differences, 42*, 597–608.

Ciarrochi, J., & Heaven, P. (2008). Learned social helplessness: The role of explanatory style in predicting social support during adolescence. *Journal of Child Psychology and Psychiatry, 49*(2), 1279–1286.

Clark, A. (2005). An early recollection of Albert Einstein: Perspectives on its meaning and his life. *Journal of Individual Psychology, 61*, 126–136.

Clark, A. J. (2009). Early recollections and object meanings. *Journal of Individual Psychology, 65*(2), 123–134.

Clark, J. (2010). Life as a source of theory: Erik Erikson's contributions, boundaries, and marginalities. In T. Miller (Ed.), *Handbook of stressful transitions across the lifespan* (pp. 59–83). New York: Springer.

Clark, M., & Arnold, J. (2008). The nature, prevalence and correlates of generativity among men in middle career. *Journal of Vocational Behavior, 73*, 473–484.

Clayson, J. (2013). Talking statistics/talking ourselves: Some constructionist lessons from the work of the psychologist

George Kelly. *Technology, Knowledge and Learning, 18,* 181–199.

Clemmens, E. R. (1987). Karen Horney, a reminiscence. In K. Horney (Ed.), *Final lectures* (pp. 107–115). New York: Norton.

Clough, S. (2009). Computerized versus paper-and-pencil assessment of socially desirable responding: Score congruence, completion time, and respondent behavior. *Dissertation Abstracts International. Section A: Humanities & Social Sciences, 4700.*

Coan, R. W. (1972). Measurable components of openness to experience. *Journal of Consulting and Clinical Psychology, 39,* 346.

Cobb-Clark, S., Kassenboehmer, S., & Schurer, S. (2014). Healthy habits: The connection between diet, exercise, and locus of control. *Journal of Economic Behavior and Organization, 98,* 1–28.

Cohen, J. B. (1967). An interpersonal orientation to the study of consumer behavior. *Journal of Marketing Research, 4,* 270–278.

Cohen, S., & Wills, T. A. (1985). Stress, social support, and the buffering hypothesis. *Psychological Bulletin, 98,* 310–357.

Cokley, K. (2002). Testing Cross's racial identity model: An examination of the relationship between racial identity and internalized racialism. *Journal of Counseling Psychology, 49,* 476–483.

Colby, D., & Shifren, K. (2013). Optimism, mental health, and quality of life: A study among breast cancer patients. *Psychology, Health & Medicine, 18,* 10–20.

Coleman, J. S., Campbell, E. Q., Hobson, C. J., McPartland, J., Mood, A. M., Weinfeld, F. D., et al. (1966). *Equality of educational opportunity.* Washington, DC: U.S. Office of Education.

Coles, R. (1998). Psychoanalysis: The American experience. In M. S. Roth (Ed.), *Conflict and culture* (pp. 140–151). New York: Knopf.

Collado, A., Felton, J., MacPherson, L., & Lejuez, C. (2014). Longitudinal trajectories of sensation seeking, risk taking propensity, and impulsivity across early to middle adolescence. *Addictive Behaviors, 39,* 1580–1588.

Collisson, B. (2013). The social projection of belongingness needs. *North American Journal of Psychology, 15,* 513–526.

Colombo, F., Balbo, M., & Baruffi, M. (2006). Subjective well-being in a sample of Italian students. *Homeostasis in Health and Disease, 44,* 34–39.

Combs, D., Penn, D., & Fenigstein, A. (2002). Ethnic differences in subclinical paranoia: An expansion of norms of the paranoia scale. *Cultural Diversity and Ethnic Minority Psychology, 8,* 248–256.

Compton, W. (2006). *An introduction to positive psychology.* Belmont, CA: Thomson Wadsworth.

Connelly, B., & Ones, D. (2010). Another perspective on personality: Meta-analytic integration of observers' accuracy and predictive ability. *Psychological Bulletin, 136,* 1092–1122.

Conner, M., & Abraham, C. (2001). Conscientiousness and the theory of planned behavior: Toward a more complete model of the antecedents of intentions and behavior. *Personality and Social Psychology Bulletin, 27,* 1547–1561.

Constantine, M., Alleyne, V., Wallace, B., & Franklin-Jackson, D. (2006). Africentric cultural values: Their relation to positive mental health in African-American adolescent girls. *Journal of Black Psychology, 32,* 141–154.

Constantinople, A. (1969). An Eriksonian measure of personality development in college students. *Developmental Psychology, 1,* 357–372.

Contarello, A., & Sarrica, M. (2007). ICTs, social thinking and subjective well-being: The Internet and its representations in everyday life. *Computers in Human Behavior, 23,* 1016–1032.

Conway, F., Magai, C., Springer, C., & Jones, S. (2008). Optimism and pessimism as predictors of physical and psychological health among grandmothers raising their grand children. *Journal of Research in Personality, 42,* 1352–1357.

Conway, M., & Holmes, A. (2004). Psychosocial stages and the accessibility of autobiographical memories across the life cycle. *Journal of Personality, 72,* 461–480.

Coolidge, F., Moor, C. J., Yamazaki, T. G., Stewart, S. E., & Segal, D. L. (2001). On the relationship between Karen Horney's tripartite neurotic type theory and personality disorder features. *Personality and Individual Differences, 30,* 1387–1400.

Coolidge, F., Segal, D., Benight, C., & Danielian, J. (2004). The predictive power of Horney's psychoanalytic approach. *American Journal of Psychoanalysis, 64,* 363–374.

Coolidge, F., Segal, D., & Estey, A. (2010). *New measure of Karen Horney's tridimensional theory in children.* American Psychological Association Convention Presentation.

Coolidge, F., Segal, D., Estey, A., & Neuzil, P. (2011). Preliminary psychometric properties of Karen Horney's Tridimensional Theory in children and adolescents. *Journal of Clinical Psychology, 67,* 383–390.

Coopersmith, S. (1967). *The antecedents of self-esteem.* New York: W. H. Freeman.

Corbett, S. (2009, September 20). The Holy Grail of the unconscious. *New York Times.*

Corby, B., Hodges, E., & Perry, D. (2007). Gender identity and adjustment in Black, Hispanic, and White preadolescents. *Developmental Psychology, 43,* 261–266.

Corr, P. (2007). Personality and psychology: Hans Eysenck's unifying themes. *Psychologist, 21,* 666–669.

Correa, T., Hinsley, A., & de Zuniga, H. (2010). Who interacts on the web? The intersection of users' personality and social media use. *Computers in Human Behavior, 26*(2), 247–253.

Costa, P. T., Jr., & McCrae, R. R. (1984). Personality as a lifelong determinant of well-being. In C. Z. Malatesta & C. E. Izard (Eds.), *Emotion in adult development* (pp. 141–158). Beverly Hills, CA: Sage.

Costa, P. T., Jr., & McCrae, R. R. (1988). Personality in adulthood: A six-year longitudinal study of self-reports and spouse ratings on the NEO Personality Inventory. *Journal of Personality and Social Psychology, 54,* 853–863.

Costescu, C., Vanderborght, B., & David, D. (2014). The effects of robot-enhanced psychotherapy: A meta-analysis. *Review of General Psychology, 18,* 127–136.

Cote, J. E., & Levine, C. (1988). The relationship between ego identity status and Erikson's notions of institutionalized moratoria, value orientation stage, and ego dominance. *Journal of Youth and Adolescence, 17,* 81–99.

Couturier, J., & Lock, J. (2006). Denial and minimization in adolescents with anorexia nervosa. *International Journal of Eating Disorders, 39,* 212–216.

Cowan, D. A. (1989). An alternative to the dichotomous interpretation of Jung's psychological functions: Developing more sensitive measurement technology. *Journal of Personality Assessment, 53,* 459–471.

Cox, A., Weed, N., & Butcher, J. (2009). The MMPI-2: History, interpretation, & clinical issues. In J. Butcher (Ed.), *Oxford handbook of personality assessment* (pp. 250–276). New York: Oxford University Press.

Cox, K., Wilt, J., Olson, B., & McAdams, D. (2010). Generativity, the Big Five, and psychosocial adaption in midlife adults. *Journal of Personality, 78*(4), 1185–1208.

Cozzarelli, C. (1993). Personality and self-efficacy as predictors of coping with abortion. *Journal of Personality and Social Psychology, 65,* 1224–1236.

Cramer, P. (1987). The development of defense mechanisms. *Journal of Personality, 54,* 597–614.

Cramer, P. (1990). *The development of defense mechanisms: Theory, research and assessment.* New York: Springer-Verlag.

Cramer, P. (2007). Longitudinal study of defense mechanisms: Late childhood to late adolescence. *Journal of Personality, 75,* 1–24.

Cramer, P. (2009). The development of defense mechanisms from pre-adolescence to early adulthood: Do IQ and social class matter? A longitudinal study. *Journal of Research in Personality, 43*(3), 464–471.

Cramer, P., & Block, J. (1998). Preschool antecedents of defense mechanism use in young adults: A longitudinal study. *Journal of Personality and Social Psychology, 74,* 159–169.

Cramer, P., & Kelly, F. (2010). Attachment style and defense mechanisms in parents who abuse their children. *Journal of Nervous and Mental Disease, 198*(9), 619–627.

Crandall, J. E. (1981). *Theory and measurement of social interest: Empirical tests of Alfred Adler's concept.* New York: Columbia University Press.

Crandall, J. E. (1984). Social interest as a moderator of life stress. *Journal of Personality and Social Psychology, 47,* 164–174.

Crawford, T., Cohen, P., Johnson, J., Sneed, J., & Brook, J. (2004). The course and psychological correlates of personality disorder symptoms in adolescence: Erikson's developmental theory revisited. *Journal of Youth and Adolescence, 33,* 373–387.

Crewsdon, J. (1988). *By silence betrayed: Sexual abuse of children in America.* Boston: Little, Brown.

Crighton, A., Applegate, K., Wygant, S., Granacher, R., & Umlauf, R. (2013). The MMPI-2 Restructured form can differentiate between pain and pain malingering. *American Psychology-Law Society Annual Conference Presentation.* http://citation.allacademic.com/meta/p_mla_apa_research_-citation/6/3/2/2/8/p632285_index.html

Crocker, J., & Luhtanen, R. (2003). Level of self-esteem and contingencies of self-worth: Unique effects on academic, social, and financial problems in college students. *Personality and Social Psychology Bulletin, 29,* 701–712.

Crocker, J., & Park, L. (2004). The costly pursuit of self-esteem. *Psychological Bulletin, 130,* 392–414.

Crockett, W. H. (1982). The organization of construct systems: The organization corollary. In J. C. Mancuso & J. R. Adams-Webber (Eds.), *The construing person.* New York: Praeger.

Crook, T., Raskin, A., & Eliot, J. (1981). Parent-child relationships and adult depression. *Child Development, 52,* 950–957.

Cross, W., Grant, B., & Ventuneac, A. (2012). Black identity and well-being: Untangling race and ethnicity. In J. Sullivan & A.

Esmail (Eds.), *African-American identity: Racial and cultural dimensions of the black experience* (pp. 125–146). Lanham, MD: Lexington Books/Rowan & Littlefield.

Crowe, M., Andel, R., Pedersen, N., Fratiglioni, L., & Gatz, M. (2006). Personality and risk of cognitive impairment 25 years later. *Psychology and Aging, 21,* 573–580.

Crozier, W., & Birdsey, N. (2003). Shyness, sensation seeking and birth-order position. *Personality and Individual Differences, 35,* 127–134.

Crump, M., McDonnell, J., & Gureckis, T. (2013). Evaluating Amazon's Mechanical Turk as a tool for experimental behavioral research. *PLoS ONE, 8*(3). http://www.plosone.org/article/info%3Adoi%2F10.1371%2Fjournal.pone.0057410

Cunningham, L. (2012, December 13). Myers-Briggs: Does it pay to know your type? *Washington Post.* https://www.google.com/#q=cunningham+myers-briggs+does+it+pay+to+know+your+type

Curry, C. (1998). Adolescence. In K. Trew & J. Kremer (Eds.), *Gender and psychology* (pp. 107–117). New York: Oxford University Press.

Custers, R., & Aarts, H. (2010). The unconscious will: How the pursuit of goals operates outside of conscious awareness. *Science, 329,* 47–50.

Dailey, M., Joyce, C., Lyons, M., Kamachi, M., Ishi, H., Gyoba, J., et al. (2010). Evidence and a computational explanation of cultural differences in facial expression recognition. *Emotion, 10,* 874–893.

Dalla, C., Edgecomb, C., Whetstone, A., & Shors, T. (2008). Females do not express learned helplessness like males do. *Neuropsychopharmacology, 33,* 1559–1569.

Dallery, J., Glenn, I., & Raiff, B. (2007). An Internet-based abstinence reinforcement treatment for cigarette smoking. *Drug and Alcohol Dependence, 86,* 230–238.

Dan, T., Jun, Z., & Ji-Liang, S. (2006). The influence factors of subjective well-being in older adults. *Chinese Mental Health Journal, 20,* 160–162.

Dana, R. (2002). Mental health services for African Americans: A cultural/racial perspective. *Cultural Diversity and Ethnic Minority Psychology, 8,* 3–18.

Daniels, D., & Plomin, R. (1985). Origins of individual differences in infant shyness. *Developmental Psychology, 21,* 118–121.

Danner, D., Snowdon, D., & Friesen, W. (2001). Positive emotions in early life and longevity: Findings from the nun study. *Journal of Personality and Social Psychology, 80,* 804–813.

Daraei, M., & Ghaderi, A. (2012). Impact of education on optimism/pessimism. *Journal of the Indian Academy of Applied Psychology, 38,* 339–343.

Darling, C., Coccia, C., & Senatore, N. (2012). Women in midlife: Stress, health and life satisfaction. *Stress and Health, 28,* 31–40.

Daugherty, D. A., Murphy, M. J., & Paugh, J. (2001). An examination of the Adlerian construct of social interest with criminal offenders. *Journal of Counseling and Development, 79,* 465–471.

Davidow, S., & Bruhn, A. R. (1990). Earliest memories and the dynamics of delinquency: A replication study. *Journal of Personality Assessment, 54,* 601–616.

Davis, P. J. (1987). Repression and the inaccessibility of affective memories. *Journal of Personality and Social Psychology, 53,* 585–593.

Dazzi, C. (2011). The Eysenck Personality Questionnaire–Revised (EPQ-R): A confirmation of the factorial structure in the Italian context. *Personality and Individual Differences, 50,* 790–794.

DeAndrea, D., Carpenter, C., Shulman, H., & Levine, T. (2009). The relationship between cheating behavior and sensation-seeking. *Personality and Individual Differences, 42,* 944–947.

Debast, I., van Alphen, S., Rossi, G., Tummers, J., Bolwerk, N., Derksen J., et al. (2014). Personality traits and personality disorders in late middle and old age; Do they remain stable? A literature review. *Clinical Gerontologist: Journal of Aging and Mental Health, 37,* 253–271.

De Brabander, B., & Boone, C. (1990). Sex differences in perceived locus of control. *Journal of Social Psychology, 130,* 271–272.

DeCarvalho, R. J. (1999). Otto Rank, the Rankian circle in Philadelphia, and the origin of Carl Rogers' person-centered psychotherapy. *History of Psychology, 2,* 132–148.

Deci, E. (2011). Self-determination theory and its relation to positive psychology. *Second World Congress of Positive Psychology Invited Speaker Abstracts.* http://psycnet.apa.org/doi/10.1037/e537892012-001

Deci, E., & Ryan, R. (2009). Self-determination theory: A consideration of human motivational universals. In P. Corr & G. Matthews (Eds.), *The Cambridge handbook of personality psychology* (pp. 441–446). New York: Cambridge University Press.

Deci, E., & Ryan, R. (2012). Self-determination theory. In P. Van Lange, A. Kruglanski, & E. Higgins (Eds.), *Handbook of theories of social psychology* (Vol. 1, pp. 416–436). Thousand Oaks, CA: Sage.

De Fruyt, F., Bartels, M., Van Leeuwen, K., De Clercq, B., Decuyper, M., & Mervielde, I. (2006). Five types of personality continuity in childhood and adolescence. *Journal of Personality and Social Psychology, 91,* 538–552.

Delevi, R., & Weisskirch, R. (2013). Personality factors as predictors of sexting. *Computers in Human Behavior, 29,* 2589–2594.

Delhey, J., & Dragolov, G. (2015, February 13). Happier together: Social cohesion and subjective well-being in Europe. *International Journal of Psychology.* http://onlinelibrary.wiley.com/doi/10.1002/ijop.12149/abstract

Delhomme, P., Chaurand, N., & Paran, F. (2012). Personality predictors of speeding in young drivers: Anger versus sensation seeking. *Transportation Research Part F: Traffic Psychology and Behavior, 15,* 654–666.

Delmonte, M. M. (2000). Retrieved memories of childhood sexual abuse. *British Journal of Medical Psychology, 73,* 1–13.

Dement, W. C., & Wolpert, E. A. (1958). The relationship of eye movements, body motility, and external stimuli to dream content. *Journal of Experimental Psychology, 55,* 543–553.

Deneui, D. (2001). Construction of a neurotic competitiveness inventory. *Program of the 73rd Annual Meeting, Midwestern Psychological Association.* http://psycnet.apa.org/index.cfm?fa=search.displayRecord&id=2E808324-C075-90B2-6502-AF81462DCC3A&resultID=1&page=1&dbTab=all&search=true

DeNeve, K., & Cooper, H. (1998). The happy personality: A meta-analysis of 137 personality traits and subjective well-being. *Psychological Bulletin, 124,* 197–229.

Denis, D. (2009). Book review: *The Cattell controversy: Race, science, and ideology,* by W. Tucker. Chicago: University of Illinois Press, 2009. *Journal of the History of the Behavioral Sciences, 45,* 390–392.

DePaulo, B. M. (1993). The ability to judge others from their expressive behaviors. In K. H. Craik, R. Hogan, & R. N. Wolfe (Eds.), *Fifty years of personality psychology* (pp. 197–206). New York: Plenum Press.

Dephilippis, D., Quintieri, P., Noble, H., Reyes, J., & Akundi, S. (2008). *Token economy reduces aggression among cognitively impaired patients in a psychiatric hospital.* American Psychological Association Convention Presentation.

De Raad, B. (2000). *The big five personality factors: The psycholexical approach to personality.* Seattle: Hogrefe & Huber.

De Raad, B., & Barelds, D. (2008). A new taxonomy of Dutch personality traits based on a comprehensive and unrestricted list of descriptors. *Journal of Personality and Social Psychology, 94*(2), 347–364.

Derks, D., Bos, A., & Von Grumbkow, J. (2007). Emoticons and social interaction on the Internet: The importance of social context. *Computers in Human Behavior, 23,* 842–849.

DeVito, A. J. (1985). Review of Myers-Briggs Type Indicator. In J. V. Mitchell, Jr. (Ed.), *Ninth mental measurements yearbook* (Vol. 2, pp. 1030–1032). Lincoln: University of Nebraska Press.

de Vries, R., de Vries, A., & Feij, J. (2009). Sensation seeking, risk-taking, and the HEXACO model of personality. *Personality and Individual Differences, 47,* 536–540.

DiClemente, C. C., Prochaska, J. O., & Gilbertini, M. (1985). Self-efficacy and the stages of self-change of smoking. *Cognitive Therapy and Research, 9,* 181–200.

Diehl, M., Chui, H., Hay, E., Lumley, M., Gruhn, D., & Labouvie-Vief, G. (2014). Change in coping and defense mechanisms across adulthood: Longitudinal findings in a European-American sample. *Developmental Psychology, 50,* 634–648.

Diener, E., & Chan, M. (2011). Happy people live longer: Subjective well-being contributes to health and longevity. *Applied Psychology: Health and Well-Being, 3,* 1–43.

Diener, E., Diener, M., & Diener, C. (1995). Factors predicting the subjective well-being of nations. *Journal of Personality and Social Psychology, 69,* 851–864.

Diener, E., Gohm, C., Suh, E. M., & Oishi, S. (2000). Similarity of the relations between marital status and subjective well-being across cultures. *Journal of Cross Cultural Psychology, 31,* 419–436.

Diener, E., Lucas, R., Oishi, S., & Suh, E. M. (2002). Looking up and looking down: Weighting good and bad information in life satisfaction judgments. *Personality and Social Psychology Bulletin, 28,* 437–445.

Diener, E., Ng, W., Harter, J., & Arora, R. (2010). Wealth and happiness across the world: Material prosperity predicts life evaluation, whereas psychosocial prosperity predicts positive feeling. *Journal of Personality and Social Psychology, 99,* 52–61.

Diener, E., Oishi, S., & Lucas, R. E. (2003). Personality, culture, and subjective well-being: Emotional and cognitive evaluations of life. *Annual Review of Psychology, 54,* 403–425.

Diener, E., & Seligman, M. (2002). Happy people. *Psychological Bulletin, 13,* 81–84.

Diener, E., Suh, E. M., Smith, H. L., & Shao, L. (1995). National differences in reported subjective well-being. *Social Indicators Research, 34,* 7–32.

Digman, J. M. (1990). Personality structure: Emergence of the five-factor model. *Annual Review of Psychology, 41,* 417–440.

Digman, J. M. (1997). Higher-order factors of the Big Five. *Journal of Personality and Social Psychology, 73,* 1246–1256.

Dignan, M. (1965). Ego identity and maternal identification. *Journal of Personality and Social Psychology, 1,* 476–483.

Dinella, L., Devita, A., & Weisgram, E. (2013). Pink fighter jets and blue tea sets: The role of toy type and toy color in adults' gender attitudes. *American Psychological Association 2013 Convention Presentation.* http://psycnet.apa.org/index.cfm?fa=search.displayRecord&id=6CE83045-0E89-35E3-FAF6-6B3C2D3FFABC&resultID=1&page=1&dbTab=all&search=true

Dingfelder, S. (2005). Closing the gap for Latino patients. *Monitor on Psychology, 36*(1), 58–61.

Dinter, L. (2000). The relationship between self-efficacy and lifestyle patterns. *Journal of Individual Psychology, 56,* 462–473.

DiRienzo, C., Das, J., Synn, W., Kitts, J., & McGrath, K. (2010). The relationship between MBTI and academic performance: A study across academic disciplines. *Journal of Psychological Type, 70*(5), 53–66.

Dithurbide, L., & Feltz, D. (2012). Self-efficacy and collective efficacy. In G. Tenenbaum, R. Eklund, & A. Kamata (Eds.), *Measurement in sport and exercise psychology* (pp. 251–263). Champaign, IL: Human Kinetics.

Doherty, A., & Kelly, B. (2010). Social and psychological correlates of happiness in 17 European countries. *Irish Journal of Psychological Medicine, 27*(3), 130–134.

Dolan, P., Kavetsos, G., & Vlaev, I. (2014). The happiness workout. *Social Indicators Research, 119,* 1363–1377.

Donaldson, G. (1996). Between practice and theory: Melanie Klein, Anna Freud, and the development of child analysis. *Journal of the History of the Behavioral Sciences, 32,* 160–176.

Donnellan, B., Trzesniewski, K., Robins, R., Moffitt, T., & Caspi, A. (2005). Low self-esteem is related to aggression, antisocial behavior, and delinquency. *Psychological Science, 16,* 328–335.

Douglas, C. (1993). *Translate this darkness: The life of Christiana Morgan.* New York: Simon & Schuster.

Downey, D. B. (2001). Number of siblings and intellectual development: The resource dilution explanation. *American Psychologist, 56,* 497–504.

Dr. Carl, G. Jung is dead at 85 (1961, June 7). Pioneer in analytic psychology. *New York Times.* https://www.google.com/#q=carl+jung+obituary

Drakopoulos, S., & Grimani, K. (2013). Maslow's needs hierarchy and the effect of income on happiness levels. In F. Sarracino (Ed.), *The happiness compass: Theories, actions and perspectives for well-being* (pp. 295–309). Hauppauge, NY: Nova Science Publishers.

Drexler, P. (2013, September 16). What your selfies say about you. *Psychology Today Onlne.* http://www.psychologytoday.com/blog/our-gender-ourselves/201309/what-your-selfies-say-about-you

Dru, V. (2003). Relationships between an ego orientation scale and a hypercompetitive scale: Their correlates with dogmatism and authoritarianism factors. *Personality and Individual Differences, 35,* 1509–1524.

Drumm, P., & Ovre, C. (2011). A batman to the rescue: A biopsychologist and bat expert worked to arm bats with miniature bombs in World War II. *Monitor on Psychology, 42,* 24–26.

Du, J., Shin, Y., & Choi, J. (2015). Convergent perceptions of organizational efficacy among team members and positive work outcomes in organizational teams. *Journal of Occupational and Organizational Psychology, 88,* 178–202.

Dubois, L., Diasparra, M., Bedard, B., Kaprio, J., Fontaine-Bisson, B., Tremblay, R., et al. (2013). Genetic and environmental influences on eating behaviors in two-and-a-half and nine-year-old children: A longitudinal twin study. *International Journal of Behavioral Nutrition and Physical Activity, 10,* Article 134. http://www.ncbi.nlm.nih.gov/pubmed/24313977

Duck, S. W., & Spencer, C. (1972). Personal constructs and friendship formation. *Journal of Personality and Social Psychology, 23,* 40–45.

Dufner, M., Denissen, J., Sedikides, C., Van Zalk, M., Meeus, W., & Van Aken, M. (2013). Are actual and perceived intellectual self-enhancers evaluated differently by social perceivers? *European Journal of Personality, 27,* 621–633.

Dumka, L., Gonzales, N., Wheeler, L., & Millsap, R. (2010). Parenting self-efficacy and parenting practices over time in Mexican American families. *Journal of Family Psychology, 24,* 522–531.

Duncan, L. E., & Agronick, G. W. (1995). The intersection of life stage and social events: Personality and life outcomes. *Journal of Personality and Social Psychology, 69,* 558–568.

Dunlop, P., Morrison, D., Koenig, J., & Silcox, B. (2012). Comparing the Eysenck and HEXACO models of personality in the prediction of adult delinquency. *European Journal of Personality, 26,* 194–202.

Dupree, L., Herrera, J., Tyson, D., Jang, Y., & King-Kallimanis, S. (2010). Age group differences in mental health care preferences and barriers among Latinos: Implications for research and practice. *Best Practices in Mental Health Care: An International Journal, 6,* 47–59.

Durgel, E., Leyendecker, B., Yagmurlu, B., & Harwood, R. (2009). Sociocultural influences on German and Turkish mothers' long-term socialization goals. *Journal of Cross-Cultural Psychology, 19,* 834–853.

Dwairy, M. (2004). Parenting styles and psychological adjustment of Arab adolescents. *Transcultural Psychiatry, 41,* 275–286.

Dwairy, M., Achoui, M., Abouserie, R., & Farah, A. (2006). Parenting styles, individuation, and mental health of Arab adolescents. *Journal of Cross-Cultural Psychology, 37,* 262–272.

Dzuka, J., & Dalbert, C. (2006). The belief in a just world and subjective well-being in old age. *Aging and Mental Health, 10,* 439–444.

Eagle, M. N. (1988). How accurate were Freud's case histories? [Review of *Freud and the Rat Man*]. *Contemporary Psychology, 33,* 205–206.

Eaton, S., Livingston, J., & McAdoo, H. (2010). Cultivating consciousness among Black women: Black nationalism and self-esteem revisited. *Journal of Black Studies, 40,* 812–822.

Eaves, L. J., Eysenck, H. J., & Martin, N. G. (1989). *Genes, culture, and personality: An empirical approach.* New York: Academic Press.

Eccles, J. S., Barber, B., & Jozefowicz, D. (1999). Linking gender to educational, occupational, and recreational choices. In W. B. Swann, Jr., J. H. Langlois, & L. A. Gilbert (Eds.), *Sexism and stereotypes in modern society* (pp. 153–192). Washington, DC: American Psychological Association.

Eckardt, M. (2006). Karen Horney: A portrait. *American Journal of Psychoanalysis, 66,* 105–108.

Eckstein, D., Aycock, K., Sperber, M., McDonald, J., Van Wiesner, V., Watts, R., et al. (2010). A review of 200 birth order studies: Lifestyle characteristics. *Journal of Individual Psychology, 66,* 408–434.

Eckstein, D., & Kaufman, J. (2012). The role of birth order in personality: An enduring intellectual legacy of Alfred Adler. *Journal of Individual Psychology, 68,* 60–61.

Edman, J., Adams, S., Park, M., & Irwin, C. (2010). Who gets confidential care? Disparities in a national sample of adolescents. *Journal of Adolescent Health, 46,* 393–395.

Edmundson, M. (2007). *The death of Sigmund Freud: The legacy of his last days.* New York: Bloomsbury.

Eissler, K. R. (1971). *Talent and genius: The fictitious case of Tausk contra Freud.* New York: Quadrangle Books.

Eklund, J., & Fritzell, J. (2014). Keeping delinquency at bay: The role of the school context for impulsive and sensation-seeking adolescents. *European Journal of Criminology, 11,* 682–701.

Ekman, P., Matsumoto, D., & Friesen, W. V. (1997). Facial expressions in affective disorders. In P. Ekman & E. L. Rosenberg (Eds.), *What the face reveals* (pp. 331–341). New York: Oxford University Press.

El-Anzi, F. (2005). Academic achievement and its relationship with anxiety, self-esteem, optimism, and pessimism in Kuwaiti students. *Social Behavior and Personality, 33,* 95–104.

Ellenberger, H. F. (1970). *The discovery of the unconscious: The history and evolution of dynamic psychiatry.* New York: Basic Books.

Ellenberger, H. F. (1978). Carl Gustav Jung: His historical setting. In H. Reise (Ed.), *Historical explorations in medicine and psychiatry* (pp. 142–150). New York: Springer.

Elliot, A. J., & Church, M. A. (1997). A hierarchical model of approach and avoidance achievement motivation. *Journal of Personality and Social Psychology, 72,* 218–232.

Elliot, A. J., Faler, J., McGregor, H. A., Campbell, W. K., Sedikides, C., & Harackiewicz, J. M. (2000). Competence valuation as a strategic intrinsic motivation process. *Personality and Social Psychology Bulletin, 26,* 780–794.

Elliot, A. J., & Sheldon, K. M. (1997). Avoidance achievement motivation: A personal goals analysis. *Journal of Personality and Social Psychology, 73,* 171–185.

Ellis, R. A., & Taylor, M. S. (1983). Role of self-esteem within the job search process. *Journal of Applied Psychology, 68,* 632–640.

Elms, A. C. (1994). *Uncovering lives: The uneasy alliance of biography and psychology.* New York: Oxford University Press.

Elms, A. C. (2010). Jung's biggest book. Book review of *The Red Book, Liber Novus,* by C. G. Jung. New York: Norton, 2009. *PsycCRITIQUES, 55*(21), Article 3.

Elson, M., & Ferguson, C. (2014). The ideological rigidity of social-cognitive theories of media violence and a response to Bushman and Huesmann. *European Psychologist, 19,* 68–75.

Emanuel, G. (2014, March 5). Post a survey on Mechanical Turk and watch the results roll in. *NPR Radio.* http://www.npr.org/blogs/alltechconsidered/2014/03/05/279669610/post-a-survey-on-mechanical- turk-and-watch-the-results-roll-in

Endo, Y., Heine, S. J., & Lehman, D. R. (2000). Culture and positive illusions in close relationships: How my relationships are better than yours. *Personality and Social Psychology Bulletin, 26,* 1571–1586.

Erikson, E. H. (1950). *Childhood and society.* New York: Norton.

Erikson, E. H. (1959). Identity and the life cycle: Selected papers [Monograph 1]. *Psychological Issues, 1.*

Erikson, E. H. (1968). *Identity: Youth and crisis.* New York: Norton.

Erikson, E. H. (1975). *Life history and the historical moment.* New York: Norton.

Erikson, E. H., Erikson, J. M., & Kivnick, H. Q. (1986). *Vital involvement in old age.* New York: Norton.

Eron, L. (1987). The development of aggressive behavior from the perspective of a developing behaviorism. *American Psychologist, 42,* 435–442.

Esnard, C., & Roques, M. (2014). Collective efficacy: A resource in stressful occupational contexts. *European Review of Applied Psychology, 64,* 203–211.

Esseilly, R., Nadel, J., & Fagard, J. (2010). Object retrieval through observational learning in 8- to 18-month-old infants. *Infant Behavior and Development, 33,* 695–699.

Esseilly, R., Rat-Fischer, L., O'Regan, L., & Fagard, J. (2013). Understanding the experimenter's intention improves 16-month-olds' observational learning of the use of a novel tool. *Cognitive Development, 28,* 1–9.

Evans, G., & Stecker, R. (2004). Motivational consequences of environmental stress. *Journal of Environmental Psychology, 24,* 143–165.

Evans, R. I. (1968). *B. F. Skinner: The man and his ideas.* New York: Dutton.

Everton, W., Mastrangelo, P., & Jolton, J. (2005). Personality correlates of employees' personal use of work computers. *Cyberpsychology and Behavior, 8,* 143–153.

Exner, J. E., Jr. (1993). *The Rorschach: A comprehensive system: Vol. 1. Basic foundations* (3rd ed.). New York: Wiley.

Ey, S., Hadley, W., Allen, D., Palmer, S., Klosky, J., Deptula, D., et al. (2005). A new measure of children's optimism and pessimism: The Youth Life Orientation Test. *Journal of Child Psychology and Psychiatry, 46,* 548–558.

Eysenck, H. J. (1980). Autobiography. In G. Lindzey (Ed.), *A history of psychology in autobiography* (Vol. 7, pp. 153–187). San Francisco, CA: W. H. Freeman.

Eysenck, H. J. (1983). A biometrical-genetic analysis of impulsive and sensation seeking behavior. In M. Zuckerman (Ed.), *Biological bases of sensation seeking, impulsivity, and anxiety* (pp. 1–27). Hillsdale, NJ: Erlbaum.

Eysenck, H. J. (1990a). Genetic and environmental contributions to individual differences: The three major dimensions of personality. *Journal of Personality, 58,* 245–261.

Eysenck, H. J. (1990b). Biological dimensions of personality. In L. A. Pervin (Ed.), *Handbook of personality: Theory and research* (pp. 244–276). New York: Guilford Press.

Eysenck, H. J. (1997). Personality and experimental psychology: The unification of psychology and the possibility of a paradigm. *Journal of Personality and Social Psychology, 73,* 1224–1237.

Eysenck, H. J., & Eysenck, M. W. (1985). *Personality and individual differences: A natural science approach*. New York: Plenum Press.

Eysenck, H. J., & Eysenck, S. (1963). *Eysenck personality inventory*. San Diego, CA: Educational and Industrial Testing Service.

Eysenck, H. J., & Gudjonsson, G. H. (1989). *The causes and cures of criminality*. New York: Plenum Press.

Eysenck, W. (2009). Personality, intelligence, and longevity: A cross-cultural perspective. *Social Behavior and Personality, 37* (2), 149–154.

Fagan, A., Wright, E., & Pinchevsky, G. (2014). The protective effects of neighborhood collective efficacy on adolescent substance use and violence following exposure to violence. *Journal of Youth & Adolescence, 43,* 1498–1512.

Faith, M. S., Wong, F. Y., & Carpenter, K. M. (1995). Group sensitivity training: Update, meta-analysis, and recommendations. *Journal of Counseling Psychology, 3,* 390–399.

Falbo, T. (1978). Only children and interpersonal behavior: An experimental and survey study. *Journal of Applied Social Psychology, 8,* 244–253.

Falbo, T., & Polit, D. F. (1986). Quantitative review of the only child literature: Research evidence and theory development. *Psychological Bulletin, 100,* 176–189.

Falk, C., Heine, S., Yuki, M., & Takemura, K. (2009). Why do Westerners self-enhance more than East Asians? *European Journal of Personality, 23*(3), 183–203.

Fallby, J., Hassmen, P., Kentta, G., & Durand-Burand, N. (2006). Relationship between locus of control, sense of coherence, and mental skills in Swedish elite athletes. *International Journal of Sport & Exercise Psychology, 44,* 111–120.

Fan, H., Lin, M., Bai, C., Huang, P., Chiang, Y., & Chiu, W. (2014). Validation of the Chinese-language brief sensation seeking scale: Implications for risky riding behaviors of parental motorcyclists and their child passengers. *Accident Analysis & Prevention, 73,* 333–339.

Fan, W., & Yan, Z. (2010). Factors affecting response rates of the web survey: A systematic review. *Computers in Human Behavior, 26,* 132–139.

Fancher, R. (2000). Snapshots of Freud in America, 1899–1999. *American Psychologist, 55,* 1025–1028.

Farley, F. (2000). Obituary: Hans J. Eysenck (1916–1997). *American Psychologist, 55,* 674–675.

Ferguson, C. (2010). A meta-analysis of normal and disordered personality across the life span. *Journal of Personality and Social Psychology, 98*(4), 659–667.

Ferguson, E. (2000). Hypochondriacal concerns and the five factor model of personality. *Journal of Personality, 68,* 705–724.

Ferguson, E. (2010). Adler's innovative contributions regarding the need to belong. *Journal of Individual Psychology, 66,* 1–7.

Ferrand, C., Martinent, G., & Durmaz, N. (2014). Psychological need satisfaction and well-being in adults aged 80 and older living in residential homes: Using a self-determination theory perspective. *Journal of Aging Studies, 30,* 104–111.

Fiebert, M. S. (1997). In and out of Freud's shadow: A chronology of Adler's relationship with Freud. *Individual Psychology, 53,* 241–269.

Findley, M. J., & Cooper, H. M. (1983). Locus of control and academic achievement: A literature review. *Journal of Personality and Social Psychology, 44,* 419–427.

Fischer, R., & Boer, D. (2011). What is more important for national well-being: Money or autonomy? A meta-analysis of well-being, burnout, and anxiety across 63 societies. *Journal of Personality and Social Psychology, 101,* 164–184.

Fisher, J. W., & Francis, L. (2013). Happiness is a thing called stable extraversion: Testing Eysenck's thesis among three samples in Australia. In F. Sarracino (Ed.), *The happiness compass: Theories, actions and perspectives for well-being* (pp. 31–36). Hauppauge, NY: Nova Science Publishers.

Fisher, J. D., & Misovich, S. J. (1990). Social influence and AIDS-preventive behavior. In J. Edwards, R. S. Tindale, & E. J. Posavac (Eds.), *Social influence processes and prevention* (pp. 39–70). New York: Plenum Press.

Fisher, S. P., & Greenberg, R. P. (1977). *The scientific credibility of Freud's theories and therapy*. New York: Basic Books.

Fisher, S. P., & Greenberg, R. P. (1996). *Freud scientifically reappraised: Testing the theories and therapy*. New York: Wiley.

Fiske, K., & Pillemer, D. (2006). Adult recollections of earliest childhood dreams: A cross-cultural study. *Memory, 14,* 57–67.

Floderus-Myrhed, B., Pedersen, N., & Rasmuson, I. (1980). Assessment of heritability for personality, based on a short form of the Eysenck personality inventory: A study of 12,898 twin pairs. *Behavior Genetics, 10,* 153–162.

Foels, R., & Reid, L. D. (2010). Gender differences in social dominance orientation: The role of cognitive complexity. *Sex Roles, 62*(9–10), 684–692.

Foley, Y., Matheny, K., & Curlette, W. (2008). A cross-generational study of Adlerian personality traits and life satisfaction in mainland China. *Journal of Individual Psychology, 64*(3), 324–338.

Fong, M., & Mashek, D. (2014, June 21). Self-esteem among Asian American undergraduates: The role of dorm connectedness. *Society for the Psychological Study of Ethnic Minority Issues Presentation*. https://center.uoregon.edu/APA/Div45/2014/program/daily_schedule.php?day=Saturday

Ford, J. G. (1991). Inherent potentialities of actualization: An initial exploration. *Journal of Humanistic Psychology, 31*(3), 65–88.

Fortuna, K., & Knafo, A. (2014). Parental and genetic contributions to prosocial behavior during childhood. In L. Padilla-Walker & C. Gustafo (Eds.), *Prosocial development: A multidensional approach* (pp. 70–89). New York: Oxford Unversity Press.

Frable, D. E. S. (1997). Gender, racial, ethnic, sexual, and class identities. *Annual Review of Psychology, 48,* 139–162.

Francis, L., & Datoo, F. (2012). Inside the mosque: A study in psychological type profiling. *Mental Health, Religion & Culture, 15,* 1037–1046.

Francis, L., Yablon, Y., & Robbins, M. (2013). Psychology of emotions, motivations and actions. In F. Sarracino (Ed.), *The happiness compass: Theories, actions and perspectives for well-being* (pp. 17–29). Hauppauge, NY: Nova Science Publishers.

Frank, T., Turenshine, H., & Sullivan, S. (2010). *Birth order's effect on personality, intelligence, and achievement: Same-family siblings*. American Psychological Association 2010 Convention Presentation. San Diego, California.

Franklin-Jackson, D., & Carter, R. (2007). The relationships between race-related stress, racial identity, and mental health for Black Americans. *Journal of Black Psychology, 33,* 5–26.

Fransella, F., & Neimeyer, R. (2003). George Alexander Kelly: The man and his theory. In F. Fransella (Ed.), *International handbook of personal construct psychology* (pp. 21–31). Chichester, England: Wiley.

Franz, C. E., McClelland, D. C., & Weinberger, J. (1991). Childhood antecedents of conventional social accomplishment in midlife adults: A 36-year prospective study. *Journal of Personality and Social Psychology, 60,* 586–595.

Frederickson, B. (2001). The role of positive emotions in positive psychology: The broaden-and-build theory of positive emotions. *American Psychologist, 56,* 218–226.

Freed, R., & Tompson, M. (2011). Predictors of parental locus of control in mothers of pre- and early adolescents. *Journal of Clinical and Adolescent Psychology, 40,* 100–110.

Freedman, D. G. (1974). *Human infancy: An evolutionary perspective.* Hillsdale, NJ: Erlbaum.

Freeman, D. (2013, March 20). B. F. Skinner, behavioral scientist who invented 'Skinner Box,' rememberd by his daughter. *Huffington Post.* http://www.huffingtonpost.com/news/bf-skinner/

Freeman, J., Rule, N., & Ambady, N. (2009). Culture shapes a mesolimbic response to signals of dominance and subordinations that associate with behavior. *Neuroscience, 47*(1), 353–359.

French, D., Olander, E., Chisholm, A., & McSharry, J. (2014). Which behavior change techniques are most effective at increasing older adults' self-efficacy and physical activity behavior? A systematic review. *Annals of Behavioral Medicine, 48,* 225–234.

French, S., & Chavez, E. (2010). The relationship of ethnicity-related stressors and Latino ethnic identity to well-being. *Hispanic Journal of Behavioral Sciences, 32,* 410–428.

French, S., Seidman, E., Allen, L., & Aber, J. (2006). The development of ethnic identity during adolescence. *Developmental Psychology, 42,* 1–10.

Freud, A. (1936). *The ego and the mechanisms of defense.* New York: International Universities Press.

Freud, S. (1901). The psychopathology of everyday life. In J. Strachey (Ed. & Trans.), *The standard edition of the complete psychological works of Sigmund Freud* (Vol. 6). London: Hogarth Press.

Freud, S. (1914). On the history of the psychoanalytic movement. In *Standard edition* (Vol. 14, pp. 3–66). London: Hogarth Press.

Freud, S. (1925). An autobiographical study. In *Standard edition* (Vol. 20). London: Hogarth Press.

Freud, S. (1940). An outline of psychoanalysis. In *Standard edition* (Vol. 23, pp. 141–207). London: Hogarth Press.

Freud, S. (1954). *The origins of psychoanalysis: Letters to Wilhelm Fliess, drafts and notes: 1887–1902.* M. Bonaparte, A. Freud, & E. Kris (Eds.). New York: Basic Books.

Freud, S. (1963). *Psychoanalysis and faith: The letters of Sigmund Freud and Oskar Pfister.* H. Meng & E. Freud (Eds.). New York: Basic Books.

Freud, S. (1985). *The complete letters of Sigmund Freud to Wilhelm Fliess, 1887–1904.* J. M. Masson (Ed.). Cambridge, MA: Belknap Press of Harvard University.

Freud, S., & Jung, C. G. (1974). *The Freud/Jung letters.* W. McGuire (Ed.). Princeton, NJ: Princeton University Press.

Frick, W. B. (2000). Remembering Maslow: Reflections on a 1968 interview. *Journal of Humanistic Psychology, 40,* 128–147.

Friedman, H., & Martin, L. (2011). *The longevity project: Surprising discoveries for health and long life from the landmark eight-decade study.* New York: Hudson Street Press.

Friedman, H. S., Schwartz, J. E., Tomlinson-Keasey, C., Tucker, J. S., Martin, L. R., Wingard, D. L., et al. (1995). Childhood conscientiousness and longevity: Health behaviors and cause of death. *Journal of Personality and Social Psychology, 68,* 696–703.

Friedman, H. S., Kern, M., & Reynolds, C. (2010). Personality and health, subjective well-being, and longevity. *Journal of Personality, 78*(1), 179–216.

Friedman, H. S., Tucker, J. S., Tomlinson-Keasey, C., Schwartz, J. E., Wingard, D. L., & Criqui, M. H. (1993). Does childhood personality predict longevity? *Journal of Personality and Social Psychology, 65,* 176–185.

Friedman, L. J. (1996). Psychological advice in the public realm in America, 1940–1970 [Review of the book *The Romance of American Psychology*]. *Contemporary Psychology, 41,* 219–222.

Friedman, L. J. (1999). *Identity's architect: A biography of Erik H. Erikson.* New York: Simon & Schuster.

Fukama, M., & Mizuochi, F. (2011). On the effect of the experience of sports activities on ego identity. *6th ASPASP International Congress on Sport Psychology, Taipei, Taiwan, November 11–13, 2011.* http://psycnet.apa.org/index.cfm?fa=search.searchResults

Funder, D. C. (2001). Personality. *Annual Review of Psychology, 52,* 83–110.

Furnham, A., Eysenck, S., & Saklofske, D. (2010). The Eysenck personality measures: Fifty years of scale development. In G. Boyle, G. Matthews, & D. Saklofske (Eds.), *The SAGE handbook of personality theory and assessment: Vol. 2. Personality measurement and testing* (pp. 199–218). Thousand Oaks, CA: Sage.

Gackenbach, J., Darlington, M., Ferguson, M., & Boyes. A. (2013).Video game play as nightmare protection: A replication and extension. *Dreaming, 23,* 97–111.

Gackenbach, J., Kuruvilla, B., & Dopko, R. (2009). Video game play and dream bizarreness. *Dreaming, 29,* 218–231.

Gafner, G. (2012). *Subliminal: How your unconscious mind rules your behavior.* New York: Pantheon.

Gaines, S. O., Jr., Marelich, W. D., Bledsoe, K. L., Steers, W. N., Henderson, M. C., Granrose, C. S., et al. (1997). Links between race/ethnicity and cultural values as mediated by racial/ethnic identity and moderated by gender. *Journal of Personality and Social Psychology, 72,* 1460–1476.

Galambos, N., Barker, E., & Krahn, H. (2006). Depression, self-esteem, and anger in emerging adulthood: Seven-year trajectories. *Developmental Psychology, 42,* 350–365.

Gale, C., Booth, T., Mottus, R., Kuh, R., & Deary, I. (2013). Neuroticism and extraversion in youth predict mental well-being and life satisfaction 40 years later. *Journal of Research in Personality, 47,* 687–697.

Ganellan, R. J. (2002). Calming the storm: Contemporary use of the Rorschach. [Review of the book *Essentials of Rorschach Assessment*]. *Contemporary Psychology, 47,* 325–327.

Ganiban, J., Saudino, K., Ulbricht, J., Neiderhiser, J., & Reiss, D. (2008). Stability and change in temperament during adolescence. *Journal of Personality and Social Psychology, 95*(1), 222–236.

Gao, X., & Maurer, D. (2010). A happy story: Developmental changes in children's sensitivity to facial expressions of varying intensities. *Journal of Experimental Child Psychology, 107*(2), 67–86.

Garcia, D., & Silkstrom, S. (2014). The dark side of Facebook: Semantic representation of status updates predict the Dark Triad of personality. *Personality and Individual Differences, 67*, 92–96.

Garcia, M. E., Schmitz, J. M., & Doerfler, L. A. (1990). A fine-grained analysis of the role of self-efficacy in self-initiated attempts to quit smoking. *Journal of Consulting and Clinical Psychology, 58*, 317–322.

Garcia, S., Tully, E., Tarantino, N., South, S., Iacono, W., & McGue, M. (2013). Changes in genetic and environmental influences on trait anxiety from middle adolescence to early adulthood. *Journal of Affective Disorders, 151*, 46–53.

Gardner, H. (1993). *Creating minds.* New York: Basic Books.

Gardner, W. L., Pickett, C. L., & Brewer, M. B. (2000). Social exclusion and selective memory: How the need to belong influences memory for social events. *Personality and Social Psychology Bulletin, 26*, 486–496.

Gaskins, S., & Paradise, R. (2010). Learning through observation in daily life. In D. Lancy, J. Bock, & S. Gaskins (Eds.), *The anthropology of learning in childhood* (pp. 85–117). Walnut Creek, CA: AltaMira Press.

Gates, L., Lineberger, M. R., Crockett, J., & Hubbard, J. (1988). Birth order and its relationship to depression, anxiety, and self-concept test scores in children. *Journal of Genetic Psychology, 149*, 29–34.

Gay, P. (1988). *Freud: A life for our time.* New York: Norton.

Gecas, V. (1989). The social psychology of self-efficacy. *Annual Review of Sociology, 15*, 291–316.

Gencoz, T., & Ozlale, Y. (2004). Direct and indirect effects of social support on psychological well-being. *Social Behavior and Personality, 32*, 449–458.

Gendlin, E. T., & Tomlinson, T. M. (1967). The process conception and its measurement. In C. R. Rogers, E. T. Gendlin, D. J. Kiesler, & C. B. Truax (Eds.), *The therapeutic relationship and its impact: A study of psychotherapy with schizophrenics.* Madison: University of Wisconsin Press.

Gendron, M., Roberson, D., van der Vyver, J., & Barrett, L. (2014). Perceptions of emotion from facial expressions are not culturally universal: Evidence from a remote culture. *Emotion, 14*, 251–262.

Gentile, B., Twenge, J., & Campbell, W. (2010). Birth cohort differences in self-esteem, 1988–2008: A cross-temporal meta-analysis. *Review of General Psychology, 14*, 261–268.

Gentile, D., Lynch, P., Linder, J., & Walsh, D. (2004). The effects of violent video game habits on adolescent hostility, aggressive behaviors, and school performance. *Journal of Adolescence, 27*, 5–22.

Gentzler, A., Oberhauser, A., Westerman, S., & Nadorff, D. (2011). College students' use of electronic communication with parents: Links to loneliness, attachment, and relationship quality. *Cyberpsychology, Behavior, and Social Networking, 14*, 71–74.

George, K., Baechtold, J., Frost, R., & Campbell, J. (2006). Sensation seeking, aggression, and reckless behavior in high school students, college students, and adults. *Perceptual and Motor Skills, 103*, 801–802.

Gerstorf, D., Ram, N., Estabrook, R., Schupp, J., Wagner, G., & Lindenberger, U. (2008). Life satisfaction shows terminal decline in old age: Longitudinal evidence from the German Socio-Economic Panel study (SOEP). *Developmental Psychology, 44*(4), 1148–1159.

Gerstorf, D., Ram, N., Goebel, J., Schupp, J., Lindenberger, U., & Wagner, G. (2010). Where people live and die makes a difference: Individual and geographic disparities in well-being progression at the end of life. *Psychology and Aging, 25*(3), 661–676.

Gerstorf, D., Ram, N., Mayraz, G., Hidajat, M., Lindenberger, U., Wagner, G., et al. (2010). Late-life decline in well-being across adulthood in Germany, the United Kingdom, and the United States: Something is seriously wrong at the end of life. *Psychology and Aging, 25*, 477–485.

Gfellner, B., & Armstrong, H. (2012). Ego development, ego strengths and ethnic identity among first nation adolescents. *Journal of Research on Adolescence, 22*, 225–234.

Giammarco, E., & Vernon, P. (2014). Vengeance and the Dark Triad: The role of empathy and perspective taking in trait forgiveness. *Personality and Individual Differences, 67*, 23–29.

Gibbons, F., Blanton, H., Gerrard, M., Buunk, B., & Eggleston, T. (2000). Does social comparison make a difference? Optimism as a moderator of the relation between comparison level and academic performance. *Personality and Social Psychology Bulletin, 26*, 637–648.

Gibson, B., & Sanbonmatsu, D. (2004). Optimism, pessimism, and gambling: The downside of optimism. *Personality and Social Psychology Bulletin, 30*, 149–160.

Gibson, S., & Dembo, M. H. (1984). Teacher efficacy: A construct validation. *Journal of Educational Psychology, 76*, 569–582.

Gieser, L., & Wyatt-Gieser, J. (2013, August 3). *Survival of the Thematic Apperception Test.* Paper presented at the American Psychological Association Convention. http://www.history-ofpsych.org/images/Division_26_APA_Convention_Program_2013.

Gillaspy, J. (2009). *Misbehavior and the relationship between the Brelands and B. F. Skinner.* American Psychological Association Convention Presentation.

Gillaspy, J., Brinegar, J., & Bailey, R. (2014). Operant psychology makes a splash-in marine mammal training (1955–1965). *Journal of the History of the Behavioral Sciences, 50*, 231–246.

Gilman, R. (2001). The relationship between life satisfaction, social interest, and frequency of extracurricular activities among adolescent students. *Journal of Youth and Adolescence, 30*, 749–767.

Gilman, R., & Huebner, E. (2006). Characteristics of adolescents who report very high life satisfaction. *Journal of Youth and Adolescence, 35*, 311–319.

Gilman, S. (2001). Karen Horney, M. D., 1885–1962. *American Journal of Psychiatry, 158*, 1205.

Givertz, M., & Segrin, C. (2014). The association between over-involved parenthood and young adults' self-efficacy: Psychological entitlement and family communication. *Communication Research, 41*, 1111–1136.

Gladwell, M. (2004, September 20). Annals of psychology: Personality plus. *New Yorker*, pp. 42–48.

Glicksman, E. (2013). Transgender today. *Monitor on Psychology, 44*, 36–41.

Glucksberg, S., & King, L. J. (1967). Motivated forgetting mediated by implicit verbal chaining: A laboratory analog of repression. *Science, 158,* 517–519.

Goby, V. (2006). Personality and online/offline choices: MBTI profiles and favored communication modes in a Singapore study. *Cyberpsychology and Behavior, 9,* 5–13.

Goldfried, M. (2007). What has psychotherapy inherited from Carl Rogers? *Psychotherapy, Theory, Research, Practice, Training, 44*(3), 249–252.

Goleman, D. (1987, August 31). B. F. Skinner: On his best behavior. *New York Times.*

Gollan, J., McCloskey, M., Hoxha, D., & Coccaro, E. (2010). How do depressed and healthy adults interpret nuanced facial expressions? *Journal of Abnormal Psychology, 119,* 804–810.

Gomez, V., Krings, F., Bangerter, A., & Grob, A. (2009). The influence of personality and life events on subjective well-being from a life span perspective. *Journal of Research in Personality, 43,* 345–354.

Gonzales-Iglesias, B., Gomez-Fraguela, J., & Luengo, M. (2014). Sensation seeking and drunk driving: The mediational role of social norms and self-efficacy. *Accident Analysis & Prevention, 71,* 22–28.

Gonzalez, H., Tarraf, W., Brady, T., Chan, D., Miranda, P., & Leong, F. (2010). Antidepressant use among Asians in the United States. *Depression and Anxiety, 27,* 46–55.

Goode, E. (2002, July 2). Researchers find that those who are happiest are less neurotic, more extroverted. *New York Times.*

Goodman, J., Cryder, C., & Cheema, A. (2013). Data collection in a flat world: The strengths and weaknesses of Mechanical Turk samples. *Journal of Behavioral Decision Making, 26,* 213–224.

Goodman, L., Smith, P., Ivancevich, S., & Lundberg, S. (2014). Actions speak louder than personalities: Effects of Facebook content on personality perceptions. *North American Journal of Psychology, 16,* 105–120.

Goritz, A. (2014). Frequency of typical dream themes in most recent dreams: An online study. *Dreaming, 24,* 57–66.

Gosling, S., Gaddis, S., & Vazire, S. (2007). *Personality impressions based on Facebook profiles.* Proceedings of the International Conference on Weblogs and Social Media.

Gosling, S., Sandy, C., & Potter, J. (2010). Personalities of self-identified "dog people" and "cat people." *Anthrozoos, 23,* 213–222.

Gosling, S., Vazire, S., Srivastava, S., & John, O. (2004). Should we trust web-based studies? A comparative analysis of six preconceptions. *American Psychologist, 59,* 93–104.

Gough, H. G., Fioravanti, M., & Lazzari, R. (1983). Some implications of self versus idealized self-congruence on the Revised Adjective Check List. *Journal of Personality and Social Psychology, 44,* 1214–1220.

Gough, H. G., Lazzari, R., & Fioravanti, M. (1978). Self versus ideal self: A comparison of five Adjective Check List indices. *Journal of Consulting and Clinical Psychology, 35,* 1085–1091.

Graham, W., & Balloun, J. (1973). An empirical test of Maslow's need hierarchy theory. *Journal of Humanistic Psychology, 13,* 97–108.

Gram, P., Dunn, B., & Ellis, D. (2005). Relationship between EEG and psychological type. *Journal of Psychological Type, 65,* 33–46.

Granello, D. (2010). Cognitive complexity among practicing counselors: How thinking changes with experience. *Journal of Counseling and Development, 88*(1), 92–100.

Graves, T. D. (1961). *Time perspective and the deferred gratification pattern in a tri-ethnic community.* Boulder: University of Colorado Institute of Behavioral Science.

Graziano, W. G., Jensen-Campbell, L. A., & Sullivan-Logan, G. M. (1998). Temperament, activity, and expectations for later personality development. *Journal of Personality and Social Psychology, 74,* 1266–1277.

Greco, A., Steca, P., Monzani, D., Malfatto, G., & Parati, G. (2015). The influence of illness severity on health satisfaction in patients with cardiovascular disease: The mediating role of illness perception and self-efficacy beliefs. *Behavioral Medicine, 41,* 9–17.

Green, B., & Griffiths, E. (2014). Birth order and post-traumatic stress disorder. *Psychology, Health and Medicine, 19,* 24–32.

Greever, K., Tseng, M., & Friedland, B. (1973). Development of the Social Interest Index. *Journal of Consulting and Clinical Psychology, 41,* 454–458.

Grey, L. (1998). *Alfred Adler, the forgotten prophet: A vision for the 21st century.* Westport, CT: Praeger.

Grice, J. (2002). Idiogrid: Software for the management and analysis of repertory grids. *Behavior Research Methods, Instruments, and Computers, 34,* 338–341.

Grieser, C., Greenberg, R., & Harrison, R. H. (1972). The adaptive function of sleep: The differential effects of sleep and dreaming on recall. *Journal of Abnormal Psychology, 80,* 280–286.

Gronerod, C., Overskeid, G., & Hartmann, E. (2013). Under Skinner's skin: Gauging a behaviorist from his Rorschach protocol. *Journal of Personality Assessment, 95,* 1–12.

Grotz, M., Hapke, U., Lampert, T., & Baumeister, H. (2011). Health locus of control and health behavior: Results from a nationally representative sample. *Psychology, Health & Medicine, 16,* 129–140.

Grubrich-Simitis, I. (1998). "Nothing about the totem meal!" on Freud's notes. In M. S. Roth (Ed.), *Freud: Conflict and culture* (pp. 17–31). New York: Knopf.

Guan, B., Deng, Y., & Luo, X. (2010). Characteristics of behavior and self-concept in psychological abused/neglected juveniles with generalized anxiety disorder. *Chinese Journal of Clinical Psychology, 28,* 334–336.

Gudmundsson, E. (2009). Guidelines for translating and adapting psychological instruments. *Nordic Psychology, 61*(2), 29–45.

Gundersen, K., Brown, M., Bhathal, P., & Kennedy, S. (2011). *Birth order perceptions: Personality differences between believers and nonbelievers.* American Psychological Association Convention Presentation. http://psycnet.apa.org/psycextra/702992011-001.pdf

Gungor, D., Bornstein, M., De Leersnyder, J., Cote, L., Ceulemans, E., & Mesquita, B. (2013). Acculturation of personality: A three-culture study of Japanese, Japanese Americans, and European Americans. *Journal of Cross-Cultural Psychology, 44,* 701–718.

Gunsung, L. (2013). *Relations between ego-resiliency, interpersonal competence, subjective well-being, and depression.* American Psychological Association Convention Presentation. Honolulu, Hawaii.

Guo-Xing, S., & Hai, Y. (2006). Subjective well-being of middle-school children. *Chinese Mental Health Journal, 20,* 238–241.

Gupta, R., Derevensky, J., & Ellenbogen, S. (2006). Personality characteristics and risk-taking tendencies among adolescent gamblers. *Canadian Journal of Behavioral Science, 38,* 201–213.

Gupta, N., Ganster, D., & Kepes, S. (2013). Assessing the validity of sales self-efficacy: A cautionary tale. *Journal of Applied Psychology, 98,* 690–700.

Gurven, M., von Rueden, C., Massenkoff, M., Kaplan, H., & Lero Vie, M. (2013). How universal is the Big Five? Testing the five factor model of personality variation among forager-farmers in the Bolivian Amazon. *Journal of Personality and Social Psychology, 104,* 354–370.

Gwandure, C., & Mayekiso, T. (2010). Predicting HIV risk using a locus of control-based model among university students. *Journal of Child and Adolescent Mental Health, 22,* 119–129.

Hackett, G. (1995). Self-efficacy in career choice and development. In A. Bandura (Ed.), *Self-efficacy in changing societies* (pp. 232–258). Cambridge, England: Cambridge University Press.

Hafner, J. L., Fakouri, M. E., & Labrentz, H. L. (1982). First memories of "normal" and alcoholic individuals. *Individual Psychology, 38,* 238–244.

Hagedoorn, M., & Molleman, E. (2006). Facial disfigurement in patients with head and neck cancer: The role of social self-efficacy. *Health Psychology, 25,* 643–647.

Hagemann, D., & Naumann, E. (2009). States versus traits: An integrated model for the test of Eysenck's arousal/arousability hypotheses. *Journal of Individual Differences, 30*(2), 87–98.

Haghayegh, S., & Oreyzia, H. (2009). Relation of aggression types according to Karen Horney's theory with negative and positive driving behaviors and accidents. *Iranian Journal of Psychiatry and Clinical Psychology, 15*(1), 81–85.

Hall, A. (2005). Sensation seeking and the use and selection of media materials. *Psychological Reports, 97,* 236–244.

Hall, C., & Van de Castle, R. (1965). An empirical investigation of the castration complex in dreams. *Journal of Personality, 33,* 20–29.

Hall, E. (1983, June). A conversation with Erik Erikson. *Psychology Today,* pp. 22–30.

Hall, M. H. (1967, September). An interview with "Mr. Behaviorist" B. F. Skinner. *Psychology Today,* pp. 21–23, 68–71.

Hall, M. H. (1968, July). A conversation with Abraham H. Maslow. *Psychology Today,* pp. 35–37, 54–57.

Hamberger, L. K., & Hastings, J. E. (1992). Racial differences on the MCMI in an outpatient clinical sample. *Journal of Personality Assessment, 58,* 90–95.

Hamermesh, D., & Abrevaya, J. (2011). Beauty is the promise of happiness? Discussion Paper No. 5600. Bonn, Germany: The Institute for the Study of Labor.

Hamm, J. (2000). Do birds of a feather flock together? The variable bases for African American, Asian American, and European American adolescents' selection of similar friends. *Developmental Psychology, 36,* 209–219.

Hampson, S., Andrews, J., Barckley, M., Lichtenstein, E., & Lee, M. (2000). Conscientiousness, perceived risk, and risk-reduction behaviors: A preliminary study. *Health Psychology, 19,* 496–500.

Hampson, S., & Goldberg, L. (2006). A first large cohort study of personality trait stability over the 40 years between elementary school and midlife. *Journal of Personality and Social Psychology, 91,* 763–779.

Hampson, S., Tildesley, E., Andrews, J., Barckley, M., & Peterson, M. (2013). Smoking trajectories across high school: Sensation seeking and hookah use. *Nicotine & Tobacco Research, 15,* 1400–1408.

Handel, R. W., & Ben-Porath, Y. S. (2000). Multicultural assessment with the MMPI- 2: Issues for research and practice. In R. H. Dana (Ed.), *Handbook of cross-cultural and multicultural personality assessment* (pp. 229–245). Mahwah, NJ: Erlbaum.

Hanewitz, W. B. (1978). Police personality: A Jungian perspective. *Crime and Delinquency, 24,* 152–172.

Hankoff, L. D. (1987). The earliest memories of criminals. *International Journal of Offender Therapy and Comparative Criminology, 31,* 195–201.

Hansel, A., & von Kanel, R. (2013). Unconscious fearful priming followed by a psychosocial stress test results in higher cortisol levels. *Stress & Health: Journal of the International Society for the Investigation of Stress, 29,* 317–323.

Hansen, E., & Breivik, G. (2001). Sensation-seeking as a predictor of positive and negative risk behavior among adolescents. *Personality and Individual Differences, 30,* 627–640.

Hanson, R. K. (1992). Thematic analysis of daily events as a method of personality assessment. *Journal of Personality Assessment, 58,* 606–620.

Happiness improves health and lengthens life, review finds. (2011, March 1). *Science Daily.*

Harber, K. D. (1998). Feedback to minorities: Evidence of a positive bias. *Journal of Personality and Social Psychology, 73,* 622–628.

Hardy, J. (2014). Dynamics in the self-efficacy/performance relationship following failure. *Personality and Individual Differences, 71,* 151–158.

Harker, L., & Keltner, D. (2001). Expressions of positive emotion in women's college yearbook pictures and their relationship to personality and life outcomes across adulthood. *Journal of Personality and Social Psychology, 80,* 112–124.

Harrington, D. M., Block, J. H., & Block, J. (1987). Testing aspects of Carl Rogers' theory of creative environments: Child-rearing antecedents of creative potential in young adolescents. *Journal of Personality and Social Psychology, 52,* 851–856.

Harrington, R., & Loffredo, D. A. (2001). The relationship between life satisfaction, self-consciousness, and the Myers-Briggs Type Inventory dimensions. *Journal of Psychology, 135,* 439–450.

Harris, B. (2011). Review of playing with fire: The controversial career of Hans J. Eysenck. *History of Psychiatry, 22,* 500–501.

Harris, D., & Kuba, I. (1997). Ethnocultural identity and eating disorders in women of color. *Professional Psychology, 28,* 341–347.

Hart, D., Atkins, R., & Matsuba, M. (2008). The association of neighborhood poverty with personality change in childhood. *Journal of Personality and Social Psychology, 94*(6), 1048–1061.

Harter, S., Marold, D. B., Whitesell, N. R., & Cobbs, G. (1996). A model of the effects of perceived parent and peer support on adolescent false-self behavior. *Child Development, 67,* 360–374.

Hartmann, E., & Hartmann, T. (2014).The impact of exposure to Internet-biased information about the Rorschach and the MMPI-2 on psychiatric outpatients' ability to simulate mentally healthy test performance. *Journal of Personality Assessment, 96*, 432–444.

Hartshorne, J. (2010, January 11). How birth order affects your personality. *Scientific American.* http://www.scientific american.com/article/ruled-by-birth-order/.

Hartshorne, J., Salem-Hartshorne, N., & Hartshorne, T. (2009). Birth order effects in the formation of long-term relationships. *Journal of Individual Psychology, 65*, 156–176.

Haslam, N. (2011). The return of the anal character. *Review of General Psychology, 15*, 351–360.

Hawi, N. (2013). Arabic validation of the Internet Addiction Test. *Cyberpsychology, Behavior, & Social Networking, 16*, 200–204.

Hawkins, R. P., Peterson, R. F., Schweid, E., & Bijou, S. W. (1966). Behavior therapy in the home: Amelioration of problem parent-child relations with the parent in a therapeutic role. *Journal of Experimental Child Psychology, 4*, 99–107.

Hayes, H., & Joseph, S. (2003). Big Five correlates of three measures of subjective well-being. *Personality and Individual Differences, 34*, 723–727.

Hazler, R. (2011). Person-centered theory. In D. Capuzzi & R. Douglas (Eds.), *Counseling and psychotherapy* (5th ed., pp. 143–166). Alexandria, VA: American Counseling Association.

Headey, B., Muffels, R., & Wagner, G. (2010). Long-running German panel survey shows that personal and economic choices, not just genes, matter for happiness. *Proceedings of the National Academy of Sciences, 107*(42), 17922–17926.

Heaven, P., & Ciarrochi, J. (2006). Perceptions of parental styles and Eysenckian psychoticism in youth. *Personality and Individual Differences, 41*, 61–70.

Heckhausen, J., & Schulz, R. (1995). A life-span theory of control. *Psychological Review, 102*, 284–304.

Heine, S., & Buchtel, E. (2009). Personality: The universal ad the culturally specific. *Annual Review of Psychology, 60*, 369–394.

Heine, S., Lehman, D., Markus, H., & Kitayama, S. (1999). Is there a universal need for positive self-regard? *Psychological Review, 106*, 766–794.

Heine, S., & Renshaw, K. (2002). Inter-judge agreement, self-enhancement, and liking: Cross-cultural divergences. *Personality and Social Psychology Bulletin, 28*, 578–587.

Heine, S., Takata, T., & Lehman, D. R. (2000). Beyond self-presentation: Evidence for self-criticisms among Japanese. *Personality and Social Psychology Bulletin, 26*, 71–78.

Hejazi, E., & Hasany, H. (2014). Identity styles, ethnic identity, and academic self-efficacy in Kurd students. *Journal of Psychology, 18*, 161–175.

Heller, D., Watson, D., & Hies, R. (2004). The role of person versus situation in life satisfaction. *Psychological Bulletin, 130*, 574–600.

Heller, M., & Haynal, V. (1997). Depression and suicide faces. In P. Ekman & E. L. Rosenberg (Eds.), *What the face reveals* (pp. 398–407). New York: Oxford University Press.

Helms, J. (1990). *Black and white racial identity: Theory, research, and practice.* New York: Greenwood Press.

Helson, R. (1992). Women's difficult times and the rewriting of the life story. *Psychology of Women Quarterly, 16*, 331–347.

Helson, R., & Klohnen, E. C. (1998). Affective coloring of personality from young adulthood to midlife. *Personality and Social Psychology Bulletin, 24*, 241–252.

Helson, R., & Srivastava, S. (2001). Three paths of adult development: Conservers, seekers, and achievers. *Journal of Personality and Social Psychology, 80*, 995–1010.

Helson, R., Stewart, A., & Ostrove, J. (1995). Identity in three cohorts of midlife women. *Journal of Personality and Social Psychology, 69*, 544–557.

Herbert, T. B., & Cohen, S. (1993). Depression and immunity: A meta-analytic review. *Psychological Bulletin, 113*, 472–486.

Herrera, N., Zajonc, R., Wieczorkowska, G., & Cichomski, B. (2003). Beliefs about birth rank and their reflection in reality. *Journal of Personality and Social Psychology, 85*, 142–150.

Hess, A., & Hess, K. (2010). *Karen Horney: An appreciation of the development of a trans-systemic theorist.* American Psychological Association Convention Presentation. San Diego, California.

Hibbard, D., & Buhrmester, D. (2010). Competitiveness, gender, and adjustment among adolescents. *Sex Roles, 63* (5–6), 412–424.

Hickman, G. (2009). Review of *Neglected Children and Their Families,* 2nd ed. *Social Work Education, 28*, 935–938.

Hilgard, E. (1987). *Psychology in America: A historical survey.* San Diego: Harcourt Brace Jovanovich.

Hill, J., Pace, T., & Robbins, R. (2010). Decolonizing personality assessment and honoring indigenous voices: A critical examination of the MMPI-2. *Cultural Diversity and Ethnic Minority Psychology, 16*, 16–25.

Hill, P., & Turiano, N. (2014). Purpose in life as a predictor of mortality across adulthood. *Psychological Science, 25*, 1482–1486.

Hillen, M., de Haes, H., Stalpers, L., Klinkenbijl, J., Eddes, E., Verdam, M., et al. (2014). How attachment style and locus of contol influence patients' trust in their oncologist. *Journal of Psychosomatic Research, 76*, 221–226.

Hines, D., Douglas, E., & Mahmood, S. (2010). The effects of survey administration on disclosure rates to sensitive items among men: A comparison of an Internet panel with a RDD telephone sample. *Computers in Human Behavior, 26*, 1327–1335.

Hintsanen, M., Puttonen, S., Tornroos, M., Jokela, M., Pukki-Raback, L., Hintsa, L., et al. (2014). Five-factor personality traits and sleep: Evidence from two population-based cohort studies. *Health Psychology, 33*, 1214–1223.

Hiroto, D. S. (1974). Locus of control and learned helplessness. *Journal of Experimental Psychology, 102*, 187–193.

Hirsh, J., Walker, K., Wilkinson, R., & Lyness, J. (2014). Family criticism and depressive symptoms in older adult primary care patients: Optimism and pessimism as moderators. *American Journal of Geriatric Psychiatry, 22*, 632–635.

Hjertass, T. (2009). Rediscovering the construct of basic anxiety. *Journal of Individual Psychology, 65*, 47–56.

Ho, M., Chen, S., & Hoffman, E. (2012). Unpacking cultural variations in peak experiences: Cross-cultural comparisons of early childhood recollection between Hong Kong and Brazil. *Journal of Happiness Studies, 13*, 247–260.

Ho, M., Chen, S., Hoffman, E., Guan, Y., & Iversen, V. (2013). Cross-cultural comparisons of adults' childhood recollections: How are peak experiences described in China and Portugal? *Journal of Happiness Studies, 14,* 185–197.

Hobfoll, S. E., Rom, T., & Segal, B. (1989). Sensation seeking, anxiety, and risk taking in the Israeli context. In S. Einstein (Ed.), *Drug and alcohol use: Issues and factors* (pp. 53–59). New York: Plenum Press.

Hofer, C., Eisenberg, N., & Reiser, M. (2010). The role of socialization, effortful control, and ego resiliency in French adolescents' social functioning. *Journal of Research on Adolescence, 30*(3), 555–582.

Hoffman, E. (1988). *The right to be human: A biography of Abraham Maslow.* Los Angeles, CA: Tarcher.

Hoffman, E. (1994). *The drive for self: Alfred Adler and the founding of individual psychology.* Reading, MA: Addison-Wesley.

Hoffman, E. (Ed.). (1996). *Future visions: The unpublished papers of Abraham Maslow.* Thousand Oaks, CA: Sage.

Hoffman, E., Kaneshiro, S., & Compton, W. (2012). Peak experiences among Americans in midlife. *Journal of Humanistic Psychology, 52,* 479–503.

Hofmann, W., Luhmann, M., Fisher, R., Vohs, K., & Baumeister, R. (2014). Yes, but are they happy? Effects of trait self-control on affective well-being and life satisfaction. *Journal of Personality, 4,* 265–277.

Holahan, C. K., & Holahan, C. J. (1987). Self-efficacy, social support, and depression in aging: A longitudinal analysis. *Journal of Gerontology, 42,* 65–68.

Holder, M., & Klassen, A. (2010). Temperament and happiness in children. *Journal of Happiness Studies, 11,* 419–439.

Holland, C., Geraghty, J., & Shah, K. (2010). Differential moderating effect of locus of control on effect of driving experience in young male and female drivers. *Personality and Individual Differences, 48,* 821–826.

Holmgren, S., Molander, B., & Nilsson, K. (2006). Intelligence and executive functioning in adult age: Effects of sibship size and birth order. *European Journal of Cognitive Psychology, 18,* 138–158.

Holtgraves, T. (2004). Social desirability and self-reports: Testing models of socially desirable responding. *Personality and Social Psychology Bulletin, 30,* 161–172.

Holtz, P., & Appel, M. (2011). Internet use and video gaming predict behavior in early adolescence. *Journal of Adolescence, 34,* 49–58.

Holzberger, D., Philipp, A., & Kunter, M. (2013). How teachers' self-efficacy is related to instructional quality: A longitudinal analysis. *Journal of Educational Psychology, 105,* 774–786.

Holzman, P. S. (1994). Hilgard on psychoanalysis as a science. *Psychological Science, 5,* 190–191.

Hoppmann, C., Gerstorf, D., Willis, S., & Schaie, K. (2011). Spousal interrelations in happiness in the Seattle Longitudinal Study: Considerable similarities in levels and change over time. *Developmental Psychology, 47,* 1–8.

Horikawa, T., Tamaki, M., Miyawaki, Y., & Kamitani, Y. (2013). Neural decoding of visual imagery during sleep. *Science, 340,* 639–642.

Horn, J. (2001). Obituary: Raymond Bernard Cattell, 1905–1998. *American Psychologist, 56,* 71–72.

Horney, K. (1926). The flight from womanhood. *International Journal of Psychoanalysis, 7.*

Horney, K. (1937). *The neurotic personality of our time.* New York: Norton.

Horney, K. (1939). *New ways in psychoanalysis.* New York: Norton.

Horney, K. (1942). *Self-analysis.* New York: Norton.

Horney, K. (1945). *Our inner conflicts.* New York: Norton.

Horney, K. (1967). The flight from womanhood: The masculinity-complex in women as viewed by men and by women. In H. Kelman (Ed.), *Feminine psychology.* New York: Norton.

Horney, K. (1980). *The adolescent diaries of Karen Horney.* New York: Basic Books. [Diaries written 1899–1911].

Horney, K. (1987). *Final lectures.* D. H. Ingram (Ed.). New York: Norton. [Lectures delivered 1952].

Hoseinzadah, A., Azizi, M., & Tavakoli, H. (2014). Social support and life satisfaction in adolescents: The mediating role of self-efficacy and self-esteem. *Journal of Iranian Psychologists, 11,* 103–114.

Howell, L., & Beth, A. (2004). Pioneers in our own lives: Grounded theory of lesbians' midlife development. *Journal of Women and Aging, 16,* 133–147.

Howell, R., & Howell, C. (2008). The relation of economic status to subjective well-being in developing countries: A meta-analysis. *Psychological Bulletin, 134*(4), 536–560.

Hsu, L., & Alden, L. (2008). Cultural influences on willingness to seek treatment for social anxiety in Chinese- and European-heritage students. *Cultural Diversity and Ethnic Minority Psychology, 14*(3), 215–223.

Huajian, C., Quipin, W., & Brown, J. (2009). Is self-esteem a universal need? Evidence from the people's Republic of China. *Asian Journal of Social Psychology, 12*(23), 104–120.

Huang, C. (2010a). Internet use and psychological well-being: A meta-analysis. *Cyberpsychology, Behavior, and Social Networking, 13*(3), 241–249.

Huang, C. (2010b). Mean-level change in self-esteem from childhood through adulthood: Meta-analysis of longitudinal studies. *Review of General Psychology, 14*(3), 251–260.

Huang, C., & Park, D. (2013). Cultural influences on Facebook photographs. *International Journal of Psychology, 48,* 334–343.

Huang, J., & Yang, Y. (2010). The relationship between personality traits and online shopping motivations. *Social Behavior and Personality, 38,* 673–680.

Huesmann, L. (2010). Nailing the coffin shut on doubts that violent video games stimulate aggression: Comment on Anderson et al. (2010). *Psychological Bulletin, 136,* 179–181.

Huesmann, L., Eron, L., Dubow, E., & Seebauer, E. (1987). Television viewing habits in childhood and adult aggression. *Child Development, 58,* 357–367.

Huesmann, L., Moise-Titus, J., Podolski, C., & Eron, L. (2003). Longitudinal relations between children's exposure to TV violence and their aggressive and violent behavior in young adulthood: 1977–1992. *Developmental Psychology, 39,* 201–221.

Huifang, Y., & Shuming, Z. (2004, July). A research on the personality types of business managers. *Psychological Science (China),* 983–985.

Hunt, C., Keogh, E., & French, C. (2006). Anxiety sensitivity: The role of conscious awareness and selective attentional bias to physical threat. *Emotion, 6,* 418–428.

Huo-Liang, G. (2006). Personality and crime: A meta-analysis of studies on criminals' behavior. *Chinese Mental Health Journal, 20,* 465–468.

Hur, Y. (2009). Genetic and environmental contributions to childhood temperament in South Korean twins. *Twin Research and Human Genetics, 12,* 549–551.

Hussain, M. (2014). The robustness of high Danish national happiness: A temporal cross-country analysis of population subgroups. *Social Indicators Research, 118,* 759–774.

Hutcheson, C., Fleming, M., & Martin, C. (2014). An examination and appreciation of locus of control in psychosis: Issues and relationships between constructs and measurement. *Journal of Psychiatric and Mental Health Nursing, 21,* 906–916.

Hutson, M. (2010). Sleep: Sweet dreams. *Psychology Today, 43* (1), 29.

Hwang, W. (2006). The psychotherapy adaptation and modification framework: Application to Asian Americans. *American Psychologist, 61,* 702–715.

Iacovino, J., Jackson, J., & Oltmanns, T. (2014). The relative impact of socioeconomic status and childhood trauma on Black-White differences in paranoid personality disorder syndrome. *Journal of Abnormal Psychology, 123,* 225–230.

Ibanez, G., Kuperminc, G., Jurkovic, G., & Perilla, J. (2004). Cultural attributes and adaptations linked to achievement motivation among Latino adolescents. *Journal of Youth and Adolescence, 33,* 559–568.

Ickes, W., Park, A., & Johnson, A. (2012). Linking identity status to strength of sense of self: Theory and validation. *Self and Identity, 11,* 531–544.

Ifcher, J., & Zarghamee, H. (2014). The happiness of single mothers: Evidence from the General Social Survey. *Journal of Happiness Studies, 15,* 1219–1238.

Isaacowitz, D. (2005a). Correlates of well-being in adulthood and old age: A tale of two optimisms. *Journal of Research in Personality, 39,* 224–244.

Isaacowitz, D. (2005b). The gaze of the optimist. *Personality and Social Psychology Bulletin, 31,* 407–415.

Iskender, M., & Akin, A. (2010). Social self-efficacy, academic locus of control, and Internet addiction. *Computers and Education, 54,* 1101–1106.

Ispas, D., Iliescu, D., Ilie, A., & Johnson, R. (2014). Exploring the cross-cultural generalizability of the five-factor model of personality: The Romanian Neo PI-R. *Journal of Cross-Cultural Psychology, 45,* 1074–1088.

Israelashvili, M., Kim, T., & Bukobza, G. (2012). Adolescents' over-use of the cyber world: Internet addiction or identity exploration? *Journal of Adolescence, 35,* 417–424.

Ivtzan, I., Gardner, H., Bernard, I., Sekhon, M., & Hart, R. (2013). Well-being through self-fulfillment: Examining developmental aspects of self-actualization. *Humanistic Psychologist, 41*(2), 119–132.

Iyer, P., Dougall, A., & Jensen-Campbell, L. (2013). Are some adolescents differentially susceptible to the influence of bullying on depression? *Journal of Research on Personality, 47,* 272–281.

Jack, R., Caldara, R., & Schyns, P. (2012). Internal representations reveal cultural diversity in expectations of facial expressions of emotion. *Journal of Experimental Psychology: General, 13,* 19–25.

Jackson, M., & Sechrest, L. (1962). Early recollections in four neurotic diagnostic categories. *Journal of Individual Psychology, 18,* 52–56.

Jacobson, J. L., & Wille, D. E. (1986). The influence of attachment patterns on developmental changes in peer interaction from the toddler to the preschool period. *Child Development, 57,* 338–347.

Jackson, T., Wang, Y., Wang, Y., & Fan, H. (2014). Self-efficacy and chronic pain outcomes: A meta-analytic review. *Journal of Pain, 15,* 800–814.

Jaffé, A. (1971). *The myth of meaning: Jung and the expansion of consciousness.* New York: Putnam.

James, S., Kavanagh, P., Jonason, P., Chonody, J., & Scrutton, H. (2014). The Dark Triad, schadenfreude and sensational interests: Dark personalities, dark emotions, and dark behaviors. *Personality and Individual Differences, 68,* 211–216.

Janarthanam, D., & Gnanadevan, R. (2014). Gender differences in ego-identity status in higher secondary students. *International Journal of Teacher Educational Research, 3,* 2319–4642.

Jasinskaja-Lahti, I., Liebkind, K., Jaakkola, M., & Reuter, A. (2006). Perceived discrimination, social support networks, and psychological well-being among three immigrant groups. *Journal of Cross-Cultural Psychology, 37,* 293–311.

Jensen-Campbell, L., & Graziano, W. G. (2000). Beyond the school yard: Relationships as moderators of daily interpersonal conflict. *Personality and Social Psychology Bulletin, 26,* 923–935.

Jensen-Campbell, L., & Malcolm, K. (2007). The importance of conscientiousness in adolescent and interpersonal relationships. *Personality and Social Psychology Bulletin, 33,* 368–383.

Jerusalem, M., & Mittag, W. (1995). Self-efficacy in stressful life transitions. In A. Bandura (Ed.), *Self-efficacy in changing societies* (pp. 177–201). Cambridge, England: Cambridge University Press.

Jeshmaridian, S. (2007). Commemorating the 100th birthday of Gordon Allport. *International Psychology Bulletin, 11*(3), 31–32.

Jiao, S., Ji, G., & Jing, Q. (1986). Comparative study of behavioral qualities of only children and sibling children. *Child Development, 57,* 357–361.

John, O. P. (1990). The Big Five factor taxonomy: Dimensions of personality in the natural language and in questionnaires. In L. A. Pervin (Ed.), *Handbook of personality: Theory and research* (pp. 66–100). New York: Guilford Press.

John, O. P., Pals, J. L., & Westenberg, P. M. (1998). Personality prototypes and ego development: Conceptual similarities and relations in adult women. *Journal of Personality and Social Psychology, 74,* 1093–1108.

Johnson, M., Rowatt, W., & Petrini, L. (2011). A new trait on the market: Honesty-humility as a unique predictor of job performance ratings. *Personality and Individual Differences, 50,* 857–862.

Johnson, R. C. (1980). Summing up [Review of the book *Personality and learning theory: Vol. 1. The structure of personality in its environment*]. *Contemporary Psychology, 25,* 299–300.

Johnson, W., McGue, M., & Krueger, R. (2005). Personality stability in late adulthood: A behavioral genetic analysis. *Journal of Personality, 73,* 523–552.

Joiner, R. (1998). The effect of gender on children's software preferences. *Journal of computer Assisted Learning, 14,* 195–198.

Jokela, M. (2010). Characteristics of the first child predict the parents' probability of having another child. *Developmental Psychology, 46,* 915–926.

Jokela, M., Bleidorn, W., Lamb, M., Gosling, S., & Rentfrow, P. (2015). Geographically varying associations between personality and life satisfaction in the London metropolitan area. *PNAS Proceedings of the National Academy of Sciences of the United States of America, 112,* 725–730.

Jokela, M., Kivimaki, M., Elovainio, M., & Keltikangas-Jarvinen, L. (2009). Personality and having children: A two-way relationship. *Journal of Personality and Social Psychology, 96*(1), 218–230.

Jokela, M., Pulkki-Rabach, L., Elovainio, M., & Kivmaki, M. (2014). Personality traits as risk factors for stroke and coronary heart disease mortality: Pooled analysis of three cohort studies. *Journal of Behavioral Medicine, 37,* 881–889.

Jonason, P., & Webster, G. (2010). The dirty dozen: A concise measure of the dark triad. *Psychological Assessment, 22,* 420–432.

Jones, E. (1953, 1955, 1957). *The life and work of Sigmund Freud* (3 vols.). New York: Basic Books.

Jones, R. L. (1994). An empirical study of Freud's penis-baby equation. *Journal of Nervous and Mental Disease, 182*(3), 127–135.

Jones, R. M., Dick, A., Coyl-Sheherd, D., & Ogletree, M. (2014). Antecedents in the male adolescent identity crisis: Age, grade, and physical development. *Youth and Society, 46,* 443–459.

Jonkmann, K., Thoemmes, F., Ludtke, O., & Trautwein, U. (2013). Personality traits and living arrangements in young adulthood: Selection and socialization. *Developmental Psychology, 50,* 683–698.

Jonsdottir, S., Arnarson, E., & Smari, J. (2008). Body esteem, perceived competence, and depression in Icelandic adolescents. *Nordic Psychology, 60*(11), 58–71.

Joo, Y., Joung, S., & Sim, W. (2011). Structural relationships among internal locus of control, institutional support, flow, and learner persistence in cyber universities. *Computer in Human Behavior, 27*(2), 714–722.

Joormann, J., & Gotlib, I. (2006). Is this happiness I see? Biases in the identification of emotional facial expressions in depression and social phobia. *Journal of Abnormal Psychology, 115,* 705–714.

Jordan-Conde, Z., Mennecke, B., & Townsend, A. (2014). Late adolescent identity definition and intimate disclosure on Facebook. *Computers in Human Behavior, 33,* 356–366.

Jorm, A. F. (1987). Sex differences in neuroticism: A quantitative synthesis of published research. *Australian and New Zealand Journal of Psychiatry, 21,* 501–506.

Joseph, S., & Linley, P. (2005). Positive adjustment to threatening events: An organismic valuing theory of growth through adversity. *Review of General Psychology, 9,* 262–280.

Judge, T., Erez, A., Bono, J., & Thoresen, C. (2002). Are measures of self-esteem, neuroticism, locus of control, and generalized self-efficacy indicators of a common core construct? *Journal of Personality and Social Psychology, 83,* 693–710.

Judge, T., Jackson, C., Shaw, J., Scott, J., & Rich, B. (2007). Self-efficacy and work-related performance: The integral role of individual differences. *Journal of Applied Psychology, 92,* 107–127.

Jung, C. (2009). *The red book: Liber novus.* New York: Norton.

Jung, C. G. (1909). The association method. In H. Read, M. Fordham, & G. Adler (Eds.), *The collected works of C. G. Jung* (Vol. 2, pp. 442, 444). Princeton, NJ: Princeton University Press.

Jung, C. G. (1923). Psychological types. In *Collected works* (Vol. 6). Princeton, NJ: Princeton University Press.

Jung, C. G. (1927). The structure of the psyche. In *Collected works* (Vol. 8, pp. 139–158). Princeton, NJ: Princeton University Press.

Jung, C. G. (1928). On psychic energy. In *Collected works* (Vol. 8, pp. 3–66). Princeton, NJ: Princeton University Press.

Jung, C. G. (1930). The stages of life. In *Collected works* (Vol. 8, pp. 387–403). Princeton, NJ: Princeton University Press.

Jung, C. G. (1947). On the nature of the psyche. In *Collected works* (Vol. 8, pp. 159–234). Princeton, NJ: Princeton University Press.

Jung, C. G. (1953). *Two essays on analytical psychology.* New York: Pantheon.

Jung, C. G. (1961). *Memories, dreams, reflections.* New York: Vintage Books.

Kagan, J. (1984). *The nature of the child.* New York: Basic Books.

Kagan, J. (1989). Temperamental contributions to social behavior. *American Psychologist, 44,* 668–674.

Kagan, J. (1999). *Three seductive ideas.* Cambridge, MA: Harvard University Press.

Kagan, J., Kearsley, R., & Zelazo, P. (1978). *Infancy.* Cambridge, MA: Harvard University Press.

Kagan, J., Snidman, N., & Arcus, D. (1992). Initial reactions to unfamiliarity. *Current Directions in Psychological Science, 1,* 171–174.

Kahneman, D., Krueger, A., Schkade, D., Schwartz, N., & Stone, A. (2006). Would you be happier if you were richer? A focusing illusion. *Science, 312,* 1908–1910.

Kahr, B. (2010). Four unknown Freud anecdotes. *American Imago, 67*(2), 301–312.

Kalichman, S. C., Johnson, J. R., Adair, V., Rompa, D., Multhauf, K., & Kelly, J. A. (1994). Sexual sensation seeking: Scale development and predicting AIDS-risk behavior among homosexually active men. *Journal of Personality Assessment, 62,* 385–397.

Kalpidou, M., Costin, D., & Morris, J. (2011). The relationship between Facebook and the well-being of undergraduate college students. *Cyberpsychology, Behavior, and Social Networking, 14*(4), 183–189.

Kanagawa, C., Cross, S. E., & Markus, H. R. (2001). "Who am I?" The cultural psychology of the conceptual self. *Personality and Social Psychology Bulletin, 27,* 90–103.

Kandel, E. (2012). *The age of insight: The quest to understand the unconscious in art, mind, and brain, from Vienna 1900 to the present.* New York: Random House.

Kandler, C. (2012). Nature and nurture in personality development: The case of neuroticism and extraversion. *Current Directions in Psychological Science, 21,* 290–296.

Kandler, C., Bleidorn, W., Reimann, R., Spinath, F., Thiel, W., & Angleitner, A. (2010). Sources of cumulative continuity in personality: A longitudinal multiple-rater twin study. *Journal of Personality and Social Psychology, 98*(6), 995–1008.

Kandler, C., Kornadt, A., Hagemeyer, B., & Neyer, F. (2014, December 29). Patterns and sources of personality development in old age. *Journal of Personality and Social Psychology.* http://psycnet.apa.org/doi/10.1037/pspp0000028

Kang, H., Chang, K., Chen, C., & Greenberger, E. (2015). Locus of control and peer relationships among Caucasian, Hispanic, Asian, and African American adolescents. *Journal of Youth and Adolescence, 44,* 184–194.

Kang, S., & Jung, J. (2014). Smartphone basic needs scale. *Computers in Human Behavior, 35,* 376–387. http://www.sciencedirect.com/science/article/pii/S0747563214001460

Kaplan, R., Atkins, C. J., & Reinsch, S. (1984). Specific efficacy expectations mediate exercise compliance in patients with COPD. *Health Psychology, 3,* 223–242.

Kaplan, R., & Saccuzzo, D. (2005). *Psychological testing: Principles, applications, and issues.* Belmont, CA: Thomson Wadsworth.

Karim, N., Zamzuri, N., & Nor, Y. (2009). Exploring the relationship between Internet ethics in university students and the big five model of personality. *Computers and Education, 53*(1), 86–93.

Kashima, Y., Kokubo, T., Kashima, E., Boxall, D., Yamaguchi, S., & Macrae, K. (2004). Cultural and self: Are there within-culture differences in self between metropolitan areas and regional cities? *Personality and Social Psychology Bulletin, 30,* 816–823.

Kasler, J., & Nevo, O. (2005). Early recollections as predictors of study area choice. *Journal of Individual Psychology, 61,* 217–232.

Kaufman, J., & Bristol, A. (2001). When Allport met Freud: Using anecdotes in the teaching of psychology. *Teaching of Psychology, 28,* 44–46.

Kaufman, M. T. (2002, September 8). Face it: Your looks are revealing. *New York Times.*

Kaufman, M., Cornish, F., Zimmerman, R., & Johnson, B. (2014). Health behavior change models for HIV prevention and AIDS care: Practical recommendations for a multi-level approach. *JAIDS Journal of Acquired Immune Deficiency Syndromes, 66,* 250–258.

Kazdin, A. E. (1989). *Behavior modification in applied settings* (4th ed.). Pacific Grove, CA: Brooks/Cole.

Kazdin, A. E., & Bootzin, R. (1972). The token economy: An evaluative review. *Journal of Applied Behavioral Analysis, 5,* 343–372.

Kean, S. (2013, July). Treasures in the attic. *Washingtonian,* pp. 47–51.

Kelly, G. A. (1955). *The psychology of personal constructs.* New York: Norton.

Kelly, G. A. (1958). The theory and technique of assessment. *Annual Review of Psychology, 9,* 323–352.

Kelly, G. A. (1969). *Clinical psychology and personality: The selected papers of George Kelly.* B. Maher (Ed.). New York: Wiley.

Kelly, T. (2010, May 14). Is the Internet the secret to happiness? *Time.* http://content.time.com/time/health/article/0,8599,1989244,00.html.

Keltikangas-Jaruinen, L., & Raikkonen, K. (1990). Healthy and maladjusted Type A behavior in adolescents. *Journal of Youth and Adolescence, 19,* 1–18.

Keltner, D. (1997). Facial expression, personality, and psychopathology. In P. Ekman & E. L. Rosenberg (Eds.), *What the face reveals* (pp. 450–452). New York: Oxford University Press.

Keniston, K. (1983, June). Remembering Erikson at Harvard. *Psychology Today,* p. 29.

Kenrick, D., Griskevicius, S., Neuberg, S., & Schaller, M. (2010). Renovating the pyramid of needs: Contemporary extensions built upon ancient foundations. *Psychological Science, 5*(3), 292–314.

Kerestes, G. (2006). Birth order and maternal ratings of infant temperament. *Studia Psychologica, 48,* 95–106.

Kernis, M. H., Paradise, A. W., Whitaker, D. J., Wheatman, S. R., & Goldman, B. N. (2000). Master of one's psychological domain? Not likely if one's self-esteem is unstable. *Personality and Social Psychology Bulletin, 26,* 1297–1305.

Kerr, N. (1984). The tyranny of the shoulds. *Perspectives in Psychiatric Care, 22,* 16–19.

Keyes, C., Shmotkin, D., & Ryff, D. (2002). Optimizing well-being: The empirical encounter of two traditions. *Journal of Personality and Social Psychology, 82,* 1007–1022.

Khan, M., Breitenecker, R., & Schwarz, E. (2014). Entrepreneurial team locus of control: Diversity and trust. *Management Decision, 52,* 1057–1081.

Khodarahimi, S. (2014, August 9). Sensation-seeking and risk-taking behaviors: A study on young Iranian adults. *Applied Research in Quality of Life.* http://www.researchgate.net/publication/264616810_Sensation-Seeking_and_Risk-Taking_Behaviors_A_Study_on_Young_Iranian_Adults

Kiang, L., Witkow, M., Baldomar, O., & Fuligni, A. (2010). Change in ethnic identity across the high school years among adolescents with Latin American, Asian, and European background. *Journal of Youth and Adolescence, 39,* 683–693.

Kidwell, J. (1982). The neglected birth order: Middle-borns. *Journal of Marriage and the Family, 44,* 225–235.

Kihlstrom, J. F. (1994). Psychodynamics and social cognition. *Journal of Personality, 62,* 681–696.

Kim, E., Hogge, I., & Salvisberg, C. (2014). Effects of self-esteem and ethnic identity: Acculturative stress and psychological well-being among Mexican immigrants. *Hispanic Journal of Behavioral Sciences, 36,* 144–163.

King, L. A., & Napa, C. K. (1998). What makes a life good? *Journal of Personality and Social Psychology, 75,* 156–165.

Kirschenbaum, H. (2009). *The life and work of Carl Rogers.* Alexandria, VA: American Counseling Association.

Kirschenbaum, H., & Jourdan, A. (2005). The current status of Carl Rogers and the person-centered approach. *Psychotherapy: Theory, Research, Practice, Training, 42,* 37–51.

Kivimaki, M., Vahtera, J., Elovainio, M., Helenius, H., Singh-Manoux, A., & Pentti, J. (2005). Optimism and pessimism as predictors of change in health after death or onset of severe illness in family. *Health Psychology, 24,* 413–421.

Klahr, A., & Burt, S. (2014). Elucidating the etiology of individual differences in parenting: A meta-analysis of behavioral genetic research. *Psychological Bulletin, 140,* 544–586.

Klein, M. H., Malthieu, P. L., Gendlin, E. T., & Kiesler, D. J. (1969). *The experiencing scale: A research and training manual.* Madison: Wisconsin Psychiatric Institute.

Klimstra, T., Hale, W., Raaijmakers, Q., Branje, S., & Meeus, W. (2010). Identity formation in adolescence: Change or stability? *Journal of Youth and Adolescence, 39*(2), 150–162.

Kloep, M., Guney, N., Cok, F., & Simsek, O. (2009). Motives for risk-taking in adolescence: A cross-cultural study. *Journal of Adolescence, 32*(1), 135–151.

Klug, H., & Maier, G. (2015). Linking goal progress and subjective well-being: A meta-analysis. *Journal of Happiness Studies, 16,* 37–65.

Knaster, C. (2013). The effect of assessee ethnicity on clinical interpretation of the MMPI-2. *Dissertation Abstracts International. Section B: Sciences and Engineering. Vol. 74 (3-BE).*

Knaster, C., & Mucucci, J. (2013). The effect of client ethnicity on clinical interpretation of the MMPI-2. *Assessment, 20,* 43–47.

Konu, A., Lintonen, T., & Rimpelae, M. (2002). Factors associated with schoolchildren's general subjective well-being. *Health Education Research, 17,* 155–165.

Kopp, R., & Eckstein, D. (2004). Using early memory metaphors and client-generated metaphors in Adlerian therapy. *Journal of Individual Psychology, 60,* 163–174.

Kosaka, Y. (2008). Developmental changes in inferiority feelings in adolescents and young adults: Important areas of the self. *Japanese Journal of Educational Psychology, 56,* 218–229.

Kosciw, J., Palmer, N., & Kull, R. (2014, April 2). Reflecting resiliency: Openness about sexual orientation and/or gender identity and its relationship to well-being and educational outcomes for LGBT students. *American Journal of Community Psychology.* http://link.springer.com/article/10.1007%2Fs10464-014-9642-6

Kosten, T. A., Ball, S. A., & Rounsaville, B. J. (1994). A sibling study of sensation seeking and opiate addiction. *Journal of Nervous and Mental Disease, 182,* 284–289.

Kotov, R., Gamez, W., Schmidt, F., & Watson, D. (2010). Linking "Big" personality traits to anxiety, depressive, and substance use disorders: A meta-analysis. *Psychological Bulletin, 136*(5), 768–821.

Koren, M. (2013, March 20). B. F. Skinner: The man who taught pigeons to play ping-pong and rats to pull levers. *Smithsonian.com.* http://www.smithsonianmag.com/ist/?next=/science-nature/bf-skinner-the-man-who-taught-pigeons-to-play-ping-pong-and-rats-to-pull-levers-5363946/

Kracke, W. (2010). Dream interpretation in the Amazon. *Journal of Developmental and Behavioral Pediatrics, 31*(4), 367–368.

Krahe, B., Busching, R., & Moller, I. (2012). Media violence use and aggression among German adolescents: Associations and trajectories of change in a three-wave longitudinal study. *Psychology of Popular Media Culture, 1,* 152–166.

Krahe, B., & Moller, I. (2004). Playing violent electronic games, hostile attributional style, and aggression-related norms in German adolescents. *Journal of Adolescence, 27,* 53–69.

Kramer, N., & Winter, S. (2008). Impression management 2.0: The relationship of self-esteem, extraversion, self-efficacy, and self-presentation within social networking sites. *Journal of Media Psychology, 20*(3), 106–116.

Kristensen, P., & Bjerkedal, T. (2007). Explaining the relation between birth order and intelligence. *Science, 316,* 1717.

Kristjansson, K. (2010). Positive psychology, happiness, and virtue: The troublesome conceptual issues. *Review of General Psychology, 14*(4), 296–310.

Kroger, J., Martinussen, M., & Marcia, J. (2010). Identity status during adolescence and young adulthood: A meta-analysis. *Journal of Adolescence, 33,* 683–689.

Kronstrom, K., Karlsson, H., Nabi, H., Oksanen, T., Salo, P., Sjosten, N., et al. (2014). Optimism and pessimism as predictors of initiating and ending an antidepressant medication treatment. *Nordic Journal of Psychology, 68,* 1–7.

Kross, E., Verduyn, P., Demiralp, E., Park, J., Lee, D., Lin, N., et al. (2013). Facebook use predicts declines in subjective well-being. *PLoS ONE, 8*(8). http://www.plosone.org/article/info%3Adoi%2F10.1371%2Fjournal.pone.0069841

Kruger, J. (1999). Lake Wobegon be gone! The "below-average" effect and the egocentric nature of comparative ability judgments. *Journal of Personality and Social Psychology, 77,* 221–232.

Krüll, M. (1986). *Freud and his father.* New York: Norton.

Kuhn, M., & Kinsky, M. (2013). *Observational learning of romantic relationship behavior in emerging adults.* American Psychological Association Convention Program. http://c.ymcdn.com/sites/www.spsp.org/resource/resmgr/conference_programs/div82013.pdf

Kulshrestha, U., & Sen, C. (2006). Subjective well-being in relation to emotional intelligence and locus of control among executives. *Journal of the Indian Academy of Applied Psychology, 32,* 129–134.

Kunzmann, U., Little, T., & Smith, J. (2000). Is age-related stability of subjective well-being a paradox? Cross-sectional and longitudinal evidence from the Berlin Aging Study. *Psychology and Aging, 15,* 511–526.

Kuo, T., & Tang, L. (2014). Relationships among personality traits, Facebook usages and leisure activities: A case of Taiwanese college students. *Computers in Human Behavior, 31,* 13–19.

Kupfersmid, J. (1995). Does the Oedipus complex exist? *Psychotherapy: Theory, Research, Practice, Training, 32,* 535–547.

Kurman, J. (2001). Self-enhancement: Is it restricted to individualistic cultures? *Personality and Social Psychology Bulletin, 27,* 1705–1716.

Lacey, H., Smith, D., & Ubel, P. (2006). Hope I die before I get old: Mispredicting happiness. *Journal of Happiness Studies, 7,* 167–182.

Lachman, M. E. (1985). Personal efficacy in middle and old age: Differential and normative patterns of change. In G. H. Elder, Jr. (Ed.), *Life course dynamics* (pp. 188–216). Ithaca, NY: Cornell University Press.

LaFountain, R. (2009). Alfred Adler's place in the field of psychology. *General Psychologist, 44*(2), 22–25.

Laird, T., & Shelton, A. (2006). From an Adlerian perspective: Birth order, dependency, and binge drinking on a historically Black university campus. *Journal of Individual Psychology, 62,* 18–35.

Lam, L., & Peng, Z. (2010). Effect of pathological use of the Internet on adolescent mental health. *Archives of Pediatric and Adolescent Medicine, 164,* 901–908.

Lam, R., & Tam, V. (2011). Correlates of identity statuses among Chinese adolescents in Hong Kong. *International Journal of Adolescent Medicine and Health, 23,* 51–58.

Lambert, C. (2007, January–February). The science of happiness. *Harvard Magazine, 109,* 26–30, 94.

Lambrecht, S., Shredl, M., Henley-Einion, J., & Blagrove, M. (2013). Self-rated effects of reading, TV viewing and daily activities on dreaming in adolescents and adults: The UK library study. *International Journal of Dream Research, 6,* 41–44.

Lang, F., & Heckhausen, J. (2001). Perceived control over development and subjective well-being: Differential benefits across adulthood. *Journal of Personality and Social Psychology, 81,* 509–523.

Lang, R., & Rispoli, M. (2015). Introduction to the special issue: Behavioral interventions to enhance academic outcomes. *Behavior Modification, 39,* 3–7.

Langan-Fox, J., & Roth, S. (1995). Achievement motivation and female entrepreneurs. *Journal of Occupational and Organizational Psychology, 68,* 209–218.

Lapan, R. T., Boggs, K. R., & Morrill, W. H. (1989). Self-efficacy as a mediator of investigative and realistic general occupational themes on the Strong-Campbell Interest Inventory. *Journal of Counseling Psychology, 36,* 176–182.

Larsen, R. J., & Kasimatis, M. (1991). Day-to-day symptoms: Individual differences in the occurrence, duration, and emotional concomitants of minor daily illness. *Journal of Personality, 59,* 387–423.

Larsson, H., Andershed, H., & Lichtenstein, P. (2006). A genetic factor explains most of the variation in the psychopathic personality. *Journal of Abnormal Personality, 115,* 221–230.

Lau, J., Rijsdijk, F., & Eley, C. (2006). I think, therefore I am: A twin study of attributional style in adolescents. *Journal of Child Psychology and Psychiatry, 47,* 696–703.

Laursen, B., Pulkkinen, L., & Adams, R. (2002). The antecedents and correlates of agreeableness in adulthood. *Developmental Psychology, 38,* 591–603.

Law, A., Logan, H., & Baron, R. S. (1994). Desire for control, felt control, and stress inoculation training during dental treatment. *Journal of Personality and Social Psychology, 67,* 926–936.

Law, D., Shapka, J., & Olson, B. (2010). To control or not to control? Parenting behaviors and adolescent online aggression. *Computers in Human Behavior, 26*(6), 1651–1656.

Le, T., Lai, M., & Wallen, J. (2009). Multiculturalism and subjective happiness as mediated by cultural and relational variables. *Cultural Diversity and Ethnic Minority Psychology, 15* (3), 303–313.

Leak, G. (2006a). Development and validation of a revised measure of Adlerian social interest. *Social Behavior and Personality, 34,* 443–450.

Leak, G. (2006b). An empirical assessment of the relationship between social interest and spirituality. *Journal of Individual Psychology, 62,* 59–69.

Leak, G., & Leak, K. (2006). Adlerian social interest and positive psychology. *Journal of Individual Psychology, 62,* 207–223.

Leatherdale, S., & Papadakis, S. (2011). A multi-level examination of the association between older social models in the school environment and overweight and obesity among younger students. *Journal of Youth and Adolescence, 40,* 361–372.

Lee, H., Offidani, E., Ziegelstein, R., Bienvenu, O., Samuels, J., Eaton, W., et al. (2014). Five-factor model personality traits as predictors of incident coronary heart disease in the community: A ten-and-a-half year cohort study based on the Baltimore Epidemiologic Catchment Area Follow-Up Study. *Psychosomatics: Journal of Consultation and Liaison Psychiatry, 55,* 352–361.

Lee, J., & Lee, R. (2014, June 20). Examining forms of discrimination and ethnic identity on adjustment. *APA Division 45, Society for the Psychological Study of Ethnic Minority Issues. Research Conference Presentation.* http://psycnet.apa.org/psycextra/517842014-001.pdf

Lee, M., Okazaki, S., & Yoo, H. (2006). Frequency and intensity of social anxiety in Asian Americans and European Americans. *Cultural Diversity and Ethnic Minority Psychology, 12,* 291–305.

Lee, Y. T., & Seligman, M. E. P. (1997). Are Americans more optimistic than the Chinese? *Personality and Social Psychology Bulletin, 23,* 32–40.

Lefcourt, H. M. (1982). *Locus of control: Current trends in theory and research* (2nd ed.). Hillsdale, NJ: Erlbaum.

Lefcourt, H. M., Martin, R. A., Fick, C. M., & Saleh, W. E. (1985). Locus of control for affiliation in social interactions. *Journal of Personality and Social Psychology, 48,* 755–759.

Leising, D., Borkenau, P., Zimmermann, J., Roski, C., Leonhardt, A., & Schutz, A. (2013). Positive self-regard and claim to leadership: Two fundamental forms of self-evaluation. *European Journal of Personality, 27,* 565–579.

Lefkowitz, M. M., & Tesiny, E. P. (1984). Rejection and depression: Prospective and contemporaneous analysis. *Developmental Psychology, 20,* 776–785.

Leonard, R., & Burns, A. (2006). Turning points in the lives of midlife and older women: Five-year follow-up. *Australian Psychologist, 41,* 28–36.

Leontopoulou, S. (2006). Resilience of Greek youth at an educational transition point: The role of locus of control and coping strategies as resources. *Social Indicators Research, 76,* 95–126.

Lester, D. (1990). Maslow's hierarchy of needs and personality. *Personality and Individual Differences, 11,* 1187–1188.

Lester, D. (2009). Cognitive complexity and personality. *Perceptual and Motor Skills,109,* 605–606.

Leung, B., Moneta, G., & McBride-Chang, C. (2005). Think positively and feel positively: Optimism and life satisfaction in late life. *International Journal of Aging and Human Development, 61,* 335–365.

Levenson, M. R. (1990). Risk taking and personality. *Journal of Personality and Social Psychology, 58,* 1073–1080.

Levinson, D. J. (1978). *The seasons of a man's life.* New York: Knopf.

Levinson, D. J. (1996). *The seasons of a woman's life.* New York: Knopf.

Lewis, C., Varvatsoulias, G., & George, W. (2012). The psychological type profile of Greek Orthodox churchgoers in London. *Mental Heath, Religion and Culture, 15,* 979–986.

Lewis, J. (2014, February 25). Internet trolls are also real-life trolls. *Psychology Headquarters, The Guardian.* http://www.theguardian.com/science/head-quarters/2014/feb/25/Internet-trolls-are-also-real-life-trolls

Leyens, J., Camino, L., Parke, R., & Berkowitz, L. (1975). Effects of movie violence on aggression in a field setting as a function of group dominance and cohesion. *Journal of Personality and Social Psychology, 32,* 346–360.

Li, F., McAuley, E., Harmer, P., Duncan, T., & Chaumeton, N. (2001). Tai Chi enhances self-efficacy and exercise behavior in older adults. *Journal of Aging and Physical Activity, 9,* 161–171.

Li, M., Mardhekar, V., & Wadkar, A. (2012). Coping strategies and learned helplessness of employed and nonemployed educated married women from India. *Health Care for Women International, 33,* 495–508.

Li, Y. (2010). Research on the relationship between self-efficacy, marital adjustment, occupational stress and subjective well-being of primary and secondary school headteachers. *Chinese Journal of Clinical Psychology, 18,* 363–365.

Libran, E., & Howard, V. (2006). Personality dimensions and subjective well-being. *Spanish Journal of Psychology, 9,* 38–44.

Lightsey, O., Burke, M., Ervin, A., Henderson, D., & Yee, C. (2006). Generalized self-efficacy, self-esteem, and negative affect. *Canadian Journal of Behavioral Science, 38,* 72–80.

Lillevoll, K., Kroger, J., & Martinussen, M. (2013). Identity status and anxiety: A meta-analysis. *Identity: An International Journal of Theory and Research, 13,* 214–227.

Lin, Y., & Raghubir, P. (2005). Gender differences in unrealistic optimism about marriage and divorce. *Personality and Social Psychology Bulletin, 31,* 198–207.

Linares, K., Subrahmanyam, K., Cheng, R., & Guan, S. (2011). A second life within second life: Are virtual world users creating new selves and new lives? *International Journal of Cyber Behavior, Psychology and Learning, 1,* 50–71.

Lindstrom, M. (2011). Social capital, political trust, and health locus of control: A population-based study. *Scandinavian Journal of Public Health, 39,* 3–9.

Lingiardi, F., & De Bei, F. (2011). Questioning the couch: Historical and clinical perspectives. *Psychoanalytic Psychology, 28,* 389–404.

Lippa, R. A., Martin, L. R., & Friedman, H. S. (2000). Gender related individual differences and mortality in the Terman longitudinal study: Is masculinity hazardous to your health? *Personality and Social Psychology Bulletin, 26,* 1560–1570.

Lischetzke, T., & Eid, M. (2006). Why extraverts are happier than introverts: The role of mood regulation. *Journal of Personality, 74,* 1127–1162.

Litwin, H. (2005). Correlates of successful aging: Are they universal? *International Journal of Aging and Human Development, 61,* 313–333.

Liu, M., & Guo, F. (2010). Patenting practices and their relevance to child behaviors in Canada and China. *European Journal of Personality, 23*(3), 153–182.

Liu, W., Rochlen, A., & Mohr, J. (2005). Real and ideal gender-role conflict: Exploring psychological distress among men. *Psychology of Men and Masculinity, 6,* 137–148.

Livingston, N., Oost, K., Heck, N., & Cochran, B. (2014). Psychology of addictive behaviors: The role of personality in predicting drug and alcohol use among sexual minorities. *Psychology of Addictive Behaviors.* http://s1.labroots.com/user/publications/detail-search/ipi/Pubmed/id/25347022/title/the-role-of-personality-in-predicting-drug-and-alcohol-use-among-sexual-minorities.

Llamas, J., & Consoli, M. (2014). Freshman struggles: Role of locus of control on intragroup marginalization and distress. *American Psychological Association.* https://education.ucsb.edu/news/2014/gevirtz-school-faculty-and-students-take-part-16-events-2014-american-psychological

Locke, E. A., & Latham, G. P. (1990). *A theory of goal setting and task performance.* Englewood Cliffs, NJ: Prentice-Hall.

Lockenhoff, C., Terracciano, A., & Costa, P. (2009). Five-factor model personality traits and the retirement transition: Longitudinal and cross-sectional associations. *Psychology and Aging, 24*(3), 722–728.

Loehlin, J. C., Horn, J. M., & Willerman, L. (1990). Heredity, environment, and personality change: Evidence from the Texas adoption project. *Journal of Personality, 58,* 221–243.

Loehlin, J. C., & Nichols, R. C. (1976). *Heredity, environment, and personality: A study of 850 sets of twins.* Austin: University of Texas Press.

Loffredo, D., & Opt, S. (2006). Argumentativeness and Myers-Briggs Type Indicator preferences. *Journal of Psychological Type, 66,* 59–68.

Loftus, E., & Davis, D. (2006). Recovered memories. *Annual Review of Clinical Psychology, 2,* 469–498.

Loftus, E., & Ketcham, K. (1994). *False memories and allegations of sexual abuse.* New York: St. Martin's Press.

Lohr, J., Olatunji, B., Baumeister, R., & Bushman, B. (2007). The psychology of anger venting and empirically supported alternatives that do no harm. *Scientific Review of Mental Health Practice, 5,* 53–64.

Loman, M., Johnson, A., Quevedo, K., Lafavor, T., & Gunnar, R. (2014). Risk-taking and sensation-seeking propensity in postinstitutionalized early adolescents. *Journal of Child Psychology and Psychiatry, 55,* 1145–1152.

Londerville, S., & Main, M. (1981). Security of attachment, compliance, and maternal training methods in the second year of life. *Developmental Psychology, 17,* 289–299.

Lonnqvist, J., Itkonen, J., Verkasaio, M., & Poutvaara, P. (2014). The five-factor model of personality and degree and transitivity of Facebook social networks. *Journal of Research in Personality, 50,* 98–101.

Loo, C. M. (1998). *Chinese America: Mental health and quality of life in the inner city.* Thousand Oaks, CA: Sage.

Lopez, I. (2008). "But you don't look Puerto Rican": The moderating effects of ethnic identity on the relation between skin color and self-esteem among Puerto Rican women. *Cultural Diversity and Ethnic Minority Psychology, 14*(2), 102–108.

Lowell, A., Viezel, K., Davis, A., & Castillo, J. (2011). *Adaptive behavior in abused and neglected children.* American Psychological Association Convention Presentation.

Lucas, R., & Diener, E. (2001). Understanding extraverts' enjoyment of social situations: The importance of pleasantness. *Journal of Personality and Social Psychology, 81,* 343–356.

Lucas, R., & Donnellan, M. (2009). Age differences in personality: Evidence from a nationally representative Australian sample. *Developmental Psychology, 45*(5), 1353–1363.

Lucas, R., & Fujita, F. (2000). Factors influencing the relation between extraversion and pleasant affect. *Journal of Personality and Social Psychology, 79,* 1039–1056.

Luce, K., Winzelberg, A., Das, S., Osborne, M., Bryson, S., & Taylor, C. (2007). Reliability of self-report: Paper versus online administration. *Computers in Human Behavior, 23,* 1384–1389.

Luhmann, M., & Eid, M. (2009). Does it feel the same? Changes in life satisfaction following repeated life events. *Journal of Personality and Social Psychology, 97*(2), 363–381.

Luyckx, K., Goossens, L., Soenens, B., Beyers, W., & Vansteenkiste, M. (2005). Identity statuses based on four rather than two identity dimensions: Extending and refining Marcia's paradigm. *Journal of Youth and Adolescence, 34,* 605–618.

Lynn, M., & Steel, P. (2006). National differences in subjective well-being: The interactive effects of extraversion and neuroticism. *Journal of Happiness Studies, 7,* 155–165.

Lynne-Landsman, S., Graber, J., Nichols, T., & Botvin, G. (2011). Is sensation seeking a stable trait or does it change over time? *Journal of Youth and Adolescence, 40,* 48–58.

Lyons, D. (2002). Freer to be me: The development of executives at midlife. *Consulting Psychology Journal: Practice and Research, 54,* 15–27.

Lyubomirsky, S. (2001). Why are some people happier than others? The role of cognitive and motivational processes in well-being. *American Psychologist, 56,* 239–249.

Lyubomirsky, S., King, L., & Diener, E. (2005). The benefits of frequent positive affect: Does happiness lead to success? *Psychological Bulletin, 131,* 803–855.

Mackavey, W. R., Malley, J. E., & Stewart, A. J. (1991). Remembering autobiographically consequential experiences: Content analysis of psychologists' accounts of their lives. *Psychology and Aging, 6,* 50–59.

Maddux, J. E. (2002). The power of believing you can. In C. R. Snyder & S. J. Lopez (Eds.), *Handbook of positive psychology* (pp. 277–287). New York: Oxford University Press.

Magnus, K., Diener, E., Fujita, F., & Pavot, W. (1993). Extraversion and neuroticism as predictors of objective life events: A longitudinal analysis. *Journal of Personality and Social Psychology, 65,* 1046–1053.

Mahalik, J. R., Cournoyer, R. J., DeFranc, W., Cherry, M., & Napolitano, J. M. (1998). Men's gender role conflict and use of psychological defenses. *Journal of Counseling Psychology, 45,* 247–255.

Mahoney, J., & Hartnett, J. (1973). Self-actualization and self-ideal discrepancy. *Journal of Psychology, 85,* 37–42.

Mahoney, J., Thompson-Lake, D., Cooper, K., Verrico, C., Newton, T., & De la Garza, R. (2015). A comparison of impulsivity, depressive symptoms, lifetime stress and sensation seeking in healthy controls versus participants with cocaine and methamphetamine use disorders. *Journal of Psychopharmacology, 28,* 50–56.

Mahoney, P. (1992). Freud as a family therapist: Reflections. In T. Gelfand & J. Kerr (Eds.), *Freud and the history of psychoanalysis* (pp. 307–317). Hillsdale, NJ: Analytic Press.

Mahoney, P. J. (1986). *Freud and the rat man.* New Haven, CT: Yale University Press.

Maier, S. F., Laudenslager, M., & Ryan, S. M. (1985). Stressor controllability, immune function, and endogenous opiates. In F. R. Brush & J. B. Overmier (Eds.), *Affect, conditioning, and cognition: Essays on the determinants of behavior* (pp. 203–210). Hillsdale, NJ: Erlbaum.

Maier, S. J., & Seligman, M. E. P. (1976). Learned helplessness: Theory and evidence. *Journal of Experimental Psychology, 105,* 3–46.

Maio, G. R., Fincham, F. D., & Lycett, E. J. (2000). Attitudinal ambivalence toward parents and attachment style. *Personality and Social Psychology Bulletin, 26,* 1451–1464.

Malcolm, J. (1984). *In the Freud archives.* New York: Knopf.

Malloy, T., Albright, L., Diaz-Loving, R., Dong, Q., & Lee, Y. (2004). Agreement in personality judgments within and between nonoverlapping social groups in collectivist cultures. *Personality and Social Psychology Bulletin, 30,* 106–117.

Manaster, G. (2006). *Adlerian lifestyle counseling* by W. Rule & M. Bishop [book review]. *PsycCritiques: APA Review of Books, 51.*

Manaster, G., & Mays, M. (2004). Early recollections: A conversation. *Journal of Individual Psychology, 60,* 107–114.

Manger, T., & Ekeland, O. (2000). On the relationship between locus of control, level of ability and gender. *Scandinavian Journal of Psychology, 41,* 225–229.

Manning, M. M., & Wright, T. L. (1983). Self-efficacy expectancies, outcome expectancies, and the persistence of pain control in childbirth. *Journal of Personality and Social Psychology, 45,* 421–431.

Maqsud, M., & Rouhani, S. (1991). Relationships between socioeconomic status, locus of control, self-concept, and academic achievement of Botswana adolescents. *Journal of Youth and Adolescence, 20,* 107–114.

Marcano, M., Michaels, D., & Pierce, J. (2014). *Fantasy proneness, perceived locus of control, and their associaton with generalized anxiety.* American Psychological Association Convention Presentation. http://psycnet.apa.org/psycextra/544492014-001.pdf

Marcia, J. E. (1966). Development and validation of ego-identity status. *Journal of Personality and Social Psychology, 3,* 551–558.

Marcia, J. E. (1967). Ego identity status: Relationship to change in self-esteem, general maladjustment and authoritarianism. *Journal of Personality, 35,* 118–133.

Marcia, J. E. (1980). Identity in adolescence. In J. Adelson (Ed.), *Handbook of adolescent psychology* (pp. 159–187). New York: Wiley.

Marcia, J. E., & Friedman, M. L. (1970). Ego identity status in college women. *Journal of Personality, 38,* 249–263.

Marcus-Newhall, A., Pedersen, W., Miller, N., & Carlson, M. (2000). Displaced aggression is alive and well: A meta-analytic review. *Journal of Personality and Social Psychology, 78,* 670–689.

Mark, G., & Ganzach, Y. (2014). Personality and Internet usage: A large-scale representative study of young adults. *Computers in Human Behavior, 36,* 274–281.

Markel, H. (2011). *The anatomy of addiction: Sigmund Freud, William Halstead and the miracle drug cocaine.* New York: Vintage.

Marker, C., & Schneider, F. (2015). Further evidence for the validity of the Need Inventory of Sensation Seeking. *Personality and Individual Differences, 77,* 41–44.

Markstrom, C., & Marshall, S. (2007). The psychological inventory of ego strength: Examination of theory and psychometric properties. *Journal of Adolescence, 30,* 63–79.

Markstrom, C., Li, X., Blackshire, S., & Wilfong, J. (2005). Ego strength development of adolescents involved in adult-sponsored structured activities. *Journal of Youth and Adolescence, 34,* 85–95.

Marrero Quevedo, R., & Abella, M. (2011). Well-being and personality: Facet-level analysis. *Personality and Individual Differences, 50,* 206–211.

Marriott, Y., & Buchanan, T. (2014). The true self online: Personality correlates of preference for self-expression online, and observer ratings of personality online and offline. *Computers in Human Behavior, 323,* 171–177.

Marshall, G. N. (1991). A multidimensional analysis of internal health locus of control beliefs: Separating the wheat from the chaff? *Journal of Personality and Social Psychology, 61,* 483–491.

Marshall, G. N., Wortman, C. B., Vickers, R. R., Jr., Kusulas, J. W., & Hervig, L. K. (1994). The five-factor model of personality as a framework for personality-health research. *Journal of Personality and Social Psychology, 67,* 278–286.

Marshall, G., Schell, T., & Miles, J. (2009). Ethnic differences in posttraumatic stress: Hispanics' symptoms differ in kind and degree. *Journal of Consulting and Clinical Psychology, 77,* 1169–1178.

Martin, C. M. (1999). A developmental perspective on gender effects and gender concepts. In W. B. Swann, Jr., J. H. Langlois, & L. A. Gilbert (Eds.), *Sexism and stereotypes in modern society* (pp. 45–73). Washington, DC: American Psychological Association.

Martin, N., & Jardine, R. (1986). Eysenck's contributions to behavior genetics. In S. Modgil & L. Modgill (Eds.), *Hans Eysenck: Consensus and controversy* (pp. 13–47). London: Falmer.

Martin-Krumm, C., Sarrazin, P., Peterson, C., & Famose, J. (2003). Explanatory style and resilience after sports failure. *Personality and Individual Differences, 35,* 1685–1695.

Maruta, T., Colligan, R., Malinchoc, M., & Offord, K. (2000). Optimists versus pessimists: Survival rate among medical patients over a 30-year period. *Mayo Clinic Proceedings, 75,* 140–143.

Masling, J. M., Rabie, L., & Blondheim, S. H. (1967). Obesity, level of aspiration, and Rorschach and TAT measures of oral dependence. *Journal of Consulting Psychology, 31,* 233–239.

Maslow, A. H. (1957). A philosophy of psychology: The need for a mature science of human nature. *Main Currents in Modern Thought, 13,* 27–32.

Maslow, A. H. (1968). *Toward a psychology of being* (2nd ed.). New York: Van Nostrand Reinhold.

Maslow, A. H. (1970a). Tribute to Alfred Adler. *Journal of Individual Psychology, 26,* 13.

Maslow, A. H. (1970b). *Motivation and personality* (2nd ed.). New York: Harper & Row.

Maslow, A. H. (1971). *The farther reaches of human nature.* New York: Viking Press.

Maslow, A. H. (1979). *The journals of A. H. Maslow.* R. J. Lowry (Ed.). Pacific Grove, CA: Brooks/Cole.

Maslow, A. H. (1987). *Motivation and personality* (3rd ed.). New York: Harper & Row.

Mason, L., Shandera-Ochsner, A., Williamson, K., Harp, J., Edmundson, M., Berry, D., et al. (2013). Accuracy of MMPI-2-RF validity scales for identifying PTSD symptoms, random responding, and genuine PTSD. *Journal of Personality Assessment, 95,* 585–593.

Mason, W., & Suri, S. (2012). Conducting behavioral research on Amazon's Mechanical Turk. *Behavior Research Methods, 44,* 1–23.

Mastekaasa, A. (1995). Age variations in the suicide rates and self-reported subjective well-being of married and never married persons. *Journal of Community and Applied Social Psychology, 5,* 21–39.

Matheny, A. P. (1983). A longitudinal twin study of the stability of components from Bayley's Infant Behavior Record. *Child Development, 54,* 356–360.

Mathew, P., & Bhatewara, S. (2006). Personality differences and preferred styles of conflict management among managers. *Abhigyan* [Asian Journal of Management], *23*(4), 38–45.

Matthews, K. A., Batson, C. D., Horn, J., & Rosenman, R. H. (1981). "Principles in his nature which interest him in the fortune of others…": The heritability of empathic concern for others. *Journal of Personality, 49,* 237–247.

Mavioglu, R., Boomsma, D., & Bartels, M. (2015, February 1). Causes of individual differences in adolescent optimism: A study of Dutch twins and their siblings. *European Child & Adolescent Psychiatry.* http://www.ncbi.nlm.nih.gov/pubmed/25638288

Maxwell, C., Garner, J., & Skogan, W. (2011, June 29). Collective efficacy and criminal behavior in Chicago, 1995–2004. *US Department of Justice (DOJ), National Criminal Justice Reference Service, (NCJRS).* https://www.ncjrs.gov/pdffiles1/nij/grants/235154.pdf

Mayes, R., & Horwitz, A. (2005). DSM-III and the revolution in the classification of mental illness. *Journal of the History of the Behavioral Sciences, 41,* 249–267.

Mazandarani, A., Aguilar-Valaje, M., & Donhoff, G. (2013). Content analysis of Iranian college students' dreams: Comparison with American data. *Dreaming, 23,* 163–174.

Mazzoni, G. A. L., Lombardo, P., Malvagia, S., & Loftus, E. (1999). Dream interpretations and false beliefs. *Professional Psychology, 30,* 45–50.

McAdams, D., & Olson, B. (2010). Personality development: Continuity and change over the life course. *Annual Review of Psychology, 61,* 517–542.

McAdams, D. P. (2001). The psychology of life stories. *Review of General Psychology, 5,* 100–122.

McAdams, D. P., Diamond, A., de St. Aubin, E., & Mansfield, E. (1997). Stories of commitment: The psychosocial construction of generative lives. *Journal of Personality and Social Psychology, 72,* 678–694.

McAdams, D. P., Hart, H. M., & Maruna, S. (1998). The anatomy of generativity. In D. P. McAdams & E. de St. Aubin (Eds.), *Generativity and adult development* (pp. 7–43). Washington, DC: American Psychological Association.

McAdams, D. P., Reynolds, J., Lewis, M., Patten, A. H., & Bowman, P. J. (2001). When bad things turn good and good things turn bad: Sequences of redemption and contamination in life narratives and their relation to psychosocial adaptation in midlife adults and in students. *Personality and Social Psychology Bulletin, 27,* 474–485.

McAdams, D. P., Ruetzel, K., & Foley, J. M. (1986). Complexity and generativity at midlife: Relations among social motives, ego development, and adults' plans for the future. *Journal of Personality and Social Psychology, 50,* 800–807.

McAdams, D. P., & de St. Aubin, E. (1992). A theory of generativity and its assessment through self-report, behavior acts, and narrative themes in autobiography. *Journal of Personality and Social Psychology, 62,* 1003–1015.

McAdams, K., & Donnellan, M. (2009). Facets of personality and drinking in first-year college students. *Personality and Individual Differences, 46,* 207–212.

McCann, S., Stewin, L., & Short, R. (1990). Frightening dream frequency and birth order. *Individual Psychology, 46,* 304–310.

McCarthy, T. (2014). Great aspirations: The postwar American college counseling center. *History of Psychology, 17,* 1–18.

McClelland, D. C. (1965a). N[eed] achievement and entrepreneurship: A longitudinal study. *Journal of Personality and Social Psychology, 1,* 389–392.

McClelland, D. C. (1965b). Toward a theory of motive acquisition. *American Psychologist, 20,* 321–333.

McClelland, D. C. (1985). *Human motivation.* Glenview, IL: Scott, Foresman.

McClelland, D. C. (1987). Characteristics of successful entrepreneurs. *Journal of Creative Behavior, 3,* 219–233.

McClelland, D. C., Atkinson, J. W., Clark, R. A., & Lowell, E. L. (1953). *The achievement motive.* New York: Appleton-Century-Crofts.

McClelland, D. C., & Boyatzis, R. E. (1982). The leadership motive pattern and long-term success in management. *Journal of Applied Psychology, 67,* 737–743.

McClelland, D. C., & Franz, C. E. (1992). Motivational and other sources of work accomplishments in midlife: A longitudinal study. *Journal of Personality, 60,* 679–707.

McClelland, D. C., Koestner, R., & Weinberger, J. (1989). How do self-attributed and implicit motives differ? *Psychological Review, 96,* 690–702.

McClelland, S. (2014a). Sexual Satisfacton Q Sort. http://psycnet.apa.org/index.cfm?fa=search.display

TestOverview&id=&resultID=&page=1&dbT
ab=&uid=9999-35430-000&isMyList=0&doi=false

McClelland, S. (2014b). "What do you mean when you say that you are sexually satisfied?" A mixed methods study. *Feminism & Psychology, 24,* 74–96.

McCoy, H., & Bowen, E. (2014, August 22). Hope in the social environment: Factors affecting future aspiratons and school self-efficacy for youth in urban environments. *Child & Adolescent Social Work Journal.* http://link.springer.com/article/10.1007/s10560-014-0343-7#page-1

McCoy, T. (2014, December 11). "Learned helplessness": The chilling psychological concept behind the CIA's interrogation methods. *Washington Post.* http://www.washingtonpost.com/news/morning-mix/wp/2014/12/11/the-chilling-psychological-principle-behind-the-cias-interrogation-methods/

McCrae, R. (2011). Personality theories for the 21st century. *Teaching of Psychology, 38,* 209–214.

McCrae, R. R., & Costa, P. T., Jr. (1985a). Openness to experience. In R. Hogan & W. H. Jones (Eds.), *Perspectives in personality* (Vol. 1, pp. 145–172).

McCrae, R. R., & Costa, P. T., Jr. (1985b). Updating Norman's "adequate taxonomy": Intelligence and personality dimensions in natural language and questionnaires. *Journal of Personality and Social Psychology, 49*(3), 710–721.

McCrae, R. R., & Costa, P. T., Jr. (1987). Validation of the five-factor model of personality across instruments and observers. *Journal of Personality and Social Psychology, 52,* 81–90.

McCrae, R. R., & Costa, P. T., Jr. (1989). Reinterpreting the Myers-Briggs Type Indicator from the perspective of the five-factor model of personality. *Journal of Personality, 57,* 17–40.

McCrae, R. R., & Costa, P. T., Jr. (1991). Adding *Liebe* und *Arbeit:* The full five-factor model and well-being. *Personality and Social Psychology Bulletin, 17,* 227–232.

McCrae, R. R., & Costa, P. T., Jr. (1997). Personality trait structure as a human universal. *American Psychologist, 52,* 509–516.

McCrae, R. R., & Terracciano, A. (2005). Universal features of personality traits from the observer's perspective: Data from 50 cultures. *Journal of Personality and Social Psychology, 88,* 547–561.

McCrae, R. R., Costa, P. T., Jr., Hrebickova, M., Urbanek, T., Martin, T., Oryol, V., et al. (2004a). Age differences in personality traits across cultures: Self-report and observer perspectives. *European Journal of Personality, 18,* 143–157.

McCrae, R. R., Costa, P. T., Jr., Martin, T., Oryol, V., Rukavishnikov, A., Senin, I., et al. (2004b). Consensual validation of personality traits across cultures. *Journal of Research in Personality, 38,* 179–201.

McCrae, R. R., Costa, P. T., Jr., Ostendorf, F., Angleitner, A., Hrebíčková, M., Avia, M. D., et al. (2000). Nature over nurture: Temperament, personality, and life span development. *Journal of Personality and Social Psychology, 78,* 173–186.

McCrae, R. R., Costa, P. T., Jr., Pedroso de Lima, M., Simões, A., Ostendorf, F., Angleitner, A., et al. (1999). Age differences in personality across the adult life span: Parallels in five cultures. *Developmental Psychology, 35,* 466–477.

McCrae, R. R., Costa, P. T., Jr., Terracciano, A., Parker, W. D., Mills, C. J., DeFruyt, F., et al. (2002). Personality trait development from age 12 to age 18: Longitudinal, cross-sectional, and cross-cultural analyses. *Journal of Personality and Social Psychology, 83,* 1456–1468.

McCrae, R. R., Yi, M. S. M., Trapnell, P. D., Bond, M. H., & Paulhus, D. L. (1998). Interpreting personality profiles across cultures: Bilingual, acculturation, and peer rating studies of Chinese undergraduates. *Journal of Personality and Social Psychology, 74,* 1041–1055.

McCullough, M. (2001). Freud's seduction theory and its rehabilitation: A saga of one mistake after another. *Review of General Psychology, 5,* 3–22.

McCullough, M., Bellah, C., Kilpatrick, S., & Johnson, J. (2001). Vengefulness: Relationships with forgiveness, rumination, well-being, and the Big Five. *Personality and Social Psychology Bulletin, 27,* 601–610.

McDaniel, M., Beier, M., Perkins, A., Goggins, S., & Frankel, B. (2009). An assessment of the fakeability of self-report and implicit personality measures. *Journal of Research in Personality, 43,* 682–685.

McHale, S., Updegraff, K., Helms-Erikson, H., & Crouter, A. (2001). Sibling influences on gender development in middle childhood and early adolescence: A longitudinal study. *Developmental Psychology, 37,* 115–125.

McLaughlin, N. G. (1998). Why do schools of thought fail? Neo-Freudianism as a case study in the sociology of knowledge. *Journal of the History of the Behavioral Sciences, 34,* 113–134.

McLeod, B. (1986, October). Rx for health: A dose of self-confidence. *Psychology Today,* pp. 46–50.

McNally, B., & Bradley, G. (2014). Driving construals: Personal construct theory in a reckless driving context. *Transportation Research Part F: Traffic Psychology and Behavior, 24,* 71–82.

McNally, R., Clancy, S., Schacter, D., & Pitman, R. (2000). Personality profiles, dissociation, and absorption in women reporting repressed, recovered, or continuous memories of childhood sexual abuse. *Journal of Consulting and Clinical Psychology, 68,* 1033–1037.

McNally, R., Perlman, C., Ristuccia, C., & Clancy, S. (2006). Clinical characteristics of adults reporting repressed, recovered, or continuous memories of childhood sexual abuse. *Journal of Consulting and Clinical Psychology, 74,* 237–242.

McNulty, J. L., Graham, J. R., Ben-Porath, Y. S., & Stein, L. A. R. (1997). Comparative validity of MMPI-2 scores of African Americans and Caucasian mental health center clients. *Psychological Assessment, 9,* 464–470.

Medinnus, G., & Curtis, F. (1963). The relation between maternal self-acceptance and child acceptance. *Journal of Counseling Psychology, 27,* 542–544.

Mehdizadeh, S. (2010). Self-presentation 2.0: Narcissism and self-esteem on Facebook. *Cyberpsychology, Behavior, and Social Networking, 13,* 357–364.

Meier, B., Robinson, M., Carter, M., & Hinsz, V. (2010). Are social people more beautiful? A zero-sum acquaintance analysis of agreeableness, extraversion, and attractiveness. *Journal of Research in Personality, 44,* 283–296.

Melamed, B. G., & Siegel, L. J. (1975). Reduction of anxiety in children facing hospitalization and surgery by use of filmed modeling. *Journal of Consulting and Clinical Psychology, 43,* 511–521.

Mellor, S. (1989). Gender differences in identity formation as a function of self-other relationships. *Journal of Youth and Adolescence, 18,* 361–375.

Mellor, S. (1990). How do only children differ from other children? *Journal of Genetic Psychology, 151,* 221–230.

Meuss, W. (2011). The study of adolescent identity formation 2000–2010: A review of longitudinal research. *Journal of Research on Adolescence, 21,* 75–94.

Meyer, G. N. (2001). Introduction to the final special section in the special series on the utility of the Rorschach for clinical assessment. *Psychological Assessment, 13,* 419–422.

Meyer, O., Zane, N., Cho, Y., & Takeuchi, D. (2009). Use of specialty mental health services by Asian Americans with psychiatric disorders. *Journal of Consulting and Clinical Psychology, 77*(5), 1000–1005.

Michikyan, M., Subrahmanyam, K., & Dennis, J. (2014). Can you tell who I am? Neuroticism, extraversion, and online self-presentation among young adults. *Computers in Human Behavior, 33,* 179–183.

Migone, M. (2013). Psychoanalysis on the Internet: A discussion of its theoretical implications for both online and offline therapeutic technique. *Psychoanalytic Psychology, 30,* 281–299,

Miletic, M. P. (2002). The introduction of feminine psychology to psychoanalysis: Karen Horney's legacy. *Contemporary Psychoanalysis, 38,* 287–299.

Milgram, N. A. (1971). Locus of control in Negro and White children at four age levels. *Psychological Reports, 29,* 459–465.

Milosevic-Dordevic, J., & Zezilj, I. (2013). Psychological predictors of addictive social networking site use: The case of Serbia. *Computers in Human Behavior, 32,* 229–234.

Milot, T., Plamondon, A., Ethier, L., Lemelin, J., St-Laurent, D., & Rousseau, M. (2013). Validity of CBCL-derived PTSD and dissociation scales: Further evidence in a sample of neglected children and adolescents. *Child Maltreatment, 18,* 122–128.

Milton, J. (2002). *The road to malpsychia: Humanistic psychology and our discontents.* San Francisco, CA: Encounter Books.

Milyavskaya, M., & Koestner, R. (2011). Psychological needs, motivation, and well-being: A test of self-determination theory across multiple domains. *Personality and Individual Differences, 50,* 397–391.

Mindess, H. (1988). *Makers of psychology: The personal factor.* New York: Human Sciences Press.

Miner-Rubino, K., Winter, D., & Stewart, A. (2004). Gender, social class, and the subjective experience of aging: Self-perceived personality change from early adulthood to late midlife. *Personality and Social Psychology Bulletin, 30,* 1599–1610.

Minkov, M. (2009). Predictors of differences in subjective well-being across 97 nations. *Cross-Cultural Research, 43,* 162–179.

Miranda, A. O., Frevert, E. S., & Kern, R. M. (1998). Lifestyle differences between bicultural and low- and high-acculturation level Latino adults. *Individual Psychology, 54,* 119–134.

Mischel, W. (1968). *Personality and assessment.* New York: Wiley.

Mischel, W. (1973). Toward a cognitive social-learning reconceptualization of personality. *Psychological Review, 80,* 252–283.

Mishali, M., Omer, H., & Heymann, A. (2011). The importance of measuring self-efficacy in patients with diabetes. *Family Practice, 28,* 82–87.

Mittal, C., & Griskevicius, V. (2014). Sense of control under uncertainty depends on people's childhood environment: A life history theory approach. *Journal of Personality and Social Psychology, 107,* 621–637.

Mogilner, C. (2010). The pursuit of happiness: Time, money, and social connection. *Psychological Science, 21,* 1348–1354.

Mohammadi, A. (2013). Relationship between family environment and parenting styles with identity status. *International Family Therapy Association's 21st World Family Therapy Congress,* Orlando, Florida. http://psycnet.apa.org/doi/10.1037/e635102013-119

Moksnes, U., Moljord, I., Espnes, G., & Byrne, D. (2010). The association between stress and emotional states in adolescents: The role of gender and self-esteem. *Personality and Individual Differences, 49*(5), 430–435.

Montag, C., Jurkiewicz, M., & Reuter, M. (2010). Low self-directness is a better predictor for problematic Internet use than high neuroticism. *Computers in Human Behavior, 26,* 1531–1535.

Moolenaar, N., Sleegers, P., & Daly, A. (2012). Teaming up: Linking collaboration networks, collective efficacy, and student achievement. *Teaching and Teacher Education, 28,* 252–262.

Morehouse, R. E., Farley, F., & Youngquist, J. V. (1990). Type T personality and the Jungian classification system. *Journal of Personality Assessment, 54,* 231–235.

Moretti, M. M., & Higgins, E. T. (1990). Relating self-discrepancy to self-esteem: The contribution of discrepancy beyond actual-self ratings. *Journal of Experimental Social Psychology, 26,* 108–123.

Morewedge, C., & Norton, M. (2009). When dreaming is believing: The (motivated) interpretation of dreams. *Journal of Personality and Social Psychology, 96,* 249–264.

Morgan, C. D., & Murray, H. A. (1935). A method for investigating fantasies. *Archives of Neurology and Psychiatry, 34,* 289–306.

Morling, B., Kitayama, S., & Miyamoto, Y. (2002). Cultural practices emphasize influence in the United States and adjustment in Japan. *Personality and Social Psychology Bulletin, 28,* 311–323.

Mosher, D. (2011, June 17). High wired: Does addictive Internet use restructure the brain? *Scientific American.* http://www.scientificamerican.com/article/does-addictive-Internet-use-restructure-brain/

Moskowitz, D. S., & Schwartzman, A. E. (1989). Life paths of aggressive and withdrawn children. In D. M. Buss & N. Cantor (Eds.), *Personality psychology: Recent trends and emerging directions* (pp. 99–114). New York: Springer-Verlag.

Motley, M. T. (1987, February). What I meant to say. *Psychology Today,* pp. 24–28.

Mroczek, D., & Almeida, D. (2004). The effect of daily stress, personality, and age on daily negative affect. *Journal of Personality, 72,* 355–378.

Mroczek, D., & Spiro, A. (2005). Change in life satisfaction during adulthood: Findings from the veterans affairs normative aging study. *Journal of Personality and Social Psychology, 88,* 189–202.

Muller, K., Beutel, M., Egloff, B., & Wolfling, K. (2014). Investigating risk factors for Internet gaming disorder: A comparison of patients with addictive gaming, pathological gamblers and healthy controls regarding the Big Five personality traits. *European Addiction Research, 20,* 129–136.

Multon, K. D., Brown, S. D., & Lent, R. W. (1991). Relation of self-efficacy beliefs to academic outcomes: A meta-analytic investigation. *Journal of Counseling Psychology, 38,* 30–38.

Munsey, C. (2010). Does marriage make us happy? *Monitor on Psychology, 41*(9), 20–21.

Murdock, N. (2008). Carl Rogers lives: Person-centered theory in the United Kingdom. [Review of the book *Humanizing psychiatry and mental health care: The challenge of the person-centered approach.* Oxford, England: Radcliffe Publishing Co. 2007]. *PsycCRITIQUES, 53*(8), Article 11.

Muris, P. (2002). Relationships between self-efficacy and symptoms of anxiety disorders and depression in a normal adolescent sample. *Personality and Individual Differences, 32,* 337–348.

Muris, P., Meesters, C., & Timmermans, A. (2013). Some youths have a gloomy side: Correlates of the Dark Triad personality traits in non-clinical adolescents. *Child Psychiatry and Human Development, 44,* 658–665.

Murray, K. M., & Johnson, W. B. (2001). Personality type and success among female naval academy midshipmen. *Military Medicine, 166,* 889–893.

Muusses, L., Finkenauer, C., Kerkhof, P., & Billedo, C. (2014). A longitudinal study of the association between compulsive Internet use and well-being. *Computers in Human Behavior, 36,* 21–28.

Myers, D. G. (2000). The funds, friends, and faith of happy people. *American Psychologist, 55,* 56–67.

Myers, D. G., & Diener, E. (1995). Who is happy? *Psychological Science, 6,* 10–19.

Myers, L., & Derakshan, N. (2004). Do childhood memories colour social judgements of today? The case of repressors. *European Journal of Personality, 18,* 321–330.

Nakamura, M. (2002). Relationship between anxiety and physical traits of facial expression. *Japanese Journal of Psychology, 73,* 140–147.

Nasser, R., & Abouchedid, K. (2006). Locus of control and attribution for poverty: Comparing Lebanese and South African university students. *Social Behavior and Personality, 34,* 777–796.

Naus, M., Philipp, L., & Samsi, M. (2009). From paper to pixels: A comparison of paper and computer formats in psychological assessment. *Computers in Human Behavior, 25,* 1–7.

Nave, C., Sherman, R., Funder, D., Hampson, S., & Goldberg, L. (2010). On the contextual independence of personality: Teachers' assessments predict directly observed behavior after four decades. *Social Psychology and Personality Science, 1*(4), 327–334.

Nebbitt, V. (2009). Self-efficacy in African American adolescent males living in urban public housing. *Journal of Black Psychology, 35,* 295–316.

Needs, A. (1988). Psychological investigations of offending behavior. In F. Fransella & L. Thomas (Eds.), *Experimenting with personal construct psychology* (pp. 493–506). London: Routledge & Kegan Paul.

Neimeyer, G. J. (1984). Cognitive complexity and marital satisfaction. *Journal of Social and Clinical Psychology, 2,* 258–263.

Nelson, D. L., & Burke, R. J. (2000). Women executives. *Academy of Management Executive, 14,* 107–121.

Netz, Y., Wu, M., Becker, B., & Tenenbaum, G. (2005). Physical activity and psychological well-being in advanced age: A meta-analysis of intervention studies. *Psychology and Aging, 20,* 272–284.

Newbauer, J., & Stone, M. (2010). Social interest and self-reported distress in a delinquent sample: Application of the SSSI and the MAYSI-2. *Journal of Individual Psychology, 66,* 201–215.

Newman, L. S., Duff, K. J., & Baumeister, R. F. (1997). A new look at defensive projection: Thought suppression, accessibility, and biased person perception. *Journal of Personality and Social Psychology, 72,* 980–1001.

Newman, L. S., Higgins, E. T., & Vookles, J. (1992). Self-guide strength and emotional vulnerability: Birth order as a moderator of self-affect relations. *Personality and Social Psychology Bulletin, 18,* 402–411.

Newman, L. S., & McKinney, L. C. (2002). Repressive coping and threat-avoidance: An idiographic Stroop study. *Personality and Social Psychology Bulletin, 28,* 409–422.

Nezami, E., Zamani, R., & DeFrank, G. (2008). Linguistic translation of psychological assessment tools. *Evaluation and the Health Professions, 31*(3), 313–317.

Nezlek, J., & Allen, M. (2006). Social support as a moderator of day-to-day relationships between daily negative events and daily psychological well-being. *European Journal of Personality, 20,* 53–68.

Nezlek, J., Kowalski, R. M., Leary, M. R., Blevins, T., & Holgate, S. (1997). Personality moderators of reactions to interpersonal rejection: Depression and trait self-esteem. *Personality and Social Psychology Bulletin, 23,* 1235–1244.

Nghe, L., & Mahalik, J. (2001). Examining racial identity statuses as predictors of psychological defenses in African American college students. *Journal of Counseling Psychology, 48,* 10–16.

Nguyen, S. (2006). The role of cultural factors affecting the academic achievement of Vietnamese refugee students. *Dissertation Abstracts International. Section A: Humanities & Social Sciences, 67,* 495.

Nicholson, I. A. M. (2003). *Inventing personality: Gordon Allport and the science of selfhood.* Washington, DC: American Psychological Association.

Niedenthal, P., Mermillod, M., Maringer, M., & Hess, U. (2010). The simulation of smiles (SIMS) model: Embodied simulation and the meaning of facial expression. *Behavioral and Brain Sciences, 33,* 417–433.

Nigg, J., John, O., Blaskey, L., Huang-Pollock, C., Willicut, E., Hinshaw, S., et al. (2002). Big Five dimensions and ADHD symptoms: Links between personality traits and clinical symptoms. *Journal of Personality and Social Psychology, 83,* 451–469.

Nikelly, A. (2005). Positive health outcomes of social interest. *Journal of Individual Psychology, 61,* 329–342.

Nolan, G. (2008). Teacher communication of unconditional positive regard (love) to students in secondary school environments. *Dissertation Abstracts international. Section A: Humanities and Social Sciences, 4978.*

Nolen-Hoeksema, S., Girgus, J., & Seligman, M. E. P. (1987). Learned helplessness in children: A longitudinal study of depression, achievement, and explanatory style. *Journal of Personality and Social Psychology, 51,* 435.

Noll, R. (1993). Personal communication.

Noll, R. (1994). *The Jung cult: Origins of a charismatic movement.* Princeton, NJ: Princeton University Press.

Noll, R. (1997). *The Aryan Christ: The secret life of Carl Jung.* New York: Random House.

Noltemeyer, A., Bush, K., Patton, J., & Bergen, D. (2012). The relationship among deficiency needs and growth needs: An empirical investigation of Maslow's theory. *Children and Youth Services Review, 34,* 1862–1867.

Norenzayan, A., & Lee, A. (2010). It was meant to happen: Explaining cultural variations in fate attributions. *Journal of Personality and Social Psychology, 98*(5), 702–720.

Noser, A., & Zeigler-Hill, V. (2014). Self-esteem instability and the desire for fame. *Self and Identity, 13,* 701–713.

Novy, D., Stanley, M., Averill, P., & Daza, P. (2001). Psychometric comparability of English- and Spanish-language measures of anxiety and related affective symptoms. *Psychological Assessment, 13,* 347–355.

Nowicki, S., & Duke, M. P. (1983). The Nowicki-Strickland life-span locus of control scales: Construct validation. In H. M. Lefcourt (Ed.), *Research with the locus of control construct* (Vol. 2, pp. 13–51). Orlando, FL: Academic Press.

Nowicki, S., & Strickland, B. R. (1973). A locus of control scale for children. *Journal of Consulting Psychology, 40,* 148–154.

Oates, J. (2012). Learning from watching. In B. Nicola & J. Byford (Eds.), *Investigating psychology: Key concepts, key studies, key approaches* (pp. 100–138). New York: Oxford University Press.

Oettingen, G., & Maier, H. (1999). Where political system meets culture: Effects on efficacy appraisal. In Y. T. Lee, C. R. McCauley, & J. G. Draguns (Eds.), *Personality and person perception across cultures* (pp. 163–190). Mahwah, NJ: Erlbaum.

Ofshe, R., & Watters, E. (1994). *False memories, psychotherapy, and sexual hysteria.* New York: Scribner's.

Ogasahara, K., Hirono, M., & Kato, S. (2013). Support for on-task behavior through a token economy system: Autistic youth who shows challenging behavior. *Japanese Journal of Special Education, 51,* 41–49.

Oishi, S., & Diener, E. (2001). Goals, culture, and subjective well-being. *Personality and Social Psychology Bulletin, 27,* 1674–1682.

Okeke, B. I., Draguns, J. G., Sheku, B., & Allen, W. (1999). Culture, self, and personality in Africa. In Y. T. Lee, C. R. McCauley, & J. G. Draguns (Eds.), *Personality and person perception across cultures* (pp. 139–162). Mahwah, NJ: Erlbaum.

Oliveira, J. (2013a). *Happiness and gratitude: A HEXACO personality structure paradigm.* American Psychological Association Convention Presentation. http://psycnet.apa.org/psycextra/603312013-001.pdf

Oliveira, J. (2013b). *Role of aggression and empathy in the Dark Triad of personality.* American Psychological Association Convention Presentation. http://psycnet.apa.org/doi/10.1037/e603302013-001.pdf

Olioff, M., & Aboud, F. E. (1991). Predicting postpartum dysphoria in primiparous mothers: Roles of perceived parenting self-efficacy and self-esteem. *Journal of Cognitive Psychotherapy, 5,* 3–14.

Olson, E., Fanning, J., Awick, E., & Chung, H. (2014). Differential trajectories of well-being in older adult women: The role of optimism. *Applied Psychology: Health and Well-Being, 6,* 362–380.

O'Neal, K., Vosvick, M., Catalano, D., & Logan, M. (2010). *Am I worth it? Loneliness, self-esteem, and locus of control: Correlates of meaning-in-life.* American Psychological Association Convention Presentation.

O'Neill, R. M., & Bornstein, R. F. (1990). Oral-dependence and gender: Factors in help-seeking response set and self-reported pathology in psychiatric inpatients. *Journal of Personality Assessment, 55,* 28–40.

Ong, E., Ang, R., Ho, J., Lim, J., Goh, D., Lee, C., et al. (2011). Narcissism, extraversion and adolescents' self-presentation on Facebook. *Personality and Individual Differences, 50,* 180–185.

Onyeizugbo, E. (2010). Self-efficacy, gender and trait anxiety as moderators of test anxiety. *Electronic Journal of Research in Educational Psychology, 8*(1), 299–312.

Orejudo, S., Puyuelo, M., Fernandez-Turrado, T., & Ramos, T. (2012). Optimism in adolescence: A cross-sectional study of the influence of family and peer group variables on junior high school students. *Personality and Individual Differences, 52,* 812–817.

Orgler, H. (1963). *Alfred Adler, the man and his work: Triumph over the inferiority complex.* New York: New American Library.

O'Riordan, S., & O'Connell, M. (2014). Predicting adult involvement in crime: Personality measures are significant, socio-economic measures are not. *Personality and Individual Differences, 68,* 98–101.

Orlofsky, J. L., Marcia, J. E., & Lesser, I. M. (1973). Ego identity status and the intimacy versus isolation crisis of young adulthood. *Journal of Personality and Social Psychology, 27,* 211–219.

Ormel, J., & Wohlfarth, T. (1991). How neuroticism, long-term difficulties, and life situation changes influence psychological distress: A longitudinal model. *Journal of Personality and Social Psychology, 60,* 744–755.

Orth, U., & Robins, W. (2014). The development of self-esteem. *Current Directions in Psychological Science, 23,* 381–387.

Orth, U., Trzesniewski, K., & Robins, R. (2010). Self-esteem development from young adulthood to old age: A cohort-sequential longitudinal study. *Personality Processes and Individual Differences, 98,* 645–658.

Ortin, A., Lake, A., Kleinman, M., & Gould, M. (2012). Sensation seeking as risk factor for suicidal ideation and suicide attempts in adolescence. *Journal of Affective Disorders, 143,* 214–222.

Osnos, E. (2011, January 10). Meet Dr. Freud: Does psychoanalysis have a future in an authoritarian state? *New Yorker,* pp. 54–63.

OSS Assessment Staff. (1948). *Assessment of men: Selection of personnel for the U.S Office of Strategic Services.* New York: Rinehart.

Overmier, J. B., & Seligman, M. E. P. (1967). Effects of inescapable shock upon subsequent escape and avoidance learning. *Journal of Comparative and Physiological Psychology, 63,* 28–33.

Overskeid, G., Gronnerod, C., & Simonton, D. (2012). The personality of a nonperson: Gauging the inner Skinner. *Perspectives on Psychological Science, 7,* 187–197.

Owen, J., & Lindley, L. (2010). Therapists' cognitive complexity: Review of theoretical models and development of an integrated approach for training. *Training and Education in Professional Psychology, 4,* 128–132.

Owen, S. (2006). Occupational stress among correctional supervisors. *Prison Journal, 86,* 164–181.

Ozer, E. M. (1995). The impact of childcare responsibility and self-efficacy on psychological health of professional working mothers. *Psychology of Women Quarterly, 19,* 315–335.

Padilla-Walker, L., Nelson, L., Carroll, J., & Jensen, A. (2010). More than just a game: Video game and Internet use during emerging adulthood. *Journal of Youth and Adolescence, 39,* 103–113.

Paige, J. M. (1966). Letters from Jenny: An approach to the clinical analysis of personality structure by computer. In P. J. Stone (Ed.), *The general inquirer: A computer approach to context analysis.* Cambridge, MA: MIT Press.

Pals, J. L. (1999). Identity consolidation in early adulthood: Relations with ego-resiliency, the context of marriage, and personality change. *Journal of Personality, 67,* 295–329.

Pancer, S., Hunsberger, B., Pratt, M., & Alisat, S. (2000). Cognitive complexity of expectations and adjustment to university in the first year. *Journal of Adolescent Research, 15,* 38–57.

Paolacci, G., & Chandler, J. (2014). Inside the Turk: Understanding mechanical turk as a participant pool. *Current Directions in Psychological Science, 23,* 184–188.

Papastylianou, A. (2013). Relating on the Internet, personality traits and depression: Research and implications. *European Journal of Counseling Psychology, 2,* 65–78.

Papazova, E., & Pencheva, E. (2008). Adolescent self-esteem and psychological type. *Journal of Psychological Type, 68*(8), 1–10.

Pappas, S. (2010, October 4). Don't worry: Happiness levels not set in stone. *Yahoo! News.*

Paris, B. J. (1994). *Karen Horney: A psychoanalyst's search for self-understanding.* New Haven, CT: Yale University Press.

Paris, R., & Helson, R. (2002). Early mothering experience and personality change. *Journal of Family Psychology, 16,* 172–185.

Park, C., Armeli, S., & Tennen, H. (2004). Appraisal-coping goodness of fit: A daily Internet study. *Personality and Social Psychology Bulletin, 30,* 558–569.

Park, D., & Huang, C. (2010). Culture wires the brain: A cognitive neuroscience perspective. *Perspectives on Psychological Science, 5*(4), 391–400.

Park, N., & Huebner, E. (2005). A cross-cultural study of the levels and correlates of life satisfaction among adolescents. *Journal of Cross-Cultural Psychology, 36,* 444–456.

Parkes, K. R. (1986). Coping in stressful episodes. *Journal of Personality and Social Psychology, 51,* 1277–1292.

Parkham, T., & Helms, J. (1985a). Attitudes of racial identity and self-esteem of black students: An exploratory investigation. *Journal of College Student Personnel, 26,* 143–147.

Parkham, T., & Helms, J. (1985b). Relation of racial identity and attitudes to self-actualization and affective states of black students. *Journal of Counseling Psychology, 32,* 431–440.

Patterson, R. (2006). The child within: Karen Horney on vacation. *American Journal of Psychoanalysis, 66,* 109–112.

Patterson, T. (2014). Early recollections and trauma in police officers. *Dissertation Abstracts International. Section B: Sciences and Engineering. Vol. 75 (1-BE).*

Patterson, T., & Joseph, S. (2007). Person-centered personality theory: Support from self-determination theory and positive psychology. *Journal of Humanistic Psychology, 47,* 117–139.

Paul, H. (2010). The Karen Horney clinic and the legacy of Horney. *American Journal of Psychoanalysis, 70,* 63–64.

Paulhus, D., & Williams, K. (2002). The Dark Triad of personality: Narcissism, machiavellianism, and psychopathy. *Journal of Research in Personality, 36,* 556–563.

Paunonen, S. V. (1998). Hierarchical organization of personality and prediction of behavior. *Journal of Personality and Social Psychology, 74,* 538–556.

Paunonen, S. V., & Ashton, M. C. (2001). Big Five factors and facets and the prediction of behavior. *Journal of Personality and Social Psychology, 81,* 524–539.

Pedersen, N. L., Plomin, R., McClearn, G. E., & Friberg, L. (1988). Neuroticism, extraversion, and related traits in adult twins reared apart and reared together. *Journal of Personality and Social Psychology, 55,* 950–957.

Pedrotti, J., & Edwards, L. (2010). *Identity incongruence, well-being, and depression among multiracial adults.* American Psychological Association Convention Presentation.

Peltzer, K., Malaka, D., & Phaswana, N. (2001). Psychological correlates of substance use among South African university students. *Social Behavior and Personality, 29,* 799–806.

Peluso, P., Peluso, J., Buckner, J., Curlette, W., & Kern, R. (2004). An analysis of the reliability of the BASIS-A Inventory using a northeastern and southeastern U.S. sample. *Journal of Individual Psychology, 60,* 294–307.

Penard, T., Poussing, N., & Suire, R. (2013). Does the Internet make people happier? *Journal of Socio-Economics, 46,* 105–116.

Pervin, L. A. (1984). *Current controversies and issues in personality* (2nd ed.). New York: Wiley.

Pervin, L. A. (2003). *The science of personality* (2nd ed.). New York: Oxford University Press.

Pesant, N., & Zadra, A. (2006). Dream content and psychological well-being: A longitudinal study of the continuity hypothesis. *Journal of Clinical Psychology, 62,* 111–121.

Peteet, B., Brown, C., Lige, Q., & Lanaway, D. (2014). Imposterism is associated with greater psychological distress and lower self-esteem for African American students. *Current Psychology: A Journal for Diverse Perspectives on Diverse Psychological Issues,* 1–10.

Peter, J., & Valkenburg, P. (2006). Individual differences in perceptions of Internet communication. *European Journal of Communication, 21,* 213–226.

Peterson, B. E. (2002). Longitudinal analysis of midlife generativity, intergenerational roles, and caregiving. *Psychology and Aging, 17,* 161–168.

Peterson, B. E., & Stewart, A. J. (1990). Using personal and fictional documents to assess psychosocial development: A case study of Vera Brittain's generativity. *Psychology and Aging, 5,* 400–411.

Peterson, B. E., Smirles, K. A., & Wentworth, P. A. (1997). Generativity and authoritarianism: Implications for personality, political involvement, and parenting. *Journal of Personality and Social Psychology, 72,* 1202–1216.

Peterson, C., & Barrett, L. C. (1987). Explanatory style and academic performance among college freshmen. *Journal of Personality and Social Psychology, 53,* 603–607.

Peterson, C., Maier, S. F., & Seligman, M. E. P. (1993). *Learned helplessness: A theory for the age of personal control.* New York: Oxford University Press.

Peterson, C., & Seligman, M. E. P. (1987). Explanatory style and illness. Special issue: Personality and physical health. *Journal of Personality, 55,* 237–265.

Peterson, C., Seligman, M. E. P., & Vaillant, G. (1988). Pessimistic explanatory style as a risk factor for physical illness: A 35-year longitudinal study. *Journal of Personality and Social Psychology, 55,* 23–27.

Peterson, C., Semmel, A., Von Baeyer, C., Abramson, L. Y., Metalsky, G. I., & Seligman, M. E. P. (1982). The Attributional Style Questionnaire. *Cognitive Therapy and Research, 6,* 287–300.

Petrosky, M. J., & Birkhimer, J. C. (1991). The relationship among locus of control coping styles and psychological symptom reporting. *Journal of Clinical Psychology, 47,* 336–345.

Phares, E. J. (1993). From therapy to research: A patient's legacy. In G. G. Brannigan & M. R. Merrens (Eds.), *The undaunted psychologist: Adventures in research* (pp. 157–171). Philadelphia: Temple University Press.

Phelps, A., & Forbes, D. (2012). Treating post-traumatic stress disorder-related dreams: What are the options? *Expert Review of Neurotherapeutics, 12,* 1267–1269.

Phillips, D. P. (1974). The influence of suggestion on suicide: Substantive and theoretical implications of the Werther effect. *American Sociological Review, 39,* 340–354.

Phillips, D. P. (1983). The impact of mass media violence on U.S. homicides. *American Sociological Review, 48,* 560–568.

Phillips, D. P. (1985). The found experiment: A new technique for assessing impact of mass media violence on real-world aggressive behavior. In G. Comstock (Ed.), *Public communication and behavior* (Vol. 1). New York: Academic Press.

Phinney, J. S., & Chavira, V. (1992). Ethnic identity and self-esteem: An exploratory longitudinal study. *Journal of Adolescence, 15,* 271–281.

Phipps, S., & Steele, R. (2002). Repressive adaptive style in children with chronic illness. *Psychosomatic Medicine, 64,* 34–42.

Piedmont, R. L. (1988). The relationship between achievement motivation, anxiety, and situational characteristics on performance on a cognitive task. *Journal of Research in Personality.*

Piekkola, B. (2011). Traits across cultures: A neo-Allportian perspective. *Journal of Theoretical and Philosophical Psychology, 31,* 2–24.

Pierre, M., & Mahalik, J. (2005). Examining African self-consciousness and Black racial identity as predictors of Black men's psychological well-being. *Cultural Diversity and Ethnic Minority Psychology, 11,* 28–40.

Pilkington, B., & Lenaghan, M. (1998). Psychopathology. In K. Trew & J. Kremer (Eds.), *Gender and psychology* (pp. 179–191). New York: Oxford University Press.

Pillay, Y. (2005). Racial identity as a predictor of the psychological health of African-American students at a predominantly White university. *Journal of Black Psychology, 31,* 46–66.

Pincott, J. (2013, March 13). Most of us live in fear of unleashing a Freudian slip. Do you? *Psychology Today.* http://www.psychologytoday.com/articles/201203/slips-the-tongue

Pinquart, M., & Soerensen, S. (2000). Influences of socioeconomic status, social network, and competence on subjective well-being in later life: A meta-analysis. *Psychology and Aging, 15,* 187–224.

Piot-Ziegler, C., Sassi, M., Raffoul, W., & Delaloye, J. (2010). Mastectomy, body deconstruction, and impact on identity: A quantitative study. *British Journal of Health Psychology, 15,* 479–510.

Pittenger, D. (2005). Cautionary comments regarding the Myers-Briggs Type Indicator. *Consulting Psychology Journal: Practice and Research, 57,* 210–221.

Plaut, V., Adams, G., & Anderson, S. (2009). Does attractiveness buy happiness? "It depends on where you're from." *Personal Relationships, 16,* 619–630.

Plaut, V., Markus, H., & Lachman, M. (2002). Place matters: Consensual features and regional variation in American well-being and self. *Journal of Personality and Social Psychology, 83,* 160–184.

Podd, M. H., Marcia, J. E., & Rubin, R. (1968). The effects of ego identity status and partner perception on a prisoner's dilemma game. *Journal of Social Psychology, 82,* 117–126.

Podlog, L., & Eklund, R. (2010). Returning to competition after a serious injury: The role of self-determination. *Journal of Sports Sciences, 28*(8), 819–831.

Pole, N., Best, S., Metzler, T., & Marmar, C. (2005). Why are Hispanics at greater risk for PTSD? *Cultural Diversity and Ethnic Minority Psychology, 11,* 144–161.

Poling, A., Weetjens, B., Cox, C., Beyene, N., Bach, H., & Sully, A. (2010). Teaching giant African pouched rats to find landmines: Operant conditioning with real consequences. *Behavior Analysis in Practice, 3*(2), 19–25.

Pollak, S., & Sinha, P. (2002). Effects of early experience on children's recognition of facial displays of emotion. *Developmental Psychology, 38,* 784–791.

Pollett, T., Dijkstra, P., Barelds, D., & Buunk, A. (2010). Birth order and the dominance aspect of extraversion: Are first-borns more extraverted, in the sense of being dominant, than later-borns? *Journal of Research in Personality, 44,* 742–745.

Porcerelli, J. H., Thomas, S., Hibbard, S., & Cogan, R. (1998). Defense mechanisms development in children, adolescents, and late adolescents. *Journal of Personality Assessment, 71,* 411–420.

Poropat, A. (2009). A meta-analysis of the five-factor model of personality and academic performance. *Psychological Bulletin, 135,* 322–338.

Postmes, T., & Branscombe, N. (2002). Influence of long-term racial environmental composition on subjective well-being in African Americans. *Journal of Personality and Social Psychology, 83,* 735–751.

Porter, S., Bhanwer, A., Woodworth, M., & Black, P. (2014). Soldiers of misfortunate: An examination of the Dark Triad and the experience of schadenfreude. *Personality and Individual Differences. 67,* 64–68.

Pozios, V., Kamban, P., & Bender, E. (2013, August 23). Does media violence lead to the real thing? *New York Times.* http://www.nytimes.com/2013/08/25/opinion/sunday/does-media-violence-lead-to-the-real-thing.html

Prelow, H., Mosher, C., & Bowman, M. (2006). Perceived racial discrimination, social support, and psychological adjustment among African-American college students. *Journal of Black Psychology, 32,* 442–454.

Prenda, K., & Lachman, M. (2001). Planning for the future: A life management strategy for increasing control and life satisfaction in adulthood. *Psychology and Aging, 16,* 206–216.

Prinzie, O., Stams, G., Dekovic, M., Reijntjes, A., & Belsky, J. (2009). The relations between parents' Big Five personality factors and parenting: A meta-analytic review. *Journal of Personality and Social Psychology, 97*(2), 351–362.

Prinzie, P., Stams, G., Dekovic, M., Reijntjes, A. H. A., & Belsky, J. (2009). The relations between parents' Big Five personality factors and parenting: A meta-analytic review. *Journal of Personality and Social Psychology, 97*(2), 351–362.

Prochnik, G. (2006). *Putnam camp: Sigmund Freud, James Jackson Putnam, and the purpose of American psychology.* New York: Other Press.

Puca, R. M., & Schmalt, H. (2001). The influence of the achievement motive on spontaneous thoughts in pre- and post- decisional action phases. *Personality and Social Psychology Bulletin, 27*, 302–308.

Pullmann, H., Raudsepp, L., & Allik, J. (2006). Stability and change in adolescents' personality: A longitudinal study. *European Journal of Personality, 20*, 447–459.

Pyszczynski, T., Greenberg, J., Solomon, S., Arndt, J., & Schimel, J. (2004). Why do people need self-esteem? A theoretical and empirical review. *Psychological Bulletin, 130*, 435–468.

Qing-Xin, S., Rong-Gang, Z., & Yan, G. (2005). Internet addiction disorder and sensation seeking of middle school and high school students. *Chinese Mental Health Journal, 19*, 453–456.

Quiery, N. (1998). Parenting the family. In K. Trew & J. Kremer (Eds.), *Gender and psychology* (pp. 129–140). New York: Oxford University Press.

Quinn, S. (1987). *A mind of her own: The life of Karen Horney.* New York: Summit Books.

Rabinowitz, P. (2005). Is noise bad for your health? *Lancet, 365* (9475), 1908–1909.

Räikkönen, K., Matthews, K. A., Flory, J. D., Owens, J. F., & Gump, B. B. (1999). Effects of optimism, pessimism, and trait anxiety on ambulatory blood pressure and mood during everyday life. *Journal of Personality and Social Psychology, 76*, 104–113.

Raine, A., Reynolds, C., Venables, P., & Mednick, S. (2002). Stimulation seeking and intelligence: A prospective longitudinal study. *Journal of Personality and Social Psychology, 82*, 663–674.

Rainey, N. (1998). Old age. In K. Trew & J. Kremer (Eds.), *Gender and psychology* (pp. 153–164). New York: Oxford University Press.

Rainville, R., & Rush, L. (2009). A contemporary view of college-aged students' dreams. *Dreaming, 19*(3), 152–171.

Ramirez-Maestre, C., Esteve, R., & Lopez, A. (2012). The role of optimism and pessimism in chronic pain patients' adjustment. *Spanish Journal of Psychology, 15*, 286–294.

Ramos-Sanchez, L., & Atkinson, D. (2009). The relationship between Mexican American acculturation, cultural values, gender, and help-seeking intentions. *Journal of Counseling and Development, 87*, 62–71.

Raskauskas, J., Rubiano, S., Offen, I., & Wayland, A. (2015, January 21). Do social self-efficacy and self-esteem moderate the relationship between peer victimization and academic performance? *Social Psychology of Education.* http://link. springer.com/article/10.1007/s11218-015-9292-z#page-2

Rauthmann, J. F., & Kolar, G. P. (2012). How "dark" are the Dark Triad traits? Examining the perceived darkness of narcissism, Machiavellianism, and psychopathy. *Personality and Individual Differences, 53*, 884–889.

Ravert, R., Schwartz, S., Zamboanga, B., Kim, S., Weisskirch, R., & Bersamin, M. (2009). Sensation seeking and danger

invulnerability: Paths to college student risk-taking. *Personality and Individual Differences, 47*, 763–768.

Rayle, A. (2005). Adolescent gender differences in mattering and wellness. *Journal of Adolescence, 28*, 753–763.

Raynor, D., & Levine, H. (2009). Associations between the five-factor model of personality and health behaviors among college students. *Journal of American College Health, 58*, 73–81.

Reid, L., & Foels, R. (2010). Cognitive complexity and the perception of subtle racism. *Basic and Applied Social Psychology, 32*, 201–301.

Reimanis, G. (1974). Personality development, anomie, and mood. *Journal of Personality and Social Psychology, 29*, 355–357.

Reio, T., & Sanders-Reio, J. (2006). Sensation seeking as an inhibitor of job performance. *Personality and Individual Differences, 40*, 631–642.

Rendon, D. (1987). Understanding social roles from a Horneyan perspective. *American Journal of Psychoanalysis, 47*, 131–142.

Rentfrow, P. (2010). Statewide differences in personality: Towards a psychological geography of the United States. *American Psychologist, 65*, 548–558.

Rentfrow, P., Mellander, C., & Florida, R. (2009). Happy states of America: A state-level analysis of psychological, economic, and social well-being. *Journal of Research in Personality, 43*, 1073–1082.

Repucci, N. D., & Saunders, J. T. (1974). Social psychology of behavior modification: Problems of implementation in natural settings. *American Psychologist, 29*, 649–660.

Resnicow, K., Soler, R. E., Braithwaite, R. L., Ben Selassie, M., & Smith, M. (1999). Development of a racial and ethnic identity scale for African American adolescents: The Survey of Black Life. *Journal of Black Psychology, 25*, 171–188.

Rettner, R. (2010, August 12). Birth order affects child's intelligence and personality. *Yahoo Live Science.*

Reuman, D. A., Alwin, D. F., & Veroff, J. (1984). Assessing the validity of the achievement motive in the presence of random measurement error. *Journal of Personality and Social Psychology, 47*, 1347–1362.

Revelle, W. (2009). Commentary: Personality structure and measurement: The contributions of Raymond Cattell. *British Journal of Psychology, 100*, 253–257.

Revelle, W., & Oehlberg, K. (2008). Integrating experimental and observational personality research: The contributions of Hans Eysenck. *Journal of Personality, 76*, 1387–1414.

Rice, B. (1968, March 17). Skinner agrees he is the most important influence in psychology. *New York Times Magazine*, p. 27ff.

Rice, T., & Steele, B. (2004). Subjective well-being and culture across time and space. *Journal of Cross-Cultural Psychology, 35*, 633–647.

Richardson, A. (2010). Facial expression theory from romanticism to the present. In L. Zunshine (Ed.), *Introduction to cognitive cultural studies* (pp. 65–83). Baltimore, MD: The Johns Hopkins University Press.

Richelle, M. N. (1993). *B. F. Skinner: A reappraisal.* Hillsdale, NJ: Erlbaum.

Riggio, R. E., & Friedman, H. S. (1986). Impression formation: The role of expressive behavior. *Journal of Personality and Social Psychology, 50*, 421–427.

Riggio, R. E., Lippa, R., & Salinas, C. (1990). The display of personality in expressive movement. *Journal of Research in Personality, 24*, 16–31.

Roazen, P. (1975). *Freud and his followers.* New York: Knopf.

Roazen, P. (1993). *Meeting Freud's family*. Amherst: University of Massachusetts Press.

Roberti, J. (2004). A review of behavioral and biological correlates of sensation seeking. *Journal of Research in Personality, 38,* 256–279.

Roberts, B. W., & Robins, R. W. (2000). Brood dispositions, brood aspirations: The intersection of personality traits and major life goals. *Personality and Social Psychology Bulletin, 26,* 1284–1296.

Roberts, B. W., Walton, K., & Viechtbauer, W. (2006). Patterns of mean-level change in personality traits across the life course: A meta-analysis of longitudinal studies. *Psychological Bulletin, 132,* 1–25.

Robins, R. W., Trzesniewski, K., Tracy, J., Gosling, S., & Potter, J. (2002). Global self-esteem across the life span. *Psychology and Aging, 17,* 423–434.

Robinson, F. G. (1992). *Love's story told: A life of Henry A. Murray.* Cambridge, MA: Harvard University Press.

Robinson, O., Demetre, J., & Corney, R. (2010). Personality and retirement: Exploring the links between the Big Five personality traits, reasons for retirement and the experience of being retired. *Personality and Individual Differences, 48,* 792–797.

Robinson, O., & Stell, A. (2014, September 19). Later-life crisis: Towards a holistic model. *Journal of Adult Development.* http://link.springer.com/article/10.1007/s10804-014-9190-5

Robinson-Whelen, S., Kim, C., MacCallum, R. C., & Kiecolt-Glaser, J. K. (1997). Distinguishing optimism from pessimism in older adults. *Journal of Personality and Social Psychology, 73,* 1345–1353.

Roccas, S., Sagiu, L., Schwartz, S. H., & Knafo, A. (2002). The Big Five personality factors and personal values. *Personality and Social Psychology Bulletin, 28,* 789–801.

Rodgers, J. L. (2001). What causes birth order-intelligence patterns? The admixture hypothesis, revised. *American Psychologist, 56,* 505–510.

Rodriguez-Mosquera, P. M., Manstead, A. S. R., & Fischer, A. H. (2000). The role of honor-related values in the elicitation, experience, and communication of pride, shame, and anger: Spain and the Netherlands compared. *Personality and Social Psychology Bulletin, 26,* 833–844.

Rofe, Y. (2006). Affiliation tendencies on the eve of the Iraq War: A utility theory perspective. *Journal of Applied Social Psychology, 36,* 1781–1789.

Rogers, C. R. (1954). The case of Mrs. Oak: A research analysis. In C. R. Rogers & R. F. Dymond (Eds.), *Psychotherapy and personality change.* Chicago, IL: University of Chicago Press.

Rogers, C. R. (1961). *On becoming a person: A therapist's view of psychotherapy.* Boston: Houghton Mifflin.

Rogers, C. R. (1967). Autobiography. In E. G. Boring & G. Lindzey (Eds.), *A history of psychology in autobiography* (Vol. 5, pp. 341–384). New York: Appleton-Century-Crofts.

Rogers, C. R. (1970). *Carl Rogers on encounter groups.* New York: Harper & Row.

Rogers, C. R. (1974). In retrospect: Forty-six years. *American Psychologist, 29,* 115–123.

Rogers, C. R. (1980). *A way of being.* Boston, MA: Houghton Mifflin.

Rogers, C. R. (1987). An interview with Carl Rogers. In A. O. Ross (Ed.), *Personality: The scientific study of complex human behavior* (pp. 118–119). New York: Holt, Rinehart & Winston.

Rogers, L. (2013). Young, Black and male: Exploring the intersections of racial and gender identity in an all-Black male high school. *Dissertation Abstracts International. Section B: Sciences and Engineering, 73.* http://psycnet.apa.org/index.cfm?fa=search.displayRecord&id=877CD6F1-BADB-27BC-B749-31521990A714&resultID=2&page=1&dbTab=all&search=true

Rogoff, B., Paradise, R., Arauz, R. M., Correa-Chavez, M., & Angelillo, C. (2003). First-hand learning through intent participation. *Annual Review of Psychology, 54,* 175–203.

Ronaldson, A., Poole, L., Kidd, T., Leigh, E., Jahangiri, M., & Steptoe, A. (2014, August 3). Optimisim measured pre-operatively is associated with reduced pain intensity and physical symptom reporting after coronary artery bypass graft surgery. *Journal of Psychosomatic Research.* http://www.ncbi.nlm.nih.gov/pubmed/25129850

Ronen, T., Hamama, L., Rosenbaum, M., & Mishely-Yarlap, A. (2014, October 8). Subjective well-being in adolescence: The role of self-control, social support, age, gender, and familial crisis. *Journal of Happiness Studies.* http://link.springer.com/article/10.1007/s10902-014-9585-5#page-2

Rose, R. J. (1995). Genes and human behavior. *Annual Review of Psychology, 46,* 625–654.

Rose, S. (2010, August). Hans Eysenck's controversial career [Review of the book *Playing with fire: The controversial career of Hans J. Eysenck,* by R. Buchanan. Oxford University Press, 2010]. *Lancet, 376,* 407–408.

Rosenbloom, T. (2006a). Color preferences of high and low sensation seekers. *Creativity Research Journal, 18,* 229–235.

Rosenbloom, T. (2006b). Sensation seeking pedestrian crossing compliance. *Social Behavior and Personality, 34,* 113–122.

Rosenthal, D. R., Gurney, M. R., & Moore, S. M. (1981). From trust to intimacy: A new inventory for examining Erikson's stages of psychosocial development. *Journal of Youth and Adolescence, 10,* 525–536.

Rosenzweig, S. (1985). Freud and experimental psychology: The emergence of idiodynamics. In S. Koch & D. Leary (Eds.), *A century of psychology as science* (pp. 135–207). New York: McGraw-Hill.

Ross, C., Orr, E., Sisic, M., Arseneault, M., Simmering, M. G., & Orr, R. (2009). Personality and motivations associated with Facebook use. *Computers in Human Behavior, 24,* 578–586.

Roth, M., & Hammelstein, P. (2012). The Need Inventory of Sensation Seeking (NISS). *European Journal of Psychological Assessment, 28,* 11–18.

Rothrauff, T., & Cooney, T. (2008). The role of generativity in psychological well-being: Does it differ for childless adults and parents? *Journal of Adult Development, 15* (3–4), 148–159.

Rotter, J. B. (1966). Generalized expectancies for internal versus external control of reinforcement. *Psychological Monographs, 80* (Whole No. 609).

Rotter, J. B. (1982). *The development and applications of social learning theory: Selected papers.* New York: Praeger.

Rotter, J. B. (1990). Internal versus external control of reinforcement: A case history of a variable. *American Psychologist, 45,* 489–493.

Rotter, J. B. (1993). Expectancies. In C. E. Walker (Ed.), *History of clinical psychology in autobiography* (Vol. 2, pp. 273–284). Pacific Grove, CA: Brooks/Cole.

Rotter, J. (2014). Julian Rotter (1916–2014). Obituary. *Social Behavior and Personality, 42,* 1.

Roussi, C., Angelosopoulou, A., & Zafiropoulou, M. (2009). Personality characteristics and profiles of Greek elementary teachers using the Sixteen Personality Factor Questionnaire (16PF). *International Journal of Adolescent Medicine and Health, 21*(3), 413–420.

Roussi-Vergou, C., & Zafiropoulou, M. (2011). 16-PF personality characteristics of Greek preschool educators. *Psychology: Journal of the Hellenic Psychological Society, 18,* 211–223.

Routh, D. (2010). The rise and fall in the scientific reputation of Carl Riggers. *Clinical Psychologist, 64*(3), 11–12.

Routh, D. (2011). Remembering George Kelly. *Clinical Psychologist, 64,* 11–12.

Routledge, C., Ostafin, B., Juhl, J., Sedikides, C., Cathey, C., & Jiangqun, L. (2010). Adjusting to death: The effects of mortality salience and self-esteem on psychological well-being, growth motivation, and maladaptive behavior. *Journal of Personality and Social Psychology, 99,* 897–916.

Rubins, J. L. (1978). *Karen Horney: Gentle rebel of psychoanalysis.* New York: Dial Press.

Rucker, D. D., & Pratkanis, A. R. (2001). Projection as an interpersonal influence tactic: The effects of the pot calling the kettle black. *Personality and Social Psychology Bulletin, 27,* 1494–1507.

Rudolph, K., & Conley, C. (2005). The socioeconomic costs and benefits of social-evaluative concerns: Do girls care too much? *Journal of Personality, 73,* 115–138.

Rudy, D., & Grusec, J. (2006). Authoritarian parenting in individualistic and collectivist groups: Associations with maternal emotion and cognition and children's self-esteem. *Journal of Family Psychology, 20,* 68–78.

Rushton, J. P., Fulker, D. W., Neale, M. C., Blizard, R. A., & Eysenck, H. J. (1984). Altruism and genetics. *Acta Geneticae et Gemellologiae, 33,* 265–271.

Russell, J. A., Bachorowski, J. A., & Fernandez-Dols, J. M. (2003). Facial and vocal expressions of emotion. *Annual Review of Psychology, 54,* 329–349.

Rutledge, P. (2013, April 18). The psychology of the selfie: How we connect and thrive through emerging technologies. *Psychology Today Online.* http://www.psychologytoday.com/blog/positively-media/201407/the-psychology-the-selfie

Ryan, R. M., & Deci, E. L. (2000). Self-determination theory and the facilitation of intrinsic motivation, social development, and well-being. *American Psychologist, 55,* 68–78.

Ryan, R. M., & Frederick, C. (1997). On energy, personality, and health: Subjective vitality as a dynamic reflection of well-being. *Journal of Personality, 65,* 529–565.

Ryan, T., & Xenos, S. (2011). Who uses Facebook? An investigation into the relationship between Big Five, shyness, narcissism, loneliness, and Facebook usage. *Computers in Human Behavior, 27,* 1658–1664.

Ryckman, R. M., Hammer, M., Kaczor, L. M., & Gold, J. A. (1990). Construction of a Hypercompetitive Attitude Scale. *Journal of Personality Assessment, 55,* 630–639.

Ryckman, R. M., & Malikiosi, M. X. (1975). Relationship between locus of control and chronological age. *Psychological Reports, 36,* 655–658.

Ryckman, R. M., Thornton, B., & Butler, J. C. (1994). Personality correlates of the Hypercompetitive Attitude Scale: Validity tests of Horney's theory of neurosis. *Journal of Personality Assessment, 62,* 84–94.

Ryckman, R., Thornton, B., & Gold, J. (2009). Assessing competition avoidance as a basic personality dimension. *Journal of Psychology: Interdisciplinary and Applied, 143*(2), 175–192.

Ryckman, R. M., Thornton, B., Gold, J., & Burckle, M. (2002). Romantic relationships of hypercompetitive individuals. *Journal of Social and Clinical Psychology, 21,* 517–530.

Ryckman, R. M., Van Den Borne, H., & Syroit, J. (1992). Differences in hypercompetitive attitude between American and Dutch university students. *Journal of Social Psychology, 132,* 331–334.

Ryon, H., & Gleason, M. (2014). The role of locus of control in daily life. *Personality and Social Psychology Bulletin, 40,* 121–131.

Salamon, M. (2011, January 11). For college students, praise may trump sex and money. *Bloomberg Businessweek.* (Online edition).

Salas, E., & Cannon-Bowers, J. (2001). The science of training: A decade of progress. *Annual Review of Psychology, 52,* 471–499.

Salem, M. (2014). Commentary on "Spiritual and religious imagery in dreams: A cross-cultural analysis." *International Journal of Dream Research, 7,* 93–94.

Salem, M., Ragab, M., & Abdel, R. (2009). Significance of dreams among United Arab Emirates university students. *International Journal of Dream Research, 2,* 29–33.

Salili, F. (1994). Age, sex, and cultural differences in the meaning and dimensions of need achievement. *Personality and Social Psychology Bulletin, 20,* 635–648.

Sammallahti, P., & Aalberg, V. (1995). Defense style in personality disorders. *Journal of Nervous and Mental Disease, 183,* 516–521.

Samreen, H., & Zubair, A. (2013). Locus of control and death anxiety among police personnel. *Pakistan Journal of Psychological Research, 28,* 261–275.

Sanna, L. J., & Pusecker, P. A. (1994). Self-efficacy, valence of self-evaluation, and performance. *Personality and Social Psychology Bulletin, 20,* 82–92.

Santos, S., & Updegraff, K. (2014). Feeling typical, looking typical: Physical appearance and ethnic identity among Mexican origin youth. *Journal of Latina/o Psychology, 2,* 187–199.

Sapouna, M. (2010). Collective efficacy in the school context: Does it help explain victimization and bullying among Greek primary and secondary school students? *Journal of Interpersonal Violence, 25,* 1912–1927.

Sarason, I. G. (1975). Test anxiety and the self-disclosing coping model. *Journal of Consulting and Clinical Psychology, 43,* 148–153.

Saric, M., & Pahic, T. (2013). Locus of control as a factor of resilience to stressful life events and a predictor of well-being. *4th ENSEC Conference, July 3–7, 2013, Zagreb, Croatia: Social and Emotional Competence in a Changing World.* http://scholar.google.hr/citations?view_op=view_citation&hl=en&user=e-mdIfAAAAAJ&citation_for_view=e-mdIfAAAAAJ:2osOgNQ5qMEC

Sasson, N., Pinkham, A., Richard, J., Hughett, P., Gur, R., & Gur, R. (2010). Controlling for response biases clarifies sex and age differences in facial affect recognition. *Journal of Nonverbal Behavior, 34,* 207–221.

Saudino, K. J., Pedersen, N. L., Lichtenstein, P., McClearn, G. E., & Plomin, R. (1997). Can personality explain genetic influences on life events? *Journal of Personality and Social Psychology, 72,* 196–206.

Saunders, J., Worth, R., Vallath, S., & Fernandes, M. (2014). Retrieval-induced forgetting in repressors: Defensive high anxious, high anxious, and low anxious individuals. *Journal of Experimental Psychopathology, 5*, 97–117.

Sayers, J. (1991). *Mothers of psychoanalysis: Helene Deutsch, Karen Horney, Anna Freud, Melanie Klein*. New York: Norton.

Scarr, S. (1968). Environmental bias in twin studies. *Eugenics Quarterly, 15*, 34–40.

Schachter, S. (1959). *The psychology of affiliation*. Stanford, CA: Stanford University Press.

Schachter, S. (1963). Birth order, eminence, and higher education. *American Sociological Review, 28*, 757–767.

Schachter, S. (1964). Birth order and sociometric choice. *Journal of Abnormal and Social Psychology, 68*, 453–456.

Schimmack, U., & Hartmann, K. (1997). Individual differences in the memory representation of emotional episodes. *Journal of Personality and Social Psychology, 73*, 1064–1079.

Schimmack, U., Oishi, S., Furr, R., & Funder, D. (2004). Personality and life satisfaction: A facet-level analysis. *Personality and Social Psychology Bulletin, 30*, 1062–1075.

Schmidt, A., & DeShon, R. (2010). The moderating effect of performance ambiguity on the relationship between self-efficacy and performance. *Journal of Applied Psychology, 95*(5), 572–581.

Schmitt, D., & Allik, J. (2005). Simultaneous administration of the Rosenberg self-esteem scale in 53 nations: Exploring the universal and culture-specific features of global self-esteem. *Journal of Personality and Social Psychology, 89*, 632–642.

Schmitt, D., Realo, A., Voracek, M., & Allik, J. (2008). Why can't a man be more like a woman? Sex differences in Big Five personality traits across 55 cultures. *Journal of Personality and Social Psychology, 94*, 168–182.

Schmitt, K., Dayanim, S., & Matthias, S. (2008). Personal homepage construction as an expression of social development. *Developmental Psychology, 44*, 496–506.

Schmitz, N., Neumann, W., & Oppermann, R. (2000). Stress, burnout and locus of control in German nurses. *International Journal of Nursing Studies, 37*, 95–99.

Schmutte, P. S., & Ryff, C. D. (1997). Personality and well-being. *Journal of Personality and Social Psychology, 73*, 549–559.

Schneewind, K. A. (1995). Impact of family processes on control beliefs. In A. Bandura (Ed.), *Self-efficacy in changing societies* (pp. 114–148). Cambridge, England: Cambridge University Press.

Schneider, A., & Domhoff, G. (2006). *The quantitative study of dreams*. http//www.dreamresearch.net/

Schneider, G., Dreisch, G., Kruse, A., Nehen, H., & Heuft, G. (2006). Old and ill and still feeling well? Determinants of subjective well-being in 60-year-olds: The role of the sense of coherence. *American Journal of Geriatric Psychiatry, 14*, 850–859.

Schneider, S. (2001). In search of realistic optimism: Meaning, knowledge, and warm fuzziness. *American Psychologist, 56*, 250–263.

Schneidman, E. S. (2001). My visit with Christiana Morgan. *History of Psychology, 4*, 289–296.

Schou, I., Ekeberg, O., Ruland, C., Sandvik, L., & Karesen, R. (2004). Pessimism as a predictor of emotional morbidity one year following breast cancer surgery. *Psycho-Oncology, 13*, 309–320.

Schou, I., Ekeberg, O., Sandvik, L., & Ruland, C. (2005). Stability in optimism-pessimism in relation to bad news: A study of women with breast cancer. *Journal of Personality Assessment, 84*, 148–154.

Schredl, M. (2006). Factors affecting the continuity between waking and dreaming: Emotional intensity and emotional tone of the waking-life event. *Sleep and Hypnosis, 8*, 1–5.

Schredl, M. (2010a). Explaining the gender difference in dream recall frequency. *Dreaming, 20*(2), 96–106.

Schredl, M. (2010b). Reading books about dream interpretation: Gender differences. *Dreaming, 20*(4), 248–253.

Schredl, M., Funkhouser, A., & Arn, N. (2006). Dreams of truck drivers: A test of the continuity hypothesis of dreaming. *Imagination, Cognition, and Personality, 25*, 179–186.

Schredl, M., & Piel, E. (2006). War-related dream themes in Germany from 1956 to 2000. *Political Psychology, 27*, 299–307.

Schueller, S., & Seligman, M. (2010). Pursuit of pleasure, engagement, and meaning: Relationships to subjective and objective measures of well-being. *Journal of Positive Psychology, 5*(4), 253–263.

Schul, Y., & Vinokur, A. D. (2000). Projection in person perception among spouses as a function of the similarity in their shared experiences. *Personality and Social Psychology Bulletin, 26*, 987–1001.

Schultz, D. P. (1990). *Intimate friends, dangerous rivals: The turbulent relationship between Freud and Jung*. Los Angeles, CA: Jeremy Tarcher.

Schur, M. (1972). *Freud: Living and dying*. New York: International Universities Press.

Schwartz, J., Buboltz, W., Seemann, E., & Flye, A. (2004). Personality styles: Predictors of masculine gender role conflict in male prison inmates. *Psychology of Men and Masculinity, 5*, 59–64.

Schwartz, S., Forthun, L., Ravert, R., Zamboanga, B. L., Umaña-Taylor, A. J., Filton, B. J., et al. (2010). Identity consolidation and health risk behaviors in college students. *American Journal of Health Behavior, 34*(2), 214–224.

Schwartz, S., Mason, C., Pantin, H., & Szapocznik, J. (2008). Effect of family functioning and identity confusion on substance use and sexual behavior in Hispanic immigrant early adolescents. *Identity: An International Journal of Theory and Research, 8*, 107–124.

Schwarz, N. (1999). Self-reports: How the questions shape the answers. *American Psychologist, 54*, 93–105.

Schwarzer, R., & Fuchs, R. (1995). Changing risk behaviors and adopting health behaviors: The role of self-efficacy beliefs. In A. Bandura (Ed.), *Self-efficacy in changing societies* (pp. 259–315). Cambridge, England: Cambridge University Press.

Schwitzgebel, E., Huang, C., & Zhou, Y. (2006). Do we dream in color? Cultural variations and skepticism. *Dreaming, 16*, 35–42.

Scoffier, S., Paquet, Y., & d'Arripe-Longeuville, F. (2010). Effects of locus of control on disordered eating in athletes: The mediational role of self-regulation of eating attitudes. *Eating Behaviors, 11*(3), 164–169.

Scollon, C., & Diener, E. (2006). Love, work, and changes in extraversion and neuroticism over time. *Journal of Personality and Social Psychology, 91*, 1152–1165.

Scollon, C., Kim-Prieto, C., & Diener, E. (2009). Experience sampling: Promises and pitfalls, strengths and weaknesses. In

E. Diener (Ed.), *Assessing well-being: The collected works of Ed Diener* (pp. 157–180). New York: U.S. Springer Science.

Scott, R., & Dienes, Z. (2010). Knowledge applied to new domains: The unconscious succeeds where the conscious fails. *Consciousness and Cognition, 29*, 391–398.

Seaton, C. (2014). The role of positive emotions and ego resilience in personal strivings. *Dissertation Abstracts International. Section B: Sciences and Engineering. Vol. 74 (10-BE)*.

Seaton, E., Caldwell, C., Sellers, R., & Jackson, J. (2010). An intersectional approach for understanding perceived discrimination and psychological well-being among African American and Caribbean Black youth. *Developmental Psychology, 4*, 1372–1379.

Seaton, E., & Yip, T. (2009). School and neighborhood contexts, perceptions of racial discrimination, and psychological well-being among African American adolescents. *Journal of Youth and Adolescence, 38*, 153–163.

Sechrest, L. (1968). Personal constructs and personal characteristics. *Journal of Individual Psychology, 24*, 162–166.

Sechrest, L. (1984). Review of J. B. Rotter's The Development and Applications of Social Learning Theory: Selected papers. *Journal of the History of the Behavioral Sciences, 20*, 228–230.

Sechrest, L., & Jackson, D. N. (1961). Social intelligence and accuracy of interpersonal predictions. *Journal of Personality, 29*, 169–182.

Seehusen, J., Cordaro, F., Wildschut, T., Sedikides, C., Routledge, C., Blackhart, G., et al. (2013). Individual differences in nostalgia proneness: The integrating role of the need to belong. *Personality and Individual Differences, 55*, 904–908.

Seeman, M., Seeman, T., & Sayles, M. (1985). Social networks and health status: A longitudinal analysis. *Social Psychology Quarterly, 48*, 237–248.

Segall, M., & Wynd, C. A. (1990). Health conception, health locus of control, and power as predictors of smoking behavior change. *American Journal of Health Promotion, 4*, 338–344.

Segerstrom, S. C. (2001). Optimism and attentional bias for negative and positive stimuli. *Personality and Social Psychology Bulletin, 27*, 1334–1343.

Segerstrom, S. C., & Taylor, S. E. (1998). Optimism is associated with mood, coping, and immune change in response to stress. *Journal of Personality and Social Psychology, 74*, 1646–1655.

Seidah, A., & Bouffard, T. (2007). Being proud of oneself as a person or being proud of one's physical appearance: What matters for feeling well in adolescence? *Social Behavior and Personality, 35*, 255–268.

Seidman, G. (2014). Expressing the true self on Facebook. *Computers in Human Behavior, 31*, 367–372.

Seiffge-Krenke, I., & Kirsch, H. (2002). The body in adolescent diaries: The case of Karen Horney. *Psychoanalytic Study of the Child, 57*, 400–410.

Seligman, M. E. P. (1975). *Helplessness: On depression, development, and death*. San Francisco, CA: W. H. Freeman.

Seligman, M. E. P. (1990). *Learned optimism*. New York: Knopf.

Seligman, M. E. P. (2002). *Authentic happiness: Using the new positive psychology to realize your potential for lasting fulfillment*. New York: Free Press.

Seligman, M. E. P., & Fowler, R. (2011). Comprehensive soldier fitness and the future of psychology. *American Psychologist, 66*(1), 81–86.

Seligman, M. E. P., & Maier, S. F. (1967). Failure to escape traumatic shock. *Journal of Experimental Psychology, 74*, 1–9.

Seligman, M. E. P., Rashid, T., & Parks, A. (2006). Positive psychotherapy. *American Psychologist, 61*, 774–788.

Seligman, M. E. P., & Visintainer, M. (1985). Tumor rejection and early experience of uncontrollable shock in the rat. In F. R. Brush & J. B. Overmier (Eds.), *Affect, conditioning, and cognition: Essays on the determinants of behavior* (pp. 203–210). Hillsdale, NJ: Erlbaum.

Sellers, R. M., Chavous, T. M., & Cooke, D. Y. (1998). Racial ideology and racial centrality as predictors of African American college students' academic performance. *Journal of Black Psychology, 24*, 8–27.

Sellers, R. M., Rowley, S. A. J., Chavous, T. M., Shelton, J. N., & Smith, M. A. (1997). Multidimensional Inventory of Black Identity: A preliminary investigation of reliability and construct validity. *Journal of Personality and Social Psychology, 73*, 805–815.

Sethi, S., & Seligman, M. E. P. (1994). The hope of fundamentalists. *Psychological Science, 5*, 58.

Shallcross, A., Ford, B., Floerke, C., & Mauss, I. (2013). Getting better with age: The relationship between age, acceptance, and negative affect. *Journal of Personality and Social Psychology, 104*, 734–748.

Shamir, B. (1986). Self-esteem and the psychological impact of unemployment. *Social Psychology Quarterly, 49*, 61–72.

Shane, S., Nicolaou, N., Cherkas, L., & Spector, T. (2010). Genetics, the Big Five and the tendency to be self-employed. *Journal of Applied Psychology, 95*(6), 1154–1162.

Shatz, S. (2004). The relationship between Horney's three neurotic types and Eysenck's PEN model of personality. *Personality and Individual Differences, 37*, 1255–1261.

Shaw, B., Liang, J., & Krause, N. (2010). Age and race differences in the trajectories of self-esteem. *Psychology and Aging, 25*(1), 84–94.

Sheldon, K., Abad, N., & Omoile, J. (2009). Testing self-determination theory via Nigerian and Indian adolescents. *International Journal of Behavioral Development, 33*(5), 451–459.

Sheldon, K., Arndt, J., & Houser-Marko, L. (2003). In search of the organismic valuing process: The human tendency to move towards beneficial goal choices. *Journal of Personality, 71*, 835–886.

Sheldon, K., Elliot, A., Kim, Y., & Kasser, T. (2001). What is satisfying about satisfying events? Testing ten candidate psychological needs. *Journal of Personality and Social Psychology, 80*, 325–339.

Sheldon, K., & Kasser, T. (2001). Getting older, getting better? Personal strivings and psychological maturity across the life span. *Developmental Psychology, 37*, 491–501.

Sheldon, K., Kasser, T., Houser-Marko, L., Jones, T., & Turban, D. (2005). Doing one's duty: Chronological age, felt autonomy, and subjective well-being. *European Journal of Personality, 19*, 97–115.

Sheldon, W. (1942). *The varieties of temperament: A psychology of constitutional differences*. New York: Harper & Row.

Shepherd, S., & Belicki, K. (2008). Trait forgiveness and traitedness with the HEXACO model of personality. *Personality and Individual Differences, 45*, 389–394.

Sher, K., Bartholow, B., & Wood. M. (2000). Personality and substance abuse disorders: A prospective study. *Journal of Consulting and Clinical Psychology, 68*, 818–829.

Shevrin, H. (1977). Some assumptions of psychoanalytic communication: Implications of subliminal research for psychoanalytic method and technique. In N. Freedman (Ed.), *Communicative structures and psychic structures* (pp. 255–270). New York: Springer.

Shim, U., Kim, H., Seung-Ju, C., Shin, C., Ryu, S., Sung, Y., et al. (2014). Personality traits and body mass index in a Korean population. *PLoS ONE, 9,* Article e90516.

Shiner, R. L. (1998). How shall we speak of children's personalities in middle childhood? A preliminary taxonomy. *Psychological Bulletin, 124,* 308–332.

Shiner, R. (2014). *Personality development in childhood and adolescence.* American Psychological Association Convention Presentation. http://psycnet.apa.org/psycextra/531012014-001.pdf

Shirachi, M., & Spirrison, C. (2006). Repressive coping style and substance use among college students. *North American Journal of Psychology, 8,* 99–114.

Shojaee, M., & French, C. (2014). The relationship between mental health components and locus of control in youth. *Psychology, 5,* 966–978.

Shostrom, E. L. (1964). An inventory for the measurement of self-actualization. *Educational and Psychological Measurement, 24,* 207–218.

Shostrom, E. L. (1974). *Manual for the Personal Orientation Inventory.* San Diego, CA: Educational and Industrial Testing Service.

Shull, R., & Grimes, J. (2006). Resistance to extinction following variable-interval reinforcement. *Journal of the Experimental Analysis of Behavior, 85,* 23–29.

Shulman, E., Harden, K., Chein, J., & Steinberg, L. (2015). Sex differences in the developmental trajectories of impulse control and sensation-seeking from early adolescence to early adulthood. *Journal of Youth and Adolescence, 44,* 1–17.

Sibley, C., Harding, J., Perry, R., Asbrock, F., & Duckitt, J. (2010). Personality and prejudice: Extension to the HEXACO personality model. *European Journal of Personality, 24,* 515–534.

Siegel, A. M. (2001). An antidote to misconceptions about self psychology [Review of the book *Kohut's Freudian Vision*]. *Contemporary Psychology, 46,* 316–317.

Siegler, I., & Brummett, B. (2000). Associations among NEO personality assessments and well-being at midlife: Facet level analysis. *Psychology and Aging, 15,* 710–714.

Silvera, D., & Seger, C. (2004). Feeling good about ourselves: Unrealistic self-evaluations and their relation to self-esteem in the United States and Norway. *Journal of Cross-Cultural Psychology, 35,* 571–585.

Silverman, L. H., & Weinberger, I. (1985). Mommy and I are one: Implications for psychotherapy. *American Psychologist, 40,* 1296–1308.

Simon, A. (2007). Sensitivity of the 16PF Motivational Distortion Scale to response bias. *Psychological Reports, 101,* 482–484.

Simon, L. (1998). *Genuine reality: A life of William James.* New York: Harcourt Brace.

Singh, T., & Choudhri, N. (2014). Early adulthood: The role of locus of control, meaning of life and subjective well being. *Journal of Psychosocial Research, 9,* 131–139.

Siribaddana, P. (2013). Personality traits of the only child, *Sciences 360.* http://www.sciences360.com/index.php/personality-traits-of-the-only-child-3045/

Skinner, B. F. (1938). *The behavior of organisms: An experimental analysis.* New York: Appleton-Century.

Skinner, B. F. (1948). *Walden two.* New York: Macmillan.

Skinner, B. F. (1953). *Science and human behavior.* New York: Free Press.

Skinner, B. F. (1958). Distinguished scientific contribution award. *American Psychologist, 13,* 729–738.

Skinner, B. F. (1967). Autobiography. In E. G. Boring & G. Lindzey (Eds.), *A history of psychology in autobiography* (Vol. 5, pp. 385–413). New York: Appleton-Century-Crofts.

Skinner, B. F. (1971). *Beyond freedom and dignity.* New York: Knopf.

Skinner, B. F. (1979). *The shaping of a behaviorist.* New York: Knopf.

Skinner, B. F. (1983). *A matter of consequences.* New York: Knopf.

Skinner, T., Hampson, S., & Fife-Schau, C. (2002). Personality, personal model beliefs, and self-care in adolescents and young adults with Type I diabetes. *Health Psychology, 21,* 61–70.

Skitka, L., & Sargis, E. (2006). The Internet as psychological laboratory. *Annual Review of Psychology, 57,* 529–555.

Sleek, S. (1998, October). Blame your peers, not your parents. *APA Monitor,* p. 9.

Slugoski, B. F., & Ginsburg, G. P. (1989). Ego identity and explanatory speech. In J. Shotter & K. F. Gergen (Eds.), *Texts of identity* (pp. 36–55). London: Sage.

Smart, E., Gow, A., & Deary, I. (2014). Occupational complexity and lifetime cognitive abilities. *Neurology, 83,* 2285–2291.

Smeekens, S., Riksen-Walraven, J., & van Bakel, H. (2007). Cortisol reactions in five-year-olds to parent-child interaction: The moderating role of ego-resiliency. *Journal of Child Psychology and Psychiatry, 48,* 649–656.

Smillie, L., Yeo, G., Furnham, A., & Jackson, C. (2006). Benefits of all work and no play: The relationship between neuroticism and performance as a function of resource allocation. *Journal of Applied Psychology, 91,* 139–155.

Smith, A., & Williams, K. (2004). R U there? Ostracism by cell phone text messages. *Group Dynamics, 8,* 291–301.

Smith, D. (2002). The theory heard 'round the world. *Monitor on Psychology, 33*(9), 30–32.

Smith, E., Bissett, D., & Russo, S. (2014). *Sensation seeking tendencies and injury patterns among Motocross athletes.* American Psychological Association Covention Presentation. http://psycnet.apa.org/index.cfm?fa=search.displayRecord&id=4CA4E0D5-F108-6F39-DFA8-567CF9EEAAEB&resultID=1&page=1&dbTab=all&search=true

Smith, J. E., Stefan, C., Kovaleski, M., & Johnson, G. (1991). Recidivism and dependency in a psychiatric population: An investigation with Kelly's dependency grid. *International Journal of Personal Construct Psychology, 4,* 157–173.

Smith, M. B. (1990). Henry A. Murray (1893–1988): Humanistic psychologist. *Journal of Humanistic Psychology, 30,* 6–13.

Smith, R. E., Ptacek, J. T., & Smoll, F. L. (1992). Sensation seeking, stress, and adolescent injuries: A test of stress-buffering, risk-taking, and coping skills hypotheses. *Journal of Personality and Social Psychology, 62,* 1016–1024.

Smith, T. B., & Silva, L. (2011). Ethnic identity and personal well-being of people of color: A meta-analysis. *Journal of Counseling Psychology, 58,* 42–60.

Solnit, A. J. (1992). Freud's view of mental health and fate. In E. E. Garcia (Ed.), *Understanding Freud: The man and his ideas* (pp. 64–77). New York: New York University Press.

Solo, C. (2015). Is happiness good for your personality? Concurrent and prospective relations to the Big Five with subjective well-being. *Journal of Personality, 83,* 45–55.

Spangler, W. D. (1992). Validity of questionnaire and TAT measures of need for achievement: Two meta-analyses. *Psychological Bulletin, 112,* 140–154.

Spann, M., Molock, S., Barksdale, C., Matlin, S., & Puri, R. (2006). Suicide and African-American teenagers: Risk factors and coping mechanisms. *Suicide and Life-Threatening Behavior, 36,* 553–568.

Spitalnick, J., DiClemente, R., Wingood, G., Crosby, R., Milhausen, R., Sales, J., et al. (2007). Sexual sensation seeking and its relationship to risky sexual behavior among African-American adolescents. *Journal of Adolescence, 30,* 165–173.

Sroufe, L. A., Fox, N. E., & Pancake, V. R. (1983). Attachment and dependency in developmental perspective. *Child Development, 54,* 1615–1627.

Stacy, A. W., Sussman, S., Dent, C. W., Burton, D., & Floy, B. R. (1992). Moderators of peer social influence in adolescent smoking. *Personality and Social Psychology Bulletin, 18,* 163–172.

Stajkovic, A., & Luthans, F. (1998). Self-efficacy and work-related performance: A meta-analysis. *Psychological Bulletin, 124,* 240–261.

Stanton, B., Li, X., Cottrell, L., & Kaljee, J. (2001). Early initiation of sex, drug-related risk behaviors, and sensation seeking among urban low-income African-American adolescents. *Journal of the National Medical Association, 93*(4), 129–138.

Statton, J. E., & Wilborn, B. (1991). Adlerian counseling and the early recollections of children. *Individual Psychology, 47,* 338–347.

Staudinger, U. M. (2001a). Life reflection: A social-cognitive analysis of life review. *Review of General Psychology, 5,* 148–160.

Staudinger, U. M. (2001b). More than pleasure? Toward a psychology of growth and strength? [Review of the book *Well-being: The foundations of hedonic psychology*]. *Contemporary Psychology, 46,* 552–554.

Staudinger, U. M., Fleeson, W., & Baltes, P. B. (1999). Predictors of subjective physical health and global well-being: Similarities and differences between the United States and Germany. *Journal of Personality and Social Psychology, 76,* 305–319.

Steca, P., Bassi, M., Caprara, V., & Fave, A. (2011). Parents' self-efficacy beliefs and their children's psychosocial adaptation during adolescence. *Journal of Youth and Adolescence, 40,* 320–331.

Steel, P. (2007). The nature of procrastination: A meta-analytic and theoretical review of quintessential self-regulatory failure. *Psychological Bulletin, 133,* 65–94.

Steel, P., & Ones, D. (2002). Personality and happiness: A national-level analysis. *Journal of Personality and Social Psychology, 83,* 767–781.

Steinberg, L., & Morris, A. S. (2001). Adolescent development. *Annual Review of Psychology, 52,* 83–110.

Stelmack, R. M. (1997). Toward a paradigm in personality: Comment on Eysenck's (1997) view. *Journal of Personality and Social Psychology, 73,* 1238–1241.

Stepanikova, I., Nie, N., & He, X. (2010). Time on the Internet at home, loneliness, and life satisfaction: Evidence from panel time-diary data. *Computers in Human Behavior, 26,* 329–338.

Stepansky, P. E. (1983). *In Freud's shadow: Adler in context.* New York: Analytic Press.

Stephan, J., Schredl, M., Henley-Einion, J., & Blagrove, M. (2012). TV viewing and dreaming in children: The UK library study. *International Journal of Dream Research, 5,* 130–133.

Stephan, Y., Boiche, J., & Le Scanff, C. (2010). Motivation and physical activity behaviors among older women: A self-determination perspective. *Psychology of Women Quarterly, 34,* 339–348.

Stephen, J., Fraser, E., & Marcia, J. E. (1992). Moratorium achievement (MAMA) cycles in lifespan identity development: Value orientations and reasoning system correlates. *Journal of Adolescence, 15,* 283–300.

Stephenson, W. (1953). *The study of behavior: Q-technique and its methodology.* Chicago, IL: University of Chicago Press.

Steptoe, A., Deaton, A., & Stone, A. (2015). Subjective well-being, health, and aging. *Lancet, 385,* 640–648.

Steptoe, A., Wright, C., Kunz-Ebrecht, S., & Lliffe, S. (2006). Dispositional optimism and health behavior in community-dwelling older people: Associations with healthy aging. *British Journal of Health Psychology, 11,* 71–84.

Sterba, R. F. (1982). *Reminiscences of a Viennese psychoanalyst.* Detroit, MI: Wayne State University Press.

Stewart, A. J., & Ostrove, J. M. (1998). Women's personality in middle age: Gender, history, and midcourse corrections. *American Psychologist, 53,* 1185–1194.

Stewart, A. J., & Vandewater, E. A. (1999). "If I had it to do over again…." Midlife review, midcourse corrections, and women's well-being in midlife. *Journal of Personality and Social Psychology, 76,* 270–283.

Stewart, G. L., Carson, K. P., & Cardy, R. L. (1996). The joint effects of conscientiousness and self-leadership training on employee self-directed behavior in a service setting. *Personnel Psychology, 49,* 143–164.

Stieger, S., & Reips, U. (2010). What are participants doing while filling in an online questionnaire: A paradata collection tool and an empirical study. *Computers in Human Behavior, 26,* 1488–1495.

Stilwell, N. A., Wallick, M. M., Thal, S. E., & Burleson, J. A. (2000). Myers-Briggs Type and medical specialty choice: A new look at an old question. *Teaching and Learning in Medicine, 12,* 14–20.

Stinson, D., Logel, C., Cameron, J., Zanna, M., Holmes, J., Wood, J., & Spencer, S. (2008). The cost of lower self-esteem: Testing a self- and social-bonds model of health. *Interpersonal Relations and Group Processes, 94,* 412–428.

Stirn, A., Hinz, A., & Braehler, E. (2006). Prevalence of tattooing and body piercing in Germany and perception of health, mental disorders, and sensation seeking among tattooed and body-pierced individuals. *Journal of Psychosomatic Research, 60,* 531–534.

Stone, A., Schwartz, A., Broderick, J., & Deaton, R. (2010, May 17). A snapshot of the age distribution of psychological well-being in the United Sates. *Proceedings of the National Academic of Sciences.* http://www.pnas.org/content/107/22/9985.full.

Story, A. L. (1998). Self-esteem and memory for favorable and unfavorable personality feedback. *Personality and Social Psychology Bulletin, 24,* 51–64.

Strano, D., & Petrocelli, J. (2005). A preliminary examination of the role of inferiority feelings in the academic achievement of college students. *Journal of Individual Psychology, 61,* 80–89.

Straumann, T. J., Vookles, J., Berenstein, V., Chaiken, S., & Higgins, E. T. (1991). Self-discrepancies and vulnerability to body dissatisfaction and disordered eating. *Journal of Personality and Social Psychology, 61,* 946–956.

Streitmatter, J. (1993). Identity status and identity style: A replication study. *Journal of Adolescence, 16,* 211–215.

Stricker, L. J., & Ross, J. (1962). *A description and evaluation of the Myers-Briggs Type Indicator.* Princeton, NJ: Educational Testing Service.

Strickland, B. (2014). Julian B. Rotter (1916–2014) [obituary]. *American Psychologist, 69,* 545–546.

Strickland, B. R. (1989). Internal-external control expectancies: From contingency to creativity. *American Psychologist, 44,* 1–12.

Strickland, B. R., & Haley, W. E. (1980). Sex differences on the Rotter I-E Scale. *Journal of Personality and Social Psychology, 39,* 930–939.

Strizhitskaya, O., & Davedyuk, E. (2014). Self-determination structure in aging: From theory to practice. *3rd Annual International Conference on Cognitive and Behavioral Psychology.* http://psycnet.apa.org/psycextra/507412014-012.pdf

Strumpfer, D. (1970). Fear and affiliation during a disaster. *Journal of Social Psychology, 82,* 263–268.

Sturman, E., Mongrain, M., & Kohn, P. (2006). Attributional style as a predictor of hopelessness depression. *Journal of Cognitive Psychotherapy, 20,* 447–458.

Suarez-Balcazar, Y., Balcazar, F., & Taylor-Ritzler, T. (2009). Using the Internet to conduct research with culturally diverse populations: Challenges and opportunities. *Cultural Diversity and Ethnic Minority Psychology, 15,* 96–103.

Suedfeld, P., Soriano, E., McMurtry, D., Paterson, H., Weiszbeck, T., & Krell, R. (2005). Erikson's components of a healthy personality among Holocaust survivors immediately and forty years after the war. *International Journal of Aging and Human Development, 60,* 229–248.

Suinn, R. (1999, March). Scaling the summit: Valuing ethnicity. *APA Monitor,* p. 2.

Suldo, S., Minch, D., & Hearon, B. (2014). Adolescent life satisfaction and personality characteristics: Investigating relationships using a five-factor model. *Journal of Happiness Studies.* http://link.springer.com/article/10.1007/s10902-014-9544-1http://link.springer.com/article/10.1007/s10902-014-9544-1

Sulloway, F. J. (1979). *Freud, biologist of the mind: Beyond the psychoanalytic legend.* New York: Basic Books.

Sulloway, F. J. (1992). Reassessing Freud's case histories: The social construction of psychoanalysis. In T. Gelfand & J. Kerr (Eds.), *Freud and the history of psychoanalysis* (pp. 153–192). Hillsdale, NJ: Analytic Press.

Sulloway, F. J. (1995). Birth order and evolutionary psychology: A meta-analytic overview. *Psychological Inquiry, 6*(1), 75–80.

Sulloway, F. J. (2007). Birth order and intelligence. *Science, 317,* 1711.

Sulloway, F. J., & Zweigenhaft, R. (2010). Birth order and risk taking in athletics: A meta-analysis and study of major league baseball. *Personality and Social Psychology Review, 14,* 402–416.

Suls, J., Green, P., & Hillis, S. (1998). Emotional reactivity to everyday problems, affective inertia, and neuroticism. *Personality and Social Psychology Bulletin, 24,* 127–136.

Summerville, K. (2010). *Antagonism of opposites: Carl Jung's legacy of analytic psychology.* American Psychological Association Convention Presentation.

Sun, P., & Anderson, M. (2012). The importance of attributional complexity for transformational leadership studies. *Journal of Management Studies, 48,* 1001–1022.

Susskind, J., Littlewort, G., Bartlett, M., Movellan, J., & Anderson, A. (2007). Human and computer recognition of facial expressions of emotion. *Neuropsychologia, 45,* 152–162.

Sutin, A. (2013). Optimism, pessimism and bias in self-reported body weight among older adults. *Obesity, 21,* 508–511.

Sutin, A., Costa, P., Wethington, E., & Eaton, W. (2010). Turning points and lessons learned: Stressful life events and personality trait development across middle adulthood. *Psychology and Aging, 25,* 524–533.

Sutton-Smith, B., & Rosenberg, B. C. (1970). *The sibling.* New York: Holt, Rinehart & Winston.

Swanbro, D. (2014). Mirror or megaphone? How relationships between narcissism and social networking site use differ on Facebook and Twitter. *Computers in Human Behavior, 29,* 2004–2012.

Swann, W., Chang-Schneider, C., & McClarty, K. (2007). Do people's self-views matter? Self-concept and self-esteem in everyday life. *American Psychologist, 62,* 84–94.

Sweeny, K., & Shepperd, J. (2010). Commentary: The costs of optimism and the benefits of pessimism. *Emotion, 10,* 750–753.

Swenson, R., & Prelow, H. (2005). Ethnic identity, self-esteem, and perceived efficacy as mediators of the relation of supportive parenting to psychosocial outcomes among urban adolescents. *Journal of Adolescence, 28,* 465–477.

Symbaluk, D. G., Heth, C. D., Cameron, J., & Pierce, W. D. (1997). Social modeling, monetary incentives, and pain endurance: The role of self-efficacy in pain perception. *Personality and Social Psychology Bulletin, 23,* 258–269.

Taforadi, R., Shaughnessy, S., Yamaguchi, S., & Murakoshi, A. (2011). The reporting of self-esteem in Japan and Canada. *Journal of Cross-Cultural Psychology, 42*(1), 155–164.

Taft, L. B., & Nehrke, M. F. (1990). Reminiscences, life review, and ego integrity in nursing home residents. *International Journal of Aging and Human Development, 30,* 189–196.

Takano, K., Sakamoto, S., & Tanno, Y. (2014). Repetitive thought impairs sleep quality: An experience sampling study. *Behavior Therapy, 45,* 67–82.

Tallandini, M., & Caudek, C. (2010). Defense mechanisms development in typical children. *Psychotherapy Research, 20* (5), 535–545.

Tamamiya, Y., & Jiraki, K. (2013). The relationship between playing digital games and recognition of facial expressions in children. *10th Asian Association of Social Psychology Biennial Conference, Yogyakarta, Indonesia, August.* http://psycnet.apa.org/psycextra/627722013-763.pdf

Tangney, J., Baumeister, R., & Boone, A. (2004). High self-control predicts good adjustment, less pathology, better grades, and interpersonal success. *Journal of Personality, 72,* 271–324.

Tavris, C. (1992). *The mismeasure of woman.* New York: Simon & Schuster.

Tay, L., & Diener, E. (2011). Needs and subjective well-being around the world. *Journal of Personality and Social Psychology, 101,* 354–365.

Taylor, J. (2009, April 30). The 2009 Time 100: Paul Eckman. *Time.* http://content.time.com/time/specials/

packages/article/0,28804,1894410_1893209_189347
5,00.html

Taylor, M. (2000). The influence of self-efficacy on alcohol use among American Indians. *Cultural Diversity and Ethnic Minority Psychology, 6,* 152–167.

Taylor, S. E., Kemeny, M. E., Aspinwall, L. G., Schneider, S. C., Rodriguez, R., & Herbert, M. (1992). Optimism, coping, psychological distress, and high-risk sexual behavior among men at risk for acquired immunodeficiency syndrome (AIDS). *Journal of Personality and Social Psychology, 63,* 460–473.

Tellegen, A., Lykken, D. T., Bouchard, T. J., Wilcox, K., Segal, N., & Rich, S. (1988). Personality similarity in twins reared apart and together. *Journal of Personality and Social Psychology, 54,* 1031–1039.

Terracciano, A., Costa, P., & McCrae, R. (2006). Personality plasticity after age 30. *Personality and Social Psychology Bulletin, 32,* 999–1009.

Terracciano, A., McCrae, R., & Costa, P. (2010). Intra-individual change in personality stability and age. *Journal of Research in Personality, 44,* 31–37.

Teti, D. M., & Gelfand, D. M. (1991). Behavioral competence among mothers of infants in the first year: The mediational role of maternal self-efficacy. *Child Development, 62,* 918–929.

Tetlock, P. E. (1983). Cognitive style and political ideology. *Journal of Personality and Social Psychology, 45,* 118–126.

Tetlock, P. E. (1984). Cognitive style and political belief systems in the British House of Commons. *Journal of Personality and Social Psychology, 46,* 365–375.

Thacker, S., & Griffiths, M. (2012). An exploratory study of trolling in online video gaming. *International Journal of Cyber Behavior: Psychology and Learning, 2,* 17–33.

Thomas, A. (1986). The New York Longitudinal Study: From infancy to early adult life. In R. Plomin & J. Dunn (Eds.), *The study of temperament* (pp. 39–52). Hillsdale, NJ: Erlbaum.

Thomas, A., Chess, S., & Korn, S. (1982). The reality of difficult temperament. *Merrill-Palmer Quarterly, 28,* 1–20.

Thompson, S. C., Sobolew-Shubin, A., Galbraith, M. E., Schwankovsky, L., & Cruzen, D. (1993). Maintaining perception of control: Finding perceived control in low-control circumstances. *Journal of Personality and Social Psychology, 64,* 293–304.

Thompson, T. (1988). Benedictus behavior analysis: B. F. Skinner's magnum opus at fifty [Review of the book *Behavior of organisms: An experimental analysis*]. *Contemporary Psychology, 33,* 397–402.

Thompson, V., & Alexander, H. (2006). Therapists' race and African-American clients' reactions to therapy. *Psychotherapy: Theory, Research, Practice, Training, 43,* 99–110.

Tobey, L. H., & Bruhn, A. R. (1992). Early memories and the criminally dangerous. *Journal of Personality Assessment, 59,* 137–152.

Tomina, Y., & Takahata, M. (2010). A behavioral analysis of force-controlled operant tasks in American lobster. *Physiology and Behavior, 101,* 108–116.

Tomlin, M., & Reed, P. (2012). Effects of fixed-time reinforcement delivered by teachers for reducing problem behavior in special education classrooms. *Journal of Behavioral Education, 21,* 150–162.

Tong, J., & Wang, L. (2006). Validation of locus of control scale in Chinese organizations. *Personality and Individual Differences, 41,* 941–950.

Torges, C., Stewart, A., & Duncan, L. (2008). Achieving ego integrity: Personality development in late midlife. *Journal of Research in Personality, 42*(4), 1004–1019.

Torges, C., Stewart, A., & Miner-Rubino, K. (2005). Personality after prime of life: Men and women coming to terms with regrets. *Journal of Research in Personality, 39,* 148–165.

Tori, C., & Bilmes, M. (2002). Multiculturalism and psychoanalytic psychology: The validation of a defense mechanism measure in an Asian population. *Psychoanalytic Psychology, 19,* 701–721.

Torres, L., & Ong, A. (2010). A daily diary investigation of Latino ethnic identity, discrimination, and depression. *Cultural Diversity and Ethnic Minority Psychology, 16*(4), 561–568.

Tosun, L., & Lajunen, T. (2010). Does Internet use reflect your personality? Relationship between Eysenck's personality dimensions and Internet use. *Computers in Human Behavior, 26,* 162–167.

Tran, X., & Ralston, L. (2006). Tourist preferences: Influence of unconscious needs. *Annals of Tourism Research, 33,* 424–441.

Triandis, H. C., & Suh, E. M. (2002). Cultural influences on personality. *Annual Review of Psychology, 53,* 133–160.

Tribich, D., & Messer, S. (1974). Psychoanalytic character type and states of authority as determiners of suggestibility. *Journal of Consulting and Clinical Psychology, 42,* 842–848.

Trice, A. (2010). Sensation-seeking and video choice in second grade children. *Personality and Individual Differences, 49,* 1007–1010.

Triplet, R. G. (1993). Book review of *Love's Story Told: A Life of Henry A. Murray.Journal of the History of the Behavioral Sciences, 29,* 384–386.

Trovato, G., Kishi, T., Endo, N., Zecca, M., Hashimoto, K., & Takanishi, A. (2014). Cross-cultural perspectives on emotion expressive humanoid robotic head: Recognition of facial expressions and symbols. *International Journal of Social Robotics, 5,* 515–527.

Trzesniewski, K. H., Donnellan, M. B., Moffitt, B., Robins, R. W., Poulton, R., & Caspi, A. (2006). Low self-esteem during adolescence predicts poor health, criminal behavior, and limited economic prospects during adulthood. *Developmental Psychology, 42,* 381–390.

Trzesniewski, K. H., Donnellan, M. B., & Robins, R. W. (2003). Stability of self-esteem across the life span. *Journal of Personality and Social Psychology, 84,* 205–220.

Tsai, M., & Tsai, C. (2010). Junior high school students' Internet usage and self-efficacy: A re-examination of the gender gap. *Computers & Education, 54,* 1182–1192.

Tskhay, K., & Rule, N. (2014). Perceptions of personality in text-based media and OSN: A meta-analysis. *Journal of Research in Personality, 49,* 25–30.

Tucker, J., Elliott, M., & Klein, D. (2006). Social control of health behavior: Associations with conscientiousness and neuroticism. *Personality and Social Psychology Bulletin, 32,* 1143–1152.

Tucker, W. (2009). *The Cattell controversy: Race, science, and ideology.* Champaign: University of Illinois Press.

Tuerlinckx, F., De Boeck, P., & Lens, W. (2002). Measuring needs with the Thematic Apperception Test: A psychometric study. *Journal of Personality and Social Psychology, 82,* 448–461.

Turkle, S. (1995). *Life on the screen: Identity in the age of the Internet.* New York: Simon & Schuster.

Turkum, A. (2005). Do optimism, social network richness, and submissive behaviors predict well-being? Study with a Turkish sample. *Social Behavior and Personality, 33,* 619–628.

Uba, L. (1994). *Asian Americans: Personality patterns, identity, and mental health.* New York: Guilford Press.

Udris, R. (2014). Cyberbullying among high school students in Japan: Development and validation of the Online Disinhibition Scale. *Computers in Human Behavior, 41,* 253–261.

Uhlmann, E., & Swanson, J. (2004). Exposure to violent video games increases automatic aggressiveness. *Journal of Adolescence, 27,* 41–52.

Umana-Taylor, A. (2004). Ethnic identity and self-esteem: Examining the role of social context. *Journal of Adolescence, 27,* 139–146.

Usborne, E., & Taylor, D. (2010). The role of cultural identity clarity for self-concept clarity, self-esteem, and subjective well-being. *Personality and Social Psychology Bulletin, 36,* 883–897.

Utsey, S., Payne, Y., Jackson, E., & Jones, A. (2002). Race-related stress, quality of life indicators, and life satisfaction among elderly African Americans. *Cultural Diversity and Ethnic Minority Psychology, 8,* 7–17.

Utz, S. (2003). Social identification and interpersonal attraction in MUDs [multi-user dungeons]. *Swiss Journal of Psychology, 62,* 91–101.

Vaidya, J., Latzman, R., Markon, K., & Watson, D. (2010). Age differences on measures of disinhibition during young adulthood. *Personality and Individual Differences, 48,* 815–820.

Valentijn, S., Hill, R., Van Hooren, S., Bosma, H., Van Boxtel, M., Jolles, J., et al. (2006). Memory self-efficacy predicts memory performance: Results from a 6-year follow-up study. *Psychology and Aging, 21,* 165–172.

Valli, K., Revonsuo, A., Palkas, O., & Punamaki, R. (2006). The effect of trauma on dream content: A field study of Palestinian children. *Dreaming, 16,* 63–87.

Van Aken, M., Denisson, J., Branje, S., Dubas, J., & Goossens, L. (2006). Midlife concerns and short-term personality change in middle adulthood. *European Journal of Personality, 20,* 497–513.

Van Boven, L. (2005). Experientialism, materialism, and the pursuit of happiness. *Review of General Psychology, 9,* 132–142.

Van de Water, D. A., & McAdams, D. P. (1989). Generativity and Erikson's "belief in the species." *Journal of Research in Personality, 23,* 435–449.

Van den Boom, D. C., & Hoeksma, J. B. (1994). The effect of infant irritability on mother-infant interaction: A growth-curve analysis. *Developmental Psychology, 30,* 581–590.

Van der Aa, N., Overbeek, G., Engels, R., Scholte, R., Meerkerk, G., & Van den Eijnden, J. (2009). Daily and compulsive Internet use and well-being in adolescence: A diatheses-stress model based on the Big Five personality traits. *Journal of Youth and Adolescence, 38*(6), 765–776.

Van der Linden, D., Scholte, R., Cillessen, A., Nijenhuis, J., & Segers, E. (2010). Classroom ratings of likeability and popularity are related to the Big Five and the general factor of personality. *Journal of Research in Personality, 44*(5), 669–671.

Van Dijk, T., Dijkshoorn, H., Van Dijk, A., Cremer, S., & Agyemang, C. (2013). Multidimensional health locus of control and depressive symptoms in the multi-ethnic population of the Netherlands. *Social Psychiatry and Psychiatric Epidemiology, 48,* 1931–1939.

Van Eeden, R., & Mantsha, T. (2007). Theoretical and methodical considerations in the translation of the 16PF into an African language. *South African Journal of Psychology, 37*(1), 62–81.

Van Hiel, A., & Brebels, L. (2011). Conservatism is good for you: Cultural conservatism protects self-esteem in older adults. *Personality and Individual Differences, 50,* 120–123.

Van Hiel, A., Mervielde, I., & De Fruyt, F. (2006). Stagnation and generativity: Structure, validity, and differential relationships with adaptive and maladaptive personality. *Journal of Personality, 74,* 543–573.

Van Hiel, A., & Vansteenkiste, M. (2009). Ambitions fulfilled? The effects of intrinsic and extrinsic goal attainment on older adults' ego-integrity and death attitudes. *International Journal of Aging and Human Development, 68,* 27–51.

Van Yperen, N. (2006). A novel approach to assessing achievement goals in the context of the 2 X 2 framework: Identifying distinct profiles of individuals with different dominant achievement goals. *Personality and Social Psychology Bulletin, 32,* 1432–1445.

Vandewater, E. A., Ostrove, J. M., & Stewart, A. J. (1997). Predicting women's well-being in midlife: The importance of personality development and social role involvements. *Journal of Personality and Social Psychology, 72,* 1147–1160.

Vandiver, B., Cross, W., Worrell, F., & Fhagen-Smith, P. (2002). Validating the Cross Racial Identity Scale. *Journal of Counseling Psychology, 49,* 71–85.

Vaughan, A., de Passille, A., Stookey, J., & Rushen, J. (2014). Operant conditioning of urination by calves. *Applied Animal Behavior Science, 158,* 8–15.

Vecchione, M., Alessandri, G., Barbaranelli, C., & Gerbino, M. (2010). Stability and change of ego resiliency from late adolescence to young adulthood: A multiperspective study using the ER89-R Scale. *Journal of Personality Assessment, 92,* 212–221.

Veenhoven, R. (2005). Is life getting better? How long and happily do people live in modern society? *European Psychologist, 10,* 330–343.

Velezmoro, R., Lacefield, K., & Roberti, J. (2010). Perceived stress, sensation, and college students' abuse of the Internet. *Computers in Human Behavior, 26,* 1526–1530.

Verkuyten, M. (2009). Self-esteem and multiculturalism: An examination among ethnic minority and majority groups in the Netherlands. *Journal of Research in Personality, 43,* 419–427.

Ventura, M., Salanova, M., & Llorens, S. (2015). Professional self-efficacy as a predictor of burnout and engagement: The role of challenge and hindrance demands. *Journal of Psychology: Interdisciplinary and Applied, 149,* 277–302.

Vetere, A., & Myers, L. (2002). Repressive coping style and adult romantic attachment style. *Personality and Individual Differences, 32,* 799–807.

Viken, R. J., Rose, R. J., Kaprio, J., & Koskenvuo, M. (1994). A developmental genetic analysis of adult personality:

Extraversion and neuroticism from 18 to 59 years of age. *Journal of Personality and Social Psychology, 66,* 722–730.

Villanova, P., & Peterson, C. (1991). Meta-analysis of human helplessness experiments. Unpublished data. (Cited in Peterson, Maier, & Seligman, 1993.)

Viner, R. (1996). Melanie Klein and Anna Freud: The discourse of the early dispute. *Journal of the History of the Behavioral Sciences, 32,* 4–15.

Visintainer, M., Volpicelli, J., & Seligman, M. E. P. (1982). Tumor rejection in rats after inescapable or escapable shock. *Science, 216,* 437–439.

Vleioras, G., & Bosma, H. (2005). Are identity styles important for psychological well-being? *Journal of Adolescence, 28,* 397–409.

Vogel, E., Rose, J., Roberts, L., & Eckles, K. (2014). Social comparison, social media and self-esteem. *Psychology of Popular Media Culture, 3,* 206–222.

Von Dras, D. D., & Siegler, I. C. (1997). Stability in extraversion and aspects of social support at midlife. *Journal of Personality and Social Psychology, 72,* 233–241.

Wagerman, S., & Funder, D. (2007). Acquaintance reports of personality and academic achievement: A case for conscientiousness. *Journal of Research in Personality, 41,* 221–229.

Wagner, J., Lang, F., Neyer, F., & Wagner, G. (2014). Self-esteem across adulthood. *European Journal of Aging, 11,* 109–119.

Waldrop, D., Lightsey, O., Ethington, C., Woemmel, C., & Coke, A. (2001). Self-efficacy, optimism, health competence, and recovery from orthopedic surgery. *Journal of Counseling Psychology, 48,* 233–238.

Walker, B., & Winter, D. (2007). The elaboration of personal construct psychology. *Annual Review of Psychology, 58,* 453–477.

Walker, R., Alabi, D., Roberts, J., & Obasi, M. (2010). Ethnic group differences in reasons for living and the moderating role of cultural world view. *Cultural Diversity and Ethnic Minority Psychology, 16,* 372–378.

Wallerstein, R. (2014). Erik Erikson and his problematic identity. *Journal of the American Psychoanalytic Association, 62,* 657–675.

Walsh, S., White, K., Cox, S., & Young, R. (2011). Keeping in constant touch: The predictors of young Australians' mobile phone involvement. *Computers in Human Behavior, 27,* 333–342.

Walters, R. H., Bowen, N. V., & Parke, R. D. (1963). *Experimentally induced disinhibition of sexual responses.* (Cited in Bandura & Walters, 1963).

Walton, K., & Roberts, B. (2004). On the relationship between substance use and personality traits: Abstainers are not maladjusted. *Journal of Research in Personality, 38,* 515–535.

Wan, W. (2010, October 11). The fundamentals of Freud come into fashion in China. *Washington Post.*

Wang, Q., Bowling, N., & Eschleman, K. (2010). A meta-analytic examination of work and general locus of control. *Journal of Applied Psychology, 95,* 761–768.

Wang, S., Shi, M., & Chen, H. (2010). Ego identity development and its relation to emotional adjustment in college students. *Chinese Journal of Clinical Psychology, 18,* 215–218.

Want, V., Parham, T., Baker, R., & Sherman, M. (2004). African-American students' ratings of Caucasian and African-American counselors varying in racial consciousness. *Cultural Diversity and Ethnic Minority Psychology, 10,* 123–136.

Warburton, J., McLaughlin, D., & Pinsker, D. (2006). Generative acts: Family and community involvement of older Australians. *International Journal of Aging and Human Development, 63,* 115–137.

Waterman, A. S. (1982). Identity development from adolescence to adulthood: An extension of theory and a review of research. *Developmental Psychology, 18,* 341–358.

Waterman, C. K., Buebel, M. E., & Waterman, A. S. (1970). Relationship between resolution of the identity crisis and outcomes of previous psychosocial crises. *Proceedings of the 78th Annual Convention of the American Psychological Association, 5,* 467–468.

Watkins, C. E., Jr. (1994). Measuring social interest. *Individual Psychology, 50,* 69–96.

Watkins, C. E., Jr., & St. John, C. (1994). Validity of the Sulliman Scale of Social Interest. *Individual Psychology, 50,* 166–169.

Watson, C. B., Chemers, M. M., & Preiser, N. (2001). Collective efficacy: A multilevel analysis. *Personality and Social Psychology Bulletin, 27,* 1057–1068.

Watson, D., Clark, L. A., McIntyre, C. W., & Hamaker, S. (1992). Affect, personality, and social activity. *Journal of Personality and Social Psychology, 63,* 1011–1025.

Watson, D., & Humrichouse, J. (2006). Personality development in emerging adulthood: Integrating evidence from self-ratings and spouse ratings. *Journal of Personality and Social Psychology, 91,* 959–974.

Watson, M. W., & Getz, K. (1990). The relationship between Oedipal behaviors and children's family role concepts. *Merrill-Palmer Quarterly, 36,* 487–505.

Watts, R., & Holden, J. (1994). Why continue to use "fictional finalism"? *Individual Psychology, 50,* 161–163.

Weber, H., Vollmann, M., & Renner, B. (2007). The spirited, the observant, and the disheartened: Social concepts of optimism, realism, and pessimism. *Journal of Personality, 75,* 169–197.

Webster, R. (1995). *Why Freud was wrong: Sin, science, and psychoanalysis.* New York: Basic Books.

Wegner, D. M., & Wheatley, T. (1999). Apparent mental causation: Sources of the experience of will. *American Psychologist, 54,* 480–492.

Wehr, G. (1987). *Jung: A biography.* Boston, MA: Shambhala.

Weinberger, D. (1995). The content validity of the repressive coping style. In J. Singer (Ed.), *Repression and dissociation* (pp. 337–386). Chicago, IL: University of Chicago Press.

Weinberger, I., & Silverman, L. H. (1990). Testability and empirical validation of psychoanalytic dynamic propositions through subliminal psychodynamic activation. *Psychoanalytic Psychology, 7,* 299–339.

Weir, K. (2012). The power of self-control. *Monitor on Psychology,* p. 43.

Weiss, A., King, J., & Perkins, L. (2006). Personality and subjective well-being in orangutans. *Journal of Personality and Social Psychology, 90,* 501–511.

Weiss, D. (2014). The relationship between Internet social networking, social anxiety, self-esteem, narcissism, and gender among college students. *Dissertation Abstracts International. Section B: Sciences and Engineering. Vol. 74 (9-BE).*

Weisse, C. S. (1992). Depression and immunocompetence: A review of the literature. *Psychological Bulletin, 111,* 475–489.

Weiten, W. (1992). *Psychology: Themes and variations.* Belmont, CA: Brooks-Cole.

Weitlauf, J. C., Cervone, D., Smith, R. E., & Wright, P. M. (2001). Assessing generalizations in perceived self-efficacy: Multi-domain and global assessments of the effects of self-defense training for women. *Personality and Social Psychology Bulletin, 27*, 1683–1691.

Wendorf, C., Lucas, T., Imamoglu, E., Weisfeld, C., & Weisfeld, G. (2011). Marital satisfaction across three cultures: Does the number of children have an impact after accounting for other marital demographics? *Journal of Cross-Cultural Psychology, 42*(3), 340–354.

Werner, N., & Bumpus, M. (2010). Involvement in Internet aggression during early adolescence. *Journal of Youth and Adolescence, 39*, 607–619.

Wernick, L., Kulick, A., & Inglehart, M. (2014). Influences of peers, teachers, and climate on students' willingness to intervene when witnessing anti-transgender harassment. *Journal of Adolescence, 37*, 927–935.

Westen, D. (1990). Psychoanalytic approaches to personality. In L. A. Pervin (Ed.), *Handbook of personality* (pp. 21–65). New York: Guilford Press.

Westen, D. (1998). The scientific legacy of Sigmund Freud. *Psychological Bulletin, 124*, 333–371.

Westerlund, M., Santtila, P., Johansson, A., Jern, P., & Sandnabba, N. (2012). What steers them to the "wrong crowd?" Genetic influence on adolescents' peer-group sexual attitudes. *European Journal of Developmental Psychology, 9*, 645–664.

Westermeyer, J. (2004). Predictors and characteristics of Erikson's life cycle model among men: A 32-year longitudinal study. *International Journal of Aging and Human Development, 58*, 29–48.

Westkott, M. (1986). *The feminist legacy of Karen Horney.* New Haven, CT: Yale University Press.

Whitbourne, S. K., Elliot, L. B., Zuschlag, M. K., & Waterman, A. S. (1992). Psychosocial development in adulthood: A 22-year sequential study. *Journal of Personality and Social Psychology, 63*, 260–271.

Whitbourne, S., Sneed, J., & Sayer, A. (2009). Psychosocial development from college through midlife: A 34-year sequential study. *Developmental Psychology, 45*, 1328–1340.

White, J., Campbell, L., Stewart, A., Davies, M., & Pilkington, L. (1997). The relationship of psychological birth order to career interests. *Individual Psychology, 53*, 89–103.

Whittaker, V., & Neville, H. (2010). Examining the relation between racial identity attitude clusters and psychological health outcomes in African American college students. *Journal of Black Psychology, 36*, 383–409.

Wichern, F., & Nowicki, S. (1976). Independence training practices and locus of control orientation in children and adolescents. *Developmental Psychology, 12*, 77.

Widom, C., Czaja, S., Wilson, H., Allwood, M., & Chauhan, P. (2013). Do the long-term consequences of neglect differ for children of different races and ethnic backgrounds? *Child Maltreatment, 18*, 42–55.

Williams, D. E., & Page, M. M. (1989). A multidimensional measure of Maslow's hierarchy of needs. *Journal of Research in Personality, 23*, 192–213.

Williams, K., & Guerra, N. (2011). Perceptions of collective efficacy and bullying perpetration in schools. *Social Problems, 58*, 126–143.

Williams, P., Suchy, Y., & Kraybill, M. (2010). Five-factor model of personality traits and executive functioning among older adults. *Journal of Research in Personality, 44*, 485–491.

Wills, T., Murry, V., Brody, G., Gibbons, F., Gerrard, M., Walker, C., et al. (2007). Ethnic pride and self-control related to protective and risk factors. *Health Psychology, 26*, 50–59.

Wilson, C. (1972). *New pathways in psychology.* New York: Taplinger.

Wilson, K., Fornasier, S., & White, K. (2010). Psychological predictors of young adults' use of social networking sites. *Cyberpsychology, Behavior, and Social Networking, 13*, 173–177.

Windsor, T., & Anstey, K. (2010). Age differences in psychosocial predictors of positive and negative affect: A longitudinal investigation of young, midlife, and older adults. *Psychology and Aging, 25*, 641–652.

Winkielman, P., Berridge, K., & Wilbarger, J. (2005). Unconscious affective reactions to masked happy versus angry faces influence consumption behavior and judgments of value. *Personality and Social Psychology Bulletin, 31*, 121–135.

Winter, D. A. (1992). *Personal construct psychology in clinical practice.* London: Routledge.

Winter, D. A. (2013). Still radical after all these years: George Kelly's *The Psychology of Personal Constructs* [book review]. *Clinical Child Psychology and Psychiatry, 18*, 276–283.

Winter, D. G. (1973). *The power motive.* New York: Free Press.

Winter, D. G. (1993a). Gordon Allport and letters from Jenny. In K. H. Craik, R. Hogan, & R. N. Wolfe (Eds.), *Fifty years of personality psychology* (pp. 147–163). New York: Plenum Press.

Winter, D. G. (1993b). Power, affiliation, and war: Three tests of a motivational model. *Journal of Personality and Social Psychology, 65*, 532–545.

Winter, D. G., & Proctor, H. (2014). Formulation in personal and relational construct psychology: Seeing the world through the clients' eyes. In L. Johnstone & R. Dallos (Eds.), *Formulation in psychology and psychotherapy: Making sense of people's problems* (2nd ed., pp. 145–172). New York: Routledge/Taylor & Francis.

Winter, S., Neubaum, G., Eimer, S., Gordon, V., Theil, J., Hermann, J., et al. (2014). Another brick in the Facebook wall: How personality traits relate to the content of status updates. *Computers in Human Behavior, 34*, 194–202.

Winterbottom, M. R. (1958). The relation of need for achievement to learning experiences in independence and mastery. In J. W. Atkinson (Ed.), *Motives in fantasy, action, and society.* Princeton, NJ: Van Nostrand.

Wirtz, D., Chie, C., Diener, E., & Oishi, S. (2009). What constitutes a good life? Cultural differences in the role of positive and negative affect in subjective well-being. *Journal of Personality, 77*, 1187–1196.

Witt, E. A., Donnellan, M. B., & Orlando, M. J. (2011). Timing and selection effects within a psychology subject pool: Personality and sex matter. *Personality and Individual Differences, 50*, 355–359.

Witt, E., Massman, A., & Jackson, L. (2011). Trend in youth's videogame playing, overall computer use, and communication technology use: The impact of self-esteem and the Big Five personality factors. *Computers in Human Behavior, 27*, 763–769.

Wittels, F. (1924). *Sigmund Freud: His personality, his teaching, and his school.* London: Allen & Unwin.

Wojcik, E. (2012). Girl Scouts' "Science of Happiness Badge" promotes positive psychology. *Monitor on Psychology, 43*(1), 11.

Wolinsky, F., Vander Weg, M., Martin, R., Unverzagt, F., Willis, S., Marsiske, M., et al. (2009). Does cognitive training improve internal locus of control among older adults? *Journal of Gerontology: Social Sciences, 65,* 591–598.

Wong, A., Shaw, G., & Ng, D. (2010). Taiwan Chinese managers' personality: Is Confucianism on the wane? *International Journal of Human Resource Management, 21,* 1108–1123.

Wong, S., Lee, B., Ang, R., Oie, T., & Ng, A. (2009). Personality, health, and coping: A cross-national study. *Cross-Cultural Research, 43*(3), 251–279.

Wong, W., & Hines, M. (2014, September 30). Effects of gender color-coding on toddlers' gender-typical toy play. *Archives of Sexual Behavior.* http://psycnet.apa.org/index.cfm?fa=search. displayRecord&id=6CED34DA-D7CA-914D-FDE1-0D6BAE4D5D74&resultID=1&page=1&dbTab=all&search=true

Wood, A., Joseph, S., & Maltby, J. (2009). Gratitude predicts psychological well-being above the Big Five facets. *Personality and Individual Differences, 46,* 443–447.

Wood, J. M., Garb, H. N., Lilienfeld, S. O., & Nezworski, M. T. (2002). Clinical assessment. *Annual Review of Psychology, 53,* 519–543.

Xian-Li, A., & Guang-Xing, X. (2006). Dream contents of modern undergraduate students. *Chinese Mental Health Journal, 14,* 57–67.

Xiang, J., & Shen, H. (2010). Defense mechanisms in college students with borderline personality disorder. *Chinese Mental Health Journal, 24,* 275–278.

Yamagata, S., Suzuki, A., Ando, J., Ono, Y., Kijima, N., Yoshimura, K., et al. (2006). Is the genetic structure of human personality universal? A cross-cultural twin study from North America, Europe, and Asia. *Journal of Personality and Social Psychology, 90,* 987–998.

Yamaguchi, S., Greenwald, A. G., Banaji, H. R., Murakami, F., Chen, D., Shiomura, K., et al. (2007). Apparent universality of positive implicit self-esteem. *Psychological Science, 18,* 498–500.

Yang, H., & Zhao, S. (2009). Psychological types of Chinese business managers. *Journal of Psychological Type, 69*(12), 157–163.

Yao, M., & Zhong, Z. (2014). Loneliness, social contacts and Internet addiction: A cross-lagged panel study. *Computers in Human Behavior, 30,* 164–170.

Yap, S., & Baharudin, R. (2015, February 4). The relationship between adolescents' perceived parental involvement, self-efficacy beliefs, and subjective well-being: A multiple mediator model. *Social Indicators Research.* http://www.researchgate.net/profile/Siew_Ting_Yap2

Yap, S., Settles, I., & Pratt-Hyatt, J. (2011). Mediators of the relationship between racial identity and life satisfaction in a community sample of African American women and men. *Cultural Diversity and Ethnic Minority Psychology, 17,* 89–97.

Ying, Y., Lee, P., Tsai, J., Yeh, J., & Huang, J. (2000). The concept of depression in Chinese American college students. *Cultural Diversity and Ethnic Minority Psychology, 6,* 183–185.

Young-Bruehl, E. (1988). *Anna Freud: A biography.* New York: Summit Books.

Yu, C. (2010). Contemporary Chinese sex symbols in dreams. *Dreaming, 20,* 25–41.

Yu, C. (2012). The effect of sleep position on dream experiences. *Dreaming, 22,* 212–221.

Yu, P., & Shu-Hua, L. (2005). The relationship between college students' attributional style, self-efficacy and subjective well-being. *Chinese Journal of Clinical Psychology, 13,* 43–44.

Zajonc, R. B. (2001). The family dynamics of intellectual development. *American Psychologist, 56,* 490–496.

Zajonc, R. B., Markus, H., & Markus, G. B. (1979). The birth order puzzle. *Journal of Personality and Social Psychology, 37,* 1325–1341.

Zanon, C., Bastianello, M., Pacico, J., & Hutz, C. (2014, July). The importance of personality and parental styles on optimism in adolescents. *Spanish Journal of Psychology, 17,* Article e47.

Zaretsky, E. (2004). *Secrets of the soul: A social and cultural history of psychoanalysis.* New York: Knopf.

Zeb, N., Naqvi, A., & Zonash, R. (2013). Big Five personality traits and ego-resilience in amputee soldiers. *Journal of Behavioral Sciences, 23,* 102–116.

Zebrowitz, L., Kikuchi, M., & Fellous, J. (2010). Facial resemblance to emotions: Group differences, impression effects, and race stereotypes. *Journal of Personality and Social Psychology, 98,* 175–189.

Zeidner, M. (1993). Coping with disaster: The case of Israeli adolescents under threat of missile attack. *Journal of Youth and Adolescence, 22,* 89–108.

Zhai, Q., Willis, M., O'Shea, B., Zhai, Y., & Yang, Y. (2013). Big Five personality traits, job satisfaction and subjective well-being in China. *International Journal of Psychology, 48,* 1099–1108.

Zhang, D., & He, H. (2010). Personality traits and life satisfaction: A Chinese case study. *Social Behavior and Personality, 38*(8), 1119–1132.

Zhang, F., & Parmley, M. (2011). What your best friend sees that I don't see: Comparing female close friends and casual acquaintances on the perception of emotional facial expressions of varying intensities. *Personality and Social Psychology Bulletin, 37,* 28–39.

Zheng, H., Ming-Yi, Q., Chun-Li, Y., Jing, N., Jing, D., & Xiao-Yun, Z. (2006). Correlated factors comparison: The trends of computer game addiction and Internet relationship addiction. *Chinese Journal of Clinical Psychology, 14,* 244–247.

Zhuo, J. (2010, November 30). Where anonymity breeds contempt. *New York Times.*

Ziegler-Hill, V., & Myers, E. (2009). Is high self-esteem a path to the White House? The implicit theory of self-esteem and the willingness to vote for presidential candidates. *Personality and Individual Differences, 46,* 14–19.

Zimmer, C. (2011, January 26). More to a smile than lips and teeth. *New York Times.*

Zimmerman, B. J. (1995). Self-efficacy and educational development. In A. Bandura (Ed.), *Self-efficacy in changing societies* (pp. 202–231). Cambridge, England: Cambridge University Press.

Zucchi, J., Bacheller, L., & Muscarella, F. (2012). *Learned helplessness and bullying: At risk for cyberbullying.* American Psychological Association Convention Presentation. http://psycnet.apa.org/psycextra/649952012-001.pdf

Zucker, A., Ostrove, J., & Stewart, A. (2002). College educated women's personality development in adulthood: Perceptions and age differences. *Psychology and Aging, 17,* 236–244.

Zuckerman, M. (1979). *Sensation seeking: Beyond the optimal level of arousal.* Hillsdale, NJ: Erlbaum.

Zuckerman, M. (1983). *Biological bases of sensation seeking, impulsivity, and anxiety.* Hillsdale, NJ: Erlbaum.

Zuckerman, M. (1990). The psychophysiology of sensation seeking. *Journal of Personality, 58,* 313–345.

Zuckerman, M. (1993). Out of sensory deprivation and into sensation seeking: A personal and scientific journey. In G. G. Brannigan & M. R. Merrens (Eds.), *The undaunted psychologist: Adventures in research* (pp. 45–57). Philadelphia, PA: Temple University Press.

Zuckerman, M. (1994a). *Behavioral expressions and biosocial bases of sensation seeking.* Cambridge, England: Cambridge University Press.

Zuckerman, M. (1994b). Impulsive unsocialized sensation seeking: The biological foundations of a basic dimension of personality. In J. E. Bates & T. D. Wachs (Eds.), *Temperament: Individual differences at the interface of biology and behavior* (pp. 219–255). Washington, DC: American Psychological Association.

Zuckerman, M. (2004). The shaping of personality: Genes, environments, and chance encounters. *Journal of Personality Assessment, 82,* 11–22.

Zuckerman, M. (2013). Biological bases of personality. In T. Howard, J. Suls, & I. Weiner (Eds.), *Handbook of psychology: Vol. 5. Personality and social psychology* (2nd ed., pp. 27–42). New York: Wiley.

Zuckerman, M., & Aluja, A. (2015). Measures of sensation seeking. In G. Boyle, D. Saklofske, & Matthews, G. (Eds.), *Measures of personality and social psychological constructs* (pp. 352–380). San Diego, CA: Elsevier.

Zuckerman, M., Buchsbaum, M. S., & Murphy, D. L. (1980). Sensation seeking and its biological correlates. *Psychological Bulletin, 88,* 187–214.

Zuckerman, M., Eysenck, S., & Eysenck, H. J. (1978). Sensation seeking in England and America: Cross-cultural, age and sex comparisons. *Journal of Consulting and Clinical Psychology, 46,* 139–149.

Zullow, H., & Seligman, M. E. P. (1985). Pessimistic ruminations predict increase in depressive symptoms. Unpublished manuscript. (Cited in D. L. Rosenhan & M. E. P. Seligman, *Abnormal psychology* (2nd ed.). New York: Norton).

Zunshine, L. (Ed.). (2010). *Introduction to cognitive cultural studies.* Baltimore, MD: Johns Hopkins University Press.

Zurbriggen, E. L., & Sturman, T. S. (2002). Linking motives and emotions: A test of McClelland's hypothesis. *Personality and Social Psychology Bulletin, 28,* 521–535.

name Index

subject Index